SHAKESPEARE SURVEY

ADVISORY BOARD

(1) Shakespeare and his Stage
(2) Shakespearian Production
(3) The Man and the Writer
(4) Interpretation
(5) Textual Criticism
(6) The Histories
(7) Style and Language
(8) The Comedies
(9) *Hamlet*
(10) The Roman Plays
(11) The Last Plays (with an index to *Surveys 1–10*)
(12) The Elizabethan Theatre
(13) *King Lear*
(14) Shakespeare and his Contemporaries
(15) The Poems and Music
(16) Shakespeare in the Modern World
(17) Shakespeare in his Own Age
(18) Shakespeare Then Till Now
(19) *Macbeth*
(20) Shakespearian and Other Tragedy
(21) *Othello* (with an index to *Surveys 11–20*)
(22) Aspects of Shakespearian Comedy
(23) Shakespeare's Language
(24) Shakespeare: Theatre Poet
(25) Shakespeare's Problem Plays
(26) Shakespeare's Jacobean Tragedies
(27) Shakespeare's Early Tragedies
(28) Shakespeare and the Ideas of his Time
(29) Shakespeare's Last Plays
(30) *Henry IV* to *Hamlet*

(31) Shakespeare and the Classical World (with an index to *Surveys 21–30*)
(32) The Middle Comedies
(33) *King Lear*
(34) Characterization in Shakespeare
(35) Shakespeare in the Nineteenth Century
(36) Shakespeare in the Twentieth Century
(37) Shakespeare's Earlier Comedies
(38) Shakespeare and History
(39) Shakespeare on Film and Television
(40) Current Approaches to Shakespeare through Language, Text and Theatre
(41) Shakespearian Stages and Staging (with an index to *Surveys 31–40*)
(42) Shakespeare and the Elizabethans
(43) *The Tempest* and After
(44) Shakespeare and Politics
(45) *Hamlet* and its Afterlife
(46) Shakespeare and Sexuality
(47) Playing Places for Shakespeare
(48) Shakespeare and Cultural Exchange
(49) *Romeo and Juliet* and its Afterlife
(50) Shakespeare and Language
(51) Shakespeare in the Eighteenth Century (with an index to *Surveys 41–50*)
(52) Shakespeare and the Globe
(53) Shakespeare and Narrative
(54) Shakespeare and Religions
(55) *King Lear* and its Afterlife
(56) Shakespeare and Comedy

Aspects of *Macbeth*
Aspects of *Othello*
Aspects of *Hamlet*
Aspects of *King Lear*
Aspects of Shakespeare's 'Problem Plays'

SHAKESPEARE SURVEY

AN ANNUAL SURVEY OF

SHAKESPEARE STUDIES AND PRODUCTION

56

Shakespeare and Comedy

EDITED BY

PETER HOLLAND

CAMBRIDGE
UNIVERSITY PRESS

PUBLISHED BY THE PRESS SYNDICATE OF THE UNIVERSITY OF CAMBRIDGE
The Pitt Building, Trumpington Street, Cambridge, United Kingdom

CAMBRIDGE UNIVERSITY PRESS
The Edinburgh Building, Cambridge CB2 2RU, UK
40 West 20th Street, New York, NY 10011-4211, USA
477 Williamstown Road, Port Melbourne, VIC 3207, Australia
Ruiz de Alarcón 13, 28014 Madrid, Spain
Dock House, The Waterfront, Cape Town 8001, South Africa

http://www.cambridge.org

First published 2003

Printed in the United Kingdom at the University Press, Cambridge

Typeface Bembo 10/12 pt   *System* LaTeX 2ε   [TB]

A catalogue record for this book is available from the British Library

ISBN 0 521 82727 2 hardback

Shakespeare Survey was first published in 1948. Its first
eighteen volumes were edited by Allardyce Nicoll.
Kenneth Muir edited volumes 19 to 33.
Stanley Wells edited volumes 34 to 52.

EDITOR'S NOTE

Volume 57 on '*Macbeth* and its Afterlife' will be at press by the time this volume appears. The theme of Volume 58, which will include papers from the 2004 International Shakespeare Conference, will be 'Writing About Shakespeare' and will be concerned both with biographical writing about Shakespeare and with approaches to Shakespeare criticism. The theme of Volume 59 will be 'Editing Shakespeare'.

Submissions should be addressed to the Editor, either as an email attachment to pholland@nd.edu or as hard copy to the Editor, *Shakespeare Survey*, at The Shakespeare Institute, Church Street, Stratford-upon-Avon, Warwickshire CV37 6HP, to arrive at the latest by 1 September 2004 for Volume 58. Pressures on space are heavy; priority is given to articles related to the theme of a particular volume. All articles submitted are read by the Editor and at least one member of the Advisory Board, whose indispensable assistance the Editor gratefully acknowledges.

Unless otherwise indicated, Shakespeare quotations and references are keyed to the modern-spelling Complete Oxford Shakespeare (1986).

Review copies should be addressed to the Editor, as above. In attempting to survey the ever-increasing bulk of Shakespeare publications our reviewers inevitably have to exercise some selection. We are pleased to receive offprints of articles which help to draw our reviewers' attention to relevant material.

P.D.H.

CONTRIBUTORS

ROBERT BEARMAN, *Shakespeare Birthplace Trust*
SARAH ANNES BROWN, *Lucy Cavendish College, Cambridge*
DYMPNA CALLAGHAN, *Syracuse University*
MICHAEL CORDNER, *University of York*
MICHAEL DOBSON, *University of Surrey, Roehampton*
DECLAN DONNELLAN, *Artistic Director, Cheek by Jowl*
MAUD ELLMANN, *King's College, Cambridge*
ANDREW HADFIELD, *University of Wales, Aberystwyth*
ANDREAS HÖFELE, *University of Munich*
PETER HOLBROOK, *University of Queensland*
RUTH MORSE, *Université Paris 7, Denis-Diderot*
STEPHEN ORGEL, *Stanford University*
PATRICIA PARKER, *Stanford University*
ADRIAN POOLE, *Trinity College, Cambridge*
ERIC RASMUSSEN, *University of Nevada*
CAROL CHILLINGTON RUTTER, *University of Warwick*
JAMES SHAW, *The Shakespeare Institute*
ALAN SINFIELD, *University of Sussex*
A. B. TAYLOR, *Swansea Institute*
ANN THOMPSON, *King's College, London*
LESLIE THOMSON, *University of Toronto*
ROBERT N. WATSON, *University of California, Los Angeles*

CONTENTS

CONTENTS

ILLUSTRATIONS

LIST OF ILLUSTRATIONS

ILLUSTRATIONS

LOOKING LIKE A CHILD – OR – *TITUS*: THE COMEDY

CAROL CHILLINGTON RUTTER

Twenty lines in to *A Midsummer Night's Dream*, when 'merriments', 'mirth' and 'pomp' have been ordered up to close off and reconcile with sportive 'triumph' the memory of the 'injuries' inflicted in the pre-history of the play by 'triumph' of a martial kind, Egeus comes crashing in upon Theseus's pre-marital tête-à-tête, fuming, spluttering, 'Full of vexation . . . with complaint / Against my child, my daughter Hermia' (1.1.22–3). Stubborn Hermia has dug her heels in, is refusing to marry her father's choice. She has eyes only for Lysander. Retaliating, the child-changed father demands 'the ancient privilege of Athens', to 'dispose' of what is 'mine' 'either to this gentleman' (Demetrius) 'Or to her death, according to our law' (41–4). 'What say you, Hermia?' asks Theseus (46). She answers: 'I would my father look'd but with my eyes' (56). But Theseus counters: 'Rather your eyes must with his judgment look' (57). That exchange, in a nutshell, formulates the impasse this most optically challenged (and challenging) Shakespeare play is going to explore, setting up a contest of looking strategies that the *Dream* is never to reconcile, only, finally, to finesse. The child Hermia wants her father to look like a child, with 'eyes' that metonymically figure desire, fancy, doting, the 'quick bright things' that dazzle and prevail upon sensible, impressionable youth (56, 149). But the father looks different, with judgment: that is, in terms the OED gives us, with 'deliberation', 'discretion', the 'faculty of judging', connecting 'judgment' back to its primary site of meaning located in the judicial, in the law. Looked at like this, their stand-off is more than a stand-off of perspective, of point-of-view; it's a stand-off of generic positions. Simply put, looking like Egeus, *A Midsummer Night's Dream* looks like tragedy; looking like the child, like comedy. We understand what the elders are objecting to: child-sight is giddy, as changeable as taffeta, as unsettled as a gad-fly, anti-authoritarian, anarchic. But it's also forgiving, restorative (both reconstructive and medicinal), saving: looking like a child is what the New Testament instructs us to achieve in order to understand grace – and salvation, the new dispensation built on the ruins of the old, codified law. Culturally, looking like a child is liberating: breaking the rules means improvising, experimenting (in what Louis Montrose would call an 'anti-structural space'[1]) with alternative cultural possibilities that just might promote cultural change. It's here that looking like a child aligns itself with theatrical looking.

Alas, poor old Egeus never does come round to Hermia's way of seeing.[2] When, on the morning after the night before, the runaways are discovered asleep in the woods and wake (seeing 'double') to talk 'amazèdly', finding their 'minds transfigured', their rivalries transformed (4.1.189, 145; 5.1.24) their sick appetites restored to health, loathing

---

[1] 'The Purpose of Playing: Reflections on a Shakespearean Anthropology', *Helios*, n.s. 7 (1980), p. 64. The term is borrowed from the anthropologist Victor Turner in *Dramas, Fields and Metaphors* (Ithaca, 1974).

[2] But see the Folio, where it's Egeus, not Philostrate, who, playing Master of the Revels, brings on the 'mirth' in Act 5, perhaps signalling a truce with comedy if not a reconciliation with his daughter.

turned to loving, in short, their world utterly changed, Egeus' world looks just the same: still stuck in Act I, still the *senex iratus*, still utterly rigid – and still saddling the play with a death-wish, clamouring, 'the law, the law' (154). Iron-ically, he, like Bully Bottom rehearsing 'Pyramus and Thisbe', seems to have no idea what kind of play he's in. Stranded inside an Ovidian narrative, but ignorant, evidently, of Ovid, he doesn't know how to read 'the plot', is unprovided with the key classical text that would inform him on the saving subject of transformation, the imperative 'change or die'. He's without a *Metamorphosis*. Now, that's just where the Roman father, Titus Andronicus, has the edge over his Athenian counterpart. I take it that *Titus* and *A Midsummer Night's Dream* are companion plays, Shakespeare as pseudo-Plutarch setting up Andronicus and Egeus as parallel lives (*Titus* has the death of Pyramus on its mind at 2.3.231). One difference is that Titus owns the better library. We may think he's slow on the up-take, that he should have thought about Philomel in Act 3, but when his copy of the *Metamorphosis* finally falls violently open at his feet in 4.1, its 'leaves' 'quote[d]' to him in the urgent actions of his daughter, he demonstrates that he knows his Ovid (45, 50). He's willing to look different. Earlier, he refused to 'see. O see' what he'd done, killing his son, Mutius (1.1.338). But confronted with the appalling metamorphosis-by-mutilation inflicted upon Lavinia, Titus 'Will . . . see it', forcing Lucius's look back when Lucius turns away: 'Faint-hearted boy, arise and look upon her' (3.1.61, 65). To Lavinia Titus says, 'Had I but seen thy picture in this plight, / It would have madded me' (3.1.103–4). Then asks, rhetorically as he thinks, because she cannot answer, 'What shall I do / Now I behold thy lively body so?' (3.1.104–5). What Titus does is what Lavinia teaches him – to look like a child, to concentrate on seeing how Lavinia looks and read-ing 'all her martyred signs', to 'wrest an alphabet' to decipher what she needs him to see (3.2.36, 44). Bizarrely, Hermia's wish, 'I would my fa-ther look'd but with my eyes', comes good in Titus – and launches the black retributive com-edy of the final act where Tamora's boys, the awful

children Chiron and Demetrius, bound, gagged, able to communicate only with their eyes, become their looks, a grotesque refiguration of 'looking like a child', served up by Titus 'trimmed' to make their mother look at them anew.

All across his work, at points of generic water-shed – points where, generically, the play could go either way – Shakespeare puts a child on stage to look, to be looked at, to focus what's at stake: my 'looking like a child' is of course a double entendre, not just what the child looks like to spectators, his image in performance, but what he's looking at, including how spectators look at him looking.[3]

---

[3] Shakespeare's scripted children are the best refutation I know of the argument advanced forty years ago by the historian of mentalités, Philippe Ariès, in *Centuries of Childhood* (London, 1962) and taken up by Lawrence Stone in *The Family, Sex and Marriage in England 1500–1800* (London, 1977) that the idea of 'childhood' was unknown in early modern European culture and that parents were affectionless because 'the very high infant and child mortality rates' made it 'folly to in-vest too much emotional capital in such ephemeral beings' (Stone, *The Family*, p. 105). Linda Pollock in *Forgotten Children* (Cambridge, 1984) and Keith Thomas in 'Children in Early Modern England' (in Gillian Avery and Julia Briggs, eds., *Children and Their Books: A Celebration of the Work of Iona and Peter Opie* [Oxford, 1989]) use contemporary documents to correct Stone's misconceptions, Thomas observing, 'Far from there having been no medieval conception of childhood, we now know that doctors, lawyers, and religious writers in the Middle Ages all recognized infancy and youth as a vulner-able, fragile period of diminished responsibility. Far from infant mortality deadening parents' sensibilities, we know that the loss of young children frequently drove them distraught [here, we might remember Ben Jonson's 'best piece of poesy' and John Chamberlain's letters]. Far from there being no affection between early modern parents and their offspring, we know that most of the moralists who urged the strict treatment of children did so because they thought that their contempo-raries were spoiling them by coddling them unduly' (p. 46). 'Childhood' was an elastic concept in the period, stretching from infancy to marriage and frequently failing to distin-guish childhood from youth, not, as C. John Sommerville observes in *The Discovery of Childhood in Puritan England* (Athens, GA, 1992, p. 15), because Shakespeare's contempo-raries 'recognized no difference', but because 'To them child-hood was a more gradual and even a longer process'. Hermia, then, is both a child and a young woman; Tamora's rapist sons are still 'boys'. This capaciousness means that Marjorie Garber is simply wrong when she remarks in *Coming of Age in*

So Edward IV holds up a baby, his heir, to show that, after three plays and fifteen acts of slaughter, the Wars of the Roses are done – then invites his twisted brother Dicky to give the infant hope a kiss (*Richard Duke of York* 5.7.33). Banquo stands in the dark, the moon down, praying the 'Merciful powers' to 'Restrain' in him 'the cursèd thoughts that nature / Gives way to in repose' (*Macbeth* 2.1.6–9), the thoughts, that, acted, would make his life, like Macbeth's, tragic 'nothing'; beside him stands his boy, holding his sword. Coriolanus, determined to burn Rome 'all into one coal' and to pack cards like a turncoat with the enemy to do so (4.7.145), faced with his child, blesses the boy's future, praying that he will be the kind of soldier who will 'stick i'th'wars / Like a great sea-mark standing every flaw / And saving those that eye thee!' (*Coriolanus* 5.3.73–5). Leontes, already feeling the killing 'infection of my brains', scans Mamillius's 'welkin' face for the antidote, the medicine, the 'childness' that 'cures... / Thoughts' that 'thick [the] blood' (*The Winter's Tale* 1.1.138, 147–8, 171–2). Cleopatra draws attention to the strange baby she suckles, that, consuming her, saves her life from tragedy as Caesar's spoil by turning her death into comic apotheosis: 'Peace, peace. / Dost thou not see my baby at my breast, / That sucks the nurse asleep?' (*Antony and Cleopatra* 5.2.303–4).

Recent film – film is, after all a 'looking medium', a medium that, as Ingmar Bergman has said, 'begins with a face'[4] – shows directors picking up Shakespeare's cues, and even elaborating them, inventing supplementary performance texts that, privileging children, invite the spectator to look like a child. Consider these film clips. First, the long tracking shot that follows Branagh's Henry V (1989) striding across the blood-mudded battlefield of Agincourt carrying over his shoulder the body of the dead baggage boy as 'Non Nobis' builds from a single voice to a wall of sound, effectively hijacking the image to translate, to incorporate child slaughter into the larger heroizing project of martial masculinity and manly sacrifice, 'dulce et decorum est...' Next, the sequence opening Richard Loncraine's *Richard III* (1996) that, following on from the credits where the title is written in

machine-gun fire, wipes out the brutal memory of war in happy images of the Yorks at play. The camera catches the little princes, naked and delightedly shrieking, chased by a nanny holding out a towel – a sequence set up to rhyme with one later that puts the younger prince in tight close-up, concentrating on the model train track running round the palace floor while behind him, voices off, the adults talk politics. Suddenly, a gigantic black jackboot comes down through the frame, the camera cutting from the child's enquiring frown to the rancidly smiling brown-shirt murderer, Tyrell. The train stops in its tracks. Next, from Baz Luhrmann's *Romeo + Juliet* (1996), the pull-back from the close-up on Juliet's open, childlike face, almost a woman's, waiting for night, waiting for Romeo, to show her sitting on her bed in a little girl's room, her shelves lined with dolls, what passes for a prie-dieu set in front of a teen-angel Madonna flanked with baby-pink cherubs; a sequence that strangely rhymes with one just before, the death of Mercutio, when the camera

---

Shakespeare that 'there are very few children in Shakespeare's plays' (1981; London, 1997), p. 30. Counting only the York princes in the tower, Macduff's and Coriolanus's sons, and Mamillius, she sees them as 'terrible infants', thinks we are 'relieved' when they 'leave the stage' and, rather bizarrely, suggests that it may 'be no accident that almost all go to their deaths' (p. 30). Her account leaves out of the reckoning most of Shakespeare's child roles: Titus's Lucius and Aaron's baby son; York's Rutland, whose blood soaks the napkin used to wipe his father's weeping face; Holofernes's Mote; Mistress Page's William and Parson Hugh's school of scholar 'fairies'; King John's nephew Arthur; Henry VIII's baby Elizabeth; the Lord's transvestite Bartholomew, 'wife' to Christopher Sly; Hippolyta's changeling child (if he's brought on stage); Falstaff's page – the same, perhaps, who, older, goes to the French wars with Nym and the rest; Benedick's boy, and Brutus's, and Mariana's; Capulet's Juliet (too young to be a bride); Henry V's baggage boys; Hamlet's Player Queen; the boy choristers in the Forest of Arden; Banquo's Fleance and the witches' weird infant prodigy that surfaces in the cauldron; Pericles's Marina and Leontes's Perdita, first babies, then girls. Then there are the notional or symbolic children: the one Julietta 'groans' with; the one Cleopatra nurses; the one Joan of Arc, at the stake, pleads; the one Helena, big bellied, promises to answer Bertram's riddle; the one Doll Tearsheet threatens to miscarry – but if she does, scoffs the Beadle, she'll deliver a cushion.
4 Quoted in Jack L. Jorgens, *Shakespeare on Film* (Bloomington, 1977), p. 23.

pulls back from his so beautiful, almost girlish, but now wrecked face to look at his dying looked at. As a sandstorm kicks up, desolating the beachscape, the camera cuts to a little black girl looking out from a beach caravan window; cuts again to a pair of grubby Chicano children staring through the mesh of the torn chain-link perimeter fence their little hands are clutching, looking, powerlessly, like children watching the big kids trash the playground. Finally, from John Madden's *Shakespeare in Love* (1998), the sequence that has Will, on his way to his shrink to cure his writer's block, stop to talk with a kid who's torturing mice, who tells him his best play is *Titus* – then tells him his own name, John Webster.

The effects these films are achieving (if only locally) are perhaps tapping in to a wider contemporary – even millennial – concern with 'childness', with negotiating the emotive subject of the child in our culture. A quick scan down the recent bestseller lists sees dozens of novels published in English on four continents, written in a genre somewhere between memoir, confession, and public record; novels that look like children, that break the adult monopoly on history, on interpreting the past, that show that we never grow out of childhood, that childhood, rather, is in-grown, novels that offer a different, 'authentic' perspective on that thing adults call 'truth' or 'the way things have to be': *Angela's Ashes*, *A Star Called Henry*, *The Road to Nab End*, *Atonement*, *According to Queenie*, *Once in a House on Fire*, *The True History of the Kelly Gang*, *Bad Blood*, *Let's Not Go to the Dogs Tonight*, *Mere*, *Two Boys*, *At Swim*, *And When Did You Last See Your Father?* As far as filmed Shakespeare goes, undoubtedly the most thoughtful contribution to this way of looking is Julie Taymor's *Titus*, released in 2000 in Britain and the United States where one board of film censors rated it 'R', the other, '18', deciding the film wasn't appropriate viewing for children – ironic, really, since Taymor's *Titus* is seen entirely through the eyes of a child.[5] I want to think through what Taymor achieves with child looking in *Titus*, but to do this, I need to start one film back, with Adrian Noble's 1996 *A Midsummer Night's Dream*, for

if, arguably, the *Dream* and *Titus* are companion plays, Noble's and Taymor's are demonstrably companion films, both of them using a child to do work for the films that has generic consequences.

Noble's *Dream*, made from his enthusiastically reviewed 1994 RSC stage production, was panned, the director-behind-the-camera slammed for thinking 'like a primitive' (*The Times*, 28 November 1996), producing something on the order of 'an ambitious film school experiment' (*Variety*, 18 September 1996).[6] It is not, however, my purpose here to kick a dead donkey; rather, to consult Noble's filmed *Dream* as a pre-text glossing of Taymor that provides important preliminary viewing. Like Noble's *Dream*, Taymor's *Titus* began in the theatre, with a production directed for Theatre for a New Audience in New York in 1994. Both film projects, then, were translation exercises working to find a film language to rewrite in visual imagery Shakespeare's dense poetic text. Both, revelling in metatextual and metacinematic discourse, declare what Mark Thornton Burnett calls their 'postmodern aspirations',[7] James Loehlin reminding us that intertextuality is 'one of the hallmarks of postmodern cinema': 'the reference to other works, genres and styles, whether as homage,

---

[5] Produced by Clear Blue Sky, the film stars Anthony Hopkins (Titus), Jessica Lange (Tamora), Laura Fraser (Lavinia), Colm Feore (Marcus), Alan Cumming (Saturninus), James Frain (Bassianus), Harry Lennix (Aaron), Angus MacFadyen (Lucius), Matthew Rhys (Demetrius), Jonathan Rhys Meyers (Chiron), Dario D'Ambrosi (Clown), Tresy Taddei (Clown's Assistant), and Osheen Jones as the Boy/young Lucius. Bah Souleymane played Aaron's baby.

[6] Made in association with BBC Channel 4 and The Arts Council of Great Britain, this production featured Osheen Jones as the Boy, Alex Jennings as Theseus/Oberon, Lindsay Duncan as Hippolyta/Titania, Barry (Finbar) Lynch as Philostrate/Puck, Desmond Barrit as Bottom, and Ann Hasson as the Head Fairy.

[7] See his 'Impressions of Fantasy: Adrian Noble's *A Midsummer Night's Dream*' in Mark Thornton Burnett and Ramona Wray, eds., *Shakespeare, Film, Fin de Siècle* (London, 2000), p. 89, for a reading that aims to 'redress' critical opinion of the film as an 'unmitigated disaster' (*The Observer*, 1 December 1996), merely 'a highbrow pantomime' (*The Sunday Times*, 1 December 1996).

parody, simple imitation or even unconscious duplication'.[8] Noble quotes children's literature (*Alice in Wonderland*, *Peter Pan*, *The Lion, the Witch, and the Wardrobe*); film (*Dorothy and the Wizard of Oz*, *Mary Poppins*, *E.T.*, *A Close Shave*); and plunders past theatre productions: Peter Brook's 1970 *Dream* most conspicuously (walking, some might say, a fine line between quotation and plagiarism), but also John Barton's (1977), Ron Daniels' (1981), Bill Alexander's (1982) all at the RSC, and Barrie Rutter's Northern Broadsides *Dream*, 1994. Taymor re-cites – mischievously – some of Noble's citations, but also *The Silence of the Lambs*, Fellini's *Satyricon* and *La Strada*, and both Jane Howell's BBC *Titus* (1985)[9] and Deborah Warner's RSC *Titus* on the Swan stage (1987) – the *Titus* that taught Taymor what our post-Tarentino generation understands very well, that laughter in this play isn't an embarrassment, an impropriety to be killed or gagged: laughter in *Titus* belongs.[10] Both Noble and Taymor are interested in toys and play, in the fantasy life of objects metamorphosing. Their films play with space (as location but also as size, as scale) and with time (as history and memory, rendered also dys-chronically, anachronistically as reverie, imagination, fantasy). They are interested in apertures (keyholes, windows, doors squeezed shut or flying open, fissures in walls and pavements, eye holes in masks) and in surfaces that work like lenses to set up complicated looking economies – rain drops, bubbles, mirrors, glass, water. And both films begin with a child, that most enduring 'part of screen mythology', the 'omnipotent tot',[11] here prompted by Shakespeare's text (the changeling child, the Indian boy in the *Dream*; young Lucius, the grandson in *Titus*) but expanded far beyond the implicit Shakespearian performance text.

I want to begin, then, by citing the opening minute of Noble's *Dream*, to observe how the camera works to capture the world of the child – a particular world, in a particular way. Starting with a shot travelling across the heavens somewhere above the clouds, accompanied by a choir that sounds like Dorothy's munchkins in Oz, the camera, cued by a key change that says 'menace', drops through the clouds, zooms through a window, and passes over the interior, a room, a *museum* rather, assembled like a material version of the Opie collection, a nursery containing the paraphernalia of an exclusive, 'proper' English Edwardian childhood. Briefly, the camera picks out a Pollock toy theatre – a replica of an antique eighteenth century stage – then finds a sleeping Boy. Shut on his pillow

---

8 '"These Violent Delights Have Violent Ends": Baz Luhrmann's Millennial Shakespeare' in Burnett and Wray, *Shakespeare, Film*, p. 124.

9 Nowhere that I have come across does Taymor acknowledge her clear debts to Howell (or Warner). Howell wants spectators to see the story from young Lucius's eyes, puts him in the frame from the opening shot: a shadow materializes as a skull before dissolving into the face of the boy (played by Paul Davies-Prowles). While she dresses Rome in period costume, she makes the boy also a modern, giving him, significantly, a pair of steel-framed spectacles to focus his looking. But she kills all the laughs that Warner later found in the play and performance, cutting Titus's 'Ha, ha, ha' – and the cook's costume.

10 As laughter, since Aristotle, has been held indecorous in tragedy, so dodging the laughs in *Titus* has been held a main – indeed, perhaps *the* main – challenge for the play's contemporary directors. Alan Dessen takes it as read that Edward Ravenscroft's eighteenth-century adaptation was finding 'solutions' for 'a series of problematic moments that continue to bedevil today's directors', and 'bedevil' because they 'elicit unwanted audience laughter' (*Titus Andronicus: Shakespeare in Performance* (Manchester, 1989), p. 9). See Dessen on Peter Brook's directing *Titus* in 1955 as a 'beautiful barbaric ritual', a reading he achieved, according to J. C. Trewin, by cutting every 'offending phrase' that threatened 'mocking laughter' (pp. 15, 22). But what if Dessen et al. are wrong? What if laughter isn't a risk to be avoided but one to be *courted* in the play? Following on from Warner, Taymor hears laughter as aurally constituting the authentic emotional territory of the tragic grotesque in *Titus*, and cues it to the laughter the play itself elicits in Titus's 'Ha, ha, ha!' (3.1.263).

11 Ruth M. Goldstein and Edith Zornow, *The Screen Image of Youth: Movies About Children and Adolescents* (London, 1980), p. xiv. 'Down through the decades in Hollywood', they continue, 'a little child has saved them – the unhappy millionaires, the gamblers with hearts of gold, the couples drifting apart, the lonely curmudgeons – saved them by falling sick, getting hurt, running away, or just giving the grown-ups a good talking to'. They cite, too, as 'another movie staple', the 'partnership between a disreputable man and a child, in which the child learns corruption from the man and the man may learn sentiment from the child' (p. 27). Both paradigms are apposite to Taymor's *Titus*.

is Arthur Rackham's illustrated *Midsummer Night's Dream*, which we can take as a *terminus a quo* for this representation: it was first published in 1908.[12]

When the camera cuts and spectators see the child walking down primary-coloured corridors, past the satyr who – Puck's avatar – guards the door, we understand that this *Dream* is his *Dream*, that, like the scene he sees when he bends down and looks through the final door's keyhole onto a magical golden room filled (seemingly) with Theseus and Hippolyta, his look is going to be the film's point of view. Later, having listened, unseen, to the lovers' plotting, the Boy, now their presumptive co-conspirator, will exit at full tilt after them out of this room, running through the yellow door then, terrifyingly, falling through the suddenly absent floorboards, dropping into space through a vortex tunnel like Alice down the rabbit hole. A quick cut to the Boy sitting up in bed screaming 'Mummy!' will be followed by a shot of him popping up through a stove pipe in a village Scout hut where, following Baden-Powell's injunction to the movement he launched in 1908 – 'Be prepared!' – a collection of superannuated Scouts distribute the parts to 'Pyramus and Thisbe', then exit into a storm. At the window, the Boy, still (always in this film) in pyjamas, watches the weather rip Peter Quince's black umbrella out of his hand, whip it up into the stratosphere, then, like saturation bombing by parachutes, return it, multiplied, transformed, floating down from a now blue sky – with fairies attached: here, all the Court parts (except Egeus) double roles in fairyland. So Philostrate returns as Puck, and Peter Quince's mob, like Aunt Em's farmhands tornado-transported from Kansas to Oz, reappear as Cobweb and Mustardseed, Peaseblossom and Mote.

As the Boy is put into play, he begins to perform work that the film needs to have done on a narrative and technical level: he is dreamer, observer, voyeur, active spectator, creative manager, agent of theatrical transformations. But enforced upon him is an adult way of looking that deprives him of childness, his look made knowing, but, curiously, simultaneously sanitized. Activating the trope of theatre-as-magic, the Boy's toy theatre

fetches up in the woods, spirited out of the nursery by Oberon's 'I know a bank where the wild thyme blows' (2.1.249), and, in a borrowing straight from Bergman's *Fanny and Alexander* (1982), the Boy collaborates with Oberon to direct the night's revels.[13] Oberon and Puck, discovering the toy theatre, bend seemingly gigantic heads level with

---

[12] Published by Heinemann in London in January, the entire de luxe edition of 1,000 copies sold out by March, along with over half of the 15,000 trade copies; new impressions followed in 1911, 1912, 1914 and 1917, and the English edition remained in print and paid Rackham royalties until the end of his life. It's no wonder, then, that Rackham's *Dream* was as common a resident in the middle-class Edwardian nursery as the clockwork lion, tin soldier, and rocking horse. While the *Athanaeum*, reviewing the *Dream*, complained that his public forced 'Mr Rackham to live in a sentimental region', where 'landscapes full of fire and vigour' were 'spoilt by the introduction of namby-pamby nymphs', *The Outlook* saw a landscape 'sprung from seed found in the fancies of Dürer'; 'trees gnarled and black and twisted'. See James Hamilton, *Arthur Rackham: A Life with Illustration* (London, 1995), pp. 167–71.

[13] I owe this citation to Tony Howard. Bergman's film opens on a toy theatre façade, the backdrop rising to reveal the face of the boy, Alexander, looking through the theatre into the camera as he reaches forward to place an additional toy figure on the set. The film is saturated with Shakespeare allusions: Shakespeare's plays are performed in the Ekdahl family's theatre where Alexander's father dies rehearsing old Hamlet's ghost, a rehearsal that continues *post mortem* with the ghost returning to haunt the son, and the mother marrying a proxy Claudius whose house becomes the children's prison. In an unpublished seminar paper Bronia Evers observes, 'The film explores the darker side of childhood from the start, contrasting the child's "theatre of the mind" (where death lurks behind the living room pot plants) with the adult construction of childhood (where children appear as angels in the Christmas play)'. For adults, 'the powerful fascination of childhood . . . rests partly on its very elusiveness'; it is 'a form of seduction' ('Shakespeare's Later Collaborators', p. 4). Quoting Bergman's film, Noble detoxifies its vision, drains it of existential menace. This being the case, to interpret power in Noble's candy-floss film as 'a matter of contest' and the Boy's 'imaginative energies' as working 'simultaneously [to] empower and enslave' – as Mark Thornton Burnett does – is to misread several key moments: there is no sense in which 'the Boy must struggle with Oberon for ownership of the puppets' strings' nor is Oberon's handling of the model figure a 'seizure' that shows him 'usurping the Boy's manipulative privileges' (Burnett, *Shakespeare, Film*, p. 91).

the miniature stage, Oberon sliding the cardboard scenery open and looking through the theatre façade – to see the Boy's gigantic face looking back. On 'seek through this grove . . .', the (now invisible) Boy reaches a huge hand forward, placing centre stage a tiny model Helena, which seems to prompt Oberon to complete his thought – 'A sweet Athenian lady' (2.1.259–60). Oberon extends his own hand across the stage, carefully picking up Helena for Puck to examine, a toy magically put into play. In the next shot, the Boy is life-sized, standing over the theatre, handling puppet strings; cutting back, the camera shows Puck and Oberon, now toy-sized like Helena, riding the wires: manipulators of dreams, manipulated by the dreamer, an idea whose potential darkness is left unexplored.

Still, this gesture puts the Boy back in charge, reverses the power dynamic set up by his earlier disconcerting discovery that he's doubling in this dream as his own alter ego: he learns that he's the very changeling child the fairy king and queen are warring over. When he was reporting Oberon's 'wrath' to Titania's punk-pink henchman as the Boy looked on, Puck fingered a raindrop off the rim of his green umbrella, blew it like a soap bubble, and magically there materialized inside it, looking back at the Boy, *himself* – or a version of himself, or indeed, a version of Kenneth Anger's changeling child in Max Reinhardt's 1935 *Dream*: in his mirror image, he's an Indian boy, wearing a turban.[14] Nothing more is made of this twinning: yet again, nothing more is made of the trope of the dreamer dreamed. But the Boy, as if to signal that he's the answer to everyone's dreams, finally is the one to break the night's hold by rolling forward Time: spectators see him pushing forward the clock in the form of a giant 'wandering moon'. In this *Dream* the child never wakes. (But then, neither do the lovers: Noble cuts to Bottom's waking straight from Titania's.) Instead, the 'changeling' is adopted into a new family whose address is a place on a stage. At the end of Peter Quince's play, which was performed on the stage of the Boy's antique toy theatre, magically grown life-sized, with the little Boy himself acting the manful stagehand, as the theatre empties, 'Pyramus and Thisbe's' actors

depart, and the lovers exit to bed, a disembodied hand in close-up is seen flipping levers backstage, dropping the curtain, dousing the lights, darkening the foyer and auditorium. A cut discovers the 'lost' Boy, not backstage where he'd been sitting in the wings, delightedly clapping Bottom's performance, but now alone in the dress circle, chin propped up on the railing, still watching. Puck steps out from behind the closed curtain, speaks his 'hungry lion' speech front-of-cloth, then turns, strides upstage, and opens a scenery door in the back wall – onto fairyland. Magically, the Boy steps into the doorway behind him, and watches as fairyland, eerily set against a full moon, travels across water toward them. Speaking his nuptial blessing on Theseus and Hippolyta's future children ('Never mole, harelip, nor scar, / . . . Shall upon their children be' (5.2.41–4)), which cuts to a close up on the 'perfect' Boy, Oberon lifts him high, like an offering or fetish, the magician literalized as the promised magic. When Puck finishes his Epilogue, speaking straight to camera, he and the Boy exit fairyland together, back through the door that opens onto the colour-filled antique stage where, crowding in behind them, the fairy world meets the stage full of mortals, Bottom now hoisting the Boy high, the whole company's trophy, before finally settling into position in slow motion, the Boy at the centre, for a family portrait – or a full company curtain call.

Introducing the Boy – who wasn't part of his original RSC production concept – as 'the mechanism', said Noble, 'for translating the theatre into film'[15] must have seemed like a canny solution to the challenge of translation. While, on the one hand, literalizing the dream wasted Shakespeare's most teasing theatrical conceit – for no one dreams

---

[14] Anger, born and raised in Tinseltown, was four years old when he played the role he called a 'decent little walk-on' in 'Warners' – not Reinhardt's – *Dream* (*Babylon II*, p. 2). Later he pursued his love-hate relationship with Hollywood by serving as its unofficial biographer, archivist of doom and dirt in *Hollywood Babylon I* and *II* (London, 1975, 1986) – an ironic afterlife for a changeling child.

[15] I'm grateful to Finbar Lynch, Puck/Philostrate in Noble's *Dream*, for recalling this.

in his *Dream* except Hermia dreaming nightmar-ishly of snakes – on the other, dreaming up the dreaming child offered Noble a place of filmic refuge, for it is at the level of the child's dream-looking that everything filmic happens in this film. (We remember, of course, that in its infancy one of the first things film learned it could do was to dream.) It's as though, as the interface between the camera and the stage, Noble slides in the face of the child, the child's looking functioning as a kind of lens or reflecting surface to focus and register magic. Looking like a child is a metonymic stand-in for the 'magic' of cinema and offers a layer of representation where the director can imagine vi-sually: where motorcycles can fly, raindrops inflate, toy theatres grow. Thus equipped, Noble goes on to produce what I want to call a 'compilation' film. First, he photographs his original theatre produc-tion virtually unchanged (with its theatre-sized act-ing and box set that looks curiously flat on screen) as though making an archive video. Then he shoots a supplementary text, framed within the unself-conscious gaze of the child, written in a film lan-guage – shot/reverse shot; close-up and reaction shot; special effects. Finally, he interleaves the two. In this process the Boy in the film stands not just as surrogate for the spectator in the theatre;[16] he stands surrogate for the process of filmmaking.

Narratively, looking like a child renders this *Dream* incoherent. Locating the Boy in the Edwar-dian nursery locates childhood in a place of nostal-gia; those toys, the nursery paraphernalia, loaded with nostalgic associations, fill in an 'authentic' *mise-en-scène* for a Merchant/Ivory film, instantiat-ing a deeply conservative, restrictive (because his-torically constituted) looking regime that Noble's opening does nothing to disrupt – by, for exam-ple, signalling itself as post-modern pastiche. Later, nervous perhaps of the (mass) audience his Ed-wardian nostalgia will alienate, Noble violates the rules of engagement that he himself has set up for the film, starts pulling in metacinematic references the Boy can't access, aimed at the multiplex gen-eration – Oberon as David Bowie's Goblin King in *Labyrinth* (1987), for example. Incomprehensi-bly, then, the Edwardian Boy is required to start

dreaming the post-modern future, not just 1980s films but 1970s, 1980s, 1990s theatres: the set he dreams up for his *Dream* belongs to Brook's *Dream* while the technology it relies on belongs to the millennium. Such citations may work at the level of stylish in-joke, but they seem unable, as Bronia Evers observes, 'to move beyond an elaborate form of collage'.[17]

Toys, Don Fleming suggests, function 'as a kind of cultural construction kit', offer ways of order-ing the 'overheard' world of adults, should be seen 'not as objects, or not only as objects' but as 'events' generating 'traffic – called "play"'.[18] But toys are also, writes David Cohen, the 'stunted hallmarks of a materialist culture' that condition children to ac-cept the adult world.[19] The fact that toys, as Roland Barthes sees, '*literally* prefigure the world of adult functions obviously cannot but prepare the child to accept them all, by constituting for him, even before he can think about it, the alibi of a Nature which has at all time created soldiers, postmen, and Vespas. Toys here reveal the list of the things the adult does not find unusual; war, bureaucracy, ugli-ness, Martians'.[20] Or indeed, in the case of the toys Noble assembles, what this adult director doesn't find unusual, the nostalgic myth of innocent child-hood. For Noble imagines a child who only wishes to play nicely and, while many of his citations fold toy, story, theatre and film in upon themselves, achieving a kind of representational closed circuitry (so that his flying Boy summons up that other fly-ing boy, remembering him in all his versions on

---

[16] As Matt Wolf shrewdly observed (*Variety*, 18 September 1996).

[17] 'Shakespeare's Later Collaborators', p. 6. I owe the Bowie citation also to Evers. I'd like to record, too, my debt to three more Warwick University undergraduates who have challenged my thinking on this film: Brent Hinks, Jonathan Heron and Irene Musumeci. I am also enormously grateful to Cathia Jenainati for acting as an unofficial research assistant on this project, who taught me how to surf the net and keep my feet dry.

[18] Don Fleming, *Powerplay: Toys as Popular Culture* (Manchester, 1996), pp. 35, 11.

[19] David Cohen, *The Development of Play* (London, 1993, second edition), p. 63.

[20] Quoted in Cohen, *The Development of Play*, p. 63.

page, stage and celluloid), Noble's citations habitually by-pass their sources' complex rendering of childhood as an elusive, menacing place. If the nursery serves frequently as the site of transfer between real and fantasy worlds – into Never Never Land, or The Thousand Acre Woods – it can work that way because the cosy domestic nursery doubles also as the terrifying space of childhood alienation and trauma, home to the uncanny where, cast in darkness, toys come alive, intruders secretly enter, and daydreams replay as nightmares. We might remember that, in the original *Peter Pan* at the Duke of York's Theatre in the Christmas season of 1904, the father of those Darling Edwardian children, Wendy and the rest, doubled as Captain Hook.[21]

Noble never seriously considers this dark territory, to explore what he only coyly flirts with in his *Dream*, the existentially terrifying hypothesis put to Alice in Looking-Glass Land that she's not the dreamer but the dreamed, that she's the Red King's fiction. He never opens up his core reference book, Rackham, to see how scarily grotesque fairyland is in the version his Boy has been reading: Rackham's Leviathan is clearly a boy-eater. Worse, considering the stories a child in 1990s multi-racial Britain might be found to tell, Noble doesn't notice that Shakespeare's *Dream*, like *Titus Andronicus* and *Antony and Cleopatra*, is also about imperial contest and the *translatio imperii*, the gradual westward shift of empire's power base.[22] The *Dream*, from Athens, looks toward the exotic, luxurious East, with its spiced air, wanton wind, yellow sands, from whence the 'lovely' changeling boy has been 'stol'n from an Indian king' – as Puck tells it – or bequeathed to the Fairy Queen as an act of devotion by the mortal mother, her 'vot'ress' – according to Titania (2.1.22, 123). But Athens looks in the opposite direction, too, toward the chaste, cold and continent West where the unseduce-able 'fair vestal', another Fairy Queen and 'imperial votress', is 'thronèd'. Like *Titus* and *Antony*, those other imperial, geographic narratives, this one is aligned along a racial axis, which Rackham certainly saw: in his illustration, the changeling child is black.[23]

Noble tidies up the nursery, nanny-like won't permit his boy to tell difficult cultural stories, or his

toys to embody, as Lois Kuznets says toys do, 'the secrets of the night' in a 'secret, sexual, sensual world' 'behind the doors of dollhouses' – or 'parents' bedrooms'.[24] The carnality Noble's stage *Dream* performed – Bottom grossly bonking Titania in a pink umbrella, a tired, Viagra-generation travesty of the Peter Brook original – was retained for the film, but this explicit adult sex practice was something no child would dream up: it exceeds the universe, the experience of the child. So, discovering there were things in his *Dream* that couldn't be made to fit the Boy's dreaming, Noble funked it: the film cuts so the child never sees what the adults get up to.

The effect is to infantilize *A Midsummer Night's Dream*, a story dreamed by a child, 'about' a child, and therefore, perhaps, for children, Noble producing a reactionary reading that, while appropriating what Brook learned from Jan Kott

---

21 Offering detailed readings of *Alice in Wonderland* and *Peter Pan* in *Child-Loving: The Erotic Child and Victorian Culture* (London, 1992), James R. Kincaid suggests that those – like Noble? – 'who imagine that the child . . . offers nostalgic "escapism", soft regression, "ease and repose from the troubles of the day", something "safe and simple", seem to have looked past the formulations of erotic Otherness in these complex images'. He sees these stories as 'dramas of perpetuation, plays of the elusive maneuverability of the child'; both stories 'are supremely indifferent to the adult's feelings and desires'; both 'are never going to let themselves down to give the adult what he wants'. Ultimately, Kincaid concludes, these are 'crisis stories' where the 'crisis' is the betrayal the child commits upon childhood by growing up (pp. 275–8). Nina Boucicault, Dion's daughter, was the original Peter Pan on stage. Cross-casting a girl to play the part of the 'cock sure' boy who refuses to grow up initiated a long theatre tradition that offered spectators Peter as a permanently, if teasingly, pre-sexual androgyne. Something of the same tease is on offer in Noble's casting of his androgynous *Dream* Boy, and is built into the story Noble directs the Boy's body (desired in this film by male and female alike) to display, only it is made 'safe and simple' by reneging on desire's abusive power. Any gesture made in this direction instantly has the punch pulled.

22 Jonathan Bate discusses this theory of 'the translation of empire' (yet another 'translation' story embedded in the *Dream*) in his Arden edition of *Titus Andronicus* (London, 1995), p. 17.

23 See the illustration facing p. 24 in the 1908 edition.

24 Lois Kuznets, *When Toys Come Alive: Narratives of Animation, Metamorphosis, and Development* (New Haven, 1994), p. 2.

and Polish theatre of the 1960s about the erotic politics inscribed in Shakespeare's adult-viewing *Dream*, first degrades then cancels that knowledge, reinstating this as the Shakespeare play that's family entertainment. And that's a genre definitively remembered in Tyrone Guthrie's 1937 Old Vic production – which put a toy theatre on stage along with the entire Sadlers Wells ballet, and, in the audience, looking like a child, the eleven-year old Princess Elizabeth and her little sister, Margaret.[25] What we see finally is Noble using the child to play out his own longing for an absent, 'never never', fantasy childhood, distorting the image of the dreaming child into an illusion that fulfils the 'wish images' of his adult nostalgia[26] – among them, surely, the fact that the Boy, a mute throughout, behaves like a well-brought-up child from the past, seen but not heard. At the level of film representation, the Boy works like an extended reaction shot, his face permanently radiant, looking like wonder. The toys in his nursery, like the objects Walter Benjamin saw in the Paris arcades of the 1850s, function as 'dream-images of the collective', objects the camera translates into so many 'commodity fetishes', dreams themselves produced as commodities – and childhood as the ultimate adult commodity fetish.[27]

Writing about what he calls 'nostalgia films' – which 'gratify . . . a desire to return' to an 'older period and to live its strange old aesthetic artefacts through once again' – Fredric Jameson diagnoses in them an inability 'today to focus our own present', as though we were 'incapable of achieving aesthetic representations of our own current experience', seeing this as a 'pathological symptom of a society that has become incapable of dealing with time and history', one 'condemned to seek the historical past through our own pop images and stereotypes about the past, which itself remains forever out of reach'.[28] Noble, re-living the *Dream* both through the 'old aesthetic artefacts' of Peter Brook and Arthur Rackham, proves incapable of imagining a *Dream* to 'focus our own present'. The sleeping child that we spectators access through the window in the film's opening sequence is finally disturbingly significant – 'looking like a child' gives

us a child with eyes wide shut, and the intertext we recognize most powerfully at this voyeuristic moment is not Barrie's *Peter Pan* but Hitchcock's *Psycho*.[29]

Four years later, in another debut film made from a stage production, Taymor's *Titus* picks up where Noble's *Dream* begins – and ends: in a nursery (of sorts), among toys, with a child, offered as a trophy of culture and representation. But this child isn't sleeping. He's looking straight at us.[30] Only, to begin with, we don't know it. For in the film's

<hr>

25 I owe this citation to Tony Howard.

26 Evers, 'Shakespeare's Later Collaborators', p. 7.

27 I am drawing upon the work of Rachel O. Moore in *Savage Theory: Cinema as Modern Magic* (Durham, 2000). Citing Benjamin's 'Arcades Project', his meditations upon 'collections of recently out-of-date objects displayed in the glass cases of the Paris arcades', she observes with Susan Buck-Morss that those objects served both as 'distorting illusion and redeemable wish-image'. Further, 'If commodities had first promised to fulfil human desires, now they created them: dreams themselves became commodities' (Moore, *Savage Theory*, pp. 76, 70).

28 Fredric Jameson, 'Postmodernism and Consumer Society' in *The Cultural Turn: Selected Writings on the Postmodern, 1983–1998* (London, 1998), pp. 8, 9, 10.

29 That Noble now mostly directs shows for children – *The Lion, the Witch and the Wardrobe* (1998), *The Secret Garden* (2000), *Chitty Chitty Bang Bang* (2002) – might be read as a career dissolving into soft focus. But he used to have a hard edge. In *Macbeth* (1988) at the RSC he used children to terrifying effect, locating in the contamination of their innocence a felt analogue to the evil circulating in the text: Macduff's flaxen-haired children, in white Victorian nightgowns, doubled as the witches' prophecies, playing a game of blind man's buff with blindfolded Macbeth and laughing through their utterance as they dodged his groping hands. In *The Winter's Tale* (1992), he staged the opening scene as Mamillius's birthday party, the little lone boy moving apart from the adults, who, captured inside a scrim box in a world of their own, in slow motion drank champagne amongst the red balloons, ignoring him as he knelt, concentrating on play, spinning a top that, turning and turning as the grown-ups talked, began to feel like Clotho's.

30 The Boy was part of Taymor's original concept both on stage and film. Seeing *Titus* as 'the greatest dissertation on violence ever written', its themes 'war, ritual, the domestic, lust, nihilism', she fixed on 'the idea of the child watching his family go at it, watching these bloodlines, these tribes, these religious rites, this whole event' as establishing the film's point

opening sequence, the camera is too close to the object that fills the frame for us to know what we're looking at, the shot dissolving from a black screen to pin-pricks of light that resolve into eyes, disconcertingly looking not out of a face but rough torn holes (see sequence 1).

As the camera pulls back and we get our bearings we find ourselves in an American kitchen, circa 1959, at a table covered with toys and after-school food, and see that we're looking at a child who's wearing over his head the kind of brown paper bag mask all of us of that vintage (which is also Taymor's) made for Halloween — a play mask that tropes masks military and theatrical, a mask, significantly, like the Greek mask, that keeps its eyes open, is unable to turn its gaze away from what appals. The lone masked 'man' at the kitchen table, it turns out, is watching another masked man — on television. The flickers of light from the screen he's watching bounce off the paper surface; he raises a hotdog to his teeth through the torn mouth-hole as we hear 'Heigh-ho Silver!' and know that, off camera, the Lone Ranger, ushered by the tooting military bugle that announces the 'good guy', is spurring his white horse, riding in with the cavalry to save the day — that most enduring trope of American history's nostalgic self-definition. But this 'toys' picnic' mobilizes other 'days' of masculine adventure and their killing technologies, simultaneously remembering an ancient world of violence and heroism while, in the post-Hiroshima Cold War era cited here, futuristically anticipating more apocalyptic ways to die: there's a platoonful of GI Joes on the table crowding out the cake, half-drunk glass of milk, mustard and ketchup bottles. There are WWII dinky toys and battery-powered action men in motion — but also gladiators and sci-fi robots. This adult-free zone shows the continuity between consumption, violence and play, and the tendency — almost a law of physics — for all of them, in performance, to exceed their texts, their rules, to go beyond. So this space transforms before our eyes into a kitchen-sink-sized impromptu theatre of cruelty as the child's play with his war toys grows violent, accelerating into frenzy. The Boy lops the head off a robot, slams the fighter plane

nose down into the cake, trashes the table, smearing it with ketchup: food becomes blood; bodies are dug into like Victoria sponge; culture gets symbolically dismembered as mayhem produces pleasure and jokey subject positions. The mechanical head on a wrecked toy whizzes around crazily 360°. This is play!

Suddenly, the Boy, twisting in pain, clutches his hands to his head as if trying to protect his ears inside the paper bag. His knees buckle. Leaping down from the chair he doubles up under the table as the kitchen window blows in, under the force of a huge explosion. From smoke and falling debris, the camera cuts to the child being pulled out from hiding by a huge man — burly, stubble-faced, he's a bizarre visual throw-back to another age, in a grubby singlet, a prize fighter's belt over leather trousers and Godot boots, a WWI fighter pilot's leather helmet on his head, the goggles up. The strongman yanks the paper mask off the Boy's head, then, cradling the sobbing child in his arms, carries him down the burning stairs (Taymor's take on Alice's rabbit hole), kicks open the front door — and steps into the past, a past absurdly animated by the boy's own violent play. In a gigantic theatre of cruelty, a Roman colosseum, the Boy is lifted up as a prize over the strongman's head, the ancient ghosts roaring approval from the dark empty tiers. Once massive, controlling the toy world, the boy is now miniaturized, the world's toy. Set on his feet, looking down, he's stunned to see one of his toys poking out of the wreckage. If this gladiator that he retrieves from the mud is a kind of psychic souvenir, it's also a monstrous prompt: the child's head swivels; the camera cuts; the gladiator *has come alive*, his mud-caked face like a mask. Behind him dozens of gladiators, exact copies of each other, are marching toward the Boy like wind-up toys in clock-work precision, the antique world descending implacably upon him.

---

of view: 'the arc of the story is the child's' and the story is 'brought to life by the boy's vision'. (Quoted from Taymor's director's commentary, *Titus* DVD, Clear Blue Sky Productions, 2000.)

1   Sequence 1: *Titus*, opening shots, directed by Julie Taymor.

1 Sequence 1: (*cont.*)

As this epic sequence proceeds – and it goes on for another three minutes – we see pairs of Roman chariots pulled by horses; warriors in authentic helmets and spears from Roman antiquity; but then, bizarrely, a squadron mounted on 1930s motorbikes followed by a company of primitive armoured personnel carriers that look like monstrous plated insects or the tin-pot tanks that patrolled Dublin at the Easter Uprising. The war treasure is ancient stuff – gold breastplates, armour, masks, chokers, chains – but it's piled into a plexi-glass coffer, which in turn is mounted on a motor-drawn cart. Seeing as the child sees – and edits keep cutting back to the child looking – we understand what he shortly discovers, that he's Titus's grand-son, Lucius, and that the past that has captured him involves not a simple time shift between 'now' and 'then'. Rather, the past is 'then', 'now', and everything in between, a temporal palimpsest that displays itself everywhere this film looks, showing the ancient world – its buildings, its monuments, its statues, its civil habits and personal protocols, its style and aesthetics – surviving in our own. This past is not 'a foreign country' where they 'do things differently';[31] it's the ground we're occupying. The primitive is the material constructing both modernism and post-modernism. With brilliant film aptitude, Taymor achieves on film using post-modern pastiche (in a later sequence, for example, when she brings Rome's factions and their ideologies into confrontation, she puts Titus on horseback, the fascistic Saturninus in a black Mussolini car, and his 'straight', clean-cut brother in a white 1950s convertible) what young Will Shakespeare achieves in his playtext using early modern pastiche. He collapses (as Jonathan Bate wonderfully observes) 'the whole of Roman history, known to him from Plutarch and Livy, into a single action',[32] making Troy, the Tarquins, Caesar and the Goths all simultaneously available to the story. As importantly, by transporting the modern child into the historic narrative Taymor mobilizes for the purposes of that narrative contemporary analyses of that history. What is the relationship between culture and violence, she asks; between subject peoples and their conquerors, the colonized and the imperialist? When does cultural practice become oxymoronic – 'irreligious piety' – redundant, require us to seek new forms? What are we doing to the children? And what are the children doing to *us*?

It's only retrospectively that we'll be able really to decipher this opening, and see the toys as more than transitional objects for ethical growth, as prostheses used, like theatre props, to 'simulate a rehearsal for real roles'.[33] We'll understand them as proleptic, cuing the film's worst – and best – moments, the child here literalizing aesthetically, in play form, the violent actions that will be repeated over and over 'for real'. So his black, comic delight as he decapitates his robot prefigures Aaron's

pleasure, presiding over Titus's joke dismemberment, and Chiron, preparing for rape, straddling Lavinia's terror-frozen torso, slicing off all the buttons down the back of her dress – Taymor's Rome, we'll see, is littered with body parts, hands, feet, arms fallen off monumental statuary. As toys become life-sized play-things so Lavinia is the 'doll' Tamora's ugly boys make their game, transforming her from Grace Kelly to Struwwelpeter, her bloody stumps turned into macabre travesties of toys, stuck with dry sticks, as surreal prosthetics.[34]

Retrospectively, too, we'll appreciate the full implication of the biggest change Taymor makes to Shakespeare's opening, starting not with politics – the election of the emperor – but with play, the play of violence, violence as play – play politicized. It is the Clown who rescues (kidnaps?) the boy. He is the strongman Zampano, straight out of Fellini's *La Strada*, and the boy is going to be meeting up with him again. The unmasking in the exploded kitchen is significant. For spectators in the know, there's the intertextual joke – the unmasked boy is the very changeling child from Noble's *Dream*, Osheen Jones. More crucially, the wordless look they exchange face to face recognizes, claims a continuity between projects, the Boy's, the Clown's, that it will take the rest of the film to decipher. Taymor sees the Clown as 'an interventionist in Shakespeare'.[35] Aligning the look

---

[31] I am, of course, quoting the famous opening of L. P. Hartley's *The Go-Between*.

[32] Bate, *Titus*, p. 17.

[33] Fleming, *Powerplay*, p. 8.

[34] Grace Kelly was Taymor's model for Lavinia; stylistically, she was looking for 'defamed, deflowered elegance' – like 'graffiti scrawled on ancient monuments' (Clear Blue Sky DVD).

[35] Taymor recognizes her debt to the Fellini not of *Satyricon* – though that's the film her wedding and orgy sequences in *Titus* call to mind – but *Amarcord*: 'I'm a caricaturist, and so was Fellini, and . . . I share Fellini's love of the human face as well as his interest in puppets, clowns, the carnival and the theatre' (Clear Blue Sky DVD). The film was shot at Fellini's old studio in Rome, Cinecittà, and, in a Felliniesque move, Taymor used one of his 'real' scenic artists to play the restorer in the workshop scene.

of this film with the look of the child she immediately complicates that alignment, attaching the Boy's look – which is going to be fixed on the Roman elite; he is, after all, one of the Andronici – to the look of the low art, plebeian Clown. This carnivalized look is the point of view Titus will finally achieve as the Clown's bizarre double much later on.

Titus's triumphal re-entry into Rome initiates the Boy into the rituals of death and blood. Young Lucius helps his grandfather heat the instruments of sacrifice; observes his father return with the basin full of Alarbus's entrails; follows as the long row of empty combat boots, what remains of Titus's dead sons, is poured, like libation, with sand. He's initiated, too, into politics. Sitting alone on the steps of Mussolini's old government building, the 'square colosseum' that will be Saturninus's headquarters, the Boy catches a stray newspaper blowing past, reads the headline, 'Death of Caesar', hears loudspeakers, and runs to join the political rally that's converging like rival football teams, later standing among the Andronici as Titus declines the election. Curious, active, keen, the kid has untroubled eyes. Until Titus kills his uncle Mutius. Then, for the first time, young Lucius turns away, can't look at his grandfather.

Earlier, I suggested that in Shakespeare's *Titus* Lavinia, after the rape, is the child who teaches Titus to look – and that's certainly how Taymor directs Anthony Hopkins and Laura Fraser. Old knowledges wiped, traumatically illiterate, Hopkins's Titus is a grizzled child, poring over Lavinia like a hard primer, trying to work out its strange letters. But Taymor also aligns Lavinia's look with the look of young Lucius, almost morphing their faces into one another – as in the sequence she elaborates out of materials from Shakespeare's 3.1 that dissolves from the family weeping at the crossroads to a face staring from a window through rain. Titus has been kneeling in the black stone-paved road, writing his sorrows in the dust, ignored by the parade of Romans and tribunes who pass him by, transporting his sons to execution for the murder of Bassianus. A long-shot sees Titus prostrate, desolate, tiny against the black pavement where four roads converge. Finally looking up from his grief, past his son, Lucius, Titus sees Marcus approaching the crossroad. He's carrying Lavinia in his arms. When her mutilation is revealed Titus says to the daughter whose face is smeared with blood, 'let me kiss thy lips' (3.1.120). But she flees his love, his touch, retreating, as if ashamed, to kneel over a pool of rain in the road, looking at her wrecked self in the water mirror. Titus follows, kneels and looks alongside her, Marcus and Lucius coming in behind, the family huddling in sorrow. The film cuts, sees their reflections in the puddle, watches as raindrops, starting to fall, break up the image, dismembering it, blurring the vision like tears in the eyes. A dissolve gives a close-up on a face. It's seen through glass, through rain running down the window pane. We think it's Lavinia – until we notice, pressed up against the glass, a hand. Then we recognize through the distorted optics the beautiful face as the Boy's. Appallingly, the moment this connection is made, suggesting that her history will be experienced also through his eyes, another is made: a series of shot/reverse shots shows the Boy looking down at what he can't yet recognize, can't yet interpret, 'black' Aaron, under a black umbrella, arriving through the storm at Titus's door where the master's not at home, turning away, then looking up, seeing the child in the window, exchanging looks that follow the child's gaze as it turns to see Lavinia brought home by his grandfather in his father's arms. Contaminating the Boy's look with Aaron's, making him unwittingly collude with the next step in the project – for Aaron has come for Titus's hand – makes this sequence almost the ugliest in Taymor's film.

After this, in a series of extraordinary moves, Taymor begins to use the look of the child to map an alternative visual education on Titus – and *Titus* (see sequence 2). Watching his grandfather utter 'sorrows deep . . . passions bottomless', a 'deluge overflowed and drowned' that covers his wait for Quintus and Martius' release – redeemed by the hand Titus has willingly urged Aaron to chop off and present to the emperor as ransom

2   Sequence 2: *Titus*, directed by Julie Taymor.

2   Sequence 2: (*cont.*)

17

(in this version, transported hygienically in a plastic zip-lock food bag) – the Boy hears something (3.1.215–16, 228). The sound of his grandfather's mighty despair is penetrated, incongruously, by the sound of the circus. Running through the courtyard the Boy flings open the gates of the villa, sees careering wildly down the road in a fog of exhaust fumes a three-wheeled 'apé' – like Zampano's in *La Strada*, an on-the-skids Mussolini-vintage delivery vehicle, its battered corrugated iron box perched on the back axle. Out of the cab climbs the Clown, carrying a loudspeaker, inviting in guttural Italian, 'roll up, roll up', as he moves disjointedly, like Charlie Chaplin, played out of synch, to the sound of the bizarre music (that could be the soundtrack to Fellini's *8 1/2*). Recognizing the Clown from the kitchen rescue brings a smile to the kid's face. He keeps smiling as the showman's assistant – a red-haired girl, like Giulietta Masina's strangely old and infantile Gelsomina – sets out stools and dances an invitation to the punters. One by one they emerge from the villa – Titus, Marcus, Lavinia, Lucius. It's comic. It's absurd. It's 'popular'. And all the time that cartoon music is playing. Until the Clown takes up a position beside his vehicle, with a sudden heave throwing up the metal shutter-siding to reveal within a scene from a pre-war travelling freak show: in front of draped velvet bunting in glass display jars, the heads of Martius and Quintus staring wide-eyed, and the neatly splayed hand of Titus Andronicus. So the Andronici are required to look at the sick joke made of their grief. The Clown's flat commiseration blares over the loudspeaker: 'Worthy Andronicus, ill art thou repaid / For that good hand thou sent'st the Emperor' (233–4). But if this is a freak show that remembers 'pop goes the weasel' decapitations in the toys' party kitchen at the beginning of the film, it's also a sideshow that prompts the child to think laterally, to go to a place that, bizarrely, looks like what he's looking at. So as one Lucius heads for the Goths and one kind of (violent) repair, the other Lucius goes elsewhere: the film cuts to a door whose glass panes are thick with sawdust, the long display windows on either side filled with a dusty jumble of heads

and hands and wings (see sequence 3). Dimly, over the Boy's shoulder, we see into a workshop, where a bearded man, shirtsleeves rolled up, sits at a battered bench among glue pots and mallets, rubbing sandpaper over wood. The Boy pushes open the door, enters – a room filled with Renaissance body parts, hanging torsos, bodiless heads, a St Sebastian without his arms, devout mannequins, eyes cast heavenwards through haloes, wingless angels, plaster moulds for hands of all sizes and benevolent gestures strung out on a washing line, a work table full of legs and feet, booted, bare, that belong to disciples and penitents, neatly laid out. These delicate, maimed statues in for restoration belong to a Rome that's a far cry from Saturninus's monumental narcissistic brutalism, a Christian Rome whose artist's material is wood, not marble; a Rome that, indebted to a tree shaped into a crucifix, acknowledges salvation through suffering, makes sense of loss through redemption, and conquers death through resurrection, capturing life, miraculously, for a divine comedy. As the camera, its movements underscored by music that could be Monteverdi's, pans across a worktable laid out with row upon row of hands, the Boy, wonderingly, calculating, passes his own hand over them, stops, picks up a hand, holds it close to his face as if measuring it. The film cuts; we see him, silhouetted against a bright sky, running into the dark doorway of the villa, carrying a box tied with string. Finding Lavinia, he puts the parcel on her lap, unties it, opens the lid, to show her, lying in wood shavings, a pair of delicate, open hands. This hauntingly poetic sequence that travels over body parts, redeeming damaged imagery from pain and gruesomeness and restoring mutilation to beauty, remembers the Clown, remembers the freak show heads in jars, remembers back to the film's beginning. But more than that, demonstrating a child's sideways understanding of what is possible, the scene looks like a child, sees in the craftsman a restorer who puts angels back together, a creative artist whose dealings with the dismembered body make it not a horror but a wonder. Giving Lavinia the gift of restoration, giving her toy hands,

Lucius makes her look like a child – but also a work of art.

In the scene that follows (3.2), as the Andronici sit down to dinner and Lavinia tries with comic awkwardness to make her hands work, and Titus, watching her fail, concentrates his looking on her, the Boy once again looks at objects skew-whiff – and thereby achieves the saving perspective (see sequence 4). In Shakespeare, 3.2 is the first of two banquets; in Taymor, we read it as one of a series, all of them replaying the boy's original kitchen spread. At this meal, a sudden loud movement from the Boy meets with Titus's rebuke: 'What dost thou strike at, Lucius, with thy knife?' 'At that that I have killed, my lord – a fly', an answer that unleashes Titus's rage: 'Out on thee, murderer! Thou kill'st my heart'. The child protests, 'Alas, my lord, I have but killed a fly' – only enraging Titus more: '"But"? / How if that fly had a father and a mother?' (3.2.52, 59, 60). Once again young Lucius has an answer, one that turns the scene around. For like Peter Brook on stage in 1955, Taymor has reassigned the fly killing; giving it to Lucius, she makes it a micro-reenactment of his earlier frenzy.[36] But more importantly for her purposes, coming into speech – for the first time, no longer a mute – Lucius constructs speech as play. He turns this dispute with his grandfather into a game: the fly, he tells him, 'was a black ill-favoured fly / *Like to* the Empress' Moor' (3.2.67–8, italics mine). So, framing killing 'as if', he teaches Titus to play. And Titus, instantly picking up the game – crying 'O, O, O!', a gleeful co-conspirator – pulps the fly with hyperbolic fury '*as if it were* the Moor' (68, 72, italics mine). The effect for the whole family is a collapse into laughter, into childness – and for the old man, a release into the serious play to come. And play he does, for the rest of the play, taking over Tamora's revenge play, recasting her players in a new plot. In Shakespeare's playtext, Marcus, the original fly-killer, comments, 'Alas, poor man! Grief has so wrought on him / He takes false shadows for true substances' (78–9). In Taymor we see him rather learning from his grandson to look like a child and play, 'minding true things by what their mockeries

be' (*Henry V*, Chorus 4). Here, the child transforms what adults look like.

For the rest of the film, young Lucius serves Titus as production assistant – or 'best boy', carrying 'toy' weapons wrapped up in schoolboy Latin tags to Chiron and Demetrius in their gothic games room underneath the palace; pulling a child's wagon through Rome's streets, knocking at doors, calling up a 'mafia' that will come to Titus's aid; finally, dressed identically to Titus in a spotless white uniform, standing under-chef at the final dinner party where Titus 'play[s] the cook' and serves up boy-pie to Tamora – a scene that's bizarrely set up by a series of cuts, from the boys-as-presumptive-carcasses, hanging naked from their heels on meat hooks in the villa's nearly dark kitchen abattoir, Titus cutting their throats then, in head shot, calmly wiping the knife on his towelling dressing gown; to a close-up on two steaming, lattice-topped pies cooling in a sunny rustic window, curtains flapping as the Sinatra-style crooner sings 'Vivere' – 'life!' – on the soundtrack; to the mid-shot entry of the guests into the formal gold dining room (5.3.203). Titus and the Boy, a bizarre apparition and a disconcerting double act, come on behind, through a red curtain yanked back, as if going on stage, Titus in his tall cook's hat performing with comic brio, dumping a slab of pie on Tamora's plate with a thud. When they happen, young Lucius is inches away from the killings, the last, performed by his father shoving a long-handled serving spoon down Saturninus's throat then pulling out his revolver. The frame freezes the mayhem – spit is caught mid-air. The sound of the shot fired triggers a zoom back: we see the table and the carnage suddenly relocated, set in long-shot in the centre of the dark Colosseum that was the original site of Titus's triumph. Only now the tiers of stone seats are full; modern faces are looking on, the camera cutting between still images, superimposing spectators' faces onto spectacle. As Marcus

---

[36] In Dessen's *Titus Andronicus*, Daniel Scuro comments that this change makes Marcus a 'nobler' figure (p. 22).

3   Sequence 3: *Titus*, workshop, directed by Julie Taymor.

20

3   Sequence 3: (cont.)

4   Sequence 4: *Titus*, fly killing, directed by Julie Taymor.

4   Sequence 4: (*cont.*)

No mournful bell shall ring her burial;
But throw her forth to beasts and birds to prey.
Her life was beastly and devoid of pity,
And being dead, let birds on her take pity.

(190–9)

Shakespeare's ending to *Titus Andronicus* concentrates on story, memory, and the obligations of survivors to *tell*: Aaron's so un-Iago-like contempt for silence – even as he's 'fastened in the earth' he's railing, ' Ah, why should wrath be mute and fury dumb?' (182–3) – is put against the assignment Lucius gives his son, to 'bear' Titus's 'tales in mind, / And talk of them when he [is] dead' – even if 'tears...choke' his utterance (5.3.164–5, 174). Shakespeare, at the end, reprises Rome's rituals: election, funeral, mourning, taking us back round to the play's beginning, the play's own past, and placing the looking child at the centre of the scene. But Taymor's film doesn't end on Shakespeare's final word.[37] She gives spectators more. Cutting young Lucius's lines remembering Titus, and those remembering his obligation to remember, Taymor severs the child from the past – but locates him on film to mark the present, to register the implications of the sentences his father, now emperor, has just pronounced. In a close-up on the adult Lucius's face, the film hangs on his last word, watches him drop his eyes after 'pity', passes into silence, then hears, off camera, an animal, or maybe an infant crying. The film cuts to the sight of Aaron's baby in the cage. Hands reach into the frame, opening the cage; a close-up on young Lucius's face shows him gazing down at the infant, then registers him, through half-closed eyes, listening to a welter of

steps to the microphone to address the 'sad-faced men, . . . of Rome, / By uproars severed, as a flight of fowl / Scattered by winds', to try to teach them 'how to knit again / This scattered corn into one mutual sheaf, / These broken limbs again into one body', the Clown is shaking out industrial-sized sheets of clear plastic, covering the bodies where they lie, securing the scene for the forensics squad – and laying a lens between us and the corpses that disturbs our focus on them (5.3.66–71). 'Now it is my turn to speak', says Lucius. 'Behold the child' (118). The camera cuts, the Clown is holding up a boy like a trophy over his head – a shot that exactly replays the opening of the film – only this time it's Aaron's baby, exposed to the view in a black metal cage. 'Give sentence on this execrable wretch', a Tribune demands (176). The child? No. The film cuts to Aaron as he's set 'breast-deep in earth': 'There let him stand, and rave, and cry for food', Lucius instructs (5.3.178–9). And threatens: 'If anyone relieves or pities him', for this 'offence he dies' (180–1). Thus, Lucius pronounces the end – an end that is about the end of pity (see sequence 5).

Some loving friends convey the Emperor hence,
And give him burial in his father's grave.
My father and Lavinia shall forthwith
Be closèd in our household's monument.
As for that ravenous tiger, Tamora,
No funeral rite nor man in mourning weed,

---

[37] The 1623 Folio *Titus*, set from Q3, ends four (lame) lines later: 'See Justice done on Aaron, that damn'd Moore / From whom, our heauy happes had their beginning: / Then afterwarde, to Order well the State, / That like Euents, may ne'er it Ruinate'. As Bate explains, these lines made their way into Q3 from Q2, set from a copy of the manuscript from which the bottom of the last page had been torn away, prompting the compositor to invent a replacement for the missing ending. In the Arden edition, Bate follows Q1's ending – and Taymor follows Bate.

5   Sequence 5: *Titus*, closing shots, directed by Julie Taymor.

5 Sequence 5: (*cont.*)

sounds in his head, baby wailing layered upon wailing as if centuries of tears echoing down the ages tracked an aural history of mankind. The crying modulates into a cacophony of sound effects, birds and bells jangling tunelessly, a soundtrack to underscore the pitilessness his father has just imagined for Tamora. Acoustically, it's as though the boy is conducting in his head a counter-textual version of all those memorial rites his father's pitiless future wants denied. And it's this future the child walks away from: lifting Aaron's baby out of the cage and holding him against his chest, he turns his back on the camera, on Rome, on us, starts his long slow-motion exit from the colosseum killing-field, a shot that symmetrically matches the film's opening and reverses it, watching for nearly three minutes as the Boy crosses the arena through an archway into the open where, as the dawn sun breaks over the horizon, the frame freezes.

In Shakespeare's *Titus*, as Bate observes, 'retribution is a matter of human, not divine will'; 'This is a world in which people make their own laws'.[38] What sort of laws, then, will people make at this ending? Does pain improve us? Do we suffer into knowledge, grow 'pregnant to good pity'? The two Luciuses are finally instructive. The child who has explored the uses of play knows on his nerve endings what the modern psychologist has also discovered, that play 'is a systemic mode of meta-communication'; and that, 'as a meta-communicative channel, play has a higher survival value than does ritual'[39] – particularly ritual violence. Taymor at the end scans the face of

---

38 p. 22.
39 Don Handleman, quoted by Cohen, *The Development of Play*, p. 14.

25

young Lucius as intently as Leontes in *The Winter's Tale* searches Mamillius's for the 'childness' that 'cures'. Making us 'look like a child' she offers us – like Titus – an alternative visual education, teaching us to 'listen visually' and transforming – metamorphically – her framing device into her film's mode of production. Requiring her spectators to look at the story through the eyes of the child she translates *Titus* into something *like* comedy, and leaves us with a comedy that, like Shakespeare's, disturbs our looking: for it is finally not the look of the child that we're left with; it's the look of Aaron's baby looking back.

COMEDY AND EPYLLION IN POST-REFORMATION ENGLAND

DYMPNA CALLAGHAN

Two species of comedy particularly disturbed prevailing political and religious mores in Elizabethan England: satire and Ovidian comedy. While the political bite and poisonously bitter aftertaste of satire constituted a pointed assault on the alleged ills of a corrupt society, Ovidian comedy, in contrast, had no agenda. Precisely *because* it eschewed moral and political purposes in favour of eroticism and myth, Ovidian comedy, although it proved more difficult to contain than satire, was as widely condemned.[1] Purged of all moral and political aims, this striking absence of purpose was perfected in the epyllion, rendering it not only a purer form of comedy, but also a supremely and irreducibly literary one. The argument I will prosecute here is that the epyllion of the 1590s – though it has suffered considerable critical neglect and misapprehension – is a complex and supremely important moment in the history of literary comedy.[2]

William Shakespeare was born a year prior to the publication of Arthur Golding's *The XV Bookes of P. Ouidius Naso, entytuled Metamorphosis...* (1565). Shaped by an unprecedented manifestation of English Christianity, Shakespeare's generation went on from an early introduction to Latin authors in the grammar schools to more profound encounters with classical paganism. In what follows, I will examine the absorption and iteration of the Roman poet Ovid in 1590s epyllia that was to be found neither in the decades that preceded it nor in those that were to follow in poetry characterized by a divorce both from didacticism and from immediately political purposes. Marked primarily by its distinctive tone – ebullient, racy, urbane and yet by turns sombre and even tragic – the epyllion's species of literary sensibility is far closer to Ovid's subtle modulations of voice in the Latin original than its precursors. In particular, I will argue that the libidinal energy carried by the comedic aspects of the epyllion renders this poetry more wholly and unapologetically literary in our modern sense, and it is so because of a certain complex but inevitable negotiation with Christianity.[3] My bigger if more tentative claim is that the species of Ovidianism that flowers in the 1590s belongs, conceptually speaking, not only in its substance, but also vitally in its comedic expression to the period's anticipation and, ultimately, its inauguration of a definitively secular modernity.

In a firmly Protestant culture, Ovid, and paganism more generally, still had a vexed relation with

---

[1] Barbara Mowat, 'A Local Habitation and a Name: Shakespeare's Text as Construct', *Style*, 23 (1989) 335–48, makes the compelling case that Shakespeare manipulates his Ovidian sources so that they seem to be based on reality and not on books.

[2] An earlier version of this article appears in Jean E. Howard and Richard Dutton, eds., *A Companion to Shakespeare, Volume IV: The Poems, Problem Comedies, Late Plays* (Oxford, 2003).

[3] See John Velz, 'Shakespeare's Ovid in the Twentieth Century: A Critical Survey', in A. B. Taylor, ed., *Shakespeare's Ovid, The Metamorphoses in the Plays and Poems* (Cambridge, 2000), pp. 181–97. Velz notes: 'Shakespeare wrote syncretically, melding Ovidian material with analogous Christian material' (187).

orthodox religion. While to modern readers it seems that nothing could be further from religious controversy than racy Ovidian verse, in early modern terms it is in fact charged with the ideological force of post-Reformation polemic.[4] Ovidian myth in the English Renaissance serves precisely as *mystères littéraires*, that is, the transfer of specifically religious rites into an emerging secular-aesthetic created by a series of shifts and displacements in social but especially religious practice. 1590s' Ovidianism demonstrates how the pagan past permits a new and specifically literary orientation towards religious discourse, ideology and practice. This is what C. S. Lewis described as 'an extension of religion, a rival of religion, and escape from religion'.[5] However, erotic Ovidian English Renaissance poems demonstrate not so much the survival of an earlier popular piety, whether pagan or Catholic, as its rearrangement and transmutation into new and ultimately secular forms.

The most notable if short-lived of these forms is the epyllion, the genre of the little epic, the erotic narrative poem, at its zenith in the 1590s. Ovid's *Metamorphoses* is itself structured as a series of epyllia, and the acme of this Ovidian tone and style is to be found in the finest epyllia of the era, Shakespeare's *Venus and Adonis* and Marlowe's *Hero and Leander*, but while the latter takes its plot primarily from the Alexandrian Greek poet Musaeus, Shakespeare's poem is Ovidian in all of its dimensions. Totally unlike its predecessors in eschewing didacticism, this new, more aesthetic and pagan conception of Ovid represents a breach with orthodox allegorical Christian interpretation of classical authors.[6] Crucially, the epyllion uses comedy as the medium through which potentially or previously sacred and moral elements are absorbed and processed into an irreducibly literary secularism. I refer here to comedy in its cosmic sense—as that which encompasses entire cycles of human existence and non-existence, not just the facts of particular lives that tend to be the purview of tragedy. And tragedy cannot help itself from having a moral purpose, or at least refrain from provoking moral reflection. From this point of view, the epyllion is not tragi-comic at all, it is, simply and very purely, comedic.

In assessing how 'the new paganism and the new secularism which accompanied the rediscovery of ancient works of literature and art'[7] came about we would do well to begin with Ovid himself. It is not too far-fetched to say that the culture of the English Renaissance began when he was born Publius Ovidius Naso in 45 BC. Ovid celebrated sex, married three times, and wrote the world's first, and surely the most eloquent, handbook on how to engage in sexual (especially adulterous) liaisons. Ovid's own society found him at least as troubling as post-Reformation England. The Emperor Augustus exiled Ovid from Rome in 8 BC to the desolate and cold region of Tomis where he died in AD 17 or 18. Ovid's 'offence' was undoubtedly to write the *Ars Amatoria*, and possibly, though less certainly, a romantic liaison with Julia, the Emperor's granddaughter, (believed in the Renaissance to be the Emperor's daughter),

---

[4] On the complexities of post-Reformation religious practice and culture see the following studies, which together pretty much cover the spectrum of historians' opinions on this topic: Eamon Duffy, *The Stripping of the Altars: Traditional Religion in England 1400–1580* (New Haven, 1992); Patrick Collinson, *The Religion of Protestants: The Church in English Society, 1559–1625* (Oxford, 1982); Peter Lake, 'Religious Identities in Shakespeare's England', in David Scott Kastan, ed., *A Companion to Shakespeare* (Oxford, 1999); Christopher Haigh, ed., *The English Reformation Revised* (Cambridge, 1996); Norman Jones, *The English Reformation: Religion and Cultural Adaptation* (Oxford, 2002); David Cressy, *Bonfires and Bells: National Memory and the Protestant Calendar in Elizabethan and Stuart England* (Berkeley, 1989).

On the assimilation of Ovid into English culture from the Middle Ages to the Renaissance, see the collection edited by Charles Martindale, *Ovid Renewed: Ovidian Influences on Literature and Art from the Middle Ages to the Twentieth Century* (Cambridge, 1988). Raphael Lyne, *Ovid's Changing Worlds: English Metamorphoses, 1567–1632* (Oxford, 2001) notes the importance of religious controversy in Golding's translation: 'Religion is a natural location for the kind of cultural mixing which is so evident in Golding's style' (69).

[5] Quoted in Maurice Evans, *English Poetry in the Sixteenth Century* (London, 1955), p. 11.

[6] William Keach, *Elizabethan Erotic Narratives* (New Brunswick, NJ, 1977), p. 33; Douglas Bush, *Mythology and the Renaissance Tradition in English Poetry* (NY, 1957), p. 72.

[7] Lily B. Campbell, *Divine Poetry and Drama in Sixteenth-Century England* (Cambridge, 1959), p. vii.

an affair famously represented on the English stage by Ben Jonson in *Poetaster*.[8] Ovid's verse narratives, whose protagonists not infrequently engage in bizarre acts of sexual perversion and turn into animals or trees and plants, were themselves metamorphosed into an often dour form of Christian didacticism. The urbane poet himself was turned into 'a ruddy country gentleman with tremendous gusto, a sharp eye on the life around him, an ear for racy speech, and a gift for energetic doggerel'.[9] Probably because the *Metamorphoses* posed an implicit challenge to Christian notions such as resurrection and redemption, translations of Ovid offer moralizing allegorical, didactic and bizarre interpretations. From this distortion it was only a short step to outright attack, though the assault on Ovid took place in the context of a more comprehensive 'war against poetry'.

> I would not wish the simple sort offended for too
> bee,
> When in this booke the heathen names of feynèd
> Godds they see.
> Which causèd them the name of Godds o[w]n
> creatures too bestowe.
> For nature beeing once corrupt and knowledge
> blynded quyght
> By *Adams* fall, those little seedes and sparkes of
> heavenly lyght
> That did as yit remayne in man, endevering foorth
> to burst
> And wanting grace and powre too growe too that
> they were at furst,
> Too superstition did decline: and drave the fearefull
> mynd,
> Strange woorshippes of the living God in creatures
> for too fynd.
>
> (Golding, 'Preface', pp. 1–10)

Ovid was Golding's last printed translation of pagan imaginative literature,[10] and the fact that he translated seven works of Calvin, the first exactly contemporary with Ovid, is something of a puzzle even though it also explains Golding's anxiety to offer Christian rationales and explanations of the mythological original.[11] However, Gordon Braden suggests 'it is more useful to take the situation as a way of defining a certain historical moment, both

in Golding's own life and in the course of English culture . . . Certainly, ca. 1567 Elizabethan society showed only early signs of its later [Protestant] cleavage, and one could hold together honorably possibilities that in time would insist on a choice'.[12]

No one could accuse Golding of undue fidelity to the original, and his prefatorial remarks smack of defensiveness, but not without cause. For while Protestantism was indeed established in England as the state religion, its precise direction had not yet been determined, made plain by the fact that the Thirty-Nine Articles of the Church of England defining Anglicanism as the state religion did not become law until 1571, six years after the English *Metamorphoses* was published. Nor was Golding at the end of this line of moral allegorical interpretation, which continued on into the seventeenth century with George Sandys's seventeenth-century translation in *Ovids Metamorphosis Englished, Mythologiz'd, and Represented in Figures* published in 1632.[13]

Yet, for all that he might have troubled Christian sensibilities, Ovid was ubiquitous.[14] What Golding signally represents is that most Ovid in the English Renaissance is so profoundly – there is no other

---

8 See Frederick Samuel Boas, *Ovid and the Elizabethans* (London, 1947), p. 2; John C. Thibault, *The Mystery of Ovid's Exile* (Berkeley, 1964), pp. 20–32.

9 Nims quoted in Gordon Braden, *The Classics and English Renaissance Poetry* (New Haven, 1978), p. 2.

10 Braden, *The Classics and English Renaissance Poetry*, p. 12. For an important recent collection on Ovid in England, see Taylor, *Shakespeare's Ovid*, esp. pp. 1–10; 15–30.

11 Braden, *The Classics and English Renaissance Poetry*, p. 8.

12 Braden, *The Classics and English Renaissance Poetry*, p. 9.

13 Raphael Lyne, 'Ovid in English Translation', in Philip Hardie, ed. *The Cambridge Companion to Ovid* (Cambridge, 2002), pp. 249–63.

14 The widespread fascination with Ovid included Thomas Howell's *The Fable of Ovid tretting of Narcissus, translated out of Latin into English meter, with a moral thereunto, very pleasaunte to rede* (1560), Thomas Peend's *The Pleasant fable of Hermaphroditus and Salmacis* from Book IV of the *Metamorphoses* (1565), William Hubbard's *The Tragicall and lamentable historie of Ceyx, Kynge of Trachine and Alcoine his wife* (1569) (Book XI), and Thomas Underdown's *Invective against Ibis* (1569). See Boas, *Ovid and the Elizabethans*, p. 4.

word for it – unOvidian, so gutted of its comically voluptuous pagan and libidinal impulses and energies as to be alien to its origins. In this Golding resembles poets like Drayton whose *England's Heroicall Epistles* (1597) were taken from Ovid's *Heroides*, and Spenser who was heavily indebted to Ovid for the plots and themes of *The Faerie Queene*. Yet the determined ideological projects (Protestant nationalism) of both these poets disqualify them from truly Ovidian status. There was, however, no doubt about the status of Shakespeare's verse as quintessentially Ovidian. Francis Meres's catalogue of English writers in *Palladis Tamia* (1598) famously claimed 'the sweet witty soul of Ovid lives in mellifluous and hony-tonged Shakespeare'.[15] Despite, then, the strenuous endeavours of Protestant translators of the *Metamorphoses* to make Ovid into a pre-Christian moralist, he remained in Latin a challenge if not a threat to Christian mores. Unlike Virgil, famously translated by Henry Howard, Earl of Surrey into English blank verse, which had the respectability of epic poetry, in the right circumstances, Ovid, from the radical Protestant perspective at least, could be dangerous.

In a far more limited way, Ovid was already available to medieval readers. The trajectory of English Renaissance Ovidianism runs from Chaucer's debt to Ovid in *The Legend of Good Women* and Gower's *Confessio Amantis*, both of which rework the Pyramus and Thisbe story in Book IV of the *Metamorphoses*. Perhaps because of the socially disruptive potential of his verse, even in the wake of an exponential increase in English translations in the sixteenth century, the *Ars Amatoria*, Ovid's cheekily avuncular advice on how to find sex in the city of Rome, was not translated until the next century as Thomas Heywood's *Love's Schoole: PVBLII OVIDII NASONIS DE ARTE AMANDI Or The Art of Love* (1625). Earlier translations, however, may have survived into the Elizabethan era: William Caxton's *Ovyd, Hys Booke of Methamorphose* (1483) and Wynkyn de Worde's *The flores of Ovide de arte amandi with theyr englysshe afore them* (1513). However, the former may never have been printed, and the latter in all likelihood was no more than a schoolbook selection of aphorisms, or purple passages commonly referred to as 'flowers', which probably had the erotic narrative juice emphatically pressed out of them.[16]

Indeed, as 'the consummate model of polished versification and rhetorical ornament' Ovid remained popular as a tool for the teaching of Latin style even though in the sixteenth century concern was expressed among those whose religious and moral sensibilities were offended by the content of the poems.[17] For example, Thomas Elyot believed a schoolboy should read Ovid for the Latin, but that the more scurrilous content should be expurgated:

I would set next unto him two books of Ovid, the one called the *Metamorphoses*, which is as much to say as changing of men onto other figure or form, the other is entitled *De fastis*, where the ceremonies of the gentiles and specially the Romans be expressed – both right necessary for the understanding of other poets. But because there is little other learning in them concerning either virtuous manners or policy, I suppose it were better that, as fables and ceremonies happen to come in a lesson, it were declared abundantly by the master, than in the said two books a long time should be spent and almost lost, which might be better employed on such authors that do minister both eloquence, civil policy and exhortation to virtue.[18]

Notably, the other work by Ovid that Elyot simultaneously recommends and warns against is the *Fasti*, the verse calendar of the religious feast days of the pagan year, which has an inherently and specifically religious theme. Other writers were more circumspect like William Webb who argued that the young should not be exposed to pagan writers

---

[15] On the importance of word play, and the ludic elements of the poem more generally, see Margaret Tudeau-Clayton, 'Stepping Out of Narrative Line: A Bit of Word, and Horse, Play in *Venus and Adonis*', *Shakespeare Survey* 53 (2000), pp. 12–24.

[16] Elizabeth Story Donno, *Elizabethan Minor Epics* (1963), p. 3; Boas, *Ovid and the Elizabethans*, p. 3.

[17] Keach, *Elizabethan Erotic Narratives*, p. 24. For a fully theorized and compelling account of the relation between Ovid and rhetoric, see Lynn Enterline, *The Rhetoric of the Body from Ovid to Shakespeare* (Cambridge, 2000).

[18] Thomas Elyot, *The Governor* in Joanna Martindale, ed., *English Humanism, Wyatt to Cowley* (Dover, NH, 1985), p. 83.

like Ovid and Martial: 'If they be prohibited from the tender and unconstant wits of children and young mindes, I thinke it is not without good reason'.[19] John Stockwood, who preached against reading erotic poems and 'a great part of Ovid' at St Paul's Cross on 10 May 1579, concurred with Webb:

And albeeit I confes that there is in some teachers such a hatred of filthines, that they overpasse such most foule places in the authors: yet who is so ignorant, he knoweth not that the nature of man is to strive most untoo that which it is most fobidden: & that boyes are most desirous too understande that place which they shal perceive their master to have overslipped, herein resembling not unfitly the nature of swine, which delite rather too wallow in the stincking mire, the[n] to ly in the sweet & pleasant grass . . . [Let] *Tibullus, Catullus, Propertius, Gallus, Martialis,* a greate parte of *Ovid,* togethir with al other filthy Poets & comedies be sent again to Rome fro[m] whence they first came . . .[20]

Since learning Latin could be dangerous in itself, some Elizabethans boasted of their ignorance as a sign of Protestant piety. Such anti-intellectualism is upbraided by Thomas Nashe: 'They contemne Arts as unprofitable, contenting themselves with a little Countrey Grammer knowledge, god wote, thanking God with that abscedarie Priest in Lincolnshire, that he never knewe what Romish popish Latine meant'.[21] Yet, even the writing of educated advocates of the reformed religion points out the dangers of literacy and especially Latinity. For example, Thomas Salter claims that Rome's glory rested precisely on its exclusion of allegedly harmful intellectual influences:

I should peradventure be suspected of some for such a one as did the same to the derogation, slander, and reproofe of learnyng, which thing I utterly denie, and yet I can alledge infinite examples to prove my proportion [proposition], as first, Roome the chiefe Citie and seate of the worldy empire, and victorious over all Nationes, I can approve and bryng in authoritie, that it hath been six hundred yeres and more without the knowledge of Letters, and also that from thence all Philosophers by publicke proclamations were exiled, as coruptors of good and vertuous life: Contrariwise, when the studie of Philosophie and Eloquence flourished therein, it loste

libertie, and finallie fell to the servitude and obedience of one man.[22]

While Salter is anxious to avoid the charge that he advocates ignorance, he is also keen to point out that tyranny may be the inevitable consequence of literacy. Salter names Ovid in particular as a danger to the Christian maiden:

But my intent is not, neither was it ever, to attribute suche evill as springeth from the mallice of wicked men, and their corupte nature, to the sacred studie of learnyng, to which I have given up my mynde so much as in me laye all my life tyme. But my purpose is to prove that in a vertuous Virgine, and modest Maiden, such use is more daungerous and hurtfull, then necessarie or praise woorthie . . . who can deny, that, seying of herself she is able to reade and understande the Christian Poetes, too wete, Prudentio, Prospero, Iuuenco, Pawlino, Nazianzeno, and such like, that she will not also reade the Lascivious bookes of Ovide.

Admittedly, Salter is anxious about all pagan verse, including Virgil and Homer, and especially so because of 'the filthie love (if I maie terme it love) of the Goddes themselves, and of their wicked adulteries and abhominable fornications'. Interestingly, there is some evidence (both fictional and actual) that Salter was correct in his assessment of women's reading habits. In Thomas Middleton's *A Mad World My Masters* (1608), a violently jealous husband, Harebrain, confiscates his wife's 'wanton pamphlets' and tries, without much success, to substitute them with a Jesuit tract, *The First Book of the Christian Exercise Pertaining to Resolution,* which he thinks more the appropriate reading matter for women:

HAREBRAIN I have conveyed away all her wanton pamphlets, as *Hero and Leander, Venus and Adonis*; oh, two luscious mary-bone pies for a young married wife.

---

[19] Quoted in Russell Fraser, *The War Against Poetry* (Princeton, 1970), p. 177.
[20] T. W. Baldwin, *William Shakespere's Small Latine & Lesse Greeke,* 2 vols. (Urbana, 1944), vol. 1, pp. 109–10.
[21] Ronald, B. McKerrow, *The Works of Thomas Nashe,* 5 vols. (Oxford, 1958), vol. 1, p. 25.
[22] Thomas Salter, *The Mirrhor of Modestie* (London, 1579) n. pag.

Here, there, prithee take the *Resolution* and read to
her a little.
COURTESAN She's set up her resolution already,
sir.
HAREBRAIN True, true, and this will confirm it
the more. There's a chapter of hell, 'tis good to
read this cold weather. Terrify her, terrify her; go,
read to her the horrible punishments for itching
wantonness . . .

(1.2.44–52)

Harebrain's recommendation of Catholic literature
implies that it is not just Protestant piety that is
an enemy to the Ovidianism which is thought to
tickle the ears of women in early modern London.
On the other hand, in 1619, Lady Anne Clifford
records that her cousin is reading Parsons's *Resolutions by Religion* (1603) and Ovid's *Metamorphoses*,[23] which suggests that these works are not
seen by every reader as mutually exclusive. For all
that, characters on stage who rail against Marlowe
and Shakespeare's epyllia were no doubt parodies
of real life figures, like Philip Stubbes who rails
against 'prophane Scheduls, sacriligious Libels and
Hethnicall pamplets of toyes and bableries, (the Authors whereof may challenge no small reward at the
hands of the devil for inventing the same) to corrupt
mens mindes, pervert good wits, allure to Bawdry,
induce to whoredome, suppresse vertue and erect
vice . . . '[24] While the diatribes against pagan poetry
seem comic to us, as they clearly did to Middleton,
it is important not to underestimate either their frequency or intensity and to understand the uneasy
coexistence (Anne Clifford's cousin not withstand-
ing) of classical paganism with Christianity.

The 'war against poetry' did not, of course originate with the English Renaissance. Plato famously
exiles poets from the Republic, Augustus banished
Ovid, and, though he was executed in 1498, the
Florentine ascetic Savonarola was a vital precursor
of Reformation antipathy to art:

There is a false race of pretended poets, who can do
naught but run after the Greeks and Romans, repeating
their ideas, copying their style and their metre; and even
involving the same deities, almost as though we were
not men as much as they, with reason and religion of our
own. Now this is not only false poetry, but likewise a
most hateful snare to our youth.[25]

Savonarola, like many later English detractors of
poetry, feared that it corrupted the young. His
concerns were not dissimilar to those of Stephen
Gosson in *The Schoole of Abuse* (1579) who saw
poetry as a poison 'which draws the mind from
virtue, and confoundeth wit' (4). Of Ovid's works
Gosson singles out the *Ars Amatoria* and Book x
of the *Metamorphoses*, Shakespeare's source for
Venus and Adonis, specifically the story of Adonis's
mother, Myrrah, who gave birth to him after
copulating with her own father. 'Many good sentences are spoken . . . and written by Poets, as orna-
mentes to beautifye their woorkes, and sette theyr
trumperie too sale without suspect' (2–3). On these
grounds, he commends Augustus's wisdom in ban-
ishing Ovid from Rome (5).

While these diatribes are all too familiar, there is
a new emphasis in Shakespeare's time on the inutil-
ity of verse over and above its lubricity.[26] '[H]onest
plain matter' is far superior to 'Poeticall additions
or faigned Allegories' according to George Wither
whose own didactic doggerel cannot be accused
of being obscured by rhetorical tropes.[27] There is
an urge toward *nuda veritas*, the naked, unadorned
truth, and a belief that such a commodity exists and
is only wilfully evaded or obscured by figurative
representation.[28] Poetry, the moralizers claimed,
obfuscates divine and scriptural truth by means
of visual images which diametrically opposed the
post-reformation iconoclastic impulse. As Ben
Jonson put it, poetry has 'correspondence to no
uses and purpose'.[29] For Gosson, this was not

---

[23] George C. Williamson, *Lady Anne Clifford Countess of Dorset,
Pembroke & Montgomery 1590–1676: Her Life, Letters and Work*
(Kendal, 1922), p. 139; see Joseph B. Collins, *Christian Mys-
ticism in the Elizabethan Age* (Baltimore, 1940), pp. 151–4.
[24] Philip Stubbes, *The Anatomie of Abuses* (London, 1583),
pp. 139–40.
[25] Quoted in Campbell, *Divine Poetry and Drama in Sixteenth-
Century England*, p. 11.
[26] Fraser, *The War Against Poetry*, p. 4.
[27] Fraser, *The War Against Poetry*, p. 17.
[28] Fraser, *The War Against Poetry*, p. 180.
[29] Fraser, *The War Against Poetry*, p. 9.

always so, and he is nostalgic for a time when poetry had a wholesome social function:

The right use of auncient Poetrie was to have the notable explytes of woorthy Captaines, the holesome councels of good fathers, and vertuous lives of predecessors set down in numbers, and sung to the Instrument at solemne feastes, that the sound of one might draw the hearers from kissing the cupp too often, the sense of the other put them in minde of things past, and chaulk out the way to do the like . . .

To this end are instruments used in battaile, not to tickle the eare, but too teach every souldier when to strike and when to strap, when to flye, and when to follow.

(7)

Only the purposeful moral and ameliorative effects of poetry are legitimate, according to Gosson. I am particularly drawn to the notion that poetry stops people getting drunk; 'kissing the cup too often'. Even the privy Council was concerned about poetry and on 21 April 1582, they issued a ban on teaching Ovid in schools:

A letter to the Commissyoners for Causes Ecclesiasticall in London that whereas there hathe bene of late a booke written in Latyn verse by one Christofer Ockland, intituled *Anglororum prelia*, . . . forasmuche as his travell therein with the qualitie of the verse hathe receyved good comendacion, and that the subjecte or matter of the said booke as his is worthie to be read of all men, and especially in the common schooles, where divers heathen poetes are ordinarily read and taught, from the which the youthe of the Realme receyve rather infectyon in manners and educatyon then advauncement in vertue, in place of which poetes their Lordships thincke fitte this booke were read and taught in grammer schooles . . . for the benefitte of the youthe and the removing of such lascivyous poetes as are commonly read and taught in the said grammer schooles, requiring them upon the receipt hereof to write their letters unto all the Busshoppes through the Realme to geve commaundement that in all the gramer and free schooles within their severall Dyoces the said bookes *de Anglorum proeliis* and peaceable government of her Majestie maye be, in place is some of the heathen poetes nowe read among them, as Ovide *de arte amandi, de tristibus*, or suche lyke . . . [30]

Three years later in 1585, the anonymous author of a speech to parliament urged revisions and clarification of a bill to prohibit the printing of 'leud, and yll bookes to be printed hereafter as also for the calling in of such bookes as be already abroad . . . as her Majeste hath doe with her coin not currant'. This writer makes a clear distinction between seditious matter and books that represent what is regarded as perhaps a more insidious form of corruption:

I will not speake of bookes sclanderous [sic] to the state, pernicious in every way, because ther be statutes to lay hold on them, and for that all of the greatest part of such come from beyond the seas and ar not prynted here.

But I mean of unprofitable and idell pamphlettes, leud and wanton discourse of love, prophane ballades, lying historie, which al tend to the corruption of manners and the expense of tyme which otherwise men would bestow in reading the scripture and other good treatiesse of morallitie . . . Is it not strang that Ovid, de arte amandi, is not only sold openly and read in the scholes for which the aughtor was punished by exile by a heathen. [31]

Another version of the bill enlarges on the iniquities of Ovid: '[S]om order might be taken also, for the cellinge in of a multitude of unprofitable, leud and lascivious discorses, by the reading wherof what hinderance hath growne to the church of God, and what an encrease in the corruptions, it is very lamentable to consider, and very strange that it is suffrable in a Christian common wealth. That scholemaster of love Ovid was banished of a heathen emperor for writing that booke and shall the same booke be salable and suffrable to be read openly in scholes, in the tyme of the gospel?'. [32]

Lamenting 'the multitude of bookes, full of all synne and abominations' that 'have nowe filled the world' Edward Dering wished that 'O that there were among us some zealous Ephesians, that bookes of so great vanity might be burned up'. [33] Similarly, one 'F. S'. complains that 'filthy

---

[30] Baldwin, 1.112; L. P. Wilkinson, *Ovid Recalled* (Cambridge, 1955), p. 429.

[31] T. E. Hartley, *Proceedings In the Parliaments of Elizabeth I* (Leicester, 1981) vol. 11, p. 40.

[32] Hartley, *Proceedings In the Parliaments of Elizabeth I*, pp. 41–2.

[33] Edward Dering, *A Brief and Necessary Instruction* (1572) A iv.

and unchast Pamphlets, (whereof the World is too full) are fitter to be burned as corrupters of youth'.[34] Only a year after Frances Meres had made what is, at least from the literary point of view, the laudatory comparison between Shakespeare and Ovid, Christopher Marlowe's translation of Ovid's *Amores* was consigned to the flames on episcopal order on 4 June 1599 at the Stationers' Hall along with a number of other 'prophane . . . sacriligious . . . and Heathenicall' works, precisely along the order of those that Stubbes had complained over ten years before.[35]

Though this was a time of censorship, it was also a moment when a fully urban and urbane poetry with a significant degree of autonomy from court and church was coming into being. Paradoxically, from Douglas Bush onwards, criticism has demonstrated a tendency to regard epyllia, no matter how technically accomplished as 'void verses', empty rhymes. That is, it has viewed these poems from exactly the standpoint of Protestant aesthetics, a trend that has only recently been modified by an interest in the Ovidianism from the perspective of gender studies and a serious interest in 'erotic gallimaufries'.[36] Clark Hulse aptly summarizes the typical description of epyllia as follows: 'By and large the poems of the minor epic genre have no great ethical import and little redeeming social value. They are by turns artificial, frivolous, arcane . . .'[37] Another critic claims, '[N]othing can deepen the significance of the poem, which appeals only to the senses.'[38] Critics have too often accepted the moralistic view of the poetry expounded in the period by its detractors, or at best have claimed, erroneously in my view, that the poems are courtly and Italianate,[39] on which grounds much fault has been found with the homely, rural and allegedly unsophisticated aspects of Shakespeare's poem. 'Shakespeare still had some heavy provincial Warwickshire loam sticking to his boots' as M. C. Bradbrook said of *Venus and Adonis*.[40] Indeed, the poem is *not* courtly. Rather, it is part of a secular amorous literature located among the wits and poets of urban London, many of whom hailed from the provinces rather than the court with its reverence for Petrarchan rhetoric.[41]

Epyllia are indeed 'artificial, frivolous, arcane' but this does not amount to superficiality or lack of intellectual depth, a realization which sharpens when these poems are viewed from the perspective

---

34 Fraser, *The War Against Poetry*, p. 178.

35 This was not however, unlike Savonarola's Bonfire of the Vanities in Florence in 1497, a public incineration, and it resulted largely from concern about satire rather than from a concern with obscenity as such. Edward Arber, ed., *A Transcript of the Registers of the Company of Stationers of London, 1554–1640* (London, 1875), vol. III, p. 677. See also Ian Frederick Moulton, '"Printed Abroad and Uncastrated": Marlowe's *Elegies* with Davies' *Epigrams*', in Paul Whitfield White, ed., *Marlowe, History, and Sexuality: New Critical Essays on Christopher Marlowe* (NY, 1998), pp. 77–90; Lynda Boose, 'The 1599 Bishop's Ban, Elizabethan Pornography, and the Sexualization of the Jacobean Stage', in Richard Burt and John Archer, eds., *Enclosure Acts: Sexuality, Property, and Culture in Early Modern England* (Ithaca: Cornell University Press, 1994), pp. 185–200. The latter essay refutes earlier notions that the burnings of 1599 were essentially an attempt to curb satire. See also Richard A. McCabe, 'Elizabethan Satires and the Bishops' Ban of 1599', *Yearbook of English Studies*, 11 (1981), 188–93.

I am deeply indebted to Peter Blaney for explaining to me the complex details of this book burning.

36 Georgia Brown, 'Breaking the Canon: Marlowe's Challenge to the Literary Status Quo in *Hero and Leander*', in Paul Whitfield White, ed., *Marlowe History and Sexuality*; Goran Stanivukovic, ed., *Ovid and the Renaissance Body* (Toronto, 2001); Enterline, *The Rhetoric of the Body From Ovid to Shakespeare*.

37 Clark Hulse, *Metamorphic Verse: The Elizabethan Minor Epic* (Princeton, NJ, 1981), p. 3.

38 L. P. Wilkinson in Philip C. Kolin, ed., *Venus and Adonis: Critical Essays* (NY, 1997), p. 429.

39 Douglas Bush, 'Venus and Adonis and Mythology', in Kolin, *Venus and Adonis*, p. 97.

40 M. C. Bradbrook, *Shakespeare and the Elizabethan Poets* (Cambridge, 1951), p. 62.

41 The period's utilization of Ovid is not then primarily an issue of the role of Ovidian myth as a plot or motif in Elizabethan poetry, or even of Ovid as an acceptable cover for explicit eroticism. Boika Sokolova, 'Erotic poems' in Michael Hattaway, ed., *A Companion to English Renaissance Literature and Culture* (Oxford, 2000), pp. 392–401, makes the case that the vogue for erotic writing began with Aretino in early sixteenth century Italian literature (393). In contrast, Keach argues: '[T]he alternative to an orthodox "Elizabethan Ovid", an Ovid made safe for the Christian reader, is not necessarily a frivolous, indulgently decorative, decadently "Italianate Ovid"', *Elizabethan Erotic Narratives*, p. 35.

of comedy. Rather these are purely literary, ornamental qualities that comport with the hieratic view of poetry available from the encounter with an Ovid freed from the necessity of reconciliation with Christian values. Writing in 1589, Thomas Nashe, for example, condemns the intellectual energy that has been wasted in reading Ovid as moral allegory by 'Gentlemen well studied in Philosophie' who 'trotted over all the Meteors bredde in the highest Region of the ayre' to reconcile 1 Corinthians 3 with 'Ovids fiction of Phaetons firing of the world'.[42] Instead, Nashe argues:

I account Poetrie, as of a more hidden & divine kind of Philosophy, enwrapped in blinde Fables and darke stories, wherein the principles of more excellent Arts and morrall precepts of manners . . . [and that] the fables of Poets must of necessitie be fraught with wisedome and knowledge.[43]

Similarly it is this quasi-mystical view of poetry that Marlowe espouses in his acknowledgement of his precursor: 'Amorous Leander, beautifull and yoong, / (Whose tragedie divine Musaeus soong)'. Musaeus sang the *tragedy* of the two lovers; but as Nashe points out in *Lenten Stuffe* (1599), it was 'a diviner Muse than he, Kit Marlow who sang their *comedy*'. This connection with mystery, the comedic, and the divine is neither merely the result of the erroneous Renaissance belief that Musaeus was the student of Orpheus, nor the accidental rhetoric of panegyric. There was, after all, classical precedent for the absorption of popular religious rites into the realm of the aesthetic, namely the Eleusinian mysteries, which entailed among other things a spiritual cult of the senses. These were rites of popular initiation, which purged participants from fear of death and admitted them to the company of the blessed. They were bound forever after by a vow of silence, which, given that we know little of these ceremonies, must have been quite effective.[44] However, as Edgar Wind has explained: 'since the sacred rites were administered to a multitude without regard to individual merit, philosophers [were] inclined to look upon them with a certain disdain'.[45] Eventually, as a result, the *mystères cultuels* were replaced by 'a figurative use of the terms and images which were borrowed from

the popular rites but transferred to the intellectual disciplines of philosophical debate and meditation'.[46]

Conventional wisdom has it, then, that the epyllion is troubling *because* it is light and frivolous, insignificant. My argument has been that it is comic in the best and most comprehensive sense. Nashe's interpretation of the value of poetry certainly suggests that there are potentially other 'hidden & divine', though crucially *not allegorical*, meanings within the apparent superficiality of verse. These 'hidden and divine' meanings are what Leonard Barkan has termed the mystical aspects of the metamorphosis, 'the mystery of the divine embedded in the real . . .'[47] While the image of metamorphosis is freighted with the magical, the mysterious, and the divine, it is simultaneously unmoored from any programmatic moral content by 'the sustained complex simultaneity of irony, humor, verbal wit, grotesqueness, and erotic pathos' of Ovidian verse.[48]

It is in its comic pathos in particular that English poetry becomes most definitively Ovidian. It is in this that these poems absorb earlier religious and iconographic impulses in the making of new secular-aesthetic via an erotic pathos that depends upon the comic inversion of typical gender roles, and especially a comically exaggerated emphasis on female power. While this phenomenon deserves a much fuller treatment than I have space to give it here, I want to examine some of its operations in the representation of Venus at the ending of *Venus and Adonis*.

The poem emphasizes female power especially in the form of sexual initiative. These are aspects

[42] Elizabeth Story Donno, 'The Epyllion', p. 75.

[43] McKerrow, vol. 1, *The Works of Thomas Nashe*, pp. 25–6.

[44] Edgar Wind, *Pagan Mysteries in the Renaissance* (London, 1958), p. 14.

[45] Wind, p. 14.

[46] Wind, pp. 14–15.

[47] Leonard Barkan, *The Gods Made Flesh: Metamorphosis and the Pursuit of Paganism* (New Haven, 1986), p. 18.

[48] Keach, *Elizabethan Erotic Narratives*, p. 24. See Barkan, *The Gods Made Flesh*, p. 17.

of pagan goddess cults and Marian piety, both already revitalized in occluded form in the figure of Elizabeth I. Yet, for most of the poem Venus manifests as a figure of comic femininity: Venus *vulgaris*, Venus *genetrix* – the reproductive and quasi-maternal wooer who urges Adonis to the joys of reproduction. Fearing Adonis dead, she is like a 'milch doe whose swelling dugs do ache' (875), sympathetic and maternal yet still carnal and animal. Such images bridge the chasm between Venus in her dolor and the more obviously comic aspects of her characterization.

On the death of Adonis, of course, Venus becomes wholly maternal, and Shakespeare offers a powerful meditation on the image of the sorrowing, lachrymose Venus; the moment when Venus becomes the *Mater Dolorosa* whose epitome and prototype was to be found in the sorrowing Mother of Christ.

> Here overcome, as one full of despair,
> She vailed her eyelids, who like sluices stopped
> The crystal tide that from her two cheeks fair
> In the sweet channel of her bosom dropped.
> > But through the flood-gates breaks the silver rain,
> > And with his strong course opens them again.
>
> O, how her eyes and tears did lend and borrow!
> Her eye seen in the tears, tears in her eye:
> Both crystals, where they viewed each other's sorrow:
> Sorrow, that friendly sighs sought still to dry,
> > But, like a stormy day, now wind, now rain,
> > Sighs dry her cheeks, tears make them wet again.
> > (955–66)
>
> Whereat her tears began to turn their tide,
> Being prisoned in her eye like pearls in glass;
> Yet sometimes falls an orient drop beside,
> Which her cheek melts, as scorning it should pass
> > To wash the foul face of the sluttish ground,
> > Who is but drunken when she seemeth drowned.
> > (979–84)

Because focus on the belly-laugh so much constricts the range of comedy I have in mind, I have deliberately not chosen the obviously 'funny bits' of the poem to make my point.

These are comically un-Petrarchan tears, and they would invariably have evoked for a Renaissance audience the image of our Our Lady of Pity. This was an image that before the destruction of icons in the Reformation was contained in every parish church, and even long afterwards it may have remained well-nigh ubiquitous in many parts of the country. As late as 1644, William Dowsing records destroying pictures and statues, including many images of the Virgin Mary, in St. Peter's church in Sudbury, Suffolk: 'We brake down . . . about an hundred in all . . . and diverse Angels'.[49] At Long Melford in Suffolk

> A fair image of our Blessed Lady having the afflicted body of her dear Son, as he was taken down off the Cross lying along on her lap, the tears as it were running pitifully upon her beautiful cheeks, as it seemed bedewing the said sweet body of her Son, and therefore named the Image of Our Lady of Pity.[50]

Many English people knew some version of the sorrows of Mary, such as those contained in the pre-Tridentine Sarum missal, *Missa Compassionis sive Lamentationis beatae Mariae Virginis.*:

> *Quis est homo qui non fleret*
> > *Matrem Christi si videret*
> > *In tanto supplico?*

[Who is there who would not weep, were he to see the Mother of Christ, in so great anguish?]

As Eamon Duffy observes, 'That question was dramatized in the vernacular in a thousand forms' well into the sixteenth century:

> I said I could not wepe I was so harde hartid:
> Shee answered me with wordys shortly that smarted,
> 'Lo! Nature shall move thee though muse be
> > converted,
> Thyne owne fadder thys nyght is deed!' – lo thus she
> > thwarted –
> > 'So my son is bobbid
> > &of his lif is robbid.

---

49 Tessa Watt, *Cheap Print and Popular Piety 1550–1640* (Cambridge, 1991), p. 173.
50 Quoted in Duffy, *The Stripping of the Altars*, p. 260.

forsooth than I sobbid,
veryifying the words she seid to me
who cannot weep may lern at mee'.[51]

The feast of Our Lady of Pity or Our Lady of Sorrows was celebrated on 15 September recalling the thirteenth Station of the Cross in which the Body of Christ is taken down from the cross. Commemoration of this image was widespread. After the terrible losses sustained in Shrewsbury in 1403 when Hotspur and his army were defeated by Henry IV, for example, Sir Roger Hussey had a chantry chapel built depicting the Blessed Virgin in mourning.

What made this image even more memorable is the *Stabat Mater dolorosa* (the standing sorrowful mother),[52] one of the greatest Latin hymns based upon the prophecy of Simeon that a sword was to pierce the heart of his mother, Mary (Luke 2:35). The hymn originated in the thirteenth century during the peak of Franciscan devotion to the crucified Christ and is attributed to Jacopone da Todi (1230–1306):

At the cross her station keeping,
stood the mournful mother weeping,
close to Jesus to the last.

Stabat Mater dolorosa iuxta crucem lacrimosa
dum pendebat Filius.[53]

In terms of the structure of Shakespeare's epyllion, it is interesting to note that there is a mirror image to this hymn, *Stabat Mater speciosa* (literally '[the] beautiful/splendid mother stood'), which echoes the joy of the Blessed Virgin Mary at the birth of Jesus. There were also images of the Virgin of Humility, suckling the child Jesus that resonate with Shakespeare's Venus as anguished milk doe.

I am not suggesting that in emphasizing its pre-Reformation resonances, we simply recapture *Venus and Adonis* as Christian parody instead of Christian moral allegory applied to Ovid that Shakespeare manages to escape. For Venus's sorrow also remains pagan, partly resembling the

uneasily comic and grotesque anthropomorphism of Io, who is transformed into a heifer, a poor cow lamenting her transformation, in the *Metamorphoses*. Io's is in fact not a complete metamorphosis but the coexistence of two conflicting human and animal identities:[54]

et conata quieri mugitus edidit ore
pertimuitque sonos propriaque exterrita voce est.
venit et ad ripas, ubi ludere saepe solebat,
Inachidas: rictus novaque ut conspexit in unda
Cornua, pertimuit seque exsternata refugit.

(I. 637–41)

and when she did assay
To make complaint, she lowed out, which did her so affray,
That oft she started at the noyse, and would have runne away.
Unto hir father Inachs bankes she also did resorte,
Where many a tyme and oft before she had been want to sporte.
Now when she lookded in the streame and sawe hir horned hed,
She was agast and from hir selfe would all in haste have fled.

(Golding I. 789–95)

The horned head here connotes not only bestial transformation (always comic), but also the virgin goddess Diana crowned by the crescent moon, in other words the vulnerable power of self-contained female sexuality. The sorrowing Venus represents not simply a secularization of literature, but rather a comic transformation of the nature of the sacred that, being purely literary, belongs to the realm of the aesthetic.

By the time George Sandys's *Ovids Metamorphosis Englished*, was published, it was probably as

---

[51] Duffy, p. 260.
[52] *Stabat* is third person singular imperfect, so it is literally, '[the] sorrowful mother stood' or 'the sorrowful mother was standing'.
[53] Trans. Edward Caswall, *Hymns and Poems, Original and Translated (1843)*.
[54] See Keach, *Elizabethan Erotic Narratives*, p. 9.

moralizing as Golding's had been nearly ninety years earlier.[55] The unparalleled literary moment represented by the comedy of the 1590s epyllia had passed.

Even comic poetry was imbued with a certain seriousness by the beginning of the seventeenth century, endowed with the moral purpose of satire, the scourge of villainy that points out the errors of the world. Notably, stage comedy had always been serious, that is, its happy endings fulfilled orthodox moral and social purposes. But now, even Ovidianism tended toward satire – Marston's *The Metamorphosis of Pigmalions Image* (1598) and Beaumont's *Salmacis and Hermaphroditus* (1602) are indicators of 'the new direction in which Ovidian poetry was tending'.[56]

In contrast, *Venus and Adonis* was comically profane by virtue of being irreducibly literary and without purpose. In this, Shakespeare's poem was closer to the Latin meaning of *profanus*, impious, unconsecrated, quotidian – precisely in the realm of comedy.[57]

---

[55] See Deborah Rubin, *Ovid's Metamorphoses Englished: George Sandys as Translator and Mythographer* (NY, 1995), pp. 1–18.

[56] Keach, *Elizabethan Erotic Narratives*, p. 119.

[57] Plautus certainly uses *profanus* in this sense.

(PETER) QUINCE: LOVE POTIONS, CARPENTER'S COIGNS AND ATHENIAN WEDDINGS

PATRICIA PARKER

We are used to telling our students that the name of Peter Quince in *A Midsummer Night's Dream* comes from carpenters' quoins or coigns, 'wedge-shaped blocks used for building purposes', at the 'corners' of houses or walls, appropriate for the carpenter who appears in a 'marriage play' concerned with constructing 'houses' of another kind.[1] But rarely is anything said of the quince itself, though it was part of a rich network of associations with marriage, sexuality, and fruitful 'issue' in the period, as well as of multi-lingual connections and metamorphic spellings that conflated it with coigns, quoyns, sexual corners or coining, and the *cunnus* or 'queynte' its sound suggests.[2]

Minsheu's *Guide unto the Tongues* (1617) situates the English 'Quince' within this suggestive interlingual network:

Quince, a kind of fruit, from French *Coing* . . . Italian *Mela cotogna, pomo cotogno*. Latin *Malum cotoneum, cydonium, Malum canum . . . Malum Lanatum* ['cottony' and 'wooly' apple], because of its wooly or downy covering. Greek *melon kudonion*, from Cydonia (a city in Crete), and *lasiomelon* ('wooly apple'), from *lasios* or *hirsutus* ('hairy' or 'rough with down') and *melon*, or Latin *pomum* ('apple'). Portuguese *Marmelo*. Spanish *Membrillo*, from *membrum*, . . . because of a certain similarity with the first pubic hairs of men and women.[3]

Minsheu's entry makes clear not only the 'cottony', 'wooly' or 'downy' covering that gave the quince its Latin and Italian names but its connection with Crete, home of the Minotaur (offspring of Pasiphae's animal lust) and the labyrinth threaded by Theseus before his abandonment of

Ariadne, all strikingly recalled within *A Midsummer Night's Dream*.[4] The entry simultaneously foregrounds the sexual associations of this downy or

---

1 See *The Riverside Shakespeare*, ed. G. Blakemore Evans, et al. (Boston, 1974), from which citations in this essay are taken, p. 225: 'Quince's name is probably a form of *quoins* or *quines*, wedge-shaped pieces of wood used in carpentry'; Harold F. Brooks's Arden 2 edition (London, 1979), p. 3, on 'Peter Quince' as 'From "quines" or "quoins": wooden wedges used by carpenters'; R. A. Foakes's New Cambridge edition (Cambridge, 1984), p. 57 ('"Quince" suggests quoins, or wedges used in carpentry'); Peter Holland's Oxford World's Classics edition (Oxford and New York, 1994) p. 148 ('Quince from "quines" or "quoins", wooden wedges used by carpenters'); Margreta de Grazia 'Imprints: Shakespeare, Gutenburg and Descartes', in Terence Hawkes, ed., *Alternative Shakespeare*, vol. 2 (London, Routledge, 1996), who notes that '"Peter" Quince finds his way into women's corners or quoins, the metal or wooden shanks used to fill up gaps', in analysing the importance of coining, stamping, the *cuneus* or wedge, and 'the mechanics of the imprint' (p. 82) to the play.

2 Important earlier discussions of some of the traditions surrounding the quince have not been reflected in editorial glossing. See especially the Revd Henry N. Ellacombe, *The Plant-Lore & Garden-Craft of Shakespeare*, 2nd edn (London, 1884), pp. 234–6; Raymond B. Waddington, 'Two Notes Iconographic on *A Midsummer Night's Dream*', *English Language Notes*, 26, no. 1 (September 1988), pp. 12–17; J. Barry Webb, *Shakespeare's Imagery of Plants* (Hastings, E. Sussex, 1991), p. 145. I have discussed some of the multilingual associations in 'The Novelty of Different Tongues: Polyglot Punning in Shakespeare and Others', in François Laroque and Franck Lessay, eds., *Esthétiques de la nouveauté à la Renaissance* (Paris, 2001), pp. 41–58, esp. 53–4.

3 John Minsheu, *Ductor in Linguas* (London, 1617), p. 437.

4 On connections with Crete (including the Minotaur and the 'bottom' or 'clue' given by Ariadne to Theseus), see Anne E. Witte, 'Bottom's Tangled Web: Texts and Textiles in

'hairy' quince in its commentary on *Membrillo* as its Spanish name from Latin *membrum* – a connection Covarrubias had already made in comparing the quince to 'el miembro genital y femineo'.[5] Both Cervantes and Gongora exploited this double-meaning *membrillo*, the latter in verses in the 1590s on '*membrillos*' as 'so many members being eaten' (and on a river as a 'great waterer of quinces'), the former in a story that features the quince as a love potion connected with '*una moresca*' or Moorish woman.[6] But even in English, quince (from French 'coing') had a sexual double meaning, figuring in a late medieval English verse whose 'Mos[s]y Quince, hanging by your stalke' is part of an address to the female pudendum.[7]

As a Cydonian 'apple' as well as a heavily scented fruit of the pear family (used to perfume Roman bed-chambers, according to a frequently cited passage from Pliny), the quince was identified not only with the golden fruit of the Hesperides and the bridal chamber of Hera and Zeus, but with the golden apples of Venus awarded by Paris.[8] Thomas Thomas's Latin Dictionary (1587) cites under '*Malum*' or 'apple' the *Malum Cydonium* or 'quince apple', while Cotgrave notes that 'the Quince hath also beene called, Pomme d'Or', or golden apple, the 'amorous apple' or 'apple of Loue', known as the 'raging, or mad, apple' or '*Pomme d'amours*' because of the madness of Eros or Cupid.[9] Venus herself was 'often represented holding a Quince in her right hand', in place of the more usual golden apple,[10] while the 'apple' thrown to a lover by the lascivious Galathea of Virgil's Third Eclogue (3.64) was identified or combined with the 'quinces' ('pale with tender down') of Eclogue 2 (2.51).[11]

In a period (and a canon) that exploits the sexual suggestiveness of the medlar and other kinds of fruit, the quince evoked in the name of Peter Quince thus joins the sexually suggestive fruit fed by Titania to Bottom ('apricocks and dewberries', 'purple grapes, green figs, and mulberries'). But the quince as a 'Cydonian apple', already identified with the golden apples of Venus, was even more specifically connected with the 'madness of Eros' or Cupid, with love potions or aphrodisiacs, and with overcoming female resistance to marriage. Emile Detienne, in describing these connections,

    A Midsummer Night's Dream', *Cahiers Elisabéthains*, 56 (October 1999), 25–39.

[5] Covarrubias, *Diccionario de la lengua castellana o espanola* (1611), 'Membrillo': 'La etimologia del membrillo traen algunos del diminutivo de la palabram membrum, por cierta semejança que tienen los mas de ellos con el miembro genital y femineo'.

[6] See Luis de Góngora, *Romances*, ed. Antonio Carreño (Madrid, 1982), no. 34 (p. 234: 'En las ruinas ahora / del sagrado Tajo, viendo / debajo de los membrillos / engerirse tantos miembros' or 'In the ruins now / of the sacred Tajo, seeing / below the quinces [membrillos or little members] / so many members being eaten') and no. 36 (p. 242, where the editor glosses '*membrillos*' by reference to Covarrubias's etymologizing and cites the '*membrillo toledano*' [or quince of Toledo] from Cervantes's *El Licenciado Vidriera* from *Novelas ejemplares*, ed. Harry Siebet). On the '*membrillo*' or quince of Cervantes's 'The Glass Graduate', see Paul Julian Smith, *Writing in the Margin: Spanish Literature of the Golden Age* (Oxford, 1988), esp. pp. 197–8; and Maria Antonia Garcés, 'The Phantom of Desire: A Cervantine Erotics' (Johns Hopkins doctoral dissertation, 1994), who comments (p. 143) that 'Toledo was celebrated for its whores, considered the best in the Peninsula'.

[7] On this 'covert description of an aged female's pudendum', see Louise O. Vasvari, 'Vegetal–Genital Onomastics in the *Libro de buen amor*' in *Romance Philology* (1988–9), p. 16; Francis Lee Utley, *The Crooked Rib: An Analytical Index to the Argument About Women in English and Scots Literature to the End of the Year 1568*, p. 213, who notes that this verse was erroneously 'ascribed by Stow to Chaucer [in Stowe's *Chaucer* of 1561]'.

[8] See Pliny, *Natural History*, Book xv. xi ('in bed-chambers also they are to garnish the images standing about the beds-head and sides'), cited here from *The Historie of the World: Commonly called, The Naturall Historie of C. Plinius Secundus*, trans. Philemon Holland, 2 vols. (London, 1635), vol. 1, p. 436; Eugene Stock McCartney, 'How the Apple Became the Token of Love', in *Transactions and Proceedings of the American Philological Association*, vol. 56 (1925).

[9] See Randle Cotgrave, 'Pomme d'or. The golden apple, amorous apple, apple of Loue; the Quince hath also been called, Pomme d'or'; 'Pomme d'amours. The raging, or mad, apple; also, the amorous apple, apple of Loue, golden apple'.

[10] Ellacombe, *Plant-Love & Garden-Craft*, pp. 234–5; Sir Thomas Browne (341) notes that we may 'read in Pierius, that an Apple was the Hieroglyphicke of Loue, and that the Statua of Venus was made with one in her hand'.

[11] See Virgil, *Eclogues, Georgics, Aeneid I–VI*, trans. H. Rushton Fairclough, revised by G. P. Goold (Cambridge, Mass, 1999), for the quinces of Eclogue 2.51 ("Come hither lovely

notes that 'The Greek word for "apple" (*mélon*)', which 'designates every kind of round fruit resembling an apple', is 'used not only for the fruit of the apple tree but for the pomegranate and the quince, which was known to the Greeks as the "Cydonian apple"'.[12] (He also connects the eating of the pomegranate by Persephone, sealing her marriage to Pluto or Dis, to the 'quince' to be eaten on the wedding night by Athenian brides, to which we will return.) In ways suggestive for the love potion of Shakespeare's marriage play, which affects not only its young Athenian lovers but the resistance of the unruly Titania, the quince was similarly identified with the golden apples of Venus used to conquer Atalanta, the Amazon-like huntress who is strikingly conflated with Hippolyta in both *Two Noble Kinsmen* and *A Midsummer Night's Dream*, the independent female whose resistance to marriage is overcome by golden apples associated with the madness of Eros in Theocritus and with being 'striken with the dart of Cupid' in Golding's *Metamorphoses*.[13] Erasmus's well-known Adage *Malis ferire* ('to pelt with apples') combines these golden apples used to overpower Atalanta not only with the 'apple' thrown by the lustful or saucy Galatea but with Virgil's downy 'quinces'.

The 'mosie' and 'most sweetly fragrant' quince also had a lively presence in contemporary continental and English herbals, which stressed (of this autumn-ripening fruit, shaped variously like 'the round apple or the more elongated pear') that its southern variety (unlike the English) was most pleasant eaten raw, that it was called in Latin *Cotoneum* because it was 'clad in a sute of white thin Coten', that it was a digestive for the 'stomach', and that, as a hirsute or 'hairy' fruit, it could be used to restore hair lost by the pox, qualities already noted in Pliny.[14] Well before *A Midsummer Night's Dream* — whose emphasis on fruitful issue extends from the 'fruitless' and 'barren' with which Hermia is threatened in the opening scene (1.1.72–3) to the blessing of Oberon on the 'issue' of the Athenian marriages at its end (5.1.401–22) — the fruitful quince was associated with pregnancy and fortunate issue, as well as with Cupid and the sexuality of Venus: Dodoens' *Histoire des Plantes*

(1557), translated into English by Henry Lyte in 1578, records (as do herbals of the 1590s) the saying of Simeon Sethi that pregnant women should eat quinces in order to give birth to wise and

---

boy . . . My own hands will gather quinces, pale with tender down', the Loeb translation pp. 34–5 of Corydon's 'Huc ades, o formose puer . . . ipse ego cana legam tenera lanugine mala'); and Eclogue 3 (Loeb pp. 42–3): 'Malo me Galatea petit lasciva puella, / et fugit ad salices, et se cupit ante videri' ('Galatea, saucy girl, pelts me with an apple, then runs off to the willows – and hopes I saw her first'). The 'apple' of the lascivious Galatea is identified as a quince or 'Cydonian apple' in the *Vertumnus* of the humanist Joan Goropius Becanus, cited in Covarrubias' *Tesoro de la lengua castellana española* (Madrid, 1611), under 'Membrillo: Juan Goropio, en su *Vertumno*, fol. 72, declarando aquel verso de Virgilio: *Malo me Galatea petit, etc., et se cupitante videri*, da a entender esto, infamando al membrillo por su forma, y concluye: *An hic non videmus clarissima indicia, cotoneum apud nos quoque eiusdem rei, cuius apud graecos symbolum fuisse, si ex eius quidem nomine vile scortum hactenus nominetur*', the *scortum* that was a familiar term for the female genitalia. See Garcés, 'The Phantom of Desire', pp. 151, 162.

[12] Marcel Detienne, *Dionysos Slain*, trans. Mireille Muellner and Leonard Muellner (Baltimore, 1979), pp. 42–3, 103, n. 125.

[13] See Golding, trans. p. 269 on Atalanta who until then 'shonnne(d) husbanding', in the story told by Venus herself in the midst of the narrative of Venus and Adonis. In Theocritus 3.40–42, the golden apples fill Atalanta with the 'madness of Eros' analysed by Detienne, who discusses the 'wild copulation' of Hippomenes and Atalanta and their subsequent metamorphosis into lions – linking this Ovidian story with those of Hippolytus and Adonis killed by the boar. On the conflation of Atalanta and Hippolyta in *MND* 5.1.111–13 and *TNK* 1.i.79, see Jonathan Bate, *Shakespeare and Ovid* (Oxford, 1993), p. 137, Lois Potter's gloss on p. 146 of the Arden 3 edition of John Fletcher and William Shakespeare, *The Two Noble Kinsmen* (Walton-on-Thames, 1997), and Eugene Waith's edition of *The Two Noble Kinsmen* (Oxford, 1994), p. 85.

[14] The quotation on its apple and pear shapes is from Rembert Dodoens, *Histoire des Plantes* (1557), translated into English by Henry Lyte in 1578; on its 'Coten' suit from Henry Buttes, *Diets dry Dinner* (1599). John Parkinson's *Paradisi in Sole: Paradisus Terrestris OR A Garden of Pleasant Flowers* contrasts the English quince that 'no man can endure to eat it . . . rawe' with the 'Portingall Apple quince' which is 'so pleasant being fresh gathered, that it may be eaten like vnto an Apple without offence'. For the quince's ability to restore hair lost by the 'mange' (as Pliny's translation renders it), see Pliny, *Natural History*, Book 23: 54.

understanding children.[15] The quince (like the mulberry) was simultaneously connected with exotic locations, including the 'Ind' of the East as well as West. Vives' *Convivium* (included among Tudor schoolboy texts) identifies it with Persia, Henry Buttes with Syria and its original Crete, while Richard Eden's translation of Peter Martyr's *De Orbe Novo*, or *The Decades of the New World* (1555) compares the 'colour' (between white and black) of inhabitants of the 'Indies' not only with the 'purple' mulberry but with the 'tawny' quince.[16]

The most striking association of 'Quince' for Shakespeare's 'marriage' play – and for what happens ultimately to its unruly women – is, however, its widespread identification in the period not only with marriage in general but with Athenian weddings in particular. Peacham's 'Matrimonium' emblem (1612), which features a man bearing a marital 'yoke' and holding a quince in his hand, glosses the 'fruitfull Quince' as the symbol of 'wedlock' that 'SOLON did present, / T'Athenian Brides, the day to Church they went', in a verse that cites 'Plutarch' as its source (see illustration 6).[17] This marital *and* Athenian quince – connected with the Lawgiver who mitigated Athens' harsh or Draconian laws – appears in no fewer than three influential Plutarch texts, all familiar well before the time of the play. Plutarch's *Life of Solon* (available in North's translation) mentions in its description of the Athenian Lawgiver's views on marriage (including that couples should not be mismatched in years or marry for property or wealth) his mandate that 'a newe maryed wife should be shut vp with her husband, and eate a quince with him',[18] in relation to problems of fruitfulness and issue. In Plutarch's *Moralia*, the section known as '*Roman Questions*' records that 'Solon in his Statutes ordeined, that the new married wife should eat of a quince before she enter into the bride chamber, to the end that this first encounter and embracing, should not be odious or unpleasant to her husband' – an influential passage on the quince as a breath-freshener for the bride which may remind us of the lines on Thisbe's 'breath' (and on 'odious' for 'odours' or 'odorous' savours 'sweet') in *A Midsummer Night's Dream* (3.1.82–5).[19]

But the most influential 'Plutarch' text for this marital and Athenian quince (also from the *Moralia* or 'Morals') was his *Conjugal Precepts* or 'Precepts of Wedlock', which prominently featured this 'quince' in the very first of its precepts. It begins with the need to combine Hermes (or pleasant speech) with Aphrodite (or sexual pleasure), in order to avoid 'conflict or quarrelsomeness' in marriage, and goes on to record that

Solon gave order and commanded that the new-wedded bride should eate of a quince before that she came in bed with her bridegroom; signifying covertly in mine opinion by this dark ceremony, that first and above all, the grace proceeding from the mouth, to wit, the breath and the voice, ought to be sweete, pleasant, and agreeable, in everie respect.[20]

---

[15] John Gerard's *The Herball or Generall History of Plants* (1597) similarly notes (p. 1264) that '*Simeon Sethi* writeth, that the woman with childe, which eateth many Quinces during the time of hir breeding; shall bring foorth wise children and of good understanding'; while Buttes's *Diets dry Dinner* records in the 'Storie for Table-talke' under '*Malum Cydonium*' or Quince '*Simeon Sethi*, counselleth women with child to eat many quinces, if they desire to haue wise children'.

[16] See Vives's *Convivium*, in *Tudor School-Boy Life: The Dialogues of Juan Luis Vives*, trans. Foster Watson (London, 1908), p. 136; and the excerpt from Eden's translation in John Hollander and Frank Kermode, eds., *The Literature of Renaissance England* (New York, 1973), pp. 44–5.

[17] *Minerva Britanna or a Garden of Heroical Deuises, furnished, and adorned with Emblemes and Impresa's of sundry natures, Newly devised, moralized, and published*, by Henry Peacham (London, 1612).

[18] *The Lives of the Noble Grecians and Romanes, compared together by that graue learned Philosopher and Historiographer, Plutarke of Chaeronea: Translated out of Greeke into French by IAMES AMYOT, Abbot of Bellozane, Bishop of Auxerre, one of the Kings priuy counsel, and great Amner of Fraunce, and out of French into Englishe, by Thomas North* (London, 1579), p. 98.

[19] *Roman Questions* is cited here from p. 872 of Holland's translation of *The Philosophie, commonlie called, the Morals written by the learned Philosopher PLUTARCH of Chaeronea. Translated out of Greeke into English, and conferred with the Latine translations and the French, by PHILEMON HOLLAND* (London, 1603). The 1623 Folio text here has 'Odours, odours', the 1600 First Quarto 'Odours, Odorous'.

[20] *Conjugal Precepts* is characterized in volume 3 of Foucault's *The History of Sexuality* (Part 5 – 'The Wife') as marking 'a changing attitude towards self and sexuality articulated by

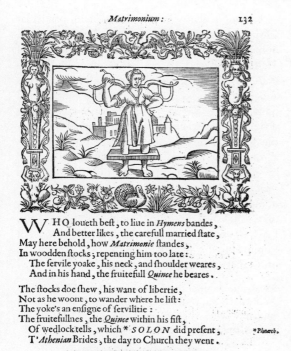

Matrimonium : 132

WHO loueth beſt, to liue in *Hymens* bandes,
And better likes, the carefull married ſtate,
May here behold, how *Matrimonie* ſtandes,
In woodden ſtocks; repenting him too late :
    The ſeruile yoake, his neck, and ſhoulder weares,
    And in his hand, the fruitefull *Quince* he beares.

The ſtocks doe ſhew, his want of libertie,
Not as he woont, to wander where he liſt :
The yoke's an enſigne of ſeruilitie :
The fruitefullnes, the *Quince* within his fiſt,
    Of wedlock tells, which * *SOLON* did preſent,   * *Plutarch.*
    T'*Athenian* Brides, the day to Church they went.

Sed

6   Matrimonium emblem by Henry Peacham, from *Minerva
Brittanna*. London, 1612.

The quince was thus associated not only with fruitful consummation on the wedding night and with
concord between bride and groom but with making the breath, and mouth, of the bride in particular
sweeter and more agreeable, counsel that Plutarch
iterates at the text's end by reminding the bride to
'haue alwaies in your mouth the good word'.

Conjugal Precepts goes on from its opening
'quince' to give other advice which resonates with
Shakespeare's *Dream*: to beware of love potions (capable of transforming a man into an 'ass'), to avoid
the lustful choice of Pasiphae, to find future husbands by the ear rather than the eye (as Hermia finds
Lysander in Act 3), to refuse expensive trifles or gifts
from suitors (as it says 'Lysander' did for his daughters), and (for wives) to imitate Phidias's statue

of the domesticated rather than the lascivious or
unruly Venus, whose foot resting on a 'turtle' sym-
bolized that wives should remain silently at home,
speaking only words agreeable to their husbands.

Plutarch's *Conjugal Precepts* exerted an enormous
influence on writing devoted to female conduct
as well as to marriage in the sixteenth century –
including Vives's *Instruction of a Christian Woman*
and Edmund Tilney's *Flower of Friendship*, which
are filled with passages from it, and Erasmus's
Conjugium or 'Marriage' Colloquy, whose English
translation in *A Mery Dialogue, declaringe the properties of Shrewd Shrews and Honest Wives* (1557) reflects
its precepts on a wife's sweet and acceptable speech
in the name of Eulalia (literally 'sweetly speaking'),
the 'honest wife' who counsels the shrewish Xan-
tippa on how to use mild words and behaviour
with her husband.[21] Solon's mandate to Athenian
brides on the eating of a quince on the wedding
night was at the same time a staple of continental
marriage treatises, which stressed that it made the
mouth more 'odorous' in every sense.[22]

writers of the early Christian era', the 'art of conjugality' that
would become 'an integral part of the cultivation of the self'.

21   See the introduction to *The Flower of Friendship: A Renaissance
Dialogue Contesting Marriage by Edmund Tilney*, ed. Valerie
Wayne (Ithaca, 1992), on the pervasive influence of Plutarch's
'Precepts' of wedlock in sixteenth-century treatments of
marriage and (p. 155) on Tilney's recall of the 'Solon' of
Plutarch's *Lives* ('Furthermore, he took awaye all joynters
and dowries in other mariages, and willed that the wives
should bring their husbands but three gownes only . . . that
man and woman should marye together for issue, for pleasure, and for love, but in no case for money'). On *De institu-
tione Christianae feminae*, by Spanish humanist Juan Luis Vives
(1523) – translated into English as *A Very Frutefull and Pleasant Boke Called the Instruction of a Christen Woman* by Richard
Hyrd before his death in 1528 – see also Diane Bornstein,
ed., *Distaves and Dames: Renaissance Treatises For and About
Women* (Delmar, New York, 1978), pp. xvii–xix. *A Mery Dialogue* is available in *Tudor Translations of the Colloquies of Erasmus* (1536–84), ed. Dickie A. Spurgeon (Delmar, New York,
1972), pp. 245–83. On Erasmus's '*Eulalia*' as 'sweetly speaking', see *The Colloquies of Erasmus*, trans. Craig. R. Thompson
(Chicago, 1965), p. 114, with Wayne's Introduction, p. 23.

22   See, for example, the 1554 Italian treatise entitled *Delle
Nozze* ('On Weddings'), from Fausto da Longiano, which
repeats Solon's precept on the eating of a quince ('un pomo

Because the *Moralia* was in Greek and not apparently available in English in its entirety until Philemon Holland's translation in 1603, it might be assumed that Shakespeare could not have known the mouth-sweetening quince of either these 'Precepts of Wedlock' or the passage of 'Roman Questions' on ensuring that the bride's breath not be 'odious' or unpleasant to her husband. This assumption, however, would be false. Within the sixteenth century, in England as in Europe, the *Moralia* was one of the most frequently cited and translated collections of 'moral' texts. *Roman Questions*, known as *Quaestiones Romanae* or *Problemata*, was available in Latin translation as early as 1477, as well as in Amyot's French translation of the whole of the *Moralia* in 1572. *Conjugal Precepts* was translated into Latin as early as 1497, and had appeared in many other Latin translations before the 1590s, as well as in multiple vernacular translations, some of which were produced for particular wedding occasions.[23] Even before Amyot's translation of the *Moralia*, these marital 'Precepts' had been translated numerous times into French, starting as early as 1535 – including a translation in 1559 occasioned by the marriage of the French Dauphin to Mary Stuart, which included an anagram of her name as its dedicatee, and another entitled *Les Regles de Mariage* by Estienne de la Boétie, composed before 1563 and published through his friend Montaigne in 1571.[24]

The *Moralia* – like Plutarch's other works – was extraordinarily popular not only on the Continent but in England, where as Martha Hale Shackford observed long ago in her study of Plutarch's English influence, 'if Sir Thomas North had not translated Plutarch's *Lives*, in 1579, there is strong probability that Shakespeare would have read the biographies in French or in Latin versions', since 'Plutarch's popularity had increased steadily in the sixteenth century until a knowledge of his *Lives* and his *Morals* was almost presupposed on the part of the reading Englishman'.[25] Debts to different parts of the *Moralia*, or 'Plutarches holesome Morrals' as they were called by Gabriel Harvey in 1592, can be seen in a wide range of English writers, including Elyot, Sidney, Gosson, Lodge, Udall, Bacon, Spenser and others.[26]

The influence of *Conjugal Precepts* in particular (along with other versions of Solon's mandated quince) was registered in England prior to *A Midsummer Night's Dream*. An anonymous English *Praise of Musicke*, in 1586, cites among the 'rites and ceremonies of marriage' the 'eating of a quince peare, to be a preparation of sweete & delightful dayes betweene the maried persons, the ioyning, of Mercury and Venus togither, as a token that love must be preferred & fostered by curteous speeches'. Perhaps most strikingly in relation to Shakespeare's exposure to this Athenian quince, Plutarch's 'Precepts of Wedlock' were not only Englished but incorporated at length into Lyly's *Euphues and his England*, in the advice of Euphues to his friend Philautus on the occasion of his marriage – which notes that

Solon gaue counsel that before one assured him-self he should be so warie, that in tying him-selfe fast, he did not vndo him-self, wishing them first to eat a Quince peare, yt is to haue sweete conference with-out brawles . . . [27]

cotogno') to make the mouth more 'odorous' (*odorato*) or sweet-smelling: *Delle Nozze. Trattato del Fausto da Longiano, in cui si leggono i riti, i costvmi, gl'instivti, le cerimonie, et le solennità di diuersi antichi popoli, onde si sono tratti molti problemi; & aggiuntiui, i precetti matrimoniali di Plutarco* (1554).

23 See the comprehensive treatment of Robert Aulotte, *Amyot et Plutarque: La tradition des Moralia au XVIe siècle* (Geneva, 1965), who cites all editions of Plutarch available in Latin and the vernaculars, including for example (Appendix 11, p. 241) a Venetian translation in 1585 by Marc'Antonio Gandino, dedicated to his nephew on the occasion of his marriage.

24 Aulotte, *Amyot et Plutarque*, esp. pp. 60–3, 348–50, and ch. 4.

25 See Martha Hale Shackford, *Plutarch in Renaissance England with Special Reference to Shakespeare* (1929), p. 5, and chs. 2–4, for the influence of individual parts of the *Moralia* and its translation in whole or in part, including the 1542 Basel Latin edition translated by various scholars, including Erasmus, Budé, Melanchthon and Poliziano and the 1570 edition of Xylander (Wilhelm Holtzman), professor of Greek at Heidelberg, who 'published the Greek text with a Latin version of all the works' (p. 17).

26 See Shackford, *Plutarch in Renaissance England*, esp. pp. 31 ff. and Gabriel Harvey, *Foure Letters and Certeine Sonnets*, Bodley Head Quarto (London, 1923), pp. 17, 41, 95.

27 For this text of Lyly – who (as Shackford comments on p. 27) was second only to North as an intermediary between

The advice given by Lyly's Euphues (who is famously figured in this text as 'Athenian' and reminds his friend that 'it is as farre from *Athens* to *England*, as from *England* to *Athens*') goes on to rehearse Plutarch's familiar conjugal precepts, including not only their advice to choose with the 'ear' rather than the 'eye' but counsel to husbands to 'suffer the wranglyngs of young maryed women' common 'in the first moneth' before they can be made more 'tractable', an influential aspect of Plutarch's text on the domesticating of 'curst wiues' that might also have influenced, directly or indirectly, plays such as *The Taming of the Shrew*.

The textual tradition identifying the 'quince' with weddings and the mandate of Solon continued well beyond the date of *A Midsummer Night's Dream* – including in an English poem by William Cartwright in 1641 on the marriage of the 'Lady Mary' to the Prince of Orange, which envisages the bride on the wedding night as 'Soft as the Wooll, that Nuptiall Posts did crowne, / Or th'Hallowd Quince's Downe, / That Ritual Quince, which Brides did eate, / When with their Bridegrooms they would treat'.[28] But the connection between the 'Quince' and weddings was also a visual commonplace by the time of Shakespeare's play. A painting by Paris Bordone is identified as a marriage portrait by the bride's picking a quince, described by Panofsky as 'the wedding fruit *par excellence*' (see illustration 7).[29] Edgar Wind likewise identifies Giovanni Bellini's *Feast of the Gods* as a wedding painting because its central female figure is shown holding a quince, 'a symbol of marriage' common in 'Venetian marriage paintings', in which 'the fruit is generally held or touched by the bride' (see illustration 8).[30] For the simultaneously marital and Athenian quince, the most widely disseminated source was Alciati's extraordinarily popular *Emblemata*, which featured a 'Quince' (or *Cotonea*) emblem that explicitly identified this 'Cydonian apple' with Solon's matrimonial mandate:

Poma nouis tribui debere Cydonia nuptis
  Dicitur antiquus constituisse Solon.
Grata ori & stomacho cum sint, ut & halitus illis
  Sit suauis, blandus manet & ore lepos.

[Solon of old is said to have ordained that quinces be given to newly-weds, since these are pleasant both to mouth and stomach. As a result their breath is sweet, and winning grace drops from their lips][31]

The emblem appeared in the massive 1621 edition complete with Hymen and Cupid (carrying a basket of quinces under a tree laden with these 'Cydonian apples') and a detailed commentary on weddings, beginning with Plutarch's *Conjugal Precepts* (see illustration 9). But right from its first appearance, in much earlier sixteenth-century editions, Alciati's 'Quince' was already the emblem of matrimony its Latin verse suggests. The 1577 edition (illustration 10), which features luscious

---

Plutarch and English readers – see John Lyly, *Euphues and his England*, in *The Complete Works of John Lyly*, ed. R. Warwick Bond (Oxford, 1902), vol. 2, p. 223. Bond observes (p. 537) of '*Euphues to Philautus*: this letter is largely borrowed from the *Coniugalia Praecepta* of Plutarch, with amplifications by Lyly . . . and some borrowings from Edmund Tylney's *Flower of Friendship*, which bears as title to the book proper, "A brief and pleasant discourse of duties in Mariage", and is itself indebted to the *Coniug. Praecepta*. From the words "Helen gaped for goods", p. 225 . . . Lyly seems to have used Xylander's translation (Basileae, 1570, fol.) ("Inhiabat opibus Helena", p. 146), from which therefore I quote'.

[28] See the reference to nuptial posts and wool in *Roman Questions*, with *Poems Written by Mr William Cartwight* (London, 1651), in *The Plays and Poems of William Cartwright*, ed. G. Blakemore Evans (Madison, 1951), p. 540.

[29] See Erwin Panofsky, *Studies in Iconology: Humanistic Themes In the Art of the Renaissance* (1939; rpt. New York, 1962), p. 163, with Figure 121 of the painting from Vienna, Kunsthistorisches Museum, no. 233; Panofsky's *Problems in Titian, Mostly Iconographic* (New York, 1969), pp. 131, 138; and for more on the quince associated with Venus and marriage, Guy de Tervarent, *Attributs et Symboles dans l'Art profane* (Geneva, 1958), p. 103.

[30] Edgar Wind, *Bellini's Feast of the Gods: A Study in Venetian Humanism* (Cambridge, Mass., 1948), pp. 36–7, 40, identifies the central mythological couple (as Neptune and Gaea or Demeter, 'the goddess holding the quince, the symbol of matrimony', 40) with Alfonso d'Este and his wife Lucrezia Borgia. The source for the painting is the story in Ovid's *Fasti* (I. 391–440 and VI: 319–48) of Priapus's interruption by the braying of Silenus's ass just as he is about to rape a sleeping nymph, an interruption for which the ass is sacrificed.

[31] Cited from Andrea Alciato, *Emblemata* (Lyons, 1550), translated and annotated by Betty I. Knott, with an introduction by John Manning (Hants, England, 1996), p. 218.

7   Allegory (Mars, Venus, Victory and Cupid) by Bordone.

pear-shaped quinces with the influential commentary of Claude Mignault, combines all three
Plutarch texts on Solon's Athenian mandate with
references to the familiar passages from Pliny on its
fragrant taste and smell, as well as its benefits for
the 'stomach'.[32]

Sixteenth-century vernacular and other versions
of Alciati's 'Quince' emblem varied between the
different Plutarch texts, as to whether this golden
Cydonian apple was a gift to both bride and groom
in Athens or just to be eaten by the bride – as
the 1549 French edition (illustration 11), for example, suggests in its recording that 'Les Coingz'
were mandated by Solon to be given 'a la nou-
uelle epouse', to render her mouth more 'odorous'
or fresh smelling ('de bone odeur') and her words
more 'modest' and 'honest'.[33] But the commentaries on Alciati's marital 'Quince' in sixteenth-
century annotated editions repeatedly stress its
relation to Plutarch's *Conjugal Precepts*, the good
words essential not just to marital concord but

to the bride in particular, as well as its value
as a breath-freshener. The *Matrimonium* emblems
of Alciati's popular collection at the same time
incorporated other influential parts of *Conjugal
Precepts*, together with the tradition connecting this
'Cydonian apple' to the golden apples of Venus associated with female sexuality, unruliness and overcoming Atalanta's resistance to marriage. One of

---

[32] *Omnia Andreae Alciati V. C. Emblemata: Cum commentariis,
qvibvs Emblematum omnium aperta origine, mens auctoris expli-
catur, & obscura omnia dubiaque illustrantur; per CLAVDIVM
MINOEM* (Antwerp, 1577).

[33] *Emblemes d'Alciat, de nouueau Trāslatez en Frāçois vers pour vers
iouxte les Latins. Ordonnez en lieux cōmuns, auec briefues exposi-
tions, & Figures nouuelles appropriés aux derniers Emblemes.* (Lyon
1549), p. 254 ('Le Coing'). One example among many of
the tradition that includes both bride and groom is provided
by the Italian *Diverse Imprese Accommodate a diuerse moralità,
con versi che i loro significati dichiarono. Tratte da gli Emblemi
dell'Alciato* (Lyon, 1549), which has 'li sposi' (or 'newlyweds').

8 Detail from *Feast of the Gods* by Giovanni Bellini.

47

9 Emblemata by Andrea Alciati. Padua 1621.

these depicts Phidias's statue of Venus holding an apple in her right hand and resting her foot on the turtle (illustration 12), an emblem of domesticity contrasted in the commentaries with garrulous, shrewish or gadding women. Another – 'On the fidelity of a wife' [*In fidem vxoriam*] – glosses the apples of Venus in the tree above its married couple (illustration 13) in a verse that features both the lascivious Galatea who threw the sexually suggestive 'apple' at her lover and the resistant Atalanta (*Scheneida* or 'Schoeneus's daughter'), who was finally conquered ('uicit') by Hippomenes her competitor-suitor, through the distracting golden apples of Venus or Cupid. The commentaries on this Matrimony emblem refer the reader both to the golden apples awarded by Paris and to the *Malis*

ferire Adage of Erasmus that combines the apples of Galatea and Atalanta with Virgil's 'quinces'.[34]

The tradition linking quinces with both sexuality and matrimony – as well as with Solon's Athenian mandate – continued in the 1593 edition of Cesare Ripa's *Iconologia*, which describes as its emblem of 'Matrimonio' a young man with a marital yoke and the quince that 'by the commandment of Solon' was presented to newlyweds in Athens, because 'it is dedicated to Venus, mother of fecundity' (as well as pleasant to the taste and 'odore' or smell). Noting that the quince appears in depictions of young lovers as well as of Venus, Ripa's 1593 edition links it both with consummation or coitus, which outside of marriage would be a 'grave sin', and with its familiar resemblance to the body's 'secret' parts ('qualche similitudine con le parti secrete del corpo'). The 1603 edition of Ripa (illustration 14) features the illustration that Peacham clearly adapted for his own 'Matrimonium' emblem of 1612, with its young man bearing the yoke of marriage and carrying the emblematic quince, accompanied by the text's reminder of Solon's Athenian mandate. In treating of the serpent or 'viper' to be placed under the married man's feet, Ripa associates the quince of 'Amor' (and the potentially excessive sexuality of the wife) with the '*malum*' (or evil) of the paradisal 'apple' itself, symbol of the first marriage as well as the Fall.[35]

'Quince' thus came with a rich set of associations in the period – with aphrodisiacs or love potions, with fruitfulness and sexuality, with exotic locations (as well as the homelier qualities of the breath-freshener and digestive for the 'stomach'), and with overcoming the Amazon-like resistance of Atalanta, who is conflated with Hippolyta in Shakespeare's marriage play as well as in *Two Noble Kinsmen*. That Shakespeare was familiar by the

---

[34] See for example the commentary by Mignault in the Antwerp 1577 edition, p. 619.

[35] See respectively *ICONOLOGIA overo Descrittione dell'Imagini Vniversali cavate dall'Antichità et da altri Luoghi* de Cesare Ripa Perugin (Roma, 1593); and the 1603 edition.

Cotonea.

EMBLEMATA.   653
EMBLEMA CCIII.

POMA nouis tribui debere Cydonia nuptis
Dicitur antiquus conſtituiſſe Sulon.
Grata ori & ſtomacho cùm ſint, vt & halitus illis
Sit ſuauis, blandus manet & ore lepos.

Plutarchus in γαμικοῖς παραγγέλμασιν ita ſcribit: Ὁ σόλων
ἐκέλευε τὴν νύμφην τῷ νυμφίῳ συγκατακλινομένην, μῆλον κυδώνιον
κατατραγοῦσαν, ἀπιτῶδρῷ ὡς ἐοικεν, ἵν᾽ ὁ δὴ τῆς ἀπὸ σόματος καὶ
φωνῆς χάρεν ἐνάρμοσον ἔναι πρῶτον καὶ ἡδεῖαν. Solon iubebat
ſponſam cum ſponſo concubituram, prius edere malum cotoneum : innuens ea re, primam quæ ore & voce initur, gratiam
concinnam debere eſſe & ſuauem . Idem in Problematis ferè
tradit. De Cotoneis Plin.15.cap.11.& 17. de eorum ſapore &
odore eiuſdem lib.cap.28.

*Cotonea cum
nouis nuptis
ederentur.*

POMA

Hede-

10   *Emblemata* by Andrea Alciati, with commentary by Claude Mignault (Claudius Minos). Antwerp, 1577.

mid-1590s with the long-standing connection be-tween quinces and weddings may be further sug-gested by the fact that the only other place in the canon where quinces appear is in the scene of preparation for Juliet's wedding to Paris, in the play that presents the correspondingly tragical version of the *amor* of Pyramus and Thisbe.

But what about the quince in relation to the carpenters' 'quoyns' or 'coigns' with which we began? Here, both similarities of sound and the metamorphic variety of early spellings collapse any distance we might anachronistically assume be-tween the fruitful quince and the quoyns, coigns,

and coins with which Quince's name has already been connected. Quince itself is spelled 'quoyne' and quincetree as 'Coyn-tree' in thirteenth- and fourteenth-century English writing, bearing the influence of French 'coing', as does the spelling of quinces as 'Coynes' in Chaucer's translation from the French of *The Romaunt of the Rose*. Quince is spelled 'quoyn' in Palgrave (153), where 'Quince tree' is 'quonynier', while the variant sixteenth-century spellings of English 'quince' make clear that 'coyns', 'quoyns' and 'quynes' could be 'quinces' as well as monetary 'coins', carpenters' 'coigns', printers' wedges or 'quoyns', and the corners,

11 Emblemes d'Alciat. Lyons, 1549.

12 Emblematum Libellus by Andrea Alciati. Paris, 1534.

coigns, or quoyns of houses and walls.[36] In relation to 'coynes' and 'corners' of all kinds, the 'quince' connected with consummation on the wedding night was thus simultaneously part of the sexually suggestive network of 'coining' and 'coigns' (including *conio, cuño,* coiner or 'wedge') and of 'con' words that included (in Florio, for example) '*coniugio,* marriage matrimonie, wedlock, copulation' and the '*conno,* womans privie parts or quaint as Chaucer calls it', which the sounding of quince as 'coynes' or 'coin-tree' suggested.

Contemporary dictionaries are highly suggestive sources for this network of contemporary cognates (including 'cognate' itself, which – as Florio comments of *cognato* – meant both related by marriage and 'cleaved or coyned'). Florio's

'Quinces' (or 'Cotogni') appear in a list that includes '*Cotone,* cotton, bumbace, a nappe or a thrum', reminding us of the cottony *Cotoneum* behind the 'Quince' who directs the Athenian 'hempen homespuns' (3.1.77), in the play whose weaver Bottom invokes the cutting by the Weaver 'Fates' of 'thread' and 'thrum' (5.1.286). But the most suggestive – and most revealing for the combination of corners, coins, and carpenters' coigns or quoyns with the simultaneously sexual and marital 'quince' – is the 'Coing' from which

36 All of these variant spellings and historical instances are readily accessible in the corresponding *OED* entries.

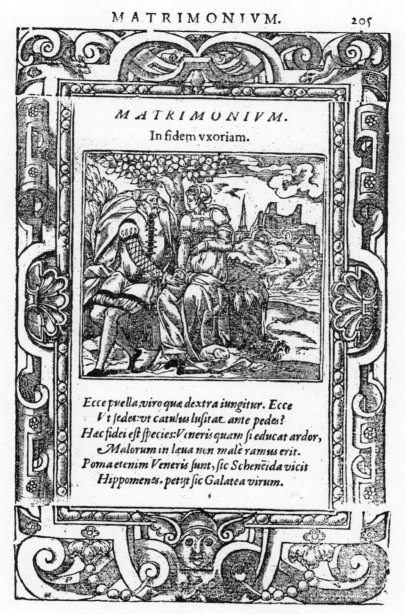

13   *Emblemata* by Andrea Alciati. Paris, 1566.

306

ICONOLOGIA

MATRIMONIO.

tenendo nella medesima mano vn cocogno, & sotto à piedi hauerà vna vipera.

Per lo giogo, & per li ceppi si dimostra, che il Matrimonio è peso alle forze dell'huomo assai graue, & è impedimento al caminare in molte attioni di libertà, essendo il maritarsi vn vendere se stesso, & obligarsi à legge perpetua, con tutto ciò è caro, & desiderabile per molti rispetti, & particolarmente per lo acquisto de' successori nelle sue facoltà, [le quali siano veri heredi della robba, & della fama, per l'honore, & credito che s'acquista nella Città, prendendosi questo carico per mantenimento d'essa, & per lo piacere di Venere che lecitamente se ne gode, però si fa con l'anello, il quale è segno di preminenza, & di grado honorato.

Il coto-

14   *Iconologia* by Cesare Ripa. Rome, 1603.

English 'Quince' itself derives, which (as Cotgrave's French–English dictionary makes clear) combines all of these into a single sound:

Coing: m. A wedge; also, a quince; also, an angle, nooke, or corner; also, a coyne, or stamp, upon a peece of coyne.[37]

'Coing' (source of the spelling of quinces as 'Coynes' and quince tree as 'Coyn-tree') is thus simultaneously a quince, a carpenter's wedge or coign, an 'angle, nooke, or corner', and the 'coyne, or stamp, upon a peece of coyne', just as the 'coignier' or quince tree in Cotgrave's definitional series is a homophone of 'Coigné' ('wedged; driuen, or knocked in; stamped, coyned'), in a list where 'Coignaufond' (driving or wedging into the

bottom or 'fond'), used by 'Rab.' or Rabelais for 'Knocking, leacherie, Venerie' (from 'Coigner. To wedge, to fasten with a wedge; to driue hard or knocke fast in, as with a wedge' as well as 'to stamp or coin'), comes immediately after 'Coignasse: f. A female Quince, or peare Quince, the greatest kind of Quince'.

The Shakespearian corpus itself exploits different parts of this homophonic network, outside *A Midsummer Night's Dream*. Kökeritz sees a sexual 'pun on *quoin* "wedge"', in Hal's 'So far as my *coin* would stretch' (*1H4* 1.2.47–56), in lines whose 'Did I ever call for thee to pay thy part?' strengthen the sexual connotations of his having 'paid all' as well as of this stretching 'coin'.[38] 'Coiner', like corner, has a sexual sense elsewhere in Shakespeare – not just in the Othello's 'keep a corner in the thing I love / For others' uses' (3.3.272–3) but in Posthumus's 'We are all bastards . . . Some coiner with his tools has made me a counterfeit' in *Cymbeline* (2.5.2–6), lines that evoke not only the monetary 'Coyne' used for consummation or coitus on the wedding night, but the cuckolding 'tool' of an adulterous phallic stamping. The 'quoin' or 'coign' that was variously 'cornerstone' and 'the external angle of a wall or building' similarly appears in the 'coigne of vantage' in *Macbeth* (1.6.7) and in the 'coign a' th' Capitol, yond cornerstone' of *Coriolanus* (5.4.1).

In Shakespeare's marriage play, 'Peter Quince' already recalls not just the one married apostle but the network of biblical 'stones' that includes the 'Peter' or 'rock' on which a different kind of structure is founded, the rejected 'cornerstone' and the 'living stones' all gathered together in the second Epistle to 'Peter' (2 Peter 2) He thus simultaneously manages to combine the fruitful 'Quince' associated with weddings in Athens, bodily 'stones', and the abjected biblical cornerstone, 'Coin' or 'coign', in a play whose artisanal (and bodily) 'Bottom' similarly recalls the 'bottom of Goddes secretes' from the Corinthians passage on

---

37 Randle Cotgrave, *A Dictionarie of the French and English Tongues* (London, 1611) [Menston, England, 1968], 'coing'.
38 See Helge Kökeritz, *Shakespeare's Pronunciation* (New Haven, 1953), p. 100.

the wisdom of the 'fool', beyond the comprehension of Greek logic or 'cool reason' and of 'the rulers of this world', including presumably Athenian rulers.

This brings us, then, to the sound of Peter 'Quince' itself and the relation of the nuptial 'present' of Shakespeare's Quince to the Athenian newlyweds (and Athenian ruler) of this 'marriage' play. We are accustomed to pronouncing the 'Qu' of 'Quince' the way anglophones rather than francophones (for example) pronounce the 'Qu' of 'Quebec'. But, in a period in which English 'quinces' were spelled 'coynes', it may well have sounded closer to the 'coingz' of its own French connections – as Kökeritz implies in his gloss on Hal's stretching 'coin' as 'quoyn' and his comments on the sounding of 'qu' as 'k' or hard 'c' in the bawdy sexual doubles entendres of 'qui's, quae's and quods' (as 'keys, case and cods') in Shakespeare's *Merry Wives* or the 'kiss kiss' of 'quis quis' in *Love's Labour's Lost*.[39] If Peter 'Quince' sounded closer to 'coigns' or French 'Coingz' than to standardized modern English 'quince', it would make even more sexually suggestive the repeated sounding of his name (as a virtual refain) in the roll call of the other suggestively named artisans (including Snug the joiner, his fellow carpenter), in the scene of the casting of the 'enterlude' to be performed on Theseus's 'wedding-day at night' (1.2.6–7), in which he advises them to 'con' their 'parts' (1.2.99–100), before their rehearsal in the Athenian woods, where (as Bottom puts it) they will rehearse more or 'most obscenely'. But whatever the sound of this Athenian artisan-director's name, all of the connotations of 'quince' as well as of wedge, coign, or 'coyne' converge in Bottom's 'First, good Peter Quince, say what the play treats on; then read the names of the actors; and so grow to a point' (1.2. 8–10) These lines exploit not only the sexual connotations of coining, driving, or wedging in (as in 'coignaufond'), but also the 'growing' (as well as genital–vegetal onomastics) already associated with the quince itself – a phallic 'growing' iterated in Lysander's amorous protestation to Helena on his 'growing' love for her instead of Hermia ('Things growing are not ripe until their

season', 2.2.117), after the love potion has transformed the object of his desire.

There is – as always – much more that could be said about the rich textual and cultural network that came to Elizabethan writers – or to the playwright of *A Midsummer Night's Dream* – bearing quinces. Both their presentation at actual weddings and the tradition of translating Plutarch's 'Precepts of Wedlock' for particular wedding occasions – may suggest that some kind of wedding occasion (actual or staged) is being evoked by Shakespeare's choice of this overdetermined name. In a very different critical direction – not of implied occasion but of the rich classical network that connected quinces with famous lovers and marital pairs, F. W. Clayton points out that the only quinces in all of Ovid appear in the story of Cephalus and Procris, an *Othello*-like tragedy of suspected infidelity and jealousy, which is comically evoked in Quince's nuptial play, in 'Not Shafalus to Procrus was so true' (5.1.198), immediately after the substitution of the notoriously unfaithful 'Helen' (197) for the paradigmatically faithful 'Hero'.[40] Even the interlingual networks we have traced do not exhaust the possibilities: Clayton himself adds, when 'quinces are ripe, *carpentur*, they'll be plucked',[41] a crosslingual connection that may seem far-fetched, until we reflect on Shakespeare's similarly interlingual metamorphosis of Ovid's *ad busta Nini* – from the story of Pyramus and Thisbe – into the English 'ninny' or fool.[42]

What might we conclude, then, of the relation of 'comedy' and 'tragedy' by the end of Shakespeare's Athenian marriage play and the 'tragical mirth' that its 'Quince' and company come 'to disfigure, or to present' (3.1.6–1) to its newlyweds in Athens? Within the matrimonial tradition

---

[39] Kökeritz, pp. 119, 331.
[40] F.W. Clayton, 'The Hole in the Wall: A New Look at Shakespeare's Latin Base for "A Midsummer Night's Dream"', The Jackson Knight Memorial Lecture, delivered at the University of Exeter, 13 June 1977 (1979), p. 9.
[41] Clayton, p. 9
[42] On *Nini* / ninny and other interlingual puns in Shakespeare and others in the period, see my 'Novelty of different tongues'.

of *Conjugal Precepts* in which Athenian quinces so prominently figured, the 'quince' identified with Athenian weddings was, as we have seen, a commonplace in the conduct literature on marriage and marital 'concord' as well as on wifely chastity, silence and obedience. From that perspective, the progression of the play as a whole, with its matrimonial ending, its language of 'concord', and a final wedding scene in which its young Athenian brides are completely silent, may suggest (as to an earlier era of critics it *did* suggest) the traditional harmonies and hierarchies produced by that trajectory, even as it raises the question for feminist and other critics of whether the very genre of such 'comedies' depends on precisely for whom they are providing a satisfying comic ending.

The quince's traditional associations with fruitful 'issue' may also seem to be perfectly echoed in this marital end, in the hoped-for 'fortunate' issue of the final 'bride bed' blessing by Oberon, who has already triumphed over Titania through the same love potion that matched Athenian 'Jack' and 'Jill'. But here, hints of the distinctly unfortunate Hippolytus who was the tragic issue of Theseus's marriage to his conquered Amazon and the echo of the ambiguous 'Not Shafalus to Procrus was so true' (5.1.109) in this final blessing ('So shall all the couples three / Ever true in loving be', 5.1. 407–8), in a play where broken oaths and infidelities have already been prominently featured, famously impart more 'discord' than 'concord' or harmony, at least in prospect. The difference between 'tragedy' and 'comedy' in this open-ended ending is itself a question of where the final punctuation, or 'stop', is placed – just as it is unclear whether Quince's nuptial offering is presented for or 'against' the happy occasion, in the performance of yet 'unbreathed'

actors whose words may be something other than (as *Conjugal Precepts* has it) 'sweete, pleasant, and agreeable, in everie respect'. The Athenian quince that was to prevent discord and sweeten the breath and mouth is echoed not only in the 'odious' of the lines on Thisbe's 'breath' in the artisans' rehearsal in the woods (where it is 'Quince' who intervenes to correct 'odious' to 'odorous' as well as 'sweet') but also in the advice to the 'dear actors' themselves (once Quince's play has been 'preferr'd') to 'eat no onions nor garlic, for we are to utter sweet breath; and I do not doubt but to hear them say, it is a sweet comedy', as Bottom puts it, just before his 'No more words . . . away!' (4.2.39–45). What Quince and company 'present' at the final Athenian wedding banquet is an 'Enterlude' (between 'after-supper and bed-time', (5.1.34)) described to Athens' ruler as the 'labor' of 'Hard-handed men that work in Athens here', who 'now have toiled their unbreathed memories / With this same play, against your nuptial' (5.1.72–5). In it, the Quince who has already made 'present' a synonym for 'to disfigure' presents their tragical mirth in a Prologue that is itself famously disfigured. The misplaced punctuation, 'points', or 'stops' of its 'sound' not 'in government' (5.1.124) transform an ostensibly intended compliment to aristocratic Athenian new-lyweds and the ruler of Athens into something very different, whose 'if we offend, it is with our good will' (108) is echoed in Puck the English actor's 'if we shadows have offended' (423), in the Epilogue to the larger play's audience that Theseus has already said no blameless play needs. Perhaps the 'Quince' of Shakespeare's 'marriage' play provides an entirely different kind of present, disfiguring as well as presenting, so to speak, an entire cultural, marital, and 'moral' tradition.

'WHEN EVERYTHING SEEMS DOUBLE': PETER QUINCE, THE OTHER PLAYWRIGHT IN *A MIDSUMMER NIGHT'S DREAM*

A. B. TAYLOR

The final version of 'Pyramus and Thisbe', the play-within-a-play in *A Midsummer Night's Dream*, is arrived at only after a series of last minute, rather frenetic changes. At the first meeting of the tradesmen in the city, their play is apparently complete; parts are assigned, and each player given his lines to learn for the rehearsal next night in the forest. However, by the time the play is performed half of the original six parts, Thisbe's mother and father, and Pyramus's father (see 1.2.56-9),[1] have disappeared without trace. When the 'company' meet in the forest, in the discussion before rehearsal begins, two new parts, 'Wall' and 'Moonshine', are added; a prologue, to be spoken by Pyramus telling the audience he 'is not killed indeed' (3.1.18), promised but never written; and curiously, the scene they rehearse never performed. At one level, this makes sense, but it also adds to the impression that the emergence of 'Pyramus and Thisbe' is somewhat chaotic. And in the middle of all this, either directly suggesting changes himself or responding to suggestions by members of the 'company', is *A Midsummer Night's Dream*'s other playwright, Peter Quince the carpenter. As his play undergoes deletion and revision which will mean his adding fifty-three new lines to the final script, itself only 133 lines in total,[2] he is remarkable for his genial tolerance and enthusiasm.

For a 'hard-handed' man, Quince is also remarkable for another thing: knowing Latin. There is ample evidence of this in his basic method in writing the play which is discussed below, but it is also obvious in incidentals like the pun on the Latin for 'left' (*sinister*) in the reference to the hole in the wall through which the young lovers communicate as 'right and *sinister*' (5.1.162 [my italics]), and the unusual reference to Pyramus as a 'juvenal' (3.1.89) from '*juvenalis*' (youthful). An Elizabethan audience would have found a carpenter knowing Latin less surprising than might be imagined. It has been calculated that, after learning the basics in the petty school, half the boys in England went on to attend free grammar schools.[3] Regardless of academic ability, then, half the boys in England would have embarked on the prescribed and rigorous study of Latin writers. Woe betide the unacademic brethren in a rigid, monolithic educational system where corporal punishment was the order of the day. When one considers the lower ability range in Elizabethan grammar schools, Jacques's picture of 'the whining schoolboy

---

This article develops and enlarges upon one of the features of 'Golding's Ovid, Shakespeare's "Small Latine", and the Real Object of Mockery in "Pyramus and Thisbe"', *Shakespeare Survey 42* (1990), pp. 53–64. It has been read in draft form by Gordon Braden, Andrew Gurr and Niall Rudd to whom I am grateful for their comments and encouragement.

[1] Reference is to *A Midsummer Night's Dream*, ed. H. F. Brooks (London and New York, 1979); reference to other works of the dramatist are to *The Complete Oxford Shakespeare*, ed. S. Wells and G. Taylor (Oxford, 1987).

[2] The 53 added lines consist of the prologue introducing the characters who take part (5.1.126–50), Wall's speech (153–63), that part of Pyramus's opening speech where 'Wall' responds to his request (172–9), Wall's lines at his exit (202–3), Lion's speech to 'You Ladies' (214–22) which the company had asked to be inserted, and Moonshine's introductory lines (235–6).

[3] M. H. Curtis, 'Education and Apprenticeship', *Shakespeare Survey 17* (Cambridge, 1964), p. 62.

with his satchel/And shining morning face, creeping like snail/Unwillingly to school' (*As You Like It* 2.1.145–7) might also serve as an emblem of the educational inhumanity of the age. With what relief such boys must have escaped school to serve an apprenticeship in the kind of trades followed by the 'rude mechanicals'; during that time they would live in their master's household and be taught not only their trade and allied subjects but also a wider, general curriculum, all, of course, in their own language.[4] The fact that their masters were legally bound to provide such instruction[5] explains why tradesmen, whether they had attended grammar schools or not, were literate. So much is evident by those in *A Midsummer Night's Dream*; Snug may be 'slow of study' (1.2.63) but he is referring to learning his part – there is no question of his not being able to read. Of course, there were also 'hard-handed' tradesmen who were gifted classical scholars and who, through circumstances, had had to discontinue their education, the most eminent example being 'the learned Ben' who began his working life as a bricklayer. But although not in that league, Quince clearly has a grammar school background.

Quince's knowing Latin explains what has surprisingly passed unremarked about his basic method: he is clearly composing his play with a copy of Ovid's *Metamorphoses* open before him at the story of Pyramus and Thisbe (iv.51–166).[6] His closeness to the Latin text is reflected in a stream of phrases translated from it word-for-word: *Dumque fugit . . . velamina lapsa reliquit* (101) becomes 'as she fled her mantle she did fall' (5.1.141); *Conveniant ad busta Nini* (88) his lovers agreeing 'to meet at Ninus's tomb' (137); *vestem . . . sanguine tinctam* (107) Thisbe's 'mantle . . . / . . . stained with blood' (272); *Ore cruentato* (104) the lion's tearing it 'with bloody mouth' (142); and *questi* (84) becomes the lovers 'make moan' (322). In addition, there is the moment ruined by Nick Bottom's Pyramus having misread the script when lions 'devouring' one of the lovers (*consumite viscera . . . /O . . . leones* 113–14; 'o lions devour me entirely') becomes 'Since lion vile hath here *deflower'd* my dear' (286 [my italics]). Moreover, the suggestion that has been made from

time to time that the problematic 'most lovely *Jew*' (3.1.89) should read 'most lovely *Juv*' [my italics][7] has viability as Quince half translating, half picking up the Latin with which Ovid introduces Pyramus, *iuvenum pulcherrimus* (55; 'the most lovely of youths' [my emphasis]).

Its closeness to Latin also explains another curious feature of Quince's play: occasionally it slips into Latin syntax. In the grammar school, boys would have been taught that this was of two kinds: 'naturall or Grammaticall order', and the more elevated 'artificiall or Rhetoricall order' (also known as 'the Order of Tully').[8] The most notable rule of 'Grammaticall order' was that adjectives followed nouns as in *puella pulcherrima*: when transposed to English, the practice sounded unnatural, for as George Gascoigne observed, 'if we should say in English a woman fayre, a house high, etc., it would have small grace, for we say a good man, not a man good'.[9] Nonetheless, although unidiomatic in English, this feature of 'Grammaticall order' occasionally appeared in Elizabethan poetry; but it

---

[4] Curtis, 'Education', pp. 61ff.

[5] By the 1563 'Statute of Artificers'; for the terms and conditions of apprenticeship which was of a minimum of seven years' duration and did not end until the apprentice was twenty-four years old, see O. Jocelyn Dunlop, *English Apprenticeship and Child Labour* (London, 1912), *passim*.

[6] Reference is to a standard sixteenth-century text of the *Metamorphoses* containing the notes of Regius, Micyllus and Petrus Lavinius, *Metamorphoseon Publii Ovidii Nasonis* (Venice, 1545). [Translations are my own.] I approach Quince's play as Jonathan Bate does, as a flawed attempt at '*translatio*' which has the tang of the schoolroom; see *Shakespeare and Ovid* (Oxford, 1993), pp. 131–3.

[7] See, for example, the footnote to 3.1.77 in R. A. Foakes's edition of *A Midsummer Night's Dream* (Cambridge, 1984).

[8] Reference is to John Brinsley's account of the teaching of Latin syntax in *Ludus Literarius or The Grammar Schoole* (1627), ed. E. T. Campagnac (London, 1917), pp. 158ff. Brinsley's account is translated from Georgius Macropedius's *Methodus de conscribendis Epistolis* which was published in London in 1595. For the widespread influence and use of the work of Macropedius (1487–1558) in the grammar school, see T. W. Baldwin, *William Shakspere's Small Latine & Lesse Greeke*, 2 vols. (Urbana, Illinois, 1944), vol. 2, pp. 256–67 and *passim*.

[9] 'Certayne Notes of Instruction' (1575), *Elizabethan Critical Essays*, ed. G. G. Smith, 2 vols. (Oxford, 1904), vol. 1, p. 53.

is heavy in Quince's play where we find 'savours sweet' (3.1.77), 'lion rough' (5.1.217), 'lion fell' (219), 'lions vile' (281), 'mantle good' (271), 'furies fell' (273), 'sisters three' (323). 'Rhetoricall order' had a small cluster of 'precepts', the first and most conspicuous of which was the location of the verb at the end of the clause or sentence; an example in Latin is *Munitissimam hostium civitatem Caesar occupavit* ('Caesar *took* the very heavily fortified town of the enemy').[10] When imposed on English, however, 'Rhetoricall order' appeared so eccentric that it does not feature elsewhere, with the exception of one group of Elizabethan writers. Led by Thomas Phaer, the early Elizabethan translators of the classics misguidedly embraced both kinds of Latin syntax in the mistaken belief that it added an epic tone to their work.[11] In this respect, where Phaer led, the others followed.[12] He occasionally but not invariably uses 'Grammaticall order' yet sometimes his taste for it can be pronounced; in the opening twenty lines of Book 3, for example, we find 'kingdome stout' (1), 'fortresse proude' (3), 'navy great' (8), 'freendship old' (19). And he is very fond of 'Rhetoricall Order'; verbs are regularly placed at the end of sentences and clauses, notwithstanding the strain on intelligibility, as in these examples from the middle of Book 3:

These tokens I thee *tell*, ... (405)
But whan approching Sicil coast the winde thee foorth *doth blow* (430)
Epirus and Italia lond, whose founder both of name King Dardan *is*, ... (528–9)
... and at Ceraunia neere our selfs we *put*
(533 [my italics])

Like 'Grammaticall order', 'Rhetoricall order' also features in Quince's play; some examples are,

And by and by I will to thee *appear* (3.1.82)
And this the cranny *is*, ... (5.1.162)
... her mantle she *did fall* (141)
... till fates me *kill* (194 [my italics])

Readers might mistake Quince's tortured syntax as part of a desperate struggle to meet the demands of metre or rhyme-scheme but, while it would be unwise to discount entirely the convenience factor,

like the early Elizabethan translators, he is basically mangling English syntax in a misguided effort to elevate his verse to epic heights.

But for all his closeness to the *Metamorphoses* and quirky syntax, Quince's Latin itself is very thin. For example, there is no lion in Ovid's story of Pyramus and Thisbe. Snug's part of 'Lion' is the result of Quince not knowing the meaning of *leaena* (iv.97, 102); as Chaucer and translators like Golding and Sandys knew, the animal that causes the tragedy in Ovid is a 'lioness'.[13] Quince was aware of the thinness of his Latin vocabulary. Translating key words in Ovid's text, he notably keeps to the beaten track, using words that had long been drilled into schoolboys such as 'chink' (5.1.175) and 'cranny' (162) for the hole in the wall through which the lovers communicate (*rima* iv.65).[14] Other slight variations on the Latin are to be accounted for by his use

10 Although there are other precepts involved in 'Rhetoricall order' (see Brinsley, *Ludus Literarius*, pp. 159ff.), in the discussion that follows, reference is confined to the distinctive first precept.

11 There are features of Spenser's poetry that also seem similar to Latin syntax but there is no reason to believe that Spenser is relevant here whereas evidence of the early Elizabethan translators' involvement in *A Midsummer Night's Dream* is explicit in Nick Bottom's long-recognized parody of Studley – 'The raging rocks,/And shivering shocks...' (1.2.27–34).

12 For convenience, illustrations are confined to Phaer. For a consideration of Phaer's influence on the syntax of the other translators, see my *Shakespeare's Ovid and Arthur Golding* (forthcoming). Reference to Phaer is to *The Aeneid of Thomas Phaer and Thomas Twynne: A Critical Edition*, ed. S. Lally (New York and London, 1987).

13 Chaucer refers in *The Legend of Thisbe* to 'a wyld lyonesse' (805), and in their translations of Ovid's poem, Golding to 'a Lionesse' (4.120), and Sandys to 'a Lyonesse'. Reference is to *The Works of Geoffrey Chaucer*, ed. F. N. Robinson, 2nd edition (Boston, 1957); *The xv Bookes of P. Ovidius Naso, entytuled Metamorphosis (1567)*, ed. W. H. D. Rouse (London, 1904; repr.1961); and *Ovid's Metamorphoses Englished (Oxford, 1632)*, ed. S. Orgel (London and New York, 1976).

14 In one of the dictionaries specially designed for use in schools, Richard Huloet's *Abcedarium Anglico Latinum* (London, 1552; revised edition 1572), for example, one finds *rima* defined as '*Chincke*, clyft, *crany*' [my italics]; and the first Latin–English dictionary for schools, *Promptorium Parvulorum* (London, 1449; five times reprinted) suggests that 'cranny' had long been the traditional translation of *rima* in English schools.

of the standard dictionary of the day, Cooper's *Thesaurus*. Where Ovid writes that Thisbe 'sits beneath the tree' (*sub arbore sedit* 95), Quince has her '*tarrying*' beneath it (147), for Cooper, besides defining '*sedere*' as 'to sit', also has it as 'to *tarie* or abyde' [my italics].[15] Indeed, Quince seems to have worked with Cooper at his elbow – and he comes unstuck by doing so when in a serene and magnanimous mood, his Pyramus nonsensically declares 'Sweet moon, I thank thee for *thy sunny beams*' (261 [my italics]). In Ovid, Quince had found the lovers' meeting took place 'by the rays of the moon' (*ad Lunae radios* 99), but nervous about his Latin and hurriedly consulting his dictionary, he had found only the stock definition of *radius* as 'A beame of the sunne'. The howler he consequently produces stems from two factors. When under pressure – an example is opening his play by ludicrously misreading his own prologue, – he gets flummoxed and has a tendency to panic. And he is under pressure here both because of his inadequate Latin, and the speed at which he works. For example, he does substantial rewrites of his play in the short space between the rehearsal and performance. So, aware of the need to press on and panicking because of his thin Latin, he has produced a line which has amused audiences ever since, and has his hero thank the moon for her '*sunny beams*'.

But the confusion goes deeper than the occasional verbal howler for he sometimes fails to grasp both large and small features of the Latin text before him. He misses, for example, the extreme youthfulness of the lovers. Details in their story in Ovid suggest Pyramus and Thisbe are not much more than children. By day, for example, both can be found playing in their gardens. It is while doing so that they discover they can communicate with each other through the fissure in the wall; at first they talk *through* the wall in 'tiny whispers' (*Murmure . . . minimo* 70), and then childishly talk *to* the wall, first chiding it as 'jealous' (*Invide* 73), then repenting to thank it for its kindness (*Nec sumus ingrati* 76; 'nor are we ungrateful'). When he first introduces the play, however, Quince tells Nick Bottom and the others that Thisbe is a 'lady' (1.2.42) and Pyramus 'a proper man' (80), a 'gen-tlemanlike man' (81), and raises no objection when Bottom suggests playing Pyramus in a beard (83ff.). His mistaking the ages of Ovid's lovers is compounded in his play when it is performed where Pyramus has become a 'knight' (5.1.266) and Thisbe a 'dame' (282).

On a lesser scale, there is Thisbe's 'mask'. When Flute objects to playing Thisbe on the grounds that he has a beard coming, Quince immediately responds 'You shall play it in a mask' (1.2.45). Editors explain this as a reference to the Elizabethan custom of ladies, wearing masks,[16] but, in the Latin text before Quince, Thisbe has her face covered. When she slips out of her father's house into the darkness to keep her fatal assignation, she has 'her face concealed' (*adoperta . . . vultum* iv.94). However, she does so not with a mask but a veil. She is wearing an *amictus*; deriving from *amicere* ('to throw round or wrap about'), this is an item of clothing she has draped about herself which could be a cloak or a veil. What shows it is a veil is the epithet used with it (*tenuis* – 'thin', 'fine') and the fact that it is in the plural form – *tenues amictus* (104). Before leaving home, such was her anxiety not to be recognized, Thisbe had thrown several thin, fine veils over her head to cover her face; presumably, as she made her way to meet Pyramus, she held these on with one or both hands, which is why being light, they are the article of her clothing that falls to the ground when she flees in panic at the sight of the lioness.

The use of 'chink' was also well established; see, for example, Peter Levins's *Manipulus Vocabulorum* (London, 1570). (Both 'chink' and 'cranny' have needlessly been identified as debts to Arthur Golding's translation of the *Metamorphoses* (1567); for details of these and other mistaken debts to Golding, see Taylor, 'Golding's Ovid, Shakespeare's "Small Latine", and the Real Object of Mockery in "Pyramus and Thisbe"'.)

[15] Reference is to Thomas Cooper's *Thesaurus Linguae Romanae & Britannicae* (London, 1565).

[16] They did so either to conceal identity or to avoid unfashionable tanned faces. Masks were oval in shape with holes for the eyes and covered either the upper or the whole face. They were made of silk or velvet, usually lined, of various colours, and sometimes held in position by an attached button which was gripped by the teeth. (See C. W. and P. Cunnington, *Handbook of English Costume in the Sixteenth Century* (London, 1954), pp. 188–9.)

(If they needed it, sixteenth-century readers would have found confirmation of Thisbe as a veiled figure in Raphael Regius' philological notes which were alongside the text in the standard edition of the *Metamorphoses* of the day, where *amictus* is rendered *velum* ('a veil').)[17] Peter Quince's Latin has let him down again; he has picked up the fact that Thisbe has her face covered, not grasped the meaning of *tenues amictus*, and simply made up his own explanation. Moreover, having done so, with the problem of Francis Flute's stubble in mind, he has extended the use of Thisbe's 'mask' from the second half of the story where there is reference to the girl having her face covered to the earlier garden scene where there is none.

Finally, his thin Latin and dictionary-dependence account for the muddle in his thinking as to what exactly 'Pyramus and Thisbe' is. He initially introduces it as 'our interlude' (1.2.5) and then when he announces the full title, despite its content, he refers to it as a 'Comedy'. The word 'interlude' for a play was being used less and less at this time, and while other plays of a tragic nature included the word 'comedy' in their title, they contained comic elements and episodes. It might sound outlandish to say it of a play that caused such hilarity over the years but there is not a vestige of comedy in Peter Quince's treatment of his subject; he intends the story to be taken for what it is, 'tragicall'. He himself unwittingly lays it open to laughter at times with an unthinking and crass insensitivity to the nuances of language as when his heroine kisses the Wall's 'stones' (188) or 'hole' (199). But consciously he devotes his energies to making sure his play is not laughed at; in rehearsal there is the effort to make sure reference is to the 'odours' and not the 'odious savours' of Thisbe's breath (3.1.79–81), and his irritated but ultimately vain attempt to avoid the schoolboy joke of his lovers meeting at 'Ninny's tomb' (5.1.200). As with his absurd attribution of 'sunny beams' to the moon, it is again his use of Cooper that accounts for the serious-minded Quince terming his play an 'interlude' and referring to it as a 'Comedy'. In the *Metamorphoses*, when Ovid first introduces the story of Pyramus and Thisbe, he refers to it as *vulgaris fabula non est* (iv.53; 'a fable not commonly known'). And when Quince turned to *fabula* in Cooper, he found it defined not only as a 'tale' but also as an '*interlude, or comedie*' [my italics]. One can only conclude that as he went about turning the story into a play, the blatantly contradictory title, 'The most lamentable comedy and most cruel death of Pyramus and Thisbe' (1.2.11–12), and the reference to an 'interlude', are his befuddled, unthinking attempts to somehow be true to what he has found in the Latin.

Besides his actors intermittently sabotaging his script (the prime example is surely Bottom's thorough confusion of the senses in 'I see a voice; now will I to the chink,/To spy and I can hear my Thisbe's face' 5.1.190–1),[18] other elements that defy Quince's efforts to produce a 'straight' play are his solutions of 'two hard things' (3.1.45). Representing 'Moonshine' (57) as a man with a thornbush, a lantern, and a dog, and 'Wall' (63) as a man with loam and plaster holding his fingers apart for a 'cranny', is well-intentioned but patently risible. It is so amateurish that the only place one could imagine such things is in a school play where the audience, in the absence of means and facilities, would perforce be called on to exercise such imaginative licence. And if the other leader of the company, Nick Bottom, is also a 'grammarian', both he and Quince could be recalling similar experiences from their own schooldays. There was and had long been a thriving tradition of staging plays in grammar schools in both Latin and English.[19]

---

[17] Accordingly, Regius also identifies the garment Pyramus finds when he arrives, *vestem* (107) as a veil (*velum*). (The Loeb translator also presents Thisbe leaving her father's house as a veiled figure, rendering *adoperta . . . vultum* (94) as 'her face well veiled'; reference is to *Metamorphoses*, ed. F. J. Miller (London, 1916; 2nd edition, repr. 1960).

[18] Cf. Bottom's even more thorough confusion of the senses in his celebrated Pauline parody: 'The eye of man hath not heard, the ear of man hath not seen, man's hand is not able to taste, his tongue to conceive, nor his heart to report, what my dream was' (4.1.209-12). (See also my 'John Hart and Bottom "goes but to see a noise"' (forthcoming)).

[19] 'While school plays were usually in Latin, English ones were not uncommon, even before Elizabeth's reign' (William

Thus, to what he found or thought he found in his play's Latin source, Quince has added a touch of romance – with the unfortunately muddled recall of famous lovers such as 'Limander' and 'Shafalus' (5.1.193 and 196). He also sought to give a flourish with a florid description of the appearance of his lovers, blithely ignorant of the indecorum of items such as 'eyes green as leeks' (322); and equally indecorous is his taste for melodramatic tragic apostrophe, 'O grim–looked night! O night with hue so black!' (168), 'O wherefore, Nature, didst thou lions frame' (280). Add the eccentricities of a cast which, in between occasionally mispronouncing the words he had written, was, with Quince's own misguided support, scrupulously devoted to destroying any vestige of dramatic illusion and, for all Quince's earnest intention for it be taken seriously, 'Pyramus and Thisbe' brings tears to the eyes of its audience for reasons other than those he intended.

This examination of the shadowy, self-effacing figure of Peter Quince reveals a playwright who like his creator, William Shakespeare, has 'small Latine'.[20] In view of the fact that 'latten' is a kind of brass, the story of Shakespeare asking Ben Jonson to 'translate' the 'Latten Spoones' he bought for a christening present for one of Jonson's children[21] suggests the dramatist's limited Latin was something of a joke between himself and his friends. What better way of sending himself up than by a caricature as a workaday playwright who is not only occasionally unsure of his English but so uncertain of his Latin that he blunders into howlers like the 'sunny beams' of the moon and the 'Comedy' of 'Pyramus and Thisbe' because in his dependence on his Latin dictionary common sense has gone out the window. But in Quince, he is caricaturing himself and exaggerating his faults. He could clearly read Latin, and did so on special occasions; writing *The Rape of Lucrece* for the Earl of Southampton, for instance, he not only used the *Fasti* for which there was no current English translation, but also consulted the Latin notes and commentary on the text by Paul Marsus in the standard edition of Ovid's poem.[22]

On the other hand, his habitual and lifelong use of translations suggests reading Latin involved some effort. William Beeston, whose father belonged to The Lord Chamberlain's Men, is reported as commenting on the matter that 'He understood Latin pretty well' – not 'very well' or 'well' but *moderately well*.[23]

If it were limited to a matter of 'small Latine', the resemblance between Quince and his creator would be of only passing interest but Quince is also an actor/playwright who takes roles in his own work in the way that Shakespeare did. In Heminges and Condell's *Comedies, Histories, and Tragedies* (1623), perhaps understandably the dramatist heads the list of 'the Principall Actors in all these Plays', but he is also listed among 'The principall Comoedians' who performed *Every Man In His Humour* in 1598, and among 'The principall Tragoedians' in *Sejanus* in 1603.[24] It may well have been his talent as an actor that initially led to his being recruited by the players; Aubrey relates hearing that as an actor in the 'Play-house', he 'did act exceedingly well'.[25] The only hint from a contemporary, however, of his range as an actor comes from John Davies of Hereford who in 1610 wrote of his playing 'Kingly parts'.[26] In 1709, Rowe claimed as the result of extensive enquiry, he played 'the

Nelson, 'The Teaching of English in Tudor Grammar Schools', *Studies in Philology*, 49 (1952), 138–9).

20 The discussion of Shakespeare that follows is based on information supplied for the most part by the dramatist himself or his contemporaries. There is minimal use of later anecdotes.

21 The story is in a manuscript by Sir Nicholas L'Estrange dated 1629–55; it is cited by S. Schoenbaum, *William Shakespeare: A Documentary Life* (Oxford, 1975), p. 206.

22 See T. W. Baldwin, *On The Literary Genetics of Shakspere's Poems and Sonnets* (Urbana, Illinois, 1950), pp. 97–9.

23 Cited by Schoenbaum, *Documentary Life*, p. 88; *OED* records the use of 'pretty well' as meaning 'moderately or tolerably well' in the sixteenth and seventeenth centuries.

24 See Schoenbaum, *Documentary Life*, pp. 147 and 150.

25 Cited by T. W. Baldwin, *The Organization and Personnel of the Shakespearean Company* (Princeton, 1927), p. 264.

26 'To our English Terence Mr. Will: Shake-speare', Epigram 159 in *The Scourge of Folly*; cited by Schoenbaum, *Documentary Life*, p. 148.

Ghost in his own *Hamlet*' and later from the disorderly notes of Oldys, the story emerged that he played Adam in *As You Like It*.[27] What evidence there is points to a character actor who had an air of *gravitas* and who specialized in playing old men. Significantly, initially Quince intends playing 'Thisbe's father' (1.2.59). In the event he takes an important but limited part, acting as 'Prologue', setting the scene for what follows just as 'The Chorus' does in *Henry V*, another role anecdotally associated with Shakespeare. There are occasions when one hears the authoritative tones of a director's voice in Shakespeare, none more so than in Hamlet's advice to the players (3.2.1–45). Such moments strengthen the probability that the dramatist limited his involvement as an actor – normally parts with which he has been associated are less than 100 lines – to attend to his more important role of 'dramatist-director of his own productions';[28] and this again takes us back to Peter Quince.

Like Shakespeare, Quince also has a reputation as both playwright and poet – 'I will get Peter Quince to write a ballad of this dream' (4.1.212–13) – and a remarkably ready facility for writing. As we have seen, he quickly rewrites substantial parts of the play in the short space between the rehearsal and performance, eliminating some characters and adding others. This was the quality of Shakespeare's writing picked out as most remarkable by Heminges and Condell in the First Folio: 'his mind and heart went together, and what he thought he uttered with that easiness that we have scarce received from him a blot in his papers'.[29] Quince, too, has a relaxed disposition and equable temperament of the kind associated with Shakespeare who was 'generous . . . in minde and moode'.[30] He rewrites quickly without complaint and is even prepared to discuss with leading members of the company which metre additional material is to be in. Finally, Quince is fond of Ovid; this shows not only in his choice of subject but also in his fondness for 'mellifluous and honey-tongued' Ovidian imagery, some of which he cannot handle properly. Shakespeare's *Venus and Adonis* had cast a spell on the young poets

of the early nineties but as the decade wore on, lush Ovidian poetry gave way to harsher satiric poetic fashions. Through Quince, his creator is himself mocking his earlier poetry, as he is his earlier drama with his tortured parody of tragic apostrophe.

And for all their appearance of amateurishness, there are moments when Quince and company appear very professional in attitude. Quince himself fulfils the offices of book-keeper and stage-keeper, retaining the master copy of the play, penning and distributing the parts complete with cues to be conned by individual actors, directing the performance, ensuring performers are ready on cue, and acting as prompter. As he additionally draws up a 'list of properties' (1.2.98) and decides on what will be the 'tiring house' for a company performing in an unfamiliar location (3.1.4), discusses forms of dialogue with his leading man, and takes a role in his own play, one is reminded of the energy Shakespeare displayed in the playhouse, and of the mockery of him as early as 1592 as a 'Johannes Factotum'.[31] Other details suggesting a professional aura are Snug being 'slow of study', an expression still used in the theatre today for tardiness in learning a part, and Bully Bottom's advice to his fellow actors to get 'good strings to your beards, new ribbons to your pumps' (4.2.33–4), and 'eat no onion nor garlic, for we are to utter sweet breath' (4.2.40–1), advice of more than usual value, given they were going to be performing in close proximity to their genteel audience.[32]

---

27 See Schoenbaum, *Documentary Life*, p. 149.

28 Baldwin, *Shakespearean Company*, p. 265.

29 John Heminges and Henry Condell, 'To the Great Variety of Readers' in the First Folio, reprinted in the *Complete Oxford Shakespeare* among the 'Commendatory Poems and Prefaces (1599–1640)', p. xxxix.

30 Davies of Hereford, *Microcosmus;* cited by Schoenbaum, *Documentary Life*, p. 205.

31 For Robert Greene's famous sideswipe at Shakespeare in *A Groatsworth of witte*, see Schoenbaum, *Documentary Life*, p. 115.

32 The reference to 'pumps' may be testimony to Bottom's conviction that their play is 'a sweet comedy' (4.2.42); for the point about breath, I am indebted to Andrew Gurr in private correspondence.

There is also the way they follow their play with a 'Bergomask dance' (5.1.352). Bergamo, a region in Italy, was famed for its rusticity and clownishness in the sixteenth century, and a 'Bergomasco', the name for a native of this region, another name for a bumpkin.[33] The 'Bergomask dance' performed by two of the 'hempen homespuns', and this is the sole use of the term in English (*OED*), was clearly a rustic, clownish dance. And at the time *A Midsummer Night's Dream* was written, professional performances in the playhouse also concluded with clownish dances. Enormously popular, and called 'jigs', these were dances usually for three or four performers who sang dialogue as they danced, periodically leaving the stage and then rejoining the action as a plot unfolded which normally centred on adultery.[34] A short, musical, scripted drama, the jig with its bawdy content and 'uncleanly handlings, gropings, and kissings'[35] delighted the groundlings and scandalized Puritans. One is not suggesting that the tradesmen's clownish 'Bergomask dance' was a jig; there is no record of its having dialogue nor would it be reasonable to hold up the action of *A Midsummer Night's Dream* while a plot unfolded. But coming where it did, immediately after their 'performance' in the place the jig normally occupied, and with Will Kemp, the great comedian and 'the most celebrated jig-maker of the age',[36] on stage playing Bottom (see below), the 'Bergomask dance' would have aroused certain expectations in the audience. It seems therefore reasonable to infer that Kemp who was famed for his dancing, with a fellow actor in the female role, did a low comedic dance which would have been in keeping with Shakespeare's 'marriage-play', perhaps a clownish parody of a courtship, wedding, and the married life that followed. This would have provided a low-life contrast to the stately matrimonial events with their fairy accompaniment that close *A Midsummer Night's Dream*. One of Shakespeare's concerns, as we shall later note, was to offset the unreality of the delicacy of his play's dramatic illusion, and the Bergomask dance, doubtless a close relative of the jig, would have helped in that cause.

Kemp is also a reminder that it is not only the resident playwright of the Lord Chamberlain's Men who is being caricatured in the burlesque. We have evidence of only two roles Kemp played, Peter (in *Romeo and Juliet*), and Dogberry;[37] but while we do not have categorical evidence that he played Bottom, there is some impressive, unremarked internal evidence. Like Richard Tarlton, whose heir he claimed to be, Kemp was ugly; in the dedication of his account of his famous morris dance from London to Norwich, *Kemps nine daies wonder*, he confesses to Anne Fitton he has 'an ill face'.[38] As we shall see, there are indications that this became a running joke in his famous jigs; and it was taken up by Shakespeare. Hence when Kemp as Dogberry, during the interview with Conrad and Borachio, starts to boast of qualities he conspicuously lacks, he begins by claiming 'I am a wise fellow...' (*Much Ado* 4.2.77–8), and then goes on to make a surprising and unexpected claim that is rather out of character for Dogberry,

33 See, for example, *Antonio and Mellida: The First Part (1602)*, ed. G. K. Hunter (London, 1965), p. 5.
34 The jig reached unprecedented heights of popularity in the latter half of the 1590s and in the succeeding decade before it declined post-1612. For the jig, see primarily C. R. Baskervill, *The Elizabethan Jig and Related Song Drama* (Chicago, 1929); useful information is also supplied by D. Wiles, *Shakespeare's Clown: Actor and Text in the Elizabethan Playhouse* (Cambridge, 1987), pp. 43ff., and P. Thomson, *Shakespeare's Professional Career* (Cambridge, 1992), pp. 133ff.
35 Wiles, *Shakespeare's Clown*, p. 45.
36 Wiles, *Shakespeare's Clown*, p. 45.
37 Kemp is named in the Q2 copy of *Romeo and Juliet*, and in the 1600 Quarto of *Much Ado About Nothing*. Apart from his two known roles, there has also been a great deal of speculation about Kemp's possible roles; see, for example, Baldwin, *The Organization and Personnel of the Shakespearean Company*, pp. 241–4; H. D. Gray, 'The Roles of William Kemp', *Modern Language Review*, xxv (1930), 261–73; and Wiles's book, while being an invaluable collection of all the known facts about Kemp, also has a speculative strand – see, for example, pp. 116–35.
38 Dedicating his pamphlet to Anne Fitton, Kemp writes '(having but an ill face before) I shall appear to the world without a face, if your fayre hand wipe not away their [i.e. his detractors'] foule colours'. Reference is to *Kemps nine daies wonder* (London, 1600).

'and which is more, *as pretty a piece of flesh as any is in Messina*' (79–80 [my italics]). At this point, one can imagine the effect of a pause and the kind of pulled face or gurney for which Kemp was famous. And exactly the same effect, plus the repetition of the same two qualities to which Dogberry laid claim, is obtained by the drugged Titania's lavish compliment to Bottom, 'Thou art as wise as thou art beautiful' (3.1.142), when under the influence of 'Love-in-Idleness', she is seeing everything upside down. Once again Kemp is centre stage, his 'ill face' puckered and screwed up, and once again Shakespeare is exploiting one of his clown's most obvious assets. And when Dogberry reflects philosophically *not* that 'Comparisons are odious' but that 'Comparisons are odorous' (3.5.15), the dramatist is inverting the joke in his earlier comedy when Bottom misreads Quince's script, 'Thisbe, the flowers of *odious* savours sweet', at which the aggrieved author moans 'Odorous! odorous!' (77–8).

There is also the amusing play on two soubriquets of which the widely travelled Kemp was fond. On 'The first daies journey' of *Kemps nine daies wonder*, he uses the first when ebulliently introducing himself, 'my selfe, thats I, otherwise called *Cavaliero* Kemp . . .' [my italics]. His fondness for the second is apparent in *Singing Simpkin* which appeared in Stationers' Register in 1595 as 'a ballad called Kemp's new jig betwixt a soldier and a miser and Sim the clown'.[39] At Kemp's appearance as Sim, the married woman with whom he is having an affair, asks, 'How is't *Monsieur* Simkin, why are you so sad?' (9 [my italics]).[40] Both soubriquets had long attached themselves to Kemp; when *An Almond For A Parrat* (1589–90), a pamphlet sometimes attributed to Nashe and part of the Martin Marprelate controversy, was dedicated to him, its writer who apparently knew him, addresses it to 'that most comicall and conceited *Cavaliere Monsieur* du Kempe' [my italics].[41] Kemp was a burly, round figure and it is ironic that when both soubriquets are used in *A Midsummer Night's Dream* in the scene in Titania's bower, they are attached not to Kemp-as-Bottom but to two beautiful, sylph-like fairies:

> BOTTOM   Give me your neaf, *Monsieur* Mustardseed. Pray you, leave your courtesy, good *monsieur*.
> MUSTARDSEED What's your will?
> BOTTOM   Nothing, good *monsieur*, but to help *Cavalery* Peaseblossom to scratch...
>
> (4.1.19–23; my italics)[42]

The joke here is akin to that in *Singing Simpkin* where Kemp who would have been at least thirty-five by the time he played the clown Sim, is referred to as a '*young sweet-fac'd* fellow' (45 [my italics]). Finally, everything about Kemp, including his spectacular morris dances, tells us that he was an attention-grabber. And his wishing to dominate the stage and be the perpetual centre of attention is hilariously sent up when Kemp-as-Bottom wants to play all the play's parts; he has already proposed crashing the gender and generic barriers by playing both the lovers ('Thisne, Thisne!' – 'Ah Pyramus my lover dear . . .' 1.2.48–9) and the Lion ('I will roar, that I will do any man's heart good . . .' 66–7) before Quince lays down the law, 'You can play no part but Pyramus' (79). Internal evidence thus points to Bottom as the most substantial role Shakespeare created for Will Kemp, the brilliant clown, and one which gave him the opportunity to take centre stage with one of 'his much loved simpletons'.[43] But at the same time, as he does in his own case, as Shakespeare exaggerates and mocks Will Kemp's faults, there is nothing but good humour. And Kemp is also offered a generous peace offering. A 'ballad' or 'ballet' was also

---

39 Wiles, *Shakespeare's Clown*, p. 51.
40 Reference is to the text of the jig reprinted by Baskervill, *Elizabethan Jig*, pp. 444–9.
41 *The Works of Thomas Nashe* ed. R. B. McKerrow in 4 vols. (London, 1905), vol. 3, p. 341.
42 For 'Cavalery' as a version of 'cavaliero', see the notes on this scene of Brook, and of P. Holland (ed.), *A Midsummer Night's Dream* (Oxford, 1994). (The name 'Bottom' taken from the weaver's ball of thread (*OED*) may also be a good-natured dig at Kemp's physical shape).
43 Thomson, *Professional Career*, p. 134.

another name for a jig[44] and when Bottom awakens from his dream and immediately resolves 'I will get Peter Quince to write a *ballad* of this dream' [my italics], Shakespeare and Kemp were much in harmony.[45]

Finally, there is one last point to be made about Peter Quince. This playwright who is concerned to the exclusion of everything else with his play and its performance, turns aside for small talk on only one occasion, for a quip on premature baldness. This was one of the few personal topics that surface in the work of Shakespeare, a writer who normally tells us very little about himself.[46] And what Quince says on this occasion, 'Some of your French crowns have no hair at all' (1.2.90), is a reference to the 'French disease', syphilis. If one accepts Katherine Duncan-Jones's suggestion that Shakespeare himself suffered from syphilis as a legacy of his life-style in London, the comment has ironic and hidden application.[47] After the appearance of the chancre in the first stage of the disease, premature loss of hair took place in the second which could happen up to three years after being infected; the third dreadful stage which could involve madness, blindness or failure of any of the vital organs took hold at any time between three and forty years following infection. There is no proof he had the disease but he had spent most of his adult life living away from his wife and family with a bohemian set. Manningham recorded the story of 'Richard III and William the Conqueror' on 13 March 1602, when both the principals involved, Burbage and Shakespeare, were very much on the scene;[48] as a member of the Inns of Court with an interest in the playhouse and players, whether this particular story was factual or not, Manningham would have known the life-style of those involved. And if Shakespeare, like Burbage, was prepared to bed the playhouse 'groupies' of his day, he was living a life that brings the promiscuous, infected 'Dark Lady' of the *Sonnets* into view (see particularly 144) and women of the sort to give their sexual partners disease. Moreover, a progressive, ultimately terminal sexual disease as a cause of the death of a man who had made his will and seems to have scrupulously prepared for his end is far more

persuasive than the 'Rhenish wine' theory. The idea that he is actually joking about having it is, of course, unthinkable. But through the mouth of his dramatic *alter ego*, he may be commenting incidentally and in a sidelong way on a matter of personal moment.

The traditional approach to the burlesque has concentrated on identifying which minor Elizabethan literary fry have been set in the literary stocks.[49] J. Thomson for his inglorious poetic assault on Pyramus and Thisbe in *A Handfull of Pleasant Delites* is very much to the fore; one or two details from the anonymous poem on the myth in *A Gorgeous Gallery* are also picked up; and from Golding's version where the translator inevitably fills his lines up with pleonastic 'do's' and 'did's',

---

[44] This was because 'ballads' (often 'ballets' in the sixteenth century (*OED*)) often incorporated singing and also a dance to interpret the words of the song, and naturally evolved into the jig. One chapter in Baskervill's *Elizabethan Jig* bears the title, 'The Simple Ballad as Jig', pp. 164–218.

[45] There is not space here to present all the internal evidence; for a fuller examination of Kemp in the role, see my 'Will Kemp as Bottom' (forthcoming).

[46] It has become traditional, for instance, to interpret the opening of Sonnet 73 as a reference to the poet's baldness:

That time of year thou mayst in me behold
When yellow leaves, or none, or few do hang
Upon those boughs which shake against the cold.

In the recent Arden edition of the *Sonnets*, the editor, Katherine Duncan-Jones, reads the lines as 'a visual analogy between an almost-leafless tree and the almost-hairless head' of Shakespeare (*Shakespeare's Sonnets* (London, 1997), p. 256).

[47] *Ungentle Shakespeare: Scenes from his Life* (London, 2001), pp. 224–6.

[48] For the entry in Manningham's diary, see Schoenbaum, *Documentary Life*, p. 152.

[49] Kenneth Muir set out the targets in his ground-breaking article, 'Pyramus and Thisbe: A Study in Shakespeare's Method', *Shakespeare Quarterly*, 5 (1954). Over the years, these have reduced in number with the elimination of Moffet by Katherine Duncan-Jones, 'Pyramus and Thisbe: Shakespeare's Debt to Moffet Cancelled', *Review of English Studies*, n. s. 32 (1981), 296–301, and Chaucer by the present writer, 'Chaucer's Non-Involvement in Pyramus and Thisbe', *Notes and Queries*, n. s. 36 (1989), 317–20.

and has his lovers thank the 'courteous' wall.[50] To these can be added the early translators for the weird Latin syntax to which they had been led by Thomas Phaer who himself is mocked for one eccentric detail with Bottom's 'hopping' heart.[51] But the whole business has proved a gigantic red herring. As well as diverting attention away from the burlesque as the culmination of the extensive and systematic subversion of the myth of Pyramus and Thisbe that threads the *Dream*,[52] it has entirely obscured the fact that the one writer who above all is being mocked is William Shakespeare. And like his Orlando, through the *persona* of Peter Quince, the playwright is largely and characteristically intent on 'chiding no breather in the world but myself' (*As You Like It* 3.2.274).

While it is the source of much genial, warm humour in the play, the dramatist's taking a place amongst the 'rude mechanicals' and portraying himself as a tradesman also inevitably evokes at some level the low esteem in which other people and he himself held players and their profession. It was not unknown for those connected with the playhouse to be referred to as 'tradesmen' during the 1590s, and such references could be scornful. In *The Second Part of The Return from Parnassus*, when Philomusus and Studioso, two Cambridge graduates, having tried most jobs and being at the end of their tether, decide as a last resort to become players, Philomusus asks reflectively, 'and must the basest trade yeeld us reliefe?'[53] There are shades here of a profession located on the wrong side of the river amid bloodsports, brothels and the dregs of London. And Shakespeare, a playwright who aspired to gentility, while living a life bound up with players and the playhouse, occasionally voiced a similarly low estimate of a profession in which 'I have gone here and there/ And made myself a motley to the view' (Sonnet 110, 1–2) and which in the opinion of others 'doth staine pure gentle bluod'.[54]

As he worked on *A Midsummer Night's Dream*, his 'first great comic masterpiece',[55] increasingly confident of his powers, Shakespeare repeatedly and teasingly sowed doubts about the credibility

of the play's poised and delicate dramatic illusion. Nowhere is this more evident than in the lines that lead up to Theseus's warning against the dangers of the imagination ('The lunatic, the lover, and the poet'), when, discussing the lovers' adventures in the forest, he declares:

> I never may believe
> These antique fables, nor these fairy toys
>
> (5.1.2–3)

He is not only proclaiming disbelief in the fairy world but in the world of ancient legend of which he and Hippolyta are a part. The audience is being reminded by the play's voice of cold reason that what they are seeing is an illusion, a 'dream', a 'trick' of the imagination, an 'airy nothing' to which 'the poet's pen' has given 'A local habitation and a name'. Wake up, they are being told, through the deconstructing voice of the play's representative of good order and rule, and you will see that this is all just make-believe, fiction, and that these people before you are only 'players' ('antics').

What this article has attempted to show is that this teasing ambivalence also extends to what might in some ways be considered the most realistic strand of the plot, the tradesmen. They are involved in proceedings for the most practical of reasons, money – their leaders coveting sixpence a day for life, and they seem to connect the play up to the everyday world. But here, too, Shakespeare

---

[50] I have changed my position on the pleonastic use of the verb 'to do' since publishing 'Golding's Ovid, Shakespeare's "Small Latine", and the Real Object of Mockery in "Pyramus and Thisbe"'.

[51] See my 'Thomas Phaer and Bottom's "hopping" Heart', *Notes and Queries*, n. s. 34 (1987), 207–8.

[52] See my 'Ovid's Myths and the Unsmooth Course of Love in *A Midsummer Night's Dream*' in *Shakespeare and the Classics*, ed. C. Martindale and A. B. Taylor, scheduled for publication by Cambridge University Press in 2004.

[53] *The Three Parnassus Plays* (1598–1601), ed. J. B. Leishman (London, 1949), 1846.

[54] John Davies of Hereford, *Microcosmus*, cited by Schoenbaum *Documentary Life*, p. 205.

[55] C. L. Barber, *Shakespeare's Festive Comedy: A Study of Dramatic Form and its Relation to Social Custom* (Princeton, 1959), p. 11.

playfully and teasingly dispels the illusion of drama by showing behind the parts of these 'hempen homespuns' are the Lord Chamberlain's Men. Peeping through the roles of the 'rude mechanicals', like Snug's face through the Lion's mask, are the faces of members of the foremost playhouse company of the age as they go about creating another, make-believe dramatic world, and recognizable among them are Will Kemp and, more intriguingly, William Shakespeare.

CULTURAL MATERIALISM AND INTERTEXTUALITY: THE LIMITS OF QUEER READING IN *A MIDSUMMER NIGHT'S DREAM* AND *THE TWO NOBLE KINSMEN*

ALAN SINFIELD

INTERTEXTUALITY

Deconstruction, appealing to the insights of Julia Kristeva, Roland Barthes and Michael Riffaterre, has sought to show that all boundaries are at best provisional, at worst false and deluding. The act of reading 'plunges us into a network of textual relations', Graham Allen expounds: 'Meaning becomes something which exists between a text and all the other texts to which it refers and relates, moving out from the independent text into a network of textual relations'.[1] The study of an author's 'sources' may be rejuvenated by ideas of 'intertextuality'. Stephen J. Lynch avers: 'The old notion of particular and distinct sources has given way to new notions of boundless and heterogeneous intertextuality'. Indeed, 'the sources themselves can be examined as products of intertextuality – endlessly complex, multilayered fields of interpretation that Shakespeare refashioned and reconfigured into alternative fields of interpretation'.[2]

Kathryn Schwarz makes a valuable historical study of ideas and images of the Amazon in early modern representation. However, she appeals also to the Derridean principle of the *supplement*:

The multiplication of statements of desire [in *A Midsummer Night's Dream*] opens those statements to interpretation: if the rhetoric of female homoeroticism sounds just like that of heteroeroticism, language, like masculinity, becomes portable, flexible in the ways that it defines and refers. A transition into heteroeroticism implies a possible transition out.

Any ascribed reading is reversible, then. 'Like Derrida's supplement, stories about Amazons both support and undermine the agendas that produce them, offering a mirror image that might turn into an entirely different picture'.[3]

The problem with deconstructive criticism is that it is excessively indeterminate: there is always a supplement – and a supplement to the supplement. So intertextuality draws us closer than we might have expected to New Criticism: the text can be demonstrated to mean ever more fully, comprising even that which it is not. Almost as with New Critical irony, the text can be both complicit and transgressive at the same time. Whereas New Criticism tended to discover one theme – the unity of text and experience – deconstruction tends to prove, over and over, the indeterminacy of text and experience.

Louis Montrose has made *A Midsummer Night's Dream* a site for major advances in the theory and the practice of an historicized and politicized criticism. He defines the critical task as 'to (re)construct an intertextual field of representations, resonances, and pressures that constitutes an ideological matrix from which – and against which – Shakespeare shaped the mythopoeia of *A Midsummer Night's Dream*'. This distinction between the play and its

---

[1] Graham Allen, *Intertextuality* (London, 2000), p. 1.
[2] Stephen J. Lynch, *Shakespearean Intertextuality* (Westport, Connecticut, 1998), p. 1.
[3] Kathryn Schwarz, *Tough Love* (Durham, 2000), pp. 220, 157.

matrix aspires to control the traffic between text and context. However, at other points Montrose allows a relatively unconfined slippage, almost in the manner of a deconstructionist. For example, he finds that 'the dominance of patriarchy' in the play 'is vulnerable to destabilization by numerous instances of dramatic contradiction and intertextual irony'.[4] This move enables Montrose to posit a more disturbing and radical *Midsummer Night's Dream* than I shall seek to disclose.

A promising way to test these ideas is to address *A Midsummer Night's Dream* (1595–6) alongside *The Two Noble Kinsmen* by Shakespeare and John Fletcher (1612–13; it derives from *The Knight's Tale* by Chaucer). In both plays there is an interruption to the nuptials of Theseus and Hippolyta. In both, further disruptions occur in the affections of marriageable young people; these become the main matters to be resolved by Theseus. Both plays feature festive presentations by lower-class people, though I do not have space to talk about them here.[5]

My goal is to use the later play to supply aspects of the ideological environment of *A Midsummer Night's Dream*, highlighting thereby the alternatives selected by each text as it actualizes different parts of their shared field of possibilities. I intend a provocative, rather than a systematic procedure; *The Two Noble Kinsmen* will be used as a lever, not as an authority. In the process, it should prove possible to clarify some of the theoretical questions that I have raised.

HIPPOLYTA'S SILENCE

The interruption at the start of *A Midsummer Night's Dream* is a commonplace instance of an endemic crisis in patriarchy: Hermia wants to marry a different man from the one that her father has chosen for her. I have described the passing of the young woman from the authority of her father to that of her husband as a 'faultline' moment in early modern gender ideology.[6] Marriage was the institution through which property arrangements were made and inheritance secured, but it was supposed also to be a fulfilling personal relationship. It was held

that the people being married should act in obedience to their parents, but also that they should love one another. Lawrence Stone observes that dutiful children experienced 'an impossible conflict of role models. They had to try to reconcile the often incompatible demands for obedience to parental wishes on the one hand and expectations of affection in marriage on the other'.[7] The faultline in official doctrine afforded one distinct point at which a woman such as Hermia (or Katherina, Juliet, Desdemona or Cordelia) might throw the system into crisis. The resolution of this disturbance – albeit by magical intervention – enables commentators to see in *A Midsummer Night's Dream* a fresh affirmation of marriage. It is often supposed that it was written to celebrate an actual union.

The interruption to Theseus's nuptials in *The Two Noble Kinsmen* is more macabre, though it again concerns the status of marriage. Three lamenting queens importune him: Creon has not allowed them to bury the remains of their defeated husbands. He is undermining the seemliness of patriarchal, warrior relations.

The representation of Hippolyta in this scene foregrounds the potential of women together. To be sure, she has lost the fight with Theseus and is hoping, rather anxiously, to build a good marriage with him. Nonetheless, her status as a great Amazon warrior is established and celebrated.

---

4 Louis Montrose, *The Purpose of Playing* (Chicago, 1996), pp. 146, 121. On the boundaries between interpretation and historicism, see Vincent Quinn, 'Loose Reading? Sedgwick, Austen and Critical Practice', *Textual Practice*, 14 (2000), 305–26.

5 Generally commentators have made only brief comparisons between the two plays. See Schwarz, *Tough Love*, pp. 236–8; Montrose, *The Purpose of Playing*, p. 130; Valerie Traub, *The Renaissance of Lesbianism in Early Modern England* (Cambridge, 2002), pp. 67, 171–2, 329–30. But see Glynne Wickham, 'The Two Noble Kinsmen or A Midsummer Night's Dream, Part II?' *The Elizabethan Theatre*, 7 (1980), 167–96.

6 See Alan Sinfield, *Faultlines* (Oxford, 1992), pp. 42–7 and ch. 2.

7 Lawrence Stone, *The Family, Sex and Marriage* (London, 1977), p. 137.

The Second Queen apostrophizes her in heroic terms:

> Most dreaded Amazonian, that hast slain
> The scythe-tusked boar; that with thy arm, as strong
> As it is white, wast near to make the male
> To thy sex captive, but that this thy lord,
> Born to uphold creation in that honour
> First nature styled it in, shrunk thee into
> The bound thou wast o'erflowing, at once subduing
> Thy force and thy affection;[8]

Hippolyta came close to defeating Theseus, the Second Queen is saying; and although it is finally natural that the man should win (Theseus is standing by), in the case of Hippolyta this is at the expense of a remarkable phenomenon. Even now, although Hippolyta may kneel in supplication before Theseus, on behalf of the Three Queens and their unburied husbands, it must be for only a moment:

> But touch the ground for us no longer time
> Than a dove's motion, when the head's plucked off.
> Tell him, if he i'th'blood-sized field lay swollen,
> Showing the sun his teeth, grinning at the moon,
> What you would do.
>
> (1.1.97–101)

Hippolyta, perhaps energized by the gruesome imagery, replies that she would as soon join the military expedition against Creon as the enterprise upon which she is embarked (that is, marriage). She threatens to defer consummation with Theseus.

If Hippolyta is largely subdued by Theseus, her sister Emilia remains thoroughly woman-centred; 'What woman I may stead that is distressed / Does bind me to her', she reassures the Third Queen (1.1.36–7). She threatens, if their pleas are ignored, never to take a husband. During the ensuing action Emilia maintains an independent stance in the face of (what we would call) harassment by Theseus. When Arcite impresses the court at a wrestling match, Theseus says Emilia might be wise to let him become her master rather than her servant. 'I hope, too wise for that, sir', she retorts (2.5.64). When Palamon and Arcite joust to win her, Theseus demands that she make herself available as the trophy: 'You are the treasure and must needs be by / To give the service pay' (5.3.31–2). She refuses.[9]

Placing the fuller evocation of female independence in *The Two Noble Kinsmen* alongside *A Midsummer Night's Dream* may help us to think about Hippolyta's attitude towards her marriage in the earlier play. As some directors have noticed (Philip C. McGuire discusses their work[10]), she has little to say in the opening scene, and what she does say scarcely indicates harmony. Theseus's first words are about how he can't wait for them to get to bed; Hippolyta's reply is that it will be quite soon enough: 'Four days will quickly steep themselves in night; / Four nights will quickly dream away the time'.[11] Mysteriously, she invokes the moon, an image of chastity. After this initial speech Hippolyta has *nothing at all to say* in the opening scene; is she perhaps dismayed by Theseus's bullying of Hermia? He doesn't consult her about the lovers' dilemma; he takes no further notice of her until he is ready to leave: 'Come, my Hippolyta; what cheer, my love?' (1.1.122). His question suggests that she is not conspicuously happy. However, she is given no voice in which to announce her recalcitrance.

Hippolyta does speak in Acts 4 and 5, but her contributions consist largely of irritable attempts to contradict or compete with Theseus. She caps his hunt with a report of another occasion, with better hounds and graced by Hercules and Cadmus. She opposes his wish to see the Mechanicals' play, and leads the mockery of the performance. Even her famous speech about how the dream of the night 'grows to something of great constancy' (5.1.26)

---

8 John Fletcher and William Shakespeare, *The Two Noble Kinsmen*, ed. Lois Potter (London, 1997), 1.1.78–85.

9 Emilia's role is stressed in Gordon McMullan, 'A Rose for Emilia: Collaborative Relations in *The Two Noble Kinsmen*', in McMullan, ed., *Renaissance Configurations* (London, 1998); Laurie Shannon, *Sovereign Amity* (Chicago, 2002), chapter 3; and Traub, *The Renaissance of Lesbianism*, pp. 172–5.

10 Philip C. McGuire, *Speechless Dialect* (Berkeley, 1985), chapter 1.

11 William Shakespeare, *A Midsummer Night's Dream*, ed. Harold F. Brooks (London, 1979), 1.1.7–8.

occurs as a refutation of Theseus's assertion that lunatics, lovers and poets are all the same.

Attending to *The Two Noble Kinsmen* may encourage a less complacent reading of *A Midsummer Night's Dream*. It draws attention to the energies that were suppressed through enforced marriage, helping us to interpret the muted and captious expression to which Hippolyta is reduced. This reading does not displace the idea of the play as a marriage celebration, but by enlarging the ideological environment it does undermine its apparently natural supremacy. However, in other aspects a comparison with *The Two Noble Kinsmen* reveals *A Midsummer Night's Dream* to be the less radical play. By 'radical', for the purposes of this essay, I mean prompting a critique of patriarchy – displaying its oppressiveness and its inability to accommodate a range of humane relations, and exploring the scope for dissident interpersonal intensities.

SAME-SEX BONDING

In *The Two Noble Kinsmen* Theseus concedes the Queens' case and goes to fight Creon, leaving his bride and the conduct of the wedding feast to his friend, Pirithous. What is striking here is how quickly the assumptions of hetero-patriarchy unravel. As soon as Theseus is out of sight the women begin to doubt the inevitability of heterosexual relations. Emilia remarks of Pirithous, as he leaves to join Theseus's army, 'How his longing / Follows his friend!' (1.3.27–8). The two men have shared many dangers, Hippolyta admits:

> Their knot of love,
> Tied, weaved, entangled, with so true, so long,
> And with a finger of so deep a cunning,
> May be outworn, never undone.
>
> (1.3.41–4)

'Their knot of love' sounds remarkably like wedlock.[12] Indeed, in Plutarch's *Lives* Pirithous, fascinated by the report of Theseus, goes to fight him, but on meeting they became sworn brothers; this is very like the battlefield betrothal of Theseus and Hippolyta.[13] But Theseus surely prefers Hippolyta,

Emilia reassures her sister, though in notably oblique phrasing: 'Doubtless, / There is a best and reason has no manners / To say it is not you' (1.3.47–9).

Emilia is moved to compare her friendship with Flavina, who died. They were young, innocent, and their feelings were reciprocal – without the tensions that evidently characterize heterosexual relations:

> The flower that I would pluck
> And put between my breasts (then but beginning
> To swell about the blossom), oh, she would long
> Till she had such another, and commit it
> To the like innocent cradle, where phoenix-like
> They died in perfume.
>
> (1.3.66–71)

It shows, Emilia declares, 'That the true love 'tween maid and maid may be / More than in sex dividual' (lines 81–2).[14]

Were she persuadable, Hippolyta admits, Emilia would 'Have said enough to shake me from the arm / Of the all-noble Theseus'; but she is confident that she rather than Pirithous holds the high throne in her husband's heart (1.3.91–6). However, Emilia sticks to her position: 'I am not / Against your faith, yet I continue mine' (lines 96–7).

Reading as a gay man, I welcome these intimations of same-sex relationships. *A Midsummer Night's Dream* appears less radical by comparison. The thought that women might live together, outside wedlock, is in the play, but in mainly negative contexts. Theseus threatens Hermia with it as the punishment for resistance to her father's will: 'For aye to be in shady cloister mew'd, / To live a barren sister all your life' (1.1.71–2). He calls it 'a vow of single life' (121) – not counting other women as

---

[12] C. T. Onions, *A Shakespeare Glossary*, 2nd edn (Oxford, 1958), p. 123.

[13] See Bruce R. Smith, *Homosexual Desire in Shakespeare's England* (Chicago, 1991), p. 31.

[14] On this last phrase, see the fascinating commentary by Peter Stallybrass, 'Shakespeare, the Individual, and the Text', in Lawrence Grossberg, Cary Nelson and Paula A. Treichler, eds., *Cultural Studies* (New York, 1992).

company. Helena speaks movingly of the erstwhile feeling between Hermia and herself:

> So we grew together,
> Like to a double cherry, seeming parted,
> But yet an union in partition,
> Two lovely berries moulded on one stem.
>
> (3.2.208–11)

Valerie Traub and Patricia Parker have remarked the intensity here.[15] Conversely, these are anxious moments for conservative criticism. C. L. Barber, for instance: 'before the scramble is over, the two girls have broken the double-cherry bond, to fight each other without reserve for her man. So they move from the loyalties of one stage of life to those of another'.[16] It was just a passing phase then.

In fact the intimacies between the girls are invoked reproachfully, in the light of Hermia's disruption of Helena's current heterosexual ambitions. Under competitive pressure they can be repudiated: 'She was a vixen when she went to school', Helena asserts (3.2.324). Hermia mentions how she and Helena would lie upon 'faint primrose beds' together, but in the context of making an assignation with Lysander (1.1.215). Helena protests to Demetrius: 'Your wrongs do set a scandal on my sex. / We cannot fight for love, as men may do' (2.1.240–41). She has forgotten that Hippolyta did just that, albeit unsuccessfully.

The deconstructive-intertextual move at this point is to allow the later play to bleed back into the earlier, sanctioning a queer reading of it, crediting it with positive-disconcerting lesbian feeling. I think, rather, that *The Two Noble Kinsmen* is reminding us of something radical that *A Midsummer Night's Dream* is ready to forget.

The boys in *The Two Noble Kinsmen* are also implicated in same-sex eroticism. Act 2 scene 2 finds Palamon and Arcite in prison together. Palamon laments the change in their circumstances. Never again will they, 'like twins of honour', exercise in arms (2.2.18). And, heaviest, Arcite adds, they will never marry and have 'The sweet embraces of a loving wife' (line 30); they will have no issue. 'This

is all our world. / We shall know nothing here but one another' (lines 40–1).

Yet there are consolations, they quickly remark. ''Tis a main goodness, cousin, that our fortunes/ Were twined together', Palamon allows (lines 63–4). Arcite agrees:

> And here being thus together,
> We are an endless mine to one another;
> We are one another's wife, ever begetting
> New births of love; we are father, friends, acquaintance,
> We are, in one another, families;
> I am your heir and you are mine.
>
> (lines 78–83)

After all, if they were at liberty a wife might part them, or business. Nothing can spoil their friendship till death. This is disconcertingly like King James's letter to George Villiers at Christmas 1623: 'And so God bless you, my sweet child and wife, and grant that ye may ever be a comfort to your dear dad and husband'.[17]

There is no equivalent to such adventurous and substantial sentiments in *A Midsummer Night's Dream*.

It is too good to be true. Perhaps Palamon and Arcite have frightened themselves with the boldness of their rhetoric. In an early variant on what Michael in *The Boys in the Band* calls the 'Christ-was-I-drunk-last-night syndrome',[18] they seize upon a glimpse of Emilia, walking in the garden below, as opportunity to reassert their heterosexual credentials. Ironically, she is talking still, now with her waiting woman, about the superiority of relations between women. Boys might love themselves, like Narcissus; they might be hard-hearted. 'They could not be to one so fair', the woman

---

[15] Traub, *The Renaissance of Lesbianism*, pp. 57–8, 64–5, 171–2, 329; Patricia Parker, *Shakespeare from the Margins* (Chicago, 1996), pp. 101–3.

[16] C. L. Barber, *Shakespeare's Festive Comedy* (Princeton, 1972), p. 130.

[17] Quoted in Smith, *Homosexual Desire*, p. 14.

[18] Mart Crowley, *The Boys in the Band* (Harmondsworth, 1970), p. 25.

replies, flirtatiously; she would not (2.2.123). They agree to lie down together:

WOMAN I could lie down, I am sure.
EMILIA   And take one with you?
WOMAN That's as we bargain, madam.
EMILIA   Well, agree then.
                                  (2.2.152–3)[19]

It is in this context of erotic female bonding that the two boys set eyes upon Emilia. First Palamon and then Arcite declares his passion for her, and they fall immediately into bitter recriminations. It does seem that Palamon sees her first, and first asserts his love, and we may infer that this prompts Arcite, producing a rivalrous triangle. Bruce Smith observes: 'Only when Palamon tells him point-blank, "You shall not love at all", does Arcite become defiant and proclaim himself the enemy of his friend'.[20] 'Who shall deny me?' Arcite demands. Palamon is incited by the challenge:

I that first saw her, I that took possession
First with mine eye of all those beauties in her
Revealed to mankind! If thou lovest her,
Or entertain'st a hope to blast my wishes,
Thou art a traitor, Arcite, and a fellow
False as thy title to her.

                                  (2.2.169–74)

This is not a replacement of male bonding by heterosexual passion, but its continuation in other terms. Observe the total failure of either man to broach the question of Emilia's wishes: she is a minor player in their game. In fact they devote far more attention to fighting each other than to wooing her. When it appears that Theseus will condemn them both to death, Palamon's plea is:

Let's die together, at one instant, Duke.
Only a little let him fall before me,
That I may tell my soul, he shall not have her.

                                  (3.6.177–9)

'Thou dost love her because thou know'st I love her', says the poet of Shakespeare's Sonnets.[21] Eve Sedgwick in Between Men develops René Girard's idea of a triangular pattern wherein male pursuit is motivated less by the qualities of the woman than by the fact that another male has chosen her; 'the bond that links the two rivals is as intense and potent as the bond that links either of the rivals to the beloved'.[22] Male bonding contributed crucially to the ties of heroism, loyalty and self-sacrifice that underpin a warrior culture; it was invaluable still in early modern England, as part of the glue for the networks of alliance, kinship and patronage through which business was conducted.[23] It was part of the system through which patriarchy organized itself. Yet, as The Two Noble Kinsmen illustrates, male rivalry could be strikingly dysfunctional.

Traces of this potential disturbance in patriarchy are less marked in A Midsummer Night's Dream than might be expected. Though Demetrius and Lysander switch the objects of their devotion arbitrarily, they pay only occasional attention to each other.

LOVELY BOYS

The intensity of same-sex bonding between both women and men in The Two Noble Kinsmen prompts some questions about sexuality. What is extraordinary in the dialogue of both the women and the men is the lack of guardedness – when Emilia says she and Flavina wanted to put the same flowers in their cleavages; when Arcite says he and Palamon are 'one another's wife, ever begetting / New births

[19] Richard Abrams elucidates the erotics of this exchange between the women in his essay, 'Gender Confusion and Sexual Politics in The Two Noble Kinsmen', in James Redmond, ed., Drama, Sex and Politics, Themes in Drama, 7 (Cambridge, 1985), p. 70.
[20] Smith, Homosexual Desire, p. 71.
[21] Sonnet 42, in W.G. Ingram and Theodore Redpath, eds., Shakespeare's Sonnets (London, 1964).
[22] Eve Kosofsky Sedgwick, Between Men (New York, 1985), p. 21.
[23] See Alan Bray, 'Homosexuality and the Signs of Male Friendship in Elizabethan England', History Workshop, 29 (1990), 1–19.

of love'. Catherine Belsey remarks how same-sex and cross-sex relations are spoken of in equivalent terms in Palamon's last words:

> Oh, cousin!
> That we should things desire, which do cost us
> The loss of our desire! That nought could buy
> Dear love, but loss of dear love!
>
> (5.4.109–12)

'Here heterosexual passion and homosocial friendship are defined in exactly the same terms: both are dear love; both are desire', Belsey observes.[24]

Such unembarrassed expressions of same-sex passion restate the question I have broached elsewhere: either same-sex practices are so remote from the minds of these people as to be off the map of potential human experience, or they are so commonplace as to be unremarkable. As Sedgwick observes, the dominant assumption in our societies is that the line between the homosexual and the homosocial must be rigorously policed. However, this is not necessarily the case in all societies. In any male-dominated society, Sedgwick adds, there will be a special relationship between male bonding and the structures of patriarchal power. But in diverse historical contexts this relationship 'may take the form of ideological homophobia, ideological homosexuality, or some highly conflicted but intensively structured combination of the two'.[25] An intriguing thought, therefore, building on the insights of Stephen Orgel and Bruce Smith, is that in early modern England male same-sex relations *were not terribly important*.[26] Traub makes a comparable case for erotic desire between women.[27] After all, in *As You Like It* and *Twelfth Night* homoeroticism is part of the fun of the wooing; but it wouldn't be fun if such scenarios were freighted with the anxieties that gay and bisexual people often experience today.

Early modern England was committed to the proposition — by no means a necessary one — that property, and all the power and authority that go with it, is legitimately held if it has passed from father to son through a recognized form of marriage. Heterosexual passion, therefore, had

large consequences. Same-sex passion became dangerous only if, as in instances such as Marlowe's *Edward II* and *The Merchant of Venice* (at least, in Portia's perception), it was allowed to interfere with other responsibilities. Plainly female assertion to the point of Amazon commitment, and the excessive bonding and crazy rivalry of Palamon and Arcite, threaten the system — to the point where the authoritarian interventions of Theseus may seem justified.

If *The Two Noble Kinsmen* suggests a significant context of companionable same-sex passion, the implications in *A Midsummer Night's Dream* may be felt most prominently not among the boys and girls, but in the devotion of Titania to a votaress of her order, and the desire of Oberon for the son. Titania's speech is evocative:

> Full often hath she gossip'd by my side;
> And sat with me on Neptune's yellow sands,
> Marking th'embarked traders on the flood:
> When we have laugh'd to see the sails conceive
> And grow big-bellied with the wanton wind;
> Which she, with pretty and with swimming gait
> Following (her womb then rich with my young
>   squire),
> Would imitate, and sail upon the land
> To fetch me trifles, and return again
> As from a voyage rich with merchandise.
>
> (2.1.125–34)

The father is scarcely needed in this marvellous pregnancy, the women are self-sufficient. For this commitment Titania has forsworn the bed of Oberon (this was the threat of Hippolyta to Theseus in *The Two Noble Kinsmen*), turning her fairy

---

[24] Catherine Belsey, 'Love in Venice', *Shakespeare Survey 44* (1992), pp. 41–53, 53.

[25] Sedgwick, *Between Men*, p. 25.

[26] Stephen Orgel, *Impersonations* (Cambridge, 1996), pp. 35–6; Smith, *Homosexual Desire*, ch. 2. See also B.R. Burg, 'Ho Hum, Another Work of the Devil: Buggery and Sodomy in Early Stuart England', in Salvatore J. Licata and Robert P. Petersen, eds., *Historical Perspectives on Homosexuality* (New York, 1985).

[27] Traub, *The Renaissance of Lesbianism*.

train into a feminized community – such as is evoked by the figures of Hippolyta and Emilia and held over Hermia as a punishment by Theseus. The chastising of this affront to patriarchy is the comic project of *A Midsummer Night's Dream*. The emblem of Oberon's power is his seizing the boy for himself.

How old is this lad? Is he old enough to be sexy? Montrose supposes that he might be at the age – around seven years old – where he would be expected to move from infancy, dominated by women, to youth.[28] This would situate Titania's dissidence as an attempt to interfere with patriarchal sequence by prolonging the boy's period within the feminized sphere of childhood. However, if he is rather older, a sexual intensity on the part of both Titania and Oberon becomes plausible:

And jealous Oberon would have the child
Knight of his train, to trace the forests wild:
But she perforce withholds the loved boy,
Crowns him with flowers, and makes him all her joy.
(2.1.24–7)

Only acute sexual infatuation, it seems to me, may plausibly move these great fairies to jeopardize the entire creation.

Other mentions of the boy do not clarify his age. Since he never appears, it may slide around, depending on the local relevance (like the age of Hamlet). Oberon calls him 'a little changeling boy' and says he wants him for a 'henchman' (2.1.120–1). Titania calls him 'the child' and 'my young squire' (2.1.122, 131). Puck calls him Titania's 'attendant' and a 'lovely boy' (2.1.21–2); 'lovely boy' is the expression used in Sonnet 126, the last of those addressed to the youth: 'O thou, my lovely boy, who in thy power / Dost hold Time's fickle glass'.[29]

Margot Hendricks describes a performance – a 'camp rendering' – in which the Indian boy appeared in his early twenties, wearing a gold lamé loincloth; in the accompanying photograph he looks pampered and sulky. Hendricks reads him as 'a rich oriental "trifle" accessible to the gaze of predominantly white audiences'.[30] Nonetheless, she doesn't credit Oberon or Titania with such

licentious appreciation of the boy. She writes of him as a child, and reads Oberon's motive as 'the manifestation of a perceived prerogative to claim possession' (p. 53). It may indeed be that; Oberon may be asserting a *droit de seigneur*.

When we started to talk about same-sex passion in the early modern period, every instance seemed a triumph for gay liberation. However, not all treatments are progressive. Gayle Rubin has shown how women are used as exchangeable property through which the bonds of men with men are secured in patriarchy.[31] Also, everywhere in the early modern period, we see a casual traffic in boys who, because they are less significant, are moved around the employment-patronage system more fluently than women. Patriarchy determined the lives of young, lower-class and outsider men, as well as women. I have remarked elsewhere how in *The Merchant of Venice* Bassanio gives new liveries to Launcelot and Gratiano for the expedition to Belmont; Jessica appears as Lorenzo's page, 'Even in the lovely garnish of a boy' (2.6.45); the young doctor (Portia) claims Portia's ring from Bassanio for services rendered.[32]

As Hendricks remarks, Titania's reference to 'th'embarked traders on the flood' and 'a voyage rich with merchandise' invites awareness of European exploitation of the Indias of spice and mine.[33] The Indian boy in *A Midsummer Night's Dream* is being traded between Titania and Oberon, neither of whom consults his preferences. Initially he is forcibly detained by Titania, then he is passed abruptly to Oberon:

---

28 Montrose, *The Purpose of Playing*, pp. 126–7, 149–50.

29 Ingram and Redpath, eds., *Shakespeare's Sonnets*.

30 Margot Hendricks, '"Obscured by dreams": Race, Empire, and Shakespeare's *A Midsummer Night's Dream*', *Shakespeare Quarterly*, 47 (1996), 37–60, 37–8.

31 Gayle Rubin, 'The Traffic in Women: Notes Toward a Political Economy of Sex', in Rayna Reiter, ed., *Toward an Anthropology of Women* (New York, 1975).

32 Alan Sinfield, 'How to Read *The Merchant of Venice* without being Heterosexist', in Terence Hawkes, ed., *Alternative Shakespeares 2* (London, 1996). The play is quoted from the edition of John Russell Brown (London, 1961).

33 Hendricks, '"Obscured by dreams"', p. 53.

I then did ask of her her changeling child;
Which straight she gave me, and her fairy sent
To bear him to my bower in fairy land.

(4.1.58–60)

They are not going hunting, then; surely this is ominously intimate; a bower of bliss! 'The mightiest kings have had their minions'.[34] Perhaps the boy will enjoy the attentions of the king of the fairies, but we don't know.

Oberon, apparently, is within his rights. It is Titania who has transgressed and must be punished. Like the Duchess of Malfi, she has chosen her partner from outside the permitted range. If she insists on challenging Oberon's privilege, then her beau must be the monstrous Bottom – who, like the boy, she swathes in flowers. A cross-class choice by women appears more dangerous for patriarchal culture than same-sex passion among boys and men. Oberon's seizing of the boy is a victory for patriarchy, not a challenge to it.

READING THESEUS AGAINST THE GRAIN

In *A Midsummer Night's Dream* a resolution of the main conflict is always available: with two boys, two girls and heterosexual ideology, we know that something will be fixed up. As it transpires, Oberon makes a genial outcome easy for Theseus. In *The Two Noble Kinsmen*, conversely, the situation appears impossible, and Theseus plainly makes it worse. His sadistic adjudication, which is not in Chaucer's version of the story, has a predictably distressing outcome for all parties. Such a violent and ridiculous closure surely brings Theseus and his system into discredit.[35] 'Is this winning?' Emilia asks (5.3.138). Patriarchy discloses its faultlines; it fails to match the intuitions of the most humane characters. (The lower-class subplot, in which the Jailer's Daughter's crazy obsession with Palamon is accommodated when a doctor and her household put up another man to impersonate him, arguably tends in the same direction.)

In the deconstructive-intertextual mode of criticism, this reading may be carried back into the earlier play. In fact some of the best commentators on *A Midsummer Night's Dream* have argued that, in the earlier play also, the destructive violence of patriarchy is exposed.

For Montrose, 'the play articulates and disseminates fragments of those socially active heterodox discourses that the politically dominant discourse seeks, with only limited success, to appropriate, repudiate, or suppress'.[36] For Parker, in a brilliant analysis, the 'harmonious ending' is 'ironized'. Disturbances radiating out from the 'misjoinings and botched constructions' of the Mechanicals make possible 'a doubled perspective on the professedly natural order of this ending, an estrangement that allows such closure to be viewed as the naturalized righting that enables the very conjunctions on which rule and governance depend'.[37]

Laura Levine, in a powerful essay, names Theseus's taking of Hippolyta a rape; his call for festivities is designed to disguise the fact:

Hippolyta, I woo'd thee with my sword,
And won thy love doing thee injuries;
But I will wed thee in another key,
With pomp, with triumph, and with revelling.

(1.1.16–19)

However, Levine finds, theatrical display only confirms 'what Theseus wants to dismiss, the reality of sexual violence'.[38] The problem with this argument is the assumption that Theseus must want to assuage his guilt. After all, in a violently male-oriented society, vaunting is at least as likely; his call for pomp, triumph and revelling doesn't sound like a man withdrawing into apologetic myths. Nor does Theseus's treatment of Hermia suggest any

---

[34] *Edward II* 1.4.390, in Roma Gill, ed., *The Plays of Christopher Marlowe* (Oxford, 1971).

[35] Theseus's tyranny is urged, against critics who have supposed that Shakespeare and Fletcher must be endorsing marriage at any cost, in Shannon, *Sovereign Amity*, ch. 3.

[36] Montrose, *The Purpose of Playing*, p. 144.

[37] Parker, *Shakespeare from the Margins*, pp. 107, 114.

[38] Laura Levine, 'Rape, Repetition, and the Politics of Closure in *A Midsummer Night's Dream*', in Valerie Traub, M. Lindsay Kaplan and Dympna Callaghan, eds., *Feminist Readings of Early Modern Culture* (Cambridge, 1996), p. 216.

relaxation of patriarchal domination. 'To you your father should be as a god', he tells her (1.1.47).

What I am trying to do, in resistance to the open-ended deconstructive mode of criticism, is maintain a sense of the ideological limits of *A Midsummer Night's Dream*. The alternatives which this play is *not choosing* lurk at the boundaries of the text, but they do not *become* the text. I agree with Montrose that the play 'may try to impose symbolic closure upon the heterodoxy to which it also gives voice, but that closure can be neither total nor final'. I argue similarly in *Faultlines*; no text can secure its own reception.[39] Notwithstanding, there are two main reasons for resisting the idea that the literary text may be able endlessly to incorporate anything that we might think about it.

First, it seems intuitively wrong and practically unhelpful to declare (in effect) that *A Midsummer Night's Dream* and *The Two Noble Kinsmen* are ultimately the same. Indeed, it is plain that for most readers and audiences *A Midsummer Night's Dream* is appropriately concluded when Puck has all the lovers paired off heterosexually, and Titania and Hippolyta have capitulated to (what I regard as) the bullying of Oberon and Theseus.

> Jack shall have Jill,
> Nought shall go ill;
> The man shall have his mare again, and all shall be
> well.
>
> (3.2.461–3)

There are, in this conventional reading, aberrant motifs and difficulties, but they are overcome by lyrical language, cunning plotting and imaginative mythology. Notions of fairies, magic, the blessing of the bridal bed, and happily-ever-after, throw over it all a charming veil of dream and enchantment. Plainly the play will bear that construction. It is entirely open to the reader, or the theatre director, to collude in the notion that love and marriage will turn out all right, so long as we do as we are told and don't ask too many questions.

Second, crediting the text even with its own negations forecloses on the space from within which one might comment on its political tendency. If *A Midsummer Night's Dream* may be inter-

preted as comprising every dissident nuance which the assiduous critic may uncover, then its conservative slant cannot be challenged; it is neither more nor less radical than any other text. I want to maintain a sense of ideological limits, so as to make apparent the choices, within the available ideological field, that constitute each play. Finally, *The Two Noble Kinsmen* draws attention to ideological limits which the earlier play accepts. The juxtaposing of two plays draws attention to the boundaries of each; while it will reveal, inevitably, the porosity of those boundaries, it will also discover their effectiveness.

Up to a point, to be sure, *The Two Noble Kinsmen* helps to supply a contextual knowledge of what *A Midsummer Night's Dream* might be; it stimulates awareness of marginal factors within the earlier play, enabling a more problematic vision of its scope. For instance, I would argue that the idea of Hippolyta's recalcitrance, prompted in part by *The Two Noble Kinsmen*, can be substantiated in the text of *A Midsummer Night's Dream*; it can work in the theatre. In other aspects, however, juxtaposing the two plays reveals that, within a complicated and largely shared cultural and political force-field, they are actualizing different ranges of ideological potential. As Jonathan Dollimore declares, 'there is a limit to which the text can be said to incorporate those aspects of its historical moment of which it never speaks'. Beyond that point, the warped and debased kind of utterance allowed to the marginal becomes, itself, an insult. 'Looking for evidence of resistance we find rather further evidence of exploitation'.[40]

Myself, I find the patriarchal figures in *A Midsummer Night's Dream* oppressive, and the same-sex relations to be the most vigorous and moving parts. If I were directing the play, I'd have Hippolyta led on in a cage, like the emperor Bajazeth defeated by Tamburlaine, and Oberon in bed with the lovely boy. To get what I regard as a happy ending I would

[39] Montrose, *The Purpose of Playing*, p. 144; Sinfield, *Faultlines*, pp. 38–51.

[40] Jonathan Dollimore, 'Transgression and Surveillance in *Measure for Measure*', in Dollimore and Alan Sinfield, eds., *Political Shakespeare*, 2nd edn (Manchester, 1994), pp. 85–6.

show the boys and girls successfully resisting the effects of Oberon's drugs, and producing some more interesting interpersonal combinations. However, it is hard to see Theseus and Oberon permitting that. Perhaps the more effective move would be to disclose the tragedy in the conventional ending. This would involve presenting the boys and girls as manifestly brainwashed and infantilized by Puck's manipulations of their minds and bodies into heterosexual pairings. Or, indeed, they could be lobotomized – reduced to the condition of the besotted Bottom. The effect, as Oberon describes it, is rather like that. His herb, crushed into their eyes, will:

> take from thence all error with his might,
> And make his eyeballs roll with wonted sight.
> When they next wake, all this derision
> Shall seem a dream and fruitless vision.
>
> (3.2.368–71)

Puck could be shown putting electrodes on to their heads; they would lose their vigour and engagement with life, and sink into marriage as into a stupor. Sustaining patriarchy is too expensive when it means tailoring passion to patriarchal ideology. Emilia's question, when Arcite has gained her at the cost of the life of his friend, is apposite here: 'Is this winning?'

However, I am aware that *A Midsummer Night's Dream* is designed to deny, rather than accommodate such ideas. Indeed, Puck encourages audience members also to think like zombies, imagining that they have but slumbered and dreamt (5.1.410–14). If I assert my own reading, I accept that it will be *against the grain*. This concept – against the grain – is very important, because it allows me to distinguish what I believe the play to be about, and how I would like it to be. I can play like a deconstructionist, but without having to forsake the evidence of scholarship, reading experience, and common sense.

'Reading against the grain' is, of course, the project proposed by Walter Benjamin. It occurs in the section of *Illuminations* where he declares: 'There is no document of civilization which is not at the same time a document of barbarism': it is be-

cause 'cultural treasures' are always coopted by the ruling elite that a historical materialist will regard it 'as his task to brush history against the grain'.[41]

To be interesting, a reading against the grain will invoke diverse nuances in the text, but it will recognize nonetheless that the text has an ideological project, to which other inferences will always be marginal. How do we know what the grain is? In the same way that we conduct any interpretation of language: by referring to our knowledge of norms and expectations as we have operated them hitherto in our life experience, picking up cues as to genre, register, subculture, tradition, and other such conventions, and watching out for irony, pastiche, jokes and mistakes. Of course, this is not a reliable procedure. But on this the deconstructionists are right: language isn't going to afford a reliable procedure. If we were to wait until we had achieved an unambiguous utterance, we would starve to death.

BEYOND THE COUPLE

A notion that appears fixed for most commentators on these plays is that it is good when people get into couples – lately even same-sex couples. Yet there is perhaps some less orthodox prompting in *The Two Noble Kinsmen*. The 'Prologue' alludes to its complicated origins: new plays are like maidens on their bridal night, and this one is well vouched for because Chaucer was the father. The husbands, then, are Fletcher and Shakespeare – both of them. Fortunately, unlike the boys and girls in our two plays, they can engage themselves with the same love object (the same play) without falling into violent dispute. The 'Prologue' speaks with undivided voice; there is another way of resolving the love triangle.

Arcite did claim, initially, that he and Palamon loved Emilia differently – one as a goddess, the other as a woman. 'So both may love' (2.2.166).

---

41 Walter Benjamin, *Illuminations*, trans. Harry Zohn (London, 1973), pp. 258–9. In *Faultlines* I offer reading against the grain as a way of challenging not only particular readings, but also the cultural authority of the Bard – which otherwise is likely to be coopted for conservative values: see pp. 16–28.

Indeed, the three lovers might have maintained all their attachments, same- and cross-gender, in a ménage à trois. Emilia lights upon this possibility. She is doing her best to think creatively, to find a non-violent (non-patriarchal) solution. She tries to prefer one boy to the other, to 'end their strife' (4.2.3), but they are both excellent. Another possibility: 'Were they metamorphosed / Both into one!' (5.3.84–5). Her most radical idea is that she might have both:

> What a mere child is Fancy,
> That, having two fair gauds of equal sweetness,
> Cannot distinguish, but must cry for both!
>
> (4.2.52–4)

However, this is forbidden; it would complicate the transmission of property. 'They cannot both enjoy you', Theseus instructs Emilia (3.6.275).

Well, they could. As Jeffrey Masten has remarked, the collaboration of Fletcher and Shakespeare echoes that of Fletcher and Francis Beaumont. They did not only write together. According to John Aubrey's *Brief Lives*, until Beaumont married an heiress in 1613 (about the date of *The Two Noble Kinsmen*), he and Fletcher 'lived together on the Banke side, not far from the Play-house, both batchelors; lay together – from Sir James Hales etc.; had one wench in the house between them, which they did so admire; the same cloathes and cloake, &c., betweene them'.[42] It doesn't matter whether they did this: it was plausible to report that they did. 'You must love one of them', Theseus asserts again. 'I had rather both; / So neither for my sake should fall untimely', Emilia replies (4.2.68–9). So every man or woman may have his or her Jack *and* his or her Jill. Of course, it won't be easy. The writer of the *Sonnets* is as jealous as Oberon when his lovely boy sleeps with his mistress.

If the ménage à trois were readily available as an option, half the plots of Elizabethan and Jacobean theatre would collapse. Yet we have diverse hints already. Achilles, Patroclus and Polyxena; Portia, Bassanio and Antonio; Rosalind, Orlando and Celia; Romeo, Juliet and Mercutio; Claudius, Gertrude and – Hamlet? Why stop at three? A foursome is proposed at the end of *The Two Gentlemen of Verona*: 'One feast, one house, one mutual happiness'.[43] Consider Orsino, Olivia, Viola, Sebastian and Antonio. If this seems far-fetched, that is an index of the extent to which we imbibe patriarchy with our Shakespeare. Reading against the grain may produce, not a more elaborate realization of the most favoured Shakespearian texts, but a critical perspective upon their ideological assumptions and, indeed, upon our own.

---

[42] John Aubrey, *Brief Lives*, ed. Andrew Clark, 2 vols. (Oxford, 1898), 1, 96. See the astute discussion of the Prologue in Jeffrey Masten, *Textual Intercourse* (Cambridge, 1997), pp. 56–62.

[43] William Shakespeare, *The Two Gentlemen of Verona*, ed. Clifford Leech (London, 1969), 5.4.171.

AS YOU LIKEN IT:
SIMILE IN THE WILDERNESS

ROBERT N. WATSON

God said, Let us make man in our image according to our likenes, and let them rule over the fish of the sea, and over the foule of the heaven, and over the beastes, and over all the earth.

(Genesis 1:26, Geneva Bible)

A Similitude is a likenesse when two thinges, or moe then two, are so compared and resembled together, that they both in some one propertie seeme like. Oftentimes brute Beastes, and thinges that have no life, minister great matter in this behalfe. Therefore, those that delite to prove thinges by Similitudes, must learne to knowe the nature of divers beastes, of mettalles, of stones, and al such as have any vertue in them, and be applied to mans life.

(Thomas Wilson, *The arte of Rhetorique*)[1]

For why should I presume to prefer my conceit and imagination, in affirming that a thing is thus or thus in its own nature, because it seemeth to me to be so; before the conceit of other living creatures, who may as well think it to be otherwise in its own nature, because it appeareth otherwise to them than it doth to me?

(Sir Walter Raleigh, 'The Sceptic')[2]

I

In the four syllables of its title, *As You Like It* contains both the words used to signal simile, and puts a 'like' as a barrier between 'you' and 'it'. From that title onward, this pastoral play is permeated with the idea of likeness, which is to say, imperfect identity – and the way that 'liking', even in apparently benign forms, necessarily imposes on its objects. Shakespeare describes the chronic nostalgia for nature as a sentimental manifestation of pyrrhonist anxieties, the suspicion that we can know things

only as we liken them, never in or as themselves. The familiar craving for a simplifying reunion with the wilderness was focused and magnified at this historical moment by urbanization, capitalism and the Protestant Reformation, each of which contributed to anxieties about mediation and the lost sensual past. The multicultural upheaval surrounding Renaissance humanism and colonialism threatened to produce a cognitive crisis by enforcing the recognition that the world is less observed than constructed, less an accessible reality than a manufactured contingency; and empirical science crystallized these epistemological doubts. Representation thus became a psychic as well as political crisis in early modern England; and theatre, as *mimesis*, amplified all these discomforts.

Elizabethan theology was enquiring about the primitive church, and shattering iconic representations. Gardening manuals boasted of reproducing Eden. Political pamphlets contrasted recent enclosure controversies and urban dystopia with a lost organic community. Philosophers wrestled with a resurgence of scepticism, philologists strove to recover an idealized textual past, Baconian scientists sought a transparent descriptive rhetoric, painters tested the limits of verisimilitude, and poets bemoaned their artistic belatedness, particularly in the rediscovered pastoral mode. The desire to recover some original and authentic reality appears to have been epidemic. The nostalgia for Paradise, for the

---

[1] Thomas Wilson, *The arte of Rhetorique* (1560), pp. 188–9.
[2] In *The Works of Sir Walter Raleigh* (New York, 1829), VIII, 551.

Golden Age, for an idealized collective-agrarian feudal England, and for a prelinguistic access to reality all coincide in fantasies of a liberating regression to garden and wilderness. If my argument jumbles together a variety of conflicting definitions of nature – as Eden, as fauna, as entropy – my excuse is that Shakespeare's play does too.

The multiple and elaborate explorations of the polarity of art and nature in *As You Like It* are mapped analogically onto a polarity of the linguistically entangled human mind and the material objects which that mind can know only partially, only by the constraints of comparison – the vocabularies and categories of mind we bring with us to carve the sensory feast into edible bites. The play sets other familiar polarities in parallel series with these, carrying considerable cultural energies: human/animal, mind/body, self/other, word/thing, signifier/signified, post-/pre-lapsarian, and even man/woman, to the extent that misogynist traditions (in our culture as well as Shakespeare's) blame women for alienating men from nature. When Marvell's 'The Garden' asserts that 'Two paradises 'twere in one, / To live in paradise alone' (63–4), the patristic resentment of Eve thinly covers the story of another fall, in which perceived nature and actual nature become irretrievably alienated, 'a green shade' never quite identical with the 'green thought' that represents it in our consciousness (48). We are postlapsarian in (among others) a post-structuralist way. How valuable, how viable, is a Miltonic 'paradise within thee' if it misrepresents a paradise that is lost – lost because it can only be misrepresented? As in *Richard II*, *Hamlet* and *The Winter's Tale*, Shakespeare's story of the fall is always partly a story about the irreversible human fall into the mediations of self-consciousness and language, whether in terms of ontogeny or phylogeny, childhood or evolution.

The pastoral genre is stubbornly artificial, as if to acknowledge that our hunger for simplicity is actually a symptom of sophistication, a self-conscious desire at once expressed and prevented by language. We gaze lovingly at ponds, but so did Narcissus; and the gates of Eden are firmly closed. *As You*

Like It begins with that originary exclusion: 'As I remember, Adam, it was upon this fashion bequeathed me . . . ' (1.1.1).[3] Efforts to bridge the gap between ourselves and nature, between our minds and reality, through simile (or perspective painting, or Protestant worship) confirm precisely the gap we are trying to erase.

The world we compose in our consciousness is never the same as the world in itself – too obvious a point to seem worth making, and yet a mote to trouble the mind's eye.[4] And it seemed to be troubling Shakespeare's vision in 1599, as he moved into a theatre called the Globe, and wrote, not only *As You Like It*, but also *Henry V*, a history play obsessed with the difference between reality and its representations. *Hamlet* – arguably the most epistemologically sceptical play of all – was probably next, a universe of rumours, forgeries, mistrusted ghosts, unanswerable questions, provocative simulations and plays within plays within plays; like a weasel, like a whale, but out there only a numinous cloud, a ghost reporting irrecoverable losses. According to the Platonic vocabulary, it was a time to acknowledge shadows; to recognize what it means to live – as Duke Senior does – in a cave.

And to die into a grave. Does it profit a man (as in Tibullus's elegies) to lose consciousness and regain a simple relationship with the material universe? 'Where is this young gallant', demands Charles the Wrestler, 'that is so desirous to lie with his mother earth?' (1.2.183–4). We may seek perfect knowledge of nature, but it knows us carnally; and (as Marvell's mower Damon discovers) throws shockingly unsympathetic welcome-home parties over our fallen bodies. Starving and freezing indeed

---

3 All citations from this play are based on the Oxford World Classics edition, ed. Alan Brissenden (Oxford, 1993). All citations from other plays are based on the Riverside Shakespeare (Boston, 1997), 2nd edn, ed. G. B. Evans et al.

4 And the eye's mind; cf. *Raleigh*, VIII, 549: 'If a man rub his eye, the figure of that which he beholdeth seemeth long or narrow; is it then not likely, that those creatures which have a long and slanting pupil of the eye, as goats, foxes, cats, &c. do convey the fashion of that which they behold under another form to the imagination than those that have round pupils do?'

bring us back to nature, as Duke Senior observes; so do snakes and lionesses. Death is in Arden, as in Arcadia; Touchstone's 'now am I in Arden' (2.4.14), may recall the ominous associations of '*et in Arcadia ego*'.[5] Our little lives are rounded with a sleep – or something like it.

II

Editors beginning with Theobald have often emended Duke Senior's 'Here feel we not the penalty of Adam' (2.1.5, Folio) to 'Here feel we *but* the penalty of Adam.' On this textual crux rests the play's most persistent question: can we redeem ourselves by returning to nature? The emendation makes sense: Duke Senior clearly *does* feel the pain of seasonal change. But other editors resist the change, for two structurally similar reasons: first, they believe that the Duke may be saying that the pain doesn't bother him because it is a good, honest, primal, outdoorsy pain, and second, they believe that they should stick to the original reading unless the sense absolutely forbids it. The defenders of the Folio's 'not' are thus like the Duke Senior they thereby preserve: they are willing to endure some discomfort for the sake of recovering what seems like the true, original, rough-hewn experience, whether of nature or of Shakespeare.

What follows from Duke Senior and his Lords proves that the penalty of Adam is fully in force; again, as the words suggest, Arden resembles Eden, but is not Eden, and the difference between likeness and identity will haunt all the play's similes, facsimiles included. The Duke here boasts how happy his displaced court is, in escaping 'painted pomp' and giving itself over completely to an authentic experience of nature. He then proves himself a liar at almost every word. The wind isn't 'chiding', it has no 'fang' to 'bite' with, and it certainly isn't a 'counsellor' seeking to 'persuade' (lines 6–11). By the time this ostentatiously alliterative speech ends six lines later, the anthropomorphizing – a pastoral symptom since the originary moment of the genre, the first line of Theocritus's first idyll – has become epidemic: the Duke is finding 'tongues in trees, books in the running brooks, / Sermons in stones,

and good in everything'. Amiens, putting the most amiable face on this, praises the Duke's ability to 'translate' his experience of untamed nature into 'so sweet a style' (19). Farmers regularly used 'stiles' to enter the animal compounds, and the Duke's translation across the human–animal boundary threatens to produce an ass-headed monster, as it does when Bottom is 'translated' in the forest of *Midsummer Night's Dream* (3.1.119); Jaques will soon assert – the pot's critique of the kettle – that to flee to nature, as Duke Senior has, is to 'turn ass' (2.5.47).

The Duke then turns his concern to the deer they hunt – 'Come, shall we go and kill us venison?' – regretting this necessary violence against the 'native burghers of this desert city' (2.1.21–3). Again he is presuming, not only anthropomorphically, but (more subtly) anthrocentrically: 'desert' defines the place by human abandonment, and the deer are not 'venison' – an animal hunted for game – until his need and aggression make them so. Even before the hunt begins, they are already no longer their animal selves, already a product for consumption by the human mouth, through the presumption of the human mind. Things are named by our need for them.

That this perceptual crime against nature is distinct from the more perceptible one becomes clear in Jaques's reaction. The Lord who reports that reaction is himself incapable of turning off the anthropomorphic switch that generates antique peeping roots, brawling brooks, and a poor 'sequestered' stag in a 'leathern coat' (this resembles the Duke's slip: 'leather' generally meant 'skin prepared for use by tanning' rather than that on a living animal) who has been hurt by 'the hunter's aim' (a revealing metonymy for an arrow). When Duke Senior asks, 'But what said Jaques? / Did he not moralize this spectacle?', the Lord replies, 'O yes, into a thousand similes' (2.1.25–45). Capturing the deer is certainly more brutal, but captioning its picture may be no less appropriative. Which has done more insidious violence to pristine nature as a collectivity,

5 See Nicolas Poussin's painting 'Les Bergers d'Arcadie' (1638–40); also Harry Morris, '*As You Like It: Et in Arcadia Ego*', *Shakespeare Quarterly*, 26 (1975), 270.

during its long siege by humanity: shooting it with a single arrow, or shattering it into a thousand similes? The question may bring Shakespearian drama into the active field of eco-criticism in a duly ambivalent way, without blunting the literary works into facile tools of social advocacy.

Jaques's projection of his own social complaints onto this animal (2.1.46–59) is interesting characterologically; what is interesting philosophically is the parallel suggestion that he could not cease to do so even if he were a sincere nature-lover – indeed, that he becomes all the more invasive the more he tries to be sympathetic. The 'bankrupt' but fashionably 'velvet' deer, abandoned by companions 'full of the pasture', does not need Jaques's tears, any more than the stream needs those of the deer (46–9). He concludes that Duke Senior's court

> Are mere usurpers, tyrants, and what's worse,
> To fright the animals and to kill them up
> In their assigned and native dwelling place.
> DUKE SENIOR And did you leave him in this
>   contemplation?
> SECOND LORD We did, my lord, weeping and
>   commenting
> Upon the sobbing deer.
>
> (61–6)

Jaques's position leaning over the stream with this deer signals the narcissistic self-involvement of his claim to care for an Other (a signal confirmed by the joke at 3.2.276–81 about Jaques seeing his own reflection in the stream as he looks for a fool). He has inserted himself in the place of the deer as assiduously, and arguably as uselessly or even tyrannically, as the hunter who will later have the hide of the deer placed over his skin and the horns of the deer placed on his head (4.2.10–11). We may indeed weep – I don't mean to belittle the empathetic impulse here – but we are always commenting as well. Jaques is, to put it politely, rather full of pasture himself.

Still, this empathetic impulse may help explain Jaques's eventual decision to 'put on a religious life' and to try to learn from 'these convertites' such as Duke Frederick who have left their former selves

behind (5.4.176–80) – a decision which seems to shock Jaques's comrades and the play's editors alike. As others arrive from court into the forest and rediscover themselves, Jaques takes the next, parallel step. Sounding oddly like the speaker of Psalm XLII, Jaques abandons his 'sensual' self (2.7.66) and averts his eyes from the facile matchings by waiting them out in Duke Senior's 'abandoned cave' (5.4.191): 'from the vulgar, civil and ordinary man he was, he becomes free as a deer, and an inhabitant of the wilderness . . . in the unpretentious rooms of the cavernous mountains, where he contemplates . . . free of ordinary lusts, and converses mostly freely with the divinity, to which so many men have aspired'.[6] This is not, however, a modern commentary on the conversion of Jaques, but instead Giordano Bruno's commentary on the transformation of Actaeon – the classical archetype of the man who saw too much, the hunter who forfeited language, and therefore community, and therefore life, because he gazed (rashly, desirously) on a divine form in a woodland stream.

III

Dressing the victorious hunter in the coat and the horns of the stag he has killed is the logical culmination, but also a brutal parody, of this effort to enter into the unmediated experience of nature, to pluck out the mystery of the hart. That costume also evokes the claim of many humanist critiques of hunters who 'setting all humanitie apart, become salvage beastes, and . . . are changed like *Acteon* into the nature of beasts'.[7] Ovid recounts that, as punishment for seeing Diana and her nymphs in their lovely nakedness, the hunter Actaeon is transformed into a hart, and (ashamed

---

[6] Giordano Bruno, *The Heroic Frenzies*, trans. P. E. Memmo, Jr. (Chapel Hill, 1964), pp. 224–5; quoted by Leonard Barkan, 'Diana and Actaeon: The Myth as Synthesis', *English Literary Renaissance*, 10 (1980), 330.

[7] Agrippa of Nettesheim, *De incertitudine*; see similarly John of Salisbury, *Polycraticus*, bk 1 ch. 4; quoted by Claus Uhlig, 'The Sobbing Deer', *Renaissance Drama*, n. s. 3 (1970), 90–1.

to return to the palace but afraid to remain in the woods) is fatally hunted by his own dogs. After citing Stesichorus's version, in which Diana sewed Actaeon 'within the skin of a Stag', George Sandys then offers his own interpretation, whereby 'Actaeon . . . puts off the minde of a man, and degenerates into a beast; while hee dayly frequents the wild woods to contend with such enemies'.[8] Indeed, Duke Senior's entire court looks oddly like the summer bachelor herd they describe.[9] By diligently blurring these boundaries, Shakespeare addresses the fear that we might (like colonizers who 'go native') lose ourselves if we engage with nature too completely.

Dizzyingly alongside this suggestion, however – in Ovid as in Shakespeare – stands a contrary suggestion that these invaders are so absorbed in Self that they can receive no true impression of the Other. Ovid's Actaeon story anticipates his Narcissus story only a hundred lines later: as in Jaques's description of the weeping deer at the water's edge, Ovid's Actaeon 'sees his features and horns in a clear pool, "Oh, woe is me!" he tries to say; but no words come. He groans – the only speech he has – and tears course down his changeling cheeks. Only his mind remains unchanged' (3.198–203). And even that is not entirely unchanged: Ovid implies that 'the secret [Actaeon] witnessed when he saw Diana bathing is the secret of self-consciousness'.[10]

Several Renaissance commentaries associate Actaeon with impudent enquiries into the secrets of nature, and Alexander Ross's version of the warning stresses that one never really escapes one's own mind anyway: 'Pry not too much into the secrets of Heaven, lest, with *Acteon*, your understanding be taken from you, and ye become a prey to the beastly imaginations of your own brain'.[11] Like Adam's, Actaeon's is a crime of presumptuous knowing; it looks ahead to the biblical warning that any mortal who looks on God directly will die. Luther calls nature 'the mask of God', and both warnings suggest that perceiving the full reality of divine creation, unfiltered by dark glasses or cognitive categories, would consume soul and synapse alike.[12] The truth hurts. The Christianizing view of Actaeon in

Pierre Bersuire's commentary in the *Ovid Moralisé* 'revives an ancient divine interpretation of the story that will reappear as Renaissance Platonism, i.e., that the hero enters upon visionary experience and as a result must perish'.[13] According to the gloss on Bruno's initial Actaeon sonnet, the hunter discovering Diana in her bath indicates the way the quester, by looking at nature, may discover ultimate beauty and truth 'in the mirror of similitudes'.[14] Bruno deems it 'impossible for anyone to see the sun, the universal Apollo and absolute light as the supreme and most excellent species; but very possible to see its shadow, its Diana, the world, the universe, the nature which is in things'; to perceive ultimate reality, free 'from the snares of the perturbing senses and the fleshly prison of matter', requires surrendering this earthly life.[15] No wonder Actaeon, in Titian's painting of 'Diana Surprised', appears to be flinching away from the sight. The godhead, according to St John of the Cross – a contemporary of Shakespeare's – is 'like to the hart wounded by thy love', but the Absolute that the soul seeks, 'she cannot receive without its almost costing her her life'.[16]

If a little knowledge is indeed a dangerous thing, total knowledge seems much more so. If it is true, as Harry Berger argues, that 'A major theme of

---

8 George Sandys, *Ovid's Metamorphoses Englished* (Oxford, 1632), p. 100; see similarly Ross, on 'Actaeon', Alexander Ross, *Mystagogus Poeticus* (London, 1648), p. 7, and Geoffrey Whitney, *Choice of Emblems*, p. 15, following Sambucus, *Emblemata* (1564), p. 128.

9 A. Stuart Daley, 'The Midsummer Deer of *As you like it*, II.i', *Philological Quarterly*, 58 (1979), 104.

10 Barkan, 'Diana and Actaeon', p. 322.

11 Alexander Ross, *Mystagogus Poeticus*, p. 7. See similarly Alexander Neckham, *De Naturis Rerum*, ed. T. Wright (London, 1863), II, p. 137.

12 Quoted by Paul J. Willis, '"Tongues in Trees"', *Modern Language Studies*, 18 (1988), 67; the simultaneously thrilling and destructive effects of LSD and other psychedelic drugs offer a modern analogue.

13 Barkan, 'Diana and Actaeon', p. 329.

14 Bruno, *The Heroic Frenzies*, p. 123.

15 Bruno, *The Heroic Frenzies*, pp. 225–6; quoted by Barkan, 'Actaeon', p. 344.

16 *The Complete Works of Saint John of the Cross*, trans. and ed., E. Allison Peers (London, 1964), II, 241.

Renaissance literature centers on techniques of withdrawal into an artificial world – a "second nature" created by the mind – where the elements of actuality are selectively admitted, simplified and explored',[17] it is also worth noting that the most sophisticated Renaissance pastorals – *As You Like It*, Andrew Marvell's 'The Garden' – recognize the real or first world as no less selectively perceived, no less necessarily simplified. The mind is its own place, and necessarily makes a pastoral retreat of an infinite universe of bustling sense-perceptions. Know the world perfectly, and you will have no mind of your own; you become a mirror, incapable of the other kind of reflection. We cannot bear to leave nature, reality or God unknown; nor can we bear to know them. Selfhood can best be defined and sustained (as in a Freudian model) by our individual blind-spots.

That 'moonish youth' Rosalind is 'like Diana in the fountain' (3.2.389, 4.1.140). Orlando stumbling across her in the forest associates him with Actaeon,[18] and does so in a way that again links men's desire toward women with human impositions on nature. As in Nonnos's fifth-century *Dionysiaca*, where 'Actaeon's hunting is made explicitly parallel to his voyeurism and to his lust for the goddess',[19] as in Petrarch's *Rime* XXIII (lines 147–60) where the object of desire transforms the poet from hunter to wandering stag, Orlando's fantasies about the disguised Rosalind link two archetypal modes of male aggression, two meanings of 'venery': hunting and lusting. He anthropomorphizes the moon as the 'thrice-crownèd queen of night', with Rosalind as a 'huntress' in her service, but he immediately betrays himself as the aggressor, imposing literature on nature even more directly than Duke Senior does: 'these trees shall be my books, / And in their barks my thoughts I'll character' (3.2.1–6).

As Duke Senior's aggression against the deer is to the more subtle and sentimental aggression of Jaques, so is Orlando's vandalism to that of the nature-loving speaker of 'The Garden':

Fond lovers, cruel as their flame,
Cut in these trees their mistress' name;
Little, alas, they know or heed

How far these beauties hers exceed!
Fair trees! wheres'e'er your barks I wound,
No name shall but your own be found.

(lines 19–24)

The oak will give him little thanks for that. In the sense that it can want anything, it wants an intact bark, and 'oak' is not its name for itself. 'Adam in a state of nature had perfect knowledge of signatures and named everything aright'[20]; the rest of us are imposers and impostors. Nature's revenge is like Diana's: making masculine aggressors self-conscious, turning the linguistic tools by which we conquer reality against us, letting slip the dogs of word, sending us into a wilderness where (Shakespeare and Marvell warn) we may hunt ourselves to death.

How appealing is any love-letter or love-lyric when it is obsessed with the lover (the human mind) and direly ignorant of the beloved (the world of nature)? The pasture could justly accuse the pastoralist as Rosalind does Orlando: of a controlling narcissism, 'as loving yourself [rather] than seeming the lover of any other' (3.2.365–6). When Touchstone responds to Orlando's verses hanging in the forest by observing that 'the tree yields bad fruit', we may suspect that Orlando's poetic fruits bear the knowledge of self and other. He lets a thousand comparisons bloom, praising Rosalind as:

Helen's cheek, but not her heart,
Cleopatra's majesty,

---

[17] Harry Berger, Jr, 'The Ecology of the Mind', *Centennial Review*, 8 (1964), p. 425.

[18] Two years later, another of Shakespeare's frustrated wooers uses a more explicit allusion to Actaeon to introduce himself (*Twelfth Night* 1.1.20–2).

[19] Barkan, 'Actaeon', p. 326, citing V, 287–551 of the *Dionysiaca*.

[20] Oswald Croll, *Basilica chymica* (1609); quoted by Hiram Haydn, *The Counter-Renaissance* (New York, 1950), p. 514; the notion was conventional. Cf. Ovid's *Metamorphoses*, trans. Arthur Golding, I, 103–4: 'Then sprang up first the golden age, which of it selfe maintainde, / The truth and right of every thing unforst and unconstrainde'. Now, in the iron age, not only is 'the loftie Pynetree...hewen from mountaines where it stood', but 'The shipman' can thereby 'hoyst his sailes to wind, whose names he did not knowe' (lines 109, 149).

Atalanta's better part,
   Sad Lucretia's modesty.
Thus Rosalind of many parts
   By heavenly synod was devised
Of many faces, eyes and hearts
   To have the touches dearest prized.

(3.2.140–7)

Similarity has become anatomy, Professor Petrarch has become Doctor Frankenstein, and the temple devoted to the worship of Rosalind herself has exploded into a junkyard of others. The homology between the anthropomorphic invasion of nature and the misogynistic shadow of Petrarchism becomes unmistakable: the beloved is anatomized, even atomized, into the vocabulary of the desiring mind.

Petrarchan lovers were constantly shattering their lovers with balms of similitude: belying women (as Shakespeare's Sonnet 130 warns) by false compare, by a blast of *blason*. Love and violence thus seem almost inseparable; you always hunt the one you love. When Rosalind hears that Orlando is 'furnished like a hunter', she says it is 'ominous – he comes to kill my heart' (3.2.237–8). And the play's references to the arrows of Cupid (1.3.1, 4.1.43, 196–8), as well as the inevitable jokes about the cuckold's horns (3.2.78, 3.3.45–57, 4.1.54–5) tie the story of hunting in the forest closely to the story of loving in the forest.

Deer-stalking provides modern law and psychology with their common term for the love that turns to possessiveness, then violence, and finally a ritual of sentimental regret. *As You Like It* has more than its share of relentless unrequited lovers: Silvius towards Phoebe, Phoebe towards 'Ganymede', Orlando towards 'Rosalind', William towards Audrey – and, I believe, most of the ardent nature-lovers towards the forest of Arden. The self-deluded, self-indulgent lovers who stalk nature produce the same dialogue that typifies erotic stalking between humans. The possessive voice says: I give you everything, you mean so much to me, you are beauty and truth, you are my soul and my destiny, I speak your name, acknowledge me. The unwilling beloveds reply, if only by a cool silence:

this is merely your fantasy, you don't really know me, you have nothing I want or need.

Orlando is thus in the tradition of Petrarch's persona and Sannazaro's Sincero: men who wander off into rustic solitude so obsessed with a lost or unachievable beloved that they populate nature with thoughts of her, imposing her name and image on everything.[21] Shakespeare's twist on that tradition is an emphasis on the way the otherness of a woman in a man's hetero-eroticism resembles and perhaps reflects an unconquerable otherness already present in nature, present in material reality itself; the pastoral retreat exposes another failed connection, this one more abstract but also more definite than unrequited human love, which is a social or psychological contingency, not a philosophical necessity. What Petrarch's 'Augustine' calls the 'traveler who cannot escape from himself'[22] is an instance of the human mind that cannot escape itself, whatever the surrounding landscape. The forest of Arden may be hard to read reliably – 'the Duke sees good, Jaques evil, Touchstone both, Corin neither'[23] – but so is everyone and everything else. Despite Ganymede's neat check-list of 'marks' for true love (3.2.356–64), inner nature remains inaccessible; despite the hunters and lovers of deer, so does outer nature.

By the time we see Orlando taking out his erotic obsession – his mourning for a lost object – on innocent natural entities, Touchstone has prepared us to ridicule that displacement:

I remember when I was in love I broke my sword upon a stone and bid him take that for coming a-night to Jane Smile, and I remember the kissing of her batler and the cow's dugs that her pretty chopt hands had milked; and I remember the wooing of a peascod instead of her.

(2.4.43–8)

Indeed, less than twenty lines after Orlando announces his own programme of pastoral displacement, the old shepherd Corin offers a flatter

---

[21] Judy Z. Kronenfeld, 'Shakespeare's Jaques and the Pastoral Cult of Solitude', *Texas Studies in Literature and Language*, 18 (1976), 451–73, discusses these precedents.

[22] Quoted by Kronenfeld, 'Shakespeare's Jaques', p. 461.

[23] Willis, 'Tongues in Trees', p. 65.

reflection of the natural world, an empiricism that stubbornly resists the imperialism of human ingenuity: he claims that 'the property of rain is to wet, and fire to burn; that good pasture makes fat sheep, and that a great cause of the night is lack of the sun; that he that hath learned no wit by nature nor art may complain of good breeding or comes of a very dull kindred'. Touchstone replies dismissively, 'Such a one is a natural philosopher' (3.2.25–30). But isn't any more active, sophisticated, interventionist way of understanding and loving nature than the shepherd's a form of stalking? Doesn't pastoralism share the dangers of Petrarchism: not just disguising verbal convention as individual emotion, but disguising aggression as submission, appropriation as donation, war as love?

IV

As You Like It depicts love and war simultaneously as natural (as in the Darwinian reading of nature) and cultural: both 'falling in love' and the 'falls' of the wrestling are called 'sports' in the play's second scene (1.2.23, 100), at once civilized ritual and mortal struggle, leaving their practitioners at once psycho-socially and physiologically 'overthrown'. Beyond these partly acculturated versions of desire and combat stand Orlando's Petrarchist lyrics and Touchstone's taxonomy of quarrelling. The calibration provokes an audience to meditate on the paradoxes of civilization elaborately simulating the wild. Touchstone himself patrols this boundary as a double agent, tending to drag the courtiers back to physical reality (3.2.85–100), while posing as an agent of high culture for the country folk (5.1.31–52). His puns repeatedly expose the thin boundary between lustful animals and literary humans, as when he tells Audrey, 'I am here with thee and thy goats as the most capricious poet honest Ovid was among the Goths' (3.3.5–6). The Ovid of the *Metamorphoses* is supremely relevant to this failure of boundaries; but (like punning itself) it is also so ostentatiously cultural as to refute the equation Touchstone proposes.

The impossibility of understanding one world from the perspective of another, and the differences that language makes, are the only points that come though decisively in Touchstone's analysis of 'this shepherd's life':

in respect of itself, it is a good life; but in respect that it is a shepherd's life, it is naught. In respect that it is solitary, I like it very well; but in respect that it is private, it is a very vile life. Now, in respect it is in the fields, it pleaseth me well; but in respect it is not in the court, it is tedious. As it is a spare life, look you, it fits my humour well; but as there is no more plenty in it, it goes much against my stomach.

(3.2.13–20)

Again here (and in the moralizing debate about court vs. country manners thirty lines later) the alienation of the sophisticate from rusticity points to the deeper alienation of the prejudicial mind from any absolute, pre-existing reality. Natural reality – as inscrutable in its judgements as the Calvinist God – has the last laugh on the quest for truth: 'You have said', remarks Touchstone, 'but whether wisely or no, let the forest judge' (3.2.117–8).

The play divides each pair of brothers into one who inhabits a court and one who inhabits the forest. Oliver du Bois is repeatedly condemned as 'unnatural' (4.3.99–125), and his liminality as he arrives in the forest brings this uneasy boundary again to our attention:

OLIVER Good morrow, fair ones. Pray you, if you know,
Where in the purlieus of this forest stands
A sheepcote fenced about with olive trees?
CELIA West of this place, down in the neighbour bottom;
The rank of osiers by the murmuring stream
Left on your right hand brings you to the place.
But at this hour the house doth keep itself.
There's none within.

(4.3.76–83)

A purlieu was a concept so ambiguous that it makes the *Oxford English Dictionary* sound like Henry

James: 'A piece or tract of land on the fringe or border of a forest; originally one that, after having been (wrongly, as was thought) included within the bounds of the forest, was disafforested by a new perambulation, but still remained, in some respects, especially as to the hunting or killing of game, subject to provisions of the Forest Laws'. Are there laws in and of the forest? Have the olive trees been cut into pieces for a fence, or do they merely serve as a fence in their living natural form? Is a sheepcote a place of nature or of culture?

Celia's reply echoes the pastoral anthropomorphism of Duke Senior. Is the bottom a neighbour, do osiers form a rank, does a stream murmur? Directional words are essential to human navigation through the landscape, even if 'west' is arbitrary – meaningless to the landscape itself – and 'left on your right hand' furthermore depends on the position of the observer. The map, as Korzybski has famously observed, is not the territory. A house does not and need not keep itself, and there is no hour there if no one is there to tell it. Time proves no more definite than space. When the disguised Rosalind asks Orlando, 'what is't o' clock?' he admonishes her: 'You should ask me what time o' day. There's no clock in the forest.' Her reply proves that time, another supposed fact of nature, actually depends on human subjectivities (3.2.290–320) – in this case, whether one is in a hurry. As Marvell asks in 'The Garden', isn't all nature a sundial that 'computes its time as well as we' (70)?

Oliver's story about coming to know himself by pursuing his fraternal likeness into the woods is at once a narrative of natural predation and defence, and a highly acculturated mythological displacement of his personal history. Food is for thought as well as for eating in this forest – no longer actually starving, Orlando was 'Chewing the food of sweet and bitter fancy' – and even the old oak is both a family tree and a human likeness, both of which Orlando encounters in the rusticated Oliver:

> OLIVER Under an old oak, whose boughs were mossed with age
> And high top bald with dry antiquity,

A wretched, ragged man, o'ergrown with hair,
Lay sleeping on his back. About his neck
A green and gilded snake had wreathed itself.

(4.3.105–9)

Are these the tree and the serpent of Genesis, or only of evolution; allegory, or only naturalistic narrative? The boys of the family named DeBois play out their crucial scene in and under this *bois*, and even the geographically surprising zoology seems partly a weird play on the suggestion of Lodge's *Rosalynde* that the Oliver character was in the forest 'thinking to get to Lions', meaning the city of Lyon.

The oak tree which looms over both Jaques's meditations on the deer and Orlando's rescue of Oliver resembles the Tree of Knowledge that looms over the fallen Eden at the end of Dante's *Purgatorio*.[24] But Shakespeare's tree offers the knowledge of Self and Other, and both scenes beneath it are mortal combats between human and animal entities that had lived harmoniously in Eden. And sometimes the tree is just a tree – or a representation of one, anyway. When, at the end of a recent outdoor production of *As You Like It*, my daughter was obsessed with whether the blades of grass climbing the facing of the low stage were real or part of the set, something beyond parental dotage allowed me to construe the question as perceptive rather than reductive: this play insistently tests the membrane separating the biological world from human artifice and illusion.

V

The play arrays the politics of race, class and gender around this distinction between what is natural and absolute, and what is imposed by human preconceptions. Rosalind's complaint that 'I was never so berhymed since Pythagoras's time that I was an Irish rat, which I can hardly remember' (3.2.170–2)

---

[24] Alice-Lyle Scoufos, 'The *Paradiso Terrestre* and the Testing of Love in *As You Like It*', *Shakespeare Studies*, 14 (1981), p. 216.

reminds us that (as the nearly universal and to-tal amnesia of infant experience indicates) a mind which has moved beyond sound into language has difficulty knowing the world outside language. Rosalind recurs to the relationship between human speech and Ireland's wildlife when she complains that the unrequited lovers sound 'like the howling of Irish wolves against the moon' (5.2.101–5). The accusation that Rosalind here participates, however obliquely and unthinkingly, in Elizabethan racism conceals a philosophical question behind a polit-ical one: isn't Rosalind here participating, how-ever obliquely and unthinkingly, in anthropomor-phism? Are either the rats or the wolves Irish, or are they only in what she calls Ireland? Spenser's *View of the Present State of Ireland* (probably drawing on Camden) mentions a belief that Irishmen 'were once every yeare turned into wolves'[25]: the bound-ary between the human and animal worlds may yield to alternation (as in Pythagorean metempsy-chosis), but not penetration or communication.

The class issue, as in Touchstone's disdain for Corin, also turns quickly into a debate about what role nature plays in defining human virtue. Or-lando's paradoxically eloquent complaint that his brother has raised 'a gentleman of my birth' like a farm animal recalls the standard pastoral motif whereby nobility shines through the most insis-tently rustic upbringing. But behind the pastoral code this time lurks a recognition that, as rusticity can never erase aristocracy, neither can it ever erase humanity:

His horses are bred better, for besides that they are fair with their feeding, they are taught their manège, and to that end riders dearly hired. But I, his brother, gain nothing under him but growth, for the which his animals on his dunghills are as much bound to him as I . . . He lets me feed with his hinds, bars me the place of a brother, and as much as in him lies, mines my gentility with my education. This is it, Adam, that grieves me; and the spirit of my father, which I think is within me, begins to mutiny against this servitude.

(1.1.10–22)

A person raised as mere domestic livestock is still

not meet, not meat, for a 'butchery' (as if to cap the point, the argument then closes with a dispute about Oliver calling Adam 'old dog' at line 77). Orlando may be stalled like an ox, but he is not an ox, any more than the hunter who is dressed like a deer becomes one. That is not just because he is the son of a nobleman, but because he is a son of Adam.

Rosalind, on the other hand, is a daughter of Eve; but gender distinction, too, is complicated by the interplay of biological base and cultural su-perstructure – and further complicated by hints that the model of base and superstructure over-simplifies a problem implicated in the interplay of a posited reality and its representations. Rosalind seeks refuge in a simile exploiting the external con-structedness of the supposedly biological category of gender:

> Were it not better,
> Because that I am more than common tall,
> That I did suit me all points like a man,
> A gallant curtal-axe upon my thigh,
> A boar-spear in my hand, and in my heart,
> Lie there what hidden woman's fear there will.
> We'll have a swashing and a martial outside,
> As many other mannish cowards have,
> That do outface it with their semblances.
>
> (1.3.113–21)

The handy-dandy game of cross-dressing – by which the audience knows that the person playing Ganymede is really female, even while know-ing that the person playing Rosalind (who plays Ganymede) is really male – shows how difficult it is either to discover or to erase the facts of biol-ogy, to end the dialogue of artificial and natural.

---

[25] Quoted by Winifried Schleiner, ''Tis Like The Howling of Irish Wolves', *English Language Notes*, 12 (1974), pp. 5–6. In George Sandys's *Ovid's Metamorphoses Englished* (Oxford, 1632), Lycaon's transformation into a wolf was merely a metaphor for a man who had been driven 'out of the Citty' and was therefore 'living like an out-law in the woods'; cf. the description of Duke Senior and his men as having been driven from the court and living 'like the old Robin Hood of England' (1.1.116).

Getting down to 'reality' is impossible, even regarding something as mundane as the qualities of pancakes and mustard, since the women (who are boys) may safely swear by their beards to the truth of something that would be a lie if they were men (1.2.59–74).

Duke Senior and Orlando both mistake identity for likeness in Rosalind:

> DUKE SENIOR I do remember in this shepherd boy
> Some lively touches of my daughter's favour.
> ORLANDO   My lord, the first time that I ever saw him,
> Methought he was a brother to your daughter.
> But, my good lord, this boy is forest-born.
>
> (5.4.26–30)

Their insight remains obstructed by the binaries of gender and class. *As You Like It* is ostentatiously concerned with the temporary obliteration of opposition, the narrowly failed effort to crush together polarities such as female and male, rich and poor, civilization and savagery. To that list I would add the polarity of the existing material world and the conceiving human mind, which builds a likeness of the world and then inhabits it.

VI

Theatre is likeness. Comedy (whether Bergsonian farce or Shakespearian romance) is about the transmission of likeness, about stock characters and breeding stock; the closing marriages stand for the likelihood of liking producing likenesses. *As You Like It* is a comedy that ostentatiously imitates two 'non-dramatic narratives, *Arcadia* and *Rosalynde*, which stress their status as imitations',[26] and representational anxieties permeate the fabric of the play. It is a likeness full of likenesses. The astonishing array of similes in *As You Like It* that cross the boundary between humans and other creatures suggests the tenacity of the impulse they reflect: the impulse of the human family to impose its familiarities, even while recognizing they are not true identities.

While there may be 'great virtue in If', in 'Like' there lies the temptation to a great sin, an appropriative violence; 'If' may be a 'peacemaker', but 'like' is a gesture of conquest – a kind of temporary occupation that stops just short of the totalitarian presumption of metaphor. The 'remarkably extensive use of "if" in *As You Like It*'[27] suggests that all the world's a hypothetical.

Similarity is the play's acknowledgment of the desire to connect, of the failure of that desire, and of the fears aroused by both the desire and the failure. The play clearly exploits anxieties (both psychoanalytic and theological) about the idea that women are almost men, but not quite; Arden is similarly similar to Eden (and seems to be at once the romantic fantasy of Lodge's Ardenne and the homely reality of Shakespeare's Warwickshire Arden). The list of *dramatis personae* includes the distracting and seemingly superfluous overlap of two men named Jaques and two named Oliver, one of whom is desperate not to recognize his brother Orlando as kin, or as the likeness of their father, the 'memory / Of old Sir Rowland' (2.3.3–4), whose name Orlando shares, but in translation. The doubling of roles in the original performance likely reinforced, and ironized, many of these imperfect overlaps. Not even 'like', Shakespeare insists, is quite like itself:

> JAQUES   Good my lord, like this fellow.
> DUKE SENIOR   I like him very well.
> TOUCHSTONE   God'ield you sir, I desire you of the like.
>
> (5.4.50–53)

In other words, he desires a like liking; he would like him to do something like like him. In the Epilogue (18), 'like' will become different yet again, taking on its archaic transitive sense of 'please'.

---

[26] Brian Gibbons, 'Amorous Fictions and *As You Like It*', in *'Fanned and Winnowed Opinions'*, ed. John Mahon and Thomas Pendleton (London, 1987), p. 57; his p. 56 notes that the pastoral genre typically 'laments the gap between representation and its imagined subject'.

[27] David Young, *The Heart's Forest* (New Haven, 1972), p. 46.

ROBERT N. WATSON

When Orlando is condemned for being like his father, Rosalind replies by likening herself to her own father, who liked Orlando's (1.2.206–23). In the following scene, she again speaks of 'liking' her father's friend's child, and when she is also accused of inherited disloyalty, she questions the 'likelihoods' of physical likeness dictating political likeness (1.3.26, 55). Celia insists she is identical to Rosalind, but she isn't; neither is Ganymede; and they aren't exactly 'like Juno's swans' either (1.3.73). Women's faults are 'like one another as halfpence are' only within the misogynist discourse Rosalind mimics as Ganymede (3.2.338).

Jaques rejects courtly compliment as 'like the encounter of two dog-apes' (2.5.22). Yet when Duke Senior seeks him out two scenes later, a lord suspects that Jaques has been 'transformed into a beast, / For I can nowhere find him like a man' (2.7.1–2). For Jaques to complain that human pride flows 'as hugely as the sea' (2.7.72) is itself an act of human pride, an appropriation of great creating nature through the presumption of simile (Rosalind chooses a similar simile in describing her affection as 'like the Bay of Portugal' at 4.1.191). Through the conventional satiric ploy of making the accusation conditional, Jaques (who repeatedly likens humans to animals in the Seven Ages speech) only replicates that presumption: 'If he be free, / Why then my taxing like a wild goose flies' (2.7.85–6).

Duke Senior declares that human adversity is 'like the toad' (2.1.13). Encountering the Duke's suave civility where he 'thought that all things had been savage', Orlando announces, 'like a doe, I go to find my faun' (2.7.107, 128–9). LeBeau provides court news 'as pigeons feed their young' (1.2.87). Touchstone derides Corin for being 'like an ill-roasted egg' (3.2.35). He then chooses not to marry a chaste woman, who is 'as your pearl in your foul oyster' (5.4.60), and therefore Jaques predicts that his marriage is doomed to warp 'like green timber' (3.3.80). Only thirty-two lines after the hunter is given the deer's 'leather skin', Ganymede dismisses Phoebe as having 'a leathern hand' (4.3.25), and adds that love has made Silvius 'a tame snake' (4.3.71). The Second Page claims that he and his partner sing 'like two gipsies on a horse' – a satyrical image reinforced (though homophonic likeness) by the First Page's claim in the previous line that 'we are hoarse' (5.3.11–14).

When Celia first describes Orlando in the forest, her similes oscillate between simple botany and romantic literature: is he 'like a dropped acorn', as she claims, or 'like a wounded knight' as she claims a moment later (3.2.227–33)? When Orlando proves unreliable, Celia subordinates his chivalric side to his biological one, comparing him to a rider who 'breaks his staff, like a noble goose' (3.4.40). Rosalind therefore says she 'had as lief be wooed of a snail' (4.1.47). But if Orlando is willing to question the romanticizing of his biological cravings, she (as Ganymede) will 'wash your liver as clean as a sound sheep's heart' (3.2.401).

Pressing Orlando to recognize some hard realities behind the time-denying love-game he is playing, Ganymede brings the natural comparisons to a crescendo:

men are April when they woo, December when they wed. Maids are May when they are maids, but the sky changes when they are wives. I will be more jealous of thee than a Barbary cock-pigeon over his hen, more clamorous than a parrot against rain, more new-fangled than an ape, more giddy in my desires than a monkey. I will weep for nothing, like Diana in the fountain, and I will do that when you are disposed to be merry. I will laugh like a hyena, and that when thou art inclined to sleep.

(4.1.134–43)

No wonder Jaques compares all the closing marital pairs to 'couples . . . coming to the ark' – the primal scene of likeness on its way to breed more likeness, again bridging (or, I suppose, boating) the gap between human and other creatures. Across the boundary between animal vulgarity and human romanticism, as much as any boundary of gender, Rosalind and Orlando play their tug-of-love. When she says, 'I thought thy heart had been wounded with the claws of a lion', he replies, 'Wounded it is, but with the eyes of a lady' (5.2.22–4).

Similitudes tell us very little when they try to leap across this boundary between cultural and biological realities: Celia teases that Orlando's hair is 'Something browner than Judas's, and Rosalind replies that 'his kissing is as full of sanctity as the touch of holy bread' (3.4.7–13). To adopt the model of transubstantiation this reply proposes: is the spiritual essence (good or bad) truly manifest in the physical realm? Are we under a traditional Catholic and Anglican dispensation whereby the similitude reflects full presence, or a radical Protestant system of representation (and Derridean system of referentiality) whereby the name or the likeness provides only a commemoration or experiential presence of the thing named or simulated? And in which of these ways do we receive the substance of the world of God?

VII

My intention is partly to challenge Foucault's argument that western culture confronted the transition from a system of resemblance to a system of difference only towards the end of the seventeenth century. But it is not my intention to follow Kierkegaard in making literature merely an occasion for philosophy: I believe the scepticism this article describes is a real and pervasive presence in Shakespeare's text. Along with the more obvious functions of *As You Like It* – popular entertainment, literary competition, social commentary – is a substantial anticipation of Locke's argument that we can know only word-definitions of physical things, never the things completely, and Kant's even later argument that we cannot know things in themselves, apart from the categories of knowledge we bring to them. The irreducible distances between likeness and identity, and between the human and the natural, are (though the term has become anathema to Shakespeare scholars) themes of the play, recurring – often in parallel – with a remarkable frequency and intricacy quite apart from any necessities of plot or realistic characterization. Nor is this insight anachronistic: St John of the Cross wrote that

a man can know nothing by himself, save after a natural manner, which is only that which he attains by means

of the senses. For this cause he must have the phantasms and the forms of objects present in themselves and in their likenesses . . . Wherefore, if one should speak to a man of things . . . whose likeness he has never seen, he would have no more illumination from them whatever than if naught had been said of them to him . . . If one should say to a man that on a certain island there is an animal which he has never seen, and give him no idea of the likeness of that animal, that he may compare it with others that he has seen, he will have no more knowledge of it . . . than he had before.

The soul must therefore find faith, in this dark cave, by some device other than simile, by some higher or more absolute form of Word.[28]

Indeed, the broadest historical implication of my argument may be that Shakespeare is heralding a huge inversion in his culture's quest for truth. For centuries – and with increasing fervour during the Reformation – that culture had prominently feared that material objects would stand between humanity and any pure encounter with the Word, the divine absolute and its intentions. *As You Like It* articulates a converse fear – increasingly visible through modern semiotics – that words stand between us and any pure encounter with absolute reality, which a secular-scientific culture assumes resides in material objects. What was anathematized as idolatry – seeing objects as important, final, efficacious in themselves rather than as media toward a higher intelligence called God – gives way to a condemnation of idols as Francis Bacon defines them: as cultural traditions, individual subjectivities and mental qualities of the species including language itself, that prevent or distort any true empirical view of the natural universe.

As You Like It depicts the folly called pastoral as merely one genre of the problem called solipsism, which revived in the same decades. Drawing on early modern anxieties about attempts to read the word of God through the world of God, and St Bonaventure's warning that the book of nature offers us only a 'trace', even saints only a 'likeness',

---

[28] *The Complete Works of Saint John of the Cross*, I, 67–8.

of the divine absolute,[29] Shakespeare begins to explore some modern anxieties about our ability to know the world itself, to move beyond simile into truth, to see the absolute face to face, as we feel we should and once did. Along with the other most brilliantly elusive writers of his time – Marvell and Montaigne – Shakespeare depicts as at once tragically and farcically futile our efforts to return to the primal feast: the symbiotic union of breast-feeding, the innocent nurturance of Eden, a renewed communion with Mother Nature.

We are, as Sir Thomas Browne noted, painfully awkward amphibians, not really at home (like the transformed Actaeon) either in nature or in culture. And, like most amphibians, like Narcissus, we spend a lot of time staring at the surface of the water. Gazing on wilderness may get us no further than gazing with similar infatuation on a human beloved – no further out of the mirrored box of self, I mean. This may be why Shakespeare caps a joke rather heavy-handedly, so that we will not miss the warning that unconquerable narcissism makes our effort to embrace nature into a dangerous folly:

JAQUES By my troth, I was seeking for a fool when I found you.
ORLANDO He is drowned in the brook. Look but in, and you shall see him.
JAQUES There I shall see my own figure.

(3.2.276–80)

If we were to go check this conclusion, we would surely see our own.

---

[29] *The Breviloquium*, in *The Works of Bonaventure*, trans. Jose De Vinck (Paterson, 1960–70), 11.12; quoted by Willis, 'Tongues in Trees', p. 66.

INFINITE JEST: THE COMEDY OF *HAMLET, PRINCE OF DENMARK*

ANN THOMPSON

This cartoon (illustration 15) appeared in the *London Evening Standard* on 16 March 2001. It is, I suppose, instantly recognizable as a reference to *Hamlet*: we know this from the man's costume, the fact that he is holding a skull, and the caption, which is clearly a parody of 'To be or not to be' (*Hamlet* 3.1.56[1]). If someone were to come across this cartoon in the archives of the *Evening Standard* in say fifty or one hundred years' time, it would still be obvious that it is a reference to *Hamlet*.

What would by then need annotation is the immediate context of the cartoon: one would need to explain that the figure represents Tony Blair, the Prime Minister of the United Kingdom at the time, and that the cartoon was published during a period when there was widespread speculation that he would call a General Election on 3 May. One would need to explain further that the object he is holding is the skull of a sheep and that the reason why he was being indecisive about the date was the epidemic of foot and mouth disease which was sweeping the country during the Spring of 2001: apart from the extent to which the election might have been seen as an unnecessary distraction at a time of national crisis, there was the practical consideration that the movements of both politicians and voters would be restricted. On the other hand, postponing the election would send a negative message to potential business investors and tourists.[2]

Hamlet is being used precisely because it has such a high recognition factor. We are sometimes told today that *King Lear* has overtaken *Hamlet* as the play generally acknowledged as 'Shakespeare's greatest tragedy',[3] but there is no single image from *King Lear* which has the recognition factor (or iconic status) of the man in black with the skull, and there is no single line from *King Lear* which is as well known as 'To be or not to be'. But where is the comedy in this cartoon? Does it lie in our perception of incongruity between the figurative allusion (high tragedy and the choice of life or death) and the literal reference (the relative unimportance of whether the election happened on 3 May or 7 June)? Foot and mouth disease was certainly not comic: does the incongruity lie rather in the contrast between the posturing politician and the animal's skull which stands in for literal and widespread destruction, both of animals and of rural livelihoods?

In addition to being somewhat puzzling, this cartoon is, from an academic (or pedantic) viewpoint, quite simply wrong. It evokes and conflates two completely different moments in the play: when Hamlet says 'To be or not to be' he is not in a graveyard or holding a skull. This most famous of

---

[1] Unless otherwise specified, quotations and references are from Harold Jenkins' Arden 2 edition (London, 1982).

[2] On the relation between the epidemic of foot and mouth disease and the timing of the 2001 General Election, see Andrew Rawnsley, *Servants of the People: The Inside Story of New Labour* (revised edn, London, 2001), pp. 466–81. To someone who asked him how he was sleeping during this period, Blair apparently replied that he 'counted sheep' (p. 471).

[3] Most notably, of course, by R. A. Foakes in *Hamlet versus Lear* (Cambridge, 1993). See also his earlier essay, '*King Lear* and the Displacement of *Hamlet*', *Huntington Library Quarterly*, 50 (1987), 263–78, and see my essay, '*Hamlet* and the Canon' in Arthur F. Kinney, ed., '*Hamlet*': *New Critical Essays* (New York and London, 2002), pp. 193–205.

"To run on May 3rd or not to run on May 3rd"

15 Cartoon by Patrick Blower, published in the *London Evening Standard* on 16 March 2001.

speeches comes much earlier in the play, at the beginning of Act 3 in the two so-called 'good' texts, earlier still in the equivalent of Act 2 in the so-called 'bad' text, the first version of *Hamlet* to be published. The skull appears in the graveyard scene in Act 5 and the words which 'should' accompany it are not 'To be or not to be' but the almost equally well known 'Alas, poor Yorick' (*Hamlet*, 5.1.178). These two iconic moments are in fact very frequently conflated in the extensive afterlife of the play in cartoons and other visual evocations, and it is not always possible to tell if the conflation is deliberate or merely erroneous. Perhaps it is simply explained by the fact that 'To be or not to be' has no

identifying prop of its own and so the skull has to be imported for us to be quite sure of the reference.

The very line 'Alas, poor Yorick!' may itself be quite simply wrong. Richard Proudfoot, senior general editor of the Arden Shakespeare, suggests that 'Yorick', like the mysterious 'Yaughan' mentioned earlier in the scene (5.1.60, but only in the Folio text), may be a phonetic spelling, in this case for a Danish name that would be more appropriately spelled 'Jurek' or 'Joerg' in a modernized text. As editors of *Hamlet* for Arden, Neil Taylor and I may well agree with this radical intervention on the part of our general editor, but would it be appropriate to adopt such a spelling when the perhaps non-existent name 'Yorick' has been canonized by 400 years of tradition? Sometimes, especially with Shakespeare, tradition forces editors to print what they consider to be incorrect – another notable example in *Hamlet* is the act division between Act 3 and Act 4 which has been placed in the middle of the closet scene since 1676. All editors since at least Samuel Johnson in 1765 deplore this as a misleading error, but virtually all follow it for the convenience of readers who are accustomed to this division. (And in any case it is arguable that Shakespeare and the other dramatists working for his company did not write plays with act divisions in mind until around 1608 when they started using the Blackfriars theatre.[4])

Yorick (or Jurek), Hamlet goes on to tell us, was 'a fellow of infinite jest'. He was a professional Fool, 'the King's jester', the King in question being Hamlet's father. In his commentary on *Twelfth Night* (forthcoming in Arden 3), Keir Elam points out that 'A dead man's delight in his jester is something of a Shakespearian topos', noting that Feste is described as 'a fool that the Lady Olivia's father took much delight in' (2.4.11n.), and comparing the Countess's reference to the clown at *All's Well That Ends Well* 4.5.63–4: 'My lord that's gone made himself much sport out of him'. All three are not only dead men but of course dead fathers. In the case of *Hamlet* it is difficult to imagine the father whom we encounter only as the Ghost enjoying (or indeed employing) such a figure, but he is affectionately recalled in Hamlet's verbal flashback, has featured in several illustrations of the play (see Edward Gordon Craig's infant Hamlet and oriental-looking Yorick[5]) and is played by the veteran comedian Ken Dodd in Kenneth Branagh's 1996 film. In all three texts he is however only mentioned for his conspicuous absence: he has been dead, Hamlet agrees with the Gravedigger in both the Second Quarto and the Folio, 'three and twenty years' (5.1.167–8). (He has been dead only 'this dozen year' in the First Quarto (16.66[6]).) This moment serves to remind us that *Hamlet*, as a play, does not contain an obvious role for a professional clown. It has been argued that this deficit was literally true of Shakespeare's acting company at the time: the Lord Chamberlain's Men

had recently lost the popular comedian Will Kempe (presumed to be the original Falstaff) and perhaps had not yet acquired Robert Armin whose earliest roles are assumed to be Touchstone in *As You Like It* and Feste in *Twelfth Night*.[7] If so, it may seem strange that Shakespeare chooses to draw attention to this deficit, not only here but also during Hamlet's first encounter with the Players in 2.2 and in his conversation with them before the performance of 'The Murder of Gonzago' in 3.2. In the earlier scene, he includes 'the clown' in his enumeration of stock dramatic characters:

He that plays the king shall be welcome . . . the adventurous knight shall use his foil and target, the lover shall not sigh gratis, . . . the clown shall make those laugh whose lungs are tickle a th' sear, and the lady shall say her mind freely – or the blank verse shall halt for't.

(2.2.318–24)

But no clown appears when the Players make their entry. In his instructions to them in 3.2 beginning 'Speak the speech, I pray you, as I pronounced it to you', it is even more evident that no clown is on stage in so far as Hamlet uses third person pronouns rather than the direct address of his first two speeches. He says:

And let those that play your clowns speak no more than is set down for them – for there be of them that will

---

[4] See Gary Taylor, 'The Structure of Performance: Act-Intervals in the London Theatres, 1576–1642', in Gary Taylor and John Jowett, *Shakespeare Reshaped 1606–1623* (Oxford, 1993), pp. 3–50.

[5] This comes from *The Tragedie of Hamlet*, text and sources edited by John Dover Wilson and illustrations by Edward Gordon Craig (Weimar, 1930).

[6] Quotations and references from the First Quarto are from the edition by Kathleen O. Irace (Cambridge Early Quartos, Cambridge, 1998).

[7] See especially David Wiles, *Shakespeare's Clown: Actor and Text in the Elizabethan Playhouse* (Cambridge, 1987), pp. 57–60. Katherine Duncan-Jones however assumes that 'Yorick' is an allusion to Richard Tarlton (*Ungentle Shakespeare: Scenes from His Life* (London, 2001)), p. 35, while Juliet Dusinberre maintains that Kempe played Touchstone in 'Topical Forest: Kemp and Martext in Arden' in Ann Thompson and Gordon McMullan, eds., *In Arden: The Editing of Shakespeare* (London, 2002).

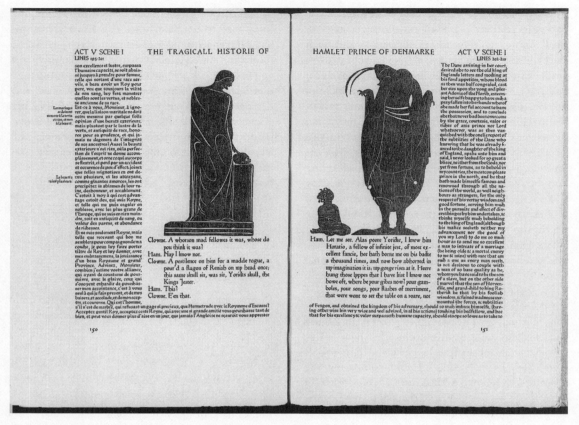

16   Illustration by Edward Gordon Craig from *The Tragedie of Hamlet*, text and sources edited by John Dover Wilson (Weimar, 1930).

themselves laugh, to set on some quantity of barren spectators to laugh too, though in the meantime some necessary question of the play be then to be considered. That's villainous, and shows a most pitiful ambition in the fool that uses it.

(3.2.38–45)

Curiously, the so-called 'bad' text continues this speech with some specific examples of precisely the ad-libbing that is being deplored. Hamlet in this text adds:

And then you have some again that keeps one suit of jests, as a man is known by one suit of apparel, and gentlemen quote his jests down in their tables before they come to the play, as thus: 'Cannot you stay till I eat my porridge?' and 'You owe me a quarter's wages', and 'My coat wants a cullison', and 'Your beer is sour', and blabbering with

his lips and thus keeping in his cinquepace of jests, when God knows, the warm clown cannot make a jest unless by chance, as the blind man catcheth a hare.

(9.21–8)

Again, his last words, 'Masters, tell him of it' (9.28), emphasize that such a clown is not present. These additional lines have found their way into some editions (notably Penguin at 3.2.43–53) and have been spoken on stage, for example by Michael Pennington, in the Royal Shakespeare Company production directed by John Barton in 1970, who commented 'The audience, lulled with familiar words, didn't half sit up'.[8]

---

8   Michael Pennington, *'Hamlet': A User's Guide* (New York, 1996), pp. 24–5.

Will Kempe was indeed famous for his improvisational comedy, and some scholars, for example Andrew Gurr, have suggested that Hamlet is voicing the view of Shakespeare's acting company which had grown tired of this sort of comedy and had decided to dispense with his services.[9] We do not however know the circumstances of Kempe's departure from the Chamberlain's Men: there has been speculation, by David Wiles, for example, that he left because Shakespeare did not write a part for Falstaff in *Henry V*, despite having promised in the Epilogue to *2 Henry IV* that he would continue the story 'with Sir John in it',[10] but one could equally well argue that his decision to leave the company was the reason for this omission – that Shakespeare responded to the fact of his departure rather than that he caused it.[11]

Whatever the truth of this, one of the consequences for *Hamlet* of the absence of an obvious actor to 'play the clown' is that the comic role is spread around amongst several performers, not least Richard Burbage as Hamlet who doubles the roles of hero and Fool. The Gravedigger himself is a clear example of a comic 'turn' which has to be sustained for the length of a single scene, not unlike the one-off clown scenes in *Macbeth* and *Antony and Cleopatra*. Molly Mahood has argued that this was in fact one of Robert Armin's first roles for the company,[12] and indeed the Gravedigger's style of prevarication is similar to that of Feste or *Macbeth*'s Porter. Other candidates for comedy in *Hamlet* include Polonius, Rosencrantz and Guildenstern, and Osric, though all of these parts can be played in a range of styles, shading from light to dark. There is a long stage tradition of doubling Polonius and the Gravedigger: many examples are recorded by Arthur Colby Sprague from 1730 onwards,[13] and it has been done most recently in London by Denis Quilley in the 2000 National Theatre production (directed by John Caird with Simon Russell Beale as Hamlet), by Bruce Myers in the 2001 Young Vic transfer of the 2000 Bouffes du Nord production (directed by Peter Brook with Adrian Lester as Hamlet) and by Alan David in the 2001 Royal Shakespeare Company production (directed by Steve Pimlott with Sam West as Hamlet).

This is one way of making up a decent afternoon or evening's work for an actor with the appropriate skills, though it may seem less appropriate if Polonius is not interpreted as a comic part.

The Gravedigger is perhaps the only unequivocally comic character in the play, and one whose presence was famously deplored by Voltaire. In response, David Garrick cut the sequence in his 1772 adaptation of *Hamlet*, claiming that he had 'rescued that noble play from the rubbish of the fifth act',[14] but even he had to acknowledge that the Gravedigger was popular with audiences, and his successors not only restored the part but, from around 1780 to 1830, enhanced the comedy with what became a traditional piece of business whereby the Gravedigger removed many layers of waistcoats, folding each one carefully, before he began his work.[15] Unlike most of the other characters who become mere butts for Hamlet to display his superior wit, the Gravedigger can hold his own in repartee (perhaps again an indication of Armin, who was himself a playwright), and performers of Hamlet can endear themselves to the audience at this point by their generosity in being prepared to play the straight man for once.

The range of possibilities for Polonius can be illustrated from an eighteenth-century

---

9 Andrew Gurr, *Playgoing in Shakespeare's London* (Cambridge, 1987), pp. 151–2.

10 David Wiles, *Shakespeare's Clown*.

11 Robert Barrie makes this point in '*Telmahs*: Carnival Laughter in *Hamlet*', in Mark Thornton Burnett and John Manning, eds., *New Essays on 'Hamlet'* (New York, 1994), pp. 83–100, p. 88.

12 M. M. Mahood, *Playing Bit Parts in Shakespeare* (1998; a revised version of *Bit Parts in Shakespeare's Plays*, Cambridge, 1992), p. 83.

13 Arthur Colby Sprague, *The Doubling of Parts in Shakespeare's Plays* (London, 1966), p. 35.

14 Garrick made this claim in a letter to Sir William Young, dated 10 January 1773; quoted in George Winchester Stone Jr, 'Garrick's long lost alteration of *Hamlet*', *PMLA*, 49 (1934), 890–921, p. 893.

15 See Arthur Colby Sprague, *Shakespeare and the Actors* (Cambridge, Mass., 1944), pp. 175–6. Mark Rosenberg notes a revival of this tradition in Toronto in 1985 (*The Masks of Hamlet* (Newark, Delaware, 1992), p. 832).

commentator, William Popple, who commented (in 1735) on what had become the traditional way of performing the character's opening lines in 1.2 when he replies to the king's question as to whether he has given his son Laertes permission to return to Paris. Polonius says

> He hath my lord wrung from me my slow leave
> By laboursome petition, and at last
> Upon his will I sealed my hard consent.
> I do beseech you give him leave to go.
>
> (1.2.58–61)

Popple notes

Here is the most simple, plain, unstudied, unaffected reply that could be given. Yet how is this spoke and acted? The eyes are turned obliquely and dressed up in a foolish leer at the King, the words intermittently drawled out with a very strong emphasis, not to express a father's concern, which would be right, but to excite laughter . . . the voice toned like the squeak of a bagpipe.[16]

Polonius at this point was not just comic but farcical. By way of contrast, Kenneth Branagh in his 1996 film, having cast Richard Briers, best known for comic parts, in the role, nevertheless presented Polonius as a sinister and hypocritical character, discovered with a prostitute in his room in 2.1 and negotiating with Reynaldo-as-pimp, memorably played by Gerard Depardieu (despite the fact that his entire part consists of about ten lines or sixty words).

Tom Stoppard's *Rosencrantz and Guildenstern Are Dead*[17] elaborates on the potential for comedy in the representation of these two characters. Shakespeare writes this into their first appearance in 2.2 when the King dismisses them saying 'Thanks Rosencrantz and gentle Guildenstern', whereupon the Queen joins in with 'Thanks Guildenstern and gentle Rosencrantz' (2.2.33–4). This can obviously be played either as a piece of courtesy whereby the Queen gives both courtiers the same degree of status, or as a correction of the King who has got the names wrong. Interestingly, her line was regularly omitted on stage from at least 1676 and the delivery of the line as a 'correction' became seen as a 'corny old joke' which later productions attempted to

avoid.[18] The traditional Anglo-American performance of the pair as Tweedledum-and-Tweedledee bunglers was not acceptable on the stages of the former Soviet Union and Eastern Europe where *Hamlet* was often seen as a play about the corruption of totalitarian states and their dependence on secret police and spies for their information: Grigori Kozintsev, for example, who directed a film of *Hamlet* in 1964, saw the moment at the end of 3.2 (after the performance of 'The Murder of Gonzago') when Hamlet attacks Rosencrantz and Guildenstern for their attempts to play upon him as if he were a pipe, as 'the most important passage in the tragedy', asserting as it does the power of the individual to remain inscrutable in the face of the operations of the state and its informers. In his book about making the film, he links this explicitly with the appearance of young Osric in the final scene: 'The first toll of Hamlet's funeral bell is the arrival of this court minor who sweeps the Elsinore parquetry with the feather on his hat . . . Hamlet is called to his death by squeaky nasal pipes. There is some sort of stupidly comic sound in the prelude to his funeral march. It is produced by an instrument that is far easier to play than a pipe – a semblance of a man, one of the generation brought up by Elsinore.'[19]

Anglo-American stage tradition has usually presented Osric as an absurdly affected courtier – a fop – and has enthusiastically developed the text's indications of stage business with his hat.[20] He is not seen as a threat to Hamlet but as the butt of his jokes, providing a last opportunity for us to see the Prince in a relaxed mode before the final duel. But, building on John Dover Wilson's suggestion that

---

[16] Quoted by Robert Hapgood in *Shakespeare in Production: 'Hamlet'* (Cambridge, 1999), p. 111.

[17] First performed in Edinburgh, 1966; published in London, 1967.

[18] See Rosenberg, *Masks*, pp. 375–6 and Hapgood, *Shakespeare in Production*, pp. 151–2.

[19] Grigori Kozintsev, *Shakespeare: Time and Conscience* (translated by Joyce Vining, London, 1966), p. 172.

[20] See Rosenberg, *Masks*, pp. 867–9 and Hapgood, *Shakespeare in Production*, pp. 263–4.

Osric as the overseer of the duel must be party to the conspiracy against Hamlet,[21] Kozintsev makes this episode ominous, with what others see as the comic inflation of Osric's language becoming an exaggerated deference to Hamlet which is sinister in its implications.[22] Osric is a representative of 'obsequious young men on the make', 'a generation which grew up with the notion that it is dangerous to think and pointless to feel'.[23]

Hamlet dismisses Polonius's taste in theatrical entertainment in 2.2. When the councillor complains that the Player's speech about the death of Priam is 'too long', Hamlet comments 'He's for a jig or a tale of bawdry, or he sleeps' (2.2.494–6). Later he describes himself, albeit ironically, as 'your only jig-maker' (3.2.123). Both of these seem interesting formulations, given that Will Kempe may have left the Chamberlain's Men late in 1599 in order to perform his famous jig as a kind of marathon from London to Norwich.

When *Hamlet* was performed at the reconstructed Globe in 2000 (directed by Giles Block, with Mark Rylance as Hamlet), it did indeed end with a jig (somewhat baffling to the audience and not repeated in 2001 for either *Macbeth* or *King Lear*), but while the performance of *Julius Caesar* that Thomas Platter saw on 21 September 1599 ended with a jig, it is entirely possible that, after the departure of their most famous jig-maker, *Hamlet* did not. The context in which Hamlet makes his claim to be 'your only jig-maker' is not at all comic: he has been aggressively obscene to Ophelia before 'The Murder of Gonzago', asking her 'shall I lie in your lap?' and so forth, and when she tries to put him off with 'You are merry, my lord', he replies:

O God, your only jig-maker. What should a man do but be merry? For look you how cheerfully my mother looks and my father died within's two hours.

(3.2.123–5)

After the play, Hamlet's elation causes him to play the role of the clown, singing and presumably dancing and asking Horatio 'Would not this . . . and a forest of feathers . . . get me a fellowship in a cry of players?' (3.2.269–72). In Peter Brook's production, Hamlet and Horatio did perform a kind of jig of

triumph at this point, though on the page Horatio is more sceptical: 'Half a share', he comments. One scholar, David Wiles, reads this as an explicit reminder that Will Kempe had sold his share in the company, and he further interprets the line in Hamlet's song, 'Thus runs the world away' as a reference to the Globe theatre: Kempe had indeed 'danced himself out of the world' in this sense, as he puts it in his account of the marathon, his *Nine Days Wonder*.[24]

In the eighteenth century Dr Johnson assures us that 'the pretended madness of Hamlet causes much mirth',[25] but modern Hamlets are rarely prepared to risk genuine laughter at Hamlet's madness. Perhaps we are less inclined to find insanity comic than our Elizabethan ancestors? Or perhaps the role of Hamlet has become somewhat restricted as it has been made more dignified and more emblematic of a rather solemn, intellectual kind of sensibility? The disarray of his dress so graphically described by Ophelia in 2.1 – 'his doublet all unbraced, / No hat upon his head, his stockings fouled, / Ungartered and down-gyved to his ankle' (2.1.78–80) – must have been literally represented on the stage in the original performances, judging by a reference in Anthony Scoloker's *Diaphantus* (1604), where a character is said to 'Put off his clothes; his shirt he only wears, / Much like mad Hamlet'.[26] By the nineteenth century the disarray was represented by minimal touches: in *Great Expectations* Charles Dickens says of Mr Wopsle as Hamlet that 'he appeared with his stocking disordered (its disorder expressed, according to usage, by one very neat fold in the top, which I suppose to be always got up

21 See John Dover Wilson, ed., *Hamlet* (New Shakespeare Series, Cambridge, 1934, reprinted 1969), note on 5.2.257, p. 253.
22 See the description of this scene in Anthony B. Dawson, *Shakespeare in Performance: 'Hamlet'* (Manchester, 1995), p. 195.
23 See Kozintsev, *Time and Conscience*, p. 171.
24 See David Wiles, *Shakespeare's Clown*.
25 Quoted in Susan Snyder, *The Comic Matrix of Shakespeare's Tragedies* (as cited in n. 40 below), p. 116.
26 C. M. Ingleby et al., *The Shakspere Allusion Book*, 2 vols., vol. 1, pp. 133–5.

with a flat-iron)'.[27] Even in the twentieth century, Mark Rylance for the Royal Shakespeare Company in 1989, directed by Ron Daniels, and again at the Globe in 2000, was highly unusual in delivering 'To be or not to be' wearing stained pyjamas or nightshirt. In a conversation between two of the most recent actors to appear in the role in London, Simon Russell Beale said to Adrian Lester 'You're madder than I am, aren't you?', to which Lester replied 'I'm backing, aren't I? I'm completely crazy'.[28] But what this meant in performance was that he drooled and dribbled extravagantly in his conversation with Polonius, only to remark 'These tedious old fools' very sanely and coldly after Polonius' exit. When I saw it, nobody laughed. Actors who have taken risks with displays of 'mad' behaviour have sometimes come unstuck, none more spectacularly than the mid nineteenth-century actor William Charles Macready who performed a famous piece of business with his handkerchief while the court audience was assembling for the play in 3.2, cued by his line 'I must be idle'. Macready, we are told,

assumed the manner of an idiot, or of a silly and active and impertinent booby, by tossing his head right and left, and walking rapidly across the stage 5 or 6 times before the footlights and switching his hankerchief – held by a corner – over his right and left shoulder alternately.[29]

This became known as the *pas de mouchoir* ('dance of the handkerchief') and Londoners flocked to see it. But when Macready was on tour in Edinburgh in 1846, Edwin Forrest, his American rival (who acted Hamlet from 1829 to 1872), was in the audience and he hissed at this point; the subsequent contest between them and their followers culminated in

an attempt to drive Macready from the stage while he was playing at the Astor Opera House in New York, in May 1849. A riot took place, the National Guard were called out, and they being attacked by the mob, fired, leaving 30 dead bodies on the ground, and wounding severely as many more.[30]

It isn't just Hamlet's madness that allows him to play the fool. Edwin Booth worried about his reaction to his first sight of his father's Ghost and his addressing it jocularly as 'boy', 'truepenny' and 'old mole', asserting 'This is not unfeeling levity but the very intensity of mental excitement'.[31] Similar problems arise in the 'closet scene' where the climactic encounter between Hamlet and his mother and the final appearance of the Ghost are bracketed between the absurd mistaking and killing of Polonius and Hamlet's jaunty exit-line: 'I'll lug the guts into the neighbour room' (3.4.214). On one level the levity has to cover the inevitable indignity of a single actor getting an adult corpse offstage – one might compare the comic treatment of Hotspur's corpse in *1 Henry IV* 5.4 – but again the last section of the scene (often cut in stage tradition) is tinged with a hysteria which seems to belie Hamlet's assertion 'That I essentially am not in madness, / But mad in craft' (3.4.189–90). This is one point at which an editor may well choose to remind readers that the hero's behaviour is even more bizarre in some of Shakespeare's sources. Thanks to the still unsurpassed work of Geoffrey Bullough, we can turn readily to the account in the twelfth century Danish History of Saxo Grammaticus in which Amleth, after killing the eavesdropper, 'cut his body into morsels, seethed it in boiling water, and flung it through the mouth of an open sewer for the swine to eat, bestrewing the stinking mire with his hapless limbs' (7.65).[32] This is a hero who has spent his time 'flinging himself on the ground and bespattering his person with foul and filthy dirt. His discoloured face and visage smutched with slime denoted foolish and grotesque madness'.[33]

---

[27] Charles Dickens, *Great Expectations* (1860–1), p. 254 in the Clarendon Press edn, ed. Margaret Cardwell, London, 1993.

[28] 'Two Hamlets Explore New Paths in an Old Terrain', *New York Times*, 8 April 2001. Obtained from *New York Times* website: http://www.nytimes.com.

[29] James Henry Hackett, *Notes . . . upon Shakespeare's Plays and Actors* (New York, 1863), p. 158.

[30] See Henry P. Phelps, *Shakespeare from the Actors' Standpoint* (New York, 1890), pp. 20–21. This actually happened during a performance by Macready of *Macbeth* (see Hapgood, *Shakespeare in Production*, p. 75).

[31] Quoted by Hapgood, *Shakespeare in Production*, p. 143.

[32] Geoffrey Bullough, *Narrative and Dramatic Sources of Shakespeare* (8 vols., London, 1957–75), vol. 7, p. 65.

[33] Bullough, *Narrative*, p. 62.

Perhaps then it is Shakespeare who is the first one to take some of the more grotesque comedy *out* of the Hamlet story? It is well known that references to an earlier Elizabethan Hamlet play seem to dismiss it as a cliché or a parody of revenge tragedy. Thomas Nashe wrote in 1589 that 'English Seneca read by candlelight yields many good sentences, as "Blood is a beggar", and so forth: and if you entreat him fair in a frosty morning, he will afford you whole Hamlets, I should say handfuls, of tragical speeches'. And Thomas Lodge referred contemptuously in 1596 to the 'pale vizard' of the ghost 'which cried so miserably at the theatre like an oysterwife, "Hamlet, revenge."'[34] Perhaps more interestingly, this tone does not alter dramatically after the staging and publication of Shakespeare's play: some of the earliest references we have to it are facetious or satirical. In *Eastward Ho*, for example, a collaborative comedy written by George Chapman, John Marston and Ben Jonson and first performed in 1605, the authors introduce a footman called Hamlet entirely, it would seem, so that someone can say to him, "Sfoot, Hamlet, are you mad?' (3.1.4.)[35] The Queen's description of the death of Ophelia is parodied in the description by Slitgut, a butcher's apprentice, of the plight of a usurer's wife who eventually survives a shipwreck in the Thames which befalls her when she is running away with her lover, Sir Petronel Flash, 'a new-made knight', who is in turn running away from his wife, Gertrude (see *Eastward Ho* 4.1.66–75). Several other allusions in this play indicate that *Hamlet* was not only well known but already available as a text inviting less than serious treatment. Thomas Dekker and Thomas Middleton's *The Honest Whore* Part 1 (1604) develops Hamlet's scene with the skull in knowing and parodic mode,[36] and tag-lines from *Hamlet* appear in a number of comedies in the first decade of the seventeenth century.

This is a point remarked upon by the editors of the *Shakspere Allusion Book*. Noting a clutch of apparently irreverent references to *Hamlet* from 1604, one of the editors, Brinsley Nicholson, comments:

This and similar quotations show the fame and reputation of Shakespere, being popularly known lines quoted or imitated for the purpose of causing a good-humoured laugh at their misappropriation.[37]

When another editor introduces an allusion with the words 'This is plainly a sneer at *Hamlet*', Alexander Dyce feels obliged to add a footnote, 'Nonsense, more compliment than sneer'.[38]

What do we make of this? We might explain it with reference to the so-called 'War of the Theatres' whereby dramatists around the turn of the century routinely attacked each others' work, but at the same time it is early evidence of a drive to send *Hamlet* up or, perhaps, as we might now say, to demystify it as a tragic icon. Interestingly, in my role as general editor of the Arden Shakespeare series, I've just been reading a draft of part of the Introduction to *Macbeth* in which Kate McLuskie notes that some of the earliest allusions to that play are similarly parodic: the appearance of Banquo's ghost becomes a comic turn in plays like Middleton's *The Puritan* and Beaumont's *The Knight of the Burning Pestle*. One of my many distinguished predecessors as an editor of *Hamlet*, George MacDonald, speculates that the habit of making jokes about *Hamlet* may even be evident in the First Folio itself. Commenting on the Folio's reading 'like the kind life-rendering politician' for the Second Quarto's 'like the kind life-rendering pelican' (4.5.146), he remarks, 'A curious misprint: may we not suspect some dull joker among the compositors?'[39]

---

34 Both cited by Harold Jenkins in the Arden 2 edition, pp. 82–3.

35 Quotations and references to *Eastward Ho* are from the Revels text edited by R. W. Van Fossen (Manchester, 1979). See also Richard Horwich, '*Hamlet* and *Eastward Ho*', *Studies in English Literature* 11 (1971), pp. 223–33 and David Farley-Hills, 'Another *Hamlet* Crux', *Notes and Queries* 243 (1998), pp. 334–6.

36 See scene 10 in the Globe Quartos text, ed. Nick de Somogyi (1998).

37 Ingleby et al., *Shakspere Allusion*, vol. 1, p. 129.

38 Ingleby et al., *Shakspere Allusion*, vol. 1, p. 200.

39 MacDonald's edition was published by Longman, London, 1885. Jesus Tronch-Perez however suggests that Laertes may be referring to a genuinely 'life-rendering politician' who would give even his blood for his country; see *A Synoptic 'Hamlet'* (Valencia, 2002), p. 289.

Of course some critics have argued that Shakespeare makes more pervasive and indeed serious use of comedy and comic structures in *Hamlet*. In her book *The Comic Matrix of Shakespeare's Tragedies*,[40] Susan Snyder focuses on the notion of multiple perspective as one of the characteristics of comedy which is endemic in *Hamlet*, but while for a character like Rosalind in *As You Like It* 'two views are better than one' and the multiple perspective gives both freedom and power, 'Hamlet's situation calls for action, and coherent action is impossible while his two apprehensions remain separate and opposed' (p. 93). Thus 'the play transmutes the comic celebration of multiplicity into an existential nightmare of competing perceptions of reality' (p. 91), since 'To perceive more truths than one is to be sure of no truth' (p. 105). Naomi Conn Liebler in *Shakespeare's Festive Tragedy*[41] reads *Hamlet* in terms of the effect on a community of the violation of ritual structures: a violation which ultimately requires Hamlet himself to become the scapegoat who has to be sacrificed to ensure the community's survival. She draws on the writings of Mikhail Bakhtin and demonstrates the relevance of work in social and cultural anthropology. Both Snyder and Liebler provoke us to reconsider our definitions of dramatic genre and to explore the boundary between tragedy and comedy which turns out to be rather permeable. They do not deny *Hamlet's* status as a tragedy but rethink tragedy itself with reference to notions of the comic and the festive.

It is perhaps surprising that *Hamlet* still has the power to work as a 'straight' tragedy given that it has been the butt of jokes for 400 years. There is an extraordinarily rich history of parodies, travesties, prequels, sequels and other comic rewritings; I'll just take three of my favourite examples from the twentieth century. In 1901 St John Hankin published in *Punch* magazine a series of comic sequels to well-known works including *Alcestis*, *The School for Scandal* and *The Lady from the Sea*.[42] In his *Hamlet* sequel, *The New Wing at Elsinore*, Horatio has seized the throne and is being visited on the battlements, amiably by Fortinbras. Horatio complains about the number of Ghosts haunting the old castle:

It's not as if we only had *one* ghost.
They simply *swarm*! There's Hamlet's father;
He walks the battlements from ten to five:
You'll see him here in half an hour or so.
Claudius, the late King, haunts the State apartments,
The Queen the keep, Ophelia the moat,
And Rosencrantz and Guildenstern the hall.
Polonius you will usually find
Behind the arras murmuring platitudes,
And Hamlet stalking in the corridors.
Alas, poor ghost! His fatal indecision
Pursues him still. He can't make up his mind
Which rooms to take – you're never safe from him![43]

Horatio takes Fortinbras to see the new wing he is having built in order to avoid the ghosts, thus baulking the original Ghost of his auditory. The workmen (former gravediggers) affect in public a laboured 'Elizabethan' witticism, admired by Horatio, dismissed as idiotic by Fortinbras. An entirely new ghost appears, Shakespeare himself, determined to haunt the new wing, declaring 'It's *mine*, I say, *my* house, *my* plot, *my* play'. Horatio is dismayed:

I shall consult with my solicitor,
And if he can't eject you from the place,
I'll sell it, ghosts and all![44]

But Shakespeare tempted posthumous collaborators precisely by leaving so many loose ends in *his* plot. J. I. M. Stewart, for example, operating under the pseudonym Michael Innes (which he had used to publish many detective novels), treated the narrative as an unsolved murder mystery in his 1949 radio talk, 'The Mysterious Affair at Elsinore'[45]: Fortinbras is criticized for destroying evidence by moving the bodies, but Innes is nevertheless able to reveal that Ophelia was secretly married to Hamlet (and

---

[40] (Princeton, NJ, 1980).
[41] (London, 1995).
[42] Published in book form as *Dramatic Sequels* edited by Herbert Farjeon (London, 1925), pp. 17–30.
[43] Farjeon, *Dramatic Sequels*, pp. 21–2.
[44] Farjeon, *Dramatic Sequels*, p. 30.
[45] Published in Rayner Heppenstall and Michael Innes, *Three Tales of Hamlet* (London, 1950), pp. 75–89.

was pregnant when she died), that Rosencrantz and Guildenstern were bastard sons of Claudius and had to be killed in order to allow Fortinbras, the real villain, to succeed, aided by his co-conspirator Horatio, whose long-awaited six-volume *Life and Letters of Hamlet the Dane* has proved a disappointment on publication, merely obfuscating the truth.

The extent of the Queen's guilt has attracted numerous authors who have written prequels to the play speculating on whether she was having an affair with her husband's brother before his death, and whether she was an accomplice to the murder. My third example is Margaret Atwood's brisk four-page rewriting of the closet scene from the Queen's point of view in 'Gertrude Talks Back' (in her collection of short fiction called *Good Bones*[46]). When Hamlet insists that his mother 'Look here upon this picture and on this', in this version of the dialogue she responds wearily

Yes, I've seen those pictures, thank you very much. I *know* your father was handsomer than Claudius . . . but I think it's about time I pointed out that your Dad just wasn't a whole lot of fun. Noble, sure, I grant you. But Claudius, well, he likes a drink now and then. He appreciates a decent meal. He enjoys a laugh, know what I mean?

(p. 16)

She tries to warn Hamlet off Ophelia:

If you ask me there's something off about that girl. Borderline. Any little shock could push her right over the edge. Get yourself someone more down-to-earth.

(p. 17)

Finally she addresses the main point:

Oh! You think *what*? You think Claudius murdered your Dad? Well, no wonder you've been so rude to him at the dinner-table! If I'd known *that* I could have put you straight in no time flat. It wasn't Claudius, darling, it was me.

(p. 18)

To return, finally to the *Evening Standard* which has supplied me with several good *Hamlet* jokes over

the last couple of years. Here is one that appeared on 19 February 2001:

A Shakespearian joke, courtesy of comedian and Radio 4 presenter Arthur Smith: 'Knock, knock. Who's there? Mandy. Mandy who? Man delights not me; no, nor woman neither, though, by your smiling, you seem to say so'.

The *Standard* did not bother to name *Hamlet*, but presumably researchers of the future will have no difficulty in identifying the last sentence, 'Man delights not me' etc. as a quotation from the play (2.2.309–10). In its Shakespearian context, it is not so much a joke as an explicit denial of a joke: Hamlet is remonstrating with Rosencrantz and Guildenstern for finding a sexual meaning in what he has just said and denying that there is anything to smile at. (Such innuendos or *doubles entendres* are of course ubiquitous in Shakespeare and often an occasion of embarrassment for editors and teachers.) But what is the joke for *Standard* readers in 2001? A researcher would need to explain at least three things:

(1) That 'Mandy' was the nickname accorded (first by *Private Eye*?) to Peter Mandelson, one of the founders of New Labour, MP for Hartlepool and erstwhile member of the government. The fact that he was sometimes referred to as 'the prince of darkness' may also be relevant.

(2) That in this context 'Man delights not me' is a reference to the fact that Mandelson is openly homosexual, but had famously tried to prevent the BBC from mentioning this (over two years earlier, in October 1998).[47]

(3) That he was in the news again in February 2001 over the favours-for-passports scandal whereby he was said to have facilitated passport applications for certain overseas businessmen.[48]

The exposition of *Hamlet* jokes begins to seem somewhat laborious at this point, so I'll end with a reference to a different play. In Shakespeare's *Troilus*

---

[46] (London, 1992), pp. 15–18.
[47] See Rawnsley, *Servants of the People*, pp. 214–5.
[48] Rawnsley, *Servants of the People*, pp. 433–62.

and Cressida, the heroine, on her first appearance, is subjected to what we would call a shaggy-dog story. Her uncle Pandarus gives a long and often inconsequential account of an encounter at the royal palace between Helen of Troy and Troilus, Cressida's would-be lover, constantly assuring her of how hilarious it was: Queen Hecuba, he insists, 'laughed that her eyes ran over'. Cressida quite deliberately refuses to understand the joke, forcing Pandarus to conclude lamely: 'But there was such laughing, and Helen so blushed, and Paris so chafed, and all the rest so laughed, that it passed'.

'So let it now', responds Cressida, 'for it has been a great while going by' (1.2.160–4).[49]

---

[49] Quotations and references from the Arden 3 text edited by David Bevington (London, 1998).

OTHELLO AND THE END OF COMEDY

STEPHEN ORGEL

Othello begins at the moment when comedies end, with a happy marriage. It begins, too, where *The Merchant of Venice* and *Twelfth Night* leave off, with the question of ethnic or social outsiders – Shylock, Malvolio – as the catalysts for the destructive elements within society. It might seem that here the terms are reversed, with the dangerous alien now the hero, while the mysterious, incomprehensibly malicious, diabolical villain is the insider, one of us. But in fact, the insider/outsider dichotomy is really a false one, because just as Shylock is essential to Bassanio's wooing, and Malvolio is essential to both Olivia's household and ultimately even to the marriage of Viola and Orsino, so is Othello essential to the safety and prosperity of the Venetian state. The tragedy is not that Othello is essential to Venice, but that Iago is essential to Othello.

We have, historically, focused on the interracial marriage as the crucial source of tension and tragedy in the play. But the larger issue in *Othello* has to do with the tragic implications not of miscegenation but of patriarchy on the one hand, and patronage or gender bonding (not limited to males in this case) on the other. I begin with the first: patriarchy is an issue that often provides both the principal motivation of comedy and a strong tragic element within it – as in the cases of Celia's villainous father in *As You Like It* and the obdurate Egeus in *A Midsummer Night's Dream*. It is on the defeat of these fathers that the comedy depends. In a strikingly ambiguous example, the death of the Princess of France's father, announced by a messenger appropriately named Mercadé ('mar-Arcady'), produces a tragic moment interrupting the comic wooing of *Love's Labour's Lost*: 'The king your father –' 'Dead, for my life!' . . . 'Worthies, away! The scene begins to cloud' (5.2.710-12).[1] This could conclude the comedy, but it does not. It is, in fact, an enabling comic event, which permits the heroine to make her own decisions. Significantly, she exercises her new authority by refusing to allow the play to conclude with the marriages of comedy, implying thereby that perhaps marriage is not such a happy ending after all.

The patriarchal imperatives are powerfully present and shrewdly finessed in *The Merchant of Venice*, where daughters are all but equated with ducats, and the triumph of romance is engineered by Portia both adhering to the letter of her dead father's will and betraying its spirit – and not incidentally turning the patriarchal tables by reducing both her father and Jessica's to their ducats. Patriarchy is specifically sidestepped in *Twelfth Night*, in which all the fathers are safely dead and their estates safely settled before the play even begins. Viola and Olivia make their own decisions about marriage, and Sir Toby's avuncular attempt to stand in the place of Olivia's father is as firmly rejected as the authority

---

For information and suggestions I am indebted to John Russell Brown, Jonathan Crewe, Suzanne Gossett, David Halperin, Peter Holland, Adrian Kiernander, Lois Potter, B. J. Sokol and John Stokes.

[1] Shakespeare quotations are from the New Pelican Shakespeare, eds. Stephen Orgel and A. R. Braunmuller (New York, 2002).

of Brabantio is in *Othello*. Indeed, there is a significant link between the two plays in the relation of Iago and Roderigo, a very sinister refiguring of Sir Toby and Sir Andrew, with Iago keeping up Roderigo's interest in Desdemona merely because it means a constant supply of ready cash for the go-between. Even here, the woman is easily convertible into a source of ducats.

If *Othello* is the next step after comedy, it is also an obvious next step after the tragedy of *Romeo and Juliet*. However admirable Romeo and Othello are (and both are presented as, in themselves, highly suitable marriage material), the question of Juliet's and Desdemona's elopement would have been a real one for Shakespeare's audience: daughters in this society *are* ducats, and the daughter was, in effect, disposing of a valuable piece of her father's property without his consent. Legally either of the women would have been perfectly entitled to make the match, since both are of age. The age of consent was twelve for women, fourteen for men. In the Canons of 1604 it was raised to twenty-one for both, but Parliament failed to pass the necessary legislation, and the age remained statutorily unchanged until the eighteenth century. It is perhaps relevant that 1604 was also the year *Othello* was first performed: the issue of parental control over marriage was being actively debated at the time. Such a marriage, therefore, raised ethical and moral issues that would have had nothing to do with the fact that Othello was black. The point here is not that daughters are at fault if they disobey or fail to consult their fathers' wishes; it is that the patriarchal system inevitably involves divided loyalties, irreconcilable, and sometimes tragic, demands. As Desdemona points out when she is summoned to account for herself before the Duke and her father, she has a double duty; the patriarchy of her father conflicts with the patriarchy of her husband. One way to view the play, as with *Romeo and Juliet*, is certainly as a moral tale about the consequences of not listening to your father. This does not imply that father always knows best; what it implies is that right or wrong, he is still your father – being wrong does not undo his authority. Inherent in patriarchy, that is, is a divided loyalty, a potentially

tragic element, always. Similarly, Shakespeare plays are full of bad kings, but they are not therefore arguments in favour of democracy: the point – often a tragic point – is that a bad king is still the king.

Nevertheless, the father is rarely simply rejected or ignored. Even in *Twelfth Night*, Viola, in determining to serve Orsino (determining in effect to fall in love with him) recalls her father talking of him with praise – she implicitly claims her father's posthumous approval for her pursuit of him. And though at the beginning of *Othello* Brabantio insists that he never had any romantic intentions for Othello and his daughter, it is nevertheless clear that Desdemona's love for the heroic Moor is an outgrowth, even an extension, of her father's – 'Her father loved me', Othello says, 'oft invited me' (1.3.128). Brabantio's assertions to the contrary notwithstanding, the marriage is presented as the logical climax to a patronage relationship, the traditional confirmation of masculine friendship – traditionally a happy ending, certainly, but one that also often constitutes the beginning of tragedy, as the comedy of Hercules's gift to Theseus of his prize, Hippolyta, leads not only to *A Midsummer Night's Dream*, but also, inexorably, to the tragedy of their offspring Hippolytus and Hippolyta's successor in Theseus's bed, Phaedra.

Consider *Othello* as a comedy. Suppose I said that this is a play about a jealous husband driven wild by the fear of being a cuckold, though his wife is in fact perfectly innocent; that the central action involves a trick played on him by a clever, malicious servant; that the crucial – and indeed, the only – piece of evidence is a missing handkerchief; and that at the end of the play the wife's innocence and the servant's trickery are both revealed to the repentant husband. I have not misrepresented the play's action at all, yet this sounds like a subject for comedy: the final sentence could very well be, 'husband and wife are reconciled, and Othello promises not to be jealous any more'.

In fact, the play tempts us with comic possibilities all the time. As with that other love tragedy *Romeo and Juliet*, nothing about it suggests the inevitability that we normally associate with tragedy. If they had only talked about it, we want to say; if

Emilia had revealed the theft of the handkerchief a little sooner; if the momentary recovery of Desdemona had lasted (I am told that this is a physiological impossibility anyway – that is, it is already a miracle; but the miracle is simply another tease) . . . and so forth. As with *Romeo and Juliet*, a significant part of the power of the play comes from how infuriatingly close it gets to not being a tragedy. We can derive a critical precept from this: what distinguishes comedy from tragedy is not the problems it deals with, but what it is willing to accept as solutions to its problems, what kind of satisfaction it is willing to deliver.

If marriage is the ultimate satisfaction of comedy, what happens next? What kind of tragic satisfaction does *Othello* deliver? Despite the fact that it opens with an elopement, it quite explicitly deprives us of the satisfaction of marriage, since on the only two nights Desdemona and Othello manage to get to bed together while they are both still alive, their lovemaking is relentlessly interrupted – it is not, in fact, even clear that the marriage has actually been consummated. Orson Welles' extraordinary film version, released in 1952, opens well after the play's conclusion, with the definitive end of the marriage, the funeral of Othello and Desdemona, in progress. Even this is interrupted, by a figure in chains being dragged to a wooden cage, into which he is thrust and then, slowly, hoisted up the sides of the castle wall, to hang from its tower as the funeral procession continues. All this takes place before even the title and credits. If we know the play, we will be aware that Iago's punishment has been meted out already. We will also be aware that, as far as poetic justice is concerned, this is all the satisfaction we will get, and that it is a satisfaction the play specifically refuses us.

But frustration clearly constitutes a good part of *Othello*'s dramatic force, and the play was from the very beginning extraordinarily popular – especially so after the Restoration, when it served as a powerful model for tragedy. The fact aroused the indignation of Thomas Rymer, who in a notorious attack published in 1693 declared that *Othello* 'impiously assumes the sacred name of tragedy',[2] but was, on the contrary, nothing but 'a bloody farce'

(p. 146). Rymer supports his judgement with one of the most detailed, and certainly the most thoroughly vituperative, analyses of the play ever undertaken. Though critics including Dryden treated it with respect, Rymer's indictment had little effect on either the theatrical repertory or the practice of criticism (far less effect, for example, than the equally moralistic arraignment of the stage by Jeremy Collier published five years later, which really did instigate certain reforms), and Rymer's attack survives in the critical literature primarily as a curiosity. T. S. Eliot, however, claimed to have been convinced by it, asserting that he had 'never . . . seen a cogent refutation of Thomas Rymer's objections to *Othello*,' and that 'Rymer makes out a very good case'.[3] Rymer's case is worth looking at: everyone remembers the famous bit about the moral being that wives should look well to their linen, but there is a great deal more in it than that (it goes on for sixty pages), and one wonders how much of it Eliot actually read.

Rymer ridicules Shakespeare from the outset for having a black hero: it is preposterous to suppose that the Venetians would 'set a Negro to be their General; or trust a *Moor* to defend them against the Turk', he says. 'With us', he continues, 'a Black-a-moor might rise to be a Trumpeter', but Shakespeare makes him a Lieutenant-General. 'With us a *Moor* might marry some little drab', but Shakespeare gives him an aristocrat's daughter (pp. 91–2). The blatant racism of this is not at all historically determined, if we think of the popularity of Oroonoko in both Aphra Behn's novel and Thomas Southerne's drama – Rymer is proud of being out of step with his society, and his point is precisely that the popularity of *Othello* indicates a significant deficiency in public morality and taste, a disregard of orthodoxy, an insufficient concern throughout the culture for principles, for correctness. This is surely one of the things Eliot must have liked about the essay – its underlying thesis is that

---

2 Thomas Rymer, *A Short View of Tragedy* (London, 1693), p. 164. Subsequent page references are in the text.

3 T. S. Eliot, 'Four Elizabethan Dramatists' and 'Hamlet', in *Selected Essays* (New York, 1950), pp. 97, 121.

of *After Strange Gods*, and if he did read beyond the handkerchief bit, both his passion for orthodoxy and his distaste for 'free-thinking Jews' would have found in Rymer a sympathetic ancestor.

There is obviously for this critic no way for the play to compensate for the ethnicity of its hero, and though Rymer is genuinely, often brilliantly, observant, much of the analysis is simply vulgar invective. The plot is declared at the outset 'intolerable and absurd' (p. 92), and it is all downhill from there. 'Nothing is more odious in Nature than an improbable lye; And, certainly, never was any Play fraught, like this of *Othello*, with improbabilities' (pp. 95–6). The latter part of this observation is quite correct – the play's deployment of improbabilities, and indeed of impossibilities, is one of its dramaturgical strokes of genius, and Rymer is the first critic to catch on to the double time scheme in the play, but it provokes only rage, not admiration.

The rage testifies to the fact, however, that the improbabilities are all too credible. Much of the time it is not Shakespeare who is being berated, but the fictional Othello, for allowing himself to be duped so easily. When Othello says 'My name, that was as fresh / As Dian's visage, is now begrimed and black/ As mine own face' (3.3.386–8) Rymer furiously scolds the hero: 'There is not a Monky but understands Nature better; not a Pug in *Barbary* that has not a truer taste of things' (p. 124) – in other words, you fool, can't you see she is innocent! Some of the discussion is clearly irrelevant, some is positively loony – Shakespeare is attacked for making Iago 'a close, dissembling, false, insinuating rascal, instead of an open-hearted, frank, plain-dealing Souldier' because that is what soldiers are really like (p. 94). (Did Eliot really read this far?) Othello's 'Farewell the tranquil mind! farewell content!' speech (3.3.348f.) is dismissed as having nothing poetical in it 'besides the sound', and is invidiously compared with the blankest of blank verse speeches from *Gorboduc* (pp. 124-5). There had been no edition of *Gorboduc* since 1590, and it is doubtful that more than a handful of readers even knew what Rymer was talking about; but it cannot be coincidental that *Gorboduc* is the only

English tragedy that Sidney, in the *Defence of Poesie*, could find to praise. It is difficult to imagine what Eliot would have considered a 'cogent refutation' of so incoherent a performance (it is quite clear why he had never seen one), but obviously all that matters is that Rymer's indignant heart was in the right place.

Rymer is interesting for my purposes precisely because of his incoherences, because he notices everything and gets the point of nothing. His sixty page tirade is sufficient witness to the fact that, for all the claims of ineptitude and incompetence, he finds the play utterly, indeed infuriatingly, compelling; and essential to his outraged fascination is a specifically generic claim, that *Othello* is not tragedy but farce. Buried beneath all the rant and rage there *is* a critical point, and something about it seems to me correct. Let us consider the famous bits (it should be emphasized that these passages constitute an infinitesimal part of the essay):

The moral, sure, [he writes,] is very instructive. First, this may be a caution to all maidens of quality how, without their parents' consent they run away with black-amoors... Secondly, this may be a warning to all good wives that they look well to their linen. Thirdly, this may be a lesson to husbands that before their jealousy be tragical the proofs may be mathematical [i.e., absolutely conclusive, like a proof in maths].

(p. 89)

So here are the morals: (1) don't marry blacks unless your parents approve; (2) count your handkerchiefs; (3) don't murder your wife unless you're sure that she is unfaithful. This comes near the beginning of the essay. By the middle, Shakespeare is being indicted for learning his craft not from the classics (or from *Gorboduc*) but from the popular theatre of his own time, mysteries and morality plays written by 'carpenters, cobblers, and illiterate fellows', who interlarded their plots with 'drolls and fooleries' to bring in the rabble (p. 111);

And it is then no wonder that we find so much farce and apocryphal matter in his tragedies. Thereby unhallowing the theater, profaning the name of tragedy; and instead of representing men and manners, turning all morality, good sense and humanity into mockery and derision.

(pp. 111–12)

Here is the conclusion, thirty pages later:

What can remain with the audience to carry home with them from this sort of poetry for their use and edification? How can it work, unless (instead of settling the mind and purging our passions) to delude our senses, disorder our thoughts, addle our brain, pervert our affections, hare our imaginations [i.e., frighten us, or make us hare-brained], corrupt our appetite, and fill our head with vanity, confusion, *tintamarre*, and jingle-jangle . . . ?

and so on in this vein for ten more lines – the invective is self-generating. The problem now is conceived in Aristotelian and Horatian terms: that *Othello* does not include the catharsis necessary to tragedy, and does not edify us, and therefore is worthless, or even vicious.

But then oddly, as the essay concludes, it turns out to be the comic elements that are all right:

There is in this play some burlesque, some humor and ramble of comical wit, some show, and some mimicry to divert the spectators; but the tragical part is plainly none other than a bloody farce, without salt or savor.

(p. 146)

It is the pretensions to tragedy that are so pernicious, unhallowing the theater, contributing to the general decay of the arts and morality, and debasing the nobility of the very category of tragedy.

What becomes clear here is that *Othello* is *the* quintessential drama for this hostile critic; it embodies everything that is trivial, dishonest, dangerous and immoral about theatre itself, and its popularity is particularly frightening because the play, as Rymer sees it, is totally irrational and should therefore be both repellent and incomprehensible. There is actually something in this, but we would want to add that a good deal of the play's power derives precisely from that deep irrationality – that deep understanding of the profoundly irrational elements in our nature – an understanding which operates not only on the characters but, through the dramaturgy, on the audience as well.

Relabelling the play, declaring it farce rather than tragedy, is the *coup de grâce* here, but why does the genre matter? Why can it not simply be a bad tragedy?[4] A century earlier Sidney, in the first real classic of English literary criticism, had had equal contempt for the improbabilities of the tragedies of his time, but these defects only make the tragedies defective; they do not banish the plays from the category: though tragedy was assumed to be the noblest of the dramatic genres, there were better tragedies and worse ones, and the bad ones were still tragedies. For Renaissance critics generally, the genres were basically a filing system, and in the most detailed and compendious of the anatomies, the *Poetics* of Julius Caesar Scaliger, many plays appear under a variety of genres – here is a characteristic passage. He begins by observing that many comedies end unhappily for some of the characters and continues:

In the same way, there are a number of happy tragedies: in Euripides' *Electra*, except for the death of Aegisthus, many people are joyful; *Ion* has a happy ending as does *Helen*. Then too, although Aeschylus's *Eumenides* contains tragic elements (such as murders and the furies), its structure is more like that of a comedy: the beginning [in *Agamemnon*] is joyful for the guard, though troubling for Clytemnestra because of her husband's arrival; then comes the murder [of Clytemnestra], and Electra and Orestes are happy; the ending is happy for everyone – Apollo, Orestes, the populace, Pallas, the Eumenides. Thus it is by no means true, as we have always been taught, that tragedy must have an unhappy ending: it need only include terrible things.[5]

There would have been no problem for Scaliger about farcical elements in *Othello*, clearly. For Rymer a century later, however, tragedy is not merely a category, it is a sacred name, and the genres constitute a hierarchy, with tragedy not simply at the top, but a divinely anointed king – there can be, in this taxonomy, no bad tragedies (in the

---

[4] The account here summarizes the more extensive treatment of the subject in my essay 'Shakespeare and the Kinds of Drama', in my collection *The Authentic Shakespeare* (London, 2002).

[5] Julius Caesar Scaliger, *Poetices Libri Septem* (Lyons, 1581), 367 [my translation].

sense that a bad tragedy is disposed of by being declared not to be a tragedy). It logically follows, however, that if tragedy is king it is always in danger of usurpation, and that is what Rymer perceives here: *Othello* not only profanes the sacred name of tragedy, it '*impiously assumes*' the name – usurps it. The trouble with thinking of dramatic genres this way, of course, is that a usurping king, like a wicked or tyrannical one, is no less the king, and the effort to dethrone *Othello* is doomed merely by definition.

What Rymer noticed, shrewdly and accurately, however, was something that for Scaliger was largely unproblematic in drama: that *Othello* works more like a comedy than like a tragedy. This is somewhat different from a point that has been observed by numerous critics of the last century, that the play is heavily indebted in its character types and situations to the *commedia dell'arte*; Rymer's invocation of the comic is structural and moral. The play is declared a farce rather than a comedy because comedy too has its civic virtues and social utility, and perhaps most important, because farce has no classical precedent; but the distinction between comedy and farce in this context is nugatory: the essential point is to remove *Othello* from the sacred category by calling it something else, and that something is comic.

II

Let us return to Rymer's three sarcastic lessons derived from the play: don't elope with a black unless your parents approve, keep track of your linens, don't kill your wife unless you're sure you're being cuckolded. What is wrong with this as a summary of the action? In fact, the only essential element of the drama that is omitted is Iago, and one of the most interesting things about Rymer's account of the play is that Iago really does not figure very significantly in it. Othello is a fool, Desdemona is a slattern and largely responsible for what happens to her, everyone is insufficiently dignified, the plot is crazy; but Iago's scheming is not a major factor in the tragedy – or farce. All the scheming, in this view of the play, is Shakespeare's. Once again, this

seems to me basically correct, and I now turn to Iago.

In the most straightforward view of the plot, Iago is the agent of all the play's destructiveness and bad faith, the source of all the tragic energy – in short, the villain. A little less straightforwardly, he is certainly still the villain, but perhaps nevertheless not the agent and source at all, but merely the catalyst, externalizing and articulating the destructive chaos that lies just beneath Othello's love and rationality, the chaos that he himself says is kept in check only by his love for Desdemona – rather like the witches in *Macbeth*, or, indeed, Lady Macbeth herself, who, however evil, are not the culprits. A lot depends on how far you want to see Iago as a classic machiavel on the one hand, or as an extension of Othello on the other. The latter might seem to be a post-Renaissance conception, but in fact the play itself questions the simple view of Iago's malign responsibility for Othello's behaviour when Emilia remarks that jealous souls 'are not ever jealous for the cause, / But jealous for they're jealous' (3.4.159–60) – Othello's jealousy is not, then, simply the creation of Iago's scheming. There is a good deal of self-interest in this piece of wisdom, of course, since Emilia herself has provided the trigger of Othello's jealousy, the handkerchief, and is covering for both herself and her husband long after she understands quite clearly the mischief she has caused; but the observation is, nevertheless, also self-evidently true, and it is a truth around which Iago designs his scheme. Villain and victim, in fact, have much more in common, understand each other much better, than husband and wife: it is clear that Iago's cynical view of women as lustful, untrustworthy and characteristically unfaithful is, when the chips are down, Othello's view also, and therefore Othello instinctively believes in Iago's honesty, not in his wife's – this is true from the first moment Desdemona's fidelity is questioned; all Iago has to say is 'I think Cassio's an honest man' (3.3.129). One could argue, indeed, that the source of the tragedy is precisely in that gender bonding – in the fact that Othello's primary loyalty is to his friend, not his wife; in the fact that Emilia chooses to betray her mistress, not her husband. But it is also possible to imagine this play without Iago: certainly all those elements of jealousy, self-dramatization, rage and barely controlled chaos that Iago elicits are aspects of Othello's character clearly articulated from the outset.

In staging the play, to make Iago a sort of allegorical extension of Othello would, of course, make for a much more complex Othello than we are used to, one that would continually raise the question of how far the play's claim that the tragedy is all Iago's fault, which is essentially a claim that jealousy is explicable and reasonable – that men get jealous because villains steal handkerchiefs and tell lies – is borne out by the action. There are two ways of reading, 'In following him, I follow but myself': as Iago's assertion of total self-interest in his relation to Othello, or alternatively, as an acknowledgement that, in a much deeper sense, they are inseparable – the bond can be construed as a love relationship, with Iago's resentment that of a scorned lover, rejected in favour of Cassio on the one hand and Desdemona on the other, a rejection all the more painful because it has been so casual (1.1.57). The jealousy, then, in the first instance would be Iago's. He presents himself again as a scorned lover when he accuses both Cassio and Othello of sleeping with his wife Emilia. This is basically the situation dramatized in the Sonnets, and if we take that sequence to be in any sense autobiographical, Shakespeare is depicting himself in Iago – Stephen Greenblatt long ago suggested, in *Renaissance Self-Fashioning*, that Iago, as the amoral manipulator and endlessly fertile improviser of plots, was a figure for Shakespeare,[6] but I am suggesting something much more psychologically and emotionally specific.

If we are thinking of Shakespeare's dramaturgy in terms of autobiography, here is another proposition: we know that Burbage played Othello, but in Shakespeare's company who played the much larger role of Iago? Iago is one of the longest roles in Shakespeare – 1020 lines, almost 250 lines longer than Othello (250 lines is the length of the entire role of Caliban). Only Hamlet, the longest role by far, and Richard III are longer; these three are the only roles that are over a thousand lines (though Henry V almost makes it, at 999). For comparison,

the whole of *The Comedy of Errors* is only 1750 lines long, and *Macbeth* just over 2000. Iago is a third of his play. Could it be a part that Shakespeare the actor wrote for himself?

Probably the answer is no; the one Shakespearian role we think we know Shakespeare played was Adam in *As You Like It*, and a much more apocryphal tradition has him as the Ghost in *Hamlet*. These stories at least suggest that the roles he took in his own plays were small ones; and John Lowin, who we know played the villainous Bosola in *The Duchess of Malfi* and the ill-tempered Morose in *Epicoene,* had joined the company in 1603, and would therefore have been available. Nevertheless the Sonnets provide an inescapable gloss on all the painful ramifications of the assumption that 'My friend and I are one' (42, 13). The identity, the interchangeability, of Othello and Iago has been a significant part of stage history for centuries, perhaps always. If the original Iago was not Shakespeare, and even if it was Lowin, did Burbage nevertheless, like Garrick, Edmund Kean, Kemble, Macready, Fechter, Irving, Edwin Booth, Olivier, even, unlikely as it sounds, Gielgud, play both roles, and were the roles, from the beginning, interchangeable; did the great actor always want to be both?[7] Virtuoso performers, starting with Edmund Kean and Charles Mayne Young, and including Macready and Samuel Phelps, Edwin Booth and Henry Irving, Richard Burton and John Neville, have even alternated the roles, sometimes from night to night, playing out, in the most literal way, 'Were I the Moor, I would not be Iago' (1.1.56). In fact, Kean, as Iago, refused to switch after he saw the first night of Young's Othello, convinced he could never equal it – Iago's envy was in this case the very essence of performance itself. The other roles that historically have been alternated are much less explosive: Richard and Bolingbroke, Hal and Hotspur, and most famously, in 1935, Gielgud

[6] Stephen Greenblatt, *Renaissance Self-Fashioning* (Chicago, 1984), p. 252

[7] Gielgud initially saw himself as Iago, and played the role in his first *Othello*. He did not play it again, and did not play Othello until thirty years later.

and Olivier switching back and forth as Romeo and Mercutio. (Bernhardt, as a footnote, played both Ophelia and Hamlet, though decades apart.)

Throughout the eighteenth and much of the nineteenth centuries, the machiavellian Iago, innately evil and an obvious extension of Richard III, often outfitted, in the absence of a hunchback, with diabolically bushy eyebrows and black wig, was standard; but from the time of Fechter and Irving, Iago has tended to be the really complex character in the play. A good deal of the cumulative effect of the drama depends on how you decide to play him. Most productions have made him complex but unattractive, saturnine, insinuating, crude, graceless – most of all, not a gentleman. In such performances, the real energy of the role goes into the villainy – it is a melodramatic energy, undeniably effective, but it simplifies the play, makes him a villain like Richard III, where his villainy is in every sense his defining characteristic. In the case of Richard III, his success is represented first as a political phenomenon, where he is supported by people who are either naively trusting or think he is horrible but will do them some good, and second – notoriously, in the wooing of Lady Anne – as a kind of mesmeric magic, because he is so obviously villainous. The problem with treating Iago this way is that such a reading does not make enough distinction between the public and the private Iago – Richard is always a villain, but until the final scene, we know much more about Iago than any of the characters do, and there has to be some reason established dramatically for why everyone finds him so implicitly trustworthy. Dramatically, making him unattractive and graceless accounts for his hostility and resentment, but does nothing to explain his extraordinary persuasiveness.

As I stage the play in my own mind, he is attractive and very charming. The only performance I have ever seen that was anything like this was Kenneth Branagh's, in the film with Laurence Fishburn as Othello. There were lots of problems with this film – Fishburn looked great, but didn't do much with the verse; Irene Jacob's English was so heavily accented that she might have been in some other play – but the Iago was a revelation:

easygoing, affable, good looking, affectionate, an instant best friend, somebody you wanted to confide in and have around. In this performance, the melodrama is saved for the soliloquies, so that Iago is completely different in public and in private. Branagh gives the film the sense of a stage performance by talking directly to the camera (rather than 'thinking' his soliloquies); he plays with the audience, taking them into his confidence, making them his accomplices, charming them, flirting with them, just as he does not so much persuade Roderigo and Cassio, but woos them.

I would even take this a step farther, and take the analogy of the Sonnets into account, making Iago an attractive gay man seriously in love with Othello, and Othello a narcissist, not at all averse to being adored, fully trusting Iago because he trusts his own attractiveness; knowing, moreover, that he does not have to promote Iago, because he is perfectly aware of his sexual power over his subordinate. (My use of the shorthand term 'gay' is anachronistic only in the sense that the term is modern; there have always been men who fell in love with other men.) The sexual dynamic here would be a two-way affair, and when, in this production of mine, Othello elicits from Iago the words of the marriage vow, 'I am your own forever', he is quite conscious of what he is doing (3.3.480). After all, throughout the play Othello is under the impression that he is using Iago, not the other way round. The fantasy of replacing Desdemona with Iago as his wife is in my production parallel to Iago's fantasy of lying awake in bed with Cassio asleep – or pretending to be – and sexually excited, taking Iago for Desdemona – or pretending to. Is Othello's fury at this solely at the idea of Cassio imagining he is in bed with Desdemona? Is the idea of Cassio actually making love to Iago no part of it? Quite possibly the answer is an indignant no, no part of it at all; quite possibly my Othello would at the very suggestion stalk off the rehearsal stage (*but why is he so angry?*); nevertheless, it is obvious that the crucial relationships in both these episodes are between the men. As in the sonnets, who knows how much is implied by 'My friend and I are one', 'I am your own forever'?

Two friends to whom I have proposed this haven't liked it; both objected that making Iago gay explains too much, that the malignity ought to be left motiveless. I am surprised that love is assumed to constitute more of an explanation than hatred; but in any case, Iago does explain at some length why he hates Othello – the problem is really that he offers too many motives, not too few. Cassio has a daily beauty in his life that makes Iago's ugly, Othello has preferred Cassio to him, Othello and Cassio have been to bed with his wife – all the explanations boil down to envy and jealousy; and as Romeo (that is, Shakespeare) says, 'Here's much to do with hate, but more with love' (1.1.174). Coleridge's point was surely that the explanations didn't really explain anything, didn't produce a *rational* motive, produced only jealousy, or hatred (or love), not that they weren't there. Romeo cites not only the inseparability of love and hate, but the motivelessness of both as well: 'Why then, O brawling love, O loving hate, / O anything, of nothing first create!' (175–6).

Some productions have in fact accounted for Iago's behaviour by suggesting that he was gay. Tyrone Guthrie in 1938 had Olivier as a homosexual Iago furtively longing for Ralph Richardson's Othello. Since the interpretation was based on Freud's view of homosexuality via Ernst Jones, there was more repression and neurotic angst than flirting, and very little satisfaction of any kind. Here is Olivier's account in his autobiography:

Tony Guthrie and I were swept away by . . . Jones's contention that Iago was subconsciously in love with Othello and had to destroy him. Unfortunately, there was not the slightest chance that Ralph would entertain this idea. I was, however, determined . . . ; we constantly watched for occasions when our diagnosis might be made apparent . . . In a reckless moment during rehearsals I threw my arms around Ralph and kissed him full on the lips. He coolly disengaged himself from my embrace, patted me gently on the back of the neck and, more in sorrow than in anger, murmured, 'There, there now, dear boy; *good* boy . . .'

In performance when Othello fell to the ground in his fit, Iago fell beside him, simulating an or-gasm – Olivier considered this 'terrifically daring'. But a trusted friend later told him she had '*no* idea what you were up to when you threw yourself on the ground', and none of the critics seemed to catch on to the fact that Iago was supposed to be queer. So they abandoned the whole theory, deciding that 'Iago just hated Othello because he was black and his superior officer'. This perfectly straightforward, perfectly straight, interpretation, however, did not work either, despite a great cast including Anthony Quayle as Cassio and Martita Hunt as Emilia. Olivier declared the production a disaster – the queer Iago was obviously not the culprit.[8] Disaster was a term that was often used of Guthrie productions, sometimes even by Guthrie.

In Terry Hands's 1985 RSC production with Ben Kingsley as Othello and David Suchet as Iago, Iago *was* widely perceived as gay, and the performance was well received, not least because by 1985 it was permissable to acknowledge that someone was gay. Hands apparently did not intend Iago to be gay, and was surprised at the reviews. David Suchet, however, in a thoughtful interview about the performance in one of the *Players of Shakespeare* volumes, says that he considered the possibility at some length. He decided that the account of the night spent with Cassio is a lie, though a significant one. He thought it quite conceivable that Iago and Cassio may in fact have been lovers, and that Othello may well be jealous of the idea that they have been to bed together – Suchet was, in short, on to my idea long before it occurred to me, and I am interested to see that an intelligent and thoughtful actor seriously considered it as a way of making the character work psychologically.[9] (Ben Kingsley, in the same volume, says nothing about any of this, and claims to have had his mind entirely on his parents' marriage, accounts of performances by Edmund Kean and Salvini, and the philosophy of Albert Camus.)

My native informant, Lois Potter, who saw the production and has total recall, has written me a

---

8 *Confessions of an Actor* (New York, 1982), pp. 105–6.
9 Russell Jackson and Robert Smallwood, *Players of Shakespeare 2* (Cambridge, 1988), pp. 192–4.

wonderful note about it which I can do no better than quote:

I did see the Kingsley–Suchet *Othello* and I think that some idea of gayness crossed my mind, mainly because of Suchet's horrified grief when Othello finally committed suicide. But this was a surprise to me, which is why it was the thing I remember best from the production; in other words, he had not come across as being in love with Othello. It was more like a cat feeling upset that the toy it has been playing with (a live mouse) has stopped moving. Or perhaps like someone suddenly realizing that there's no longer any purpose to his life. Both actors said they weren't playing the character as gay, but that reviewers did tend to think that there was a gay subtext. It also struck me that no one was remotely interested in the Desdemona (Niamh Cusack).

That last bit seems to me very much to the point. Potter then goes on with a comment on the Olivier Iago, about which she has written:

My suggestion was that audiences weren't used to seeing gay behaviour depicted onstage before 1968 except in a comic context, and thus actors didn't have a shorthand by which to communicate it.[10]

By the end of the twentieth century, we have had an openly gay Mercutio who goes partying in drag in Baz Luhrmann's 1996 *Romeo + Juliet*. My students like this, and when I asked what they liked about it one young woman explained that 'cool gay guys are really neat'. Apparently more than half the audience of the American version of *Queer as Folk* is straight, or at least, identifies itself as such to telephone interviewers. I want my Iago to be a really cool gay guy, an Iago who is all the more dangerous because both Othello and more than half the audience find him attractive.

III

Iago is the play's villainous schemer, but the principal, enabling scheme is not his. Credit for discovering the double time scheme in *Othello* is always accorded to two ingenious Victorian critics, Nicholas Halpin and John Wilson, writing in *Blackwood's* in 1849; but they were merely the first critics

to treat it systematically and consider it a good idea. It is all in Rymer, and drives him into a frenzy.

Here, briefly, is the point.[11] Time in the play goes very fast; the action, in fact, is almost uninterrupted. Act 1 covers the night of the elopement and the Council scene. Othello and Cassio go to Cyprus the next morning, and Desdemona, Iago and Emilia follow in however long you want to imagine it takes them to get ready and make the voyage – this would be a minimum of a couple of weeks (Cassio says they have come unusually fast, a week earlier than they were expected). So there is that one gap, two weeks or so, when Othello and Cassio are on Cyprus, and Desdemona, Iago and Emilia are on their way. From the time they reach Cyprus the action again is continuous, through the night of Desdemona's arrival, the next day, and that night, which is the night of the murder (the usual estimate is thirty-three hours). The momentum is important because the whole credibility of Iago's plot depends on speed – clearly if Othello ever gets a chance to compare notes with anyone, the scheme will fall apart, as it does as soon as the literal notes are produced from the slain Roderigo's pocket.[12]

But, if you take that aspect of the play seriously, the play as a whole will be a mass of impossibilities, just as Rymer says it is. When, in this thirty-three hours, was the adultery supposed to have taken place? Othello left Venice on his wedding night, taking Cassio with him – this is the man he believes has been cuckolding him. When? In order to prevent the audience from noticing this, Shakespeare uses some brilliant sleight of hand, compelling our belief in the plot through references to action that there's no time for in the time of the play. For example, Iago's story about the night that he spent in bed with Cassio, when Cassio took him for

[10] See Lois Potter, *Shakespeare in Performance: Othello* (Manchester, 2002), p. 92

[11] I am in part summarizing my own account in the Introduction to John Sutherland and Cedric Watts, *Henry V, War Criminal?* (Oxford, 2000).

[12] Or perhaps not slain, another tease: at 5.2.309 he is 'the slain Roderigo', but at 5.2.327-8 'even but now he spake, / After long seeming dead'.

17　The Mediterranean in 1595. Detail of the map of Europe in the Mercator-Hondius atlas of 1623.

Desdemona – during the whole time of the marriage Cassio has been in Cyprus with Othello, and Desdemona has been with Iago in Venice or on a ship; there was no night Cassio and Iago could have spent together. Or Cassio talking about how Bianca runs after him, and threw herself at him 'the other day' (4.1.132) and Othello overhearing this thinks he is talking about Desdemona – *what* other day? The only other day was yesterday, which is the day she arrived. Or the whole opening of 4.2, where Othello questions Emilia about whether she has seen Desdemona and Cassio together, and a long period and a number of occasions are alluded to. The reason this works is that we are treated just the way Othello is, persuaded parenthetically, not given time to ask any questions or compare notes. Not, of course, entirely without resistance: I have already alluded to the famous story of the man leaping up during the death scene shouting 'You fool, can't you see she's innocent?'

The story is no doubt apocryphal, but it is unique to this play. There are no parallel stories of audience members trying to stop the blinding of Gloucester or reminding Albany that he has forgotten about Lear and Cordelia.

This treatment of time is not at all unique to this play. There is a similar instance in *Love's Labour's Lost*, for example, where Jaquenetta is declared to be pregnant by Armado two days after their first meeting; but it is generally a comic dramaturgy, and the audience is in on the joke – nobody ever leaps up from the stalls to explain to Armado that he cannot be the father. But comedy in *Othello* is the device of villainy, and to my knowledge, nowhere else is it employed so systematically. There is an especially subtle example of the device in the scene where Othello is recalled to Venice because the Turks have been defeated, and Cassio is appointed in his place. The defeat took place only the day before – Othello arrives victorious from the battle just after Desdemona and Iago land. How long does it take for the news of the victory to travel from Cyprus to Venice, and then for the Venetian emissaries to travel back to Cyprus?

Illustration 17 is a detail of Mercator's map of the Mediterranean, drawn in 1595. Venice is at the upper left, Cyprus is the large island at the lower right. Travelling by ship, the distance is about 1600 miles each way. A really fast ship of the period (I am informed by a sailing expert friend) had a maximum speed of 7 knots, a little more than 8 miles an hour – this is with everything working out right, good winds from the right direction, calm sea; and it would be unlikely to have perfect sailing conditions for the whole voyage in both directions. The absolute minimum time for this voyage in one direction would be nine days; the round trip would take almost three weeks, allowing for time in Venice to deliver the news, get new instructions, replenish the ship. We are taught by the history of theatre not to question such conventions; and this is one of the moments that make us think there is much more time in the play than there really is. The distance represented on this map, the space of this geography, is precisely the period of time when Desdemona and Cassio are supposed to be carrying on together, the time between Desdemona's arrival and Othello's recall to Venice. This is the time of, the space for, Iago's scheming. But the deception is not being practised on Othello by Iago, it is being practised on us by Shakespeare. Shakespeare is the *real* villain in this play, and we are the willing dupes.

SHAKESPEARE AS A JOKE: THE ENGLISH COMIC TRADITION, *A MIDSUMMER NIGHT'S DREAM* AND AMATEUR PERFORMANCE

MICHAEL DOBSON

Nicky Watson and I moved house in the summer of 2002, and since this was I think the tenth time we've wound up doing so since we were married, the feeling of shame and humiliation which overwhelmed us as our miscellaneous worldly goods were exposed to the view of the removers was pretty familiar. This time, though, the sensation was made a little more specific. Among the crack team of musclebound Vikings who arrived on the great day to throw our worldly goods into boxes and then throw those boxes into a lorry was one trainee, who had yet to learn the complete, silent, non-judgemental tact that must necessarily characterize anyone who aspires to a long-term future in that demanding service trade. Carrying yet another box of books and a stone bust towards the lorry through the blazing heat of the day, this mover met my eye and raised his eyebrows. 'Like Shakespeare, do we, sir?', he asked. The tone wasn't primarily of mockery: it was intended to express pity, though it came out with a strong poorly camouflaged undertone of derision. It was as if he had found ten bookshelves detailing all the railway engine numbers currently in service on Network South-East, or several complete sets of ankle bells and a hobby horse. Back in the late 1980s and early 1990s, several of us were publishing books all about how William Shakespeare became the great figure of authority which he remains for English-speaking culture, and I suppose one of the incidental questions I want to raise in this article, during this short examination of the strange interrelations between Shakespeare and the traditions of English comedy and of English professionalism since his death, is simply this: who

did we think we were kidding? It's an odd but unmistakeable fact about Shakespeare's current status in his erstwhile homeland that although England is a country which prides itself on its comedy, and regards Shakespeare, who specialized in comedy, as its national writer, the Shakespeare of popular culture is generally a good deal more joked against than joking, less witty in himself than the cause that wit is in others. The main thing everyone knows about Shakespearian comedy – with one key exception, which I'll be coming to in due course – is that it isn't funny.

In the year 2000, for example, while the invitees to the International Shakespeare Conference were in Stratford celebrating the millennium by talking about Shakespeare and religion, a handful of other people were doing so by visiting the Millennium Dome at Greenwich, where they were all shown a specially made video. This was a belated, one-off reunion episode of Richard Curtis's television series *Blackadder*, called 'Blackadder Back and Forth' in which Rowan Atkinson's present-day Blackadder travelled into the past in a time machine, visiting, among other familiar destinations, the court of Miranda Richardson's Elizabeth I. In one tiny, offhand vignette, culminating in the sort of vindictive slapstick in which Atkinson specializes, Blackadder met an apologetic-looking, black-clad Shakespeare, played by Colin Firth, and, on ascertaining his identity, knocked him down with a swift punch to the jaw – this was a punishment, Blackadder explained, for all the suffering that would be inflicted in his name on the generations of schoolchildren who would be forced 'to spend hours in classrooms, trying to find a single joke in *A Midsummer Night's Dream*'. The main gag here, of identifying Shakespeare solely with his posthumous role in the National Curriculum and then taking it out on him in person, was reinforced by the casting: a year after the release of *Shakespeare in Love*, this scapegoated fall-guy of a Shakespeare wasn't even played by Joseph Fiennes but was instead impersonated by the member of that film's cast who had played its pompous unsmiling dupe and scapegoat, Lord Wessex. It's not a very interesting joke, I agree, but it is nonetheless striking that if Shakespeare is a figure of authority at all in the context of this sort of popular comedy, it is only a petty, schoolmasterly, killjoy authority, like that of Malvolio. Indeed, having floored Shakespeare as retribution in advance for his role in the school syllabus, Blackadder subsequently chastised him for threatening the mass-market cinema's usual provision of cakes and ale, delivering a violent kick in the shin with the line 'and that's for Ken Branagh's endless four-hour uncut *Hamlet*'. This looks like a rather shrill Jonsonian shorthand for the shin-centred punishment to which Malvolio is himself subjected, those humiliating yellow stockings.

But then the gulling of Malvolio, we are often told, is a joke closer in spirit to the work of Jonson than to the rest of Shakespearian comedy anyway, and the fact that Shakespeare should wind up at the sharp end of this particular Jonsonian gag is perfectly in keeping with a familiar account of Shakespeare's influence on the development of English comedy since the seventeenth century. According to this account, that influence has been approximately zero. The advent of the actress in 1660 permanently ruined Shakespeare's signature boy-dressed-as-girl-dressed-as-boy motif, so that Pepys famously found *Twelfth Night* 'but a silly play', just as he regarded *A Midsummer Night's Dream* as 'insipid and ridiculous': and although Davenant borrowed Beatrice and Benedick in 1662 for the first of many recyclings in Restoration comedy (in *The Law Against Lovers*), the mainstream of English comic drama remained profoundly Jonsonian. The typical English comedy, according to the anthologists at any rate, is socially realistic, set in the present, and

laced with greater or lesser degrees of topical satire: the line runs from *The Alchemist* through *The Man of Mode* through *The School for Scandal* and down to *London Assurance* and thence, ultimately, to the farces of Ray Cooney or the television sitcoms of Ray Galton and Alan Simpson, or, most Jonsonian of all, John Cleese and Connie Booth, the writers of *Fawlty Towers*. The only Shakespearian comedy that approximately fits this pattern – with lots of farcical incident, an English setting, cuckoldry jokes, and foreigners with silly accents – is *The Merry Wives of Windsor*, which was accordingly the one set of Shakespearian jokes which the Restoration and eighteenth century more or less got. Hence that period's only attempt to write a new Shakespeare comedy – instead of rewriting the old ones so as to cure them – is William Kenrick's feeble emulation of *The Merry Wives*, *Falstaff's Wedding* (1766). Nor is it only in stage comedy that Shakespeare loses out to Jonson in this customary account of their afterlives: in the novel, Dickens, for all his Shakespearian allusions, is far more visibly influenced by Jonson than by Shakespeare when it comes to actually getting laughs, and despite his interest in the Gadshill episode in *1 Henry IV* (detailed by Adrian Poole elsewhere in this volume), his main funny borrowing from Shakespeare is only the unsexed, innocent version of Falstaff at the centre of his early hit *The Pickwick Papers*.

This predominance of Shakespeare's rival comedian was so obvious that it had already been recognized, in 1786, by a pig. In the anonymous novel *The Story of the Learned Pig*, the performing animal of the title narrates its own history: this whole conceit is a joke about a minor contemporary celebrity of the fairgrounds and even the salons, which had been trained to spell out words using cards. (The firm Bowles and Carver issued a rather snide print of this beast, in which he is obediently laying out the word 'pork'.) The pig, like Feste, subscribes to the doctrine of metempsychosis, and in *The Story of the Learned Pig* he tells everything he can remember about his previous lives. In one of his pre-swinish incarnations, in the time of Elizabeth I, he was, he tells us, a man called Pimping Billy, and as this dubiously professional William he came to know another one, to his cost: '[Shakespeare]', re-counts the pig, 'has been father'd with many spu-rious dramatic pieces [,] *Hamlet, Othello, As You Like It, The Tempest* and *Midsummer Night's Dream* for five: of all which I confess myself to be the author'.[1] This now-familiar crack, the knowingly outrageous claim that Shakespeare used a ghost-writer, looks to us like a joke about the Author-ship Controversy, even though it was made sixty years before the Authorship Controversy even hap-pened.[2] But more to the point, it is here pioneered in the person of an explicitly Jonsonian character, since Pimping Billy is, so he tells us, the son of Cob, the kipper-obsessed water-carrier of *Every Man In His Humour*.

Set aside by the comic playwrights of succeed-ing generations in favour of his less romantic rival, accused of plagiarism by a Jonsonian pig, and doomed ultimately to feature in the national con-sciousness as a physically maltreated Malvolio, this Shakespeare, according to the familiar piece of lit-erary history I've outlined, plays a fairly minor role in the making of the modern English sense of humour – as well he might, since the very term smacks more of Jonson than of Shakespeare. But to accept this verdict as the whole truth about Shakespeare's influence on subsequent native com-edy, as many literary historians do, is to ig-nore another tradition entirely, and one in which Shakespeare plays a fundamental role – even if it is a role which once more, as in the case of Colin Firth's honorary Malvolio, winds up with Shakespeare in contemporary popular culture posthumously be-coming the butt of one of his own best jokes. There isn't a very good analytical vocabulary for describ-ing this alternative tradition, which is one reason it so often disappears from critical discussion: it is much easier to identify it solely by its instances. It is related to literary satire, but it pushes parody to such extremes in pursuit of surreal bathos and non-sense for their own sakes that no familiarity with the original objects of its satire is required to enjoy it, and the term 'burlesque' doesn't quite seem to get it right. Hence while the moralistic Victorian school-room poems which Lewis Carroll transformed into 'You are old, Father William' and 'Speak roughly to

your little boy' have long been forgotten, Carroll's verses remain utterly themselves, just as the un-listening narrator and mad speculations of 'The White Knight's Song' are hilarious even for people who haven't been forced to study Wordsworth's 'Resolution and Independence'. Similarly, long after Restoration heroic tragedy had been laid aside, the comic drama most often quoted and al-luded to in the writings of the eighteenth-century literati is Buckingham's *The Rehearsal*, with its behind-the-scenes look at parodied feats of stage bombast which have become independently mag-nificent achievements of unmeaning.[3] Closer to the present day, the supremely imaginative leaps of illogic performed on radio by *The Goon Show* still delight people who have never read the John Buchan or Sapper thrillers which its nominal plots so frequently send up; and its closest televisual de-scendant, *Monty Python's Flying Circus* – for which John Cleese will be remembered far more grate-fully than for the more orthodox and Jonsonian *Fawlty Towers* – managed to please audiences even in North America, for whom the unknown local contexts of its once-part-topical sketches became themselves part of the delightfully baffling weird-ness of the whole programme. For every *The Way of the World*, in fact, there has usually been a *Chronon-hothonthologos* or a *Hurlothrumbo*. The really inter-esting and distinctive bits of English comedy have nothing to do with Jonsonian social realism at all, however ingeniously, as I shall show, social realism may seek to reclaim them.

This less explicable strain of comedy, too, dates back at least as far as the Renaissance: one of its first recognizable fully fledged exponents was John Taylor, the Water Poet, and he knew exactly where he had picked it up from. Even if Pepys dismissed *A Midsummer Night's Dream* in the 1660s, and even if

---

[1] *The Story of the Learned Pig* ('By an Officer in the Royal Navy') (London, 1786), p. 38.

[2] On this point, see Samuel Schoenbaum, *Shakespeare's Lives* (2nd edn, Oxford, 1991), pp. 396–7.

[3] See, for example, the annotations to Donald Burrows and Rosemary Dunhill, eds., *Music and Theatre in Handel's World: The Papers of James Harris, 1732–1780* (Oxford, 2002).

the Restoration and eighteenth-century stage was only rarely willing to see all its different strands performed at once,[4] one particular section of that play was still regularly quoted and alluded to right down to the seventeenth century and beyond, and nowhere more tellingly than by the Water-Poet.[5] I quote from the introduction to his celebrated and much-imitated pamphlet of 1622, ostensibly a parody of Sir Thomas More but really a specimen of a far less utilitarian sort of comedy. That pamphlet is called 'Sir Gregory Nonsence His Newes from No Place':

At last he laughed in the Cambrian tongue, and began to declare in the Utopian speech what I have here with most diligent negligence Translated into the English language, in which if the Printer hath placed any line, letter or sillable, whereby this large volume may be made guilty to be understood by any man, I would have the Reader not to impute the fault to the Author, for it was farre from his purpose to write to any purpose, so ending at the beginning, I say as it is applawsefully written and commended to posterity in the Midsummer nights dreame. If we offend, it is with our good will, we came with no intent, but to offend, and show our simple skill.[6]

Regardless of the fate of the rest of *A Midsummer Night's Dream*, or of the rest of the Shakespeare canon, 'Pyramus and Thisbe' and its rehearsals have remained ever since Taylor's time the one chunk of Shakespeare almost guaranteed to get laughs – though it often does so in contexts, like this one, far removed from the supposed mainstream of English humour. This is the bit of Shakespeare that has been performed not only by the likes of Charles Kean or the RSC but by the Crazy Gang, and indeed by those four loyal disciples of the Goons, the Beatles, who in honour of Shakespeare's 400th birthday in 1964 played it as a sketch on a television special. (The Pyramus was Paul; Ringo was Lion, John, Thisbe; George, suitably enough, was Moonshine; and Trevor Peacock made a guest appearance as Wall). It is with the independent fate of 'Pyramus and Thisbe', and its role in the production of Shakespeare's own current joke status, that the remainder of this paper will be concerned, and that fate is inextricably bound up with another phe-

nomenon well-nigh invisible to orthodox literary and dramatic history, and that is the development of English amateur theatre.

Taylor doesn't quote very precisely from Quince's prologue, but then for a nonsense pamphlet to quote a nonsensical prologue too accurately wouldn't really make any sense. Noel Malcolm, glossing this passage in his important anthology *The Origins of English Nonsense* (1997), calls it 'a parody of the prologue to *Pyramus and Thisbe*' (137), but this isn't really right: as Richard Schoch remarks in passing of *Pyramus and Thisbe* in his excellent study of nineteenth-century Shakespearian burlesque, *Not Shakespeare*, it is very difficult to parody or burlesque something which is already parody or burlesque.[7] But if 'Pyramus and Thisbe' *is* primarily a piece of literary or theatrical satire, as this implies, then what precisely is it a satire on? Most commentators have assumed that the verbal mannerisms of the mechanicals' script were intended as a burlesque on specific contemporary plays which Shakespeare's audience might recently have seen on the professional stage, but if that were the case, then we might reasonably expect its jokes to have died the death long ago. But they haven't, and in any case no one has yet succeeded in identifying which plays Shakespeare was sending up, if he was. As Peter Holland puts it in his Oxford edition of *Dream*, 'the object of the burlesque does not appear to be straightforwardly the work of rival companies or indeed of Shakespeare's own' (89). The over-arching joke, then, we might assume, must instead be less against the script than

---

[4] On this aspect of the play's performance history, see especially Peter Holland's Oxford edition (1994), pp. 99–100, and his '*A Midsummer Night's Dream*, 1660–1800: Culture and the Canon', in P. Faini and V. Papetti, eds., *Le forme del teatro: Saggi sul teatro elisabettiano e della Restaurazione* (Rome, 1994), pp. 201–46.

[5] As well as the instances I discuss here, the *Shakspere Allusion Book* cites examples from Sharpham (1607), Gee (1624), Sampson (1636), Gayton (1662) and Marvell (1673).

[6] In Noel Malcolm, ed., *The Origins of English Nonsense* (London, 1997), pp. 154–5.

[7] Richard W. Schoch, *Not Shakespeare: Bardolatry and Burlesque in the Nineteenth Century* (Cambridge, 2002), p. 148.

against the social circumstances under which it is so badly performed, a jibe at amateur drama *per se*, the absurd and incongruous social and intellectual aspirations of those real-life Elizabethan artisans who liked to play at being heroes and gentlemen. The paradox here, though, is that in Shakespeare's time no such practices seem quite to have existed. Although the *Records of Early English Drama* volumes provide rich evidence of ambitious dramatic activities within gentry households, and although members of the lower classes might form professional troupes[8] or even find themselves performing high tragedy in the Navy,[9] 'workers', as Holland puts it, 'seem never to have acted classical Ovidian plays like "Pyramus and Thisbe"...nothing like a bunch of workers attempting their own adaptation of a play on "Pyramus and Thisbe" had ever been seen in England' (91–2).

What instead appears to happen over the course of its reception history is that 'Pyramus and Thisbe' itself calls into being the social institution which it presciently ridicules: starting life as a flight of surreal fancy, a piece of nonsense-drama, it only becomes more-or-less realistic social satire through accidentally begetting the particular artisan-class form of amateur drama of which, in 1595, it finds the very idea ludicrous. There may not have been non-professionals doing 'Pyramus and Thisbe' before *Dream*, but there certainly have been ever since, and these Bottom wannabes start appearing around the play remarkably early. In 1646, James Shirley's masque *The Triumph of Beauty* plagiarizes Bottom and his fellow-actors wholesale, as a crew of thespian shepherds led by the thinly disguised Bottle: this whole work, says the printed edition, was 'personated by some young *Gentlemen*, for whom it was intended, at a private recreation'.[10] Further down the status hierarchy from these closet aristocratic masquers, just the mechanicals' scenes were culled from *Midsummer Night's Dream* at around the same time by the actor Robert Cox, and they were printed in 1661 as *The Merry Conceited Humours of Bottom the Weaver*. This playlet, says the title page, is proof that am dram is alive and well among the lower ranks, having been 'lately, privately, presented, by several APPRENTICES for their

harmless recreation'. An introductory letter from the Stationer to the Reader offers this text's ability to generate non-professional theatre as one of its chief recommendations: 'this...we know may be easily acted, and may be now as fit for a private recreation as it hath formerly been for a public'. Some sort of evidence that this droll did indeed catch on among amateurs, even among schoolchildren, is provided by Nahum Tate's adaptation of Jonson, Chapman and Marston's *Eastward Ho!* twenty years later. In *Cuckold's Haven* (1685), the usurer Security is endowed with an incongruous enthusiasm for amateur dramatics, and while holding forth on the subject he experiences a sudden vivid flashback, half quotation and half plagiarism, to his youth as a schoolboy Bottom:

Why, I will act thee a better Play my self. What wilt thou have? The Knight of the Burning Pestle? Or, the doleful Comedy of *Piramus* and *Thisbe*? That's my Master-Piece;

---

[8] An instance often misleadingly cited as evidence that there were indeed real-life Quinces and Bottoms in Shakespeare's time is that of Richard Cholmeley's Men, the company of Catholic ex-shoemakers who toured the North Riding of Yorkshire from the later 1590s through 1609, but the scale of their dramatic engagements suggests that these were in fact itinerant professionals who had given up what we might anachronistically call their day jobs: as Charles J. Sisson put it, with an unconscious Shakespearian pun,

It is clear that we must beware of applying to all such provincial companies, even if they were shoemakers by trade, the satire in Shakespeare's picture of the rude mechanics...in fact the probability is that their theatrical profession was their sole occupation throughout the year.

Charles J. Sisson, 'Shakespeare Quartos as Prompt-Copies, with some account of Cholmeley's Players and a new Shakespeare allusion', *Review of English Studies*, 18 (1942), 129–43: 136–7.

[9] Cf. the famous instance of shipboard performances of *Hamlet* and *Richard II* on William Keeling's ship the *Dragon* off Sierra Leone in 1607. The story of non-professional performance among the military and in colonial contexts, however, is a separate (though intriguingly related) chapter of theatrical history to the development of English amateur drama in the classic civic form which 'Pyramus and Thisbe' seems to adumbrate.

[10] *The Dramatic Works and Poems of James Shirley*, eds. William Gifford and Alexander Dyce, 6 vols. (London, 1833), vol. VI, p. 317.

when *Piramus* comes to be dead, I can act a dead man rarely, *The rageing Rocks, and shivering Shocks, shall break the Locks of Prison Gates; and* Phoebus *Carr shall shine from Far, to make and mar the foolish Fates.* Was not that lofty now? Then there's the Lion, *Wall* and *Moonshine,* three Heroick Parts; I play'd 'em all at School. I roar'd out the Lion so terribly, that the Company call'd out to me to roar again.[11]

Tate at least seems to think that his audience in 1685 will be able to imagine that a contemporary usurer might have been in 'Pyramus and Thisbe' when at school, even if he has apparently failed to detect the jokes just as signally as would Lord Blackadder.

It was the aristocratic strain in non-professional theatre, however, which held most prominence over the ensuing century, temporarily slowing the momentum of this apparent progression, in the footsteps of Shakespeare's mechanicals, towards something we would still recognize as standard English village amateur dramatics. Instead of amateur performance appearing to be, as in these last two seventeenth-century examples, a case of lower-ranking men or boys aspiring towards the status of professional players or of the more elevated amateurs who staffed the court masque, the eighteenth century amateur theatre was primarily the province of aristocrats slumming it among the players, building private theatres in their country houses and then inviting London stage celebrities down to play supporting roles to their own and their families' heroic posturings in front of the neighbours.[12] This vogue for upper-class, country house am dram had already begun to come down in the world by the time Austen depicted it in *Mansfield Park* (1814), but a sense of where the boundaries fell between the respectably professional and the sordidly mercenary, between the properly disinterested and the merely amateurish, is well delineated by a play written at the height of the craze in the 1780s. In James Powell's *Private Theatricals* (1787), Alderman Grubb, father of the ingenue Lucy, has recently married a second and very stage-struck Lady Grubb, who has spoiled his country estate by putting marble busts of Jonson and Shakespeare in his favourite grotto and

renaming his hermitage 'Prospero's Cave'. Furthermore, she has built a stage in his drawing room, and with the help of some London professionals she is busily presiding over some Quince-style rehearsals of *Romeo and Juliet*, with Lucy as Juliet. It is at last revealed even to Alderman Grubb that the actor who has been playing Romeo is really Juliet's forbidden suitor Villars, but, in the inevitable reconciliation scene, Villars, forswearing his assumed profession with contempt, assures his future father-in-law that he is neither a mere actor nor a supporter of Lady Grubb's chosen hobby:

Forgive, Mr Alderman, the stratagems of love, I am no player (tho' in its proper place, an enthusiast in the art). And I think the present rage for theatrical private performances, has grown to a ridiculous pitch, and is productive of much mischief to the morals of society, by admitting the loose and profligate (who are a scandal to the age) into the houses of virtue, whose reputation and honor they generally endanger.[13]

Powell, the writer of this pious speech, even makes the same social disclaimer for himself: scorning to be identified either as a professional playwright or as a corrupted dilettante, he has this work 'Printed and sold by the Author', namely 'James Powell (of the Custom House)' – neither mechanical nor hack, but a civil servant and a gentleman.

Remarkably, Shakespeare's mechanicals, thus excluded from the social circles of contemporary am dram but still hungry for a referent, turn pro for the duration of the eighteenth century. In Richard Leveridge's *Pyramus and Thisbe, a comic masque* (1716) and John Frederick Lampe's *Pyramus and Thisbe, a mock opera* (1745), Bottom and co. are patronized not for being amateurs but

---

[11] Nahum Tate, *Cuckolds-Haven: or, An Alderman No Conjurer* (London, 1685), p. 16.

[12] See especially Sybil M. Rosenfeld, *Temples of Thespis: Some Private Theatres and Theatricals in England and Wales, 1700–1820* (London, 1978).

[13] James Powell, *The Narcotic and Private Theatricals* (London, 1787), p. 35. Appropriately, the only recorded performance of this play was given by respectable amateurs, the Lymington Players in Hampshire, in 2000.

for being mere professionals, transformed from volunteer Athenian actors into hired Italian theatre musicians. Their amputated scenes dwindle to close topical parody of *opera seria*, anticipating the parody of Italian grand opera with which Benjamin Britten would endue them in his own operatic *Dream* in 1960. It is only in the nineteenth century, with the advent of the 'spouting clubs' – artisan associations which met above pubs to indulge both in political rhetoric and in literary recitation – and with the related enthusiasm among Chartist groups for using Shakespeare as a vehicle for the raising of working-class consciousness, that amateur drama again comes to fit the social pattern mocked in advance by *Midsummer Night's Dream*.[14] Non-professional theatre comes again to be associated with lower-class aspirations of all kinds, especially in the burgeoning manufacturing towns of the North of England. The first formally institutionalized am dram group in Britain, the Manchester Athenaeum Dramatic Society, 1847, performed more Shakespeare than anything else in pursuit of its stated aims, viz. 'to cultivate a taste for standard dramatic literature and poetry and to be a source of mutual improvement to its members'.[15] Quince, surely, would happily have signed such a charter. Hence when a nineteenth-century young man of the upper class shows an enthusiasm for am dram in a comedy, it is emphatically construed as a piece of reprehensible downward mobility rather than the emulation of an aristocratic vice, and Bottom is explicitly invoked as the hobby's damning defining instance. In T. W. Robertson's play *M.P.* (1870), the parliamentarian of the title, Dunscombe Dunscombe, learns that his son is planning to go in for amateur theatricals in a big way, and they have a memorable argument on the subject. 'See what Shakespeare . . . thinks of the amateur actor', urges Dunscombe. 'Look at him in the *Midsummer Night's Dream* – the Weaver Bottom – a conceited, pragmatical, imbecile idiot!' 'And see how Shakespeare rewards him!', counters his son. 'Who falls in love with this idiot and imbecile? Titania, Queen of the Fairies'. But Dunscombe has a riposte to this:

Yes, sir. And do you know why? Because Puck, before he shows this broken-brained weaver to Titania, raises him in the scale of intellect from an amateur actor to a donkey. Shakespeare knew that as a donkey he was presentable at the fairy court – as an amateur actor the thing was too impossible.[16]

Nevertheless, *A Midsummer Night's Dream* would go on serving as an inspiration to others than young Dunscombe, particularly in the earlier twentieth century. During the forgotten glory days of what was called the Little Theatre, between the wars, for instance, am dram was seriously offered as a civic humanist antidote to all forms of totalitarianism. Reconnecting the masses with a new, disinterested forum of public culture, undiscredited by either the war or the Depression, am dram, in the hands of idealists such as Barry Jackson, had now attained the status of a 'movement'. In its grandiose two-volume manifesto and how-to guide, *The Theatre and Stage* (edited by Harold F. Downs, 1934), this development was again read back onto Shakespeare in a way that retrospectively turned the 'Pyramus and Thisbe' scenes into a piece of benign and well-intentioned social realism:

The amateur movement of [Shakespeare's] day – in one of its less exalted manifestations – comes in for some pointed yet not unsympathetic satire in the clown scenes of *A Midsummer Night's Dream*. Bottom and his troupe of 'rude mechanicals' suggest that amateur acting . . . had spread, as in our own day, to the ranks of the 'workers'.

(1, 3)

In fact, as we've seen, it hadn't, or at least not in any such classical literary mode as that attempted

---

[14] See *The Life of Thomas Cooper written by himself* (London, 1875), cited in Jonathan Bate, *The Genius of Shakespeare* (London, 1997), pp. 214–15.

[15] On this group and its successors, notably the Stockport Garrick Society, see Adrian Rendle, *Everyman and his Theatre: A Study of the Purpose and Function of the Amateur Theatre Today* (London, 1968), pp. 8–10; George Taylor, *A History of the Amateur Theatre* (Melksham, 1976), p. 38.

[16] T. W. Robertson, *M.P.* (1870; London, 1966), 326–7. Schoch discusses part of this dialogue as an instance of the impossibility of admitting that Shakespeare himself wrote burlesque: Schoch, *Not Shakespeare*, pp. 146–8.

by Bottom and his peers. But this passage's desire to hold up Elizabethan drama as a model of a participatory national culture equally available to all remains intensely familiar to anyone who grew up in the lost, post-war 'New Elizabethan' age, and a rather poignant one to remember. These amateur-acting workers are furthermore urged to perform Shakespeare's 'poetic comedy' 'for the sake of what they can learn', even though their audiences 'may not like what they do' (1, 349): if they offend, clearly, it should be with their good will. In such non-professional *Dream*s as these, of which there are still dozens every English summer,[17] the whole production itself can at last serve as the willing real-life object of the play's own satire.

In this long series of attempts to give Bottom a referent, then, so that his endlessly popular play-within-the-play can be got back into the perceived mainstream of English comedy as an orthodox piece of Jonsonian realist satire, he and his colleagues have metamorphosed from nonsensical Ealingesque hypothesis to Italian musicians to retrospectively invented Elizabethan champions of cultural egalitarianism. It is as such, perhaps, that this process has most decisively rubbed off on their creator, leaving him the derided and déclassé figure perceived, despite the best efforts of the Little Theatre Movement, by today's removals men. Shakespeare, too, has regularly been construed as just such a champion, and invocations of his genius, that which transcends the merely professional, are always liable to turn him into merely a special kind of amateur – an aspiring Bottom who can give every trueborn Englishman hope of cultural entitlement. Back in eighteenth and nineteenth-century poetry and criticism, characteristically, Shakespeare was regularly depicted as an uneducated Warwickshire rustic with an untaught enthusiasm for the drama, who in youth fell asleep beside the fairy-haunted Avon and saw the future outpourings of his genius in a dream, past the wit of any lesser man to say what dream it was. (This is how he is depicted, for example, in Charles Somerset's play *Shakspeare's Early Days*, 1829, and as late as 1886 Franklin Harvey Head's *jeu d'esprit* 'Shakespeare's

Insomnia and the Causes Thereof' claims that 'Pyramus and Thisbe' was the boy Shakespeare's first play, and amateur at that, 'played by himself and Nicholas Bottom and Peter Quince and others', in a barn, for the delectation of the townsmen'.)[18] I have written elsewhere about Enlightenment culture's desire to identify Shakespeare with Bottom, particularly in depictions of his dealings with the Fairy Queen, Elizabeth.[19] But I want to close with a contemporary example of the Shakespeare-as-Bottom trope, this one played deliberately as a joke. The most fully developed Shakespeare joke carried out in book form in recent years has been Patrick Barlow's *Shakespeare: The Truth* (1993). It is written by one of the two members of the comedy troupe The National Theatre of Brent, and it is written in the person of Barlow's inept alter ego, Desmond Olivier Dingle, a lower-middle-class self-appointed expert on everything who is also an incorrigibly bad amateur actor who insists on having all the best parts. The book is described on its cover as 'Desmond Olivier Dingle's *controversial exposé*, including family tree, props list, complete history of the English language, handy acting tips, tourist guide to Stratford, glossary *and* special feature: "Shakespeare's Unknown Wives"'. On the cover appears Dingle, bewigged and made up as Shakespeare despite his signature metal-framed rectangular spectacles: a sad figure, haunted by poetic visions he can't quite understand, playing an

---

[17] The most recent survey, the Central Council for Amateur Theatre's *Amateur Theatre in Great Britain* (London, 1989), estimated that there were 6,500 societies, with a membership of more than 700,000, playing to audiences totalling more than 16 million annually. These figures exclude school and university drama. I would estimate the percentage of performances of plays by Shakespeare at something approaching 20 percent of this activity, and of the canon, *A Midsummer Night's Dream* is easily the most frequently produced play.

[18] The claim is made in a letter from this allegedly real Bottom to Shakespeare, demanding a share of the profits from *A Midsummer Night's Dream*. The work is reprinted in Maurice O'Sullivan, Jr., ed., *Shakespeare's Other Lives: Fictional Depictions of the Bard* (Jefferson, NC, 1997), pp. 68–79: 75.

[19] See Michael Dobson and Nicola Watson, *England's Elizabeth: An Afterlife in Fame and Fantasy* (Oxford, 2002), pp. 128–33.

am dram Shakespeare. If you come upon a copy of this work, and if this is not the first time that you have read an article in *Shakespeare Survey*, do take a good look: this humiliated enthusiast for an incomprehensible lost cause, with a status somewhere between train-spotter and morris-dancer, is precisely the figure that removals men see when they look at your bookshelves. Rather than a Malvolio in agony, this particular popular culture Shakespeare is a Bottom in pain – which is perhaps just preferable to merely being, as nowadays seems more usual, a pain in the bottom.

FALSTAFF'S BELLY, BERTIE'S KILT, ROSALIND'S LEGS: SHAKESPEARE AND THE VICTORIAN PRINCE

ADRIAN POOLE

We can all see ourselves in Shakespeare. But if you were the Prince of Wales you'd be bound to take a particular interest in Hal – and therefore in Falstaff. Imagine therefore that you're Albert Edward Prince of Wales, familiarly known as Bertie, that you're eleven years old, that it's the Christmas holidays of 1852, that Charles Kean and his troupe are giving a command performance of *Henry IV, Part I* at Windsor Castle for your mum and the rest of the family. And that Falstaff makes you laugh. Many years later the actor playing Prince Hal will recall your reaction to 'the scene where Falstaff boasts of his bravery with his shield and buckler'. Like this:

The Royal heir to the throne of England became so engrossed with the comicality of the scene (admirably played by Bartley) that he was carried away completely. He wore a tartan dress, and as tears of laughter rolled down his cheeks in his ecstasy, he rolled up his tartan and at the same time rubbed his knees with great gusto. His sister, the Princess Royal, saw with horror the innocent impropriety, and never shall I forget her terrified glance round the room. However, finding that all were intent upon the scene, she gave one vigorous tug at the tartan, which restored propriety and brought the happy boy to a sense of the situation.[1]

What futures lay ahead of them. The Princess Royal would marry the Crown Prince of Prussia and give birth to a boy called Willy, the future Kaiser. Her brother Bertie would wait and wait as Prince of Wales for almost fifty years before ascending the throne for a mere nine-year stint as King Edward VII. His mother had dreamed he might be the first King Albert. But as Henry James noted,

he was bluntly known as 'fat Edward', and, with slightly more wit, as Edward the Caresser.[2]

But back to the shameless boy and his kilt. I take the anecdote to symbolize all sorts of strife in Victorian culture. Keeping the body at bay is hard work. It's a constant battle to stop happy boys getting engrossed, feeling ecstasy, lifting up their dresses and rubbing their knees with gusto. You'll need more than one vigorous tug at the tartan. Like other Victorian boys intent on happiness and prone to impropriety, poor Bertie's whole upbringing consisted of tugs at the tartan from his father and mother and their surrogates, plus the odd birching. No wonder he became addicted to the pleasures of the flesh, especially after his father Prince Albert's death in 1861 when his mother renounced the world and committed her eldest son to a state of permanent freezing reproof. She had never much cared for Bertie, and now the shock of his first sexual transgression had killed his father, so she liked to believe. This Prince of Wales found himself cast as a Hal who could never be forgiven. So why not just carry on misbehaving?

To understand the Victorian Falstaff we need to go back to the Regency years and an earlier Prince of Wales. Or to be less exact, we need to consider the whole turbulent era marked by Uncle George. That is, the period of nearly fifty years marked by the coming of age of the future George IV in 1783,

---

[1] Fred Belton, *Random Recollections of an Old Actor* (London, 1880), pp. 159–60.
[2] Stanley Weintraub, *The Importance of Being Edward: King in Waiting 1841–1901* (London, 2000), p. 390.

his accession to the Regency in 1811 and to the throne in 1820, and his death in 1830. In a sense this era was continued up to the young Victoria's coronation by his brother's brief intervention as William IV. When someone suggested to Queen Victoria that she might be bringing up her son and heir too strictly she answered: 'Remember, there is only my life between his and the lives of his Wicked Uncles'.[3] It was not only his mother who was troubled by the comparison, especially with Wicked Uncle George. It was clearly implied in the prayer uttered by Canon Sydney Smith in the Sunday sermon at St Paul's just after his birth, and explicitly voiced by the anonymous author of the pamphlet Who Should Educate the Prince of Wales? two years later in 1843.[4] As he neared the age of thirty, the satirical magazine Tomahawk had a cartoon of him as Hamlet swearing to the ghost of Uncle George, 'I'll follow thee'.[5] In 1867 readers of The English Constitution would have thought of their own Prince of Wales as Walter Bagehot reflected on the moral to be drawn from his predecessor the Prince Regent's example, that 'All the world and all the glory of it, whatever is most attractive, whatever is most seductive, has always been offered to the Prince of Wales of the day, and always will be. It is not rational to expect the best virtue where temptation is applied in the most trying form at the frailest time of human life'.[6] Which is rational and generous.

For the Victorians Falstaff is associated with the Regency era in two main ways. Both are dominated by images of 'liberty', but one is menacing, libidinous and libertine, while the other is comforting, regressive and luxurious. One is overtly political in its attendance on royalty and the idea of the monarch-in-waiting, the great expectations invested in him and the threat of privilege abused. The other is more ostensibly personal in its memories of childhood and good times, especially of eating and drinking and rubbing your knees with gusto. This is notably true for writers of the generation of Thackeray and Dickens, born respectively in 1811 and 1812, for whom the Regency and post-war years were profoundly associated with Shakespeare's great figure of conviviality. The shade of Falstaff presides over the eating and drinking essential to the conduct of most (male) literary life in the middle decades of the century. The young Tennyson and his Cambridge friends regularly swapped Falstaffian banter, accusing each other of being 'gross and fatwitted', and so on.[7] It's no coincidence that one of the founders of Punch (in 1841) and its long-serving editor, Mark Lemon, should have played Falstaff in Dickens's uproarious production of The Merry Wives in 1848. (The cast included Dickens as Shallow and Mary Cowden Clarke as Mistress Quickly.)

The role played by Falstaff in Dickens's imagination is a rich and complex one.[8] There is the obsession with Gadshill. There are the chimes at midnight that gave him the title of his second Christmas book. There is the stimulus provided by Mistress Quickly and Falstaff to the Trial of Bardell against Pickwick (specifically the scene in 2 Henry IV, Act 2, scene 1), and the more diffused associations between Pickwick and the Windsor Falstaff.[9] For at least one reviewer however it was not Pickwick but Sam Weller who 'made old England more

---

3 Weintraub, p. 33.

4 Weintraub, pp. 4, 6.

5 Reproduced by Allen Andrews, The Follies of King Edward VII (London, 1975), p. 101. Tomahawk was the pseudonym of Arthur à Beckett, son of one of the original staff of Punch. The magazine ran for three years from 1867, and featured some mild anti-royal satire. On 7 March 1868, under the title 'A Princely Programme', it contrasted the Shakespeare once played at Windsor with the vulgar fare now sponsored by the Prince of Wales at Sandringham, including can-cans, poses plastiques and choruses such as 'Rumti-tiddyti-bow-wow-wow' by the Jolly Dogs' Choir and a Finale consisting of 'Grand Steeple-chase over the Furniture by the Entire Company (Lady riders up)' (vol. 11, p. 96).

6 Walter Bagehot, The English Constitution, ed. Miles Taylor (Oxford, 2001), p. 50.

7 See The Letters of Alfred Lord Tennyson, eds. Cecil Y. Lang and Edgar F. Shannon, Jr, vol. 1 (Oxford, 1982), pp. 70, 96, 145.

8 See Valerie L. Gager, Shakespeare and Dickens: The Dynamics of Influence (Cambridge, 1996).

9 See John Glavin, 'Pickwick on the Wrong Side of the Door', Dickens Studies Annual, 22 (1993), 1–20. Glavin has a suggestive line of thought about the way Pickwick 'miscarries from Falstaff...' and offers to 'misread the entire novel along a template of The Merry Wives' (pp. 3, 4).

"merrie" than it had ever been since Falstaff drank, and roared, and punned, at the Globe Theatre'.[10] For another, Falstaff provided a model for the immortality to which the Wellers and the Pecksniffs, the Swivellers and the Micawbers had soared, 'immortals of lesser note, and more of mortal mixture, but still of the same lineage with Falstaff'.[11] To Dickens himself Falstaff was a name for the power of performance to melt the world around him. Like the grim person who entered the theatre, so he told an audience in 1863, 'a mere figure of snow, but who gradually softens and mellows' until his face 'realizes Falstaff's wonderful simile of being "like a wet cloak ill laid up"'.[12]

Falstaff was no less important to Dickens's great rival, the creator of 'that fat *gourmand*' Jos Sedley.[13] One of Thackeray's illustrations to *Vanity Fair* (1847–8) shows Jos as a Falstaff entertained by Becky Sharp's Doll Tearsheet. In his 'Memorials of Gormandising' Thackeray muses approvingly on the legend that Shakespeare died of a surfeit brought on by carousing with a literary friend from London: 'And wherefore not? Better to die of good wine and good company than of slow disease and doctor's doses'.[14] Recall that the new King Henry advises Falstaff to 'Leave gormandizing'.[15] As for Hal and his father, 'Tom Eaves' is credited with these sardonic reflections in *Vanity Fair*, à propos Lord Steyne and Gaunt House: 'Take it as a rule . . . the fathers and elder sons of all great families hate each other. The crown prince is always in opposition to the crown or hankering after it. Shakespeare knew the world, my good sir, and when he describes Prince Hal . . . trying on his father's coronet, he gives you a natural description of all heirs-apparent'.[16] Thackeray's full treatment of the Hal–Falstaff relationship however is in *Pendennis* (1848–50), where the Major plays Falstaff to his nephew's Prince. The Major yearns for the days 'of the wild Prince and Poyns', a phrase which recurs in *The Newcomes* (1853–5) and *The Adventures of Philip* (1861–2).[17] The Major is the bad mentor who promotes all Pen's shallowest ambitions, until the climactic chapter LXX ('Fiat Justitia') in which Pen turns on his uncle and says in effect 'I know thee not old man'.

Perhaps the most poignant celebration of this early Victorian nostalgia for the roistering Regency comes from a man lampooned by Thackeray in this same novel as Captain Shandon. Some twenty years older than Thackeray and Dickens, William Maginn was a prodigally gifted and fatally dissipated contributor to *Blackwood's* and to the *Fraser's Magazine* he helped to found in 1830. 'Barring drink and the girls, I ne'er heard of a sin:/Many worse, better few, than bright, broken Maginn'. Thus the kindly epitaph from John Gibson Lockhart after his death in 1842.[18] In the late 1830s Dickens extracted from Maginn a series of eight papers on Shakespeare.[19] The first of these is an extraordinary elegy to a Falstaff that is also a painful self-portrait. Falstaff's deep hidden melancholy is not be confused with Jaques's shallow posturing, says Maginn, for the iron has not entered into Jaques's soul, as it has into Falstaff's. And the resemblance between Falstaff and Sir Toby Belch is merely superficial: 'they are as distinct as Prospero and Polonius' (505). Falstaff's real affinity is with the Macbeth who despairs at the thought of the things that should accompany old age and will never do so for him. 'The comic Falstaff says nothing on the subject': and yet, 'neglect, forgotten friendships, services overlooked,

---

[10] *Fraser's Magazine* (December 1850), in *Dickens: The Critical Heritage*, ed. Philip Collins (London, 1971), p. 245.

[11] Mowbray Morris, *Fortnightly Review* (1 December 1882), in *Dickens: Critical Heritage*, p. 611.

[12] Speech to the Royal General Theatrical Fund (4 April 1863), quoted by Gager, *Shakespeare and Dickens*, p. 300.

[13] *Vanity Fair*, ed. John Sutherland (Oxford, 1983), p. 66

[14] 'Memorials of Gormandising. In a Letter to Oliver Yorke, Esq. By M. A. Titmarsh', *Fraser's Magazine* (June 1841), 724.

[15] *2 Henry IV*, 5.5.53 (*The Riverside Shakespeare*, ed. G. Blakemore Evans, 2nd edn (Boston, 1997)).

[16] *Vanity Fair*, p. 592.

[17] In *The Newcomes*, vol. 1, chs. 10 and 28, and *The Adventures of Philip*, vol. 1, ch. 7.

[18] William Maginn, *Miscellanies* (London, 1885), vol. 1, p. xviii.

[19] First published as 'Shakspeare Papers. – No. I: Sir John Falstaff', and 'No. II: Jaques', *Bentley's Miscellany*, 1 (May 1837), 494–508, and (June 1837), 550–60. Reprinted, along with papers on 'Romeo', 'Midsummer Night's Dream – Bottom the Weaver', 'His Ladies – Lady Macbeth', 'Timon of Athens', 'Polonius' and 'Iago', in *Shakspeare Papers: Pictures Grave and Gay* (1859).

shared pleasures unremembered, and fair occasions gone for ever by, haunt him, no doubt, as sharply as the consciousness of deserving universal hatred galls the soul of Macbeth' (501). Yet it is not only Falstaff's melancholy with which Maginn identifies. He conceives of a Hal who is truly spellbound by Falstaff, and in the great scene of repudiation he imagines that it is only by the skin of his teeth that the young King manages to turn 'the old master-spirit' away.[20] He mustn't let Falstaff get a word in edgeways. One lightning repartee and Falstaff would not have been packed off to prison but invited to the coronation dinner. Hence for the King, 'His only safety was in utter separation... He was emancipated by violent effort'. And yet – 'did he never regret the ancient thraldom?' (497) It takes violence, it seems, or a vigorous tug at the tartan, to escape from being a happy prince, enthralled and engrossed, and become a sad grown-up monarch.

Only a lonely brooding reader could turn Falstaff into Macbeth, and Maginn was predictably cutting about the crudity of theatrical Falstaffs. For the sharpest possible contrast we could turn to the leading American exponent of the role in mid-century, James H. Hackett. Hackett was thoroughly provoked by the lofty reception accorded his Falstaff at Drury Lane in 1840. The *Times* reviewer particularly got his goat by opining of Falstaff that 'With all the bold outline and full-facedness of a coarsely painted Dutch clock, he has all the delicate organization of a Geneva watch; and hard is it for the actor to avoid marring some part of the fine machinery'.[21] Rubbish, said Hackett. Why all the palaver about Falstaff's inner workings? He's not Hamlet for God's sake. And as for all this English deference to his gentility... The man is just a rogue, 'with no amiable or tolerable quality to gloss or cover his moral deformity, except a surpassingly brilliant and charming wit, and a spontaneous and irresistible flow of humour'. The nub of the matter is that 'the character was designed for stage-effect';[22] you just have to do the lines.

Nothing could be further from Maginn's impassioned reading, and I'd suggest that the difference between them marks something more than the usual rivalry between performer and reader.

The quality of the rift anticipates the receding of Falstaff as a powerful imaginative source and resource, from about 1860 onwards. It's as if Falstaff's body and spirit become too sharply dissociated from each other, or his belly and his wit, or the public performance and the private reading. Up until 1860 Falstaff has enjoyed an almost unchallenged supremacy as the most imaginatively vital of Shakespeare's comic creations. But for the last forty years of the century he is superseded by a figure in whom the body and spirit seem to be less sharply, more intriguingly and hence desirably at odds with each other. The kind of liberty that Falstaff promises (or threatens) now seems to belong to the past; Rosalind's belongs to the future.[23]

By the time Thackeray died in 1863 Falstaff was suffering a comparative eclipse. In 1857 a writer

---

[20] Maginn writes: '... if the thing be not done on the heat, – if the old master-spirit be allowed one moment's ground of vantage, – the game is up, the good resolutions dissipated into thin air, the grave rebuke turned all into laughter... The king saw his danger: had he allowed a word, he was undone. Hastily, therefore, does he check that word; "Reply not to me with a fool-born jest;" forbidding, by an act of eager authority, – what he must also have felt to be an act of self-control, – the outpouring of those magic sounds which, if uttered, would, instead of a prison becoming the lot of Falstaff, have conducted him to the coronation dinner, and established him as chief depositary of what in after days was known by the name of backstairs influence' (496–7).

[21] James H. Hackett, *Falstaff: A Shakesperean [sic] Tract* (London, 1840), p. 7.

[22] Hackett, *Falstaff*, p. 11.

[23] The story I'm sketching about the subsidence of Falstaff and ascendancy of Rosalind corresponds to some extent with the fortunes of 'humour' and 'wit' in the Victorian period, as described by Robert Bernard Martin in *The Triumph of Wit: A Study of Victorian Comic Theory* (Oxford, 1974). Martin contends that 'As a general pattern, it might be said that comedy during the reign of Queen Victoria changed from sentimental comedy to the comedy of wit and paradox' (p. 3). He sees a key point of transition in the late 1860s, 'when we find the reviewers and critics becoming increasingly restive about the state of comic writing. Wit and intellectual comedy had been universally agreed upon as arrogant, cold, and unpoetic, but when they had almost disappeared in practice, the suspicion grew that they might be a cool refreshment from the sticky and unrelieved sentimentality of what had been passing as comedy' (p. 38).

in the *Athenaeum* commented disparagingly on a painting of 'Falstaff promising to marry Dame Quickly' exhibited at the Royal Exhibition, that Falstaff 'is not a mere walking stomach with just soul enough to suit his flesh and keep it from turning to carrion before its time; but an Epicurean gentleman, shrewd, careless, witty, suspicious of too much virtue, and a moral cosmopolite, sociable from his birth, – a character grown impossible since taverns have become extinct'.[24] But by 1857 many were beginning to suspect that it might be impossible to have too much virtue. Richard Altick notes a sharp falling off after 1860 in visual representations of the Falstaff plays.[25] The London theatres had seen a plethora of performances through the 1840s and 1850s of *1 Henry IV* and the *Merry Wives* (*2 Henry IV* being always of course more of a rarity). Falstaff was a role particularly associated with Samuel Phelps at Sadler's Wells, from 1846 (*1 Henry IV*) and 1848 (*Merry Wives*) onwards. Witty, intelligent, perhaps lacking in exuberance, but widely acclaimed. Theodore Fontane thought the Eastcheap Falstaff his greatest role.[26] Phelps was still playing the Windsor Falstaff in 1874, but productions of all the Falstaff plays dwindle markedly after 1860, and it is only with the advent of Beerbohm Tree at the end of the century that they pick up again. Tree started his association with the *Merry Wives* in 1888 and with *1 Henry IV* in 1896 (both at the Haymarket), though he had notably more success with the former.

Of course the popularity of the Windsor Falstaff has always been confined to the theatre and to performance. From the 1890s through to the Great War, the Englishness of the figure and the play become more marked. It's symptomatic that Tree should have mounted a revival starring Ellen Terry and Madge Kendal as Mistress Page and Mistress Ford to coincide with the new King's coronation in the summer of 1902.[27] And in 1911 Reginald Buckley's alarmingly racist account of 'the Stratford movement' hailed the Merry Wives as 'a fair picture of what England was and might well become again without deterioration'.[28] Outside the theatre the Windsor Falstaff had attracted the scorn of critics

and scholars through the nineteenth century from Hazlitt to Dowden and beyond.[29] He was simply not the same man as his 'immortal' namesake. This trend culminates in Bradley's rapturous essay, where he hails the 'immortal' Falstaff as 'a character almost purely humorous', for whom 'happiness' is too weak a word: 'he is in bliss, and we share his glory', and clinchingly: 'The bliss of freedom gained in humour is the essence of Falstaff'.[30] But like many influential literary critics Bradley is out of date and touch with the creative writers and visual artists for whom Falstaff had subsided as an imaginative source and resource from about 1860 onwards. From that time on his true creative afterlife will be, thanks to Verdi, Elgar, Holst and Vaughan Williams, not in words and images so much as in music.[31]

However through the later decades of the nineteenth century there is a continuing interest in the model provided by Falstaff and Hal. It belongs to a theatre with which we have now become all too

---

[24] *Athenaeum* (23 May 1857), 667.

[25] Richard D. Altick, *Paintings from Books: Art and Literature, in Britain, 1760–1900* (Columbus, Ohio, 1985), p. 260.

[26] Shirley S. Allen, *Samuel Phelps and Sadler's Wells Theatre* (Middletown, Conn., 1971), pp. 181–2.

[27] Hesketh Pearson notes that Terry was then fifty-five, Kendal fifty-three and Tree himself in his fiftieth year 'but they romped through the play like children' (*Beerbohm Tree: His Life and Laughter* (London, 1956), p. 130).

[28] Reginald R. Buckley, *The Shakespeare Revival and the Stratford-upon-Avon Movement* (London, 1911), p. 116.

[29] See Jeanne Addison Roberts, 'The Windsor Falstaff', *Papers on Language and Literature*, 9 (1973), 202–30. Note that she identifies, in distinction from this dominant trend, a group of critics who reunite the two Falstaffs: they acknowledge 'a "decline" in *The Merry Wives* but believe it to be dictated by the exigencies of plot or setting or by moral imperatives' (214).

[30] A. C. Bradley, 'The Rejection of Falstaff', in *Oxford Lectures on Poetry* (London, 1909), pp. 260, 261, 262.

[31] Giuseppe Verdi's opera *Falstaff* (1893); Edward Elgar's symphonic poem *Falstaff* (1913); Gustav Holst's one-act musical interlude *At the Boar's Head* (1925); Ralph Vaughan Williams' opera *Sir John in Love* (1929). Lyric Falstaffs based on *The Merry Wives* that precede Verdi's masterpiece include operas by M. Balfe (London, 1838), O. Nicolai (Berlin, 1849) and A. Adam (Paris, 1856). Mention should also be made of Robert Nye's uproariously 'Rabelaisian' novel *Falstaff* (London, 1976).

familiar – a theatre of 'celebrity' created by the 'media'. Here the comparison and contrast with the Regency period is instructive. There were the real perceived connections, especially in the early years of Victoria's reign, with the bad old Prince of Wales, and the traditions of political satire and caricature about which Jonathan Bate has written so well.[32] From the mid-1780s on that Prince had mixed with a group of dissolute prominent Whigs including Fox, Sheridan and Hanger, and the caricaturists lost no time in identifying them with Falstaff, Bardolph and Pistol – and Mrs Fitzherbert with Doll Tearsheet. In 1788 Gillray gives to an enormous Falstaff-Fox the lines, for example, 'The Laws of England are at my commandment'. When the Prince broke with the Whigs in the 1790s there were hopes that he would turn into a King Henry V. In 1853 the parallel with Prince Hal was still vivid for the writer in *Blackwood's* who commented that Shakespeare had foreseen it all, and that 'The scene between Henry the Fifth and Falstaff has been acted in every court of Europe, where the acquaintance began in the tavern'.[33]

But there is always the fear (and desire), touched on by Maginn, that King Henry may *not* repudiate Falstaff. Even worse, that the Prince may simply *become* Falstaff. This had been one way of lampooning the Prince Regent, and in the later decades of the nineteenth century, as Bertie's girth started to emulate that of his wicked uncle, the Shakespearean parallels return with their question: will this prince rise to become King Henry or degenerate into Falstaff?[34] Disraeli was not the only one to think of him as 'our young Hal'.[35] In 1876 Samuel Beeton and some henchmen published an enormous verse drama entitled *Edward the Seventh*.[36] This was the last of a series of satires beginning with *The Coming K—* in *Beeton's Christmas Annual* for 1872. Modelled on Tennyson's *Idylls*, this featured the amorous exploits of 'Guelpho the Gay' (that is, the Prince of Wales, drawing on the family name of Guelph). The Beetons' biographer rightly judges it 'much too topical to be comprehensible in the twentieth century'.[37] It was followed in 1873 by *The Siliad* which included characters such as Gladimennon and Dudizzy and conversa-

tions between Victoria and Guelpho: it sold like hot cakes. *Edward VII* is much the most substantial of the three, and deserves Weintraub's praise of it as 'a remarkable *tour de force* of foreshadowing and fancy'.[38] It takes as its guiding motif the parallel with Shakespeare's Hal, providing Prince Guelpho with dubious cronies called Hardolph, Quoins and Palstaff. (A *Key* was published as a sixpenny pamphlet which identifies the real persons concerned.) There's a scene in Act II which parodies the one in *2 Henry IV* when Hal takes the crown from his sleeping father. Here the Prince sees the sleeping Queen's account books and is appalled to discover how much money she's hoarding to spend on yet more memorials to her idolized 'Albor'. The whole drama is hostile to 'Queen Victa' and sympathetic to her son and heir. This becomes particularly blatant in the later Acts (there are no less than seven) which project the narrative into the future. These send the Prince and his bohemian friends to war in India and Egypt against the Russians and the Germans, providing Bertie with the military career he had always craved in reality and been denied by his mother. The Prince becomes King Henry before Agincourt; a defeated Russian general is made to shout 'A horse, a horse, Siberia for a horse!' (p. 86); on receiving news of the death of a friend, the Prince starts playing Hamlet in the graveyard, 'Alas, poor Charlie! A most genial soul, / The king of jokers, infinite in jest; / ... How we shall miss him at the Malborrow, / And sigh to see his pipes, his cues, his chair – ' (p. 89). He is also given a more

---

[32] Jonathan Bate, *Shakespearean Constitutions: Politics, Theatre, Criticism 1730–1830* (Oxford, 1989), pp. 75–84.

[33] *Blackwood's Magazine* (January 1853), 105.

[34] Recalling the new King Henry's great speech about turning away his former self, Weintraub notes that this was just what the Victorian Prince failed to do, and that his biography of Edward is about 'his former self' (p. xiv).

[35] Weintraub, *The Importance of Being Edward*, p. 209.

[36] Samuel was the husband of the famous Mrs Beeton (née Isabella Mary Mayson), who died in 1865 at the age of twenty-eight, having bequeathed to posterity her phenomenally best-selling *Book of Household Management*.

[37] Nancy Spain, *Mrs Beeton and Her Husband* (London, 1948), p. 233.

[38] Weintraub, *The Importance of Being Edward*, pp. 251–2.

chilling speech about how the ills of contemporary England have all been caused by idleness, opulence and Jews, and what we all need is a damned good war. Most striking of all is the news at the end that the Queen has abdicated, leaving her son to a clinching identification with Shakespeare's King Henry and a close mimicking of his 'reformation' speech. As if.

One more Shakespearian reference before we leave the Prince. On his fiftieth birthday in 1891, *Punch* offered an obsequious testimony to the distance between this Prince of Wales and Wicked Uncle George. A cartoon and brief dramatic sketch depict the Prince visiting with Mr Punch the Old Boar's Head tavern. The Shade of Falstaff enters from behind the Arras and starts bantering with them. He's impressed. Punch seems to be his heir: 'If to be old and merry be a sin, then thou, PUNCH, art but a latter-day JACK thyself'. The Prince gives his seal of approval: 'Bating the grossness, and retaining the humour without the humours, thy comparison is not so wholly unapt, Sir JOHN'. How times have changed, and Princes with the times, old Falstaff exclaims: 'No marvel i' faith, that heirs-apparent are so improved, when such a Momus and Mentor in one as PUNCH supersedeth such a Silenus-Mercury as poor old tun-bellied, pottle-pot-loving, though loyal, jocund and jape-enjoying JACK FALSTAFF!' And so on, with unction. The cartoon that heads this scene clinches the double identification of Falstaff not only with Punch but also with a Prince of Wales who is clearly Falstaff's upright, regal descendant. This is Falstaff Reformed: forget about Hal.

So by 1891 the threat has been rebuffed that this Prince of Wales would indeed follow Uncle George and plunge the monarchy back into the turbulent Regency past. Britain had seen some spasms of republican fervour, especially around 1870 with the violent turmoil across the Channel. But by the end of Victoria's reign the British monarchy was morphing into a new kind of 'show' to which the Prince of Wales's frankly hedonistic life made a powerful contribution. A Hal who turns into a Falstaff? Well let him, why not? For the laws of England are *not* under his commandment. They are not his business. The business of monarchy is now simply to represent some collective ideas of wealth and prestige, their pleasures and their pains, even or especially if around 1901, it meant looking fat and being known as Edward the Caresser.

Let me turn now briefly to Rosalind's legs – and the Forest of Arden. The Victorians took a vast and varied interest in all Shakespeare's women and Rosalind was by no means their unchallenged favourite. Anna Jameson includes her as the last and in some ways the least of her four 'Characters of Intellect', after Portia, Isabella and Beatrice.[39] Fanny Kemble called Portia her 'favouritest of all Shakespeare's women',[40] and amongst women readers from 1830 to 1900 Portia would probably have topped the poll, as she did quite literally in 1887 when the *Girl's Own Paper* ran a contest among its readers for essays on 'My Favourite Heroine from Shakespeare'.[41] But in width of appeal to readers and theatre-goers both male and female throughout the period, and to creative writers and artists in its later decades, so I'd hazard, Rosalind emerges as the most vital, complex and inspiring female figure, Juliet's comic counterpart – and Falstaff's successor.

Why? Because Rosalind offers a new dream of liberty. In terms of performance the role poses a challenge comparable to that posed by Falstaff, in that it seems to require and certainly invites a physical exuberance, a showiness, a zest for effect. Thus Hackett's Falstaff, and also at much the same time, Louisa Nisbett's Rosalind at Drury Lane in 1842, admired for her 'exhilarating animal spirits',[42] in the tradition of the saucy lackey and romping hoyden popularized by Dora Jordan. One of Nisbett's best roles was Lady Gay Spanker in Boucicault's

---

[39] Anna Jameson, *Characteristics of Women, Moral, Poetical, and Historical*, 2 vols., 4th edn (London, 1846), 1, pp. 143–54.

[40] Frances Anne Kemble, *Records of a Girlhood*, quoted in Julie Hankey, 'Victorian Portias: Shakespeare's Borderline Heroine', *Shakespeare Quarterly*, 45.4 (Winter 1994), 435.

[41] Tricia Lootens, *Lost Saints: Silence, Gender, and Victorian Literary Canonization* (Charlottesville and London, 1996), p. 104.

[42] Westland Marston, *Our Recent Actors* (1890), quoted in Donald Mullin, *Victorian Actors and Actresses in Review* (Westport, Conn. and London, 1983), p. 356.

IT was the eve of the New Year, the Year of Grace 1892, and Mr. PUNCH, musing deeply upon the manifold duties opening upon him with his opening Volume, nodded over his cigar, drowsed, and dreamed a dream of the Old Days and of the New, "in visionary vagueness strangely blent." The substance of that suggestive Vision he thus dramatically sets forth :—

SCENE—*Eastcheap. A Room in the Boar's Head Tavern.*   *Enter Prince* ALBERT EDWARD *and Mr.* PUNCH.

Prince. After you, Mr. PUNCH!

Punch. Though you be but Prince of WALES, yet are you the King of Courtesy!

Prince. Well quoted, i' faith! Verily this shadowy precinct smacks of antiquity, and suggesteth Shakspearian tags.

18   Punch, the Prince, and the Ghost of Falstaff (26 December 1891).

London Assurance. But in 1842 Nisbett epitomized an old Regency spirit that was no longer to everyone's taste. When she fell ill Macready replaced her with Helen Faucit, who offered a new kind of inwardness – pensive, modest, sensitive – something closer to the Rosalind a reader might imagine in private.[43] It became her signature role. Whereas the Falstaff imagined by Maginn was barely compatible with performance, the Rosalind provided by Faucit

43 See Charles H. Shattuck's note on 'Two Rosalinds' in *Mr Macready produces 'As You Like It': A Prompt-Book Study* (Urbana, Ill., 1962), pp. 54–7. Shattuck writes: 'The fact was that the character of Rosalind was just at this point passing through the final stage of metamorphosis from an eighteenth-century hoyden, a comic breeches part, into the sentimental 'womanly woman' so cherished throughout Victorian times. One might pinpoint the transition as occurring in this very season and production . . .' (p. 54).

could hold together the rival demands for 'show' and for 'inwardness'. An 1845 reviewer of her Rosalind uses terms that decisively distinguish her from that coarse old extrovert Regency past: 'This softness and delicacy we never saw more beautifully represented ... the caprice of the part never more ethereally embodied'.[44] 'Ethereally' is the key word, one that no Falstaff will ever attract (except perhaps through music). Faucit became a good friend of George Eliot's, and when she retired from the stage she committed to print her images of the Shakespearian women she had played – Rosalind, Portia, Juliet, Imogen and others.[45]

But Faucit was not happy about showing her legs, and she argued with Macready over the costume he wanted her to wear for Imogen. Other Victorian actresses had much less compunction, especially towards the end of the century. The flamboyant Ada Rehan for example, who realized 'as no other actress can', said one reviewer in 1890, 'the humour of Rosalind, the bubbling, effervescing frolic and fun'.[46] In fact one is struck by the sheer diversity of successful Rosalinds on both sides of the Atlantic, from Faucit and Nisbett and Ellen Tree and Charlotte Cushman to the Mary Scott-Siddons who provoked from the young Thomas Hardy in 1867 his poem 'To an Impersonator of Rosalind', to Madge Kendal, Helena Modjeska, Mary Anderson, Ada Rehan (who also excited Hardy in the 1890s), Julia Marlowe and Julia Neilson.[47] And let us not forget the Lillie Langtry who made Rosalind her favourite role when she took to the stage in 1882 after her affair with – the Prince of Wales.

His big belly and her lovely legs: Falstaff and Rosalind. In the theatre Rosalind shares with Falstaff a tension between 'physique' and 'wit', the outward, fleshed, spectacular show, and the spirit, the *esprit* that keeps winning through it. As Falstaff's belly is the sign of his corporeality, so are Rosalind/Ganymede's legs of his or hers. Both Falstaff's body and Rosalind's are a mystery – what is your substance, whereof are you made? – but Rosalind's is crescent and Falstaff's senescent. Falstaff's wit seeks in vain to resist or deny the degeneration of his body, while Rosalind's generates

new uses for hers. Where Falstaff's belly is a sign of unbridled appetite, Rosalind's legs are a sign of sexual independence, of indeterminacy, of performativity, of promise.

For theatre-goers and readers alike from the 1870s onwards Rosalind embodied the best of dreams. In 1885 W. E. Henley waxed lyrical about the heroine of George Meredith's *Diana of the Crossways*. It was of Rosalind she most reminded him: 'For such a union as she presents of capacity of heart and capacity of brain, of generous nature and fine intelligence, of natural womanhood and more than womanly wit and apprehensiveness, we know not where to look save among Shakspeare's ladies, nor with whom to equal her save the genius of Arden'.[48] A casual phrase, that last, but the space of which Rosalind is the 'genius' is an essential part of her allure. The period in which the play has sustained a special ascendancy in the British theatre can be dated fairly precisely to the forty years from 1871 to 1911.[49] Joseph Knight was excited by the Haymarket production of 1876 to this rapturous vision of Rosalind's domain:

Nowhere else in literature are the real and the Arcadian so harmoniously united. That enchanted ground of Arden is at once fairyland and home. Its denizens are influenced by passions such as our own. They yield to joys and sorrows with which we sympathise, and are, in all respects, our counterparts. Yet the world is one in which the baser part of our nature falls off or is purified ... The world is

---

44 *Athenaeum* (8 November, 1845), quoted in Mullin, *Victorian Actors*, p. 182.

45 Helen Faucit, *On Some of Shakespeare's Female Characters* (London, 1885). More generally, see Carol Jones Carlisle, *Helen Faucit: Fire and Ice on the Victorian Stage* (London, 2000).

46 A. B. Walkley, quoted in Mullin, *Victorian Actors*, p. 377.

47 See Patty S. Derrick, 'Rosalind and the Nineteenth-Century Woman: Four Stage Interpretations', *Theatre Survey*, 26.1 (May 1985), 143–62.

48 *Meredith: The Critical Heritage*, ed. Ioan Williams (London, 1971), p. 259.

49 I am indebted to Richard Foulkes, 'Touchstone for the Time: Victorians in the Forest of Arden', in *Victorian Shakespeare: Theatre, Drama, Performance*, eds. Gail Marshall and Adrian Poole (Basingstoke, forthcoming).

Love's world, and Love is lord of all. In the presence of that great potentate, prince and peasant are equal.[50]

Few peasants are likely to have been in the audience for Lady Archibald Campbell's celebrated *al fresco* production at Coombe House in 1884 (and again, 1885).[51] But who would not wish to be a 'denizen' of such a realm, where all differences are magically resolved? No wonder Shaw hated the play.

Both fairyland and home. The differences between the Victorian Falstaff and the Victorian Rosalind can be focused in the contrast between the forests of Windsor and Arden, between Herne's Oak and the Greenwood tree. One is the site of old Falstaff's shame, the other of young Rosalind's game. As the century progressed the 'greenwood' or 'wildwood' became an increasingly attractive and complex image for artists of all kinds. Not that it is a simple space, any more than it is in Shakespeare's own play (or plays – the wood of *A Midsummer Night's Dream* as well, of course). Think of the way George Eliot lures Gwendolen Harleth into imagining herself as Rosalind, and then punishes her narcissistic fantasy.[52] Think of the way the greenwood is shadowed by darker woods and more fatal trees in Thomas Hardy's fiction.

Or compare Tennyson and Wilde in the 1890s. In Tennyson's late play *The Foresters* (written 1881, published and performed 1892) Shakespeare's wild woods support a staging of the Robin Hood story infused with all sorts of fantasies of loss, Englishness and patriarchy restored.[53] There is some curious cross-dressing: Robin Hood disguises himself as an Old Woman to escape from Prince John, and Maid Marian dresses up as her brother in the armour of the Redcross Knight. She is also crowned Queen of the Wood. Ada Rehan told the author that she felt the 'beauty and simplicity and sweetness' of the role, 'which makes me feel for the time a happier and a better woman'.[54] But she must have had far more fun as Rosalind/Ganymede. *The Foresters* belongs very firmly to the men, to Robin himself (who turns into Prospero in his farewell speech to the woods),[55] and to the returning King Richard (who at one point bursts in on the scene like the famished Orlando). The closing song begins: 'Now the King is home again, and nevermore to roam again, . . . '.

These are not exactly the fantasies explored by Oscar Wilde, whose enthusiastic review of the Coombe House production recalled the transvestite performance in Théophile Gautier's 1835 novel *Mademoiselle de Maupin*.[56] Rosalind is one of the several identities with which Wilde's own Dorian Gray falls in love. Or is it the costume?

---

[50] Joseph Knight, *Theatrical Notes* (London, 1893), pp. 95–6, cited by Foulkes.

[51] Lady Archibald played Orlando to Eleanor Calhoun's Rosalind; the production was directed by E. W. Godwin. See John Stokes, *Resistible Theatres: Enterprise and Experiment in the Late Nineteenth Century* (London, 1972), pp. 47–50. Foulkes points out that Lady Campbell's inspired many subsequent outdoor productions.

[52] *Daniel Deronda* (1876), vol. 1, bk 2, ch. 14.

[53] The play is sub-titled 'Robin Hood and Maid Marian'. Tennyson said that as in his other plays he had 'sketched the state of the people in another great transition period in the making of England' (*Alfred Lord Tennyson: A Memoir by His Son*, 2 vols. (London, 1897), vol. 2, p. 173).

[54] Quoted in *The Letters of Alfred Lord Tennyson*, vol. 3 (Oxford, 1990), p. 441.

[55] Thus Robin Hood:

> Our forest games are ended, our free life,
> And we must hence to the King's court. I trust
> We shall return to the wood. Meanwhile, farewell
> Old friends, old patriarch oaks. A thousand winters
> Will strip you bare as death, a thousand summers
> Robe you life-green again. *You* seem, as it were,
> Immortal, and we mortal. How few Junes
> Will heat our pulses quicker! How few frosts
> Will chill the hearts that beat for Robin Hood!

Marian responds with this more optimistic note:

> And yet I think these oaks at dawn and even,
> Or in the balmy breathings of the night,
> Will whisper evermore of Robin Hood.
> We leave but happy memories to the forest.
> We dealt in the wild justice of the woods.

(*The Works of Tennyson*, ed. Hallam, Lord Tennyson (London, 1913), p. 840)

[56] Wilde's review is in the *Dramatic Review* (6 June 1885); see John Stokes, '"Shopping in Byzantium": Oscar Wilde as Shakespeare Critic', forthcoming in *Victorian Shakespeare*, eds. Marshall and Poole.

When she came on in her boy's clothes she was perfectly wonderful. She wore a moss-coloured velvet jerkin with cinnamon sleeves, slim brown cross-gartered hose, a dainty little green cap with a hawk's feather caught in a jewel, and a hooded cloak lined with dull red. She had never seemed to me more exquisite.[57]

More dangerously, in 'The Portrait of Mr W. H.' Erskine confides in the narrator that Cyril Graham 'was the only perfect Rosalind I have ever seen'.[58] Nina Auerbach suggests that 'for England's homosexual elite', the bold cross-dressing heroine became 'a symbol of visionary liberties their own country forbade'.[59]

As for princes, finally, and the dream of liberty. No one dreams of being Hal, but Hal is not Shakespeare's only prince, thank God. There's a Danish one, and there's one in effect in the Forest of Arden. If you have to be a prince, or want to be a prince, then Rosalind/Ganymede might be the one to go for. At least that's the blithe view of it. I said that Falstaff's liberty belonged to the past and Rosalind's to the future. But depending where we stand we can look forward to the Falstaff we might still become and we can look back to the Rosalind we'll now never be. Let's look back with regret then at two late-Victorian Rosalinds that might have been. As you contemplate Lord Ronald Gower's Shakespeare Monument in the Memorial Gardens in Stratford-upon-Avon, it strikes you that Lady Macbeth, Falstaff and Hamlet could do with another figure of youthful promise to complete their dysfunctional family quartet. It seems a pity that for his aspiring prince Gower chose a boyish Hal rather than an androgynous Rosalind.[60] Secondly: Ellen Terry counted it one of the great disappointments of her life that Irving never let her loose in the Forest of Arden. In her old age she confessed that she went on studying Rosalind, 'rather wistfully'.[61] What a shame that she never got to show off her legs and her wit in the role she was made for – and make *everyone* rub their knees with gusto.

---

[57] Oscar Wilde, *The Picture of Dorian Gray* (1891), in *Collins Complete Works of Oscar Wilde*, Centenary Edition, ed. Merlin Holland (Glasgow, 1999), p. 65.

[58] *Collins Complete Works*, p. 305. First published in *Blackwood's* in 1889, the tale was expanded by Wilde into a longer version that was not printed until 1923. I am indebted to a forthcoming paper by Russell Jackson, 'Oscar Wilde and Shakespeare's Secrets'.

[59] Nina Auerbach, *Ellen Terry: Player in Her Time* (London, 1987), p. 232. Did anyone think of comparing Wilde and Bosie to Falstaff and Hal – the young man's father, the Marquess of Queensberry, for instance? I note the relevance of Robert Sawyer's discussion of Swinburne's interest in the relations between Falstaff and Hal in his unpublished PhD dissertation, 'Mid-Victorian Appropriations of Shakespeare: George Eliot, A. C. Swinburne, and Robert Browning' (University of Georgia, 1997), in the abstract of which he writes: 'Chapter three examines A. C. Swinburne's Shakespearean criticism, arguing that Swinburne's critique anticipates by one hundred years the recent homoerotic reading of *1 Henry 4*; at the same time that masculine identities were being refashioned in England, Swinburne's criticism opens a space for a re-examination of the relationship between Falstaff and Hal. Thus Swinburne escalates the queering of Shakespeare, a significant contribution that is overlooked in the recent discussion of emerging notions of masculinity in the Victorian period'.

[60] Some have thought Gower the model for Lord Henry Wotton in *The Picture of Dorian Gray*. This is uncertain, but Wilde certainly delivered the eulogy at the unveiling of the Stratford monument (originally sited behind the Memorial Theatre) in 1888. See M. Kimberley, *Lord Ronald Gower's Monument to Shakespeare*, Stratford-upon-Avon Papers, III (Stratford-upon-Avon, 1989).

[61] See Auerbach, *Ellen Terry*, pp. 230–7.

THE SIXTH ACT: SHAKESPEARE AFTER JOYCE

MAUD ELLMANN

In Oscar Wilde's *The Picture of Dorian Gray*, Sir Henry Wotton complains that women never let go of their old love affairs. At a recent dinner-party he was dismayed when one of his ex-lovers tried to drag out a romance that he had wisely buried in a bed of asphodel. Although she insisted he had spoiled her life, Wotton observed that she ate an enormous dinner, so he did not feel any anxiety. 'But women never know when the curtain has fallen', he declares.

They always want a sixth act, and as soon as the interest of the play is entirely over they propose to continue it. If they were allowed their own way, every comedy would have a tragic ending, and every tragedy would culminate in a farce. They are charmingly artificial, but they have no sense of art.[1]

As usual in Wilde, this criticism against women is really a compliment in disguise – for no one could be more addicted to sixth acts than the charmingly artificial Oscar. *De Profundis* is one of the longest postscripts ever written to a played-out love affair, and it makes a devastating tragic ending to what should have been a bedroom farce. Similarly, Wilde's story 'The Portrait of Mr W. H.' adds a sixth act to Shakespeare's love-life, outing the Bard after the curtain has fallen on his sexuality. Like *Dorian Gray*, 'The Portrait of Mr W. H.' is a story about three men and a picture, in which one friend after another falls for the contagious theory that the *Sonnets* were dedicated to one Willie Hughes, supposedly a fetching boy-actor at the Globe. The sixth act of this comedy ended in tragedy at the Old Bailey when Edward Carson cross-examined

Wilde. 'I believe you have written an article to show that Shakespeare's sonnets were suggestive of unnatural vice', he barked. 'On the contrary I have written an article to show that they are not. I objected to such a perversion being put upon Shakespeare'. When Carson proposed that the 'affection and love of the artist of Dorian Gray might lead an ordinary individual to believe that it might have a certain tendency', Wilde replied that he had 'no knowledge of the views of ordinary individuals'. 'Have you ever adored a young man madly?' Carson demanded. 'I have never given adoration to anybody except myself', Wilde declared. Thoroughly defeated in Shakespearian expertise, Carson changed the subject to rent boys, and Wilde's brilliant stand-up comedy routine was brutally transformed into a passion play.[2]

Basil Hallward, the painter of Dorian Gray, makes the famous observation that 'every portrait that is painted with feeling is a portrait of the artist, not of the sitter'.[3] This phrase 'a portrait of the artist' provided Joyce with the title of his first completed novel. His second novel, *Ulysses*, paints an updated portrait of the artist, but also offers an alternative sixth act to *Hamlet*, the play that Stephen Dedalus interprets as a portrait of the artist Shakespeare. Nora Barnacle Joyce once said of her husband's anxiety of influence: 'Ah, there's only one man he's got to get the better of now, and

---

[1] Oscar Wilde, *The Picture of Dorian Gray* (1881; London, 2000), p. 99.
[2] See Richard Ellmann, *Oscar Wilde* (London, 1987), pp. 421–2.
[3] Oscar Wilde, *Dorian Gray*, p. 9.

that's that Shakespeare!'[4] Both *Ulysses* and *Finnegans Wake* try to get the better of Shakespeare, and especially to out-Hamlet Hamlet by composing extra comic acts to Shakespeare's masterpiece. In Stephen's theory of *Hamlet*, expounded in the 'Scylla and Charybdis' episode of *Ulysses*, Joyce transforms Shakespeare's Danish tragedy into an Irish farce, a treacherous act of 'scandinavery', as he puts it in *Finnegans Wake*.[5] By domesticating 'Patrick W. Shakespeare', Joyce found himself unwillingly in league with Freud, who brings the tragic themes of incest and revenge in *Hamlet* down with a bump into the bourgeois family.[6]

This essay is about the sixth acts that Joyce wrote to Shakespeare – the hardest act to follow. But I'd like to linger for a moment on Wilde's idea that the sixth act changes tragedy into comedy, and comedy into tragedy. Does this imply that the categories are reversible? Comedy was the theme of the International Shakespeare Conference of 2002, but it was striking that the first paper to be offered was on *Hamlet*. The next paper (to quote its author's email) was 'on those well-known comedies *Romeo and Juliet* and *Titus Andronicus*'. The third was on *Othello*. Does this mean we critics are in league with Henry Wotton's women, determined to add sixth acts to Shakespeare's plays that turn the tragedies into comedies? Would we need to hold a conference on tragedy in order to solicit papers on comedy? If Wotton's women have no sense of art, they do show a keen sense of the permeability of academic categories. In my view, the sixth act is the countertendency built into the preceding five, the comedy implicit in the tragedy, the tragedy implicit in the comedy.

In Edmund Burke's *A Philosophical Enquiry into the Origin of our Ideas of the Sublime and Beautiful*, there is a telling moment when he hints that the comic is the flipside of the tragic. Obscurity, Burke argues, is essential to the terrible, for objects grow in the dark, but shrink in the clear light of day. 'A clear idea is . . . another name for a little idea', he contends. The sublimity of the *Book of Job* depends upon the 'terrible uncertainty of the thing described'; yet even the clearest painting of the torments of Hell makes Burke wonder if the artist

actually intended something ludicrous – one thinks of Bosch's funny little monsters gobbling bouquets of body-parts.[7] Similarly tragic drama is always haunted by the possibility of a carnivalesque reversal of the solemn into the absurd. The psychoanalytic writer André Green has argued that drama is the art of 'the misheard and the misunderstood'.[8] Whether such misunderstanding leads to comedy or tragedy often hinges on the minor details rather than the major themes: Romeo and Juliet are victims of bad timing, Desdemona of a mislaid handkerchief. In contrast to Greek tragedy, where downfall is determined from the outset, Shakespearian tragedy relies on elements of accident and error more readily associated with the art of farce. Hamlet, with his bumbling and clowning, behaves like a character from farce who has blundered onto the wrong stage, unleashing comic mayhem into the inexorably plotted universe of tragedy. Richard Curtis' parody 'The Skinhead *Hamlet*' brings out the slapstick humour already implicit in the play, especially in scenes such as the accidental murder of Polonius – 'Fuck! I thought it was that other wanker', Hamlet curses – or the drinking of the poisoned chalice: 'Fucking odd wine!'[9]

On the other hand, romantic comedy also has its tragic side. What E. M. Forster described as the 'idiotic use of marriage as a finale' has much the

4 As recalled by Frank Budgen, according to Clive Hart in *Structure and Motif in 'Finnegans Wake'* (Evanston, Ill., 1962), p. 163.
5 James Joyce, *Finnegans Wake* (1939; London, 1964), p. 47, line 21. Henceforth cited as *FW*, followed by page and line numbers.
6 James Joyce, *Ulysses* (1922; Harmondsworth, 1986), ch. 12 ('Cyclops'), p. 244, lines 190–1. Henceforth cited as *U*, followed by chapter and line numbers.
7 Edmund Burke, '*A Philosophical Enquiry into our Ideas of the Sublime and the Beautiful' and Other Pre-Revolutionary Writings*, ed. David Womersley (London, 1988), p. 106.
8 André Green, 'Prologue: The Psychoanalytic Reading of Tragedy', Prologue to *The Tragic Effect: The Oedipus Complex in Tragedy*, trans. Alan Sheridan (Cambridge, 1979), rpt. in Maud Ellmann, ed., *Psychoanalytic Literary Criticism* (London, 1994), p. 41.
9 Richard Curtis, 'The Skinhead Hamlet: Shakespeare's play translated into modern English', in *The Faber Book of Parodies*, ed. Simon Brett (London, 1984), pp. 318, 320.

same effect in comedy as the use of death in tragedy, which is arguably idiotic too.[10] Both the romantic and the tragic endings show that love and death, or Eros and Thanatos, are not the opposites they seem, but alternative versions of the will to closure. If sexual union were the object of romantic comedy, the show would be over in five minutes. What sustains the play is distraction from attraction: distraction releases what attraction binds. Distraction is not unique to comedy, however, but also plays a crucial part in Shakespeare's tragedies. In an obvious sense the comic subplots in the tragedies provide a distraction from impending doom – the gravedigger in *Hamlet* turns death itself into a distraction, a ghoulish entertainment for the groundling in us all. But there are also stranger moments of distraction, such as the ending of *King Lear*, when everyone's attention is momentarily distracted from Cordelia and her wildly distracted father.

'Distraction' – a term I borrow from Christopher Pye's brilliant new work on Shakespearian drama – has many meanings, some of which I've just deployed.[11] The term derives from the Latin 'distrahere', which means to pull asunder, and therefore represents the countermovement of attraction, which derives from 'attrahere', meaning to drag or draw in. In common usage, a distraction is an entertainment, usually of a lightweight and light-hearted kind. To create a distraction is to divert attention from the scene of action, to lure the viewer into focusing on the gratuitous. Distraction means absentmindedness, but to be driven to distraction is to lose one's mind entirely – distraction is a synonym for madness or hysterico passio. This is the sense in which the term is used most frequently in Shakespeare – in Hamlet's 'distracted globe', for instance – although 'distracted' can also mean 'distraught', without the imputation of insanity.[12]

In *Alice in Wonderland* the Mock Turtle recommends distraction as a key ingredient of a well-rounded education, which should include 'Reeling and Writhing, of course, to begin with . . . and then the different branches of Arithmetic: Ambition, Distraction, Uglification, and Derision'.[13] (This speech gave Joyce one of his favourite recipes for the concoctions in *Finnegans Wake*.) Adorno, on the other hand, condemns distraction or 'deconcentration' as a pernicious side-effect of modern mass culture. 'Deconcentration is the perceptual activity which prepares the way for the forgetting and sudden recognition of mass music'. Listeners who can no longer 'stand the strain of concentrated listening . . . surrender themselves resignedly to what befalls them, with which they can come to terms only if they do not listen to it too closely'.[14]

Adorno's disapproval of distraction resembles T. S. Eliot's condemnation of the 'twittering world' of modernity: a world of 'Tumid apathy with no concentration . . .' in which people are 'Distracted from distraction by distraction'.[15] Yet Eliot himself (whom Joyce nicknamed 'the Bishop of Hippo') was also well aware of the pay-offs of distraction, both in poetry and in religious faith.[16] Eliot's famous proposition that 'genuine poetry can communicate before it is understood' implies a distracted reader, whose intellect remains on stand-by while image and sonority pervade the mind.[17] Distraction also furnishes the necessary precondition for a state of grace – 'the distraction fit, lost in a shaft of sunlight'. Revelation never comes to those who concentrate. 'Wait without hope', 'wait without love', 'wait without thought', Eliot counsels, for hope and love and thought always focus on the

---

[10] E. M. Forster, *Aspects of the Novel* (1927; Harmondsworth, 1970), p. 45.

[11] Christopher Pye's previous works include *The Regal Phantasm: Shakespeare and the Politics of Spectacle* (London, 1990) and *The Vanishing: Shakespeare, the Subject, and Early Modern Culture* (Durham, NC, 2000).

[12] *Hamlet*, ed. Cyrus Hoy (New York, 1963), I. v. 97.

[13] Lewis Carroll, *Alice in Wonderland*, ch. 9, in *The Annotated Alice*, ed. Martin Gardner (London, 2001), p. 102.

[14] Theodor W. Adorno, 'On the Fetish Character in Music and the Regression of Listening', in *The Culture Industry: Selected Essays on Mass Culture*, ed. J. M. Bernstein (London, 1991), p. 43.

[15] Eliot, *Burnt Norton* (1935), part III, in *Four Quartets, Collected Poems 1909–1962* (London, 1963), pp. 192–3.

[16] See Richard Ellmann, *James Joyce* (1959; New York, 1982), p. 495.

[17] Eliot, *Dante* (1929), in *Selected Essays* (London, 1951), p. 238.

wrong things.[18] We must stop focusing in order to receive the blessing from beyond. In a paradox typical of Eliot, distraction is both the curse of modern life and the source of its redemption – God comes only to those with Attention Deficit Disorder.

The greatest evangelist for distraction among modern critics is Walter Benjamin. In his famous essay 'The Work of Art in the Age of Mechanical Reproduction', Benjamin takes issue with the 'ancient lament that the masses seek distraction whereas art demands concentration from the spectator'. He points out that 'a man who concentrates before a work of art is absorbed by it', whereas 'the distracted mass absorbs the work of art'.[19] In contrast to Adorno, who deplores distraction as a form of bondage, Benjamin perceives it as a form of mastery, arguing that the 'distracted mass' actively consumes the image, whereas the concentrating connoisseur is passively consumed *by* it. Distraction therefore frees the masses from the tyranny of the artwork, shattering its aura or cult status, and by implication empowers them to overthrow the mental tyranny of capitalism.

Whatever we think of this Brechtian voodoo, whereby changes in perception of the artwork have the power to overcome false consciousness, Benjamin goes on to offer some provocative ideas about distraction, particularly in relation to the movies. He writes:

Reception in a state of distraction, which is increasing noticeably in all fields of art and is symptomatic of profound changes in apperception, finds in the film its true means of exercise. The film with its shock effect meets this mode of reception halfway. The film makes the cult value recede into the background not only by putting the public in the position of the critic, but also by the fact that at the movies this position requires no attention. The public is an examiner, but an absent-minded one.[20]

This to my mind is a more enticing description of distraction, in that it suspends the question of mastery – an obsessive question in aesthetic theory from Burke onwards – by placing neither the spectator nor the film in the position of control. The film does not command the full attention of the audience, yet on the other hand the audience does not command the film, but cultivates what Wordsworth called 'wise passiveness'. Benjamin's notion of distraction corresponds to Roland Barthes's conception of the reading process, which he describes as a form of 'drifting', a suspension of the triumphant, heroic, muscular type of pleasure, even a kind of stupidity: 'I am not necessarily *captivated* by the text... [reading] can be an act that is slight, complex, tenuous, almost scatterbrained...'.[21] Thus distraction, which Adorno sees as dumbing-down, is reconceived by Benjamin and Barthes as an enlightening stupidity.

Barthes's notion of scatterbrained reading is tailor-made for Joyce's stream-of-consciousness technique, in which the reader drifts through Bloom's distractions, fishing the odd recognition out of the flux. Adorno's objection to distraction is that it diverts attention from the whole; the same could be said of Bloom's interior monologue, which can only be absorbed *in bits* – an obsolete meaning of distraction, by the way, is scattering, dispersion. Bloom is arguably 'the most absent-minded character in world literature', as Franco Moretti has observed, and the effect of this distraction is to open possibilities.[22] What makes us happy when we read Bloom's monologue, despite its undercurrent of pain, is the sense it conveys of the 'actuality of the possible as possible' (*U* 2:77). The constant bombardment of the senses, far from dulling the mind or producing what Georg Simmel called a 'blasé attitude', awakens Bloom's imagination and resourcefulness, transforming him into the

[18] Eliot, *The Dry Salvages* (1941), part V, *East Coker* (1940), part III, in *Four Quartets*, pp. 213, 200–1.

[19] Walter Benjamin, 'The Work of Art in the Age of Mechanical Reproduction', in *Illuminations*, ed. Hannah Arendt, trans. Harry Zorn (London, 1999), p. 232.

[20] Benjamin, 'The Work of Art', pp. 233–4.

[21] William Wordsworth, 'Expostulation and Reply'; Roland Barthes, *The Pleasure of the Text* (1973), trans. Richard Miller (Oxford, 1975).

[22] Franco Moretti, *Modern Epic: The World System from Goethe to García Márquez*, trans. Quintin Hoare (London, 1996), p. 137.

wily Odysseus of city life.[23] Thus Bloom's distraction is a way 'to avoid being overwhelmed by the big world that is concentrated in the big city'.[24]

This resistance to bigness is also a resistance to tragedy, for comedy celebrates the little guy who just keeps going. Joyce argued that comedy is more 'perfect' than tragedy in that it makes for joy where tragedy makes for sorrow, the sense of 'possession' in the one being superior to the sense of 'privation' in the other.[25] Slavoj Žižek makes a similar point in psychoanalytic terms. He argues that tragedy and comedy both rely on 'the gap between the impossible Thing and an object, part of our reality, elevated to the dignity of the Thing, functioning as its stand-in'. If this is so, then comedy distracts our attention from the big Thing, awesome and unattainable, and diverts us to the little thingummies that keep us going. In the graveyard scene in *Hamlet*, for example, the gravedigger distracts us from the Big Death by playing with the little death embodied in a grinning skull. Žižek goes on to say:

It is not enough, however, to claim that comedy mobilizes the gap between the Thing and the ridiculous object occupying its place; the crucial feature is, rather, that both comedy and tragedy involve kinds of immortality, albeit opposed. In the tragic predicament, the hero forfeits his earthly life for the Thing, so that his very defeat is his triumph, conferring sublime dignity upon him, while comedy is the triumph of indestructible life – not sublime life, but opportunistic, common, vulgar earthly life itself . . . the stuff of comedy is this repetitive, resourceful popping-up of life – whatever the catastrophe, no matter how dark the predicament, we can be sure in advance that the little fellow will find a way out.

For this reason Žižek proposes that the ultimate comic scene is the fake death.[26] There are a number of tragedies that contradict this view, most notably *Romeo and Juliet*, but it is clear that Joyce realized the comic potential of the fake death in *Finnegans Wake*, its title borrowed from a vaudeville song in which the corpse of Tim Finnegan rises from its coffin, revived by a shot of whiskey, and joins in the general merriment: 'Lots of fun at Finnegan's Wake', goes the chorus. And fun is the purpose of Joyce's 'funferall' (*FW* 13: 15, 111: 15). When asked about the layers of meaning to be explored

in *Finnegans Wake*, Joyce said, 'No, no, it's meant to make you laugh'. 'I am only an Irish clown, a great joker at the universe'. 'In risu veritas', he improved on the old adage.[27]

Finnegans Wake could be seen as the sixth act that adds a comic encore to the tragic death, for the hero of the *Wake* is always dying and reviving, just as an actor fakes his death night after night, only to rise again with the next curtain-call. The *Wake* also resists death by defying closure through the use of puns: here the infinite possibilities of Bloom's monologue are packed up into the portmanteau or verbal suitcase. Open up the portmanteau and meanings scatter or 'distract' themselves like mischief from Pandora's box. Of course, one could argue that the puns in *Finnegans Wake* resist closure to the point of total opacity – for Joyce as for Shakespeare, the pun was the fatal Cleopatra for which he lost the world, and was content to lose it. When a critic complained that it was trivial to write a book in puns, Joyce replied that some of the puns were trivial, but others were 'quadrivial'.[28]

In different ways, both *Ulysses* and *Finnegans Wake* distract us from closure and from tragedy. They also create a distraction from Shakespeare, a decoy that diverts our gaze from the literary father to the son. Yet to overthrow the father Joyce elicits the ruses of distraction already built into Shakespeare's works: the puns, the diversions, the deliria. Throughout his work Joyce attempts to 'shakespill' his precursor, to 'Shakhisbeard' and overcome his 'Shikespower', by using the same

[23] Georg Simmel, 'The Metropolis and Mental Life', in *The Sociology of Georg Simmel*, trans. Kurt H. Wolff (Glencoe, Illinois, 1950), pp. 413–14.

[24] Moretti, *Modern Epic*, p. 137.

[25] James Joyce, Paris Notebook (1903), in *The Critical Writings of James Joyce*, ed. Ellsworth Mason and Richard Ellmann (New York, 1959), p. 144; see also Richard Ellmann, *James Joyce*, p. 120.

[26] Slavoj Žižek, *Did Somebody Say Totalitarianism? Five Interventions in the (Mis)use of a Notion* (London, 2001), pp. 81–5.

[27] Richard Ellmann, *James Joyce*, p. 703.

[28] Eugene Jolas, 'My Friend James Joyce', in *James Joyce: Two Decades of Criticism*, ed. Seon Given (New York, 1948), p. 24.

methods as the 'Great Shapesphere'.[29] Stephen Dedalus' famous disquisition in the National Library, where 'he proves by algebra that Hamlet's grandson is Shakespeare's grandfather and that he himself is the ghost of his own father', deploys a number of distractions (U 1: 555–7). First Stephen attempts to distract his audience from Shakespeare's work into his life, thus turning literary criticism into gossip, or unmasking the nosiness that drives interpretation. Then he distracts attention from the hero of the play on to the secondary figure of the father's ghost. If Shakespeare chose to play the Ghost at the Globe, he must have identified himself with the dead father rather than the living son. It follows that Ann Hathaway must have been the guilty queen. Senior to her husband by some years, Ann must have overborne the young Will Shakespeare in a cornfield: hence the magnificent pun, 'If others have their will Ann hath a way' (U 9: 256–7). Later she betrayed her husband by committing adultery with his two brothers, Edmund and Richard, the names of two of the worst villains in the Shakespeare canon. Stephen has no explanation for Iago, however, a significant omission that returns to haunt him in the Circe episode. Meanwhile Shakespeare also made the mistake of sending Mr W. H. to act as go-between with the Dark Lady, but the young rogue ran off with her himself. At this point Shakespeare's rage against wife, mistress and boyfriend commingled in a whirlpool and generated the fury of the tragedies. If the late comedies breathe a spirit of reconciliation, it is because of the birth of a granddaughter, immortalized in the redemptive figures of young girls such as Miranda and Perdita.

Stephen knows his theory is preposterous and admits he doesn't believe in it himself, although he also asks the Lord to *help* his unbelief – but then again he doesn't believe in the Lord either. Nonetheless his theory adds a sixth act to *Hamlet* that turns the tragedy into 'a French triangle' or a bedroom farce (U 9: 1064–78). At another point in the same chapter Stephen ponders the question of debt, and although his immediate concern is with financial debt, he is equally preoccupied with his literary debts to Shakespeare. Remembering

the pound he owes AE, the mystic codename of George Russell, Stephen thinks: 'Wait. Five months. Molecules all change. I am other I now. Other I got pound'. Nonetheless he also knows that 'I am I by memory': despite the molecular decomposition of the body, a thread of memory connects the I that borrowed to the I that owes. Such continuity is rather an expensive luxury: 'A E I O U', Stephen concludes (U 9: 205–13).

By acknowledging this financial IOU, Stephen implicitly acknowledges his literary borrowings, especially those that he has scrounged from Shakespeare. This is more explicit in another passage about molecules, where Stephen says:

As we, or mother Dana, weave and unweave our own bodies...from day to day, their molecules shuttled to and fro, so does the artist weave and unweave his image. And as the mole on my right breast is where it was when I was born, though all my body has been woven of new stuff time after time, so through the ghost of the unquiet father the image of the unliving son looks forth.

(U 9: 376–81)

This passage bristles with literary thefts, particularly from the famous Conclusion of Pater's *Renaissance*, but the clue to Shakespeare is the mole. The mole on Stephen's right breast refers to Imogen's 'cinque-spotted' breast in *Cymbeline* (2.2.38), as well as to Hamlet's speech about the 'vicious mole of nature' in the soul. Most importantly, however, it alludes to the ghost of Hamlet's father, the 'old mole' under the floorboards of the stage, the ghost who cries, 'Remember me' – a cry that reverberates through Joyce's work, ultimately gender-bending into the 'mememormee' or mammary memory of *Finnegans Wake*, with its echo of Dido's terrible lament 'Remember me' in Purcell's *Dido and Aeneas*.[30]

The image of the unliving son is Hamnet, the son of Shakespeare's body, who died at Stratford, according to Stephen, so that his namesake Hamlet might live forever. But this potential son is also Joyce himself, already looking forth through

[29] FW 161: 31; 177: 32; 47: 19; 295: 4.
[30] U 9: 474; Hamlet 1.4.24; 1.5.170, 91; FW 628: 14.

Shakespeare's eyes. Joyce attempts to overcome the mole, forget the father, by shuttling the molecules of Shakespeare's work; but as Stephen says, 'That mole is the last to go': the mark or 'penmark' of Shakespeare constantly reprints itself in Joyce, particularly in his reincarnations of the Prince of Denmark.[31] Shakespeare is the mole of debt that cannot be obliterated by the molecules of change. So it's clear that Joyce had no choice but to obey the literary father's dread command, 'Remember me'. He remembered him all right, though he dismembered him as well.

A case in point occurs in the 'Circe' episode, where distraction crescendos into madness. Even Joyce was driven to distraction by this chapter as its 'dreadful performance' grew ever 'wilder and worse and more involved' until he complained, 'Circe has turned me too into an animal'.[32] At one point in the whirlwind of hallucinations, Bloom and Stephen look into a mirror where instead of discovering their own reflections, they find themselves confronted with the face of Shakespeare. The vision appears when Stephen's friend Lynch says, 'The mirror up to nature', echoing Hamlet's instructions to the players – an abracadabra that serves to conjure up the master-spirit of the theatre.

LYNCH (*points*) The mirror up to nature. (*he laughs*) Hu hu hu hu hu! (*Stephen and Bloom gaze in the mirror. The face of William Shakespeare, beardless, appears there, rigid in facial paralysis, crowned by the reflection of the reindeer antlered hat rack in the hall.*)

SHAKESPEARE (*in dignified ventriloquy*) 'Tis the loud laugh bespeaks the vacant mind. (*to Bloom*) Thou thoughtest as how thou wastest invisible. Gaze. (*he crows with a black capon's laugh*) Iagogo! How my Oldfellow chokit his Thursdaymornun. Iagogogo! [....] (*with paralytic rage*) Weda seca whokilla farst.

(*U* 15: 3819–53)

This Shakespeare is the beardless boy ravished in a cornfield by Ann Hathaway, who later gave him cuckold's horns, here represented by the antlered hatrack. Because Othello also thinks himself a cuckold, we find his molecules shuttling to and fro with those of Hamlet in this passage. 'How my Oldfellow chokit his Thursdaymornun' is 'how my Othello choked his Desdemona', but Othello here becomes the murderous father, rather than the husband, choking his son Joyce, who was born on a Thursday morning, or his son Stephen, also born on a Thursday and therefore doomed to exile – for Thursday's child has far to gogogo, as Joyce echoes the old nursery-rhyme. Another possible reading is that Joyce himself is the murderous oldfellow who chokes all the creatures that he brought into existence on the morning of Thursday 16 June 1904 – the morning of *Ulysses*.

Shakespeare's rigidity suggests erection, which seems to contradict the innuendoes of castration in the passage, except that Shakespeare lost his sexual confidence when he was ravished by an older woman in a cornfield: 'he will never be a victor in his own eyes after or play victoriously in the game of laugh and lie down . . . No later undoing will undo the first undoing' (*U* 9: 457–9). Overcome by Ann Hathaway regardless of his 'will' or volition, his 'will' or desire was precociously aroused, and young Will Shakespeare was emasculated by his own potency. He avenged himself in his 'last will intesticle', in which he left his wife his 'secondbest bed' – a phrase that echoes through *Ulysses*, and may even be encrypted in that garbled line from *Hamlet*: 'Weda seca whokilla farst' – that is, 'None wed the second but who killed the first'.[33] This pun on farce and first also reappears in *Finnegans Wake*, as in the 'farced epistol to the hibruws' (*FW* 228: 33–4), suggesting that the very notion of a first is farcical: everything is secondhand, belated, plagiarized. While Marx said that history repeats itself, the first time as tragedy, the second as farce, Joyce suggests that all writing is rewriting, the old tragedies 'farced' into new comedies.[34]

[31] *U* 9: 391; *FW* 606: 26; 301: fn5; 421: 18.

[32] *Selected Letters of James Joyce*, ed. Richard Ellmann (New York, 1975), p. 271; *Letters of James Joyce*, vol. 1, ed. Stuart Gilbert (1957; New York, 1965), p. 146.

[33] *FW* 413: 17; *Hamlet* 3.2.164.

[34] Karl Marx, *The Eighteenth Brumaire* (1852), in Terry Eagleton and Drew Milne, eds., *Marxist Literary Theory: A Reader* (Oxford, 1996), p. 35.

'Rigid in facial paralysis', Shakespeare's stiffness offers an amusing contrast to the notion of mobility suggested by 'Iagogo' and 'Iagogogo'. This is the laugh of the eunuch or 'black capon', but it also refers to the one great Shakespearian villain left out of Stephen's theory – Iago. Has Iago escaped or gone a-gogo by eluding the snares of psychobiographical criticism? Or, given that Iago is the Spanish form of James, is it the author who is saying I'm a-going? Is he going into exile or going to the toilet in baby-talk: I-agogogo...? Who knows? What interests me, however, is that Joyce associates Iago with mobility, because it's true that without Iago the story of Othello would have no go in it. Iago is the principle of distraction or interference that gets things going, unbinds paralysis, unleashes narrative. He's the go-go-go-between who distracts attention from the leading players, while distracting the attraction that binds them to each other. A jokester turned demon, he represents the agency through which the tragedy could have turned into a farce, and *Othello* could have ended up like *Così Fan Tutte*. Instead Iago stage-manages a sixth act in which the romantic comedy of marriage is transformed into a tragedy of errors. The French term for interference on the telephone line, '*parasitage*', encapsulates the role of Iago and that of other panders, go-betweens, and middlemen in Shakespeare's work: those parasites who depend upon the principals yet also interfere with the teleology of plot, creating a distraction from the central drama. Both male and female, both comic and tragic, the parasite deconstructs dualities, whether of gender or of genre. In this sense the parasite represents the sixth act built into the preceding five, the dangerous supplement that overturns the distinction between tragedy and comedy.

Perhaps the reason why Joyce identifies himself with Iago/James in the mirror-scene – *I-agogo* – is that he sees himself as a parasite on Shakespeare's work, interfering with the transmission of the master's word. In *Finnegans Wake*, this interference takes the form of a stammer or 'hasitatense', reminiscent of Shakespeare's stammer in 'Circe' – 'Iagogogo' (*FW* 296: fn4). It is Humphrey Chimpden Earwicker, the guilty father of *Finnegans Wake*,

who suffers from this speech-impediment, which represents the telltale trace or 'wake' of his original sin in Phoenix Park. His 'hasitatense' harks back to Hamlet's hesitancy, his inability to act on time, or to sense the tense pressure of what Joyce called the 'pressant' tense (*FW* 221: 17). What is the time to act? Hamlet asks himself again and again. Has it a tense? Joyce's puns on hesitancy also refer to the famous letter forged by Lester Piggott in which Charles Stuart Parnell ordered the Phoenix Park murders of 6 May 1882, when two high-ranking English ministers were stabbed to death by the Invincibles. It was the misspelling of the word 'hesitency' [sic] that led to the exposure of the forgery.

Joyce boasts about his own forgeries throughout *Finnegans Wake*, describing his double Shem the Penman as a forger and plagiarist, 'covetous of his neighbour's word', and especially covetous of 'shaggspick's' promiscuous words (*FW* 172: 30; 177: 32). Jim the Penman was an Irish forger – Joyce called himself Jim the Punman – and Shakespeare was also famously accused of plagiarizing other playwrights in order to create the 'only shake-scene in a country'.[35] According to Shem's jealous brother Shaun the Postman, Shem the Penman is a low-down sponger who won't get a job. 'His jymes is out of job, would sit and write': the time is out of joint, and James would rather sit and write than set it right (*FW* 181: 29–30). His workshop of filthy creation has 'soundconducting walls', so that he can eavesdrop on other people's speech, and it is 'persianly literatured' with 'quashed quotatoes' and 'messes of mottage' (*FW* 183: 9–10, 22–3). Like Hamlet, he's got an 'eatupus complex', indulging in incestuous cunnilinguistics underneath the 'squirtscreen' of his octopus-ink; and he also eats too much, bulimically devouring and regurgitating other people's words (*FW* 128: 36, 186: 7).

35 *The Letters of James Joyce*, ed. Richard Ellmann, vol. 3 (New York, 1966), p. 157; see also Adaline Glasheen, *Third Census of 'Finnegans Wake'* (Berkeley, 1977), p. 145; Robert Greene's *Groatsworth of Wit*, cited by Vincent Cheng in *Shakespeare and Joyce: A Study of Finnegans Wake* (Gerrards Cross, 1984), p. 92.

Shakespeare is what Shem eats for breakfast. As Vincent Cheng has pointed out, the *Wake* is full of puns on Shakespeare and breakfast: hamlet and eggs, 'secondbest buns', and 'homelettes' – that is, little men, hamlets and omelettes.[36] (Jacques Lacan adopts the 'hommelette' as his model of the human subject: an eggy mess whose boundaries can only be solidified within the frying-pan of the Symbolic Order.) Often the breakfast menu involves a choice between shakespill and bacon – that is, Francis Bacon, contender for the authorship of Shakespeare's plays, and his demented champion Delia Bacon (no relation). There's also a Viconian recipe for scrambled eggs: 'eggburst, eggblend, eggburial, and hatch-as-hatch can' (*FW* 614: 32–3). After pigging out on 'shakespill and eggs', Shem shits his shakefest out again throughout the long night of *Finnegans Wake*, when he writes with his own excrement on 'the only foolscap available', his own body (*FW* 161: 31, 185: 35–6). But Shem also aspires to out-Shakespeare Shakespeare: 'he would wipe alley english spooker, multiphoniaksically spuking, off the face of the erse' (*FW* 178: 6–7). He would wipe any English speaker, any of the spooks of the English literary tradition, even the one who played the spook in *Hamlet*, off the face of the earth, or the Irish arse, with a multiphonic, multivoiced spuke – speech, puke and spunk – a spuke all of his own.

In conclusion, Joyce parasites Shakespeare in order to create a distraction from the masterwork, a sixth act that turns Shakespearian drama upside-down and bottom up, the face of tragedy reversed into the erse of comedy. Among other things, *Finnegans Wake* is Bottom's dream, a dream of bottoms written by the bottom, a Rabelaisian fantasia of bottoms-up. As a parasite, Joyce's role is to unbind the constipation of the masterwork – Iagogogo! – in order to unleash its infinite jest.

---

[36] *FW* 586: 18; 59: 31; 121: 32. See also Cheng's discussion of 'Shakespearean Breakfasts' in *Shakespeare and Joyce*, pp. 101–6.

THE RETURN OF PROSPERO'S WIFE: MOTHER FIGURES IN *THE TEMPEST*'S AFTERLIFE

SARAH ANNES BROWN

Fresh as a rose in spring. And laid out in my coffin. He had built it himself, my husband. Yes, he did. Always had a gift for shaping things. Couldn't have been a more stylish coffin in the country. Handle bars in silver, and the lining of silk from end to end. He'd prepare my body himself; white veil and the lace nightgown in black. Wouldn't have any other shade but black. Transparent, so that I showed all through. God, how frightened I would be sometimes. The way he watched over me; watched over his corpse. After he had made me ready for burial, he would wait by his coffin, and watch over me. The only pleasure he would have of me.[1]

The Tempest has exerted a consistently strong influence on readers and audiences. Plays once well known and admired, such as *King John* and *Henry VIII*, are now seldom performed, whereas others, such as *Titus Andronicus*, were little appreciated until the twentieth century. But *The Tempest*'s high status within the corpus has never seriously been questioned, and this prominence is reflected in the large body of creative works – novels, poems, plays and films – where its influence is strongly felt. If we trace the play's creative afterlife it soon becomes clear that critics' recent preoccupation with issues of race, sexuality and gender have long been anticipated. In particular the play's two absent mothers – Sycorax and Prospero's wife – can be identified as surprisingly potent presences, not simply in recent novels such as Marina Warner's *Indigo* and Gloria Naylor's *Mama Day*, but in two of the very first creative responses to the play, Jonson's *The New Inn* and Fletcher's *The Sea Voyage*. This paper is an attempt to chart the complex fortunes of *The Tempest*'s mother figures from the play's contemporary reception to the present day.

In an influential essay[2] Stephen Orgel discusses Miranda's mother's near absence from *The Tempest*, recalled only to reassure Miranda of her legitimacy. Orgel goes on to suggest that Sycorax can be read as a kind of surrogate for Prospero's dead wife, an idea that may be illuminated by Luce Irigaray's account of attitudes towards maternity in western culture. In 'The Bodily Encounter with the Mother' she counters Freud's oedipal version of the family romance, identifying a contrasting impulse towards symbolic matricide:

The murder of the mother results, then, in ... the burial of the madness of women – and the burial of women in madness – and the advent of the image of the virgin goddess, born of the father and obedient to his law in forsaking the mother.[3]

Irigaray's observations are consistent with Janet Adelman's analysis of mother figures in Shakespeare's late plays: 'in the plays of paternal recovery, the mother must be demonized and banished before the father's authority can be restored'.[4] According to Adelman's reading of the play (and

---

[1] George Lamming, *Water with Berries* (Trinidad, 1973). The speaker is the wife of the novel's 'Prospero'.
[2] Stephen Orgel, 'Prospero's Wife', *Representations*, 8 (1984), 1–13.
[3] *The Irigaray Reader*, ed. Margaret Whitford (Oxford, 1991), pp. 37–8.
[4] Janet Adelman, *Suffocating Mothers: Fantasies of Maternal Origin in Shakespeare's Plays, Hamlet to The Tempest* (New York, 1992), p. 193.

Irigaray's model of family relationships) Prospero's wife *becomes* Sycorax on some level; the demonized mother figure is inserted into the textual gap left by the dead wife. Many of the texts discussed below play with this hidden connection between the virtuous and invisible Mrs Prospero and the demonic virago Sycorax; the parallel may be used to re-empower *The Tempest*'s women or to reaffirm the need for matricide and the occlusion of all women except Miranda, the 'virgin goddess' of Irigaray's model who, as Stephen Orgel reminds us, is symbolically reborn of the father.[5]

> Under my burden groaned; which raised in me
> An undergoing stomach, to bear up
> Against what should ensue.
>
> (1.2.156–8)

In one of the very earliest responses to *The Tempest* the metamorphosis of Mrs Prospero into Sycorax is unexpectedly reversed.[6] Ben Jonson's *The New Inn* has traditionally been viewed as one of Jonson's failed late works, his 'dotages'.[7] Its hero Goodstock, really the disguised Lord Frampul, lives in exile as landlord of the New Inn; Prospero-like, he watches the antics of his customers as though they were but his puppets:[8]

> and if I have got
> A seat to sit at ease here, i'mine inn,
> To see the comedy . . .
>
> (1.4.131–3)[9]

We learn that he has been estranged from his wife for many years, apparently because of his anger at her inability to bear him sons. She deserted him, taking with her their younger daughter, Letitia. Lord Frampul in turn abandoned his remaining daughter Frances, leaving her in an unusually independent position – she is a single woman of property, Lady Frampul in her own right in the absence of either parents or husband.

It is through the apparently marginal character of an old Irish nurse that the transformation of Sycorax back into Prospero's wife is effected. The host may think he knows more than any other character but in fact it is the nurse who holds the key to the play's final mysteries. She affects to belong to

a despised colonized race (the Irish, whose stereotypical presentation has been associated by Vaughan and Vaughan with the character of Caliban[10]), and Frampul treats her with contempt – 'she's a wild Irish born, sir, and a hybrid' (2.6.26); she came to the inn as a beggarwoman encumbered with a son, Frank, whom Frampul bought from her and raised as his own. This 'son' turns out to be Frampul's missing younger daughter, and the nurse none other than his estranged wife. Miranda's shadowy dead mother has been reinvented as a survivor, determined to secure her children's happiness. By reversing the original model whereby Prospero's wife became subsumed by Sycorax and thus demonized, *The New Inn* dramatically overturns the original's matricidal urge. The metamorphosis from Nurse to Lady Frampul takes place before our eyes, and could be read as a sign of the play's refusal to demonize the mother.

She is not the only character whose presentation subverts the family dynamic of *Tempest*. The young Lady Frampul, Frances, has been brought up independently of her parents in the pride of rank and riches. She has not, Miranda-like, shared her father's exile, but has instead learned self-reliance. In that she can be capricious and wilful she is perhaps criticized by the text, yet our overwhelming impression is of a young woman who is both attractive and powerful, no dutiful, dependent daughter but

---

[5] The play's lack of women is also discussed by Ann Thompson in 'Miranda, Where's Your Sister: Reading Shakespeare's *The Tempest*' in *Shakespeare: The Tempest: New Casebooks*, ed. R. S. White (1999) pp. 155–66.

[6] The connections between *The New Inn* and Shakespeare's late plays have been widely acknowledged. See for example Anne Barton, *Ben Jonson, Dramatist* (Cambridge, 1984) p. 281.

[7] A recent discussion of the play by Richard Harp is included in the *Cambridge Companion to Ben Jonson*, eds. Richard Harp and Stanley Stewart (Cambridge, 2000), pp. 93–6.

[8] A recent analysis of the connections between Prospero and Lord Frampul is offered by John Lee in 'On Reading *The Tempest* Autobiographically: Ben Jonson's *The New Inn*', *Shakespeare Studies (Japan)*, 34 (1996), 1–26.

[9] Ben Jonson, *The New Inn*, ed. Michael Hattaway (Manchester, 1984).

[10] Alden T. Vaughan and Virginia Mason Vaughan, *Shakespeare's Caliban: A Cultural History* (Cambridge, 1991), pp. 141–2.

a woman who is in charge of her destiny. She is in fact a Prospero as much as a Miranda figure, and inherits Frampul's sense of life as theatre. When Pru her maid objects to her passing an old dress on to the players Lady Frampul answers: 'Tut, all are players and but serve the scene' (2.1.39).

Like Prospero she uses others to orchestrate her pageant, exalting Pru to a mistress of ceremonies whom all must obey. Pru decrees that her mistress should favour her admirer Lovell, but only for two hours. Here, as in *The Tempest*, the slipperiness of the boundary between theatre and reality is foregrounded. To love for two hours signifies, in theatrical terms, a love that will last until the curtain drops, and thus forever. This ambiguity colours the 'court of love' over which Pru presides. Lady Frampul appears to be swayed by Lovel's discourse but Pru's commentary – 'Excellent actor, how she hits this passion!' – suggests dissimulation (3.2.209). (Yet, even if Lady Frampul is 'sincere' Pru's words are true if applied to the boy who represents her.)[11]

But as well as allowing Jonson to indulge his fondness for moments of metadrama, this inset play directed by Pru acts as a potent counter to Prospero's own direction of the 'fair encounter of two most rare affections' between Miranda and Ferdinand.[12] He too utters a gleeful aside, delighted that the affair is progressing according to his script:

> It goes on, I see
> As my soul prompts it. (*To Ariel*). Spirit, fine spirit,
> I'll free thee
> Within two days for this.
>
> (1.2.423–5)

Pru, by contrast, is delighted by Frances's skill, by her ability to act. Whether acting or in earnest Frances, unlike Miranda, is not being manipulated by any force within the play. Even Pru's direction, because she is a subordinate female friend, has little power over her. Taking the roles of both Prospero and Miranda, Frances's autonomy in love matches her unusual and significant status as 'femme sole'.[13]

In a slightly later dramatic response to *The Tempest*, Fletcher's *The Sea Voyage*, the mother figure

is more strikingly re-empowered.[14] The plot is motivated by two separate shipwrecks. The first, which seems to have taken place some ten years before the action begins, separated Sebastian and his nephew Nicusa from the women of their party. Although all the survivors inhabit the same island when the play begins, the men's and women's domains are mutually inaccessible and neither party knows of the other's survival. The second shipwreck brings to (the male) shore Albert, an attractive pirate, together with his kidnapped love, the chaste Aminta, as well as an assortment of male friends and followers.

Most of the negative elements to be found in *The Tempest*'s *dramatis personae* – ambition, savagery, avarice – seem to be coded as masculine on Fletcher's island (although lust afflicts both sexes pretty equally). This is signalled through Fletcher's starkly concrete interpretation of the tantalizing indeterminacy of Prospero's island. In *The Tempest* the island seems fertile or barren according to the deserts of each castaway. Fletcher's island is more essentially split into two halves, one completely desolate where a stray rat constitutes a feast, the other fruitful and pleasant. The two surviving males of the wreck malinger on the barren side of the island whereas their female companions have been marooned quite separately on the fertile side. Neither Sebastian nor Nicusa seems particularly deserving of such a dismal exile, yet if we read this play refracted through *The Tempest* some shadow of the wicked nobles' dissatisfaction with the island

---

[11] Harriet Hawkins observes that 'throughout *The New Inn* Jonson coaches the audience to consider plot and character in terms of theatrical practices, in relation to conventions which produce dramatic illusion', 'The Idea of a Theater in Jonson's *The New Inn*', *Renaissance Drama*, 9 (1966), 205–26, p. 206.

[12] William Shakespeare, *The Tempest* (Oxford, 1998), 3.1.74–5. All subsequent references are to this edition.

[13] Her legal position is discussed by Helen Ostovich in 'Women's Friendship in *The New Inn*', *The Ben Jonson Journal*, 4 (1997), 1–26.

[14] A useful account of the play, and its debt to Shakespeare, is included in Gordon McMullan's *The Politics of Unease in the Plays of John Fletcher* (Amherst, 1994), pp. 235–54.

may affect our perception of them, and thus perhaps of men as a whole in Fletcher's play. The association of Sebastian and Nicusa with negative forces from *The Tempest* is reinforced when we see them through the eyes of the sea's more recent victims:

TIBALT   I have heard of sea-calves.
ALBERT   They are no shadows sure, they have
        legs and arms . . .
AMINTA   Are they men's faces?
TIBALT   They have horse-tails growing to 'em,
        Goodly long manes.

(1.3.95–9)[15]

The castaways' grotesque, non-human appearance recalls both Caliban's own beastly exterior and the monstrous creatures of whom Gonzalo has heard tell (3.3.46–7).

The masculine half of the island continues to bring out the worst in its inhabitants; the new victims start to quarrel over a hoard of treasure, allowing Sebastian and Nicusa to steal their (still seaworthy) boat and make a getaway. Aminta, the only female among the newly shipwrecked, tries to make peace and is later nearly eaten by the starving sailors for her pains. (This descent into cannibalism recalls *The Tempest*'s Caliban by association even though there is no suggestion in the play that he lives up to his name.) McMullan suggests that the sailors' behaviour parodies or critiques travel writers who made cannibalism the preserve of those 'savage' non-Europeans with whom dramas of sea voyage were more usually concerned.[16] But within the context of the play's treatment of the sexes cannibalism can be seen as another sign of male fallibility. Certainly the play's men seem more quarrelsome than the women, and less able to form a happy social order away from society's conventions. For the women, though by no means perfect, have formed a workable Amazonian society, safe if sterile:

this place yields
Not fauns nor satyrs, or more lustful men.
Here we live secure,

And have among ourselves a commonwealth
Which in ourselves begun, with us must end.

(2.2.14–18)

Clarinda, daughter of the island's 'governess' Rosellia, the play's Prospero figure, forms part of a tradition of virgin innocence displayed for the amusement of male spectators from Dryden to *Forbidden Planet*. But the effect of an interdict on male companionship is modified when it derives from a female parent. When Rosellia discovers Clarinda embracing the handsome pirate Albert she exclaims, 'unhand this monster'. When Prospero similarly deprecates the appearance of Ferdinand we interpret his desire to mislead Miranda rather differently (*Tempest* 2.1.482–4). His apparent attempt to make his daughter think Ferdinand ugly can be read as a move to protect her innocence, or simply as a device to prolong the courtship and enflame their mutual love, but similar expressions from Rosellia seem more unequivocally hostile towards men. As Prospero is a man, we do not interpret his animadversions on Ferdinand as a slander on his own sex. And when he prescribes chastity we trace his anxiety to the conditions of a patriarchal society where a man's honour lay in his wife's keeping. (Although perhaps facetious, Prospero's only reference to Miranda's mother in the play articulates male anxiety about inheritance and legitimacy.) But Rosellia aligns the qualities she hopes for from her daughter with those she aspires to herself:

Child of my flesh
And not of my fair unspotted mind . . .

(2.2.182–3)

Because she is a woman her strictures against men allow her to appeal to a shared experience of female suffering:

Have I not taught thee
The falsehood and the perjuries of men?
On whom but for a woman to show pity
Is to be cruel to herself. The sovereignty

---

[15] *Three Renaissance Travel Plays*, ed. Anthony Parr (Manchester, 1995).
[16] McMullan, *The Politics of Unease*, pp. 151–2.

Proud and imperious men usurp upon us
We confer on ourselves, and love those fetters
We fasten to our freedoms.

(2.2.186–92)

Rosellia is refreshingly unconcerned about Clarinda's virgin knot; far from fetishizing chastity she seems to see it as an incidental contingency of independent life for women, and indeed later gives permission for all her ladies (including her daughter) to cohabit with the shipwrecked sailors for a month, retaining any female issue.

Although a light-hearted play which ends with the breaking up of the Amazonian colony and Rosellia's reunion with her husband, *The Sea Voyage*'s subversive undercurrents are undeniably present, still more strikingly so if we read the play through *The Tempest*.[17] The location of Sebastian and Nicusa, for example, is less likely to be ascribed to mere chance by the reader who remembers that all Shakespeare's undeserving lords *perceived* Prospero's island to be similarly unwelcoming. The improbability of two adjacent pieces of land being so very different might contribute to the impression that Fletcher's seascape, like Shakespeare's, is in some sense a mindscape as well. Similarly a reader of *The Tempest*, able to trace clear links between Rosellia and Prospero, might recall how the latter had been responsible for the shipwreck and wonder whether Rosellia is in any sense responsible for her husband's fate. Fletcher's presentation of her as the devoted wife of a loving husband is somehow at odds with her passionate embrace of Amazonian society and her warning to Clarinda with its searing attack on male treachery. Here, at least temporarily, the daughter's alliance is with her mother rather than her father. Adrienne Rich writes: 'Revision – the act of looking back, of seeing with fresh eyes, of entering an old text from a new critical direction – is for women more than a chapter in cultural history: it is an act of survival'. As far as *The Tempest*'s own *Nachleben* goes it would seem that the first steps towards such a 're-vision' were taken by men.[18] Although both texts discussed so far feature strong female characters it is the way they appear to enter into a dialogue with *The Tempest* which

makes them amenable to subversively feminist readings. Interpretive indicators are hidden in the gap between each later play and *The Tempest*, and the plays' treatment of women, particularly mothers, is modified for readers and spectators who recognize the Shakespearian presence in *The New Inn* and *The Sea Voyage*.

In two later works which owe similar debts to *The Tempest*, *The Magic Flute* and Mary Shelley's *Lodore*, opposing ideological positions on maternity are dramatized more overtly. Each text could be said to deceive the reader, *The Magic Flute* by presenting us with a 'Prospero's wife' who is transformed into Sycorax, *Lodore* by first championing the eponymous Prospero-like hero, before shifting his power and moral authority to his initially shadowy female relatives. In both works a young girl is taken from her mother by a father (or in Sarastro's case a father figure); whereas Shelley encourages the reader to become increasingly doubtful about the father's custody rights, *The Magic Flute* promotes this apparently cruel action as an absolute necessity.

The similarities between *The Magic Flute* and *The Tempest* have long been noted: among their many shared motifs are a barbarous servant who tries to rape the heroine and a hero who must undergo trials to prove his worth.[19] Yet again the mother figure has been reinstated in a pivotal role. Although she is not Sarastro's wife, there is a symbolic marital link between them because Sarastro inherited quasi-paternal responsibility for Pamina after her father's death. At first, *The Magic Flute* appears to champion the Queen of the Night as a wronged mother, desperate for Prince Tamino to rescue her daughter Pamina from the 'evil' Sarastro. (The librettist, Emanuel Schikaneder, was almost certainly influenced by *Lulu oder die Zauberflöte*, a tale pub-

---

17 The final note of unease is noted by McMullan, *The Politics of Unease*, p. 254.
18 Adrienne Rich, *On Lies, Secrets, and Silence: Selected Prose* (New York, 1979), p. 35.
19 The connection is discussed briefly by E. J. Dent in *Mozart's Operas: A Critical Study* (1913; rpt Oxford, 1991), p. 262.

lished in 1789, in which the mysterious fairy queen is a force for good.[20]) Yet when we finally encounter Sarastro he asserts the justice of his actions, and the remainder of the opera reinforces our sense of his virtue while demonizing the Queen of the Night. Her chaotic female magic is contrasted with masculine wisdom:

That evil woman vaunts her power; she thinks to dazzle and delude the people with her degraded superstitions, and utterly to destroy this our temple of Nature, Reason, and Wisdom.[21]

Irigaray's 'family romance' unfolds not, as in *The Tempest*, before the curtain opens, but in front of the audience's eyes. Yet we do not have to read *The Magic Flute* as simply a misogynist text. Even though Sarastro's version of events proves correct the opera is 'many voiced' in the Bakhtinian sense, and could be interpreted as a dramatization of the way male voices prevail in narrative.[22] Sycorax's voice has been swiftly silenced but not, as in *The Tempest*, omitted altogether. And if we see this as the triumph of a masculine over a feminine narrative, perhaps little traces remain of an outcome more favourable to the Queen. Tamino can only succeed in his trial by using the flute and bells she gave him at the opening of the opera.[23] It is also significant that Papageno allows Tamino to think it was he who slew the serpent – when in fact it was the Queen's three ladies. In this early episode the woman's version prevails and Papageno is silenced as a punishment for his deceit; perhaps we should take this as a hint that men do not always tell the truth.

Another character who problematizes a monolithic reading of the opera is the African Monostatos. At the end of the opera his alliance with the Queen of the Night seems to confirm her status as the evil 'Sycorax' of the story. Yet in Act I, as Sarastro's servant, he is only prevented from killing Pamina by the entrance of Papageno. And later it is the Queen of the Night, not Sarastro, who prevents Monostatos from raping her daughter. His position of power over her does not reflect well on his master's judgement. Again, it almost seems as though the opera is being wrenched away from its original

trajectory when Sarastro suddenly denounces the slave, and Monostatos defects to his master's mortal enemy.

The opera, like the texts discussed earlier, acquires an additional edge if we remember *The Tempest*. Tamino is 'right' to ignore Pamina while he undergoes his trials, but his rigid silence and obedience to the fatherly authority of Sarastro might be unfavourably contrasted with the less dutiful but more human Miranda who disobeys her father's wishes to comfort Ferdinand.[24] Fletcher and Jonson could be said to question *The Tempest* by reprising its central themes within a less patriarchal dramatic context. By invoking *The Tempest* within a more rigidly patriarchal framework *The Magic Flute*, it might be argued, questions itself.

Mary Shelley's *Lodore* could be read as a reversal of the pattern established in *The Magic Flute*.[25] This is one of her later works; it is less sensational

---

[20] This source is discussed by Robert Spaethling, 'Folklore and Enlightenment in the Libretto of Mozart's *Magic Flute*', *Eighteenth-Century Studies*, 9.1 (1975), 48–9.

[21] *The Magic Flute*, trans. Edward J. Dent (Cambridge, 1911), p. 28.

[22] A practical explanation has been offered for the libretto's apparent move from the Queen to Sarastro. It is sometimes claimed that Schikaneder had intended that the opera, like *Lulu*, should feature a good fairy and an evil enchanter, but changed his plot half way through because it would have been too close to a rival show, Joachim Perinet's *Der Fagottist, oder die Zauberzither*. See Spaethling, 'Folklore and Enlightenment in the Libretto of Mozart's *Magic Flute*', pp. 61–3; E. M. Batley, *A Preface to the Magic Flute* (London, 1969), pp. 114–6; Jane K. Brown, 'The Queen of the Night and the Crisis of Allegory in *The Magic Flute*', *Goethe Yearbook*, 8 (1996), 142–56; Brigid Brophy, *Mozart the Dramatist* (London, 1964), pp. 144–62.

[23] This oddness is pointed out by Spaethling: 'Why do flute and glockenspiel aid the lovers in their ordeals while those who gave the magic instruments, the Queen and her ladies are cast down in damnation?' 'Folklore and Enlightenment in the Libretto of Mozart's *Magic Flute*', pp. 45–67, pp. 47–8.

[24] This unattractive episode is noted by Brophy, *Mozart the Dramatist*, pp. 162–3.

[25] Recent discussions of this comparatively neglected novel include Richard Cronin's 'Mary Shelley and Edward Bulwer: *Lodore* as Hybrid Fiction', in *Mary Shelley's Fictions: From Frankenstein to Faulkner*, ed. Michael Eberle-Sinatra (Basingstoke, 2000), pp. 39–54.

than *Frankenstein*, and draws on her experiences of disrupted families. When we first meet him, the eponymous hero is set up as a modern Prospero, an exile alone with his daughter Ethel in the wilds of North America. But Lodore's motives are increasingly called into question, and both his moral authority and his Prospero role are usurped by his daughter, his sister and his estranged wife.

When the novel opens Lodore's exile is simply a mysterious given which allows his daughter to be brought up in rural simplicity. We infer that his long absence from home has some connection with his failed marriage, yet must wait many chapters before the mysteries of his early life are revealed. Although he has no special powers, Lodore possesses an aura of mystery and his comfortable home was built 'like magic'.[26] The circumstantial affinities between him and Prospero are further suggested by the epigraph to chapter 3, a quotation from the first act of *The Tempest*:

> MIRANDA   Alack, What trouble Was I then
> to you!
> PROSPERO   O, a cherubin
> Thou wast that did preserve me.
>
> (1.2.151–3)

The parallel is again made when Lodore asks Ethel whether she remembers their former life in England. Like Miranda, her memories are cloudy: '"It may be the memory of a dream that haunts me", she replied, "and not a reality; but I have frequently the image before me, of having been kissed and caressed by a beautiful lady, very richly dressed"' (80). The mother figure, missing from Miranda's memories, is here troublingly invoked; no explanation for her absence is offered by Lodore, though Ethel assumes she has died. Only later do we learn that, although Cornelia has been guilty of stubborn pride, Lodore is equally to blame for their separation.[27] It soon becomes apparent that Shelley feels some misgivings about Lodore's education of Ethel; he teaches her to place all her dependence on her father, rather than to think for herself: 'active in person, in mind she was too often indolent, and apt to think that while she was docile

to the injunctions of her parent, all her duties were fulfilled. She seldom thought, and never acted, for herself' (67).[28]

But although the novel may be characterized by a movement away from Lodore in favour of his estranged Lady, the characters are morally nuanced – Lodore has many attractive qualities and Cornelia's behaviour is flawed. Mary Shelley's ambivalence towards her characters is inscribed in the novel's many echoes of *The Tempest*. Although it could be argued that the novel opens with a male Prospero in charge and gradually shifts control to his wife, Shelley's attitude towards powerful women is more equivocal than such a summary would suggest.

The first female Prospero we learn of in the novel is Lodore's mother-in-law, Lady Santerre. Her name suggests her homeless, wandering state, deprived of home and income not by political machinations but by the inheritance laws of a patriarchal society. At thirty-four, Lodore is rather old to play Ferdinand, but the storm which introduces him to Cornelia, living in 'exile' with her mother in rural Wales, casts him in that role. But despite Cornelia's beauty, Lodore is not so easily enthralled as Ferdinand; we learn that he might never have proposed 'but that Lady Santerre was at hand to direct the machinery of the drama' (98). In her ability to control the young couple she is later referred to as a 'magician' (100). Because of her controlling role as sole parent the reader may already have aligned her with Lodore himself, and his later powerful influence over Ethel. This negative female Prospero, Lady Santerre, suggests an ideology similar to that of *The Magic Flute*; power in women's hands is

---

[26] Mary Shelley, *Lodore* (1835; rpt Ontario, 1997), p. 54.

[27] Sharon L. Jewell discusses the importance of mother/daughter relationships in the novel in 'Mary Shelley's Mothers: The Weak, The Absent, and The Silent in *Lodore* and *Faulkner*', *European Romantic Review*, 8.3 (1997), 298–322.

[28] The novel's emphasis on parenting is analysed by Charlene E. Bunnell in 'Breaking the Tie that Binds: Parents and Children in Romantic Fiction', in *Family Matters in the British and American Novel*, eds. Andrea O'Reilly Herrera, Elizabeth Mahn Nollen, Sheila Reitzel Foor (Bowling Green, Ohio, 1997), pp. 31–53.

almost certain to be misapplied – a benevolent father-in-law is one thing, an interfering mother-in-law quite another.[29] But Shelley reveals some ambivalence in her attitude towards gender and power; she deplores the influence of Lady Santerre, and particularly Cornelia's inability to benefit from her husband's manly guidance. Yet we have already been encouraged to perceive this guidance as itself flawed; he later fails to nurture Ethel's self-reliance and moral firmness.

The next female Prospero we encounter is Ethel herself. She first experiences such power when her admirer, Whitelock, made her feel 'like a magician holding for the first time a fairy wand' (75), and later her reciprocated passion for Villiers, her future husband, animated her 'with such a spirit as may be kindled within the bosom of an Enchantress, when she pronounces the spell which is to control the movements of the planetary orbs' (238). Such a comparison might recall Prospero's alter ego, Medea, and remind us of the 'feminine' ends achieved by the enchantress's magic: to capture and secure the love of a husband. If it seems odd that *Lodore*'s Miranda figure should usurp Prospero's role, we might remember how much more of a Medea Miranda is than Prospero, defying her father's interdicts in order to help her lover succeed in his tasks. Later Ethel is more explicitly aligned with Medea: 'she . . . felt indeed that Medea, with all her potent herbs, was less of a magician than she, in the power of infusing the sparkling spirit of life into one human frame' (295). In shifting Prospero's powers away from Lodore and onto his female relations, Shelley has also rendered those powers more feminine – Medea's necromancy has been transmuted into the ability of a loving woman to raise the spirits of her husband. But although an infinitely more positive 'female Prospero' than Lady Santerre there is nothing subversive or threatening about Ethel's role: this is Prospero as 'angel of the house'. Her mother will wear the father's mantle with more assertive authority.

Lady Lodore's survival distinguishes her from Prospero's shadowy wife. Rather than being a docile martyr to her maternal function, Cornelia is a more threatening type of absent mother. She feels little initial interest in Ethel, orders her to be removed when she makes a noise, and is happy to separate from her temporarily when she journeys to the country. Whereas Prospero is deprived of his male birthright, temporal power, Cornelia's female prerogatives of wife- and motherhood are taken from her. It is Ethel who makes the first tacit link between Cornelia and Prospero. She is sure that her mother is no 'Medea' (273). As *The Tempest* is an established subtext in the novel, any reference to the enchantress might recall Prospero's own use of the Ovidian Medea's incantations. This allusion again reflects the text's ambivalence toward women; we are invited to compare her with Medea while assured (through the reliable heroine) that to compare them would be slander.

A similar equivocation is suggested by the next pairing of her with Medea. Still distrustful of her character, Villiers sneers that 'she must be a Medea, in more senses than the obvious one' (372), when he reads that she has stirred his solicitor – Medea's rejuvenating power is suggested – to disentangle him from debt, not realizing that it is her own financial sacrifice which will accomplish his relief. But despite his sarcasm Lady Lodore is just such a positive Medea, giving new life to her desolate daughter. Medea's multiple significance – she is powerful, at times even benevolent, yet she murdered her own children – mirrors Shelley's uncertainties about the less dramatically unmaternal Lady Lodore.

As Cornelia grows in self-knowledge and maturity she is presented as a spiritual castaway, in exile in the heart of fashionable society:

The tide of life is ebbing fast! I had fancied that pearls and gold would have been left by the retiring waves; and I find only barren, lonely sands! No voice reaches me from across the waters – no one stands beside me on the shore! Would – O would I could lay my head on the spray-sprinkled beach, and sleep for ever! (355)

---

[29] Anne K. Mellor observes that she conforms to 'the sexist stereotype of the domineering and insensitive mother-in-law', *Mary Shelley: Her Life Her Fiction Her Monsters* (London, 1989), p. 190.

She both acknowledges and dismisses her husband's Prospero powers, asserting that 'a mightier storm than any he could raise has swept across me since, and laid all waste' (355). When she finally decides on a path of great self-sacrifice for the sake of her child, Cornelia seems to conquer the perplexities of Prospero's isle at the same time as she conquers her distaste for her son-in-law Villiers and her reluctance to cultivate her daughter; like Prospero, she has replaced bitterness with mercy: 'a new light shone on the tedious maze in which she had been lost; a light – and she blessed it – that showed her a pathway out of the tempest and confusion into serenity and peace' (369). Her flaws, like Prospero's magic powers, have been buried in the sea – Shelley quotes *Richard III*, but we might also think of Prospero's renunciation of his book when we learn that Cornelia's past errors are 'in the deep bosom of the ocean buried' (371). Her decision to return to the 'exile' of Wales, whence Lodore had taken her, parallels Lodore's earlier self-imposed exile in Illinois. Although both Lord and Lady Lodore are rather quixotic characters, her exile is undertaken for nobler purposes than his. Shelley is quick to remind us that her undramatic choice of retreat does not detract from her exile's bleak prospects: 'her state of banishment would be far more complete than if mountains and seas only constituted its barriers'(385).

The novel's final and most surprising Prospero is Lodore's elder sister, a retiring figure whose exile is described in the novel's opening chapter, for her residence is in a 'secluded nook' in 'the flattest and least agreeable part of the county of Essex' (49). She is amiable towards all except her sister-in-law, Cornelia, whom she views most unjustly as solely responsible for her marriage's breakdown. When Cornelia is drawn to her husband's childhood home and lodges in a cottage near Longfield, Mrs Fitzhenry is in the same position as Prospero, for her enemy has joined her exile. Her feelings for Cornelia are presented in extreme terms: 'Her violence might almost seem madness; but all people who live in solitude become to a certain degree insane' (427). But she

conquers the memory of her brother, a false or at least a faulty Prospero, and embraces the original Prospero's choice of mercy and forgiveness.

Critics have noted that the novel's title *Lodore* misleads the reader; when the 'eponymous' hero dies at the end of the first volume we realize that 'Lodore' signifies the whole family, not merely the husband.[30] Similarly the dynamic away from a masculine to a feminine presentation of Prospero can be read in quasi-feminist terms, a corrective to the ostensible message of *The Magic Flute* and indeed *The Tempest*. Yet there are limitations to this 're-vision' of *The Tempest*. Lady Lodore is increasingly invested with symbolic power and authority as the novel's principal female Prospero. Yet this authority must be bought at a price; Cornelia has to develop maternal tenderness, and display that most conventionally approved of feminine virtues, self sacrifice, before she inherits the mantle of her husband.

So far we have seen Prospero's supremacy challenged by avatars of his dead wife and by feminized versions of Prospero himself. But Sycorax's presence has been less potent, more negative: the Queen of the Night becomes more Sycoraxian (through her increasingly overt evil and her liaison with Monostatos) as her power declines, and the Irish Nurse casts off a Sycorax mask in order to take up her proper role as Lady Frampul. It might be countered that any feminine Prospero (such as Cornelia or Rosellia) is always in some sense a Sycorax because of the covert bond between the enchanter and the witch. (Both were exiled to the same island, both had a single child, both practised magic, both exploited the powers of Ariel.)[31] But the connection, if it is there, has not been exploited by any of the texts so far considered. Until comparatively recently, literary references to Sycorax were rare and almost uniformly negative. In Colley Cibber's 1709 play, *The Rival Fools*, an unattractive elderly woman is called a 'Sycorax' (2.1.150), and

---

[30] The title is discussed by Lisa Vargo in her introduction to the novel, p. 22.

[31] The link is discussed by, for example, Orgel, 'Prospero's Wife', p. 27.

James Brunton Stephens, in 'A Picaninny', refers to the mother of a pretty Aborigine child as 'that haggard Sycorax that bore thee'.[32]

However, modern writers have increasingly been drawn to the marginalized figure of Sycorax. A prominent recent example of her rehabilitation can be found in Marina Warner's retelling of the play in her novel, *Indigo*.[33] Here Sycorax is a native Carib inhabitant of a small island in the West Indies which is just beginning to be affected by the slave trade. Yet again the novel's message is strongest for readers who can identify it as a corrective re-vision of Shakespeare. Warner seeks to expose the limitations of a western colonial perspective by, as it were, revealing the true facts which lie at the heart of *The Tempest*'s warped retelling of events.

Sycorax mirrors Prospero's – and Medea's – feat of waking sleepers from their graves by digging up the body of a drowned African slave because a sudden intuition tells her a living baby has been buried with her. Here and elsewhere a motif from *The Tempest* is revived and transformed in order to reflect on the miseries caused by colonization and slavery; thus Warner's is a dialectical imitation of *The Tempest*, turning the play back upon itself to take issue with its (perceived) ideological bias. The drowned slaves themselves are the subject of a harshly parodic response to Ariel's 'full fathom five' song (1.2.400–8); the lovely, lapidary metamorphoses described by Ariel become the thoroughly demystified and natural metamorphoses of violent death:

Others had lost extremities, become shorn of nose and trimmed of fingers by nibbling fish, others were missing heads, arms and legs; one was a floating head on its own, with long curly hair, like a human octopus. (79)[34]

Warner makes a pointed comment on the long lived evils of the slave trade by referring to the corpses as the sea's 'strange fruit' (80), an echo from Billie Holiday's song describing another century's racial outrages.

The rescue of Dulé, the drowned slave's child, complements Ariel's evocation of beauty salvageable even from death, yet also works against *The Tem-* *pest*, for this boy, her foster son, will be enslaved by the white settlers and called Caliban. But before the colonists arrive Dulé is joined in the household by another exile, an Indian girl from the mainland, Ariel. Far from being Sycorax's prisoner, Ariel is dearer to her than her natural children (105). The 'cloven pine' in which Shakespeare's Ariel was confined is here transformed into a sanctuary, Sycorax's own tree house, raised to avoid predators (1.2.279).

Sycorax is as protective of Ariel as Prospero is of Miranda, resenting her liaison with Everard, just as Prospero feared his daughter's 'dalliance' with Ferdinand (4.1.51). As in *The Sea Voyage* the shared sex of parent and child modifies the meaning of this protectiveness. Sycorax has no objection to her adoptive daughter enjoying sex with her own kind, but is horrified that she has been chosen by Everard, one of a group of white men who injured her, deforming her into the hoop described in *The Tempest* (1.2.260). (This deformity, perceived as a visible sign of her evil in Shakespeare, here becomes a badge of oppression.) Prospero's threat that 'barren hate' (4.1.19) will separate the lovers if they give way to lust becomes an actual curse in *Indigo* on her foster daughter's miscegenous offspring:

The child in your belly isn't a human child. I've changed him – your son, I know it is a son. For it will be a whelp you carry, a small, red-furred beast with sharp teeth and

---

[32] James Brunton Stephens, *The Poetical Works* (Sydney, 1902), p. 173.

[33] Marina Warner, *Indigo or, Mapping the Waters* (London, 1992). The treatment of Sycorax in *Indigo* is analysed by Tobias Döring in 'Chains of Memory: English-Caribbean Cross-Currents in Marina Warner's *Indigo* and David Dabydeen's *Turner*', in *Across the Lines: Intertextuality and Transcultural Communication in the New Literatures in English*, ed. Wolfgang Kloos (Amsterdam, 1998), pp. 191–204; Caroline Cakebread, 'Sycorax Speaks: Marina Warner's *Indigo* and *The Tempest*', in *Transforming Shakespeare: Contemporary Women's Re-Visions in Literature and Performance* (Basingstoke, 1999). Kate Chedgzoy *Shakespeare's Queer Children: Sexual Politics and Contemporary Culture* (Manchester, 1995), pp. 123–9; Julie Sanders in *Novel Shakespeares: Twentieth-Century Women Novelists and Appropriation* (Manchester, 2001), pp. 132–50.

[34] The drowned slaves are discussed by Cakebread, 'Sycorax Speaks', pp. 219.

sharper claws that will grow up a bear, a fox, who knows? Some kind of savage creature. Like its father, and he will mangle you.

(170–1)

This picture of a savage child overturns the racial implications of *The Tempest*. His white blood means the child is somehow less than human, not a baby but a 'whelp'. In *The Tempest* it is Caliban who is referred to as 'freckled whelp' (1.2.285).

After her death Sycorax's spirit comes closest to Shakespeare's Prospero as she echoes his Medea speech (5.1.33–57), not wishing to abjure magic, but rather to use her powers to turn back time and prevent the white men's incursions:

Oh airs and winds, you bring me stories from the living, rustle of leaves and heave of branches, you speak to me of pain, and you, streaming magma from the belly of Adesangé and cold rivers too, spouting from down below…HEAR ME!…Turn back your currents in their course. the stiff breeze and the gentle wind, pull back the tide and send the sun, the moon, and the stars spinning in the churn of the heavens – so that we can return to the time before this time'.

(212)

By thus refracting the words and actions of Prospero through Sycorax Warner builds a tension of sameness and difference between the worlds of *Indigo* and *The Tempest*, combatting the latter's presentation of both race and gender. Her words also perhaps undermine Prospero's authority by suggesting that, even if Prospero's interest in magic predated his exile, his present expertise is Sycorax's legacy. (Rather similarly, in *Forbidden Planet*, the function of Sycorax is given to the Krell, Altair's previous inhabitants, whose superior development allows Morbius access to greatly advanced technology.)

Marina Warner is neither completely uncritical of Sycorax nor entirely unsympathetic towards Everard and his men. She herself has a Caribbean inheritance,[35] but through her relationship with a colonizer – the seventeenth-century Thomas Warner – rather than the colonized, and the novel ends with a liaison between Miranda (the novel's twentieth-century, predominantly white, heroine) and a black actor, George. Warner concludes by coopting *The Tempest*'s image of lovers playing chess as an emblem of a harmonious interracial match (5.1.174–80):

They had begun play. Their openings were well-tried, unadventurous. But these same familiar moves would take them in deep: face to face and piece by piece they would engage with each other so raptly that for a time they would never even notice anyone else outside looking in on the work they were absorbed in, crossing the lines, crossing the squares, far out on the board in the other's sea.

(395)

Gloria Naylor's is a more clearly partisan vision. *Mama Day* is one of this African-American novelist's best-known works; it contains two Sycorax figures, one a long dead slave, Sapphira Wade, who ensured that her owner-husband willed the isle of Willow Springs to her and her fellow slaves, the other her descendant, the 'Mama Day' of the title, though her real name is Miranda.[36] In the texts examined so far female characters have clawed back status and presence by usurping the role of Prospero. *Lodore* and *The New Inn*, for example, at first replicate *The Tempest*'s own balance of power, weighted heavily towards Prospero, but conclude by dethroning him from this position of authority. Even in *Indigo*, which contains no single compelling Prospero figure, Sycorax is constructed in implicit counterpoint to him. But Naylor is more radical than this; it is as though she is trying rather to erase the memory of Prospero altogether, refusing to invoke him even antagonistically.

Like Sycorax, Sapphira had power over the elements: 'She could walk through a lightning storm without being touched; grab a bolt of lightning in

[35] She reflects on this background in 'Between the Colonist and the Creole: Family Bonds, Family Boundaries' in *Unbecoming Daughters of the Empire*, eds. Shirley Chew and Anna Rutherford (Sydney, 1993), pp. 199–204.

[36] In 'Rainbows of Darkness' Valerie Traub uses *Mama Day* to illustrate how 'African-American authors negotiate the plots, conventions, and politics of Anglo-European cultural traditions'. *Cross-Cultural Performances: Differences in Women's Re-Visions of Shakespeare*, ed. Marianne Novy (Urbana, Illinois, 1993), p. 150.

the palm of her hand...' (3). And, like Sycorax, though more dramatically, she eluded the death penalty, 'escape[d] the hangman's noose, laughing in a burst of flames'(3). Her crime was murdering Bascombe Wade, the novel's occluded Prospero figure. Here the exploitative white European lost the battle to the transgressive African female long before the novel's action begins. As in *Lodore*, it is the father, not the mother, who is banished from the text. In a tacit riposte to Prospero's control over language, so resented by Caliban, Sapphira's power is nonverbal or preverbal – 'Sapphira Wade don't live in the part of our memory we can use to form words' (4).

Naylor's novel doesn't confront *The Tempest* as directly as Warner's. In fact she denies that it particularly influenced *Mama Day*, citing instead works such as those of her fellow African-American Zora Neale Hurston.[37] These competing literary influences – white male, black female – parallel the opposed forces of Prospero and Sycorax. Naylor's championing of Sycorax within the text – her refusal to acknowledge that Prospero is an enemy to be reckoned with – is mirrored by her sense of literary community with other black women writers. Most critics do identify a link with *The Tempest* however; the heroine, Cocoa, seems to voice Naylor's own refusal to owe too great a debt to Shakespeare when she writes:

Just proves that Shakespeare didn't have a bit of soul – I don't care if he did write about Othello, Cleopatra, and some slave on a Caribbean island. If he had been in touch with our culture, he would have written somewhere, 'Nigger, are you out of your mind?'

(64)

And we can perhaps discriminate between a writer, such as the Martinican Aimé Césaire for example, whose treatment of Shakespeare is so cleverly and thoroughly oppositional to *The Tempest* as to constitute a kind of homage, and Naylor who allows a few echoes of the play – and surely the periphrastic allusion to Caliban is just a little *too* casual – into her novel, but keeps them fully subordinate to her own freewheeling imaginative vision of a Black American island.

A humorous episode, poking fun at a son of the island, a college boy turned sociologist, can be read as an emblem of Naylor's refusal to subordinate her novel to *The Tempest*, even antagonistically. The young academic wants to account for the use of the phrase '18 & 23', used to describe anything mysterious or momentous on the island.

he done still made it to the conclusion that 18 & 23 wasn't 18 & 23 at all – was really 81 & 32, which just so happened to be the lines of longitude and latitude marking off where Willow Springs sits on the map. And we were just so damned dumb that we turned the whole thing round. Not that he called it being dumb, mind you, called it 'asserting our cultural identity', 'inverting hostile social and political parameters'.

(7–8)

In fact the expression is derived from the date on which Sapphira murdered Bascombe Wade. The islanders evolve their own ways of talking about the world, without feeling the need to invert or subvert the terms used by the dominant white culture. And neither does Naylor need to keep up a continuous pattern of response to *The Tempest* in her novel. Its teasingly elusive presence in the play is a sign of Sycorax's liberation from Prospero.[38] Mrs Prospero may be happy to wrest power from Prospero on *The Tempest*'s own terms, but Sycorax has to abandon the play entirely if she wants to regain control. In the other intertexts discussed here it is vital to be aware of exactly what each author is doing with *The Tempest*; in *Mama Day* it is just as important to know what she's *not* doing.

It would be misleading to suggest that a clear trajectory can be charted whereby Sycorax is

---

[37] See James R. Andreas, Sr, '"Signifying" on *The Tempest* in Gloria Naylor's *Mama Day*', in *Shakespeare and Appropriation*, eds. Christy Desmet and Robert Sawyer (London, 1999), p. 104; Sanders, *Novel Shakespeares*, pp. 186–8.

[38] James R. Andreas, Sr thus perhaps suggests a greater (or different) debt to Shakespeare than Naylor owes when he asserts that the novel 'systematically turns *The Tempest* upside down'('"Signifying" on *The Tempest*', p. 106). Peter Erickson has a stronger sense of her independence, noting that 'Shakespeare does not assimilate Naylor; Naylor assimilates Shakespeare', in *Rewriting Shakespeare, Rewriting Ourselves*, ed. Peter Erickson (Berkeley, 1991), p. 145.

increasingly empowered and favoured in later responses to the play. In particular it may be noted that a number of recent works by male writers do not follow their seventeenth-century forebears in creating interesting, powerful and sympathetic living mothers from the play's maternal traces. In Derek Jarman's film version, for example, Sycorax is a grotesque figure who forces Ariel to fall in with her lewd commands.[39] She is more impressive in Edwin Morgan's 'From the Video Box', but scarcely positive:

> She reigns,
> Bitch-queen, batch-quern, grinds out
> Pure nature, calves icebergs, makes archipelagos,
> And I saw her suddenly in a final shot
> Solid with her thighs around the world,
> Frowning at a thousand twangling instruments
> That to her were neither here nor there.
>
> (330–6)[40]

Here her female ability to create is awe-inspiring but it is a purely natural power quite divorced from the European, male culture of Shakespeare's 'twangling instruments'.

Two of the most hostile late twentieth-century treatments of Sycorax respond to different patterns of resemblance within *The Tempest*. Disney's *The Little Mermaid* draws out the suggestive parallels between Sycorax and Miranda's dead mother, while in Ted Hughes's *Birthday Letters* Sycorax is presented as an evil female Prospero.

The Little Mermaid encourages us to dwell on the similarities in theme and setting between Andersen's story and *The Tempest* by naming its heroine Ariel. The heroine's mother is an even more shadowy figure here than in *The Tempest*; her absence is never an issue. Therefore the significance of Ursula the sea witch as an evil mother figure is still more pronounced, particularly as we learn she formerly lived in the palace, although she has been banished for many years. She is an object of horror for all the sea creatures: 'she's a demon, she's a monster' exclaims Sebastian the courtier crab. It would seem that the sea king, Triton, simply replaced her as ruler, but the possibility that they

ruled *together*, that, like Lady Lodore, she is a repudiated wife, is never denied. The presentation of Ursula accords with Irigaray's account of the demonization of the mother; Ariel approaches her gloomy abode through a decidedly vaginal tunnel, and the witch's caressing manner apes that of an affectionate mother for she addresses her as 'my dear sweet child'.[41] Ariel's approach to Ursula signals her disobedience to her father and paves the way for Triton's own temporary subjection to the witch. Eventually, Prince Eric kills her by sailing a boat with a broken prow into her distended belly, destroying the film's disturbing site of motherhood.[42] Here, more than in *The Tempest* or any other later text, are the figures of Sycorax and Miranda's mother most fused together, as though in total rejection of the maternal function. Even *The Magic Flute* offers a less negative take on the play's mothers than this post-feminist revision.

Once again, Irigaray's writings provide a suggestive commentary on this demonization of the mother:

The problem is that, by denying the mother her generative power and by wanting to be the sole creator, the Father, according to our culture, superimposes upon the

---

[39] Chantal Zabus and Kevin A. Dwyer note that Jarman's 'cultural conservatism inevitably goes hand in hand with a professed lack of concern for the post-colonial potentialities of the play'. '"I'll be wise hereafter": Caliban in Postmodern British Cinema', in *Constellation Caliban: Figurations of a Character*, eds. Nadia Lie and Theo D'haen (Amsterdam, 1997), p. 272.

[40] Morgan, 'From the Video Box', *Collected Poems* (Manchester, 1996).

[41] See Richard Finkelstein's 'Disney Cites Shakespeare: The Limits of Appropriation', in Desmet and Sawyer, *Shakespeare and Appropriation*, pp. 179–96.

[42] Finkelstein notes that 'the triumph of Eric and Ariel, the creations of a large patriarchal corporation, over Ursula is the disciplining of the female "fatness" she represents' (p. 189). Coppélia Kahn's observation that the late plays 'mirror anxiety about – and even disgust at – desire, female sexuality, and procreation' is equally true of Disney's *Little Mermaid*. 'The Providential Tempest and the Shakespearean Family', in *Representing Shakespeare: New Psychoanalytic Essays*, eds. Murray M. Schwartz and Coppélia Kahn (Baltimore, 1980), p. 220.

archaic world of the flesh a universe of language [langue] and symbols which cannot take root in it except as in the form of that which makes a hole in the bellies of women and in the site of their identity.

(41)

Sycorax appears twice in the works of Ted Hughes; the two poems reflect opposed perspectives on the enchantress and suggest Hughes's own ambivalence towards female power. In the earlier poem, 'Prospero and Sycorax', Sycorax is associated with females who have suffered at the hands of men. Earlier I referred to Orgel's suggestion that Sycorax and Caliban can be seen as ghostly surrogates for the missing members of Prospero's family, and here Hughes perhaps hints at a possible liaison, Brady Bunch style, between the two 'half families', a possibility which, to Sycorax's regret, Prospero has rejected:

> She knows, like Ophelia,
> The task has swallowed him.
> She knows, like George's dragon,
> Her screams have closed his helmet.[43]

Here Hughes moves from a conventional feminine victim to a feminized monster, equating her difference of sex with her difference of kind (of race or even species) as equivalent barriers, which Prospero might have overcome, and perhaps even did for a while, before eventually finding it easier to revert to conventional type:

> She knows, like God,
> He has found
> Something
> Easier to live with –
>
> His death, and her death.

We can perhaps infer that her death is literal, his a moral or spiritual demise brought about by his refusal of an alliance with Sycorax. Stephen Greenblatt wrote of the Spanish destruction of the Aztecs: 'For a moment you see yourself confounded with the other, but then you make the other become an alien object, a thing, that you can destroy or incorporate at will'.[44]

As the melancholy vocalizer of the poem, Sycorax engages the reader's sympathy. Yet in Hughes's later 'Setebos', which alludes to his relationship with Sylvia Plath, Sycorax becomes a hostile figure.

> Your mother
> Played Prospero, flying her magic in
> To stage the Masque, and bless the marriage,
> Eavesdropping on the undervoices
> Of the honeymooners in Paris
> And smiling on the stair at her reflection
> In the dark wall.[45]

By feminizing Prospero and identifying him with Sylvia's mother, Hughes taps into the covert suggestion of parity between Prospero and Sycorax. Prospero's knowing stage management of the romance is given a more sinister edge here with the description of her 'smiling on the stair at her reflection/in the dark wall'. This reflective moment hints at some darker alter ego – Sycorax? – sharing a moment of complicity with Prospero. Again, the twentieth-century male writer seems far less open to female creativity and control than some of his predecessors. Jonson's imperious Frances and energetic Pru are attractive stage manager figures; even Lady Santerre, though perhaps just as unappealing as Sylvia's mother, is presented within a social context which encourages the reader to feel some sympathy for her interference in her daughter's marriage.

The affinity between Hughes's feminine Prospero and Sycorax is strengthened by his description of the latter's brooding presence:

> Sycorax,
> The rind of our garden's emptied quince,
> Bobbed in the hazy surf at the horizon
> Offshore, in the wings

43 Ted Hughes, *New Selected Poems 1957–1994* (London, 1995).
44 Stephen Greenblatt, *Marvelous Possessions: The Wonder of the New World* (Oxford, 1991), p. 135.
45 Ted Hughes, *Birthday Letters* (London, 1998). The poem is discussed by Erica Wagner in *Ariel's Gift: Ted Hughes, Sylvia Plath and the Story of Birthday Letters* (London, 2000), pp. 151–2.

Of the heavens, like a director
Studying the scenes to come.

She has usurped Prospero's role of writer and director: as the poem's title, 'Setebos' intimates, in this *Tempest* the forces of darkness have the upper hand. This realignment of Sycorax and Prospero as similar if not identical characters perhaps suggests a deeper hostility to female power on Hughes's part, including the poetic power of his wife:

> The laughter
> Of Sycorax was thunder and lightning
> And black downpour. She hurled
> Prospero's head at me . . .

Such hostility is scarcely surprising when we recall Hughes's disgusted description of Goddess as Sow (of whom Sycorax is an avatar) in *Shakespeare and the Goddess of Complete Being*. 'Her combination of gross whiskery nakedness and riotous carnality is seized by the mythic imagination, evidently, as a sort of uterus on the loose . . . a woman-sized, multiple udder on trotters'.[46] Hughes's concluding vision of Sycorax's triumph might seem to disassociate her from the poem's female Prospero, and to suggest that the latter is a positive force. Yet one senses that the defeated Prospero is male and that Sylvia's mother is a mere usurper, indistinguishable from her supposed opponent, Sycorax. The reforming stance of a vision such as Mary Shelley's in which the mother is reclaimed as a sympathetic

and powerful, though feminine, presence, and the radical approach of *Mama Day* which erases Prospero and celebrates Sycorax, may be contrasted with Hughes's own response, which presents us with a Sycorax as negative as Shakespeare's. Indeed, she is more negative, for 'Setebos', unlike *The Tempest*, offers us no subtle invitations to question and reconstruct the surface statements of Shakespeare's complex play.

The persistence of *The Tempest*'s mothers, absent presences at best, is surprising, yet may be partly determined by the symbolic force of the play's island setting. In *Islands* John Fowles suggests that, *pace* Donne, we are all islands, with the sea as our 'evolutionary amniotic fluid, the element in which we too were once enwombed, from which our own antediluvian line rose into the light and air'.[47] The maternal is thus embedded in the play, and symbolic and ultimately inconclusive battles between Prospero and *The Tempest*'s absent mothers are a prominent feature of its creative reception. The emergence of Sycorax as a force for good in at least some twentieth-century texts is perhaps the most significant development in this ongoing struggle. But as 'Setebos' demonstrates, Prospero is far from beaten yet.

---

[46] Hughes, *Shakespeare and the Goddess of Complete Being* (London, 1992), p. 11.
[47] John Fowles, *Islands* (London, 1978), p. 12.

DIRECTING SHAKESPEARE'S COMEDIES: IN CONVERSATION WITH PETER HOLLAND

DECLAN DONNELLAN

Declan Donnellan is joint Artistic Director of Cheek by Jowl. He was born in England of Irish parents in 1953, read English and Law at Queens' College, Cambridge and was called to the Bar at the Middle Temple in 1978. With designer Nick Ormerod, he formed Cheek By Jowl in 1981; the group has since been described by *Time* magazine as 'one of the ten great theatre companies in the world'. For Cheek by Jowl he has directed nine Shakespeare productions, including an all-male *As You Like It* (1991; revived 1994), *Measure for Measure* (1994), *Much Ado About Nothing* (1998), and, in collaboration with the Maly Theatre, St Petersburg, *The Winter's Tale* (1999). He has won several awards in Paris, Moscow, New York and London including the Olivier Award for Outstanding Achievement in 1991. His first book *The Actor and the Target* was published in 2002. He directed the inaugural production of *King Lear* for the RSC Academy in 2002.

PETER HOLLAND In 1999 you directed a production of *The Winter's Tale* with the Maly Dramatic Theatre of St Petersburg which toured in England playing in Russian. I wondered about your experience of directing a Russian company in the play. What made you pick *The Winter's Tale* as the play you wanted to do with them?

DECLAN DONNELLAN I picked *The Winter's Tale*, just as I picked *King Lear* to direct for the RSC Academy in 2002, because it is a play I had always wanted to do, something which I think is very important for the people I'm working with: that I

actually want to direct the play that I'm doing – which doesn't necessarily have to be the case. I was very lucky to be asked to direct a show by Lev Dodin, the artistic director at St Petersburg; they wanted me to do some Shakespeare and I thought the company would be rather good because they're mostly in their forties. The Maly has this rather fantastic company, most of whom are about my age now – quite a good age for doing Leontes and so on, a sort of parental age and an age for looking back. It's rather difficult to do *The Winter's Tale* in Britain where we depend so much on young companies for all sorts of reasons. I would rather see a young man playing King Lear than a young man playing Leontes, which I would find difficult to justify – there's just something different about the weight; I suppose it's a question of sensibility.

It was fascinating working with them because, for one thing, the process was very slow. I don't speak Russian, so we had to work through an interpreter. There are downsides because we used a translation by Pyotr Gnedich who is a great translator and a contemporary of Pushkin's but, for example, the line 'Look down and see what death is doing' was translated as 'Look, she's turned quite cold' – so many merry hours got wasted in rehearsal.

My best translation story is when I was doing *Macbeth* in Finland [in 1986] and I was doing the big scene between him and her (1.7) and if you notice in that scene they go 'I', 'thou', 'I', 'thou' – there are some 'you's in there – and then suddenly 'we': 'If we should fail?' 'We fail? But screw your courage to the sticking place and we'll not fail' (1.7.59). If memory serves me correctly it is the first time 'we' is used in that scene[1] and I spent hours rehearsing this with these two very fine actors at The National Theatre of Finland. 'Ei' is 'No' in Finnish and so you're completely lost; it's not an Indo European language and you've no idea where the verb comes or anything. Only after hours did I discover that 'If we should fail?' had been translated as 'But what will happen if it doesn't work?'

Problems of translation are often to do with subtle bowdlerization to make things sound better. I think that one of the reasons that Shakespeare is a great writer is that he knows that words don't work and you have to know that words don't work before you can write properly because it's believing that words work perfectly that gets us into so much trouble. I think the truly great writers – and it's great not having to justify myself because I'm not an academic and so I can be as opinionated as I like! – know that words are for writers like knitting with tree trunks – to do important but delicate work, all we have are crude tools.

A word can be a symptom of something and it can be a cause of something. I think that we have to go back to roots but we have to keep reminding ourselves that words don't work. So that the great mistake is to think that, when Lear says 'Who is it that can tell me who I am?' (1.4.230), the words are doing what he wants them to. It's very important to understand that everything we do is a failure because it is only an approximation to what we would have preferred to have done. Classics come with a dangerous authority, classic status may lead us to believe the writer is articulate and that the writer writes precisely what he, she or the characters want. This is particularly pronounced in forms like the French alexandrine where the double line may imply a sense of perfection – *'that is all I wanted to say, that, exactly that, no more and here's a rhyme to prove it!'* It is more useful to imagine that Shakespeare, Corneille and Pushkin are great writers precisely because they know that they can't write that well.

Put another way, what a character is trying to do is much more sophisticated, much more full of feeling, much more elemental, much more complex than any words that the character may actually use. Not only the alexandrine can give the impression of something that's perfectly packaged, the great lines of Shakespeare (like 'man, proud man, / Dressed in a little brief authority', *Measure for Measure*, 2.2.117–18) can give us the impression that these magnificent words in some way do what they are supposed to because Shakespeare is an articulate writer. I think that is wrong – I hate to use that word but I will. These expressions, these means of communication, are fantastic precisely because the author *knows* they don't work perfectly, that they are inadequate to express feeling. We know that perhaps no words are as important as 'I love you' and that no words are as banal as 'I love you' and that expressing myself by words is crude – I didn't say 'useless' but 'crude'. Just because words don't work does not mean we should stop using them. Perfectionism is merely a vanity.

The actor must not feel cowed by the reputation of the words but I am not talking about perversity for its own sake, I am not talking about Cordelia running around and sticking her head in a toilet.

The great danger is that we'll imagine that there is a one-on-one mapping, that the words perfectly parallel what we feel or what we are trying to achieve. It is not a rule that as the stakes go up the more articulate we become. It is a more useful principle that the more the situation matters, the more we *may* be able to tell the truth precisely by acknowledging our lack of articulacy. I find it interesting to think of Shakespeare as being a great writer precisely because he understands both his own limitations and the limitations of words. He understands his own dissarticulacy – if that word exists.

PH And yet it's striking that two of your most brilliant and best-known productions of Shakespeare comedies, *As You Like It* (Cheek by Jowl, 1991) and *Much Ado About Nothing* (Cheek by Jowl, 1998), have at their centres three characters, Rosalind,

---

[1] DD's memory has not served him quite correctly: Macbeth uses it earlier 'We will proceed no further in this business' (1.7.31) – PH.

Beatrice and Benedick, who are, on the surface at least, extraordinarily articulate, that they appear able to use language.

DD It's interesting to look at them as they have one of many elements in common: they sometimes use words, wit, articulacy, in order to lie. The words become a shield rather than a means of communication. Beatrice and Benedick, of course, use their wit to hide their feelings. I think one of the most foolish ways of looking at Beatrice and Benedick is that you direct them as if they are witty, sophisticated people. They'd *like* to be witty, sophisticated people, they would *prefer* to be witty, sophisticated people. When you do the play you have to infer and not merely float on the surface, by swallowing all the press releases that the characters issue about themselves. As we know from politics, the louder the abuse the bigger the lie. The more we sell our identities, the more that Beatrice sells herself as not being interested in men, as someone who really doesn't find Benedick as amusing and attractive as everybody else does, the more we can imply that the opposite *also exists*. But the same is true through all of the plays. We can assume how much Goneril and Regan love Lear, how much Edmund loves Gloucester; that's what's so painful, the fact we have to hold conflicting feelings in our heads.

But to return to Beatrice and Benedick, we can use our articulacy to separate ourselves from each other, just as we can even use sex to be less intimate with somebody; we can actually use words to deny communication with other people.

The other thing to remember about text – which is what we deal with – is that they're only words. We do not need to be Freud to know that deeds count more than words and we should always look at what people do rather than what they say. Hamlet doesn't go to Wittenberg and he doesn't kill Claudius and that's much more important than what he says about it. What really matters about Hamlet is that he doesn't kill Claudius: that's the central (non-)event of the play.

When Rosalind dresses up as a boy the thing she most wants in the world is Orlando not to recognize her and think she's somebody else and think she's not a woman, to think she's a man. What she *least* wants is for Orlando not to recognize her and think she's a boy. It's both at the same time – it's not half and half. To be actually not recognized by the person that loves you isn't very nice. That's got to be given its weight. The director's responsibility is to the text but to honour the text you also have to honour the story that precipitates the text and if the two seem to clash then you have to give precedence to the story. This may lead you to some very interesting choices. Because the words, of course, aren't the truth. The words that we use are much more to do with what we want to be the truth than what actually is the truth, so that when we say 'My sweet Lord' or 'My dear Lady' it's not so much a description of the truth, it's what you want to be the truth. It actually means something political, with a very, very small 'p'; when we speak it changes the situation. When we speak, we speak to change the world; we don't speak to give expression to our feelings. Our feelings may express themselves through what we do but the actor, for example, cannot express his or her feelings – what the actor can do is try to change the world and let those feelings affect how that changing of the world happens. Maybe you better get me back to Shakespearian comedy.

PH I don't think you're at all far away from Shakespearian comedy! If we go back to your *As You Like It*, what of course that production was most visibly and immediately apparently about was the fact that you used an all-male cast. Many of us had seen the one at the National Theatre some years earlier; that production seemed, to me at least, to be more mocking than serious while yours had an extraordinary seriousness about what the consequences for gender were. I wonder if you could talk about the decision to do the play with an all-male cast.

DD I know the plays that I direct very well but at the same time I've got to un-know the plays in order to direct them. It's just the same as the way the actor has to forget the rehearsal in performance because if you see an actor remembering the rehearsal in performance you won't actually feel or understand anything. You've got to forget to know.

Nick and I decided we wouldn't do it with an all-male company unless we could find an actor to play Rosalind. And had we not found Adrian Lester we would have had women in those roles. Theatre is far more pragmatic on the inside!

Of course I had no idea of the effect of this all-male production. I had a missionary zeal to avoid the British pantomime tradition or to fall into that more sort of Mediterranean sort of *travestie* – the whole drag queen tradition and I didn't want to go down that path at all. So we had very puritan rehearsals about how to try as well as we could not to satirize the characters but to see from within what was happening, to see what the characters see. My fears when we set out on it were in that middle scene when Rosalind as Ganymede plays the girl for Orlando. So it's a boy dressed as girl dressed as boy dressed as a girl and there's one point when there are four different genders present at one time. What I didn't want and hoped wouldn't happen was that it would be like a clever and ironical exercise that would deprive the audience of feeling because they would be watching something that was a little bit arch and cold. I was delighted that that wasn't the case, that people said that what was extraordinary was that they were able to hold those things in their heads and were encouraged to feel *more*. As if irony and feeling are not only compatible but also that they are mutually *dependent*.

Irony is rather difficult to define; it gets mixed up with sarcasm. But one of the things about irony that can get extended into camp is to do with a distance from the feeling. The problem for a human being is that there is always distance from feeling, that we're never quite in feeling as much as we'd like to be. We can infer this from the way people sell us products on the television because most products are sold to us on the basis that if we only drive this motor car or suck this chocolate bar then we will be released into a world of unalloyed, pure, unironic feeling. Great writers understand that we are emotionally illiterate, that we're all fully equipped with a set of feelings, we just give them funny names because we don't much like the look of many of them: envy

we can pretend is rage and desire we can pretend is envy and loneliness we can pretend is hunger and we have many, many different feelings at the same time that we don't add up. One of the things that a work of art does is that it helps to name a feeling. An act of torture, as Elaine Scarry has written about, takes the name away from feeling, it takes the names away from thought and in a way one of the things that a Shakespearian play does is, in a community, to help us: we think 'I've seen that too, I've been there too, I've felt that too.' It gets named and just that humble process of naming makes us feel just a little bit less lonely and we can participate with other people because we understand that what we have in common with them is our otherness, that we see that we're as mad as they are and they're as mad as we are. What strikes me always as being so perverse is when we try to stereotype the living characters of Shakespeare – that Juliet must be pretty, that Romeo must be unimaginative – because it's in those moments of strangeness, oddness, weirdness and lunacy that we most connect with them, and that we most feel connected to humanity.

PH There was in your *As You Like It* a remarkable effect that whatever the emotion was that was being generated between characters it was dissociated from gender. What was being offered was desire between one human being and another, not a representation of a particular sexuality.

DD Yes, I think that's one way of looking at it. On the other hand I always felt that I didn't want to desexualize the play. It's important also that for Rosalind it's not a question of being half man/half woman but actually a question of being all woman so that you can be all man, and all man so that you can be all woman. In other words, that there isn't a hermaphrodite or androgyne mean, a narcissistic limbo where the sexual organs completely disappear and you don't need to have sex with anybody. It would actually be quite the reverse of this creature that's all man, all woman, all desiring and all desired, and not some sort of narcissistic 'closed-circuit'. It was very important for me that the guy who played Rosalind was male, because I think that it's only by being fully male that he can become fully female, and the other way round, that these two things aren't as opposite as we think.

PH One last question, about endings. You found a brilliant solution in *The Winter's Tale* to the extraordinary problem of how you resolve an action by bringing Mamillius back into a frozen moment of time in the court, led by Time herself, to look at the faces and forgive his father. It was absolutely overwhelming.

DD There is a problem with all generations: we never show enough respect to the young. The most important character for me in *The Winter's Tale* is Mamillius – I mean, they kill the little boy! Hermione and Leontes working out their destinies are far less important. They kill the little boy between them, and that to me is the most important event. I really wanted to make him central because we all forget about Mamillius by the end when everyone's celebrating 'It's OK'. It's not OK!

DANIEL YANG I'm a professional director. Since you have done *As You Like It* with an all-male cast, were you really trying to be different or were you inspired by something in the text for you to make that decision?

DD You should never try to be different. You should never try to be original because originality is none of our business. All we can do is do the best that we can. In a way I have to ignore all tradition when I direct a Shakespeare play. My aim is to treat the audience as if they are two things: one is bright and the other is ignorant. Because that's the frame of mind I try to put myself in when I read the play and put the play on. I don't think there is anything patronizing about it. I absolutely try to ignore all tradition because it's like trying to be original. When I open my eyes I've created a work of art because I've invented the world inside my head and it will be unique. As soon as I try to be original then I actually end up destroying the uniqueness that has been given to me. But to get

Juliet actually to see Romeo and vice-versa, the Romeo that *that* Juliet sees, and the Juliet that *that* Romeo sees and the way I see the words and the way they see the words and feel them; that is unique whether we like it or not. The world I see is specific whether I like it or not, the world is changing whether I like it or not and I have to go with the flow. What I have to do is try not to blind myself to the ever-changing uniqueness of an ever 'renewing' creation – that's what I have to do, but it's not very easy.

Before I direct a play I may have ideas, which are very dangerous things, as they tend to come from the head rather than the heart. I remember when I directed *The Tempest* I had this wonderful idea (I was very pleased with myself) that when Miranda says 'O, brave new world', she should slug Prospero, because it is actually the most wicked lie. There's something profoundly evil to tell young people 'You wait! You'll see! They're all arseholes!'

Anyway I had this great idea and it didn't work! So we didn't do it. Theatre is far more practical than we imagine.

PENNY GAY You've spoken very affectingly about the language and what it can't do. Can I ask you about the other aspect of comedy – physical comedy, slapstick – how do you see them fitting into your work?

DD I love them but I have no taste and my partner Nick Ormerod has less. So I love scenes like the clown scenes in *The Winter's Tale*. We set the second one in a customs hall which is very Russian, with the characters asking for their visas and so on. We were doing prat-falls on rhythms of three – you turn, you turn, you turn and you fall – and people going in one door and coming out of another. We were all killing ourselves laughing and one of the Russian actors looked at me and said 'Declan and Nick, how do you know so much about the Russian sense of humour?'

HERB WEIL Could you give us some examples of the ways plays change during rehearsal?

DD Before I directed *As You Like It* I never much liked it and before I directed *Much Ado* I thought I adored it and I had to live with both of them for nine months. *As You Like It* I loved more and more as a play and *Much Ado* I loathed more and more as a play – the more you actually start to really pay *Much Ado* the respect of finding out what is happening in it the more appalling it becomes. I still hear lines in *As You Like It* and think we completely missed the point. One of the reasons why I direct Shakespeare is because if you are going to live with a play for eight or nine months you want to make sure you've got a pleasant travelling companion and Shakespeare you can just get to know and get to know and get to know. Now *Much Ado* I started to find more and more negative but the joy that started to come out of *As You Like It* increased and increased.

In rehearsal you're not trying to find, conceptually, something that's right. What we have to do is find things that are alive. So it is quite possible for me to make a work of theatre and for me to not like it. Why should I like it? As long as it's alive, even though I may not like it. It's not in my control.

I think *Much Ado* was fairly alive but I just didn't much like it. I hated what it said about that triple relationship of two men [Don Pedro and Claudio] using a woman [Hero] to stabilize themselves. The more you start to look at it the more you realize there's just something very unpleasant at the play's heart. Actually as a gay man I found it rather homophobic. But actually, the more I went into it, the more we just went down that path to pay the respect of going 'if that, then this; if this, then that'. It is just like going into a sort of little tunnel down to hell. Afterwards I thought that, maybe, other interpretations which I have sneered at in the past, that were more superficial and leg-kicking, were actually rather better. But there are certain respects that the play doesn't bear because there is such a bitter heart to it.

CAROL RUTTER Given the mode of original performance and subsequent performance and original sexuality and subsequent sexuality and the sexuality of the text and textuality of sexuality and so on, is it time for you to direct an all-male *Taming of the Shrew*?

DD I've been thinking about that an awful lot. I think an all-male *Taming of the Shrew* would be wonderful because it would be so offensive and it's only when it starts to be offensive that you know that somehow it might be biting – because of course art is, normally, a little bit offensive. The opposite of offensive is inoffensive in a way and there's nothing worse than a work of art that is inoffensive.

LAURIE MAGUIRE When you directed *A Midsummer Night's Dream* for Cheek by Jowl in 1985, shortly after the Royal Wedding, the actor who played Theseus did a rather fine Prince Charles impersonation. At what stage in directing comedy, does topicality enter your thought process as opposed to generalized relevance?

DD Yes, we did actually characterize Theseus as Prince Charles. I remember thinking during the tour that it was a terrible idea – and I also remember not being able to prise it away from the actor.

PH What of Alonso in your production of *The Tempest* who became Alonza, and who many people read as Margaret Thatcher?

DD Yes, and in Bucharest as Elena Ceaucescu. That's to do with projection because it's a woman in power.

PH And with a handbag.

DD All women in power have handbags. Imelda Marcos had several! Anyway, I'd quite like to do *Midsummer Night's Dream* again and *not* do that with Theseus – I was young!

'TO SHOW OUR SIMPLE SKILL': SCRIPTS AND PERFORMANCES IN SHAKESPEARIAN COMEDY

MICHAEL CORDNER

In 1982 the actor Derek Jacobi was in Stratford-upon-Avon to play three roles – Prospero, Benedick and Peer Gynt – for the Royal Shakespeare Company. During that summer he had several abrasive encounters with academics, who criticized some of the line-readings he used as Benedick. One disliked his almost trademark habit of elongating selected vowel sounds and told him that this trait was more appropriate to a stand-up comic than a leading Shakespearian actor. Another regretted a moment in Benedick's Act 2 soliloquy, as he absorbs the news that a love-lorn Beatrice is allegedly pining away for him. In modernized texts the words in question (*Much Ado About Nothing* 2.3, 212–13) characteristically read as follows: 'Love me? Why, it must be requited'. Which Jacobi had the temerity to convert into: 'Love me! Why? It must be requited'. So the disagreement hinged on whether a single three-letter word, 'why', should here be regarded as an interjection-cum-exclamation or an interrogative – an issue less trivial than might at first appear, since contrary judgements about it can generate radically different performances of the soliloquy.

Jacobi remained riled by his scholarly inquisitors when he recalled these incidents in an interview three years later. They epitomized for him the gulf in understanding which can open up between stage and study. His account of that divide is unashamedly partisan. On one side he positions actors who, like Jacobi himself, are dedicated to speaking words written four hundred years ago 'as if they've entered your brain at that moment and you've decided to say them', and who are ea-ger, via devoted 'detective work', to 'find out new meanings for the lines, meanings that are attractive mentally to me, that are stimulating'. On the other side he ranks the hidebound custodians of the sacred texts, willing to authenticate only a narrow range of meanings and swift to brand all other interpretations as illegitimate. He questions the evidence on which the scholars erect their certainties. With regard to that dispute about the difference between a comma and a question-mark, for instance, Jacobi insists that 'we don't actually know what the punctuation was', a fact which instills in him 'a healthy disrespect for' the punctuation editors impose. Throughout the interview Jacobi asserts the authority of his hard-won experience as an actor against his academic critics' inclination to assume that only their own mode of expertise has authority in this field.

Theatre audiences loved Jacobi's reading. One of the greatest of modern actors, Paul Scofield, has said that he relishes playing comedy, because 'to make an audience laugh is a special happiness for an actor, a confirmation of mutual understanding'.[1] The brilliant economy with which Jacobi bestowed an unexpected inflection on a single word is a vivid example of such a moment of 'mutual understanding'. Like all the best comic effects, this one was immediately funny *and* had longer-term consequences. It overturned the expectations set up by the preceding conversation between Don Pedro,

---

[1] Garry O'Connor, *Paul Scofield: The Biography* (London, 2002), p. 24.

167

Leonato and Claudio, which identifies Benedick's pride as the main obstacle to Beatrice's happiness. As Benedick testifies, 'they say I will beare my selfe proudly, if I perceiue the loue come from her' (2.3, 213–15).[2] Many Benedicks follow that cue and make this soliloquy the moment when that arrogance begins to be dismantled; whereas Jacobi's startled, self-distrustful 'Why?' abruptly revealed that his Benedick suffered from a profound disbelief in his ability to attract and deserve another's love. His friends' masquerade would have its desired effect, but for reasons quite different from those they smugly predicted. A tiny textual adjustment had transformed the shape of the role.

In the process, Jacobi – in 1982 something of a specialist in the impersonation of self-analytical introverts and loners, but not successful lovers[3] – had established a productive kinship between his new acting assignment and his most recent successes. His reading was not, however, so neatly tailored to his own gifts as to render it uninteresting to other actors, some of whom have subsequently paid it the sincerest form of compliment – plagiarism. Mark Rylance, who was in the 1982 Stratford company and played Ariel to Jacobi's Prospero, borrowed 'Love me! Why?', when he played Benedick, with a Belfast accent, in a London production eleven years later;[4] and the chain of inheritance continues to grow, the latest example of which I am aware being provided by David Tennant's Benedick in the recent BBC Radio 3 production.[5]

A line-reading can have a vigorous contemporary stage life and yet be remote from anything scholars accept as a plausible early modern meaning. Is that the case here? Neither Quarto nor Folio follows that crucial 'why' with a question mark. In both the passage reads: 'loue me? why it must be requited:', which also means that in neither is 'why' succeeded by the comma, or begun with the capital letter, familiar from most modern editions. Modernizing editing works from distrust of the authority of Quarto and Folio punctuation and accordingly grants itself the license to repunctuate boldly. At many points this involves interventions at least as radical as Jacobi's improvisation. 'Why',

that apparently innocent word, is frequently the subject of such editorial adjustments. As Norman Blake has demonstrated, the variety and ambiguity of the ways in which the word was deployed in early modern English, as an interrogative and as a discourse marker, make its specific function in many Shakespearian passages difficult – in some cases, impossible – to determine definitively.[6] If modernizing editors conceded authority to the original punctuation, then they could logically argue that the lack of a question mark in Quarto and Folio at this point is decisive. But, since this is not their position, it has to be difficult for them entirely to rule out the possibility that 'why' might here be interpreted as an interrogative. Reading it as such offends against no rule of early modern English. Syntactically, Jacobi's line-reading fits as neatly with the surrounding phrases as the conventional interpretation does. So, on what grounds, a puzzled actor may persist in asking, can the experts decree that this tempting possibility is absolutely inadmissible?

The conversations which infuriated Jacobi happened two decades ago. Much has changed since. Shakespearian scholarship has become more attentive to the plays' origins as scripts for performance, and all the major series of Shakespeare texts currently in progress profess performance-friendly goals undreamt of by Ardens 1 and 2. Which leaves

---

[2] Shakespearian quotations in this article, unless otherwise identified, derive from the 1623 First Folio.

[3] In 1982, Jacobi's most internationally celebrated triumph had been in the title-role of the 1975 BBC TV series *I, Claudius*. On stage he had recently played the leading role in Nicolai Erdman's *The Suicide* in New York. While still performing Benedick for the Royal Shakespeare Company in 1983, he added another variation on this kind of part to his repertoire – Rostand's Cyrano de Bergerac.

[4] Peter Holland, 'Shakespeare Performances in England, 1992–1993', *Shakespeare Survey 47* (Cambridge, 1994), p. 193.

[5] This production, directed by Sally Avens, was broadcast on Radio 3 on 23 September 2001 and is now available on audiocassette (ISBN 0563 535334) and CD (ISBN 0563 535342).

[6] Norman Blake, '*Why* and *What* in Shakespeare', in Toshiyuki Takamiya and Richard Beadle, eds., *Chaucer to Shakespeare: Essays in Honour of Shinsuke Ando* (Cambridge, 1992), pp. 179–93.

me wondering why neither of the recent editions of *Much Ado About Nothing* – in the New Cambridge and Oxford Shakespeare series[7] – acknowledges the interrogative possibility here. The only edition which does refer to it is John F. Cox's in the 'Shakespeare in Production' series from Cambridge University Press, where the general editorial brief requires that the annotation include 'the fullest possible stage histories'. Ironically, Cox credits its invention to Rylance, not Jacobi.[8]

This general neglect is the more curious, given that Jacobi's interview appeared in no less canonical a periodical than *Shakespeare Quarterly* and was presented by the interviewer, John F. Andrew, as in tune with the growing recognition by some scholars that 'they can learn at least as much from watching an actor like you as they can from working in the library'.[9] In effect, he offered the interview as an example of the kind of material on which a remodelled scholarly practice might be built – one which fostered and relished a closer, mutually advantageous interchange between stage and study.

Richard Proudfoot, the senior general editor on Arden 3, has recently described how contemporary editions avowedly find their 'patrons' in 'the *actors*, students, teachers and others who will buy their editions' (emphasis mine).[10] This identification of actors as one of the key constituencies of readers for Shakespeare editions is welcome. But what does it imply for the ways in which the plays have traditionally been edited? The question has prompted scarcely any systematic debate. Yet it cannot be taken for granted that minor modifications to usual practice will be sufficient. Should a contemporary edition of *Much Ado About Nothing* acknowledge Jacobi's reading of this passage? If not, on what grounds would that decision be reached? Jacobi's 'healthy disrespect' for scholars' punctuation indicates that he did not believe editions in 1982 were addressed to his professional needs. How may that situation best be remedied in 2003 and beyond?[11]

Choice of phrasing and inflection is absolutely central to the actor's art – a fact which makes a Shakespeare edition's use of punctuation especially sensitive. As Jonathan Crewe has observed, modernizing punctuation 'constitutes the most ubiquitous and least heralded form of editorial intervention in the Shakespearean text'. Accordingly, he concludes, this 'fact calls for commensurate critical engagement'[12] – an engagement the subject has almost never received.

W. W. Greg's momentous, and massively influential, distinction between 'substantive' readings 'that affect the author's meaning or the essence of his expression' and 'accidentals', including punctuation, that affect only the 'formal presentation' of the text has been crucial here.[13] The unstable nature of this distinction has caused persistent difficulties for those who seek to defend it.[14] It has also attracted radical criticism from scholars who consider it fundamentally unsound. A characteristically firm statement of the latter position is offered by Morse Peckham:

Punctuation does not merely '"affect" an author's meaning'. Without punctuation it is frequently impossible to decide on that meaning. Punctuation is not a form or dress of substantives, something different from words. It is

---

7 Edited, respectively, by F. H. Mares (Cambridge, 1988) and Sheldon P. Zitner (Oxford, 1993).
8 William Shakespeare, *Much Ado About Nothing*, ed. John F. Cox (Cambridge, 1997), p. 140.
9 John F. Andrews, 'Derek Jacobi on Shakespearean Acting', *Shakespeare Quarterly*, 36 (1985), 134–40.
10 Richard Proudfoot, *Shakespeare: Text, Stage and Canon* (London, 2000), p. 28.
11 I have explored other aspects of the problems involved in making Shakespeare editions fully responsive to theatrical issues in two previous articles: 'Annotation and Performance in Shakespeare', *Essays in Criticism*, 46 (1996), pp. 289–301, and 'Actors, Editors, and the Annotation of Shakespearian Playscripts', *Shakespeare Survey* 55 (2002), pp. 181–98.
12 Jonathan Crewe, 'Punctuating Shakespeare', *Shakespeare Studies*, 28 (2000), p. 25.
13 W. W. Greg, 'The Rationale of Copy-Text', *Studies in Bibliography*, 3 (1950–1), p. 21.
14 See, for example, the difficulties in which Cyrus Hoy, 'On Editing Elizabethan Plays', *Renaissance and Reformation*, 8 (1972), finds himself when exploring this topic, and which finally lead him to the unhappy expedient of inventing the category of 'semi-substantive' for cases where he finds it impossible to deny that differences in punctuation do affect meaning (p. 91).

part of speech. Juncture, pitch, and stress are inseparable components in the semantic continuum of the spoken language. Their signs are punctuation.[15]

Despite such strictures, Greg's distinction still exercises a powerful influence on modern Shakespearian editing.

As a result it remains normal for editors to collate all verbal adjustments to copy-text, but to emend the punctuation silently, in all but extremely exceptional cases. Prefatory statements about the modernizing policy followed in particular volumes tend to be concise to the point of uncommunicativeness. A characteristic example from a recent edition ventures only the following about how it has reshaped the punctuation in its sole authoritative source-text:

The Folio punctuation is the compositors' rather than Shakespeare's, but it is generally sensitive, if somewhat heavy by modern standards. Changes to it are necessarily numerous, and only those which affect meaning are collated, as at 4.3.104.[16]

This seems inadequate to me. In effect, it treats the subject as too insignificant or self-evident to warrant a more detailed statement. Yet it begs a number of important questions. Why, for example, are the changes 'necessarily numerous'? What are these 'modern standards' which are casually invoked, but not defined? And what criteria of 'meaning' were in play while the crucial decisions were made about whether or not a particular adjustment to punctuation affected 'meaning'? At the very least, we may conclude, contemporary editorial practice on this issue lacks transparency.

Joseph Moxon, author of the first English manual on printing-house practices, observed, in an often quoted passage, that it was the compositor's 'task and duty . . . to discern and amend the bad Spelling and Pointing of his Copy'.[17] From which principle derives the assumption that punctuation in any printing of a Shakespeare play will have been subject to such regularizing interventions. As a result, it becomes impossible to identify any particular habit of punctuation as incontrovertibly characteristic of Shakespeare's own practice or deriving from his manuscript.

In a provocative article in 1977 Michael Warren accordingly argued that Shakespearian editors must always remain aware 'how little of substance we have to depend on in our judgments, how little we really *know* about the relation of any extant text to the author's original'. Quarto and Folio punctuation may well be scribal and/or compositorial; but, in the end, it remains all we have. It is therefore, in Warren's view, an illusion to believe that scholarship can remove it and reveal with objective clarity the syntactical structures it allegedly obscures. Warren insists that 'the alteration of punctuation is an act of interpretation in itself', and that 'our modern punctuation also has rhetorical implications, and its intrusion inevitably affects the phrasing and, especially for the actor, the intonation of the speech'. He concludes that 'the most innocent modernization may preclude an alternative interpretation, or alter a rhythmic pattern'.[18]

Warren's intervention prompted Stanley Wells to an interesting response in his *Modernizing Shakespeare's Spelling*. For Wells, it is axiomatic that 'the punctuation of the control-text would often bewilder or mislead a modern reader, and must be altered in a modern-spelling edition'.[19] So, while conceding some of Warren's detailed points, Wells remains wedded to a project the legitimacy of which Warren ultimately questions. If one's key aim is that Shakespeare's work should be as widely read as possible, then the modernizing project, it can be argued by its proponents, has proven success on its side. It is also unlikely that publishers

[15] Morse Peckham, 'Reflections on the Foundations of Modern Textual Editing', *Proof*, 1 (1971), p. 124. Cf. Stephen Orgel, 'What is an Editor?', *Shakespeare Studies*, 24 (1996), pp. 24–5.
[16] William Shakespeare, *As You Like It*, ed. Alan Brissenden (Oxford, 1993), p. 88.
[17] Joseph Moxon, *Mechanick Exercises on the Whole Art of Printing*, ed. Herbert Davis and Harry Carter (London, 1962), p. 192.
[18] Michael J. Warren, 'Repunctuation as Interpretation in Editions of Shakespeare', *English Literary Renaissance*, 7 (1977), pp. 156–7.
[19] Stanley Wells and Gary Taylor, *Modernizing Shakespeare's Spelling, with Three Studies in the Text of 'Henry V'* (Oxford, 1979), p. 31.

will henceforward resolve only to issue facsimiles of the earliest printings. As John Jowett has remarked, experience to date suggests that 'only a dedicated minority of any critical persuasion is in practice prepared to abandon the seductively usable modern edition and read their Shakespeare in photographic facsimiles of the original quartos and Folio'.[20] This, however, proffers the most powerful of reasons for asking searching questions about how modernizing editing is currently carried out.

Wells does not underrate the practical difficulties confronting the modernizing editor or the tentative, speculative nature of some of the logic on which he or she must depend. Ultimately, Wells tends to envisage a diversity of modernizing practices, with editions of the same play diverging in accordance with the conscientious – but, in key ways, essentially subjective – exercise of each editor's judgement. He illustrates this via an example from *Coriolanus* 1.1, 187–98 – Caius Martius's eruption, which begins (in the First Folio), 'Hang 'em: They say?' Surprisingly, Wells does not reproduce the 1623 version of the speech, but instead gives us the Arden 2 and New Penguin modernizations of it.[21] He lists some of the differences between them, which are considerable. His overall attitude is permissive. He has, he says, no desire to establish one as 'preferable to the other', but merely 'to point to the interpretative effect of punctuation, whether it is derived from a control-text or not, and to suggest that the editor should have firm confidence in the authenticity of the control-text's punctuation before he commits himself to attempting to convey its effect to the modern reader'.[22]

His chosen example, however, raises concerns to which this concluding formulation provides no answer. Here are the opening lines in the speech according to the First Folio text:

> Hang them: They say?
> They'l sit by th'fire, and presume to know
> What's done i'th Capitoll: Who's like to rise,
> Who thriues, & who declines: Side factions, & giue out
> Coniecturall Marriages, making parties strong,
> And feebling such as stand not in their liking,

Below their cobled Shooes. They say ther's grain enough?

The First Folio punctuation draws attention to the echo which links 'They say' in Martius' first line with 'They say ther's grain enough' in the last line quoted by using a question mark to conclude both. One might argue that this tactic – whether authorial or not – helpfully pinpoints a key piece of rhetorical patterning, to which an actor should ideally respond while plotting a performance of the speech. This does not, of course, mean that he would voice the two phrases identically, merely that the latter 'They say' should be spoken so as to allude to, and build on, its predecessor.

Question marks are frequently used in early modern printing where we would employ exclamation marks. So the modernizing editor needs to consider whether these two phrases are best treated as exclamations or as questions. Wells's specimen editions, however, both see the need to make a further intervention, but disagree on how best to execute it. The Arden 2 version reads 'They say!' in the first line, but 'They say there's grain enough?' for the echo phrase, whereas the New Penguin text retains the first as 'They say?', while converting the latter into 'They say there's grain enough!'[23] Neither collates these changes, nor attempts to justify them in a note. Nothing, therefore, in their editions alerts the reader to the alterations they have introduced nor to the existence of alternative ways of interpreting and voicing the lines.[24]

---

20 John Jowett, 'After Oxford: Recent Developments in Textual Studies', in W. R. Elton and John M. Mucciolo, eds., *The Shakespearean International Yearbook 1: Where Are We Now in Shakespearean Studies?* (Aldershot, 1999), p. 74.

21 Edited, respectively, by Philip Brockbank (London, 1976) and G. R. Hibbard (Harmondsworth, 1967).

22 Stanley Wells and Gary Taylor, *Modernizing Shakespeare's Spelling*, p. 33.

23 In comparing the two editions' handling of the 'They say' lines, Wells mistakenly speaks of 'F's exclamation mark after "They say"' (p. 32).

24 The two most recent major editions of the play – the Oxford Shakespeare, edited by R. B. Parker (Oxford, 1994) and the New Cambridge, edited by Lee Bliss (Cambridge, 2000) – both echo the New Penguin repunctuation. Unlike the

I can deduce no reasons for either change, beyond the personal (and perhaps transitory) preferences of the two editors. Certainly nothing in the syntactical organization of the speech favours one possibility over the other. In effect, these editors are functioning as directors, moulding the words to fit the interpretation they currently favour. I cannot conceive that, if challenged, either would have argued that the version they offer is the only extrapolation possible from the available data. The problem is that nothing in their editions makes that clear. Such diversity may be stimulating for those who own more than one version of a play and are alert to the disagreements they act out. But for readers who will only ever consult a single version of a particular work the text before them is likely to acquire prescriptive authority, *unless* the editor has taken systematic steps to counter that effect.

It would be easy to supply a host of examples illustrating the recurrent nature of this problem in modernized texts of Shakespeare. For our present purposes, however, let one further instance stand in lieu of many others. It occurs in the first Viola/Olivia encounter in *Twelfth Night*, 1.5, a scene to which I will also return later. The 1994 Oxford Shakespeare text, edited by Roger Warren and Stanley Wells, provides this version of Viola's final speech in this scene:

> I am no fee'd post, lady, keep your purse.
> My master, not myself, lacks recompense.
> Love make his heart of flint that you shall love,
> And let your fervour like my master's be
> Placed in contempt. Farewell, fair cruelty.

(1.5. 274–8)

The Oxford Shakespeare provides notes on 'fee'd post' (line 274), 'Love' (line 276), and 'his heart of flint that you shall love' (line 276), but the collation records no editorial adjustments to the First Folio text, the only authoritative source for the play. The latter provides the following version of these lines:

> I am no feede poast, Lady; keepe your purse,
> My Master, not my selfe, lackes recompence.
> Loue make his heart of flint, that you shall loue,

And let your feruour like my masters be,
Plac'd in contempt: Farewell fayre crueltie.

The 1994 modernization reorders the speech in a familiar fashion. The First Folio punctuation, for example, connects the second half of the first line with the speech's second line as an interlinked unit of thought, suggesting as its meaning '*I* don't need payment from you, it's my master who has not been rewarded for his service' – a reading easy for an actor to convey. The Oxford Shakespeare re-sorts the sequence and makes the first line firmly end-stopped, so that 'keep your purse', now linked to the clause which precedes it, spells out the implication of 'I am no fee'd post' with a vigorous and blunt imperative which for the moment obliterates the social divide between messenger and countess – a rudeness reinforced by the emphatic end-line pause on which the remodelled punctuation insists. This too is an option easy to realize in performance.

The crucial question has to be what it was about the First Folio version which rendered its alteration indispensable. No issues of comprehensibility are raised by the 1623 pointing. Each of the clauses is readily understandable as punctuated in the First Folio; but their interrelationships, *and hence, pace Greg, their cumulative meaning*, are significantly reinvented by the Oxford Shakespeare repunctuation. Why then was it deemed necessary? The 1623 punctuation may well be compositorial, and an editor might legitimately wish to underline that it therefore has no special legislative force. Other performance extrapolations from these words are perfectly legitimate. But the 1623 version is evidently coherent and playable, and the version substituted for it can possess no claim to superior authenticity or theatrical persuasiveness. In addition, the silent way in which the substitution has been made renders it 'impossible for readers to read through the editorial punctuation to that in the Folio to see

---

Oxford Shakespeare, the New Cambridge does, however, collate the alteration.

whether a different reading may have been possible'.[25]

How then can it be justifiable to perform such changes without overt acknowledgement? In addition, what satisfactory rationale could be provided for the routine, *ad hoc* alteration of texts in this manner? This instance clearly does not fit Wells's criterion of a passage where 'the punctuation of the control-text would often bewilder or mislead a modern reader' and where adjustment therefore becomes imperative in a modernized edition. Instead, it looks perilously like the introduction of change merely for change's sake; and, as such, it has to be deeply problematic. Every time an editor repeats the traditional mantra that they have 'modernized spelling and punctuation without annotation, unless they affect meaning'[26] and then proceeds to make wholesale, and undeclared, alterations to the punctuation in this way, they seriously mislead their readers about the nature and import of the changes they have introduced.

Armed with Jacobi's bracing scepticism about editorial punctuation, an actor can coolly disregard such distractions. But Jacobi's attitude cannot be taken to be the one usual in the theatre. Juliet Stevenson, for example, a highly intelligent actress, has expressed her respect for 'the structure of Shakespeare's language', and particularly his 'metre – that basic ten-syllable iambic pentameter line', and argued that 'you have to observe what he's doing with them, not as an end in itself but because they give you so many clues'. The latter, she reports, are to be discovered in 'his rhythms, his pauses, his punctuation'.[27] Stevenson is clearly unaware that we do not possess Shakespeare's punctuation, and that the Penguin edition, for example – at the date of her remarks the series the Royal Shakespeare Company recommended and used in rehearsals – deploys punctuation systems unlike any in use in late Elizabethan and early Jacobean England. Teaching guidebooks often display the same misplaced trust in the authority of the punctuation in the text before them.[28] Current editorial procedures make such misunderstandings more or less inevitable.

Stephen Greenblatt expressed a desire to speak with the dead.[29] Shakespearian actors encounter another fate. They have to speak with language composed by the dead, to which they strive to give living meaning. This confronts them with major technical challenges. These difficulties are caused not only by the unfamiliarity of early modern vocabulary and syntax, but also by the remarkable velocity and density of the plays' rhetoric and by the often intricate formal properties which underpin the dialogue's organization. Modern acting training does not equip its students to confront complex verse structures with ease and command.[30] Here, it might seem, is terrain where the scholar could enter into tactful, yet constructive, dialogue with the performer, especially since an edition's preparation involves a host of decisions which impact materially on the understanding of those structures. The

---

[25] N. F. Blake, *Shakespeare's Language: An Introduction* (London and Basingstoke, 1983), p. 121.

[26] William Shakespeare and John Fletcher, *Henry VIII, or All is True* (Oxford, 1999), ed. Jay L. Halio, p. 63.

[27] Carol Rutter, *Clamorous Voices: Shakespeare's Women Today* (London, 1988), p. 42. Stevenson specifically acknowledges the powerful influence on her thinking of 'Cis Berry, the RSC's voice teacher' (p. 43). In her widely used books, Cicely Berry displays little concern about the issues under discussion here. In *Text in Action* (London, 2001), her most recent publication, for instance, she makes the following insouciant statement about her choice of Shakespeare texts: 'please note that all the extracts bar one are taken from the Penguin editions, as that is what we use at the RSC. The one exception is *Timon of Athens*, which is taken from the Arden Shakespeare. Punctuation in Shakespearean texts does vary depending on the publisher, and different punctuation may confuse an exercise' (p. 273).

[28] See, for example, Rex Gibson, *Teaching Shakespeare* (Cambridge, 1998), p. 167; Jean Benedetti, *Stanislavski and the Actor* (London, 1998), pp. 88–92.

[29] Stephen Greenblatt, *Shakespearean Negotiations: The Circulation of Social Energy in Renaissance England* (Oxford, 1988), p. 1.

[30] For two sample illustrations of the kinds of difficulty this can cause, cf. Kristina Bedford, *'Coriolanus' at the National: "Th'Interpretation of the Time"* (Selinsgrove, 1992), pp. 142 and 350–1, and Carole Zucker, *Figures of Light: Actors and Directors Illuminate the Art of Film Acting* (New York, 1995), p. 184.

problem is that, here too, editors are accustomed to do their work invisibly, far from the gaze of critical scrutiny. At the very least, greater explicitness from them about their practices would be helpful to readers. It might also in time modify editorial practice, since explaining what one customarily does can lead one to question why one has been doing it that way.

The editorial habit of secrecy can extend to suppressing all mention of alternative theories to the one the present editor favours. The Oxford Shakespeare *Twelfth Night* provides an illustration of this in its treatment of the concluding couplet of Viola's exit speech in 1.5, which in the First Folio reads as follows:

> And let your feruour like my masters be,
> Plac'd in contempt: Farewell fayre crueltie.

The Arden 2 *Twelfth Night*, which appeared before the Warren / Wells edition, stays loyal to the First Folio at this point and glosses its decision with the following note:

I follow Turner in keeping F's punctuation, which rightly stresses the rhyme-word; he paraphrases 'let your fervour be like my master's, that is, held in contempt'.[31]

Basic scansion also suggests a stress on that concluding 'be'. Reinforcing that expectation with the argument from the rhyme, in my view, makes the logic of the Arden 2 comment pretty unassailable.[32] Removing the comma, as most modernized editions puzzlingly do, I would argue, both misreads the couplet metrically and reinvents its meaning, implying for the latter: 'May your fervour, like my master's for you, be scorned'. Such a debatable decision may suggest that sensitivity to metrical values, and their performance consequences, is not always the priority it should be in modern Shakespearian editing.[33] The Oxford Shakespeare's ignoring of the Arden 2 decision is especially odd. Editors clearly have every right to disagree with their predecessors' actions. But one might expect some explanation of why Arden 2's note justifying its fidelity to the First Folio punctuation has been judged unconvincing. Again, the silence with which an intervention with important implica-

tions for performance has been executed leaves the reader underinformed and arguably misled.

If editors, like actors, need to be attuned to textual minutiae, both also need to be alert to larger structural patterns and their performance implications. Decisions on points of detail can have major ramifications for the larger progress of a scene. Here too the first Viola/Olivia encounter provides us with an interesting case-study. In the remainder of this paper I want to concentrate on the relevant sequence from that scene and, especially, on one brief, pivotal moment in it. In the process I will sample some recent writing about it by both actors and academics, while also exploring how editors have handled it.

The duel between Viola and Olivia begins in prose. When Viola buttresses her offer to recite the speech in Olivia's praise she professes to have learned by heart with the boast that ''tis Poeticall', Olivia blocks the threatened move with the firm put-down: 'It is the more like to be feigned' (1.5 187–8). So, for the moment, verse seems to be stigmatized as a medium from which neither truth-telling nor plain-speaking is to be expected. Which raises the stakes for the players, since this scene is itself destined to move into verse in its later stages.

How to negotiate that transition is inevitably much on the mind of those who perform it. For Emma Fielding, who played Viola for the Royal Shakespeare Company in 1994, the graph of development was clear:

I loved playing this scene: the staccato prose beginning, when Viola wants clarity; then it grows as the speech turns to the poetry of blank verse, the only form that can

---

[31] William Shakespeare, *Twelfth Night*, ed. J. M. Lothian and T. W. Craik (London, 1975), p. 36. Arden 2 is reacting against the precedent of Arden 1 – edited by Morton Luce (London, 1906) – which here altered the First Folio reading in the style favoured by Warren and Wells.

[32] If a modernizing editor felt the use of a comma here to be inappropriate to modern conventions, then an obvious alternative punctuation would be: 'And let your fervour like my master's be – / Placed in contempt'.

[33] For some provocative thoughts on this subject, see Carol M. Sicherman, 'Meter and Meaning in Shakespeare', *Language and Style*, 15 (1982), pp. 169–92.

really cope with Viola's heart-burning passion. It turns from prose and the prosaic – Are you really the lady of the house? – to the soaring poetry of the 'willow cabin' speech.[34]

This account, however, foreshortens events, since Viola makes the move into verse earlier than the 'Make me a willow Cabine' speech (257–65). Fielding does not, therefore, tell us how she reckons the moment of transition itself should be handled.

In his recent book on the play, Michael Pennington, who has both directed *Twelfth Night* and acted in it, only pauses to remark directly on the change of mode from prose to verse when he reaches Viola's 'I see you what you are, you are too proud: / But if you were the diuell, you are faire' (239–40), again a step or two too late. At that point, however, he observes:

The imagery is darkening, and, its emotions cranked up a notch, the dialogue is breaking mutually into verse – with a sense of surrender, the release we feel when we finally start telling the truth.[35]

This is more circumstantial than Fielding's description – also, more overheated in its implicitly orgasmic metaphor. But is it accurate? Is 'the dialogue' here really 'breaking *mutually* into verse'? If this implies that the two characters move into verse simultaneously, then it is inaccurate. Viola makes the move first; Olivia initially refuses to follow suit. Exactly when she finally concedes to verse is a question on which, as we shall see, experts differ.

Another experienced player, Janet Suzman, does not believe that Olivia responds to 'I see you what you are' in verse. Indeed, she contrasts Viola, at this point, 'in the searing fire of poetry' with 'Olivia in an increasingly sober prose', though the only speech which seems a possible candidate for the latter description is the brief 'How does he loue me?' (243). For her the moment when 'Olivia, to her credit, catches the new seriousness' comes as 'she condescends, as it were, to poetry, and meets Viola's intensity with an equal burst of frankness'. Suzman's language repeatedly associates authenticity of emotion and freedom of expression with verse – an association which, she is certain, will also work its effect on the play's spectators. Thus,

she reports, it 'is with some relief that we encounter a truthful Olivia', when, at last released into verse, she begins her 'Your lord does know my mind' excursion.[36]

Patsy Rodenburg, the influential voice teacher, has also mapped this scene in detail. On Viola's first use of verse – after Olivia's ''Tis in grain sir, 'twill endure winde and weather' (227) - she remarks that 'It is at this moment that Viola moves into verse and speaks so directly. Her next four lines flow regularly and with great ease and freedom'. So, similar ideas about an almost automatic link between verse and 'ease and freedom' seem to be operating here. She judges that Olivia's entry into verse occurs at the same point as Suzman had identified for it; but she characterizes it differently: 'Suddenly Olivia moves into verse. Although her thoughts all start at the beginnings of lines, only two are regular – she is struggling to find form'. Rodenburg then stumbles into bathos with the surmise that 'Maybe she hasn't felt the need to speak verse for some time'! Lucidity, however – Olivia's, that is – wins out, since 'Nonetheless, her thoughts are well argued'.[37]

I want to add to our four theatrical witnesses two academic ones, beginning with a scholar interested in the way in which early modern actors prepared their performances. In her book on the history of rehearsal from Shakespeare's time to Sheridan's, Tiffany Stern underlines the scarcity of anything we would call full rehearsal in the early modern playhouses. Much of an actor's preparatory work was perforce done solo. He also received his role via the medium of a cue-script, in which were written merely his own lines and the briefest of cues for each of his contributions – a habit which persisted in British theatre until the mid twentieth

---

[34] Helen Fielding, *Twelfth Night; or, What You Will* (London, 2002), p. 18.

[35] Michael Pennington, *'Twelfth Night': A User's Guide* (London, 2000), p. 68.

[36] Janet Suzman, *Acting with Shakespeare: The Comedies* (New York, 1996), pp. 102–3.

[37] Patsy Rodenburg, *Speaking Shakespeare* (London, 2002), pp. 321–2.

century. From this Stern draws far-reaching conclusions. Since actors learned 'their own fragment in isolation from the story that surrounded it', they 'did not have a natural sense of the play as a whole; a fact that was reflected...in the way they performed when together'. She emphasizes that what resulted might seem accident-prone and imperfect to later eyes. She cannot, however, quite let go of a model of authorial control. She insists that dramatists 'composed for learning of this kind, and the parts they produced contained the information needed for solo practice'.

As her prime example of this phenomenon Stern cites Olivia's cue-script for her 1.5 meeting with Viola. Explore the information such a document would convey to the eyes of an Elizabethan actor, she asserts, and 'the actual moment at which the love is engendered is clear: the moment when Olivia's part switches from prose to verse (ironically with the words, 'Your Lord does know my mind, I cannot loue him', (*TN* 549), the very words with which Olivia denies her love for Orsino)'.[38]

For a number of reasons this seems highly questionable to me. It works from an unargued premise – that is, that, as a key priority, the player of Olivia must communicate to the audience the metamorphosis of her feelings *during* the stage enactment of her interview with Viola. Why should we accept such a premise? If we did not bring such a preconception with us, would anything in the scene itself suggest it? Some critics have implicitly made a similar assumption, as when Bertrand Evans, for instance, tracked Olivia's progress in the later stages of 1.5 thus: her 'attitude changes in the course of 100 lines from haughty scorn to flirtatious interest and finally to love'.[39] Others have been more cautious. Gary Taylor, for instance, surmises that 'the full meaning and pattern of the scene probably only strike us when she's alone, when they strike her'.[40] Such a reading certainly protects Viola, who may otherwise end up looking naive and slow-witted as Olivia's transformation is unmistakably conveyed to the audience, but remains bafflingly indecipherable to her. It is noteworthy that Shakespeare has not here employed a revelatory aside, the classic device – as with Claudius's sudden confession of fratricidal guilt in *Hamlet* 3.1. 52–6 – to allow such information to be communicated without compromising the standing of other characters simultaneously on stage. This may be evidence that ensuring the audience were immediately aware of what Olivia was experiencing was not a high priority for him during the encounter with Viola. Olivia's following soliloquy can be left to take care of that. Similarly, unless the actor already assumes – or perhaps has been instructed by some process other than the cue-script itself – that this is the task which faces him, would he ever deduce it from the nature of Olivia's speech at this point – an itemized assessment of Orsino's qualities? Despite Stern's attempt to draw dramatic irony from its very inappropriateness, this is scarcely the obvious language in which to reveal the onset of an erotic obsession with Cesario. For Stern, the simple fact of the transition from prose to verse is indisputably 'an actor's stage direction' signalling the onset of passion, an enormous leap of faith in which it is difficult to join her. One might ask, as a *reductio ad absurdum*, whether, when Viola earlier moves from prose to verse, we should draw a matching conclusion and deduce from this revelatory moment the burgeoning of an otherwise unexpressed passion for Olivia.

Once again the academic reading – this time one avowedly attempting to retrieve a more realistic sense of early modern theatrical practicalities – ends up unacceptably narrowing down the interpretative possibilities of Shakespeare's words. Stern professes a major debt to Patrick Tucker, a theatre director who has long been committed to experimenting with directing Shakespeare from the earliest printings of the plays.[41] In his own recent book

---

[38] Tiffany Stern, *Rehearsal from Shakespeare to Sheridan* (Oxford, 2000), pp. 64–5.

[39] Bertrand Evans, *Shakespeare's Comedies* (Oxford, 1960), p. 121.

[40] Gary Taylor, *Moment by Moment in Shakespeare* (Basingstoke, 1985), p. 77.

[41] Tiffany Stern, Introduction to *Rehearsal from Shakespeare to Sheridan*, p. v.

Tucker visits this same scene. Some of his suggestions overlap with Stern's. He too emphasizes the 'gear change in the scene', as Olivia converts into verse. But, although he mentions the idea that this could be the moment when 'she falls in love with' Viola, he cites that as only one possible reading and explicitly allows for the equal validity of other interpretations.[42] His commentary lacks at this point the prescriptiveness of Stern's.

Another scholar, Peter Thomson, views the theatrical demands of *Twelfth Night* differently. He concludes that it 'is written for ensemble playing'. He points, for example, to the absence of a single 'big' part, and that eight actors are assigned '150 lines or more', with the largest role, Sir Toby Belch's, only notching up 401 lines. He notes that this 'spread and distribution of lines are unique [among Shakespeare's scripts], even in those plays written for performance in the years around 1601'. He deduces that 'Shakespeare's belief in his fellow-actors was rising high in 1600/1601'.[43]

Nothing in Thomson's findings denies the information on which Stern mounts her case – that, for instance, group rehearsal was scarce, that much preparation for performance was solitary, etc. But missing from Stern's account is Shakespeare's necessary belief, as Thomson conceives it, that his actors could and would respond to the novel challenge he was setting them – one which posited in them a capacity, *however they may have prepared for performance*, to collaborate and interact purposefully once they were gathered on the Globe stage. Without such faith, in Thomson's view the experimental design of *Twelfth Night* is inexplicable. A professional dramatist would be writing without intelligent care for the capacities and propensities of the actors who were due to realize his script, and who were responsible for its commissioning.

Whatever the resulting 'ensemble playing' may have been like, it will clearly have been very different from the carefully premeditated organization of ensemble aimed at by contemporary directors like Peter Stein or Trevor Nunn. It will perforce have had rough-hewn qualities which modern rehearsal methods tend to eliminate. But this is not the same as saying that early modern audiences watched a line-up of performers pursuing their own narrow agendas, as decreed by the meagre evidence provided by their cue-scripts. One of the most polished English farce actors of the English stage in the early to mid-twentieth century, Robertson Hare, acted from cue-scripts for the majority of his working life. When he later had a regular part in a television comedy series, he was disturbed by being given the entire script for a half-hour episode. It contained too much information for him. So, according to one of his fellow actors, Hare used to write out a cue-script for himself for each episode 'in immaculate copperplate writing'. He 'couldn't work in any other way'.[44] Yet Hare was renowned for the security, speed and inventiveness of his responses in fast-moving scripts where extended speeches were exceedingly rare. Dependence on a cue-script does not, therefore, rule out vivid, fast-thinking, creative responsiveness to group interaction during performance.

Once in front of an audience, Elizabethan players, like Robertson Hare, needed to be listening alertly and capable of absorbing information as the performance evolved. The player of Olivia might indeed be anticipating the moment when his dialogue moved from prose to verse, but as a result he was more likely to register the fact, *however belatedly he discovered it*, that the shift into verse is initiated by Viola and that Olivia at first resists it. Her delayed concession to verse derives its dramatic potency from that fact. Any reading of the scene which ignores this is untrue to the structure of the scene Shakespeare has crafted for the actors he knew so intimately. Similarly, no history of rehearsal can be adequate unless it brings fully into play the nature of the scripts being rehearsed.

Our four witnesses from the theatre view the scene with greater complexity. But all of them insistently associate the move into verse with

---

[42] Patrick Tucker, *Secrets of Acting Shakespeare: The Original Approach* (London, 2002), p.144.

[43] Peter Thomson, *Shakespeare's Theatre* (London, 1983), pp. 98–9.

[44] Kate Dunn, *Exit Through the Fireplace: The Great Days of Rep* (London, 1998), p. 123.

truth-telling and the direct expression of authentic feeling. In their fixation with this idea, none takes seriously into account the dialogue's earlier playing with the idea of poetry – specifically, poetic encomium – as a mode of communication where feigning is to be taken for granted. This prelude surely has to have repercussions for the moment when verse finally becomes the scene's idiom.

We have noted uncertainty among our theatrical witnesses about exactly when Olivia begins to speak verse. This should be precisely the kind of issue on which illumination can be sought from a play's editors. Quarto and Folio lineation often receives adjustment in modern editions. At certain points the lineation may, for example, have come adrift from anything we recognize as apt line divisions, and as a consequence intervention may seem indispensable. The problem which unfortunately may then arise is that editors can differ widely in the solutions they silently adopt for the agreed problem. Another kind of challenge – one which arises recurrently in *Twelfth Night* – involves the First Folio's habit of justifying to the left when printing what may be the second portion of a divided verse line. Sometimes – especially in relatively early plays – the adjustment to modern lay-out conventions at such points can be uncontroversial. At others trickier decisions can be involved, and passages which some construe as prose may end up being highjacked into unconvincing verse-layouts, with the whole process once again being performed silently.

This first Viola/Olivia meeting includes a number of points where tricky decisions of this kind are required of editors. One of them is identified in the notes to the Oxford Shakespeare edition. It affects the conclusion of the 'willow Cabine' speech. In the First Folio the passage reads as follows:

> O you should not rest
> Betweene the elements of ayre, and earth,
> But you should pittie me.
>   Ol. You might do much:
> What is your Parentage?

The last three clauses here have prompted various competing modernizations in recent editions. Arden 2, for example, offers:

> But you should pity me.
> *Olivia.*   You might do much.
>   What is your parentage?

Herschel Baker's Signet Classic edition,[45] however, favours this solution:

> But you should pity me.
> *Olivia.* You might do much. What is your parentage?

The Oxford Shakespeare declines to enter the competition and prints the following:

> But you should pity me.
> OLIVIA You might do much.
> What is your parentage?

Its accompanying note contains much that is illuminating and stimulating:

Three broken verse lines; either the first two or the last two could form a complete verse line. Perhaps Olivia, entranced by the power of Viola's speech, says *You might do much* at once, completing Viola's line; or perhaps there is a pause after *pity me*, indicating Olivia's absorption in a different way, with Olivia's two sentences forming one verse line. Or maybe the three broken lines are intentional, with a second pause after *You might do much*, before Olivia asks, *What is your parentage?* This would help to emphasize the significance of the question, for Olivia is actually asking whether Viola/Cesario is of the rank to qualify as a potential husband, and thus unmistakably expressing her interest in 'Cesario' for the first time. These broken lines may also be what Viola refers to later when she says that Olivia spoke 'in starts, distractedly' (2.2.21).

This note is valuably frank about the fact that the enigma bequeathed to us by the First Folio is strictly insoluble, and that this exchange as we have received it accordingly accommodates a number of different performance realizations, including more possibilities than are listed here. Refraining from

---

45 William Shakespeare, *Twelfth Night; or, What You Will*, ed. Herschel Baker (New York, 1965), p. 57.

adjusting the layout, while exploring some of the acting options in a note, therefore seems by far the best solution here. In the process, the reader and performer are alerted to the potential acting significance of the missing beats in these lines. The note implicitly works from an important presupposition about the rhythmic potency of this kind of verse in early modern performance. The quality of attention it will have elicited from spectators is taken to be sufficiently alert and attuned for them to register that the expected completion of the line patterning has not been fulfilled here, and that this fact therefore becomes an important weapon in the actor's hands.[46]

The Oxford Shakespeare edition's tactics here are an invaluable innovation in the annotation of *Twelfth Night*. From which moment of celebration I must ungratefully move on to regret that its editors are not equally communicative about the issues involved in all the other such moments in this scene. Here, for example, is the First Folio text of a moment a little earlier in 1.5, 241–5:

> O such loue
> Could be but recompenc'd, though you were crown'd
> The non-pareil of beautie.
> *Ol.* How does he loue me?
> *Vio.* With adorations, fertill teares,
> With groanes that thunder loue, with sighes of fire.

The metrically incomplete – or should that be defective? – penultimate line here has sometimes been commented on by editors, with radical differences of opinion between them. For the Oxford Shakespeare, 'This is a four-foot line (unless *adorations* is trisyllabic), but not metrically defective'. Warren and Wells offer a number of comparisons from elsewhere in the play and suggest that 'Perhaps Viola pauses in mid-line so as to give Orsino's *adorations* as much weight as possible'. Arden 2, on the other hand, deems the line defective and notes that it is consequently 'impossible to recover Shakespeare's text except by conjecture', which, in the nature of the case, can never be verified. The two editions are, however, at one in simply insisting on the correctness of the version they

prefer. Neither even acknowledges the existence of alternative opinions on the issue. Do readers not deserve to be more fully briefed?

Whatever view one may favour on the defectiveness or otherwise of this line, no one doubts that Viola is speaking verse here. But is Olivia? The Oxford Shakespeare modernizes the first part of this exchange as follows:

> O, such love
> Could be but recompensed though you were
>   crowned
> The nonpareil of beauty.
> OLIVIA   How does he love me?

In this they follow a well-settled pattern for modern editions and accordingly feel no need to collate their adjustment to lay-out or to defend it in a note. If they are right, then this becomes the moment when Olivia moves finally into verse. A first thought might be that the most obvious motivation for a surrender to verse on 'How does he loue me?' would not be an access of truth-telling and free speaking, as some of our performers wish the abandoning of prose to signal, but a potent reaffirmation of the narcissism of which Viola has several times accused her. Part of a repeated pattern, therefore, it would not provide a turning-point for the scene as a whole.

But is 'How does he loue me?' indisputably the conclusion of a verse line? Despite the editorial consensus, Patsy Rodenburg automatically takes it to be a prose speech,[47] an assumption in which she is joined by Tiffany Stern, who works directly from the First Folio.[48] Given what is potentially riding on this moment, it seems reasonable to ask editors to be explicit about the reasoning which guides their practice here. But, once again, the operation is performed in silence, and no explanations are forthcoming. I can imagine no satisfactory justification for this, despite the fact that it is common practice.

---

[46] Cf. Coburn Freer, *The Poetics of Jacobean Drama* (Baltimore, 1981), pp. 28–61.

[47] Patsy Rodenburg, *Speaking Shakespeare*, p. 322.

[48] Tiffany Stern, *Rehearsal from Shakespeare to Sheridan*, p. 65.

Regular scansion for the alexandrine the editorial tradition favours would generate an odd pattern of emphases: 'The *nonpareil* of *beauty*. / *How* does *he* love *me*?' Does this fit the dramatic context? Viola has been evoking Orsino's adoration for Olivia and insisting it demands reciprocation. She has not spoken directly of the feelings Olivia either has or should have for Orsino. So the natural stress pattern here would seem to be not 'what are the feelings *he* has for *me*', which implies a contrast with an immediately preceding discussion of *her* feelings for *him*, but, rather, '*How* does he *love* me?', which would fluently cue Viola's answer: 'With adorations, fertile tears...' On this view, the editorial consensus may create more problems than it solves. Is the layout it silently imposes really a plausible one?

If we regard these six words as prose, however, then Olivia's obstinacy persists a little longer, and her concession to verse would finally arrive with 'Your Lord does know my mind'. Here too it is difficult to discern the traces of emotional authenticity and frank self-expression which our theatrical witnesses persistently wish should characterize Olivia's venturing into the novel realm of verse. In this version, her first verse utterance lists and acknowledges, in orderly fashion, Orsino's admirable public qualities, but firmly registers, 'I cannot loue him' (251). Not obviously the urgent language of fresh, revelatory feeling. So, the usual question from the actors inevitably recurs. Why here?

Daniel Seltzer has penned a vivid portrait of his ideal moment of Shakespearian performance as that rare occasion when you 'feel...a breathing of life back and forth between two people who are really listening to each other, whose actions might really cause a reaction, whose words – be they verse or prose, elegantly or ill-spoken – are inhabited with cause, with inner needs, with – in short – an understanding of the life of the text which can only be the result of exposure and time, as well as of talent and training'.[49] This is a rapt evocation of desired perfection, not an image of everyday theatrical reality. But, in my imagined circumstances of early modern performance, the capacity to listen carefully and respond intelligently to what is heard moment-

by-moment remains a *sine qua non* for a successful performer. In this encounter, indeed, Shakespeare has also made that ability intrinsic to the manoeuvres of his two major characters. Thus, when Maria attempts to dismiss Viola with the contemptuous 'Will you hoyst sayle sir, here lies your way', her intended victim improvises a brusquely unanswerable response, which throws Maria's nautical metaphor back in her face: 'No good swabber, I am to hull here a little longer' (194-5). Similarly, Olivia immediately picks up on Viola's claim that what she needs to say would be 'to your ears, Diuinity; to any others, prophanation' and, as a consequence, mischievously treats her first lines when they are alone together as if they were the beginning of a sermon (207–8). Alacrity in absorbing and acting upon the stimuli offered by an interlocutor's briefest use of simile or metaphor is the basic currency of this scene and requires from its performers a matching agility.

An Olivia listening alertly to his fellow player will remember the moment when Viola abandoned prose. It followed Olivia's removal of her veil with the question, 'Is't not well done?' (224-5). Viola responds to that with a retort which mingles praise and mockery of her rival's pride: 'Excellcatly done, if God did all' (226). Olivia holds her ground with ''Tis in graine sir, 'twill endure winde and weather' (227). After which Viola ventures into verse with ''Tis beauty truly blent, whose red and white, / Nature's own sweet, and cunning hand laid on' (228–9) and proceeds to deduce from this beauty a procreative argument, in the manner of Shakespeare's sonnets, for Olivia's agreeing to marry Orsino (230–1). This in turn provokes from a stubbornly prose-bound Olivia an ironic inventory of the items which compose her beauty (233–8). So Viola's shift into verse occurs on a compliment – slightly formal perhaps, also perhaps an implicit apology for the aggression in 'if God did all', but offered, it would seem, unironically. A performer playing Olivia may therefore find it

49 Daniel Seltzer, 'Acting Shakespeare Now', *Mosaic*, 10 (1977), 73.

provocative that her own matching move into verse is plotted to come as she repudiates Viola's accusation of pride by testifying to the merits of the man the latter rebuked her for undervaluing and scorning. And the inventory form in which this first verse utterance is couched echoes – and perhaps compensates for – the sarcastic prose inventory of her own physical properties with which she answered Viola's first verse improvisation. The symmetries which link the two moments are rendered the more piquant by the fact that, as she thus justifies herself to Viola, so she stops resisting the latter's pull towards verse. In addition, the earlier rejection of poetic encomium as 'like to be feigned' rhymes neatly with the fact that Viola and Olivia move into verse as each modifies the mood of her contributions by praising, respectively, Olivia's beauty and Orsino's virtues.

Such intricate planning placed rich resources before Shakespeare's actors. I do not presume to risk speculating in any detail about what they may have made of these riches in performance. Consecutive early modern performances may even have diverged radically in the ways in which they realized possibilities from the menu Shakespeare had presented to them. What I cannot believe is that their acting would have been utterly unresponsive to the way in which Shakespeare has rendered resonant and complex the negotiations which accompany the scene's turn into verse.

My last few paragraphs imply that our modern actors' persistent equation of verse with free feeling and truth-telling may be too monochromatic to catch the subtlety of its uses in this scene. There is surely, at the very least, the possibility here for an interesting, potentially productive dialogue between study and stage. Even the oft-cited 'willow Cabine' speech scarcely offers a direct expression of Viola's emotions. She sketches in it what she would do if she were Orsino and sought Olivia's hand. The vitality with which she plots this hypothetical wooing belies the passivity of her relation to her own plight. Actors may invite their spectators to sense behind the 'willow Cabine' speech the pressure of Viola's own unfulfilled – and perhaps unfulfillable – desires. They may even emu-

late Peggy Ashcroft's taking of the cry "Olivia" at its climax 'as a hastily remembered substitution for the "Orsino" that possesses her own thoughts'.[50] Yet in this comedy 'with no straightforward wooing scenes'[51] Viola's self-expression is only mistily glimpsed at one remove behind an adroit rhetorical masquerade, in which she responds to Olivia's cue, 'Why, what would you?', with an impromptu display of eloquence, which identifies her as an ideal courtly ambassador and perhaps worthy of a countess's interest in 'his' own right. This is a scene in which hierarchical expectations are repeatedly overturned, so that a messenger imperiously exceeds the decorum of 'his' role, frequently seizes the initiative in speech, and interrogates – even castigates – 'his' social superior. In the process, 'he' becomes an object of interest – ultimately, amorous interest – in 'his' own right for that social superior. The messenger inadvertently becomes the message.

We have seen Warren and Wells assuming that, when Olivia says, 'You might do much: What is your Parentage?', she 'is actually asking if Viola/Cesario is of the rank to qualify as a potential husband, and thus unmistakably expressing her interest in "Cesario" for the first time'. This is one way in which these words are sometimes now performed. But this reading is clearly not the only possibility. A go-between has just performed the task assigned 'him' with superb aplomb and eloquence. A countess applauds 'his' sure-footed conduct with praise which prophesies the possibility of a glorious career ahead of 'him' ('You might do much') and then asks the inevitable early modern question: whether the gifts 'he' has just displayed are inherited or acquired ('What is your Parentage?'). A player making this the primary meaning of these phrases of Olivia's could also decide to hint that other, more covert imperatives give them additional resonance; but s/he might also choose not to

---

50 Richard David, 'Shakespeare in the Waterloo Road', *Shakespeare Survey* 5 (1952), p. 124.
51 Lois Potter, *'Twelfth Night': Text and Performance* (Basingstoke, 1985), p. 16.

do this and instead postpone the moment of truth-telling about the transformation of her feelings until Olivia's imminent soliloquy. Shakespeare's words will here, as so often elsewhere, abide a variety of performance embodiments.

As will be clear, my own instinct is that Olivia's move into verse comes on 'Your Lord does know my mind'. Given the state of the surviving evidence, however, absolute certainty on this issue, as on many other such moments in Shakespeare's scripts, looks unobtainable. Which reinforces our urgent need for editions which avoid 'premature closure'[52] in such circumstances and are explicit about what editors are doing and why they are doing it as well as about the nature of the evidence from which they are working. Anything less entails in the end systematic misrepresentation of the true situation. It also serves to reinforce the gulf between study and stage. In the rehearsal room pragmatic day-by-day reality demonstrates the susceptibility of words upon the page to different – even sometimes radically opposed – vocalizations. Only by conceding this, and acting wholeheartedly upon its implications, can an open-minded, mutually profitable dialogue with ambitious and intelligent actors such as Jacobi be made possible.

The prize for the most elegantly crisp contribution to *The Oxford Companion to Shakespeare* has to go to Eric Rasmussen's entry on punctuation. I quote it in its entirety:

A coherent system of punctuation, which did not exist in the classical or medieval periods, was probably first mandated by Renaissance printers. Given the almost complete absence of punctuation in Shakespeare's contribution to the *Sir Thomas More* manuscript, some scholars have concluded that punctuation marks in the printed texts of his plays are probably the compositors' rather than Shakespeare's. And yet, the humour of Peter Quince's prologue in *A Midsummer Night's Dream* (5.1.108–17) depends upon its deliberate mispunctuation: as Theseus observes, 'This fellow doth not stand upon points' (5.1.118).[53]

Quince's accident-strewn performance is clearly a crucial test-case. It seems safe to surmise that a playwright scripting such a moment will need to be precise in indicating on paper the failures of syntactical comprehension which afflict his earnest Athenian performer. But this does not mean that his notation of all the other speeches in the same play will inevitably display identical characteristics. This may indeed be the subject of a neat actors' in-joke here. To mimic the 'simple skill' (5.1.110) – for which read 'incompetence' – of his amateur competitor the professional performer requires in this unusual instance an amplitude of punctuation his own well-honed craft skills render redundant elsewhere.

This is not to propose that cue-scripts were wholly unpunctuated. But nor have we any evidence that they were pointed with the thoroughness or consistency necessary to provide a comprehensive map of the linguistic intricacies the early modern actor had to unpack and then communicate in performance. The early modern actor did not therefore simply follow 'points' inscribed on paper for his guidance. He actively identified – and also, inevitably, in the process fashioned – such 'points'.[54]

Phrasing is central to the player's art, and it always involves choices. Different decisions about which words to link with, and balance against, other words can transform the intellectual and emotional force of a speech. No system of committing words to paper can ever wholly fetter the actor's freedom of choice in this respect. As Richard Sennett has remarked, 'the performing arts always have this problem with a text: the degree to which

---

[52] Leah S. Marcus, *Puzzling Shakespeare: Local Reading and its Discontents* (Berkeley, 1988), p. 46.

[53] Michael Dobson and Stanley Wells, eds., *The Oxford Companion to Shakespeare* (Oxford, 2001), p. 359.

[54] In early modern practice the words for punctuation marks were also often used to designate the phrases the latter separated out. Thus, 'comma', for instance, in addition to its now familiar meaning, also meant 'a group of words in a sentence' (Alan Cruttenden, 'Intonation and the Comma', *Visible Language*, 25 (1992), 55). *OED*, similarly, lists as the relevant meanings of 'period' in the sixteenth and seventeenth centuries: 'A complete sentence', 'A full pause such as is properly made at the end of a sentence', and 'The point or character that marks the end of a complete sentence' (*sb.* 10 and 11).

a language of notation is adequate to a language of expression'.[55] Scripts which are lightly and intermittently punctuated, however, concede a much wider licence to players in this respect than ones where the punctuation is emphatic and detailedly directive. It seems clear towards which end of this spectrum Shakespearean cue-scripts must have been located.

As we have seen, the First Folio layout in Viola and Olivia's 'But you should pittie me. / You might do much: / What is your Parentage?' sets us an insoluble puzzle. If early modern printing had no way of clarifying such tangles (or if compositors in 1623 saw no need to attempt to do so), what chance is there that the original manuscript or cue-scripts were any more decisive? Peter Thomson spoke of Shakespeare's 'belief in his fellow-actors in 1600/1601'. This must have entailed ceding to them as their professional due a large element of freedom in determining how they realized his words in performance. We should not seek to be more prescriptive in our dealings with actors than Shakespeare himself chose or, as far as we can judge, cared to be.

---

[55] Richard Sennett, *The Fall of Public Man: On the Social Psychology of Capitalism* (New York, 1976), p. 198.

JOHN SHAKESPEARE'S 'SPIRITUAL TESTAMENT': A REAPPRAISAL

ROBERT BEARMAN

The document known to us as John Shakespeare's 'Spiritual Testament', allegedly discovered during repairs in the 1750s to the roof of the house in which he once lived, is perhaps the greatest weapon in the arsenal of those who maintain that Shakespeare's father remained a practising Catholic; and, if he did, that his son must at least have been reared in the Catholic faith. Moreover, it has been claimed, John's subscription to this 'testament' can be dated to 1580 or 1581, the years of the Jesuit mission into England, led by Edmund Campion and Robert Parsons, thus bringing the Shakespeare family, during William's formative years, into close contact with dangerous Catholic conspirators.[1] However, there are difficulties to overcome if we are to accept the document's authenticity, let alone its Jesuit associations; and even if we could, this would not establish that Shakespeare remained loyal to the Catholic church in later years. Be that as it may, it is the purpose of this essay to subject the 'Spiritual Testament' to close critical examination in an effort to determine whether it can indeed be safely used in the debate over Shakespeare's religious beliefs.[2]

Firstly, what is John Shakespeare's 'Spiritual Testament'? In the form in which it has come down to us it is a declaration of faith in fourteen articles, each of which professes itself to be the belief of John Shakespeare, revealing at the same time the fact that he is a practising Catholic.[3] Article 4, for example, reads 'I will also pass out of this life armed with the last sacrament of extreme unction', and Article 12, I John Shakespeare . . . pray and beseech all my dear friends . . . for fear notwithstanding least by reason of my sinnes I be to pass and stay a long while in purgatory, they will vouchsafe to assist and succour me with their holy prayers . . . especially with the holy sacrifice of the masse, as being the most effectuall meanes to deliver soules from their torments and paines.

The last, Article 14, concludes dramatically:

I am grateful to those who have read this paper in its various drafts and in particular for helpful comments by Susan Brock, Katherine Duncan-Jones, Mairi MacDonald and Stanley Wells.

[1] This theory, most recently, and enthusiastically, championed by Richard Wilson in an article in the *Times Literary Supplement* (19 December 1997, 11–13), is uncritically repeated by Anthony Holden in *William Shakespeare: His Life and Work* (London, 1999), 53–62. Although it depends on the absolute authenticity of the spiritual testament, this is not an issue which either author really addresses.

[2] The evidence has been subject to very little critical study in recent years, and the most detailed review is still that of J. H. de Groot, *The Shakespeares and the Old Faith* (New York, 1946), pp. 64–110. James G. McManaway, in his 'John Shakespeare's "Spiritual Testament"', *Shakespeare Quarterly*, 25, iii (1967) 197–205 (reprinted in James G. McManaway, *Studies in Shakespeare, Bibliography and Theatre* (New York, 1969), pp. 293–304) provides more textual evidence but does not analyse it closely. S. Schoenbaum, in *William Shakespeare: A Compact Documentary Life*, revised edn (Oxford, 1987), pp. 45–55, and *Shakespeare's Lives* (Oxford, 1991), pp. 80–1, reviews the evidence but introduces no new material and remains characteristically cautious.

[3] The text is most conveniently available, in facsimile, in S. Schoenbaum, *William Shakespeare: A Documentary Life* (Oxford, 1975), pp. 41–3. For the source of this facsimile, see note 5.

I, John Shakespeare, have made this present writing of protestation, confession and charter in presence of the Blessed Virgin Mary, my angell, guardian and all the celestiall court as witnesses hereunto, the which my meaning is that it be of full value now, presently and for ever with the force and vertue of testament, codicill and donation in cause of death, confirming it anew, being in perfect health of soul and body, and signed with my own hand, carrying also the same about me; and for the better declaration hereof, my will and intention is that it be finally buried with me after my death.

To determine authenticity is not straightforward, as the manuscript containing this supposed declaration is lost. Its existence is first recorded in a letter of 14 June 1784 and is last heard of on 12 March 1790.[4] Its text is therefore only known to us from copies made at that time. Firstly, there is a printed version prepared by Edmond Malone from the alleged original then in his possession and published in November 1790, in his 'Historical Account of the English Stage', part of his edition of Shakespeare's plays (hereafter referred to as C1).[5] The second copy survives as a manuscript, made by March 1790 by the Stratford poet and wheelwright, John Jordan (hereafter C2).[6] There is an important difference between the two: whereas Jordan's version (C2) forms a continuous text, Malone's version (C1) is in two parts (for reasons which will become apparent), with a break half way through Article 3, the second (longer) part appearing in the main body of the printed volume and the first as an appendix to it.[7]

The circumstances surrounding the creation of these two versions form an important prelude to establishing the authenticity (or not) of the lost original and must be rehearsed in some detail. The first contemporary reference to the original occurs in an unpublished letter of 14 June 1784 from John Jordan to the editor of the *Gentleman's Magazine*, clearly accompanying a copy of the 'Testament' which has not survived.[8] In it, he explained that 'there are two sentences and a half lost at the begginning', that it had been discovered by Joseph Moseley, a bricklayer,

some years ago, under the tileing of the house where the poet was born, and carefully by him preserved till he most generously gave me the original manuscript the

8th day of June 1784, where any gentleman who chuses to call on me shall be welcome to the perusal.

As we shall see, the editor was said to have rejected the document as spurious and we have to wait until October 1789 for it to resurface. From 1788, Edmond Malone had been in correspondence with the vicar of Stratford, James Davenport, concerning details of Shakespeare's genealogy. Then, in a letter of 8 October 1789, Malone had asked Davenport to extend his researches into the Corporation archives.[9] In a reply, undated but written before 15 October, Davenport reported that, when he had made application to the mayor to consult the Corporation records,

Mr [John] Payton, one of the aldermen, was present, and related the following odd circumstance: one Moseley, a bricklayer, in repairing a few years ago the old house in which our poet was born found a small paper book concealed between the raftering and the tiling. This book he shewed to Mr Payton who, expressing a wish to have it, the man gave it to him. I have just seen this book and it appears to be the confession of our poet's father's faith drawn up by himself, and by which it appears he was a strict Roman Catholic. If you have any curiosity to see

---

4 See notes 8, 14.

5 William Shakespeare, *Plays and Poems*, 10 vols. in 11 (London, 1790), 1, pt. 2, pp. 162–6, 330–1.

6 Birmingham Reference Library (BRL) 2510, 56–60. A manuscript copy of this by James Saunders, c. 1826 (Shakespeare Birthplace Trust Records Office (SBTRO), ER 1/91, ff. 56–61), was edited and published by J. O. Halliwell in 1865 in *Original Memoirs and Historical Accounts of the Families of Shakespeare and Hart . . . down to this present year 1790* (London, 1865), pp. 71–8. Saunders made careful notes of the differences between it and 'another copy', which, on examination, proves to be Malone's printed version. See also note 16.

7 See note 5.

8 Published by J. O. Halliwell in his *Outlines of the Life of Shakespeare*. The only one of the seven editions to include it, or any mention of the 'Spiritual Testament', was the last, published in 1887 (London), 2 vols, II, p. 399, but I have not been able to trace his source.

9 *The Correspondence of Edmond Malone, the Editor of Shakespeare, with the Rev. James Davenport, D.D., Vicar of Stratford-on-Avon*, ed. J. O. Halliwell (London, 1864), 42–3. The originals of these have not survived but Halliwell was able to use copies made by R. B. Wheler in 1814: (SBTRO), ER 1/9, ff. 129–51.

this [he concludes], Mr P. I doubt not will permit me to send it to you for your inspection.[10]

On 15 October, Malone wrote to confirm that he would indeed like to peruse the manuscript.[11] It was clearly sent, for on 21 October Malone wrote again raising questions about its authenticity.[12] He thought that the handwriting post-dated John Shakespeare's death in 1601 by at least thirty years, and was unhappy about some of the spellings which he thought insufficiently 'ancient'. He speculates that perhaps this could be explained by its having been written by a hitherto unknown John Shakespeare the younger, William's elder brother. He thought the punctuation so perfect that he assumed Davenport or Payton had done it: also whether they might have added the Roman numerals at the beginning of each article. He laments the loss of the first leaf (as earlier reported in Jordan's letter to the *Gentleman's Magazine*) and wonders whether it can still yet be traced. He asks Davenport whether Moseley was still alive, how long he had had the document in his possession before he gave it to Payton, whether Payton had paid anything for it, and whether Thomas Hart, the owner of the house at the time, knew anything about it. He also complains about the difficulty he had had transcribing the last page due to the faded ink – particularly a phrase in Article 13 which he had read as 'like a charge in a censore' – and then asks: 'are the contents of a censor called anywhere in the sacred writings its charge?'

Davenport's reply survives as an undated draft.[13] He reported that:

Moseley the bricklayer has been dead about two years. He was a master bricklayer but usually worked together with his men. He bore the character of an honest, sober, industrious man, and no doubt found the manuscript in the manner before described. His daughter remembers him finding it, and that he showed it at the time to many of his neighbours. Some of them have been applied to and they say the beginning was wanting when they saw it. He had it in his possession several years before he gave it to Mr Payton. Mr P. informs me that he was showing the old house to some friends as the man was passing by, who mentioned the circumstances of finding this paper, and on Mr. P's wishing to see it, he fetched it and at

his desire readily gave it him. He asked nothing for it. The man was much employed, I find, in the building and repairing a house for Mr Payton's father. This may be the reason of his giving it him so readily. Mr Thomas Hart has heard the man speak about finding it. The numerals were not made, nor the pointing done by either Mr Payton or me. It is exactly in the same state in which it was given to Mr P . . . The handwriting and spelling of this paper, I confess, struck me as more modern than the era when our Poet's father died.

Malone's reply, if there was one, has not survived but some five months later, on 12 March 1790, he wrote to Davenport: 'I return the paper you were so good as to transmit to me some time ago, and beg you will accept of my best thanks'.[14] In his previous letter, Malone had referred to the 'testament' as a 'paper' and it would therefore seem fairly likely that this was also the item referred to in this later communication. If it were, this is the last we hear of the original.

Malone, sufficiently reassured by Davenport's report, decided to include a copy of the manuscript in the prefatory volume of his edition of Shakespeare's plays, currently going through the press, together with the account Davenport had given him of its discovery. He adds a physical description – a small paper book once of six leaves but the first of which was now missing – and dates its discovery to 'about twenty years ago'.[15] He also qualified his doubts about the date of the handwriting by claiming a sufficient similarity with examples 'now before me' of William Alleyn's and John Ford's.

However, shortly before 10 March 1790, Malone received a packet from John Jordan, the Stratford wheelwright and self-taught poet and antiquarian. Jordan had got wind of Malone's interest in Shakespeare and had sent him a copy of his collections on the Shakespeare/Hart

---

[10] SBTRO, ER 88, f. 34.
[11] *Correspondence of Malone with Davenport*, p. 44.
[12] *Correspondence of Malone with Davenport*, pp. 44–7.
[13] SBTRO, ER 88, ff. 36–36v.
[14] *Correspondence of Malone with Davenport*, p. 47.
[15] Shakespeare, *Plays and Poems*, Edmond Malone, ed., I, pt 2, pp. 162–6.

family.[16] Much to Malone's surprise, it included a complete transcript of the 'testament' (C2), including the hitherto missing Articles 1 and 2 and the first part of Article 3, the whole introduced with a note to the effect that it was 'found on the 29th day of April 1757'. On the face of it, then, the original could not have been lacking its first leaf when Jordan made his copy.

Malone wrote immediately to Jordan to ask for an explanation.[17] As he understood it, the document had been discovered minus its first leaf: 'How, then, have you made a copy of the first two articles and part of the third? When was your copy made, and from whom did you obtain the original?' He adds, from some gossip he must have picked up: 'And did you, some years ago, send a copy of this paper to the printer of the Gentleman's Magazine?'

Jordan replied on 19 March.[18] He said the will was given to him in June 1785[19] by Moseley, the bricklayer who said he had found it in 1757. 'I observed to him that the beginning was wanting; he answered it was, but it was perfect when he found it'. Moseley had also told him he had showed it to Payton, who had read it and returned it to him, and then had gone on to tell Jordan that it had been knocking around in his house until then. In response to Jordan's request that he would be 'glad to have it perfect', Moseley had then agreed to search for the missing page. Since then, Jordan goes on to say, he had shown it to a number of people, including the bookseller, James Keating, to whom he had given a copy. The Reverend Joseph Greene, rector of Welford and headmaster of the Stratford grammar school, 'a gentleman possessed with much classical knowledge and antiquarian sagacity', had declared it a forgery, but advised him to send it to the editor of the Gentleman's Magazine. This he had then done, but with the response we have already noted. In the autumn of 1786, Jordan continues, Moseley had asked to have the document back so that he could show it to someone else. He said he would return it but had not done so and, when Jordan had asked for its return, Moseley said he had given it instead to Payton. Jordan had again raised the issue of the missing leaf, and Moseley again said he would hunt for it. Jordan then goes on to say

that two years later, in September 1788,[20] he had looked in on Moseley, who was ill; Moseley had produced the missing leaf which he had allowed Jordan to copy. He hung onto the original, with the intention of passing it to Payton. However, he had died in December, which, Jordan assumed, was the reason for his having failed to do so. It was inscribed, at the top, so Jordan claimed: 'found the 29 of April 1757'.

Malone was not entirely satisfied with this account and wrote to Jordan again on 25 March.[21] From this we learn that the document he had seen comprised five leaves, 'tacked together by a thread the size of the eighth part of a sheet and the upper part of the last page but one, almost illegible'. This would put it at octavo size, about seven by five inches. He then quizzed Jordan about the appearance of the missing leaf, asking him whether it matched the format of the document he had seen and whether he recalled a similarity between the handwriting. To this letter, Jordan appears not to have replied, but this does not appear to have upset Malone in any way, who wrote again on 31 March firing off another string of questions on other subjects for which he required answers, but making no mention of the will.[22] Indeed, he went out of his

---

[16] Jordan's original manuscript is now BRL 2510. On Malone's death it passed to James Boswell, and, when he died, it was sold by auction in 1826 to John Merridew, a Warwick bookseller. It was seen and copied at this point by James Saunders (see note 7) but then passed into the collection of William Staunton of Longbridge. In 1868 it was, according to Halliwell, 'difficult of access' (Original Memoirs and Historical Accounts of the Families of Shakespeare and Hart, pp. v–vi). It was acquired by Birmingham Reference Library in March 1870.

[17] Original Letters from Edmond Malone, the Editor of Shakespeare, to John Jordan, the Poet, ed. J. O. Halliwell (London, 1864), 7–8. The originals of most of these are at SBTRO, ER 1/15.

[18] Folger Shakespeare Library W. B.17, printed in Halliwell, Outlines, 11, pp. 400–2.

[19] This is inconsistent with his statement, in his letter to the Gentleman's Magazine of 14 June 1784, that he had received it from Moseley on 8 June of that year (above, p. 185).

[20] Another inconsistency, as Moseley had died in January that year (below, p. 201).

[21] Letters from Malone to Jordan, pp. 11–12.

[22] Letters from Malone to Jordan, pp. 13–21.

way to sympathize with Jordan on the matter of the latter's straitened circumstances, promising to help him if he could. We may conclude, then, that Malone, faced with the pressing decision of whether or not to include the contents of this first leaf in his book, had decided in its favour. Even so, he was too late for it to appear except as an appendix, to which he added the note that he had since been 'furnished with the introductory articles from the want of which I was obliged to print this will in an imperfect state'.[23]

Six years later, he back-tracked. Over the winter of 1794/5 William Henry Ireland had announced the discovery of a major cache of papers relating to Shakespeare: deeds, papers, letters, even an unpublished play called *Vortigern*, arrangements for the performance of which, at Drury Lane, were almost immediately made. Malone, however, was suspicious and began his own investigation, the result of which was published in March 1795.[24] He exposed the 'discoveries' as outrageous forgeries and Ireland, and his unfortunate father, Samuel, were condemned to permanent disgrace. One of the fabrications Malone seized on was another Profession of Faith, this time by William Shakespeare. Malone concluded that it was merely based on the version of John's which he himself had published in 1790, but then went on to say that he was now convinced, by other papers in his possession, that he had in any case been mistaken over the earlier testament, and that it had not been written by John at all, nor by any member of the poet's family.[25] He promised he would make clear why he believed this in his projected 'Life of Shakespeare', but, as this never appeared in the form he intended, and the papers to which he referred never unearthed, we do not know why he changed his mind. Be that as it may, Malone's retraction and the earlier pronouncements of forgery by the editor of the *Gentleman's Magazine* and Joseph Greene were enough to discredit the document for over a hundred years.

By the early twentieth century, however, it was becoming clear that there was more to the 'Spiritual Testament' than had at first been imagined. The pioneer in its rehabilitation was Herbert Thurston,

who, as early as 1882, had expressed his firm conviction that the text was authentic.[26] His confidence was eventually rewarded, in 1923, on his discovery of a printed Spanish version of what was clearly a very similar document, published in Mexico in 1661.[27] The authorship of this version was attributed to Charles Borromeo, archbishop of Milan, who had died in 1584.[28] With the author now identified, further copies were more easily traced, a manuscript version, again in Spanish, dating from about 1690, a printed version in Romansch published in 1741, five other Spanish versions published in Mexico, one undated of the seventeenth century, and the other four published between 1708 and 1797, and one in Italian, though attributed to Borromeo's confessor, Alexander Sauli, occurring in an appendix to an 1878 edition of the *Vita de Beato St Alessandro Sauli* by Francesco Saverio Maria Bianchi (1743–1815). A testament in French 'on the same lines' has also been identified.[29] Even greater excitement was aroused on the discovery, in 1966, in a book of devotions acquired by the Folger Shakespeare Library, of a printed English version of this text, published

[23] Edmond Malone, *Shakespeare, Plays and Poems*, I, pt 2, pp. 330–1.

[24] Edmond Malone, *An Inquiry into the Authenticity of Certain Miscellaneous Papers and Legal Instruments* (London, 1796).

[25] Malone, *An Inquiry*, pp. 198–9.

[26] Herbert Thurston, 'The Religion of Shakespeare', *The Month*, 26 (May, 1882) 1–19, esp. 4–6. See also Herbert Thurston, 'The Spiritual Testament of John Shakespeare', *The Month*, 118 (Nov. 1911), 487–502.

[27] Herbert Thurston, 'A Controverted Shakespeare Document', *The Dublin Review*, 148, Oct.–Dec. (1923), 161–76.

[28] *Testamento O Ultima Voluntad del Alma . . . Ordenado por San Carlos Borromeo, Cardenal del Santa Praxedis, y Arcobispo de Milan.*

[29] For these see Thurston, 'Controverted Shakespeare Document', 166–7; de Groot, *Shakespeares and the Old Faith*, pp. 80–1; McManaway, 'John Shakespeare's "Spiritual Testament"', 198–9. The Italian version is of particular interest in casting doubt on the authorship, although I have not traced the source from which it was copied into the 1878 edition. Its introduction reads: 'Testamento Spirituale in Apparecchio alla Morte Dettato dal Beato Alessandro Sauli a San Carlo Borromeo suo penitente'.

in 1638.[30] Another English edition, published in 1635, was later reported at Oscott College. This is also included in a composite volume, the first item of which is a copy of Geronymo Gracian's *The Burninge Lampe*. This was noted by A. F. Allison and D. M. Rogers in 1956, but the Borromeo testament overlooked.[31]

By comparing Malone's text of the lost 'John Shakespeare' version with the English versions of the 1630s, it was now possible to demonstrate that, by and large, they were the same and that the former thus had a serious claim to authenticity. There was, however, one major exception to this close similarity: the first two and a half articles, missing from the document as first supplied to Malone, but included in Jordan's copy, are completely different. In other words, although the main text is sufficiently close to other formularies to warrant its being taken seriously, the first two and a half articles are clearly revealed as a forgery. And when we recall the train of events which led to the complete text reaching Malone's hands it is not difficult to detect when this forgery occurred. The general understanding had always been that the 'Testament', when discovered, was already lacking its first leaf. It was manifestly in this state when Jordan provided a copy for the *Gentleman's Magazine* on 14 June 1784.[32] Quite why he, or an associate, decided to 'improve' the version by supplying the first two and a half articles we do not know. His version of the will occupies pp. 56–60 of the volume of notes which he sent to Malone in March 1790, but it is not clear whether he had compiled this specifically for Malone (it was certainly not at his request as its arrival was a surprise) or whether it had been some years in preparation.[33] We may also surmise that Jordan was unaware that Malone had been sent the original or he might have hesitated in supplying a version which he knew would raise awkward questions. His tortuous and inconsistent explanation of the anomaly which he subsequently had to give has all the hallmarks of guilty evasiveness (an impression not dispelled by the fact that Moseley, the only witness, was by then dead) and, with the knowledge that we now have that these first clauses are indeed a fabrication of some sort, it is difficult not to conclude that Jordan was the culprit. We may also note that by the time the document reached Malone, it seems to have been deliberately distressed. He had complained, as we have seen, about the difficulty of reading the last page, rendering one particularly obscured passage as 'like a charge in a censore'. The correct reading, as the printed versions now make clear, was 'like a sharp cutting razor', a form of words which Jordan, as his copy shows, had had no difficulty in reading only a year or two before.

The fact that these opening articles are forged does not, of course, automatically invalidate the possible authenticity of the remaining (and greater) part of the text. It does, however, cast a shadow which must be dispelled if we are to regard the source as an authoritative one. It is, for instance, unsafe to claim that the document was discovered on 29 April 1757. According to Jordan, this information was on the first leaf, which it is now clear he never saw. On reflection, this early date is in any case unlikely, presupposing an interval of twenty-seven years between the alleged discovery of an item of such importance and its being made public (when Jordan wrote to the *Gentleman's Magazine*). In fact, in his letter, Jordan dated the discovery to 'some years ago'. Davenport, as we have seen, had put it at just 'a few years ago' and Malone had eventually come down in favour of 'about 1770'. There is also the rather odd fact that the owner of the property from 1778, Thomas Hart, could not corroborate the story. Malone, it will be remembered, had asked Davenport whether Hart knew anything about the discovery, to which he had replied only that 'Mr Thomas Hart has heard the man [Moseley] speak about finding it'.[34] It might also strike

---

[30] McManaway, 'John Shakespeare's "Spiritual Testament"', 197–205. See STC 5645.5

[31] A. F. Allison and D. M. Rogers, *A Catalogue of Catholic Books in English Printed Abroad or Secretly in England, 1558–1640* (1956), no. 366. This version is now STC 12144.5. It was reprinted as volume 140 of *English Recusant Literature* (Menston, 1973).

[32] Above, note 8.

[33] Above, notes 6 and 16.

[34] SBTRO, ER 88, f. 36.

one as suspicious that Davenport's enquiries had neither identified another witness to the actual discovery nor revealed the major part which Jordan had played in the affair.

If we move beyond this and propose that the whole document is a fabrication, there would seem to be only one explanation: that in the 1770s someone had come across a defective copy of the printed English version of the testament, lacking its first page or two, and had conspired to turn it into a Shakespeare document, copying John's name into each article. However, before examining how likely this might be, we must first look more closely at what the two printed versions we have can tell us, one published in 1635 (hereafter referred to as A) and the other in 1638 (hereafter B), when set against the copies of the manuscript version (C1 and C2).[35] We must first observe that they are not 'stand-alone' editions. B was published with a similar tract, the *Contract of the Soul*, which takes up the first forty-one pages of the volume in which it occurs. Version A comes third in a similar compilation, not beginning until page 126 of the volume. They must therefore have been derived from an earlier version, or versions. Another obvious point is that, word for word, they, and C, are so similar that they cannot be independent translations from the original, which, one must suppose, was in Italian.[36] A typical shared phrase which could hardly have been arrived at independently occurs in Article IX, when the testator thanks God for so far not taking him out of this life 'even then when I was plunged in the durty puddle of my sinnes', followed in Article X by 'I am willing, yea I do infinitely desire'.[37] Yet it is also clear, on comparing A more closely with B, that there are significant differences between them. Excluding those of spelling, punctuation, capitalization and abbreviation, some seventeen substantive differences occur. The most obvious are in the preamble and Articles 1 and 2, where A has four complete phrases omitted in B. In Article 4, B lists the six senses as 'seeing, speaking, tasting, touching, smelling, hearing', whilst A has them in a different order − 'seeing, speaking, tasting, smelling, hearing, touching'. In Article VI, A has the clumsy phrase, 'pardoned many as great sinners as myselfe',

compared to B's 'many grievous sinners'. At the end of Article 7, the testator asks God not to forsake him, in B, in that 'grievous and painful conflict', but in A in that 'grievous and painful agony'. A also concludes with a longer list of prayers which should then be said than are recommended in B. In the final protestation, a typographical error in A ('in cause of death') is rendered in B, correctly, as, 'in case of death'. Similarly, the phrase in Article IV, given in A as 'anoynt any senses', reads better in B as 'anoint my senses'. On the other hand, another typographical error at the end of Article 14, 'change to the (*recte* be) made by me', occurs in both A and B.

These differences could be explained in two ways: either B was simply a new edition of A, or A and B were independently derived from a common parent. On balance, the former seems more likely. The phrases which occur only in A might well have been dropped by the editor of B in the belief that this would be an improvement. Changing 'as great sinners as' to 'grievous sinners', and correcting 'any senses' to 'my senses' and 'cause' to 'case', could have been done for the same reason. But it is his apparent failure to spot the other typographical error in A ('the' instead of 'be') which is the most persuasive argument in favour of regarding B as a new edition of A.

Comparing Jordan's and Malone's copies of the lost manuscript version (C1 and C2) with A and B is not entirely straightforward as we have to allow for the fact that either of them could have made mistakes in their transcriptions. However, it

---

[35] The four texts are available from the author.

[36] The English versions are clearly based on a translation from the Italian one (see note 29). Although this in turn could have been translated from Latin, it would seem more likely that Italian was the language of the original text.

[37] 'Dirty puddle' is, if the Italian version of the testament is accepted as the original text (see note 29), a rather unsatisfactory translation of 'fango' (mire), and surely not one that two independent translators would have given. Similarly, the word 'coffin' (in 'the amorous *coffin* of the side of Jesus Christ': Article 13), occurring in both A and B, is a translation of 'caverna', again an unlikely rendering by independent translators.

is again clear, firstly, as has already been pointed out, that by and large the wording is so similar that the manuscript could not have been an independent translation but must have been copied from the same, or very similar, printed version on which A and B are based, albeit inserting John Shakespeare's name into each clause. Indeed, in one case, the creator of C can be seen to be copying in just this fashion: in his haste to insert 'I John Shakespeare' into the opening of Article VIII, but not immediately understanding the syntax, he wrote: 'Item I John Shakespeare by virtue of this present testament I doe pardon'. Secondly, a comparison of the substantive differences between A and B with their rendering in C reveals a clear bias. This comparison can only be done in eleven of the seventeen instances cited above, as six of the differences between A and B occur in the opening section for which Jordan, as we have seen, had fabricated his own version. But in these eleven, C follows A in eight cases and B in only one, the other two being irrelevant in this enquiry.[38] Differences in spelling, though naturally less conclusive, reveal the same pattern. In the section where a comparison with C can be made, there are fifty-two spelling differences between A and B. Of these C follows A on twenty-seven occasions and B on only nine, with the remainder inconclusive.

This would seem to place C closer to A than B, and, if forgery was committed, it was clearly not done by using the later B as a template. Nor would this have been likely. The forgery theory would involve the discovery of a printed version with its first page or two missing, hardly likely in the case of B which is only known to us as the middle section of a larger book. However, if A and C are closer to the original translation, there is a further consideration, namely that there are (excluding the insertion of the name John Shakespeare into every clause) seventeen substantive differences between C and A–B. Five of these differences involve words in A–B missing in C, perhaps to be explained by poor copying. In nine other cases, however, the differences involve words which are found only in C, suggesting an independent copying from a common parent. These mostly relate to the word 'do', inserted more consistently in C than in A–B, after

the personal pronoun 'I' at the opening of each article. Also of interest, in Article 13, is the word 'last' found before 'will' in C but not in A–B. In Article 14 there are significant differences involving extra as well as fewer words: 'I commend my soul and body, my life and death, and I beseech him' in C, as opposed to 'I commend my soul, my body, my life and my death, and I beseech him' in A–B. Of even more significance is the correct rendering of 'change to *be* made by me' in Article 14 which, due to a typographical error referred to above, is given as 'change to *the* made' in both A and B. In Article 4, C has the correct '*my* senses', rendered incorrectly as '*any* senses' in A but corrected in the later B. The phrase, '*cause* of death' in A is, however, repeated in C.

What can we conclude from this textual examination? Firstly, although A (1635), B (1638) and C (uncertain) have a very great deal in common, and can therefore hardly be independent translations of Borromeo's original text, they are not all simply copies of one another. A, being in any case included in a composite volume, must have been drawing on an earlier source. The substantive differences between it and B suggest that the latter may have been no more than a reissue. Moreover, although C is closer to A than B, it has some material which is found in neither. This suggests that it was probably taken from a 'free-standing' copy pre-dating both A and B. As no copies of this have survived, there is no way of knowing how many editions of this were produced but the differences are not so great that C and A could not have been taken from the same one.

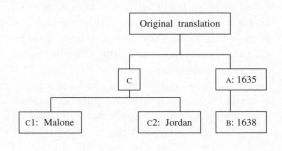

[38] They occur in the instructional sentences at the end of the testament which C omits completely.

The question which must now be resolved is whether the manuscript copy C (since lost) was indeed made for John Shakespeare before his death in 1601 or whether a 'free-standing' printed version was discovered in the eighteenth century, lacking its first page or two, and a fraud perpetrated by copying it out and inserting John Shakespeare's name into each article.

The case for C being genuine – that it is a pre-1601 manuscript copy of a printed version circulating by that date – would, of course, be greatly improved if there was independent evidence that such a printed copy existed. A case has been made that copies were in circulation as early as 1580, but a close examination of the evidence on which this claim depends does not bear this out. It is based on the following train of events.[39] Borromeo's testament was most probably written, it is claimed, in the period 1576–8 when plague was ravaging his city of Milan. In May 1580, Borromeo had received Edmund Campion and Robert Parsons at Milan before they set out on their Catholic mission to England. In June 1581, William Allen, rector of the English College at Rheims wrote, in Latin, to Alphonsus Agazarri, rector of the English College in Rome, reporting that Father Robert Parsons, now in England, 'wants three or four thousand or more of the testaments, for many people desire to have them'. On the face of it, it may not seem an unreasonable proposition that these 'testaments' might have been the Borromeo document, and it has therefore been suggested that Parsons and Campion had gone into England later in 1580, armed with a supply of copies of Borromeo's testament which had been so quickly exhausted as to prompt a request for several thousand more, and that one, albeit a manuscript copy, had come into John Shakespeare's hands at that time. This has been further elaborated in recent times into claims that Campion actually met John Shakespeare at Lapworth, that he had personally given him a copy of the will there, that the Shakespeares then became implicated on the arrest of Campion in the summer of 1581, and that William Shakespeare, under the alias William Shakeshaft, had been sent off to Lancashire, to spend time in the Catholic household of Alexander Hoghton of Hoghton Tower.[40]

However, a reading of this letter in the context of other events does not provide a sound basis on which to speculate in this fashion. Firstly, there is the consideration that Borromeo's authorship is by no means proven, the only Italian version attributing it to his confessor, Alessandro Sauli.[41] There are also at least two different interpretations of this reference to 'testaments', one more likely than the other but both more plausible than the claim that it refers to an otherwise unrecorded (at least by this date) English translation of the Borromeo text.

First, a case could be made out that this phrase might be in some way connected with the controversy then surrounding the notorious double apostate, John Nichols, whose activities, as related by Parsons to Allen had filled the part of Allen's letter immediately preceding the reference to 'the testaments'.[42] 'People are already universally tired of him [Nichols]', Allen had written, 'and I imagine that he will be soon tripped up, especially when the abjuration of heresies [i.e. Protestantism] which he made at Rome in the Inquisition comes to England. For I have received the authentic copy of it which you sent containing his whole recantation and have sent it to Father Robert in England. Father Robert desires three or four thousand or more of the testaments as many people wish to have them'.[43] There is nothing inconsistent with

---

[39] First set out clearly by de Groot, *Shakespeares and the Old Faith*, pp. 85–90. His sources will be cited later.

[40] Wilson, *TLS*, 19 December 1997, 11–13; Holden, *William Shakespeare*, pp. 53–62. For a recent discussion on the unlikelihood of Shakespeare's migration to Lancashire, see Robert Bearman, '"Was William Shakespeare William Shakeshafte?" revisited', *Shakespeare Quarterly*, 53, 1 (2002), 83–94.

[41] Above, see note 29.

[42] The letter is given in full, in translation, in Richard Simpson, *Edmund Campion, a Biography*, revised edn. (London, 1896), pp. 293–7. For the Latin versions from which it was taken, see note 43. For Nichols (as Nicholls), see *DNB*, 60, 441–3. The controversy is documented in a pamphlet war, summarized in Peter Milward, *Religious Controversies of the Elizabethan Age* (London, 1977), pp. 52–4.

[43] Simpson, *Edmund Campion*, p. 294. The translation can hardly be faulted but Simpson made the final sentence the start of

linking this last phrase with Parsons' efforts to discredit Nichols. The first stage in this campaign had been his publication of his *Discoverie of J. Nichols* earlier that year. This had ended with a section: 'new information from Rome', brought by 'an honest, discreet and learned gentleman' who testifies that Nichols's boasts about his first recantation, which had involved preaching before the cardinals, are false.[44] At the time of publication, however, there was clearly no documentary proof of this first recantation; this messenger had told Parsons about a search for this in the archives of the Inquisition, to the abstraction of ten sheets of paper, copied word for word by public notaries, and the common seals also 'of the office was added unto it'. However, this document, Parsons then explains, had been forwarded elsewhere for further authentication and was 'not yet come unto my handes' and 'the printer being not able to staye, nor I certaine how soone it will come', he had gone ahead with publication on the testimony of the messenger. Surely we must associate this delayed documentary proof with 'the original . . . in which his entire recantation was contained', mentioned above, which passed through Allen's hands, on its way from Rome to Parsons in June; and, as there is no paragraph, nor even a sentence, break between the reference to this document concerning Nichols's recantation and Parsons's request for multiple copies of the 'testaments', we might also reasonably propose that they could relate to one and the same thing and that what Parsons was so anxious to obtain were copies taken from these proofs or evidences.[45]

However, although this may seem a more likely proposal than that this reference to testaments refers to the Borromeo text, there is a second, even more convincing alternative. There survives another seventeenth-century copy of Allen's letter, in which the critical phrase is rendered: 'tria vel quatuor millia aut etiam plura ex testamentis anglicis, cum illa a multis desiderenter'.[46] The inclusion here of the additional word 'anglicis' immediately suggests a reference to the Catholic (or Rheims) translation of the Bible. It is customary to dismiss this argument on the grounds, firstly, that this (or, at least, the New Testament) was not published until

March 1582, secondly, that to suggest that such a quantity of books could be smuggled into England is 'preposterous', and, thirdly, that there would have been no point in Allen writing to Rome about such a request.[47] These arguments, however, overlook the circumstances in which the Rheims Bible was produced. The translation was the brainchild of William Allen, rector of the College at Rheims, conceived in the mid 1570s as the only effective way of dealing with the alleged heresies to which the Protestant versions had given rise.[48] The translation was entrusted to the noted scholar, Gregory Martin, recalled to Rheims in April 1578, who began work on 16 October following.[49] The task was completed, remarkably, in less than two years, as the Rheims Annual Report, covering the period June 1579 to July 1580 makes clear: 'there is also

---

a new paragraph, which it is not in the document he was copying – nor is it even punctuated as a new sentence – and by doing so he has allowed it to be taken out of context by those who would prefer it to mean something else. It must be acknowledged, of course, that the document from which Simpson was working (in fact, two near identical copies: Public Record Office (PRO), SP12/149, nos 51, 52; ff. 122–4; ff. 126–8) was only a contemporary copy of Allen's letter. For a printed version of the Latin text, see for convenience the source cited in note 46.

44 *A Discouerie of J. Nicols, Minister, Misreported a Jesuite. wherein is contayned a ful answere to his recantation* (STC 19402), unpaginated.

45 Assuming, that is, that Allen used *ex testamentis* instead of the more usual *ex testimoniis*. The documentation disproving Nichols's claim to have preached in Rome was eventually published following his arrest and imprisonment (and third recantation) at Rheims in February 1583: *A True Report of the Late Apprehension of John Nicols Minister, at Roan*, Rheims 1583: STC 18537.

46 The text is printed in *The Letters and Memorials of William Cardinal Allen*, ed. T. F. Knox (London, 1882), pp. 95–8, from the Archives of the Society of Jesus in Rome, ms. Anglia 8, fol. 23. I am very grateful to Thomas McCoog for checking this reference for me and for the suggestion that the copyist may have been Christopher Grene (1629–97).

47 De Groot, *Shakespeares and the Old Faith*, 88; McManaway, 'John Shakespeare's "Spiritual Testament"', 199, n. 8.

48 J. J. Pollen, 'Translating the Bible into English at Rheims', *The Month*, 160 (1922), 141–54.

49 *The First and Second Diaries of the English College, Douay* (London, 1878), p. 145.

complete but not yet published a very Catholic translation into the vernacular of the Bible . . . there are some other books written both in Latin and in English, and now ready for the press, but there is no opportunity of printing them'.[50] On their journey from Rome to England, Parsons and Campion may indeed have been Borromeo's guests at Milan in May; but in June they had also passed through Rheims and would have known of the existence of this translation, ready for the press.[51] Doubtless Allen would also have told them, as the Rheims Annual Report goes on to inform us, that 'our people most earnestly beg and expect this book from us'.[52] It is hardly wild speculation to suggest that some nine months later Parsons's urgent request for multiple copies of English testaments, 'for many people desire to have them', refers to this impending publication. Strong evidence for his concern over the delay in publication is also to be found in the principal reason Parsons gave for his decision to return to France in August: his wish to discuss with Allen the hastening of the publication 'of the edition of the New Testament translated into English . . . at Rheims . . . For this work and for the expenses of printing, Father Parsons had procured a thousand gold crowns from certain Catholic gentlemen'.[53]

As to the doubt that such a quantity of books could ever have been assembled and dispatched, we must recall that Parsons's writings are full of claims of how thousands of recruits were rallying to the Catholic cause. Indeed, the same letter which reports his request for multiple copies of the 'testaments' also includes Campion's claim that the number of Catholics in England had increased by 20,000 over the past twelve months.[54] It is therefore hardly surprising, even if this figure is a hopeful approximation, that Parsons should be looking for a very substantial number of copies of what, to him, would be the Jesuits' main weapon in their battle against Protestant heresies. The Rheims New Testament did eventually prove to be a sizeable volume (about 400 quarto leaves) but there is also good evidence for the import of other large but less important volumes in quantities of one thousand and more: in 1584, for instance, one of Walsingham's agents reported that a thousand copies of Richard Hopkins' recent translation of Luis of Granada's *Of Prayer and Meditation* were ready for import into the country, to be distributed in London and other places, together with 1,500 copies of a new translation of Diego de Estella's *Contempte of the World*, destined for London and 'the north', 600 copies of 'Reynolds book against Fulke in defence of the newe testament, and the discovery', and no less than seven thousand 'catechismes, golden Letanies and Jesus psalters'.[55] There is also no doubt of Parsons' conviction that the publication of books and their widest possible dissemination was the key to the battle for men's souls. Several thousand copies of the New Testament would hardly, in the light of this, seem overambitious.

As to the alleged unlikelihood of Allen, in Rheims, writing to Agazzari in Rome about these 'testaments', this can simply be accounted for by the need for papal approval. Quite when Allen applied for this is not clear, though his petitions seeking permission postdate the completion of the translation (summer 1580), and presuppose that the translation would require checking by experts.[56]

---

[50] *The Douay College Diaries . . . 1598–1654, with the Rheims Report, 1579–80*, ed. Edwin H. Burton and Thomas L. Williams, Catholic Record Society (CRS), 11 (1911), pp. 558, 565.

[51] 'The Memoirs of Father Persons' (Part 1), ed. J. H. Pollen, in *Miscellanea II*, CRS, 2 (1906), 26, 197, 199.

[52] *The Douay College Diaries . . . 1598–1654*, pp. 558, 565.

[53] 'The Memoirs of Father Persons' (Part 2), ed. J. H. Pollen, in *Miscellanea IV*, CRS, 4 (1907), 96.

[54] Simpson, *Edmund Campion*, p. 296.

[55] PRO, SP12/175/74. Hopkins's translation is either STC 16907 (Paris, 1582), an octavo of 331 leaves, or STC 16908 (Rouen, 1584), a duodecimo of 346 leaves. The translation of *Contempt of the World* is STC 10541 (Rouen, 1584), a duodecimo of 272 leaves. 'Reynold's book' is probably STC 20632: William Rainolds, *A refutation of sundry reprehensions . . . to deface the late English translation, and catholike annotations of the new Testament* (Paris, 1583), though this is not ostensibly 'against Fulke', presumably William Fulke's 1583 attack (STC 11430) on the Catholic translation of the New Testament. On this exchange, see also Milward, *Religious Controversies*, pp. 46–8.

[56] Translated in Pollen, 'Translating the Bible', 146–9.

Some funding might also have been requested for the project. Delays extending into 1581 might therefore be expected and Parsons's impatience, and Allen's letter to Agazzari thus simply explained. In the event, the translation, of the New Testament only, was not to appear for another eighteen months, lack of money being again cited as the reason for delay.[57]

Whilst there is no proof positive that Parsons's request for three or four thousand English testaments relates to his need either for evidence in his current war with Nichols or, more likely, for copies of the Rheims New Testament, there is very strong circumstantial evidence that it could relate particularly to the latter, whereas for the claim that it might be the Borromeo testament there is none except the fact that Parsons and Campion had visited Borromeo on their way to England. On balance, any attempt to authenticate John Shakespeare's 'Spiritual Testament' on the grounds of Parsons's request must therefore surely fail in the face of more likely explanations.

If this is accepted, other things become easier to explain, or need not be explained at all. Parsons has left detailed accounts of how he and Campion went about their work, but nowhere is there mention of distributing copies of Borromeo's testament, or seeking subscriptions to it. We are simply faced now with the question of whether it is likely that, some time before 1601, when John died, a manuscript copy, the only one to have survived, was made from a printed version of which no copy has similarly ever come to light, and that it just happened to be subscribed to by the father of perhaps the most famous of all Englishmen.

That a 'stand-alone' printed copy in English did probably exist prior to 1635, when the earliest known version, based on it, was published, has already been demonstrated.[58] But, without the circumstantial evidence to fall back on that such copies existed in England from 1580, or at all until the 1630s, it now requires a much greater leap of faith to accept that John Shakespeare might have come into contact with one. Despite claims that Borromeo's writings generally, and his 'Spiritual

Testament' in particular, were highly influential, it is difficult to substantiate even this in a convincing manner. In 1611, John Heigham published, as one of Six Spiritual Books, 'Certaine Advertisements teaching men how to lead a Christian Life, written in Italian by the Right Honorable Cardinal Borromeus and now first translated into English'.[59] In the preface, however, Heigham feels the need to explain who Borromeo was. He also draws attention to his canonization in 1610, the result of a campaign launched in 1603 by Borromeo's cousin and successor as archbishop of Milan, Federico Borromeo, suggesting that it was this event which had prompted the translation of a work first published, it seems, as long ago as 1580.[60]

It has also been suggested that echoes of the 'Spiritual Testament' can be found in other English texts of the 1580s. Whilst a general similarity of sentiment might well be expected (and this was the reason why earlier apologists for the 'John Shakespeare' version believed it to be authentic), it is far more difficult to establish that Borromeo's tract was actually used as a model by other writers. A prayer ('A Protestation to be made in times of sickness') included in Gaspar Loarte's *Essercitatio della vita christiana*, first translated into English in 1579,[61] does indeed have striking similarities to Article I of the Borromeo testament.

But this does not mean that the former was based on the latter. No first edition of Loarte's *Essercitatio* appears to have survived but, as he died in 1578,

---

57 *The Letters and Memorials of William Cardinal Allen*, 109; *The New Testament of Iesvs Christ, Translated Faithfvlly into English* (Rheims, 1582) (STC 2884), preface; Pollen, 'Translating the Bible', 150.

58 Above, p. 190.

59 Not in STC.

60 *Ricordi di Monsign. Illustriss. Borromeo, cardinale di Santa Prassede & Arciuescouo di Milano. Per il uivere christiano ad ogni stato di persone* (Rome, 1580). News of Borromeo's canonization was also the occasion of one of the earliest references to him in English state papers: *Calendar of State Papers, Domestic (CSPD), James I, 1603–1610*, p. 641.

61 *The Exercise of a Christian Life, Written in Italian*, 1579: STC 16641.5

Loarte	Borromeo
I protest here before Almightie God my maker and Redeemer, before the blessed virgin Marye, and al the whole Court of heauen, namely, before my Gardian Angel, and al you that are here assistant about me, that, by Gods grace, I minde to liue and dye in this faith I have here protested, according as the holy Catholike and Romane Church vnderstandeth it, and I wil euermore, by Gods grace, remain in the vnion of the bodie of this Churche, vnder the head our Lord and Sauiour Iesus Christe, and his Vicar here in earth. And if anie word that sounded contrary hereto, should by dotage escape out of my mouth, I protest here, that it is not mine, but onely that which I have aboue protested.	First, I heere protest, and declare in the sight, & presence of Almighty God, Father, Sonne, and holy Ghost, three Persons, & one God; and of the B.V. Mary, and of all the holy Court of Heauen, that I will liue and dye obedient vnto the Catholike, Romaine, & Apostolicke Church firmely belieuving all the twelue Articles of the Fayth taught by the holy Apostles, with the interpretation, & declaration made thereon by the same holy church, as taught defined & declared by her. And finally I protest, that I do belieue all that, which a good & faithfull Christian ought to belieue: In which faith I purpose to liue & die. And if at any time (which God forbid) I should chance by suggestion of the diuell to do, say, or thinke contrary to this my beliefe, I do now for that time, in vertue of this present act, reuoke, infring, & annull the same, & will that it be held for neither spoke, or done by me.

it is very unlikely that he could have based it on Borromeo's testament, if, as is generally supposed, this was written during the outbreak of plague in Milan during the years 1576–8.[62] What the similarity more likely establishes is a common Italian source. Another prayer, one 'for the sicke person to saye after his beleefe', included in the earliest edition of a *Manual of Prayers newly gathered ovt of many diuers famous authours as well auncient as of the tyme present*, first published in 1583,[63] is also alleged to include borrowings from articles 1 and 7 of Borromeo's Testament.

Here again, however, the similarity may be no more than a reflection of contemporary Catholic piety, examples of which have been identified in such works as the first complete printed edition of the *Sarum Horae*, published in 1494. This contains 'Two devoute prayers in Englysshe', one of which protests 'here before thi maieste that I will lyve and deye in thys fayth and continue all my lyfe',[64] the other 'that I will lyue and deye in the fayth of the Holy chirch our moder'. The second also, like the Testament, seeks to protect the supplicant from any backsliding in times of sickness:

Yf adventure bi ony temptacion, deception, or variacyon comyng by sorowe or peyne or seknesse or by ony feblenesse of body; or by ony other occasion whatsoever it be, that I falle of declyne in peril of my soule, or preiudyce of my helth or in errour of the holy faith catholike ... that errour wyth my power I resiste and here renounce.

In any case it is not easy to accept, if this anonymous entry in the *Manual of Prayers* (most of the other prayers in the compilation are attributed to their authors) were indeed based on a clause in the Borromeo testament, that it could have so quickly qualified for consideration.

The evidence we have then (or rather do not have), far from establishing that Borromeo's works were well known and circulating in England from the 1580s, suggest the complete opposite. For the *Spiritual Testament* itself there is not even a surviving

[62] And if, indeed, he wrote it: above, n. 29.
[63] STC 17263.
[64] *Horae Beatae Mariae Virginis or Sarum and York Primers with Kindred Books*, ed. Edgar Hoskins (London, 1901), p. 113. The prayers are printed in William Maskell, *Monumenta Ritualia Ecclesiae Anglicanae*, 2 vols. (London, 1846), II, pp. 262–3.

Manual of Prayers	Borromeo
O Almightie and mercyfull Iesu, I protest before thee and before all the courte of heauen, that I haue a will and desire to finishe my lyfe in this fayth, wherein of necessitie euery childe (obediente to our Mother the holye Church) ought to dye. Further my sweete Sauiour I protest to beleeue wholly and vniuersally all that which is conteined in the Catholicke fayth, and that which is a true faithful Christian ought to beleeue: that if it happen by the assaults of the deuil, or by violence of sicknes, I come to thinke, say or doe anything contrary to this purpose, I doe reuoke it at this present & protest that I gyue no consent to any such thought, word, or worke	First, I heere protest, and declare in the sight, & presence of Almighty God, Father, Sonne, and holy Ghost, three Persons, & one God; and of the B.V. Mary, and of all the holy Court of Heauen, that I will liue and dye obedient vnto the Catholike, Romaine, & Apostolicke Church firmely belieuving all the twelue Articles of the Fayth taught by the holy Apostles . . . Item, I protest by this present Writing, that I will patiently endure, & suffer all kind of infirmity, sicknesse, yea & the paine of death it selfe: wherin if it should happen, which God forbid, that through violence of paine & agony, or by subtility of the Diuell, I should fall into any impatience, or temptation of blasphemy, or murmuration against God or the Catholike Fayth, or giue any signe of bad example, I do henceforth, & for that present repent me, & am most hartily sorry for the same

sixteenth-century copy in Italian, let alone English, and no known example of any of his work available in English before the translation of his *Certaine Advertisements teaching men how to lead a Christian Life* in 1611. Moreover, whilst copies survive of most of the books, some quite obscure, which were reported as being smuggled into England from the 1580s, there has yet to be discovered even a reference to Borromeo's Spiritual Testament being one of them, despite its alleged popularity;[65] and, although it might be tempting to seize on any reference to a 'testament' in order to contradict this, it has been demonstrated above that such allusions almost certainly apply to the Bible in its various translations.

Given the extreme unlikelihood of John Shakespeare, or any of his contemporaries, for that matter, ever having come into contact with an English version of Borromeo's Testament, it is now time to address the issue of whether the document which came to light in Stratford, already established as forged in its opening clauses, was, in fact, a hoax in its entirety. Brought to light in the 1780s, at a time when Shakespearian folklore was being

converted into fact and spurious Shakespeare relics were being sold to unsuspecting visitors, the possibility that this was the case is now surely much more likely.

Such a hoax would have involved the discovery of a 'free-standing' copy of the early printed text lacking its first few leaves or so, and the making of a manuscript copy in a manner to persuade the reader that it was John Shakespeare's personal statement. As this forgery (if such it was) is lost to us, are there any indications in the copies which have survived that this might have been the case?

Very little, of course, can be expected in the way of anachronisms as the forger was copying an authentic text. He may have made one slip,

---

[65] It is not included, for instance, in John Gee's long list of 'Popish Bookes lately dispersed in our kingdom', an appendix to his *The Foot of the Snare* (see note 68). For the record, none of Borromeo's works in any language have been noted in contemporary private English libraries (information from the *Private Libraries in Renaissance England Project*; E. S. Leedham-Green, *Books in Cambridge Inventories*, 2 vols. (Cambridge, 1986)).

however. We have already examined the substantive differences between A–B and C and have concluded, in the case of words omitted in C, or where words appeared in C but not in A–B, that C was taken from a slightly different, and earlier, version. But there is one variation which cannot be so easily explained, the distinctly modern-sounding 'when I least thought of it' in C (Article 9) where A–B has 'when I least thought thereof'. This may seem far from conclusive, but there are other oddities. Firstly, we may note that, according to the instructions to the testator at the beginning of the printed texts of the testament (known to us now but not to the presumed forger as this portion was lost), the testator was directed to insert his name into the first article only, and then in a blank space at the end. The instruction to sign at the end is repeated before this blank space. However, the forger, not knowing of the first instruction, may have thought it would look odd to have the conclusion starting 'I, John Shakespeare' in this way without inserting 'John Shakespeare' after 'I' at the beginning of each article as well. More suspicious is the final line. After the request that the testament be buried with the testator, the 1635 version continues: 'Having made the foresayd protestations & subscription, he may say deuoutly the ensuing prayers, Pater Noster, Ave Maria, Credo. Jesu son of David have mercy on me. Amen'. We do not know quite how this option was presented in the 'free-standing' version but, if it was given as advice, then clearly the forger could not copy it into the customized version he was concocting for John Shakespeare without revealing that he was just copying from a formulary. At the same time, however, he seems to have misunderstood that these words indicated the titles of prayers. He thus concludes simply, but inexplicably, with the words 'Pater Noster, Ave Maria, Credo. Iesu son of David, have mercy on me. Amen'. It is this last clause which also states that the testator intends to carry this testament 'continually about me: and for the better declaration herof, my will and intention is that it be finally buried with me after my death'. That no such English 'free-standing' printed copy of the testament has ever come to light suggests that this is, in fact, what happened in most cases, and makes John Shakespeare's alleged behaviour (immediately hiding it in the roof of his house to escape detection during the hunt for Jesuits and then never retrieving it) rather hard to believe.

Another problem the forger would have encountered was the bracketed space left in Clause 10 for the insertion of, as the preamble to the 1635 version puts it, the names of saints 'to whome they have speciall Deuotion'. C has the name Saint Winifred inserted here but in a clumsy way 'together with these other Saints and Patrons [Saint Winifride], all whom I invoke and beseech'. Surely nobody copying out the will specifically for John Shakespeare would have included these brackets in his copy, and it would also have been odd for this contemporary copyist to have failed to change the syntax from plural to singular when John could only come up with one. Those who believe the document genuine and that it is to be dated to around 1580 have developed a theory that the shrine of St Winifrid, at Holywell, four miles north-west of Flint, was linked to the Jesuit mission of 1580, the episcopal head of which, Thomas Goldwell, had secured from the Pope confirmation of indulgences granted by Martin V to pilgrims visiting it. However, as the link between the testament and the Jesuit mission is now in serious doubt, the proposition that members of the Jesuit mission suggested this name to John is redundant; and we may legitimately wonder instead why his choice fell on a female saint and not, as would have been usual for a man, on a male one. On the other hand, if the forger was copying a 'free-standing' version of the formulary subscribed to by an English Catholic in the 1620s or 1630s, there would be nothing surprising for him to have found that it included the name of St Winifrid as an object of special devotion. In 1629, despite official disapproval, 1,400 lay Catholics and 150 priests were said to have assembled there, and accounts of several miracles also date from this period.[66]

Believers in the document's authenticity also have to explain why it is in manuscript, rather than

---

[66] Below, p. 200.

printed form, especially as they wish to link it with the thousands of copies allegedly requested by Parsons in 1581. Their solution is to propose that the printed copies had not yet arrived from France and that, in John Shakespeare's case, a manuscript version therefore had to be prepared. This, however, does not explain the oddity to which attention has already been drawn,[67] namely, the syntactical error which occurs at the opening of Article VIII – 'I John Shakespeare by virtue of this present testament I doe pardon'. As the rest of the text is almost identical to the printed versions, albeit from the 1630s, the obvious explanation of the writer's mistake would therefore surely have to be that he was, in fact, copying from, and inserting words into, such a printed text and, in his haste, introduced the words 'John Shakespeare' at the wrong point. In other words, there would have to have been printed copies available in England after all and that the laborious (and inexplicable) task of copying out one for John was made more so by inserting extra words into each clause when there was no need to do so. That this is what happened is not, of course, absolutely impossible but is surely a much less likely explanation than one of fraudulent manipulation of a formulaic text at a later date in an attempt to link it firmly with John Shakespeare's name.

There is one final point which might arouse suspicion. The incomplete version which Malone saw and published (C1) started half way through article 3 with four asterisks (indicating, presumably, an indecipherable word or a lacuna) and the words 'at least spiritually'. These same words also occur at the top of a page of B (the 1638 version). On the face of it, this remarkable coincidence would seem to confirm that a defective copy of a free-standing text had indeed been found and copied out from the top of the first surviving page. However, there are two objections to this. Firstly, one would have expected the copy to have survived from the top of a recto (or right hand) page for the simple reason that if a verso (left-hand) page had survived, then the previous recto-numbered page one would have been on the back of it. But in the 1638 version (B) the words 'at least spiritually' are at the top of page 50, a left-hand page. Moreover, C is closer not to B

but A, which has completely different pagination. We will therefore have to wait for the discovery of a 'free-standing' copy of the 'testament' to explore this issue further. However, this coincidence of pagination does allow certain deductions to be made. B occupies a further fifteen pages (seven and a half leaves), whereas C comprises only two thirds of this (ten pages on five leaves). In B, the first two and half articles (missing from C) occupy four pages (two leaves): on the proportions established above, we would thus expect C to have been short by nearly three pages: in fact, Malone, from the appearance of the document before him, believed that it lacked only a single leaf.

What, therefore, may we conclude? An incomplete manuscript, purporting to be the 'Spiritual Testament' of John Shakespeare, was circulating in Stratford in the late 1780s. This had allegedly been discovered some ten years earlier in the roof of Shakespeare's birthplace. Although it was rejected as spurious by the editor of the *Gentleman's Magazine* and by the Reverend Joseph Green, Edmond Malone was at first persuaded that it was genuine, but then five years later, for reasons unknown, also rejected it. More than a hundred years later, the discovery of English formularies, published in 1635 and 1638, for a very similar document, established that the manuscript version must have had a printed ancestor common to all three. These discoveries also proved that the missing section of the will, as supplied to Malone by Jordan, was a forgery, and cast serious doubt on the date of the discovery of the manuscript, attributed in that section only to 1757. If the manuscript was genuine it would, of course, have to have been taken from a printed version published prior to John Shakespeare's death in 1601. Claims that such copies were circulating in their thousands in 1580/81, brought to England by Campion and Parsons, now seem, on examination, to have little or no foundation. Indeed, no printed English translation is known earlier than 1635, though clearly one or more must have existed. We are also faced with John's now inexplicable

[67] Above, p. 191.

decision to hide the document in the roof of his house when the whole point of the document was for the testator to carry it round with him even into the grave. An alternative to the document's authenticity is a hoax involving the discovery of a damaged 'free-standing' printed version, and the passing off of it as a genuine expression of John Shakespeare's faith, by copying it out, at the same time inserting John's name into each clause. In this process, some minor slips were made, none of them conclusive enough on its own to prove forgery, but, when considered with the others, cumulatively sufficient to indicate it.

For this to be plausible, however, two questions remain. Firstly, how likely is it, given that no free-standing printed copies of the document are now known to exist, that one came to light in the third quarter of the eighteenth century, thus giving rise to the idea of a hoax, a copy, moreover, that presumably had St Winifrid's name inserted at the appropriate point? This latter point raises no real difficulties. St Winifrid's Well, at Holywell, gushing forth on the site of her miraculous recovery from decapitation, had become a popular place of pilgrimage during the late mediaeval period. An attempt was made at the Dissolution to suppress the cult, but pilgrimages continued, coming into particular prominence in the 1620s, much to the disgust of John Gee who reported in 1624 that 'once every year ... many superstitious papists of Lancashire, Staffordshire and other more remote counties go in pilgrimage, especially those of the feminine and softer sex, who keep their rendezvous, meeting with divers priests their acquaintance'.[68] This is confirmed, as we have seen, by evidence of 1629 when the claim was made that 1,400 or 1,500 laity, including nobility and gentry, with their priests visited the site on her feast day;[69] and in 1633 the bishop of St Asaph felt moved to report to the archbishop of Canterbury on the 'number and boldnes of Romish recusants' and their 'frequent concourse ... to Holywell' which 'hath longe been complained of wthout remedy'.[70] That some unknown recusant should insert special thanks to St Winifrid in his or, more probably, her copy of the

Borromeo testament should therefore come as no surprise. Indeed, a record of some fifty cures at the well over the period 1556 to 1674 contains a disproportionate number of south Warwickshire examples: Eleanor Calve, for instance, a 34-year-old woman from Tysoe suffering, in 1640, from a 'veery great sickness ... so that her body consumed all away, no substance ... appering in her but the skin and bone'; Francis Reeves, a tenant of the Throckmortons, cured in 1655 of complications after breaking his leg 'which was blistred and festred from his anckle to the knee'; and Dorothy Hopkins from Wootton Wawen, aged twenty, who in 1667 obtained relief from 'a painefull distemper in her body' comprising 'pimples or hollow swellings abiout the bignesse a pease in several places of her body'. Robert Whetston and Robert Hill, pilgrims in 1668, came from Bromsgrove, just over the border into Worcestershire.[71] However, the very rarity of free-standing copies of this tract suggests that those who subscribed to the formula did indeed carry it with them to their last resting places. One macabre possibility, therefore, is that a copy could have been recovered from a coffin or a grave some 150 years later. This would explain its damaged condition. Until the middle of the eighteenth century, human remains were routinely dug up to make room for more burial space, and the bones consigned to charnel houses: a discovery of this sort would therefore not be as unlikely as it would be today.

The second related question concerns the identity of the forger and his motivation. It is fairly clear

---

[68] *The Foot out of the Snare* (London, 1624), 38 (STC 11704).

[69] *CSPD, Charles I, 1629–31*, p. 87. For efforts, in 1617, 1626 and 1636–7, to hinder these pilgrimages, see David Thomas, 'Saint Winifred's Well and Chapel, Holywell', *Journal of the Historical Society of the Church in Wales*, 8 (1958), 15–31, esp. 22; *CSPD, Charles I, 1625–26*, p. 464; *1636–37*, pp. 87–8; *Acta Sanctorum*, November 1, p. 738.

[70] Lambeth Palace ms. 943, fol. 249. For a similar, and 'usuall', complaint, in 1636, see fol. 271, when Lady Vaux of Harrowden, Northamptonshire, was singled out for special mention.

[71] *Analecta Bollandiana*, 6 (1887), 306–52, esp. 331, 338, 345–7; *Acta Sanctorum*, November 1, 740–4, esp. 743–4.

that Jordan was deeply involved in the fabrication of the first two and half articles and that he lied to Malone about how he had come by them. But was it he who manipulated the remaining, and larger portion, and what, precisely, had been Moseley's role in the deception? It is difficult to cast the poorly documented Moseley in the role of an active forger. His place of birth is uncertain but he was of Stratford in November 1753 when he married Mary Hurdis there. The couple had three daughters, born between 1757 and 1762.[72] In 1765, Joseph (and his household of six) was living in Henley Street ward, probably in Windsor Street, an area characterized by small rented dwellings.[73] In 1783, there are signs of increasing prosperity when, as a mason, he took on a lease of a larger property in Henley Street, to hold for the lives of his daughters, Sarah and Molly.[74] He made his will (again as mason) on 4 January 1788 and was buried a week later.[75] His personal goods were valued at less than £100 and his signature, even allowing for ill health, does not exhibit developed literacy skills. If forgery was committed, then, clearly it was not by him, even though, as Davenport's enquiries revealed, he must have been implicated. Jordan, on the other hand, today enjoys the not undeserved reputation of inventor, or at least ardent propagator, of Shakespeare legend, his more notorious impositions – the 'identification' of Mary Arden's House, for example[76] – albeit dating from the early 1790s. Earlier, he had laboured, unsuccessfully, to break into the world of middle-class antiquarianism. Increasing financial problems, it would seem, then tempted him into a more profitable line of business, escorting gullible visitors around Shakespeare's town, regaling them with stories which doubtless increased the pleasure of their visit but which also provided him with a valuable income, and acting as middleman in the sale to them of spurious relics.[77] It would certainly not have been out of character for such a man to have perpetrated a fraud of the kind proposed, especially as it is almost certain, as we have seen, that he forged at least the opening sections of the 'testament'. Moseley presumably became involved either because it was he who had come across the damaged template on which the forgery was based or because Jordan required a builder's testimony to explain how the document came to light. To have attempted to associate the forged document with Shakespeare himself would have been difficult as his Stratford home – New Place – was no more; but it would still have been possible to link it with his father as the old family home in Henley Street was still standing. As Shakespeare's genuine will had also been discovered by that time, but not his father's (who, in fact, may have died intestate), John may also have appealed as a more likely target.

This essay cannot claim to have established with certainty that forgery did indeed take place. However, it has been demonstrated that the 'spiritual testament' cannot, without very considerable qualification, be used to indicate John Shakespeare's religious views and that to associate it with the English Mission of 1580 cannot be justified. It is not only detailed textual analysis and close examination of the available evidence which has led to this conclusion; for, in the final assessment, it is the sheer unlikelihood of this document being genuine which should put us on our guard. Proven to be a forgery in part, and coming to light at a time when other impositions were being made on a gullible public, we are nevertheless asked to believe that this, the only 'stand alone' English copy ever found, and of a text which is not recorded in England before 1635, just happened to have belonged to a member of the Shakespeare family and that it was preserved because John Shakespeare hid it, against the instructions to which he was subscribing, in the roof of his house where it was conveniently discovered,

---

[72] Parish registers, Holy Trinity Church, Stratford-upon-Avon.

[73] SBTRO, ER 1/8, p. 525 (Stratford census, 1765).

[74] SBTRO, ER 3/1431.

[75] SBTRO, DR 148/1/367; parish registers.

[76] For conclusive evidence that this identification was fabricated, see N. W. Alcock, with Robert Bearman, 'Discovering Mary Arden's House: Property and Society in Wilmcote, Warwickshire', *Shakespeare Quarterly*, 53 (2002), 53–83, esp. 53–8.

[77] For Jordan, see Schoenbaum, *Shakespeare's Lives*, pp. 131–4 and my contribution to the new *DNB* (forthcoming).

inexplicably damaged, over 150 years later. To overcome the prejudice which this inevitably provokes, convincing material evidence is required, and this has not been forthcoming. Instead, the circumstantial arguments which have been offered in support of its authenticity turn out, on examination, to have little substance and certainly do not outweigh the apparent evidence of forgery which a detailed study of the text, and of the events surrounding its 'discovery', reveals. In short, it has, in our present state of knowledge, very little to contribute to the debate over Shakespeare's religious views.

SHAKESPEARE AS A FORCE FOR GOOD

PETER HOLBROOK

The disease of Victorian England was claustrophobia –
there was a sense of suffocation, and the best and most
gifted men of the period, Mill and Carlyle, Nietzsche and
Ibsen, men both of the left and of the right, demanded
more air and more light.
(Isaiah Berlin, 'John Stuart Mill and the Ends of Life')[1]

> For sweetest things turn sourest by their deeds;
> Lillies that fester smell far worse than weeds.
> (William Shakespeare, Sonnet 94)[2]

For two decades now Shakespeare scholars have
been busy exposing the use of this writer in the le-
gitimation of various oppressive regimes – sexual,
imperialist, racial, class, and so on. To put it crudely:
as World's Most Canonical Author, Shakespeare has
become synonymous with the Establishment.[3] Not
a few Shakespeare critics would now agree with
William Hazlitt that Shakespeare 'had a leaning to
the arbitrary [i.e. anti-democratic] side of the question'[4] – or, perhaps, would ruefully second Walt
Whitman's accusation that, his 'dramas' being 'the
superbest poetic culmination-expression of feudalism', Shakespeare had nothing to offer democra-
cies.[5]

George Orwell once said some authors were
'worth stealing', a truth demonstrated by both left
and right attempting to claim them as their own.[6]
But many left-wing Shakespearians now concur
with their ideological opponents that this writer
naturally – or, at least, regularly – suits a conservative agenda. Michael Bristol's summary of what
he calls 'the contemporary oppositional critique' of
Shakespeare is fair. 'Recent research', he says,

1 Isaiah Berlin, 'John Stuart Mill and the Ends of Life' (1959),
   in Four Essays on Liberty (Oxford, 1969), p. 198.
2 Shakespeare's Sonnets, ed. Katherine Duncan-Jones (London,
   1997).
3 For Alan Sinfield Shakespeare has become 'in part at least,
   a shrine for Establishment values': 'Heritage and the Market, Regulation and Desublimation', in Political Shakespeare:
   Essays in Cultural Materialism, ed. Jonathan Dollimore and
   Alan Sinfield, second edn (Manchester, 1994; first pub. 1985),
   p. 255. He says: 'In education Shakespeare has been made to
   speak mainly for the right'; see his essay 'Give an account of
   Shakespeare and Education, showing why you think they are
   effective and what you have appreciated about them. Support
   your comments with precise references'; Political Shakespeare,
   p. 159. Terence Hawkes writes: 'By the end of the first quarter
   of the twentieth century, largely as a result of . . . educational
   processes . . . Shakespeare had . . . become . . . a pillar of the existing social and political order in Britain'; see Meaning by
   Shakespeare (London, 1992), p. 48. In That Shakespeherian Rag:
   Essays on a Critical Process (London, 1986) Hawkes observes
   that '[a]s a central feature of the discipline we call "English"',
   Shakespeare's plays 'form part of that discipline's commitment – since 1870 in a national system of education – to the
   preservation and reinforcement of what is seen as a "natural"
   order of things' (p. 68).
4 William Hazlitt, 'Coriolanus', in Characters of Shakespeare's
   Plays (1817); William Hazlitt: Selected Writings, ed. Jon Cook
   (Oxford, 1991), p. 345.
5 Walt Whitman, Democratic Vistas (published 1870 but dated
   1871) in Walt Whitman: Poetry and Prose, ed. Justin Kaplan
   (New York, 1996), p. 957n; the first part of Democratic Vistas, from which this quotation is taken, was published in
   Galaxy in 1867. Edward Dowden quoted Whitman's remark
   that Shakespeare was 'incarnated, uncompromising feudalism in literature', in Shakspere: A Critical Study of his Mind
   and Art, third edn (London, n.d.; originally published 1875),
   p. 319.
6 'Charles Dickens' (1939), The Penguin Essays of George Orwell
   (Harmondsworth, 1984), p. 41.

has been concerned with demonstrating how [Shakespeare] has been enlisted by a social and economic regime to serve the interests of a white, Christian, middle-class, predominantly male and heterosexual mainstream . . . [and thus with] exposing the function of Shakespeare in furthering class or gender domination and social discipline.[7]

Of course the situation is more complex than my remarks so far suggest, Cultural Materialist critics, for example, demonstrating the ways Shakespeare is a *disputed* object of political struggle.[8] But while many scholars have uncovered a democratic Shakespeare,[9] full-blown Bardolatry, such as numerous radicals of the past espoused, is distinctly out of fashion among progressive Shakespearians, tending indeed to be associated with the cultural right.[10] Their author's membership of the Establishment makes many Shakespeare scholars unhappy, placed as they are in the position of offering at best mealy-mouthed defences of him or, perhaps even more depressing, of seeing their job as guarding the young from his influence (showing how bad he is despite the poetry). We have virtue, but the Devil has the best tunes.[11]

This predicament reminds me of the one Richard Rorty describes in a recent essay, 'The Inspirational Value of Great Works of Literature'.[12] Rorty thinks academics in English Departments have traded an upbeat attitude about their objects of study (something their less sophisticated counterparts once enjoyed) for a dry, joyless, knowing one borrowed from Foucault: thus we now 'interrogate' rather than celebrate great authors. But, he believes, this mindset is of dubious political value, cutting itself off from the inspiration to be derived from past cultural achievements and engendering a spirit of hopelessness, in which history reveals only the triumph of barbarians.

Left-wing Shakespeare scholars would enjoy greater peace of mind if they could aver proudly that Shakespeare had not always been cosying up to reactionaries. They would sleep better if he had sometimes helped along liberty, justice and equality – the ideals of what Rorty, following Emerson, calls the party of hope.[13] While Harold Bloom is wildly wrong to dismiss out of hand politically

[7] Michael D. Bristol, *Big-Time Shakespeare* (London, 1996), p. 25. On sexual politics, cf. R. S. White's statement that contemporary feminists attack 'Shakespeare's plays as repositories of male, heterosexual attitudes which have harmed subsequent generations of women and gay men'; he cites Jacqueline Rose, Lisa Jardine, and Dympna Callaghan; see 'Shakespeare Criticism in the Twentieth Century', in *The Cambridge Companion to Shakespeare Studies*, ed. Margreta de Grazia and Stanley Wells (Cambridge, 2001), p. 292. Earlier feminists were possibly more disposed to admire Shakespeare. Phyllis Rackin says: 'The heroines of Shakespeare's middle comedies were especially attractive to the feminist critics of the 1970s, when it seemed important to mobilize Shakespeare's authority in the service of our own political goals. In the 1980s, however, a more pessimistic picture emerged as scholars marshaled historical evidence to demonstrate the pervasiveness of patriarchal beliefs and practices and discredit the optimistic feminist readings of the 1970s as unhistorical'; see her 'Misogyny is Everywhere', in *A Feminist Companion to Shakespeare*, ed. Dympna Callaghan (Oxford, 2000), p. 44. If Rackin is correct, contemporary feminists in this regard reflect a broader trend among emancipation-minded critics to find that Shakespeare does not play on their side.

[8] 'The text is always a site of cultural contest', Sinfield, *Faultlines: Cultural Materialism and the Politics of Dissident Reading* (Oxford, 1992), p. 49. Hence colonized peoples can use Shakespeare (or canonical western culture generally) to think critically about their subjugation (p. 261). Ania Loomba and Martin Orkin remark that while 'Colonial masters imposed their value system through Shakespeare . . . colonized peoples often answered back in Shakespearean accents'; 'Introduction: Shakespeare and the Post-colonial Question', in *Post-Colonial Shakespeares*, ed. Loomba and Orkin (London, 1998), p. 7. This 'oppositional' Shakespeare is often allowed for by radical critics (though mostly as a wan theoretical possibility, devoutly to be wished for rather than robustly believed in). But the *tone* of recent 'committed' criticism is overwhelmingly of the 'J'accuse!' kind – which explains why it so often leaves the radical Shakespeare-lover feeling despondent and restless (terrible to find out the nasty truth about one's beloved).

[9] Jonathan Bate's pioneering work is central here: see *Shakespearean Constitutions: Politics, Theatre, Criticism, 1730–1830* (Oxford, 1989), on radical uses of Shakespeare by Hazlitt and others, and, for a book which takes up the topic of Shakespeare's cultural politics in many different contexts, *The Genius of Shakespeare* (New York, 1997). In *Engaging with Shakespeare: Responses of George Eliot and Other Women Novelists* (Iowa City, 1998) Marianne Novy explores how female novelists 'have . . . appropriat[ed] some Shakespearean characters and some aspects of Shakespeare's cultural image for women' (p. 1). I am grateful to Jean Howard for drawing my attention to Novy.

motivated criticism of Shakespeare – for such criticism has produced *knowledge* about conservative uses of the poet – he is right to feel that much of it has a resentful air and a depressing effect.[14] Here, then, is a prediction: if we persist in convincing ourselves that Shakespeare has mainly been deployed for – mainly lends himself to – oppressive, anti-human ends, we will find it harder and harder to like him, and this irrespective of how much we adored him in the past, when we were blinded to the horrible truth. Soon enough, we will begin to feel about Shakespeare as he claimed to feel (in his *Sonnets*) about his once-idealized young man. Who wants that?

Fortunately, an affirmation that Shakespeare has been on the side of the party of hope is certainly possible. We need not deny – I do not – that Shakespeare has been and is put to oppressive uses (for example national chauvinism) to claim another, positive side to his reception.[15] Shakespeare enthusiasm has often been on the side of the angels. An oppositional or libertarian Shakespeare is especially prominent in the nineteeth century, when Romantic adulation of this author was at its height. (That ardent Shakespearian Victor Hugo famously defined Romanticism as 'liberalism in literature').[16] There is an uplifting story to be told about what we might call 'progressive Bardolatry' in this period: the passion for Shakespeare among liberals, socialists, radicals, bohemians, feminists, sexual dissidents, national liberationists and social reformers. Remembering this story can make even some pillars of the Shakespeare Establishment back then seem less heartily blimpish than they might otherwise appear.

Take A. C. Bradley, whose *Shakespearean Tragedy* is now almost a century old (published in 1904, it drew on lectures delivered at Liverpool, Glasgow and then Oxford, where Bradley was Professor of Poetry from 1901–6). As Katherine Cooke and G. K. Hunter have shown, Bradley belonged to a broadly progressive current in late nineteenth-century English society.[17] He was a disciple of the Oxford teetotaller, social reformer, and Hegelian T. H. Green, who is sometimes credited with laying the theoretical foundations

[10] Thus White on how Hawkes 'dismantles the institutions of English education and criticism to explain the ways in which "the canon" and "bardolatry" have . . . give[n] legitimacy to social attitudes which are implacably conservative' (p. 290); for relevant quotations from Hawkes himself, see n. 3 above.

[11] Some sense of the discomfort progressive Shakespearians nowadays feel about their author can be gauged from Callaghan's introduction to her *Feminist Companion*. Discussing the cultural historian Margaret King's call to feminist scholars to turn away from 'the grand monuments' of (masculine) high culture to focus on 'the objects most associated with' women, those 'spun, woven, sewn, embroidered by female hands', Callaghan observes that this exhortation places the feminist Shakespearian in a difficult position 'if the object of feminist inquiry is "women" of the late sixteenth and early seventeenth centuries, then Shakespeare, undoubtedly the grand monument of literary studies, would seem to offer only a very oblique bearing on the subject' (p. xii). In so far as feminists continue to study Shakespeare they have, in my view rightly, rejected the essentialism, not to say fundamentalism, implicit in King's position. My point is simply that the queasy sense that, *as a progressive*, one might have chosen a better author to study than Shakespeare is now common among scholars and university teachers (and on a great variety of grounds: feminist, anti-colonial, anti-racist, anti-elitist . . .).

[12] In *Achieving our Country: Leftist Thought in Twentieth-Century America* (Cambridge, Mass., 1998).

[13] Rorty, *Achieving our Country*, p. 139.

[14] Bloom attacks the ideological, 'anti-elitist', anti-canonical bent of contemporary academic criticism which, he claims, threatens to 'expel' Shakespeare from the universities: *Shakespeare: The Invention of the Human* (New York, 1998), pp. 9, 17, and *passim*. I reviewed his book adversely in *The Australian's 'Review of Books'* (April, 1999); nonetheless, the notion that contemporary progressive critics now regularly display at the least a certain suspicion towards Shakespeare does seem justified.

[15] On the national chauvinist Shakespeare, see Sinfield's discussion of a British armaments manufacturer's invocation of the poet in a magazine ad (*Faultlines*, pp. 1–4); he cites G. Wilson Knight's association of Shakespeare with an ideal of English Empire (p. 6). Such evidence makes one agree that Shakespeare has 'been a key imperial site where ideology is produced' (p. 28). For arguments linking Shakespeare with imperialism see Stephen Knight, 'In the Golden World: Shakespeare and the Pedagogy of Power', in *Shakespeare's Books: Contemporary Cultural Politics and the Persistence of Empire*, ed. Philip Mead and Marion Campbell (Melbourne, 1993), p. 115; Simon During, 'Transporting Literature: Relations between Metropolitan and Colonial Literary Cultures During the Settlement Period', *Shakespeare's Books*, p. 61; Michael Dobson, *The Making of the National Poet: Shakespeare, Adaptation, and Authorship, 1660–1769* (Oxford, 1992), p. 227.

of the British welfare state. (Green was the intellectual leader of the so-called New Liberals, who abandoned their predecessors' extreme laissez-faire-ism.)[18] As an undergraduate Bradley's circle included Swinburne (who declared 'the author of *King Lear*...a spiritual if not a political democrat and socialist')[19] and he was a life-long friend of the anti-imperialist propagandist and Greek scholar Gilbert Murray.[20] I don't, however, wish here to explore Bradley's politics but rather another aspect of his Shakespeare writing: what we might call his moral latitudinarianism. I want to show how he used Shakespeare in a way that helped foster individualistic, emancipatory tendencies in Victorian civilization. Bradley's Shakespeare criticism runs against the moralism of his era. He wanted more air and light, to quote from one of my epigraphs. What's more, I don't think his use of Shakespeare in this way was atypical. Shakespearianism (and Elizabethanism more generally) is at this time frequently associated with an oppositional outlook on society and a relativizing one on morality.

To show even a part of this story, however, I have to go back in time, to the unavoidable figure of J. S. Mill, especially the Mill of *On Liberty*, published in 1859.

As everyone knows, the nineteenth century saw pervasive anxiety about the disappearance of individuality in an anonymous, herd-like society.[21] Hazlitt wrote in 1813 that 'our distinguishing characteristic [is] the want of all character'.[22] Seventy years later the Renaissance scholar and behind-the-scenes campaigner for homosexual law reform, John Addington Symonds, invoked the oppressiveness of mass society when he wrote, in *Shakespeare's Predecessors in the English Drama*, that during the Age of Elizabeth 'The characters of men were harshly marked, and separated by abrupt distinctions. They had not been rubbed down by contact and culture into uniformity'.[23] Such diverse figures as Marx, Nietzsche, Emerson, Herbert Spencer, Oscar Wilde (in *The Soul of Man under Socialism*, for instance) are equally preoccupied with the future of individuality. I suggest Shakespeare plays a part in this concern, both as an embodiment

of creative genius and as the inventor of energetic, idiosyncratic individuals who implicitly rebuke the bland conformity of modern people.[24]

---

[16] Quoted in Lillian R. Furst, *Romanticism* (London, 1969; repr. 1973), p. 3. By 'liberalism' Hugo meant the popular, anti-absolutist politics of the French Revolution. In *William Shakespeare* (1864) he wrote that 'The Revolution...is the source of the literature of the nineteenth century' and that 'romanticism and socialism are the same fact'; see the translation by Melville B. Anderson (Chicago, 1899; first pub. 1886), pp. 374, 373. For Hugo's radical reading of Shakespeare, see Bate, *Genius*, pp. 235–9.

[17] See Hunter's article on Bradley in *The New Dictionary of National Biography* (forthcoming); I am grateful to Professor Hunter for showing me proofs. See also Katherine Cooke, *A. C. Bradley and his Influence in Twentieth-Century Shakespeare Criticism* (Oxford, 1972) and Hunter's 'A. C. Bradley's *Shakespearean Tragedy*', in his *Dramatic Identities and Cultural Tradition: Studies in Shakespeare and his Contemporaries* (Liverpool, 1978).

[18] See F. A. Hayek, 'Liberalism' (1973), *New Studies in Philosophy, Politics, Economics and the History of Ideas* (London, 1978), p. 130.

[19] A. C. Swinburne, *A Study of Shakespeare* (London, 1920), p. 175. According to Edmund Gosse's Preface, Swinburne began his essay in 1874 and published instalments in the *Fortnightly Review* in 1875 and 1876; it appeared in book form in 1880. On Bradley's undergraduate acquaintances, see Hunter, *New DNB*; these included John Addington Symonds, mentioned below.

[20] Gilbert Murray, *An Unfinished Autobiography, with Contributions by his Friends*, ed. Jean Smith and Arnold Toynbee (London, 1960), p. 96.

[21] For W. H. Greenleaf the 'tension between libertarianism and collectivism' was the essential structure of British politics in the nineteenth century and after; see his *The British Political Tradition*, 3 vols. (London, 1983–), 2, p. xi; he quotes J. S. Mill arguing in 'Civilization' (1836) that modern society tended to make 'the importance of the masses...constantly greater, that of individuals less' (2.106). For a fascinating, polemical treatment of aspects of this topic at the latter end of the period, see John Carey, *The Intellectuals and the Masses: Pride and Prejudice among the Literary Intelligentsia, 1880–1939* (London, 1992).

[22] 'On Modern Comedy', *Selected Writings*, p. 101.

[23] John Addington Symonds, *Shakespeare's Predecessors in the English Drama*, new edn (London, 1906; first pub. 1883), p. 23.

[24] Hazlitt said that '[e]ach of [Shakespeare's] characters is as much itself, and as absolutely independent of the rest...as if they were living persons, not fictions of the mind'; 'Shakespeare', *Selected Writings*, p. 328. On the same page he speaks of Shakespeare's 'individuality of conception'.

The pre-eminent figure here is Mill. He was passionately committed to protecting individuality and autonomy, not just from the State but from public opinion and custom. Favouring what he called 'different experiments of living', he proposed 'that free scope should be given to varieties of character, short of injury to others'.[25] The quotations are from the chapter of *On Liberty* entitled 'Of Individuality, as One of the Elements of Well-Being'. Mill was influenced by Wilhelm von Humboldt, from whose *The Limits of State Action* he took the epigraph to *On Liberty*.[26] The German had championed human self-realization and (as J. W. Burrow summarizes it) 'different styles of life' and 'cultural diversity'.[27] As he wrote: 'that on which the whole greatness of mankind ultimately depends [is] individuality of energy and self-development'.[28] Mill takes over Humboldt's obsession with 'originality' and makes of it a criterion for social policy. He knows the moralist's argument against originality – moral laws are by their nature universal – and, unlike Nietzsche, he does not scorn morality as a ruse of the weak to hobble the strong. But he does argue, rather like Nietzsche's friend Burckhardt, whose *The Civilization of the Renaissance in Italy* appeared a year after *On Liberty*, that the energy of free individuals is a social boon, even if purchased at a cost to morality. Burckhardt thought Renaissance individualism had inaugurated *modern* ethics: 'In itself [individualism] is neither good nor bad, but necessary; within it has grown up a modern standard of good and evil – a sense of moral responsibility – which is essentially different from that . . . familiar to the Middle Ages'.[29]

Central to *On Liberty* are the concepts 'character' and 'energy'. In a healthy society vigorous and diverse personalities flourish; Mill, no less than Nietzsche, writes in the shadow of a crushing moralism in contemporary civilization:

To say that one person's desires and feelings are stronger and more various than those of another, is merely to say that he has more of the raw material of human nature, and is therefore more capable, perhaps of more evil, but certainly of more good. Strong impulses are but another name for energy. Energy may be turned to bad uses; but more good may always be made of an energetic nature,

than of an indolent and impassive one. Those who have the most natural feeling, are always those whose cultivated feelings may be made the strongest. The same strong susceptibilities which make the personal impulses vivid and powerful, are also the source from whence are generated the most passionate love of virtue, and the sternest self-control. It is through the cultivation of these, that society both does its duty and protects its interests: not by rejecting the stuff of which heroes are made, because it knows not how to make them . . . Whoever thinks that individuality of desires and impulses should not be encouraged to unfold itself, must maintain that society has no need of strong natures – is not the better for containing many persons who have much character – and that a high general average of energy is not desirable.[30]

This passage from *On Liberty* seems written under the impress of just those vivid, distinctive, passionate individualities great tragedy displays. Mill's use of the literary word 'hero' is telling; so is his vision of personalities whose potential for good is as strong as for evil. The passage recalls Mill's Romantic solicitude for genius expressed in other of his writings. Thus in a review of his friend and liberal ally George Grote's *History of Greece* (1846–56) he quotes a long passage from Grote on individuality in ancient Athens:

The national temper was indulgent in a high degree to all the varieties of positive impulses: the peculiar promptings in every individual bosom were allowed to manifest themselves and bear fruit, without being suppressed by external opinion, or trained into forced conformity with some assumed standard . . . Within the limits of the law, . . . individual impulse, taste, and even eccentricity, were accepted with indulgence . . .

---

[25] See *'On Liberty' and Other Essays*, ed. John Gray (Oxford, 1991), p. 63.

[26] See the editor's introduction to Wilhelm von Humboldt, *The Limits of State Action*, ed. J. W. Burrow (Cambridge, 1969), p. vii. The book was published in 1854, written 1791–2.

[27] Humboldt, *Limits*, pp. xxiii and xxiv.

[28] Humboldt, *Limits*, p. 17.

[29] Jacob Burckhardt, *The Civilization of the Renaissance in Italy* (1860), trans. S. G. C. Middlemore, 2 vols. (New York, 1929, repr. 1975), 2, p. 443.

[30] Mill, *On Liberty*, pp. 66–7.

Mill comments:

The difference here pointed out between the temper of the Athenian and that of the modern mind, is most closely connected with the wonderful display of individual genius which made Athens illustrious, and with the comparative mediocrity of modern times. Originality is not always genius, but genius is always originality; and a society which looks jealously and distrustfully on original people – which imposes its common level of opinion, feeling, and conduct, on all its individual members – may have the satisfaction of thinking itself very moral and respectable, but it must do without genius.[31]

Mill's insistence on the importance of originality in life is no less vehement than Nietzsche's. Key is the idea (again, with literary overtones) of *character*. 'At present', laments Mill in *On Liberty*, 'individuals are lost in the crowd' while 'public opinion . . . rules the world'. The tyranny of 'collective mediocrity' means that people have '[t]heir thinking . . . done for them . . . through the newspapers'.[32] Implicit is a contrast between the present (newspapers, levelling mass culture) and more poetic, romantic, heroic epochs. Thus Mill's concession to the moralists that 'There has been a time when the element of spontaneity and individuality was in excess, and the social principle had a hard struggle with it. The difficulty then was, to induce men of strong bodies or minds to pay obedience to any rules which required them to control their impulses'.[33] The historical argument brings to mind Nietzsche's celebration of the Renaissance as an age of powerful, immoral drives, epitomized for him most attractively in the ferociously cruel soldier, tyrant, and murderer Cesare Borgia.[34] Of course, Mill may have had in mind the Middle Ages, or some other supposedly barbarous past. But it is at least as likely that he was thinking of Shakespeare's time. We have to recall the impact on him of what he called 'the Germano-Coleridgian school' which, he thought, had founded the 'philosophy of human culture'. Chief among this school was the historicist proto-anthropologist, cultural theorist, and Bardolater, J. G. Herder.[35] Herder sparked Goethe's love of Shakespeare, and there is an intriguing connection between the birth of cultural historicism

with Herder and the emergence of a Romantic Shakespeare cult in Germany and England.[36] Mill summarizes Herder's perspective as follows:

The culture of the human being had been carried to no ordinary height, and human nature had exhibited many of its noblest manifestations, not in Christian countries only, but in the ancient world, in Athens, Sparta, Rome; nay, even barbarians, as the Germans, or still more unmitigated savages, the wild Indians, and again the Chinese, the Egyptians, the Arabs, all had their own education, their own culture; a culture which, whatever might be its tendency upon the whole, had been successful in some respect or other. Every form of polity, every condition of society, whatever else it had done, had formed its type of national character. What that type was, and how it had been made what it was, were questions which the metaphysician might overlook, the historical philosopher could not.[37]

Herder's anthropological relativism – every culture is valuable because unique – was individualism extended to peoples.[38] There is no one way of living well. The Germans are not obliged to live like the French, the Indians like the English. Mill's position is more subversive than it may at first appear: it is not an enormous leap from his and Herder's

---

[31] See J. S. Mill, 'Grote's *History of Greece*' (1853) in vol. 11 of *The Collected Works of John Stuart Mill*, 23 vols.; this vol. ed. J. M. Robson, intro. by F. E. Sparshott (Toronto, 1978), pp. 320, 320–1.

[32] Mill, *On Liberty*, p. 73.

[33] Mill, *On Liberty*, p. 67.

[34] 'We misunderstand the beast of prey and the man of prey (for example, Cesare Borgia) thoroughly, we misunderstand "nature", as long as we still look for something "pathological" at the bottom of these healthiest of all tropical monsters and growths . . .'; Nietzsche, *Beyond Good and Evil* (1886), section 197, in *Basic Writings of Nietzsche*, trans. Walter Kaufmann (New York, 1966; repr. 1992), pp. 298–9.

[35] See *Mill on Bentham and Coleridge*, intro. by F. R. Leavis (Cambridge, 1980; first pub. 1950), pp. 129, 130, 131. 'Bentham' appeared in 1838, 'Coleridge' in 1840.

[36] For this suggestion, see my 'Shakespeare at the Birth of Historicism', in *The Touch of the Real: Essays in Early Modern Culture*, ed. Philippa Kelly (Crawley, Western Australia, 2002).

[37] Mill, *Mill on Bentham and Coleridge*, p. 132.

[38] See Guido de Ruggiero, *The History of European Liberalism*, trans. R. G. Collingwood (Boston, 1959; translation first pub. 1927), pp. 222, 223.

commitment to personality to the self-fashioning advocated by a Nietzsche or Foucault, as described recently by Alexander Nehamas in his *The Art of Living*:

...the art of living [which] is the subject of this book...is the least universalist of all. According to it, human life takes many forms and no single mode of life is best for all. Philosophers like Montaigne, Nietzsche, and Foucault articulate a way of living that only they and perhaps a few others can follow. They do not insist that their life is a model for the world at large...This...art of living is aestheticist...As in the acknowledged arts, the aim is to produce as many new and different types of works – as many different modes of life – as possible, since the proliferation of aesthetic differerence and multiplicity, even though it is not often in the service of morality, enriches and improves human life.[39]

Mill frets that 'life' is in danger of being 'reduced...to one uniform type'; that the modern 'ideal of character...is to be without any marked character' and to 'desire nothing strongly'.[40] In the Coleridge essay he deplores 'the relaxation of individual energy and courage' and the 'passionless insipidity' of modern society.[41] The Coleridgean provenance of the idea suggests, again, an implicit distinction between the Age of Shakespeare and the present.

What I am interested in is how notions of Shakespeare's life, times and works inform Victorian culture critique. In the eighties Symonds would invoke the Elizabethans in a Millian condemnation of the repressive uniformity of the present – partly to legitimate 'uranian', or homosexual, desire. (Describing the recklessness of Renaissance men, he observed that they 'carved Madonna and Adonis on the self-same shrine, paying indiscriminate devotion to Ganymede and Aphrodite...'[42]) 'Already', wrote Mill, 'energetic characters on any large scale are becoming merely traditional...But it was men of another stamp than this that made England what it has been...'[43] But who (besides Chaucer) for English criticism at this time is the master contriver of character? Despite Mill's patriotic rhetoric there is, haunting *On Liberty*, a Shakespeare who is less the National Poet than the genius of 'experiments of living'. Variety is precious to

Mill. But again, what poet or period is more associated in English criticism with 'variety' (Chaucer, who gave us 'God's plenty',[44] is perhaps the sole exception) than Shakespeare and the Elizabethans – in Romantic literary history, a race of giants? And to go back to Mill's point about energy for evil as well as good: what figures in the Romantic tradition in which I am placing Mill are more resplendent in this regard than Shakespeare's tragic heroes?

Shakespeare, I am suggesting, underwrites Mill's experimental approach to life. He was lauded as the poet of the most varied portrayal of human life (with 'the largest and most comprehensive soul', as Dryden put it)[45] and so imaginatively, at least, satisfies Mill's desire for the 'richest diversity' of 'human development' (the words are from *On Liberty*'s epigraph). Shakespeare is traditionally the poet of *experience* – the unruly genius before whom neoclassical theory beats a retreat – and as such may appear to sponsor Mill's ethical empiricism. It might even be said he comes to stand for the irregularities of life itself. Thus in 1858 Walter Bagehot, in an essay entitled 'Shakespeare – The Individual', likened him to the liberal, non-dogmatic English constitution: 'there are no straight lines in nature or Shakespeare'; the poet's nature is opposite to that of a '*doctrinaire*'.[46] Mill does not go as far as Burckhardt or Nietzsche, who cheerfully accept evil as inseparable from real personality. But we should not miss his apparent *lack of concern* whether the selves produced by his 'experiments in living' are moral.[47] Just as Shakespeare, according to Samuel

---

39 Alexander Nehamas, *The Art of Living: Socratic Reflections from Plato to Foucault* (Berkeley, 1998), p. 10.

40 Mill, *On Liberty*, pp. 82, 77.

41 Leavis, *Mill on Bentham and Coleridge*, p. 105.

42 Symonds, *Shakespeare's Predecessors*, p. 24.

43 Mill, *On Liberty*, pp. 77–8.

44 'Preface to the Fables', *Essays of John Dryden*, 2 vols., ed. W. P. Ker (Oxford, 1900), 2, p. 262.

45 'An Essay of Dramatic Poesy', *Essays of John Dryden*, 1, p. 79.

46 Walter Bagehot, 'Shakespeare – The Individual', in *Estimates of Some Englishmen and Scotchmen* (London, 1858), pp. 232, 225; see also pp. 244–5.

47 See Stefan Collini, *Public Moralists: Political Thought and Intellectual Life in Britain, 1850–1930* (Oxford, 1991), p. 102.

Johnson, seemed to write 'without any moral purpose',[48] so Mill relishes individuality *for its own
sake*. (Similarly, Bagehot opposed Shakespeare to
'religionist[s] . . . possessed of a firm and rigid persuasion that you must leave off this and that, stop,
cry, be anxious, and, above all things, refrain from
doing what you like, for nothing is so bad for any
one as that'; by contrast Shakespeare, he said, expresses 'a sense of freedom'.)[49] Mill is a founder
of the modern ethic Charles Taylor describes as
'expressive individuation': the conviction that the
'differences' between individuals 'lay the obligation
on each of us to live up to our originality'.[50] I have
suggested that Shakespeare – as himself a genius and
as the creator of strong personalities – guarantees
this project.[51]

I want now to return to Bradley's *Shakespearean
Tragedy*, and suggest that that book, like *On Liberty*,
entertains the notion that some individualities,
though immoral, are desirable because original.[52]

Stefan Collini, to whose accounts of nineteenth-
century intellectual life I am greatly indebted, has
adduced Bradley's *Shakespearean Tragedy* as an example of the concern in Victorian political discourse
with the idea of character.[53] Certainly a theme of
Bradley's criticism is what we might call the Millian
one of the decay of personality. At the end of a 1909
lecture, Bradley declared his allegiance to the Romantic period: 'I believe', he writes, 'in that Age':

Every time . . . has the defects of its qualities; but those
periods in which, and those men in whom, the mind is
strongly felt to be great, see more and see deeper . . . than
others. Their time was such a period, and ours is not.
And when the greatness of the mind is strongly felt, it
is great and works wonders. Their time did so, and ours
does not. How should it? From causes totally unknown to
us, it seems that after about 1840 for many years scarcely
any men of the highest genius, if any, were born in this
country or elsewhere on the earth.[54]

The passage sounds like a reprise of Mill's criticism
of a heavy, self-thwarting, absolutistic morality
that he believed had produced the 'pinched and
hide-bound', 'cramped and dwarfed' subject all
too typical of his century.[55] In Bradley we feel
the grip of this moralism relaxing. Mill wrote, and

Bradley's *Shakespearean Tragedy* seems not to deny,
that 'Pagan self-assertion is one of the elements of
human worth, as well as Christian self-denial'.[56]
Bradley finds in Shakespeare's tragedies a critical
object that helps him think his way outside the
constricting morality of his day. As seems often to
happen in the period, the plays (or Shakespeare
himself, or, as with Symonds, 'Elizabethanism' –
his word) are used in a self-liberating project.[57]

---

[48] Samuel Johnson, 'Preface to Shakespeare' (1765), *Johnson on
Shakespeare*, ed. Walter Raleigh (Oxford, 1908; repr. 1968),
p. 21.
[49] Bagehot, 'Shakespeare', p. 269.
[50] Charles Taylor, *Sources of the Self: The Making of the Modern
Identity* (Cambridge, Mass., 1989), pp. 376, 375.
[51] For the role of Shakespeare in forming the Romantic ideal
of original genius, and for the ideal's potentially radical social
implications, see Bate, *Genius*, pp. 157–86.
[52] As suggested, this is a Nietzschean theme. In *Nietzsche: Life
as Literature* (Cambridge, Mass., 1985) Alexander Nehamas
stresses 'Nietzsche's view that character is important independently of its moral quality' (pp. 192, 191–9). Literature,
including Shakespeare, helped Nietzsche formulate his belief
that we should value strong personalities even if they are immoral (p. 193). As Nehamas summarizes his thinking: in the
case of 'the great literary villains, figures like Richard III (in
Shakespeare's version) . . . we freely place our moral scruples
in the background' (p. 192). On Nietzsche and Shakespeare
generally, see my 'Nietzsche's *Hamlet*', *Shakespeare Survey, 50*
(1997), pp. 171–86.
[53] Collini argues that political thinkers in the period were frequently preoccupied with the effects on individual character of social and economic arrangements: see pp. 91–5; for
Bradley, pp. 96–7. Mill needs to be understood as one such
thinker: see H. S. Jones, *Victorian Political Thought* (London,
2000), p. 35.
[54] A. C. Bradley, 'English Poetry and German Philosophy in
the Age of Wordsworth', in his *A Miscellany* (London, 1929),
p. 138.
[55] Mill, *On Liberty*, p. 69.
[56] Mill, *On Liberty*, p. 69.
[57] Symonds uses the word 'Elizabethanism' in 'A Comparison of Elizabethan with Victorian Poetry', in *Essays Speculative and Suggestive*, third edn (London, 1907; first edn 1890),
p. 372. In the same essay he finds the 'characteristic of Elizabethan poetry' to be 'freedom, adolescence, spontaneity;
mainly freedom' (p. 370; see also 371). Symonds's attitude
towards Elizabethan poetry is connected to a general celebration of the age as one in which 'Thought and action
were no longer to be fettered. Instead of tradition and pre-
scription, passion and instinct ruled the hour. Every nerve

Something at any rate of Mill's impatience with ethical rigorism – indeed a liberal, individualistic, historicist spirit – informs Bradley's Shakespeare writings. He rejects moralizing interpretations. In 1902 he denied that Shakespeare's characters are simply 'good' or 'bad':

This is one of our methods of conventionalising Shakespeare. We want the world's population to be neatly divided into sheep and goats, and we want an angel by us to say, 'Look, that is a goat and this is a sheep', and we try to turn Shakespeare into this angel. His impartiality makes us uncomfortable: we cannot bear to see him, like the sun, lighting up everything and judging nothing.[58]

He rejoices in Falstaff as an image of 'freedom' and 'the enemy of ... everything respectable and moral'.[59] It is true that *Shakespearean Tragedy* discovers a 'moral order' in the plays:[60] the conflict in each is a division in the play-world's moral substance. But, notably, this substance encompasses what we might take to be non-moral qualities. An expansion of the 'good' takes place, in a move against the moralism Mill excoriated: 'Let us understand by these words [i.e., good and evil], primarily, moral good and evil, but also everything else in human beings which we take to be excellent or the reverse'.[61] Like Mill, Bradley is hardly a frank immoralist à la Nietzsche. But his (or his Shakespeare's) morality includes traits richer and more variegated than those traditional ethics valorizes.

For Bradley, the essence of the plays – and this is in the tradition of the Victorian preoccupation with the need to develop character, as Collini shows – is personality: each play's 'action is essentially the expression of character'.[62] But the nature of this character

is exceptional, and generally raises [the hero] in some respect much above the average level of humanity. This does not mean that [the hero] is an eccentric or a paragon. Shakespeare never drew monstrosities of virtue ... His tragic characters are made of the stuff we find within ourselves and within the persons who surround them. But, by an intensification of the life which they share with others, they are raised above them ... [63]

'The tragic hero with Shakespeare, then', he writes, 'need not be "good", though generally he is "good"'

and therefore at once wins sympathy in his error. But it is necessary that he should have so much of greatness that in his error and fall we may be vividly conscious of the possibilities of human nature'.[64] Note the language of self-development ('possibilities of human nature') reminiscent of Mill. Bradley rejects the religious approach to Shakespeare ('the Elizabethan drama was almost wholly secular')[65]

---

was sensitive to pleasure bordering on pain, and pain that lost itself in ecstasy. Men saw and coveted and grasped at their desire ... Not conformity to established laws of taste, but eccentricity betokening emergence of the inner self, denoted breeding ... Everyone lived in his own humour then, and openly avowed his tastes ... Instead of curbing passions or concealing appetites, men gloried in their exercise. They veiled nothing which savoured of virility; and even conversation lacked the reserve of decency which civilised society throws over it'. See Symonds, *Shakespeare's Predecessors*, pp. 23–4. Rather inconsistently, but perhaps strategically, Symonds presents 'the moral teaching' of Elizabethan drama to be in the main 'unexceptionable'; the dramatists' 'tone is manly and wholesome; the moral sense is not offended by doubtful hints, or debilitated by vice made interesting ... What is bad, is recognised as bad, and receives no extenuation' (p. 65). But that view is in some tension with Symonds's final chapter on Marlowe, which stresses his lawlessness and libertinism (pp. 466, 486); on p. 491 he discusses how 'Hero and Leander' shows Marlowe 'mov[ing]' in a hyperuranian region, from which he contemplates with eyes of equal adoration all the species of terrestial loveliness'; this may not, however, be a 'sexual' passion. Shakespeare is seen to have 'completed and developed ... that national embryo of art' Marlowe first created (p. 484).

[58] Bradley, 'The Rejection of Falstaff' (1902) in his *Oxford Lectures on Poetry*, second edn (London, 1909), p. 255.

[59] Bradley, 'Rejection', p. 262.

[60] A. C. Bradley, *Shakespearean Tragedy: Lectures on 'Hamlet', 'Othello', 'King Lear', 'Macbeth'* (London, 1952; first pub. 1904; second edn 1905), pp. 30–31.

[61] Bradley, *Shakespearean Tragedy*, p. 33.

[62] Bradley, *Shakespearean Tragedy*, p. 19; for Collini, see n. 53 above.

[63] Bradley, *Shakespearean Tragedy*, pp. 19–20.

[64] Bradley, *Shakespearean Tragedy*, p. 22.

[65] Bradley, *Shakespearean Tragedy*, p. 25; see also Bradley, *The Nature of Tragedy with Special Reference to Shakespeare: A Paper Read Before the Warrington Literary and Philosophical Society, 19 February 1889* (London, 1889): '... the special significance of Shakespeare's tragedies in literary history lies in this: that they contain the first profound representation of life in modern poetry which is independent of any set of religious ideas' (pp. 25–6).

but he also repudiates the *moral* response to tragedy altogether:

... the ideas of justice and desert are, it seems to me, in *all* cases ... untrue to our imaginative experience. When we are immersed in a tragedy, we feel towards dispositions, actions, and persons such emotions as attraction and repulsion, pity, wonder, fear, horror, perhaps hatred; but we do not *judge*. This is a point of view which emerges only when ... we fall back on our everyday legal and moral notions. But tragedy does not belong ... to the sphere of these notions ... [66]

Such complicating attitudes are everywhere in Bradley's writings. In an 1889 lecture on 'Poetry and Life' he wrote that

An ordinary 'moral' point of view is far simpler and narrower than a dramatist's point of view ... [The latter] shows you Antony destroyed by his passion, but it shows him also exalted by it ... [Poetry can show us that the] right thing may involve a real loss, the wrong thing may have something really desirable about it ... [67]

Such remarks do not contain the whole of Bradley's thinking about tragedy but do present Shakespearian tragedy as sitting awkwardly with conventional morality. His focus on the hero expresses his belief that, as he writes in 'Hegel's Theory of Tragedy', 'The importance given to subjectivity ... is the distinctive mark ... of modern art'.[68] The modern 'interest in personality', he says,

explains the freedom with which characters more or less definitely evil are introduced in modern tragedy ... The passion of Richard or Macbeth ... is egoistic and anarchic, and leads to crimes done with a full knowledge of their wickedness; but to the modern mind the greatness of the personality justifies its appearance in the position of hero.[69]

It is important to recognize that Bradley is on the moderns' side and, like Mill, willing to risk the evil in heroes for the sake of their individuality. The hero's death, he writes, elicits in us 'A rush of passionate admiration, and a glory in the greatness of the soul' – amoral responses.[70] In tragedy, he argues, '"good" ... means anything that has spiritual value, not moral goodness alone, and "evil"

has a similarly wide sense'.[71] Here again we notice how terms of praise and blame are made helpfully fuzzier: Shakespearian tragedy instances different kinds of (non-moral) good – the results of what Mill had called different experiments of living.[72] 'Is there not ... good in Macbeth?', Bradley asks. And immediately qualifies: 'It is not a question merely of moral goodness, but of good'.[73] In a note he writes, in very Millian language: 'Our interest in Macbeth may be called interest in a ... personality full of matter'.[74]

L. C. Knights succeeded in ridiculing the whole Bradleyan 'stress upon "personality"'.[75] But perhaps his charge that Bradley neglected to see that a Shakespeare play is above all a poetic structure to which the characters are merely subordinate is, in the end, slightly beside the point: logically compelling as his case is, Knights failed to see that Bradley's Shakespeare criticism doesn't aim just to 'get it right' (though it often does that) but also wants to 'make a difference'. Knights couldn't see (or, perhaps, couldn't identify with) the dissenting cultural agenda behind Bradley's apparently naïve 'stress upon "personality"'.

---

[66] Bradley, *Shakespearean Tragedy*, pp. 32–33.

[67] Bradley, *Poetry and Life: An Inaugural Address Delivered in the University of Glasgow, November 8, 1889* (Glasgow, 1889), pp. 18–19.

[68] Bradley, 'Hegel's Theory of Tragedy' (1901), *Oxford Lectures*, p. 77.

[69] Bradley, 'Hegel's Theory', p. 78. Hunter notes that for Bradley Shakespeare's tragic characters raise 'questions about the intertwining of good and evil'; see Hunter, 'Bradley's *Shakespearean Tragedy*', p. 282.

[70] Bradley, 'Hegel's Theory', p. 84.

[71] Bradley, 'Hegel's Theory', p. 86.

[72] In a 1915 lecture on 'International Morality: the United States of Europe', Bradley wrote that 'Moral goodness, ... though a large part of the best life, is not the whole'; see *The International Crisis in Its Ethical and Psychological Aspects: Lectures Delivered in February and March 1915 by Eleanor M. Sidgwick, Gilbert Murray, A. C. Bradley, L. P. Jacks, G. F. Stout, and B. Bosanquet* (London, 1915), p. 50.

[73] Bradley, 'Hegel's Theory', p. 87.

[74] Bradley, 'Hegel's Theory', p. 88.

[75] L. C. Knights, 'How Many Children Had Lady Macbeth?' in his *Explorations: Essays in Criticism Mainly on the Literature of the Seventeenth Century* (London, 1963; first pub. 1946), p. 37.

At times, the lectures on *Macbeth* in *Shakespearean Tragedy* have a strangely Nietzschean elation to them, with Bradley stressing the admiration the heroes inspire despite their immoral nature. Readers gaze 'at Lady Macbeth in awe, because though she is dreadful she is also sublime'; he finds the language of the play displays 'a peculiar... energy, even violence'.[76] 'Energy', a favourite word for Mill we recall, is fundamental to his analysis. Lady Macbeth and Macbeth are 'two great terrible figures, who dwarf all the remaining characters... Both... inspire... the feeling of awe'. He dismisses moralizing readers: 'The way to be untrue to Shakespeare here, as always, is... to conventionalise, to conceive Macbeth, for example, as a half-hearted, cowardly criminal, and Lady Macbeth as a whole-hearted fiend'.[77] Lady Macbeth's 'inflexibility of will', her 'sheer force of will', overwhelm one: 'However appalling she may be, she is sublime'.[78] He credits her with a kind of revaluation of all values:

one sees that 'ambition' and 'great' and 'highly'... are to her simply terms of praise, and 'holily' and 'human kindness' simply terms of blame. Moral distinctions do not in this exaltation exist for her; or rather they are inverted: 'good' means to her the crown and whatever is required to obtain it, 'evil' whatever stands in the way of its attainment.[79]

One can't help noticing the exaltation in Bradley's own prose when he describes Lady Macbeth. Like Mill, he flirts with ethical individualism. The quasi-Nietzschean language informs the earlier *Nature of Tragedy with Special Reference to Shakespeare* (1889):

[T]he tragic character must be raised above the common level. This does not mean that he must be necessarily *good* or lovable... [T]he essential point is not goodness but power; and power may be intellectual or mere power of will just as well as moral power.

We sympathize morally, says Bradley, with the opponents of, for example, Richard III, Macbeth, Cleopatra, or Napoleon – but we are in 'awe' of the bad tragic character's 'gifts' which 'however used, are glorious'; we recognize that these 'splen-

did gifts or energy are the material of a character that might be not only splendid but great'.[80] It is not quite my intention to present Bradley as an Oxford Zarathustra, though it *is* intriguing that Nietzsche's ideas were circulating in literary circles in England from the mid-nineties, and it is certain Bradley had (by 1915, at any rate) read Nietzsche.[81] In any case, and wherever it came from, the language of such passages – 'will', 'awe', 'energy', 'power' – might give us pause: surely it can serve oppression just as well as liberty? Terry Eagleton reminds us that antinormative thought is hardly always and everywhere emancipatory.[82] And yet in Bradley's case I think it is evident that this language of 'will', etc. is deployed *against* a moralism in the nineteenth century that he finds cramping and stifling.

My point has simply been that Bradley's Shakespeare is directed against social conformism – that the critic conscripts the poet into the emancipationist side of a culture war. The spirit of Bradley's book, which declares on every page allegiance to Shakespeare's ethical freedom and individualism,

---

76 Bradley, *Shakespearean Tragedy*, p. 332.
77 Bradley, *Shakespearean Tragedy*, pp. 349, 349–50.
78 Bradley, *Shakespearean Tragedy*, pp. 366, 367, 368; for this exalted language of the will see also p. 371: 'The greatness of Lady Macbeth lies almost wholly in courage and force of will'.
79 Bradley, *Shakespearean Tragedy*, pp. 369–70.
80 Bradley, *The Nature of Tragedy with Special Reference to Shakespeare*, pp. 13–14, 14.
81 As Patrick Bridgwater observes, Havelock Ellis wrote the 'first extended sympathetic essay in English' on Nietzsche in *The Savoy* in 1896; see *Nietzsche in Anglosaxony: A Study of Nietzsche's Impact on English and American Literature* (Leicester, 1972), p. 12; 'in the years 1896–99... there were countless... reviews of [Nietzsche's] work in the British press' (p. 14). Ellis reprinted the essay in his *Affirmations* (second edn, London, 1915; first pub. 1898). He notes that 'For Shakespeare... [Nietzsche's] admiration was deep' (*Affirmations*, p. 43 [1926 reprint]). In the 1915 lecture on 'International Morality', Bradley expressed his dislike of Nietzsche as a champion of force, while acknowledging that Nietzsche was, though not 'by any means a great philosopher... a man of genius, with a poetic imagination and an admirable style' (p. 77).
82 Terry Eagleton, *The Illusions of Postmodernism* (Oxford, 1996), p. 56.

reminds me of nothing so much as Edmund Gosse's *Father and Son*, published three years after *Shakespearean Tragedy*. Like Bradley, Gosse was born into a deeply (even fanatically) religious family; and for him, as, I suspect, for Bradley, literature was an escape route from the narrowness of that background. Gosse's father 'prided himself on never having read a page of Shakespeare'.[83] Gosse's painful break with his father's unbending puritan faith was a life-and-death struggle, he believed, for 'self-sufficiency' and 'individualism'; and the book closes with him claiming 'a human being's privilege to fashion his inner life for himself'.[84] It is a very inspiring story. And Shakespeare critics can, I think, take heart from the story I have been telling, about Shakespeare's appeal to liberal, dissident, anti-conformist, anti-Establishment milieux in the nineteenth century. Occasionally, at least, he has been a force for good, and one good in particular: freedom.

---

[83] Edmund Gosse, *Father and Son: A Study of Two Temperaments*, ed. William Irvine (Boston, 1965; first pub. 1907), p. 151.
[84] Gosse, *Father and Son*, pp. 224, 227.

TIMON OF ATHENS AND JACOBEAN POLITICS

ANDREW HADFIELD

What exactly is the relationship between Shakespeare's plays and their political significance? It is clear that large political issues determine the form and content of the plays he wrote, even if their political focus and direction often appear enigmatic to commentators.[1] It surely cannot be a coincidence that Shakespeare's history plays, all of which date from the 1590s (except the late collaboration *Henry VIII*), deal extensively and obsessively with the question of the monarch's legitimacy and the problem of the succession. These were the issues that dominated political discussions and literary representations of Elizabeth, who actively forbade her subjects to talk openly about her – and their – future.[2] After 1603, Shakespeare produced a number of plays that deal with the matter of Britain – *King Lear*, *Macbeth* and *Cymbeline* – suggesting that his use of history had altered along with the new issues raised by James's reign.[3] James's accession undoubtedly transformed the political agenda: certain approaches and burning issues were put to one side or disappeared altogether, and others came to the fore and assumed a vital new importance.

In this essay I want to argue that after Elizabeth's death Shakespeare accepted the legitimacy of the new king, even if he had feared his accession while the queen was still alive[4] However, it would be quite wrong to assume that supporting the right of the monarch to rule meant uncritically celebrating his reign, as has often been argued.[5] Rather, the political significance of Shakespeare's plays lies in their often critical representations of the monarch, making them part of a long tradition of humanist works keen to advise and correct the monarch through providing counsel. Or, more likely, represent how the monarch might be advised if he wished to take advice through the act of showing theatre audiences how things were going wrong at court.[6]

---

[1] For an eloquent argument that Shakespeare's politics are too elusive to pin down, see Blair Worden, 'Shakespeare and Politics', *Shakespeare Survey 44* (1991), pp. 1–15. Earlier versions of this essay were given at the Dept. of English, University of Glasgow and the Centre for Seventeenth-Century Studies, Durham University, in November 2001. I would like to thank the audiences there for their helpful comments and questions which improved this published version.

[2] Helen Hackett, *Virgin Mother, Maiden Queen: Elizabeth I and the Cult of the Virgin Mary* (Basingstoke, 1995), ch. 6.

[3] For further discussion, see Andrew Hadfield, *Shakespeare, Spenser and the Matter of Britain* (Basingstoke, 2003), chs. 3, 10.)

[4] See Katherine Duncan-Jones, *Ungentle Shakespeare: Scenes from his Life* (London, 2001), ch. 7; Howard Erskine-Hill, *Poetry and the Realm of Politics: Shakespeare to Dryden* (Oxford, 1996), ch. 3.

[5] For examples of such readings, see Josephine Waters Bennett, *Measure for Measure as Royal Entertainment* (New York, 1966); David L. Stevenson, 'The Role of James I in Shakespeare's *Measure for Measure*', *ELH*, 26 (1959), 188–208; Henry N. Paul, *The Royal Play of Macbeth : When, Why and How it was Written by Shakespeare* (London, 1950).

[6] See, for example, Greg Walker, *Plays of Persuasion: Drama and Politics at the Court of Henry VIII* (Cambridge, 1991); L. K. Born, 'The Perfect Prince: A Study in Thirteenth- and Fourteenth-Century Ideals', *Speculum*, 3 (1928), 470–504. I hope it is clear that I am not trying to conflate the significance of the performance of court entertainments and the development of the public stage, but trying to show important similarities between the two.

James himself made the case that a monarch should avoid flatterers and promote useful subjects who could provide helpful advice. While refusing to grant his subjects any right to challenge or circumscribe the king's actions, James explicitly advised his son, Prince Henry, to choose his court carefully and not to promote flatterers to positions of responsibility and power because of the crucial role in government that advisers would play:

But specially take good heed to the choice of your servants, that ye preferre to the offices of the Crown and estate: for in other offices yee have onely to take heede to your owne weale; but these concerne likewise the weale of your people, for the which yee must bee answerable to God. Choose then for all these Offices, men of knowen wisedome, honestie, and good conscience, well practised in the points of craft, that yee ordaine them for, and free of all factions and partialities; but specially free of that filthie vice of Flatterie, the pest of all princes, and wracke of Republickes . . . I fore-warned you to be at warre with your owne inward flatterer, how much more should you to be at war with outward flatterers, who are nothing so sib to you, as your selfe is by the selling of such counterfeit wares, onely preassing to ground their greatnesse upon your ruines.[7]

In the political world according to James, the king's advisers and political servants play a crucial role, even if they have no say in determining the actions of the king in a free monarchy. Throughout his political works, James stresses the need for the monarch to obey the laws he has established and to serve as an example to his people who will then copy him: 'for people are naturally inclined to counterfaite (like apes) their Princes maners' (p. 155). *Basilikon Doron*, fittingly enough, opens with a clear distinction between the 'lawfull good King' and 'an usurping Tyran', 'the one acknowledgeth himselfe ordained for his people . . . the other thinketh his people ordeined for him, a prey to his passions and inordinate appetites' (p. 155). The king had a duty to listen to advice and not surround himself with those – flatterers – who would fail to save him when he went wrong and would actually assist in turning him into a tyrant. In *The Trew Law of Free Monarchies*, James is clear that as

'Gods Lieutenant in earth', the king makes the laws not his subjects, but that 'although hee be above the Law, will subject and frame his actions thereto, for examples sake to his subjects, and of his owne free will'.[8]

James made sure that his key works, including *Basilikon Doron* and *The Trew Law of Free Monarchies*, were published in a new edition before he arrived in England in May 1603.[9] There could be no excuse for any of his literate and influential new subjects being ignorant of his political views. If James was seeking to reassure his English subjects that they had nothing to fear from his views, he was also paving the way for any possible battle with parliament.[10] In *Basilikon Doron*, James referred to parliament as 'the Kings head Court', which should only meet when the king judged that the time was right to make new laws (p. 156). The first parliament of his reign opened on 19 March 1604. James made a speech outlining his view of his role as a divinely ordained king who would serve as the head of the kingdom, while they made up the body.[11]

It is clear that whatever disagreements James had with the representatives of his subjects, his political vision left ample room for vigorous discussion and that he was prepared – at least, in theory – to take advice from trusted councillors.[12] Furthermore, he was at pains to stress this crucial aspect of his philosophy in his writings and make them available for all who wanted to read them. Francis Bacon enthused

---

7 James I, *Basilikon Doron* in *The Workes* (1616) (Hildesheim, 1971), pp. 137–89, at p. 169. Subsequent references to this edition in parentheses in the text.
8 James I, *The Trew Law of Free Monarchies*, in *Workes*, pp. 191–210, at pp. 200, 203.
9 Roger Lockyer, *James VI and I* (Harlow, 1998), p. 34.
10 Lockyer, *James VI and I*, p. 35.
11 The text of the speech is conveniently reproduced in King James VI and I, *Political Writings*, ed. Johann P. Somerville (Cambridge, 1994), pp. 132–46.
12 Lockyer, *James VI and I*, p. 27. Lockyer points out that 'James was amenable to learned argument'. For a wider discussion, see J. P. Somerville, *Politics & Ideology in England, 1603–1640* (London, 1986); Glenn Burgess, *The Politics of the Ancient Constitution: An Introduction to English Political Thought, 1603–1642* (Basingstoke, 1992).

that *Basilikon Doron* 'falling into every man's hand filled the whole realm as with a good perfume or incense before the King's coming in, for being excellently written and having nothing of affectation'. Bishop Montagu was equally fulsome in his praise and evaluation of the wide readership of the same work: 'What applause had it in the world . . . how did it enflame men's minds to a love and admiration of his Majesty beyond measure'.[13]

Moreover, James was keen to be seen as a patron of art and literature. He adopted an existing troop of players, The Lord Chamberlain's Men, making them the King's Men, and had numerous plays performed at court throughout his reign. He helped to establish the masque as a vital form of court entertainment through the appointment of Inigo Jones and Ben Jonson, as set designer and masque writer respectively, and he also encouraged the preaching of sermons so that they became 'the pre-eminent literary genre at the Jacobean court'.[14] It is true that there were times when James appears to have been more keen on the appearance rather than the content of the entertainment in question – especially masques – and he could be impatient if there was more verbiage than action on stage.[15] He was also quick to censor any work that exceeded the boundaries of what could legitimately enter the public realm. As King of Scotland he took offence at Edmund Spenser's *The Faerie Queene*, which represented his mother, Mary Queen of Scots, in an unfavourable light; he called in Sir Walter Raleigh's *History of the World*; and he was keen to demonstrate his power as a monarch through a series of book burnings throughout his reign.[16] However, James was quite capable of promoting and censoring the same authors at different points. He took umbrage at the anti-Scots jibes and sneers at his plans for uniting the kingdoms in Jonson, Chapman and Marston's *Eastward Ho*, and may also have been instrumental in having Ben Jonson called before the Privy Council to explain the significance of *Sejanus his Fall* at the very start of his reign.[17] Nevertheless, Jonson became a key figure at court soon afterwards.[18] Some years later (1616), James was scandalized by John Barclay's satirical *Corona Regia* and its unfavourable portrait of kings, but later (1622),

wanted another work made more widely available, presumably because he approved of its political and moral sentiments.[19]

The evidence would suggest that James was keen to use and extend the venerable tradition of literature of counsel at court, encouraging lively debate and sponsoring performances and texts that he thought were of political value. The list of plays that were staged by the King's Men, many of which were performed at court as surviving dramatic records indicate, shows that James was certainly not averse to seeing plays that questioned and challenged his conception of how the monarch should behave and, often explicitly, his conception of kingship.[20] For example, Barnabe Barnes's rabidly anti-Catholic *The Devil's Charter* was performed at court in January and February 1607. This was undoubtedly part of a reaction to the Gunpowder Plot of two years earlier, but was clearly at odds with James's general policy of extending

---

[13] D. Harris Wilson, *King James VI and I* (London, 1956), p. 166.

[14] Gurr, *Shakespearian Playing Companies*, chs. 6–7; Martin Butler, 'Ben Jonson and the Limits of Courtly Panegyric', in Peter Lake and Kevin Sharpe, eds., *Culture and Politics in Early Stuart England* (Basingstoke, 1994), pp. 91–115; Peter McCullough, *Sermons at Court: Politics and Religion in Elizabethan and Jacobean Preaching* (Cambridge, 1998), p. 125.

[15] See the descriptions in Robert Ashton, ed., *James I by his Contemporaries: An Account of his Career and Character as seen by some of his Contemporaries* (London, 1969), pp. 237–44.

[16] Richard A. McCabe, 'The Masks of Duessa: Spenser, Mary Queen of Scots, and James VI', *ELR* 17 (1987), 224–42; Robert Lacey, *Sir Walter Raleigh* (London, 1975), pp. 365–7; Cyndia Susan Clegg, 'Burning Books as Propaganda in Jacobean England', in Andrew Hadfield, ed., *Literature and Censorship in Renaissance England* (Basingstoke, 2001), pp. 165–86.

[17] Blair Worden, 'Ben Jonson among the Historians', in Lake and Sharpe, eds., *Culture and Politics*, pp. 67–89; David Riggs, *Ben Jonson: A Life* (Cambridge, Mass, 1989), ch. 7; Ben Jonson, *Sejanus his Fall*, ed. W. F. Bolton (London, 1966), introduction, p. xii.

[18] See Richard Dutton, *Licensing, Censorship and Authorship in Early Modern England* (Basingstoke: Palgrave, 2000), ch. 6.

[19] *HMC 75: Downshire Manuscripts, VI, Papers of William Trumbull, Sept. 1616–Dec. 1618*, pp. 211–12. I owe this reference to Rebecca Moss.

[20] Complete listings of the plays performed at court are given in Gurr, *Shakespearian Playing Companies*, pp. 304–5, 386–93.

tolerance to loyal Catholics, enshrined in the Oath of Allegiance passed in the House of Commons in the session immediately prior to the performance of Barnes's play.[21] And, although it was probably not performed at court, the King's Men were also responsible for producing Jonson's controversial *Sejanus his Fall*, and, later, *Catiline his Conspiracy*.[22]

A culture of lively critical debate existed in court literature, as it did elsewhere in James's realm (notably parliament, for all James's emphasis on the Divine Right of Kings).[23] Shakespeare's plays written after 1603 concentrate far less on the legitimacy of the monarch than they had done before, and far more on the behaviour of the monarch as a ruler in office. In doing so they are generally simultaneously more supportive of monarchy as an institution and equally – if not more – critical of the monarch's conduct as the works written in the 1590s.

Timon of Athens, a play only occasionally read in terms of contemporary politics, illustrates a number of issues relating to the practice rather than the theory of James's reign.[24] The play is most frequently read as an inferior *King Lear*, and dates from around the same period, although I would like to argue for a later date – 1608 – than has often been proposed (see below).[25] The plot shows how the profligate generosity and susceptibility to flattery of a wealthy Athenian enable him to squander his vast fortune and give away his riches to a series of undeserving, petty-minded citizens. As a result of their short-sighted greed, the citizens leave Athens open to the invasion of the exiled general, Alcibiades. Timon, now a troglodyte hermit and dedicated misanthrope, pays Alcibiades's army from a horde of gold that he has just discovered and refuses to listen to the pleas of the senators. It is only when Alcibiades learns of Timon's death that he rethinks his plan to take revenge against his and Timon's enemies in Athens, although his last lines are open to a number of interpretations and do not necessarily guarantee peace.

As with many of Shakespeare's plays produced at court for James, there are frequent occasions when the behaviour of one of the central characters re-

sembles that of the king.[26] While Timon is still enjoying the illusion of his wealth and the popularity it brings him, unaware that his coffers are actually empty, he is told by his steward, Flavius, that Lord Lucullus wishes to hunt with him and has presented him with 'two brace of greyhounds' (1.2.187). Greyhounds were expensive and important animals used in hunting, which was James's favourite pastime, as was frequently noted by his contemporaries. M. de Fontenay, envoy to James from his mother, Mary Stuart, observed back in 1584 that 'He loves the chase above all the pleasures of this world, living in the saddle for six hours on end, running up hills and down dales with loosened bridle'.[27] James became notorious for refusing to attend to matters of state when it did not suit him and spending his time hunting at one of his – or his subject's – country retreats.[28] In 1603, James's nine-year-old son, Prince Henry, was represented with Sir John Harington symbolically sheathing his sword after cutting the head off a deer by the court painter, Robert Peake. Next to him are the chief animals used by the hunter, his horse and his dog. The tableau is a sign of how significant hunting was as the official sport of James's court, and as

---

[21] Notestein, *House of Commons*, pp. 146–8; Lockyer, *James VI & I*, ch. 6.
[22] Gurr, *Shakespearian Playing Companies*, pp. 299–300; Jonson, *Sejanus his Fall*, introduction, pp. xi–xii; Riggs, *Ben Jonson*, pp. 176–7.
[23] Lockyer, *James VI & I*, pp. 159–77.
[24] Three important recent articles are Robert S. Miola, 'Timon in Shakespeare's Athens', *Shakespeare Quarterly*, 13 (1980), 21–30; John M. Wallace, '*Timon of Athens* and the Three Graces: Shakespeare's Senecan Study', *Modern Philology*, 83 (1985–6), 349–63; Coppélia Kahn, '"Magic of Bounty": Timon of Athens, Jacobean Patronage, and Maternal Power', *Shakespeare Quarterly*, 38 (1987), 34–57.
[25] It is usually suggested that it was written c. 1607–8. See *Timon of Athens*, ed. H. J. Oliver (London, 1959), introduction, pp. xl–xlii. On *Timon* as an inferior *King Lear* see Nicholas Grene, *Shakespeare's Tragic Imagination* (Basingstoke, 1992), p. 147; John Dover Wilson, *The Essential Shakespeare* (Cambridge, 1932), p. 131.
[26] For an incisive discussion, see Kahn, '"Magic of Bounty"', pp. 41–50.
[27] Ashton, ed., *James I by his Contemporaries*, p. 2.
[28] Lockyer, *James VI & I*, p. 200.

a symbolic activity denoting manly achievement, physical prowess and power over nature.[29]

Shakespeare's reference to hunting in *Timon of Athens* is therefore automatically pointed, especially when it is made clear in the second act that Timon is reluctant to turn from the pleasures of the hunt to deal with the pressing business of sorting out his bills and debts to the despair of his steward (2.2.1–8). Elsewhere in his work hunting is explicitly associated with tyranny, when, for example, Prospero hunts Caliban in *The Tempest*, or, as we witness a bloody 'ritual of death and dismemberment', in *Titus Andronicus* and *Julius Caesar*.[30] It is hard to believe that the audience failed to make the connection between Timon at this point in the play and the behaviour of their king.[31] In the lines that follow the offer of Lord Lucullus – which, we know, has only been made in anticipation of a greater gift in return from Timon – Flavius delivers a lengthy aside showing that he realizes the folly of his master's actions:

> He commands us to provide, and give great gifts,
> And all out of an empty coffer;
> Nor will he know his purse, or yield me this,
> To show him what a beggar his heart is,
> Being of no power to make his wishes good.
> His promises fly so beyond his state
> That what he speaks is all in debt; he owes for ev'ry
>   word:
> He is so kind that he now pays interest for't[.]
>   (190–7)

Timon then proves his steward right, and compounds the error in a significant manner: ''tis not enough to give: / Methinks I could deal kingdoms to my friends, / And ne'er be weary' (218–20).

Timon's words seem to point the reader towards an obvious metaphorical significance of the word 'state' (195), transforming it from its meaning as an individual's wealth or fortune into another common usage in early modern English political language, that of the realm or nation.[32] Shakespeare makes it clear that the significance of the metaphor and its vehicle are reversible: Timon may be figuratively dealing in kingdoms in giving away gifts to friends and promising to bestow rewards on

flatterers beyond his state, but the real king of England was accused by contemporaries of literally doing just that.

The essayist Francis Osborne provides a graphic link between James and Timon via a story about the Lord Treasurer, Sir Robert Cecil.[33] The story may well be apocryphal, but, whether true or not, it does date from the time that the play was written, as Sir Robert Carr, the king's favourite, was described as being in the 'flower of his favour before he had either wife or beard'.[34] Carr came to London in the wake of James in 1603, was knighted in 1607, and married in 1613.[35] Cecil became Lord Treasurer in spring 1608 when the earl of Dorset died. If there is a connection between *Timon* and the following anecdote – and I think it likely that there is – then the play was probably written/performed in mid–late 1608.

Osborne alleges that the Lord Treasurer, Sir Robert Cecil, worried about James's lavish gifts to Carr, laid out the sum of £20,000, which James had given to his favourite

upon the ground in a roome through which his majesty was to passe: who, amazed at the quantity, as a sight not unpossibly his eyes never saw before, asked the treasurer whose money it was, who answered, 'Yours, before you gave it away;' whereupon the king fell into a passion,

---

[29] For commentary, see Edward Berry, *Shakespeare and the Hunt: A Cultural and Social Study* (Cambridge, 2001), pp. 1–3; Roy Strong, *Henry Prince of Wales and England's Lost Renaissance* (London, 1986), p. 114.

[30] See Berry, *Shakespeare and the Hunt*, chs. 3, 7 (quotation at p. 94).

[31] Commentators appear not to made this connection, although Rolf Soellner alludes to a link between Timon and James: *Timon of Athens: Shakespeare's Pessimistic Tragedy* (Columbus, Ohio, 1979), p. 124.

[32] See the *OED* definition, p. 3025, no. 29.

[33] For details of Osborne's importance as a source for the life of James, see Lockyer, *James VI & I*, pp. 2–4. The anecdote is alluded to in Alvin Kernan, *Shakespeare, the King's Playwright: Theater in the Stuart Court, 1603–1613* (New Haven, 1995), pp. 126–7.

[34] Cited in Ashton, ed., *James I by his Contemporaries*, p. 69.

[35] Lockyer, *James VI & I*, p. 168; David Lindley, *The Trials of Frances Howard: Fact and Fiction at the Court of King James* (London, 1993), ch. 4.

protesting he was abused, never intending any such gift: And casting himselfe upon the heap, scrabled out the quantity of two or three hundred poundes, and swore he should have no more. However, it being the king's minion, Cecil durst not provoke him farther than by permitting him only the moiety.[36]

Osborne's anecdote shows how James only begins to understand the nature of money when he is confronted with the reality of it in the form of a huge pile. The lesson reduces James to a greedy miser, scrabbling in the pile to save his wealth from disappearing. The miser was frequently represented on stage by figures such as Shylock, who laments the loss of his gold more than his daughter (*Merchant*, 2.8.15–6), and Barabas in Marlowe's *The Jew of Malta*.[37] Even after this humiliation, Cecil cannot face curtailing the king's expenditure as he would wish and the king is too foolish to control his finances of his own accord. The last lines suggest that Cecil should really have refused to allow James to give Carr any money at all, but he dared not go that far because of the king's attachment to his favourites. The further implication is that it was commonly understood that Carr should not have been given anything at all, that James favoured him because he could not see his faults. Put another way, the relationship between James and Carr was that between a doting monarch and a flatterer.

The image of the undignified, prostrate James sorting through his displayed wealth may well be signalled in Shakespeare's stage image of Timon digging for roots and finding gold. Timon, his wealth dissipated, has now left Athens and is searching for the most basic meal that the earth can provide him. Instead he discovers gold, exactly what he has left Athens to avoid, and so he curses the precious metal, which he now sees as the root of all evil, sent to tempt him:

> Gold? Yellow, glittering, precious gold?
> No, gods, I am no idle votarist.
> Roots, you clear heavens! Thus much of this will
> make
> Black, white; foul, fair; wrong, right;
> Base, noble; old, young; coward, valiant.
>   . . . this

> Will lug your priests and servants from your sides,
> Pluck stout men's pillows from below their heads.
> This yellow slave
> Will knit and break religions, bless th'accurs'd,
> Make the hoar leprosy ador'd, place thieves,
> And give them title, knee and approbation
> With senators on the bench.

> (4.3.26–38).

As is well known, this passage was praised by Karl Marx for its penetrating insight into the nature of money, as the fetishized commodity which possessed 'the property of buying everything, by possessing the property of appropriating all objects' and so mediating – falsely – between mankind and nature.[38] Whatever its value as a philosophical statement it is clear that Timon's impassioned and angry reaction to his former worldly status is simply an inversion of his previous error, rather than a solution to the problem of his myopia. Timon allows his reaction to gold to determine his existence; in Athens he fails to notice that it distorts and undermines the ideal friendships he thinks he is establishing; in the woods he fails to understand that his undue trust in the benign effects of wealth have now led him to turn against mankind and become '*Misanthropus*' (4.3.54). The naive community of the *polis* has been replaced by a body politic in which Timon and Apemantus snarl at each other, and Timon either repels intruders into their world or does what he can to bring the outside world to his level of misery.[39]

James, in Osborne's anecdote, also lets money dominate his life and also fails to grasp its essential nature. He either uses it to promote his favourites, satisfying his whims and enhancing his glory and status as ruler, or, horrified at his foolishness, seeks to protect his hoard. In desperately flinging himself

---

[36] Cited in Ashton, ed., *James I by his Contemporaries*, p. 69.

[37] A further analogue is Malbecco in Edmund Spenser's *The Faerie Queene*, Book II, canto x.

[38] Karl Marx, *Economic and Philosophic Manuscripts* (1844), cited in Karl Marx and Frederick Engels, *On Literature and Art* (Moscow, 1976), p. 135.

[39] On the significance of the Athenian setting of the play, see Miola, 'Timon in Shakespeare's Athens'.

on top of his heap of gold James abandons the regal dignity of the monarch, something he was obsessed with protecting in his writings. Just as Timon fails to learn the lesson of his folly, so does James, illustrating his fallible nature as a man, sharply at odds with his image of himself as a divinely appointed ruler. Both Timon and James illustrate Marx's point that money determines the relationship between mankind and the wider world.

Anthony Weldon's description of James's character in his *The Court and Character of James I* also makes James sound very similar to Shakespeare's Timon:

He was very liberall of what he had not in his owne gripe, and would rather part with 100 *li.* hee never had in his keeping then one twenty shillings piece within his owne custody; he spent much, and had much use of his subjects purses, which bred some clashings with them in parliament . . . and truly his bounty was not discommendable, for his rising favourites was the worst[.][40]

Weldon's critique of James, not published until 1650, is based on his support for the parliamentary cause. It situates James's alleged inadequacies within a greater battle between the king and the institutions which represent the people and guarantee their liberties and their rights. In *Timon of Athens*, the profligacy of Timon and his ill treatment by his friends and dependants ultimately leads to disaster for the city-state, Timon's disillusionment helping to fuel the revenge of Alcibiades. Timon later refers to his remaining stock of gold as 'thou sweet king-killer' (4.3.384), again making a link between the play and the incumbent monarch (especially, given that the Gunpowder Plot did nearly succeed in killing the king only two years earlier).

The play ends with lines of studied ambiguity. Alcibiades, on hearing of Timon's death, appears to rethink his plans for sacking Athens, but the sense of his words is cryptic: 'bring me into your city, / And I will use the olive branch with my sword, / Make war breed peace, make peace stint war, make each / Prescribe to other, as each other's leech' (5.4.81–4). The lines appear to mean that Alcibiades regards war and peace as symbiotic rather than opposite states of existence, both necessary for the public

good as he sees it. However they are interpreted, the lines sound like a deliberate parody of James's self-fashioned image as the 'rex pacificus', the astute ruler capable of steering his subjects clear of the danger of destructive conflict.[41] Given that Timon's profligacy helps to secure the rise of Alcibiades, Shakespeare's play seems to be suggesting that a lack of control over the distribution of favours and gifts and the encouragement of a spendthrift culture in the body politic may undermine the legitimate aims of the governors.

Timon's riches undoubtedly fuel careless and dangerous profligacy, just as James's assumption that the financial strictures placed on him as King of Scotland would be ended when he got his hands on England's bounty earned him the enmity of some of his powerful subjects.[42] But the even more pernicious political effect of his attitude to wealth was the encouragement of flatterers, precisely the sort of courtiers and advisers James had urged Prince Henry to avoid in *Basilikon Doron*. *Timon* contains seventeen references to flattery and flatterers, more than any other Shakespeare play (*King Lear*, the work closest in style and scope to *Timon* contains seven; *Coriolanus*, which can be read as a companion play based on Plutarch, twelve).[43] In the first scenes in the play, the 'churlish philosopher', Apemantus, detects the malign effects of Timon's foolish actions, and refuses to join in the festivities he organizes. Timon reproaches Alcibiades that he 'had rather be at a breakfast of enemies than a dinner of friends' (1.2.75–6), which Alcibiades deliberately turns into a cannibalistic image, reminiscent of the gory cycle of revenge represented in a play such as *Titus Andronicus*, or the violent aristocratic honour and dysfunctional family relationships displayed in *Coriolanus*: 'So they

---

40 Cited in Ashton, ed., *James I by his Contemporaries*, p. 14. On Weldon, see Lockyer, *James VI & I*, pp. 2–4.

41 Wilson, *King James VI and I*, ch. 15; Ashton, ed., *James I by his Contemporaries*, ch. 8.

42 Lockyer, *James VI & I*, pp. 78–80. See also Kahn, '"Magic of Bounty"', pp. 42–7.

43 See John Bartlett, *A Complete Concordance to Shakespeare* (London, 1997, rpt. of 1894), p. 539.

were bleeding new, my lord, there's no meat like 'em; I could wish my friend at such a feast' (77–8). Timon's witty antithesis is immediately transformed from a comic remark to a tragic irony. Apemantus, who aspires to be a self-sufficient cynic, completes the philosophical gloss, before a hypocritical guest proves the point and Timon shows that, despite the evidence at his disposal, he is still living in the enclosed comic world he has created for himself:

APEM   Would all those flatterers were thine enemies then, that then thou mightst kill 'em – and bid me to 'em.

FIRST LORD. Might we but have that happiness, my lord, that you would once use our hearts, whereby we might express some part of our zeals, we should think ourselves for ever perfect.

TIM. O no doubt, my good friends, but the gods themselves have provided that I shall have much help from you: how had you been my friends else?

(80–8)

The dramatic irony of this exchange is straightforward: Timon refuses to leave the festive world that he has created and confront the truth that Apemantus, by no means an ideal friend, has shown him. Once again, the need for the powerful and mighty to listen to counsel they may not want to hear is highlighted, precisely the point made in Osborne's anecdote. Timon allows money to determine his relationship with his fellow man, something that is as true of his social existence after his descent into poverty as it was before. Apemantus, who is one of the few Athenians capable of giving Timon good counsel, gives up after the banquet scene when his comments go unheeded, and decides simply to resort to abuse. He concludes that advising a man like Timon is pointless: 'O that men's ears should be / To counsel deaf, but not to flattery' (1.2.250–1). The James who wrote *Basilikon Doron* would obviously have agreed, but the James observed by Francis Osborne and Anthony Weldon would have been too obsessed with using his imagined fortune to promote adoring favourites to take proper heed.

The Athenian setting is clearly also relevant to a political reading of the play, given the importance of Athens as the city-state where European political thought was conceived.[44] John Lyly, in *Euphues: The Anatomy of Wit* (1579), had represented Athens as an allegorical form of Oxford, deliberately drawing a parallel between the two centres of philosophical and political speculation. Given Shakespeare's knowledge of Lyly's comedies and the immense popularity of *Euphues*, it can be assumed that Shakespeare would have known of this precedent.[45] *Timon* makes use of the story of the famous misanthrope, Timon, contained in a variety of sources, but the story of Alcibiades is undoubtedly more important for reconstructing the political context of the play.[46] Alcibiades was a talented but unscrupulous Athenian who ignored the splendid education he received at the hands of his tutors, Pericles, the founder of the democratic Athenian constitution, and the good will of Socrates. Indeed, it was partly owing to Alcibiades that Pericles's plans to unite Greece as a democratic federation of states was abandoned and gave way to the revival of the imperialist designs of the Peloponnesian War. When he was summoned back to Athens to face trial for his violent crimes he fled to Sparta and supported revolts against Athens until he was recalled, serving the city as a military commander, before he was banished again and eventually assassinated by his many enemies.

---

44 See Harry V. Jaffa, 'Nature and the City: *Timon of Athens*', in John E. Alvis and Thomas G. West, eds., *Shakespeare as Political Thinker* (Wilmington, Delaware, 2000), pp. 177–201, at pp. 199–200; Miola, 'Timon in Shakespeare's Athens'. Nicholas Grene suggests otherwise and claims that Athens 'is an indeterminate place with the vaguest of classical associations' (*Shakespeare's Tragic Imagination*, p. 126). It is true that Shakespeare's representation of Athens lacks the historical and geographical specificity of his representation of Rome, but this does not mean that we can assume that Athens has no significance as a location.

45 See G. K. Hunter, *John Lyly: the Humanist as Courtier* (London, 1962), p. 59.

46 For details of the sources, see Geoffrey Bullough, *Narrative and Dramatic Sources of Shakespeare*, vol. VI (London, 1966), ch. 3. Bullough suggests that Shakespeare made use of Lyly's *Campaspe* (pp. 339–45).

Shakespeare would have known the story of Alcibiades possibly from reading Thucydides's *History of the Peloponnesian War*, an English translation of which was published in 1607 when he was probably at work on *Timon*.[47] It is more likely that he used North's Plutarch, given that he was going through what one critic has termed his '"Plutarchian" transitional period' between the great tragedies and late romances.[48] As Plutarch twins his 'Life of Alcibiades' with that of 'Caius Martius Coriolanus', the source of *Coriolanus*, written within a year of *Timon*, it is hard to believe that Plutarch's comments on Alcibiades do not have a central relevance to Shakespeare's play.

Plutarch represents Alcibiades as a charismatic figure, a bold warrior and leader, as well as a persuasive orator, but ultimately shows him to be addicted to pleasure and having no firm control over his undoubted talents. Alcibiades's essentially savage nature shows through in a story about a wrestling bout in his youth:

One day wrestling with a companion of his, that handled him hardly, and thereby was likely to have given him the fall, he got his fellow's arm in his mouth, and bit so hard, as he would have eaten it off. The other feeling him bite so hard, let go his hold straight, and said unto him: 'What, Alcibiades, bitest thou like a woman?' 'No marry do I not', quoth he, 'but like a lion.'[49]

The cannibalistic image can be related to our initial impression of Alcibiades in *Timon*, keener to breakfast on his enemies than with his friends. Plutarch is clearly emphasizing Alcibiades's viciousness and the fact that the educational training he receives from Pericles and the friendship of Socrates can only transform him to a limited extent. It is equally significant that one of Alcibiades's chief vices is vanity and he is highly susceptible to flattery, a word North uses frequently throughout his narrative. The story of Alcibiades's youth is that of a battle between vice and virtue. Socrates labours heroically to keep him away from 'strangers, seeking to entice him by flattery' and nurture his 'natural inclination to virtue' (p. 90). He generally succeeds, but on occasions his love of 'lust and pleasure' triumph and

Alcibiades is 'carried away with the enticements of flatterers' (p. 92).

The adult Alcibiades is an equally ambiguous figure, sometimes leading the Athenians to heroic victories against all odds; at others, threatening to undermine the city-state. Plutarch emphasizes the problematic relationship between the flawed general and the democratic body politic of Athens. Plutarch describes Alcibiades's plan to invade Sicily, a cherished dream of the Athenians in suitably pointed terms: 'the only procurer of the Athenians, and persuader of them . . . was Alcibiades; who had so allured the people with his pleasant tongue, that upon his persuasion, they built castles in the air' (p. 104). Alcibiades and the people of Athens have a symbiotic relationship: if he leads them astray through his dangerous oratory, they recognize that he is vital to their success. His second banishment, soon before his murder, is generally recognized as a disaster, as the military successes Alcibiades achieved disappear:

The Athenians found themselves desolate, and in miserable state to see their empire lost . . . they began together to bewail and lament their miseries and wretched state, looking back upon all their wilful faults and follies committed: among which, they did reckon their second time of falling out with Alcibiades, was their greatest fault. So they banished him only out of malice and displeasure, not for any offence himself in person had committed against them[.] (p. 134)

Timon links together the story of Timon with the story of Alcibiades to produce a moral fable that has a political dimension.[50] The play, just like Plutarch's 'Life of Alcibiades', chronicles the failure of both citizens and leaders who between

[47] Thucydides, *History. Tr. into Englishe* (1607) [translator anon.]. A previous translation by T. Nicolls had appeared in 1550.
[48] A. D. Nuttall, *Timon of Athens* (Boston, 1989), p. xix.
[49] Plutarch, 'Life of Alcibiades', in *Selected Lives of the Noble Grecians and Romans*, trans. Thomas North, ed. Judith Mossman (London, 1998), pp. 87–136, at p. 88. Subsequent references to this edition in parentheses in the text.
[50] On *Timon* as a fable, see Wallace, '*Timon of Athens* and the Three Graces'.

them manage to undermine the state they inhabit. Timon fails to see that he is squandering his wealth because he is too foolish to see that his utopian ideal of friendship is actually based on the cash nexus he imagines is purely a reward for good fellowship. Alcibiades is banished because he cannot control his aggressive nature. His appeal for an equitable conception of the law based on mercy ('For pity is the virtue of the law, / And none but tyrants use it cruelly' (3.5.8–9)) does not sit well with the cause he pleads:

> It please time and fortune to lie heavy
> Upon a friend of mine, who in hot blood
> Hath stepp'd into the law, which is past depth
> To those that, without heed, do plunge into't.
> He is a man, setting his fate aside,
> Of comely virtues;
> Nor did he soil the fact with cowardice
> (An honour in him which buys out his fault)
> But with a noble fury and fair spirit,
> Seeing his reputation touch'd to death,
> He did oppose his foe[.]
>
> (10–20)

Alcibiades's conception of justice and mercy is so warped – suggesting that anyone who fairly owns up to a crime should be excused is hardly a reasonable principle of jurisprudence – that it is obvious that he is as unsuited for legal as Timon is for financial office.[51]

However, if Alcibiades has his faults, his banishment by the senate for pleading the case of a fellow soldier who has served Athens in its military campaigns rather too vigorously is also unjust and short-sighted. His plan to loose his army of 'discontented troops' (116) on Athens is a potent threat and one that makes a definite allusion to a central fear of Elizabethan and Jacobean societies that had terrifying experiences of demobbed, unpaid armies wandering the countryside in search of the basic means of existence. Alcibiades's threat takes this fear a stage further.[52] There is an obvious sense of poetic justice when the deputation of senators try to entice Timon back to Athens, presumably so that his new-found wealth can help to fund an army to defend Athens against Alcibiades. Timon is given an abject apology when the senate, 'which doth seldom / Play the recanter' (5.1.144–5), admits that it has treated Timon with a 'forgetfulness too general gross' (143), and now offers him 'absolute power' (161). Timon suggests that hanging themselves on the tree outside his cave will prevent further misery.

Timon cannot be reduced to a simple political allegory and it has often been suggested that it is a hybrid, experimental work, possibly written in collaboration with Thomas Middleton, and perhaps never even produced on stage in Shakespeare's lifetime.[53] Nevertheless, the fact that it is not simply a political work and cannot be decoded as an allegory of Jacobean politics in 1608, does not mean that the play has no political charge nor that it does not contain allegorical representations which can easily be identified (such as Timon's profligacy and that of James).[54] While Timon and Apemantus are arguing in the woods, Apemantus tells Timon that he would give the world to the beasts, because he is so disgusted with the society made by men. Timon produces an elaborate analysis based on Apemantus's hypothesis to show the savage and competitive nature he sees as the essence of Athenian society:

If thou wert the lion, the fox would beguile thee; if thou wert the lamb, the fox would eat thee; if thou wert the fox, the lion would suspect thee, when peradventure thou wert accus'd by the ass; if thou wert the ass, thy dulness would torment thee, and still thou liv'dst but as a

---

[51] On Alcibiades as a furious anti-Stoic figure, see Wallace, 'Timon of Athens and the Three Graces', p. 361.

[52] See A. L. Beier, *Masterless Men: The Vagrancy Problem in England, 1560–1640* (London, 1985), pp. 93–5.

[53] Grene, *Shakespeare's Tragic Imagination*, p. 147; *Timon of Athens*, ed. Karl Klein (Cambridge, 2001), introduction, pp. 61–6; Nuttall, *Timon of Athens*, ch. 3; Luke Wilson, *Theaters of Intention: Drama and the Law in Early Modern England* (Stanford, 2000), pp. 177–83.

[54] The political charge of a Jacobean play for the public stage might be usefully contrasted to contemporary court masques, such as those which reflect on the significant incidents in the life of Frances Howard; see Lindley, *Trials of Frances Howard*, pp. 17–19, 58–60, *passim*.

breakfast to the wolf; if thou wert the wolf, thy greediness would afflict thee, and oft thou shouldst hazard thy life for thy dinner.

(4.3.329–36)

Apemantus articulates the inescapable moral they have already come to: 'the commonwealth of Athens is become a forest of beasts' (349–50).[55]

The arguments of each misanthrope owe much to traditional representations of men as animals in beast fables, most importantly, those of Aesop and Lucian, which Ben Jonson used to spectacular effect in *Volpone* (1605–6), a play that was part of the repertoire of the King's Men between 1603 and 1608, and so would have been performed by the same actors who performed *Timon*.[56] However, the choice of the beasts, the fox, the lion and the wolf, recalls Machiavelli's famous advice that a prince must know how to act like a beast if he is to retain power and govern effectively:

For heerby hee [Machiavelli] gaue to understand, that a prince ought to shew himselfe a man and a beast together. A prince then being constrained well to know how to counterfet the beast, hee ought amongst all beasts to chuse the complexion of the Fox, and of the Lyon together, and not of the one without the other: for the Fox is subtill, to keepe himselfe from snares, yet he is too weake to guard himselfe from wolves: and the Lion is strong enough to guard himselfe from wolves, but hee is not subtill enough to keepe himselfe from nets: A man must then bee a Foxe to know all subtilties and deceits, and a Lyon to bee stronger, and to make wolves afraid.[57]

Machiavelli's point is that a prince need not keep his word to his subjects. In the bestial world of modern politics, honour and trust are not principles that can be followed or valued.[58] Elsewhere Machiavelli asserts that a Prince 'ought not to trust in the amitie of men' because they are 'full of ingratitude, variable, dissemblers . . . and covetous of gain . . . So that a prince which leaneth upon such a rampire, shall at the first fall unto ruine'.[59] Few maxims apply more obviously to both James and Timon.

Shakespeare would have probably known Machiavelli from Innocent Gentillet's refutation of

The Prince, popularly known as the *Anti-Machiavel*, translated into English in 1577 by Simon Patericke, and eventually published in 1603 (the quotations are from Patericke's translation of Gentillet), which included a translation of most of *The Prince* and extracts from *The Discourses*.[60] In linking the plot of Timon the misanthrope to the story of Alcibiades, *Timon* forges a bond between morality fable and political narrative (a link already implicit in the form of Plutarch's *Lives*). The argument of Gentillet's treatise is similar. His aim was to resist the amoral political world he saw in Machiavelli's writings and show that in a just society the right thing to do is the right thing to do, putting political discourse back onto a moral basis. For Gentillet a prince must not only appear but be devout and he must certainly always keep his word (pp. 92–9, 222–7).

Timon can be read as a play which represents the political world according to Machiavelli as a brutal fact. Athens, for all its philosophical sophistication, lurches chaotically from one extreme to another. Thucydides, the main source for its history, shows Athens veering between the perils of democracy and those of tyranny.[61] Shakespeare's Athens is in a state of degenerate chaos where flattery determines

---

55 See Miola, 'Timon in Shakespeare's Athens', p. 26.

56 Gurr, *Shakespearian Playing Companies*, p. 304. On *Volpone* and beast fables, see Douglas Duncan, *Ben Jonson and the Lucianic Tradition* (Cambridge, 1979), ch. 7. John M. Wallace argues that *Volpone* and *Timon* 'are competitive studies of the same subject': '*Timon of Athens* and the Three Graces', p. 350.

57 Innocent Gentillet, *A Discourse upon the Meanes of Wel Governing and Maintaining in Good Peace, A Kingdome, or other principalitie . . . Against Nicholas Machiavell the Florentine*, trans. Simon Patericke (1602) (New York, 1969), p. 222.

58 For comments on Shakespeare and Machiavelli as a representative of 'modern politics', see John E. Alvis, 'Introductory: Shakespearean Poetry and Politics', in Alvis and West, eds., *Shakespeare as Political Thinker*, pp. 1–27.

59 Gentillet, *Discourse*, p. 218.

60 For analysis, see Felix Raab, *The English Face of Machiavelli: A Changing Interpretation, 1500–1700* (London, 1965), pp. 56–7; Quentin Skinner, *The Foundations of Modern Political Thought*, 2 vols. (Cambridge, 1978), I, pp. 250–1.

61 Thucydides, *The History of the Peloponnesian War*, trans. Rex Warner and M. I. Finley (Harmondsworth, 1972), *passim*.

master–servant relations, the law has lost its impartiality and become subject to the whims of a ruling elite who own it. Force ultimately holds sway in this world of beasts, not men. In such a society the choice is between joining the corrupt body politic or retreating to the woods and becoming a misanthrope. Shakespeare implies that Machiavelli's conception of the world may be undesirable but true; Gentillet's desirable but false. The play's political message would appear to be that James in England, just like Timon in Athens, will need to adapt his relationship to others and his political practice to survive in such a world. In essence, he must become rather more realistic in his political ambitions and perceptions of others. *Timon* is not wholly negative in its implications, although it has usually proved somewhat relentless as a piece of theatre.[62] The play ends with Alcibiades about to conquer Athens, an uncertain moment which presages disaster in the short term, but in the longer term the audience knows that Athens will become the bedrock of European thought. The implication is that people can learn from their mistakes, and the malign influences that cause a society to degenerate can be corrected. Perhaps, Shakespeare may have thought, this applied especially to a philosopher king like James keen to encourage lively debate at his court.

---

[62] For stage history, see *Timon*, ed. Klein, introduction, pp. 35–52.

MAN, WOMAN AND BEAST IN TIMON'S ATHENS

ANDREAS HÖFELE

'From *Grecia* in olde time did almost all famous things come. [The Greeks] were the authors of ciuilitie vnto the Westerne nations', George Abbot, author of *A Brief Description of the Whole World*, asserts in 1599.[1] Athens, in particular, Peter Heylyn concurs, some two decades later,[2] 'was a famous Vniuersitie, from whose great cisterne, the conduit pipes of learning were dispersed over all *Europe*' (209–10). And Roger Ascham maintains that 'in that one Citie, in memorie of one aige, were mo learned men [...] than all tyme doth remember, than all place doth affourde, than all other tonges do conteine'.[3] The contrast, however, between such glories of the past and a far from glorious present could not be more striking. As Heylyn observes:

The people were once braue men of warre sound Schollers, addicted to the loue of vertue, and ciuill of behauior, for which vertues other nations were by them scornfully tearmed *Barbarians* a name now most fit for the *Grecians*, being an inconstant people vnciuill, not regarding learning, as hauing not one Vniuersitie in it, and in a word wholy degenerate from their ancestours.

(204–5)

It seems most fitting that the one play in the Shakespearian Folio which carries Athens in its title should hinge upon a similar lapse from civility into barbarism, from metropolitan plenitude in 'all famous things' to a wilderness where cave-dwelling and digging for roots are the order of the day. In Shakespeare's lifetime Athens itself had all but disappeared from Western consciousness. Captured by the Turks in 1456/8, it so entirely fell into

oblivion that the Tübingen humanist, Martin Crusius, had to prove in 1573 that it actually still existed: a small provincial town by the name of Setine. It is almost as if Timon's curse against his native city had come true; as if 'antique fable' and contemporary history were converging in the final, emblematic image of the play, a grave 'upon the very hem o'th'sea' (5.4.66),[4] an epitaph destined to be erased by 'the turbulent surge' of the waves (5.1.2/7), a name and memory heading for extinction. Across the time gap, across the divide between fictional and factual topography, the extra-mural territories of the Shakespearian Wild[5] thus merge into the dim regions of the Ottoman Empire. 'Greece, the Mother of Arts and Sciences',[6] had become a no-go area for Western travellers, inaccessible except for some Venetian strongholds along its insular fringe.[7] This is reflected in the pictorial representation of Europe as Elizabeth I in a Dutch map of 1598, 'where the queen's left arm forms England and Scotland, her right, Italy, and her

---

[1] *A Brief Description of the Whole Worlde* (London).

[2] *Microcosmus, or, A Little Description of the Great World* (Oxford, 1621).

[3] *The Scholemaster* (1570), John Mavor (ed.) (New York, 1967), p. 51.

[4] All quotations from Karl Klein's Cambridge edition of *Timon of Athens* (Cambridge, 2001).

[5] Cf. Jeanne Addison Roberts, *The Shakespearean Wild: Geography, Genus, and Gender* (Lincoln, London, 1991).

[6] Peter Heylyn, *Microcosmus*, 204.

[7] Between 1450 and 1670 we have no first-hand Western traveller's account of Athens.

body, the mass of the continent'.[8] Greece, located in the nether regions of her anatomy, where the anthropomorphic dissolves into the merely geomorphic, is clearly marked as lying outside the fold of Elizabeth's ample, protective skirt.

The dual construction of Athens in these textual and pictorial representations as, on the one hand, matrix and acme of Western civilization and, on the other, that civilization's barbaric opposite, is fundamental also to Timon's Athens, the location of a singularly disjointed, 'dual' play and a deeply troubled vision of man.[9] It is the nature of that trouble as it encroaches upon his masculinity and human-ness[10] alike that will be the subject of this essay.

In no other Shakespeare play is the male quite so overwhelmingly overrepresented as in *Timon* – to the all but total exclusion of women. Apart from two cameo appearances – the Amazon dancers in the first part (1.2.127–53), Alcibiades's whores in the second (4.3.49–177) – female characters are conspicuously absent. When they do appear it is in groups – generically rather than individually, as part of a service industry catering exclusively to men, thereby enhancing, rather than diminishing, the play's homosocial, all-male setting. Yet in spite – or indeed precisely because – of the absence of an external Other, man's opposites in terms of gender and species – woman and beast – are all the more powerfully operative from within. They turn out to be inhabiting the very core of his identity.

In its combination of all-male company, the glorification of friendship and a festive Athenian setting, the opening of the play presents a situation reminiscent of the *locus classicus* of these ingredients, Plato's *Symposium*.[11] The two texts even share one of their *dramatis personae*, the volatile Alcibiades, whose intrusion threatens to disrupt the *symposium* at Agathon's house just as it does Shakespeare's senatorial Athens (as well as the somewhat frangible cohesion of the play itself). *Timon of Athens* holds, as it were, a distorting mirror up to the *Symposium*, rendering the idealizations of the Platonic paradigm in radically anti-idealistic disfiguration. To be effective, such disfiguration has first to call up

the norms which it will then proceed to unsettle. Just as much as the *de casibus* pattern of Timon's downfall requires as its point of departure the fabulous affluence of the big spender, the play's anti-idealistic drive can only gather its downward momentum from such elevated notions of man as those promoted by the 'diuine Philosophers' of Athens (Heylyn, *Microcosmus*, p. 205). Initially, therefore, Timon must be presented as a veritable paragon of mankind, 'A most incomparable man, breath'd, as it were, / To an untirable and continuate goodness' (1.1.9f.). But such excellence cannot long remain unquestioned in a play that announces its characteristically contrary dynamics in almost its very first line: 'how goes the world?' asks the Poet. 'It wears, sir, as it grows' (1.1.2f) is the Painter's answer. A similarly telling hint occurs in the dialogue between Merchant and Jeweller some fifteen lines later. The subject is a jewel to be offered to Timon:

> MERCHANT: 'Tis a good form.
> JEWELLER: And rich. Here is a water, look ye.
> (1.1.17f.)

'Water', as editors tell us, is a technical term meaning 'lustre', but it may also be taken to suggest a

---

8 Jodi Mikalachki, *The Legacy of Boadicea: Gender and Nation in Early Modern England* (London, New York, 1998), p. 20. For a reproduction of the map, see p. 23.

9 The duality of the play extends, and has often been ascribed to the possibility of double authorship – a hypothesis first advanced by Charles Knight in 1842 and a bone of contention ever since, witness e.g. the opposite conclusions drawn in the 1986 Oxford *Complete Works* and the 2001 Cambridge edition of the play.

10 A term introduced by Erica Fudge 'to represent the qualities which [are] propose[d] as specific to the human'. Erica Fudge, *Perceiving Animals: Humans and Beasts in Early Modern English Culture.* (Basingstoke, 2000).

11 To my knowledge, A. D. Nuttall is alone in even mentioning the *Symposium* in connection with a discussion of *Timon* (*Timon of Athens.* Harvester New Critical Introductions to Shakespeare (Hemel Hempstead, 1989), p. 79). For a brief assessment of the influence and transformation of the Platonic doctrines of love in the fifteenth and sixteenth centuries see Peter Burke, *The European Renaissance: Centres and Peripheries* (Oxford, 1998), pp. 206f.

corrosive fluidity at the very heart of what seems firm and fixed: an erosion of 'form' into 'flow' introducing the play's characteristic mode of 'wear'. Thus, while Timon's towering ascendancy over other men, as well as his seemingly inexhaustible fortune, seem to hold promise of endless *growing*, the erosive flow of *wearing* has already set in. The Painter's portrait of Timon may proclaim its subject's robust masculine 'form' – 'How this grace / Speaks his own standing!' (1.1.30f.) – but such manly uprightness cannot long withstand the levelling pull of counterforces gathering head even in the adulation of Timon's flatterers. Thus, when the Poet follows the Painter with a description of his own offering to his patron, the Lord Timon, Coppélia Kahn argues, is reduced to the role of a baby, first fed, then spurned by, the almighty mother, Fortune. In this, one of the key passages of the play (1.1.64–90), Timon allegorically figures as Fortune's favourite, outclimbing all his rivals 'that labour on the *bosom* [my italics] of this sphere' (68), that is, who are trying to get to the top of Fortune's 'high and pleasant hill' (65). Not only the word 'bosom' but also '[t]he image of [Timon] "bowing his head against the steepy mount" suggests', so Kahn argues, 'a baby with its head on its mother's breast'.[12] While this 'core fantasy [. . .] of maternal bounty and maternal betrayal' (p. 35) focuses on Timon's receiving of gifts, his prodigal giving, Janet Adelman suggests, invokes a different, aggressively male, fantasy of self-generating abundance, in which Timon usurps the female prerogative of nurturance.[13] Diverging from both these readings, Jody Greene maintains that

the 'monstrous image' of Timon's 'bounty' is not mammary but phallic; the 'shower' of gifts which his followers 'drink' is not lactic but seminal; and the obliging tongues which flatter Timon in a feast of verbal usury derive figurative sustenance not from his breast but from his 'fontem [sic!] liberalitatis.' The fantasy of bounty which determines the first half of the play is thus not figured as a jealous desire for the sustaining powers of the maternal breast but as a dream of inexhaustible male potency to which the Lords and their 'Athenian minion' greedily subscribe.[14]

Although Greene supports the case for a consistently phallic subtext with an impressive amount of textual evidence,[15] I would still like to suggest an alternative reading that is neither exclusively 'mammary' nor exclusively 'phallic'. My point is precisely that this distinction collapses in the play, swept away, as it were, by a veritable 'orgy of feeding and breeding' (Greene, 'You Must Eat Men', p. 184) and the well-nigh ubiquitous prevalence of fluids. As both Kahn and Greene have remarked, fluidity is the characteristic mode of Timon's transactions with his sycophantic friends. While 'He pours it out' (1.1.275), they 'Rain sacrificial whisperings in his ear, [. . .] and through him / Drink the free air' (1.1.83–5). Passing the cup around ritualistically confirms this liquid bonding:

TIMON let the health go round.
SECOND LORD Let it flow this way, my good lord.
APEMANTUS Flow this way? A brave fellow. He keeps his tides well. Those healths will make thee and thy state look ill, Timon.

(1.2.53–7)

Timon's narcissistic pride in his own liquidity is unmistakable. But as he indulges this masculine fantasy of inexhaustible spending power, his masculinity is already undergoing the process of being liquidated. The text introduces an ironic double perspective. What Timon wishes to see as acts of manly generosity can just as well be perceived as progressive stages in a continual unmanning. The transformation already hinted at in the dialogue between Painter and

---

[12] Coppélia Kahn, '"Magic of bounty": *Timon of Athens*, Jacobean Patronage, and Maternal Power', *Shakespeare Quarterly*, 38 (1987), 34–57; p. 37.

[13] Janet Adelman, *Suffocating Mothers: Fantasies of Maternal Origin in Shakespeare's Plays, 'Hamlet' to 'The Tempest'* (New York, London, 1992), pp. 165–74.

[14] Jody Greene, '"You Must Eat Men": The Sodomitic Economy of Renaissance Patronage', *GLQ: A Journal of Lesbian and Gay Studies* (1994), 163–97, p. 186.

[15] Even though some of her examples – the allegedly phallic meaning of 'roots', for instance – may rely a little too heavily on Partridge's inflationary inventory of sexual connotations.

Poet is confirmed by Cupid in his announcement of the masque:

The best five senses acknowledge thee their patron, and come freely to gratulate thy plenteous bosom

(1.2.119–21)

The patron turns matron. Timon's one-upmanship, his insistence on always out-spending other men,[16] lands him in the position of the breastfeeding mother. The phallic 'dream of inexhaustible male potency' (Greene, 'You Must Eat Men', p. 186) blends into – it actually begets – the nightmare of emasculation.

The terms, as well as the operational principle, of Timon's transmutation are clearly grounded in the physiology of the one-sex body as detailed by Thomas Laqueur, 'a physiology of fungible fluids and corporeal flux' effectuating '[e]ndless mutations'.[17] In describing '[t]he complex network of interconvertibility implicit in the physiology of one sex' (p. 37), Laqueur frequently employs a vocabulary of economic exchange. 'Interconvertibility' itself suggests currency transaction. Elsewhere he speaks of an 'economy of fungible fluids' (p. 36) or even a 'free-trade economy of fluids'. The same metaphorical connection, or trope, pervades *Timon of Athens*. More precisely, the trope is reversed. Where Laqueur translates physiological into economic terms, the play converts the economics of Timon's expenditure, his ceaseless 'flow of riot' (2.2.3) into terms of bodily consumption. The transactions of the Athenian gift economy are consistently projected into the fluidly metamorphic medium of his body. Like Polonius, Timon ends up at a feast 'Not where he eats, but where he is eaten' (4.3.19). This reversal from active to passive confirms his emasculation, already manifest in his change from patron to matron. Instead of feeding his guests, they feed on him. As the cynic Apemantus remarks:

What a number of men eats Timon, and he sees 'em not! It grieves me to see so many dip their meat in one man's blood; and all the madness is, he cheers them up too.

(1.2.39–41)

The orality evoked in these lines is sacrificial as well as sexual. It suggests both fellatio and the Eucharist. Dipping their meat in his blood, Timon's guests perform a parody of the Lord's Supper.[18] But over and above these sexual and religious associations the passage clearly also suggests cannibalism.[19] That is, after all, what 'eating men' literally means. The monstrosity of 'debosh'd' intercourse broadens out into the monstrous image of humanity preying on itself. This image grounds, and recurs in, the frequent references to animals which occur throughout the play and particularly in its latter half. 'Uncover, dogs, and lap' (3.6.82), the bankrupt Timon snaps at his guests who are gathered for one more, final feast, where instead of meat and 'blood' only lukewarm water awaits them. False, ingrateful friends turn, not into swine, the most common emblematic representation of ingratitude,[20] but into fawning, greedy dogs and rapacious wolves. Cannibalism may in actual fact be no more common among animals than among men, but it seems inevitably to evoke images of predatory beasts. As Kenneth Burke puts it: 'We are invited to think of eating, not as the pleasant

---

16 Most conspicuously in 1.2.8–13 where he refuses Ventidius's offer of repaying his debt.

17 Thomas Laqueur, *Making Sex: Body and Gender from the Greeks to Freud* (Cambridge, Mass. 1990), p. 35.

18 Cf. Jarold W. Ramsey, 'Timon's Imitation of Christ', *Shakespeare Studies* (1966), 162–73; also Winifred M. T. Nowottny, 'Acts IV and V of *Timons of Athens*', *Shakespeare Quarterly*, 10 (1959), 493–7.

19 A motif connected with the Timon tradition since at least Lucian's *Dialogue of Timon*, written in the second century AD cf. Geoffrey Bullough, ed., *Narrative and Dramatic Sources of Shakespeare*, vol. VI (London, New York, 1966), p. 265: 'Even when the poor wretch was having his liver eaten by so many vultures, he thought they were his friends and well-wishers, who took pleasure in consuming it because of the love they bore him. When they had finally eaten him down to the bone, and sucked the marrow, they left him dry and stripped from top to toe [. . .]'

20 Cf. R. Allott, *Wits Theater of the little World* (London, 1599), p. 226: 'Of Ingratitude [. . .] most rightly figured in swine, who eate the Acorns, but neuer looke vp to the tree'.

gratifying of a peaceloving appetite [...] but as rending, tearing, biting, destroying. Eating here is the rabid use of claws and jaws, a species of hate'.[21] Just as the shape of man conceals the beast within, civilization, embodied in the city, harbours a wilderness: 'the commonwealth of Athens is become a forest of beasts' (4.3.349f.), its inhabitants are identified as 'those wolves' (4.1.2).

Conventionally, such animal imagery provides a ready-made lexicon of moral emblems whose didactic effect depends on a double transposition. Human traits must first be projected onto suitable animals (the brave lion, the sly fox, the false serpent) before they can then be re-projected onto humans. Only rarely will such crossings of the species boundary even hint at a possible slippage of category distinctions. The zoomorphic signifier is safely and predictably contained by the anthropocentric perspective. Up to a point, this also holds true for *Timon*. Apemantus, for example, labelled as the cynical, or dog-like, philosopher, could be almost said to impersonate, as well as articulate in his speeches, such moral emblematics. And when Timon in his last encounter with Apemantus musters a whole menagerie of emblematic animals, he has cribbed their meanings straight from the moralizing, anthropomorphic zoology of the medieval bestiaries:

APEMANTUS What things in the world canst thou nearest compare to thy flatterers?

TIMON Women nearest, but men – men are the things themselves. What wouldst thou do with the world, Apemantus, if it lay in thy power?

APEMANTUS Give it the beasts, to be rid of the men.

TIMON Wouldst thou have thyself fall in the confusion of men, and remain a beast with the beasts?

APEMANTUS Ay, Timon.

TIMON A beastly ambition, which the gods grant thee t'attain to. If thou wert the lion, the fox would beguile thee; if thou wert the lamb, the fox would eat thee; if thou wert the fox, the lion would suspect thee, when peradventure thou wert accus'd by the ass; if thou wert the ass, thy dulness would torment thee, and still thou liv'dst but as a breakfast to the wolf; if thou wert the

wolf, thy greediness would afflict thee, and oft thou shouldst hazard thy life for thy dinner; wert thou the unicorn, pride and wrath would confound thee and make thine own self the conquest of thy fury; wert thou a bear, thou wouldst be kill'd by the horse; wert thou a horse, thou wouldst be seiz'd by the leopard; wert thou a leopard, thou wert germane to the lion, and the spots of thy kindred were jurors on thy life. All thy safety were remotion, and thy defence absence. What beast couldst thou be that were not subject to a beast? And what a beast art thou already, that seest not thy loss in transformation!

APEMANTUS If thou couldst please me with speaking to me, thou mightst have hit upon it here; the commonwealth of Athens is become a forest of beasts.

TIMON How has the ass broke the wall, that thou art out of the city?

(4.3.322–48)

The conventional figures are all there in this passage, but they are, I would propose, only cited, spoken in implied quotation marks, as it were. For Timon at this stage has moved well beyond them. By reeling off the clichés of a hackneyed animal emblematics he is rebuffing Apemantus's offer of a shared world view: that men are really beasts. But isn't this precisely Timon's own position, explicitly stated in an encounter just prior to this dialogue?

ALCIBIADES What art thou there? Speak.

TIMON   A beast as thou art.

(4.3.49–50)

The answer, it seems to me, is that in his rejection of mankind Timon has far more radically bestialized himself than Apemantus ever has or ever will. The cynic's railing is toothless, his dog-philosophy mere barking. For all his churlish behaviour and animal nickname, he remains safely within the bounds of humankind, socially accepted as a kind of jester. Timon, by contrast, has moved beyond the pale,

---

[21] Kenneth Burke, '*Timon of Athens* and misanthropic gold', in Burke, *Language as Symbolic Action* (Berkeley, 1966), p. 123.

adopting the habit and habitat of beasts. Dissevering all ties to his own 'kind', he has taken

> to the woods, where he shall find
> Th'unkindest beast more kinder than mankind.
>
> (4.1.35–6)

Thus Apemantus's accusation that Timon is just plagiarizing him (4.3.201) misses the mark. Timon clearly outmatches his rival, who is therefore right in saying:

> The middle of humanity thou never knewest, but the extremity of both ends.
>
> (4.3.307–8)

This reproach hits home. As excessive now in his misfortune as when he lived 'But in a dream of friendship' (4.2.34), Timon serves as the perfect illustration of Aristotle's famous dictum, famously quoted in Bacon's essay 'Of Friendship': 'Whosoever is delighted in solitude is either a wild beast or a god'.[22] At least one Elizabethan version of Timon's story makes no bones about deciding the alternative. William Painter entitles the twenty-eighth novella in his *Palace of Pleasure* (1566) 'Of the straunge and beastlie nature of Timon of Athens, enemie to mankinde'.[23] Compared to Timon, Apemantus is only a poseur, his intention of turning all mankind into beasts mere rhetoric. It is worth noting that it is precisely over a question of rhetoric that the distance between him and Timon emerges:

APEMANTUS What things in the world canst thou nearest compare to thy flatterers?
TIMON Women nearest, but men – men are the things
   themselves.

> (4.3.322–4)

Where Apemantus is expecting a trope, an adroit rhetorical turning of men into figurative beasts, Timon refuses to call men anything but men: not even the misogynist commonplace will quite do – it has to be 'the things themselves'. This rejection of metaphor evinces a much more fundamental questioning of man's ascendancy than any of Apemantus's facile analogizing. Timon's bestialization has indeed proceeded to extremity, expelling him not only from 'the middle of humanity', but even across 'the borders of the human'.[24] The perspective is reversed, man radically decentred by being looked at, as it were, from the other side of the species boundary. Michel Foucault describes just such a reversal in *Madness and Civilization*:

In the thought of the Middle Ages, the legions of animals, named once and for all by Adam, symbolically bear the values of humanity. But at the beginning of the Renaissance, the relations with animality are reversed; the beast is set free; it escapes the world of legend and moral illustration to acquire a fantastic nature of its own. And by an astonishing reversal, it is now the animal that will stalk man, capture him, and reveal him to his own truth.[25]

The extremism of Timon's bestial misanthropy may be madness. Madness is, in fact, the epithet generally applied to his behaviour from the moment he begins to rage at his ungrateful friends: '[H]is wits / Are drown'd and lost in his calamities' (4.3.89–90). But Timon's madness has a clear-sighted, almost clairvoyant, quality to it, not unlike that of the mad Lear. It is the kind of madness Foucault finds erupting in the apocalyptic visions of Bosch, Thierry Bouts, Dürer and Grünewald, visions 'of the world where all wisdom is annihilated', where 'the beast is set free' with a vengeance, and man is forced to recognize that 'the animal that haunts his

---

[22] Francis Bacon, *The Essays or Counsels Civil and Moral*, ed. Brian Vickers (Oxford, 1999), p. 59. Robert Burton cites a somewhat different version: 'Homo solus aut deus, aut demon: a man alone is either a saint or a devil', in *The Anatomy of Melancholy* (London, New York, 1932), vol. 1, p. 248.

[23] William Painter, *The Palace of Pleasure* (London, 1929), vol. 1, p. 92. Cf. also Burton, *Anatomy*, vol. 1, pp. 248f: 'These wretches do frequently degenerate from men, and of sociable creatures become beasts, monsters, inhuman, ugly to behold, *misanthropi*; they do even loathe themselves, and hate the company of men, as so many Timons [. . .]'.

[24] Cf. the title of a collection of essays edited by Erica Fudge et al., *At the Borders of the Human: Beasts, Bodies and Natural Philosophy in the Early Modern Period* (Basingstoke, London, 1999).

[25] *Madness and Civilization*, trans. Richard Howard (London, 1987), p. 21.

nightmares and his nights of privation is his own nature' (p. 23). Timon's apostrophe to the 'common mother' earth discloses just such a nightmare vision:[26]

> Common mother, thou
> Whose womb unmeasurable and infinite breast
> Teems and feeds all; whose self-same mettle,
> Whereof thy proud child, arrogant man, is puffed
> Engenders the black toad and adder blue,
> The gilded newt and eyeless venomed worm,
> With all th'abhorrèd births below crisp heaven
> Whereon Hyperion's quick'ning fire doth shine;
> Yield him, who all the human sons do hate,
> From forth thy plenteous bosom, one poor root.
> Ensear thy fertile and conceptious womb;
> Let it no more bring out ingrateful man.
> Go great with tigers, dragons, wolves and bears,
> Teem with new monsters, whom thy upward face
> Hath to the marbled mansion all above
> Never presented.
>
> (4.3.179–94)

This invocation of the mother recalls the other prominent image of maternal power in the play, the Poet's allegory of Fortune in Act 1. But its emphasis on monstrous plenitude also brings to mind Timon himself in his 'flow of riot', his own 'maternal' prodigality. The very words which were then addressed to him, now recur in his own appeal to mother Earth: 'thy plenteous bosom' (1.2.121 and 4.3.188).

Emasculation and bestialization, the dual threat to the status of man, can thus be perceived to operate in collusion. In the exchange of gifts for flattery they become interdependent. The bestial rapacity of Timon's friends thrives on at the same time as it is the cause of Timon's effeminization. Indeed the assault on humanness may be conceived in terms of the same fluidity as the lapse from masculinity. In Apemantus's diagnosis, Timon's fall into beast-like behaviour is clearly gendered, the product of 'A poor *unmanly* melancholy' (4.3.205; my italics). Mark Breitenberg has shown that melancholy, in Galenic physiology an excess of fluid, 'becomes the overarching term for anything imbalanced or excessive – whatever is not normal',[27] 'a repository for those elements deemed contrary to a specifically masculine vision of social order and individual rationality' (p. 38). In *Timon of Athens*, this contrariness appears in the double figure of woman and beast. The play's action shows the progress of civilization in reverse. In his lapse from masculinity and humanness Timon undoes the cultural work on which the ascendancy of Athens was built.

But if the dual nightmare of emasculation and bestialization is one of the shaping fantasies of the play, we might ask if there is not also room for an alternative fantasy. If Timon's 'magic of bounty' (1.1.6) overflows the limits of properly regulated manhood, could this not hint at a fusion of male and female conceived as neither a lapse into abject otherness[28] nor as the hegemonial annexation of that otherness which is suggested by Janet Adelman? Could it perhaps hint at something altogether outside the binary logic of these bleak alternatives? Intriguing as it may be, such a possibility is tenuous at best. For whatever utopian fantasy the play may offer is beleaguered, circumscribed and finally erased by overwhelming counterrealities.

Economically, Timon's 'Flow' comes 'all out of an empty coffer' (1.2.191), his 'great flow of debts' (2.2.136) resulting in a complete drying-up, 'the ebb of [his] estate' (2.2.135). Inextricably bound up with the economic flow is the flow of emotions – a connection which is most graphically obvious in the exchange of tears between Timon and his friends:

---

[26] Foucault expressly links the madness in Shakespeare and Cervantes to those earlier visions: 'Doubtless, both testify more to a tragic experience of madness appearing in the fifteenth century, than to a critical and moral experience of Unreason [beginning with Erasmus] developing in their own epoch' (31).

[27] Mark Breitenberg, *Anxious Masculinity in Early Modern England* (Cambridge, 1996), p. 37.

[28] As Laura Levine explains in her study of effeminization in anti-theatrical pamphlets and Shakespearian drama: 'In a general way, for these texts, femininity seems to be the default position, the otherness one is always in danger of slipping into, so nobody ever thinks of it as *needing* to be maintained or performed'. Laura Levine, *Men in Women's Clothing: Anti-Theatricality and Effeminization, 1579–1642* (Cambridge, 1994), p. 8.

TIMON O what a precious comfort 'tis to have so many
like brothers commanding one another's fortunes. O
joy's e'en made away ere't can be born! Mine eyes can-
not hold out water, methinks. To forget their faults,
I drink to you.
APEMANTUS Thou weep'st to make them drink,
Timon.
SECOND LORD Joy had the like conception in our
eyes.
And at that instant like a babe sprung up.

(1.2.93–9)

This confluence of male tears overflows the boundaries separating genders as well as individuals:
it results in the bringing forth of a baby. But
any reciprocity in this exchange of tears – and
of 'one another's fortunes' – is, as Apemantus
points out, illusory. Timon's spontaneous over-
flow meets with mere show, with nothing more
than the proverbial crocodile's tears which are
well established in the emblematic zoology of the
period:

[. . .] such is the nature of the Crocodile, that to get a man
within his danger, he will sob, sigh & weepe, as though he
were in extremitie, but suddenly he destroyeth him. Others say, that the crocodile weepeth after he hath deuoured
a man. How soeuer it be, it noteth the wretched nature of
hypocriticall harts, which before-hand will with fayned
teares endeuour to do mischiefe, or els after they haue
done it be outwardly sorry [. . .][29]

The tears of the flatterers, signifiers not of true generosity but of 'hypocriticall harts', expose Timon's
utopia of universal brotherhood as but another instance of that 'debosh'd' intercourse which the play
consistently castigates as effeminate.

But a strikingly different picture emerges when
Timon encounters Flavius, his faithful steward, in
act 4. This scene also hinges upon the shedding
of tears, triggered this time, however, by 'honest
grief' (4.3.462). In a world of falsehood, Flavius'
tears mark him out as the 'One honest man' (490)
precisely because he behaves like and therefore, in
Timon's perception, becomes a woman:

TIMON What, dost thou weep? Come nearer,
then I love thee,

Because thou art a woman, and disclaim'st
Flinty mankind, whose eyes do never give
But thorough lust and laughter.

(4.3.475–8)

Timon's almost Lear-like moment of anagnorisis
singularly valorizes woman as the sole source and
exemplar of humanness. The gender binary which
throughout the play serves as the norm by which
lapses into effeminacy are measured is thus suddenly
emptied of all force. And at the same time maternity, hitherto associated with images of 'the whorish mother' Fortune (Kahn, 'Magic of Bounty',
p. 35) and 'monstrous generativity' (Adelman, *Suffocating Mother*, p. 173), receives full credit as a positive agency in the lineage of man:

TIMON Let me behold thy face. Surely this man
Was born of woman.

(486f.)

Of the two arguably most powerful readings of the
maternity theme in *Timon*, one, that by Coppélia
Kahn,[30] ignores the passage entirely, while the
other – Janet Adelman's[31] – reduces it to virtual in-
significance. Timon's 'ab/whoring of women is too
insistent', Adelman argues, 'to be easily recupera-
ble' (p. 174) Whether the adverb 'easily' adequately
reflects the weight of the Flavius encounter in the
overall scheme of the play is open to question.

Timon's sudden departure from his habitual
misogynist vituperation would seem in fact to make
the Flavius encounter all the more striking. After the meeting with Alcibiades and his mistresses
Phrynia and Timandra, in which the 'ab-whoring'
of women escalates into a paroxysm of disgust; after the subsequent confrontations with Apemantus
and the 'Banditti', in which the bestial replaces the
whorish as the epitome of human depravity, the
encounter with Flavius constitutes something like
a final moment of truth, a last chance of reconciliation, even of redemption. The moment does
pass. Yet it does so, not, I would argue, because

---

[29] Edward Topsell, *The Historie of Serpents* (London, 1608).
[30] Cf. above, note 12.
[31] Cf. above, note 13.

the case it presents for a non-vituperative vision of feminized humanity is lacking in weight or persuasiveness, but because Timon's unrelenting progress towards self-annihilation cannot be halted, let alone reversed, by the single exception of a Flavius.[32] Just as *King Lear* might, but does not, end with the reunion of the father with his one good daughter, *Timon of Athens* might, but does not, end with the reunion of the prodigal patron with his one faithful servant. Awaiting each of the two protagonists once they have moved past these unrealized happy endings is a prospect even more deeply troubling than the troubled negotiation of gender. What propels each play to its catastrophe is predicated not on the man–woman binary but on the opposition of man and beast. Ultimately at stake in both plays is the equivocal essence of humanness itself. In *King Lear*, the final undoing of the human paradoxically takes the form of a categorical affirmation of 'man's distinctive mark'.[33]

> I cannot draw a cart, nor eat dried oats.
> If it be man's work, I'll do't.
>
> (5.3.39f)[34]

It is with this chillingly casual remark that the captain, commissioned by Edmund to kill the captive Cordelia and her father, embarks on the final, most horrendous outrage. Throughout the play human

depravity has been classified as bestial, but this ultimate atrocity conspicuously resists that classification. 'Man's work' is strictly sui generis; it cannot be blamed on his bestial other.

Timon arrives at a similar conclusion. His hate and avoidance of his own kind, which culminates in his withdrawal into beast-like, that is, speechless, death – although this is accompanied by the unmistakably human gesture of a written epitaph[35] – oscillate in perpetual ambiguity between the notion of man-as-beast and the even more devastating recognition that all such analogizing is futile because men, after all, 'are the things themselves'.

---

[32] G. Wilson Knight (*The Wheel of Fire* (London, 1949), p. 228) suggests that Timon manages to keep up his 'pilgrimage of hate' because 'with an afterthought, [he] suspects Flavius of mean motives'. But lines 516ff. indicate that Timon finally abandons this suspicion.

[33] The formulation is from Robert Browning's 'A Death in the Desert'; cf. also Manfred Pfister '"Man's Distinctive Mark"; Paradoxical Distinctions between Man and his Bestial Other in Early Modern Texts', in: E. Lehmann, B. Lenz, eds., *Telling Stories: Studies in Honour of Ulrich Broich on the Occasion of his 60th Birthday* (Amsterdam, 1992), pp. 17–33.

[34] *King Lear*, ed. R. A. Foakes, The Arden Shakespeare (Walton-on-Thames, 1997).

[35] It is also attended by the unresolved riddle of who actually buries Timon; he can hardly be assumed to have interred himself.

ROUGH MAGIC: NORTHERN BROADSIDES AT WORK AT PLAY

CAROL CHILLINGTON RUTTER

I

Unless I do it me self no bugger's going to ask me to play Richard III, are they? They want it posh. They want it Received Pronunciation.[1]

That was the unmistakably Northern-voiced soundbite Barrie Rutter gave the London critic who travelled to Yorkshire in June 1992 to preview the inaugural production of his new company, Northern Broadsides, named, pointedly, to deliver what it promised in performance: 'verbal attack'. Voices like Rutter's have never been cast as Shakespeare's royals, at least not at the Royal Shakespeare and National Theatres; hence his audacious (some said barmy) decision to declare theatrical UDI, to set up a company where he and his working-class Northern accent would be entitled to play the hunchback king. As things turned out, however, when it came to the performance, Rutter's Richard sounded different even before he opened his mouth. It was his footfall that produced the play's original bizarre acoustic, an uneven, slurred silence broken by a percussive clomp as he limped the full length of his impromptu stage, a concrete-floored boatshed on Hull marina. On his good foot Rutter was wearing a shoe; on the gammy twisted one, the sort of wooden clog every spinner or weaver in the north of England wore in the mills a couple generations back and fishworkers on Hull docks, Rutter's father among them, still did in the 1960s – the sort of clog that functioned not just as industrial footwear but class apparatus and cultural marker. Eyes fixed on the ground, Rutter's halting Richard in his army surplus bomber jacket

seemed merely to be passing through the traverse playing space, trailing the family party of Yorkist revellers that had already disappeared behind the queen in her too-tight frock, fur coat and stiletto heels. But then he turned, raking dangerous inspection across the audience on either side, and began:

> Now is the winter of ower disconn-tent
> Med glory-uss summmer by this sunn'o'York.

The voice was like the clog on the concrete, rough, percussive, arresting, yet strange to the ear, for Rutter's Richard was speaking Shakespeare as Shakespeare's Richard never spoke on a London or Stratford stage, in a Northern voice pitched to claim Shakespeare's 'elite' text for 'popular' speech and his royal roles for working-class aspirants. Reviewing this *Richard*, Irving Wardle called it 'a thrilling departure in classical performance' and pointed to 'some extraordinary things' that 'happen to the lines' as 'Elizabethan English comes into Yorkshire close-up'. The production, he wrote, 'needs to be seen in London' (*Independent on Sunday*, 25 July 1992). In December it was – and savaged by John Peter in *The Sunday Times* as 'karaoke theatre', and worse, 'superfluous'. 'To hear Richard say that he is "scarce half made oop"', wrote Peter, 'adds nothing either to him or to Shakespeare' (13 December 1992). For Michael Arditti in the *Evening Standard*, Rutter's aim – 'to destroy the hegemony of Oxford vowels' – put

---

[1] Quoted in Sarah Hemming, *Independent*, 10 June 1992.

19   Rude mechanicals play Pyramus and Thisbe in *A Midsummer Night's Dream*. Oldham Mill 1994 (l to r: Francis Lee, Owen Shaw, Paul McCrink, Andrew Whitehead, John Branwell, Roy North, T. C. Howard).

'regional actors back where they began: as comic relief' (11 December 1992).[2]

Ten years on, Northern Broadsides has survived mauling to emerge as Britain's gutsiest, wittiest, and certainly most clamorous touring Shakespeare company, an impressive list of productions to its credit, all starting with UK tours – *The Merry Wives* (1993; India tour and London, 1994); *A Midsummer Night's Dream* (1994; international tour and London, 1996); *Antony and Cleopatra* (1995; international tour, 1997); *Twelfth Night* (1999); *Romeo and Juliet* (Europe and USA, 1997); *King Lear* (1999); *Much Ado About Nothing* (UK and Germany, 2000); *King John* (2001, in a double bill with the revived *Merry Wives*); *Macbeth* (UK and Germany, 2002). Along the way, Broadsides has picked up a tidy collection of awards,[3] travelling as far afield as Rio de Janeiro (1996), Carnuntum (1995), New Delhi (1993) and Delphi (1995) to play

[2] Other metropolitan reviewers responded differently. See, for example, Aleks Sierz ('none of the plummy, tight-arsed home county accents normally associated with the bard', *Tribune*, 18 December 1992); Carole Woddis ('redress the oh-too-southern domination of vowel sounds in the Shakespeare canon', *What's On*, 16–30 December 1992); Michael Wright ('mushroomy vowels and earthy modulations . . . breathe new life into familiar lines worn out with years of RADA-accented abuse', *Time Out*, 16–30 December 1992); and Charles Spencer ('I confess I thought it sounded dotty, but the weird thing is it works . . . Shakespeare sounds terrific in authentic Northern voices. The flattened vowels, dropped aspirates, and use of words like owt and ee . . . give the language a real immediacy and speed' (*The Daily Telegraph*, 14 December 1992). Having seen both *Richard III* and *The Merry Wives* Jeffrey Wainwright understood Rutter's aim: 'This is emphatically not Shakespeare with a northern *accent*, but Shakespeare in a northern *voice*, with all the bodily depth, personal and cultural rootedness the word implies'(*Independent*, 16 June 1993). For Wainwright, 'To hear "I know a bank where the wild thyme blows" in the scoops of Barrie Rutter's Yorkshire is

20 Ægypta Capta played to watching Caesar as burlesque prologue to *Antony and Cleopatra*. The Viaduct Theatre 1997 (l to r: John Elkington, Andrew Whitehead, Matthew Booth, Paul Gabriel, Andrew Cryer [back to camera]).

in what Rutter calls 'non-velvet' spaces: that original boathouse in Hull, a disused wool–combing shed at Salts Mill, the subterranean viaduct, now the company's home, at Dean Clough in Halifax, Skipton's Cattle Market, the Tower of London, the (reconstructed) Bankside Globe, and – a concession to 'poshness' – the RSC's Swan.[4] The company has restaged Tony Harrison's *Trackers of Oxyrhynchus* (West Yorkshire Playhouse, 1998) and *The Mysteries* (playing *The Passion* at Easter in 1997 and 1998 and the trilogy as *The Millennium Story* in January, 2000). It has collaborated with Harrison on *Poetry or Bust* (Salts Mill, 1993) and *The Labourers of Herakles* (Delphi Drama Olympics, 1995) while simultaneously commissioning a steady flow of new work. From Blake Morrison came a triumphant 'Northern' translation of Kleist's *The Broken Jug* (Northern Broadsides' *Cracked Pot*, West Yorkshire Playhouse,

not an exciting novelty, it just sounds right' (*Independent*, 10 September 1994). Today, Rutter considers John Peter a stout supporter of the company – which includes noticing when they get things wrong.

3 Naming Rutter joint Stage Actor of the Year with Simon Russell Beale, both for *Richard III*, in the *Independent on Sunday Annual Review of Theatre 1992* Irving Wardle considered that they had 'reclaimed the role from the last lingering grasp of Olivier'. Other awards include: Time Out Magazine (1993); Manchester Evening News Theatre Award (1994); British Regional Theatre Award (1995); Prudential Award for the Arts (1996); Manchester Evening News Awards (1996); Liverpool Echo Arts (2000). In the 1994 Shakespeare Globe awards Broadsides won the Tyrone Guthrie Award for Best Production for *A Midsummer Night's Dream*.

4 For complete documentation of Northern Broadsides' production history see the company's website: www.northern-broadsides.co.uk. Playing *Richard III* at the Tower for Shakespeare's birthday in April 1994 was undoubtedly the company's greatest political and performance coup, the invitation being unprecedented. The cobbled yard in front of the Queen Elizabeth Tower was the playing space, the White Tower,

1995; UK tour 1996) and a hauntingly poetic *Oedipus* (UK tour 2001; in a double bill with the revived *Cracked Pot*). From Sir Antony Caro came the set designs for a starkly muscular and architectural *Samson Agonistes* (Viaduct Theatre, 1998). Ted Hughes made the company his theatrical executor, leaving Northern Broadsides his final play, *Alcestis* (world premiere, and UK tour, 2000).[5] In June 2000 Rutter won the prestigious 'Creative Briton' award and £100,000 prize money for the company.

Still, John Peter's swipes and Michael Arditti's sneers niggle. Rutter's original Northern Richard was undoubtedly a gimmick, a way one 'upstart' actor saw of legitimating his plebeian access to 'royal' Shakespeare: Richard gave Rutter the one role in the canon that 'naturally' talked Northern.[6] (As Shakespeare gimmicks go, it wasn't all that far-fetched: the authentic Richard of history, born and bred in the North, lived most of his adult life at his castle seat in Middleham.) A dozen productions later, however, Broadsides has outgrown gimmicks. But the company refuses to concede anything of its founding manifesto, its dedication to playing classic texts in a Northern voice, to making Verona as naturally a suburb of Barnsley as Barnes, and the Nile a river that runs through Leeds before emptying into the Thames – and to breaking the 'southern' stranglehold on Shakespeare. Actors employed by Northern Broadsides are native Northern speakers.[7] Clearly, the Northern voice is no gimmick. So what do Rutter's 'oop-starts' add to Shakespeare? Does the Northern voice reveal anything new in Shakespeare and his roles that enriches the text in return? To try to answer these questions I want to map the eventful history of this company. My intention at this stage is not to judge the company's work but to schedule it, to put on record an account of the company's origins and declared self-image, its 'self-legitimation crisis', that positions Northern Broadsides as a cultural phenomenon in a rapidly changing Britain – this, as a preliminary to the more important business of reading the company's work in performance which can follow. Like other 'minority' companies in Britain – Talawa, Tara Arts, Monstrous

Regiment – Northern Broadsides began with a mission, with something to prove, with a perceived history of prejudice and discrimination to overturn – which just may explain, initially at least, the self-justifying aggression of the company's combative artistic director. As I see it, Northern Broadsides tells us plenty about Shakespeare, but even more about 'SHAKESPEARE', that iconic figure who stands at the centre of what Terence Hawkes calls 'Bardbiz', focusing the on-going British culture war (reported initially fifty years ago by Richard Hoggart in *The Uses of Literacy*) over the ownership of 'Littererchewer' and the arts, elitism and the popular, Shakespeare as playwright for the 'toffs' or the 'plebs'.[8] As the hegemonic assumptions expressed by Peter and Arditti demonstrate, there has been no recent de-commissioning of traditional weapons in Britain's class war-of- words, whose

---

behind, in constant view of the audience; Richard stood on the walls, Bible in hand, looking down on the Lord Mayor, to counterfeit the deep tragedian; and the Keepers fed the ravens early to make sure they didn't interrupt Shakespeare.

5 Both *Alcestis* and *Richard III* were recorded for transmission on Radio 3.

6 In a *London Evening Standard* interview (4 December 1992) Rutter stated, 'It's an unapologetic attempt to get inside the castle keep of received pronunciation, to let actors do classical work in their own voices and not be told what they can or cannot do'.

7 The catchment area for the Northern voice is wide in Rutter's audition practice, extending from Newcastle to Nottingham, Liverpool to Hull, Barrow to Stoke – and taking in, on a handful of occasions, North Wales, Northern Ireland, South London, and even South Warwickshire. Casting at Broadsides is conducted as in any other UK company including the RSC and National: at the discretion of the director, which is to say that it is wholly discriminatory in favour of the production and the company's house style.

8 In particular, see 'Playhouse-Workhouse' in Hawkes's *That Shakespeherian Rag* (London, 1986), pp. 1–26 and 'Bardbiz' in *Meaning By Shakespeare* (London, 1992), pp. 141–53; and in Hoggart's seminal work, '"Them" and "Us"' (London, 1957), pp. 62–85. In personal correspondence dated 1 April 2001 Hawkes calls accent the 'dirty secret' at the heart of British class politics and comments upon the 'wholesale cultural and linguistic cleansing' 'brutally undertaken' during the nineteenth century 'in Wales, Ireland and – interestingly – in areas of England itself where many a rough-hewn Caliban felt the cutting edge of Prospero's plan'.

divisions, exaggerated in the 1980s by Thatcherite policies designed to bulldoze a North–South divide somewhere around Derby, continue to plague.

II

Poetry's the speech of kings. You're one of those
Shakespeare gives the comic bits to: prose!
(Tony Harrison, 'Them & [uz]')[9]

Northern Broadsides was Rutter's brainchild, but the company's demon godfather was Tony Harrison, the Leeds-born poet of *The Loiners* and *Continuous* who happens also to be probably the finest theatre poet England has produced since Shakespeare. Through his working with Harrison at the National Theatre in the 1980s Rutter formulated the attitude to his own voice which became the basis of his company's politics of expression.[10]

Harrison himself freely admits that his poetry began as an act of revenge against an English teacher, the one who informed him, an eleven-year-old working-class lad on one of the scholarships reserved for the 'plebs' to the 'poshest' of the grammar schools in Leeds, that his Northern voice was wrong for poetry. For 'Poetry's the speech of kings'. Poetry requires 'RP', 'Received Pronunciation': 'We say [ʌs] not [uz]', the teacher witheringly told him. (And 'that shut my trap', for, as Harrison remembers in 'The Rhubarbarians', his schoolboy accent was so thick it tied his tongue in knots around 'glottals' that 'glugged like poured pop'.) Still, even marked out as a 'barbarian' by a speech impediment that made him one of 'them', not one of '[ʌs]', and culturally disqualified him from taking any of the major speaking parts in 'our glorious heritage', Harrison was equipped for *something*: those 'comic bits', the 'prose'. Circa 1949, then, as he reports in 'Them & [uz]', young Harrison got his chance with Shakespeare – and 'played the Drunken Porter in *Macbeth*'.

Rutter's route to Shakespeare was less humiliating. Ten years younger than Harrison, he grew up alongside Hull's fish docks on Hessle Road, a grimy working-class district whose back-to-back two-up, two-down terraces Richard Hoggart remembers permanently clad in a 'pall of cooking fish-meal'.[11] His standard demotic was the same 'barbarian' street slang Harrison records in 'Me Tarzan': '*Off laikin*', '*off tartin*', '*off to t'flicks*'. No scholarship boy, Rutter managed to scrape a place at one of the Labour Government's new-model, post-war grammar schools, their remit, to open up 'elite' education to the working classes. There, at sixteen in 196[] he got *his* chance with Shakespeare – and played Macbeth in *Macbeth*.

By the time the poet and the player met twenty years later, however, Rutter knew that nobody but a Hull Grammar School saw him as next casting for any of Shakespeare's kings. He had notched up two full seasons with the Royal Shakespeare Company, two RSC world tours, and a number of critically acclaimed performances in minor roles, among them a truculent sod of a First Citizen in *Coriolanus* (1977), a Dick the Butcher who clearly relished turning men into meat in *Henry VI* (1977), and a goggle-eyed Lollio who stole *The Changeling* (1979) notices. Even so, his director, Terry Hands, thought a voice like his should be thinking about a future in TV soaps and variety, not in 'serious' work on the classics.

Rutter decamped to the National Theatre to join Bill Bryden's company at the Cottesloe for a revival of Tony Harrison's *The Passion* (1980), a project that eventually grew into the three-part *Mysteries*, culled, adapted, and new-scripted from the medieval York, Wakefield, and Chester cycles, performed in 'authentic' Northern voices – some of them acquired only as far north as the NT's rehearsal rooms. The following year Harrison's stunning translation of *The Oresteia* opened at the National Theatre. Scripted for masks and an all-male company, *The Oresteia* specified Northern voices (this time, real ones), needed, said Harrison,

---

9 Reprinted in Carol Rutter, ed., *Tony Harrison: Permanently Bard* (Newcastle upon Tyne, 1995), pp. 33–4.

10 About their first meeting Rutter comments, 'Here was a man who wrote for a voice like mine . . . the gods had smiled down on me' (Jackie McGlone, *The Glasgow Herald*, 19 December 1992).

11 Richard Hoggart, *The Uses of Literacy* (Fair Lawn, N.J., 1957) p. 75.

to produce the percussive, consonant-heavy sound required to 'carry the traffic' his Aeschylus script had to deliver through the open mouths of the tragic masks. Written in a language imitative of the original Greek, a language knotted with the musculature of Beowulf's English, this script was designed to release savage energies. Politically, it did something more. Putting his Northern *Oresteia* on to the NT stage, Harrison inserted his 'marginal' barbarian voice into the very centre of elite Establishment culture and roused the ghost of humiliated memory once again – this time to mock it. For in *his* theatre poetry, *Northern* voices produced 'the speech of kings'. (As it happened, Northern voices produced the 'comic bits' too – but in Harrison even the 'comic bits' are poetry.)

If performing Harrison's theatre poetry in *The Mysteries* and *The Oresteia* was for Rutter like taking remedial tutorials in the cultural crash course recited by the poet's schoolboy self in 'Them & [uz]', Rutter's next Harrison project completed his education. Harrison wrote for him the part of the phallically deflated Silenus in *The Trackers of Oxyrhynchus* (1988), a modern satyr play built around a fragment of Sophocles' *Ichneutai*. Here again, cultural grudge was Harrison's topic as he set his clog-dancing chorus of tumescent rowdies in head-on collision with privileged culture's aloof apparatchiks. Silenus told the story of Marsyas, who was flayed alive on Apollo's orders to punish him, a mere satyr, for presuming to retrieve and learn to play the aulis, which the god had discarded. Seeing Marsyas as an appalling metaphor for contemporary cultural practices, Harrison used his 'low art' satyrs to critique what he saw, depressingly, as the cultural status quo in post-Thatcherite Britain: the division of art into 'high' and 'low' and the mystification of culture by an Apollonian elite bent on excluding the 'plebs' from 'patrician' pleasures (theatre, opera, ballet – and Shakespeare). In Harrison's view, 'nob' appropriation of the arts produced 'yobs', alienated cultural vandals who wrecked what they'd been denied. But for Rutter, it was not the world premiere of *Trackers* in the ancient stadium in Delphi or even the transfer to London and the National that changed the direction of his professional life, but

the play's restaging, two years later, at Salts Mill, three miles north of Bradford. For the first time, brought 'home' to Yorkshire, *Trackers* met an audience who shared its voice, who heard the satyrs speaking not as 'Them', but as '[uz] [uz] [uz]', an audience who occupied the very ideological space of conflict the play explored – and stood their ground. They weren't going to be fobbed off with elitism's cultural leavings, its 'comic bits' and pieces. They wanted poetry. For Rutter, the 'sheer affinity' between the popular voice of the audience and the popular voice Harrison found and released in the classic text 'was a revelation'. And more, fired an ambition: after Sophocles, to reclaim Shakespeare for the popular voice. Starting with *Richard*.

III

People know very well that certain sorts of speech cut off a person forever from getting more than three or four pounds a week all their life long – sorts of speech which make them entirely impossible in certain professions.

(George Bernard Shaw)

'No-buddy talks like dat'.

Some Like It Hot [12]

Why did Shakespeare *need* reclaiming? When was he captured for high culture and taught to speak RP? And when did Shakespeare performance start exploiting regional accent as 'comic relief'? Like so much else that happened to Shakespeare, the project of cultural appropriation began with the Victorians – who were also the ones to reinvent regional accent as a class marker of inferiority.

Before 1870, regional accent certainly operated as a marker of difference, but on a horizontal or spatial scale – that is, measuring proximity to, or remoteness from, what was seen as the centre of culture – not on a vertical scale of social exclusion. English theatre started making fun of English speaking almost the moment it started speaking English, Englishmen lampooning each other ('them what talk funny' vs. '[uz] what don't') across

---

[12] Quoted in Albert C. Baugh, *A History of the English Language* (New York, 1957), p. 380; MGM, directed by Billy Wilder, 1959.

regional boundaries, which are also, in England, cultural faultlines. Significantly, the ridicule was reciprocal, a two-way traffic: in the late fifteenth-century *Second Shepherd's Play* the con-man is exposed when he tries to talk 'posh' to his Yorkshire cronies, who let him know he can 'sett' his fake 'sothren tothe' 'in a torde' (lines 214–16).[13] Already heard (and mocked) as 'nice', Southern English managed to trump its rivals with technology thanks to William Caxton's printing press, set up in London in 1476, as, over the next hundred years, the dissemination of print culture that revolutionized communications established the linguistic usages of London as standard written English.[14] At the same time, while the ordinary people of England went on speaking their regional dialects in their distinctive regional accents, London speech, specifically 'of the shires lying about London within 60 miles and not much more', as George Puttenham observed in *The Art of English Poesie* (1589),[15] gradually achieved authority as 'correct' speech, the linguistic apparatus that identified the metropolitan elite, a minority culture, embedded in the mass population, that comprised the Court, the gentry, the educated: Puttenham's sixty miles took in Oxford and Cambridge. Some of Elizabeth's courtiers, however, never adopted London standard pronunciation – Walter Raleigh probably kept a West Country tongue in his head to his dying day.[16]

On Shakespeare's stage – he was, after all, a Warwickshire provincial who had to acquire whatever metropolitan skills he came to possess – speech gags worked as much to invert as to instantiate urban elitism, the courtier as likely to be clobbered as the clown. So when Touchstone sits down with William in Arden or Falstaff with Shallow in an orchard in Gloucestershire, the joke is certainly on the rustic, mocked for slow wit and slow speech, but equally on the courtier, shown up in speech as over-sophisticated, superfluous, a verbal decadent run to fat on easy living, a waterfly or potential Osric brought close to linguistic melt-down by the frustration of a wit too ingenious for the work-a-day world. The Court in Shakespeare is the locus of refinement, but equally, of corruption and hypocrisy. Marking distance from this Court, re-

gional accent distances the speaker from both kinds of courtliness: if the 'hempen homespun' is a clot-pole, he is also unvarnished, a man of plain-speaking integrity. So in *King Lear*, as men lose power – sexual, political, cultural – they lose language, adopting 'accents' they 'borrow' (1.4.1) as protective disguise but use to ideological effect, becoming dissonant in an acoustic court world divided by the division of the kingdom. The voice of the yokel, Kent's blunt Caius, Edgar's Kentish peasant and West Country churl, monitors the Court's 'large' speech, registering that decency and pity survive in the kingdom – only banished to its remotest corners, to the far side of Lear's heath. About early modern Shakespeare, then, Tony Harrison's English teacher was wrong: poetry is not the prerogative 'speech of kings' and neither is the clown a prose moron.

But that English teacher was *right* about late Victorian Shakespeare. For in or about September 1870, English accent changed – or rather, how English accent was heard.[17] Led by Dr Arnold

---

[13] A. C. Cawley, ed., *Everyman and Medieval Miracle Plays* (London, 1974).

[14] For this history, I am indebted to John Honey's excellent *Does Accent Matter?: The Pygmalion Factor* (London, 1991), especially pp. 12–37.

[15] Quoted by Honey, *Does Accent Matter?*, p. 15.

[16] Honey, *Does Accent Matter?*, p. 17, quotes John Aubrey (b. 1621) in his *Brief Lives* (A. Powell, ed., (London, 1949), p. 324) who claims to have heard it from a judge who, as a youth, knew Raleigh personally: 'notwithstanding so great mastership in style, and his conversation with the learnedest and politest persons, yet he spake broad Devonshire to his dying day'.

[17] Honey sees 1870 as the watershed year when the Rugby programme had produced sufficient critical mass of those speaking standard accent to qualify the trend as socially transformative. Earlier generations who went through the public school system and even on to Oxford and Cambridge 'went on speaking with marked traces of local accents all their lives', even men at the centre of national power and prestige who 'lived out their public careers in London': Robert Walpole (Eton, Cambridge), the first British Prime Minister, went to his grave sounding 'like a Norfolk squire'; Disraeli said the fifteenth Earl of Derby (Rugby, Cambridge), Foreign Secretary in the 1860s and 1870s, spoke 'Lancashire patois'; Gladstone (Eton, Oxford) always retained traces of his

at Rugby School, from 1828 a programmatic revolution in education had produced, by 1870, a group of some fifty socially selective, like-minded public schools who were now uniformly turning out what John Honey calls 'the new caste of "public school men"', their 'emergence constituting a major development in British social history'.[18] For the identifying badge of this new elite was accent, 'PSP' (or 'Public School Pronunciation' as it came to be called). A socially engineered discourse if ever there was one, it was the prototype of Received Pronunciation. Now accent was heard no longer simply as a regional marker but as an index of *class* that instantly authenticated a speaker as one of the 'tribe', and just as instantly marked the social inferior for social exclusion. 'PSP' identified Britain's officer and professional classes; it was the accent heard in college rooms, pulpits, Parliament, at high tables – and among social aspirants who, as Honey observes, advertised their identification with the privileged cultural corps d'élite and its values by painstakingly erasing their own accents and ventriloquizing the voice of 'culture'.[19] Where other nations would use race, Britain employed accent to effect cultural apartheid, dividing the privileged from the working classes to such an extent that, by 1912, G. B. Shaw could observe, 'It is impossible for an Englishman to open his mouth without making some other Englishman hate or despise him'.[20]

In the 1880s and 1890s, increasing pressure was brought to bear, much of it by schools' inspectors, to extend PSP down into elementary schools, a state-organized system of mass elementary education having been instituted in 1870. In 1889, a Whitehall directive outlined 'the correct method of teaching vowel sounds'; teacher-training colleges 'offered instruction in elocution'. So did Anglican theological colleges. In 1916, one grammar school in the Midlands that aspired to public school status went about eradicating 'pleb' accents by requiring boys to spend the first period each morning chanting a designated vowel sound – the sort of ritual practice 'Them & [uz]' shows still survived at Leeds Grammar School into the 1950s: '*E-nun-ci-ate!*' In Birmingham in 1918 the promotional squib on a 'teach yourself' elocution manual

claimed it contained the class accent equivalent of the miracle cure.[21] In 1921, the Newbolt Report on the teaching of English in state schools made it 'emphatically the business of the elementary school to teach all pupils' to 'speak standard English'. And continued: 'The great difficulty of teachers in elementary schools in many districts is that they have to fight against the powerful influence of evil habits of speech contracted in home and street. The teacher's struggle is thus not with ignorance but with perverted power'.[22] Mobilizing language that makes class accent a communicable disease or social perversion, the phonetic strain of other infections picked up on the streets whose terraces constituted a kind of evil anti-empire, Newbolt saw standard English as a value worth fighting for: in its terms, class accent prefigured class war. Not insignificantly, perhaps, the Newbolt committee included not just grammarians but an expert on language in literature, Professor Caroline Spurgeon of University College, London, whose influential book on *Shakespeare's Imagery and What It Tells Us* would appear in 1935. One of Spurgeon's contentions would be that 'it is chiefly through his images' that a poet, 'to some extent unconsciously, "gives himself away"'.[23] Evidently, what images did for the poet, class accent did for the rest of mankind. Education had to be evangelical.

In effect, however, from the 1920s, the responsibility for grafting RP on to the British body politic passed from the education system to the new

---

Liverpool Lancashire accent (Honey, *Does Accent Matter?*, p. 24). The schoolboy Harrison in 'Them & [uz]' achieves an epiphany when he learns some of this pre-Arnoldian history, and that Keats spoke Cockney and Wordsworth rhymed 'matter' with 'water'.

[18] Honey, *Does Accent Matter?*, pp. 26–7, considers its impact 'understated and even disregarded in many modern textbooks about this period'.

[19] Honey, *Does Accent Matter?*, p. 28.

[20] Preface to *Pygmalion* in G. B. Shaw, *Androcles and the Lion; Overruled; Pygmalion* (New York, 1916).

[21] Honey, *Does Accent Matter?*, pp. 29, 31, 30.

[22] Quoted by Ken Worpole, 'Scholarship Boy', in Neil Astley, ed., *Tony Harrison* (Newcastle-upon-Tyne, 1991), p. 65.

[23] Quoted in Gary Taylor, *Reinventing Shakespeare* (London, 1990), p. 258.

mass media: the BBC, founded in 1922, set up an Advisory Committee on Spoken English in 1926, chaired first by the Poet Laureate, Old Etonian Robert Bridges, then by George Bernard Shaw. From the first, the voice the BBC presented spoke RP – by official policy. Thirty years later, BBC television (followed shortly by commercial TV) adopted the same policy. Reaching its first mass audience in Queen Elizabeth II's coronation year (1953), television in the next decade entered household after household in Britain, bringing with it the version of English it promoted as 'correct', 'proper', 'educated', 'smart'. Non-standard accents did feature in radio and television, indeed, were convenient character giveaways stereotyping the booby, the hayseed, the primitive, subalterns and the lower orders from below stairs, blue-ish comedians. The weather could be reported in regional accents, and gardeners' questions answered; so could documentaries and social dramas on inner-city deprivation. In BBC radio's longest-running soap, the tenant farming Grundys were cast in 'rural Borsetshire' accents; the landowning farmers, the Archers, spoke 'posh'. As 'BBC English', broadcast on the Home Service and exported globally on the World Service, established itself as the authentic voice of English speaking, accent was functioning as ideology: RP became 'invisible'; only non-standard speakers had 'accents'. 1950s Britain, then, contained 'two cultural nations: those *with accents*, and those even more absurdly styled as *without accents*'.[24] RP's hegemony would remain unchallenged until the 1960s.[25]

Meanwhile, on a parallel track of appropriation, the Victorians, Edwardians and post-war Elizabethans of the 'Second Elizabethan Age' did for Shakespeare what they had done for spoken English, recruiting, mystifying, institutionalizing, handing Shakespeare over to academics and experts, and ultimately, in the theatre, reserving him to a minority audience, a spectatorly corps d'élite. It is a history Gary Taylor has exhaustively documented: in 1864, the publication of the first academically produced and printed edition of Shakespeare (just as, in another part of the forest, PSP was completing its conquest of schoolboy demotic);[26]

in 1874, the foundation of the New Shakespere Society (its aim, wrote F. J. Furnivall in his invitational prospectus, to apply to Shakespeare the kinds of investigations 'our geniuses of Science' were using to 'wrest . . . her secrets from Nature');[27] by 1887, the availability of over eighty schools editions of individual plays, making Shakespeare the subject of twice as many textbooks as any other English author.[28] Installed on the schools syllabus as a set text from the 1880s, by the 1890s Shakespeare was fixed as the core author of the newly devised university English Literature syllabus.[29] At both addresses, schoolboys and undergraduates had learned to read poetry in RP. Shakespeare, too, was 'naturally' dubbed into the accent of the elite – having already been recruited to selecting that elite: from 1855 he featured on the competitive Indian Civil Service examination.

This thoroughly institutionalized Establishment Shakespeare increasingly belonged to readers, not spectators, but readers who heard his voice in a

---

[24] Neal Acherson, *Observer*, 6 April 1986, quoted by Honey, *Does Accent Matter?*, p. 1.

[25] As recently as 1981 Robert Burchfield's *The Spoken Word: A BBC Guide*, written for in-house staff instruction, began: 'In what follows it is assumed that the speaker uses Received Standard English in its 1980s form. The form of speech recommended is that of a person born and brought up in one of the Home Counties, educated at one of the established southern universities, and not yet so set in his ways that all linguistic change is regarded as unacceptable'. Quoted by Worpole, 'Scholarship Boy' p. 67.

[26] Edited by three Cambridge dons (and printed by Cambridge University Press) the Globe or 'Cambridge' Shakespeare represented 'the first serious intrusion of academics into the history of Shakespeare's reputation' (Taylor, *Reinventing Shakespeare*, p. 186). It became the standard text for over a century. Oxford University Press followed with the Oxford Shakespeare in 1868.

[27] Taylor, *Reinventing Shakespeare*, p. 165.

[28] Taylor, *Reinventing Shakespeare*, p. 184.

[29] University College London had a chair in English Literature and History by 1828; Trinity College, Dublin, from 1867. At Cambridge, English belonged to the Board of Medieval and Modern Languages, founded in 1878, until the English tripos was devised in 1921. At Oxford, the Merton Professorship was established in 1884 and university examinations in English instituted in 1893 (Taylor, *Reinventing Shakespeare*, p. 194).

particular register.[30] By the end of Victoria's reign, Taylor observes, 'theatre mattered less to the dominant consciousness of Shakespeare' than it had 'in the two preceding centuries'.[31] Subsequent generations of academic readers alienated Shakespeare even further from the playhouse, seeing, as L. C. Knights did, his plays not as potential performances but as 'dramatic poems': 'We start with so many lines of verse on a printed page which we read as we should read any other poem'.[32] As poetry, practised by modernist poets, became 'difficult', 'a superior amusement', so Shakespeare, too, in the 1920s and 1930s became difficult. It was given to be understood that his ambiguities and allusions, his complexities of imagery and subtleties of reference were really only accessible to a cultural elite, the literary heirs to Elizabethan England's discerning theatrical elite to whom (in this modernist fashioning that mapped its own cultural divisions on to the early modern past) Shakespeare addressed his best, elevated work – as against the plebs in the pit to whom he tossed down bawdy like apples to apes. As it happened, Britain's latter-day hairy apes were being catered for elsewhere, at the 'movies', while live theatre shrank into smaller auditoriums with distinctly smaller audiences, dwindling into a minority cultural experience.

The Shakespeare who played to this elite audience in the West End or at the Old Vic or Stratford's Memorial Theatre in the 1930s and 1940s spoke the class accent of its audience; indeed, since before the turn of the century, had been *groomed* to speak that accent. LAMDA (the London Academy of Music and Dramatic Art) began training actors in 1861, just when Arnold's Rugby project was poised for triumph and three Cambridge dons were settling down to their editing project; RADA (the Royal Academy of Dramatic Art), attached to Beerbohm Tree's Her Majesty's Theatre, in 1904; the Central School of Speech Training and Dramatic Art at the Albert Hall in 1906. Elocution, defined as 'poetic speech', was the core curriculum drilled into generations of aspiring thesps by the redoubtable Miss Elsie Fogerty at Central (among them, Laurence Olivier and Peggy Ashcroft, both first termers in 1924), while at RADA, the playwright

of *Pygmalion*, clearly thinking of actors as among those permanently 'cut off' by 'certain sorts of speech' from any job paying 'more than three or four pounds a week', endowed actors' training at the Royal Academy.[33] By the mid-1930s on the metropolitan stage the cultivated voice of Shakespeare, and the voice cultivated par excellence *for* Shakespeare, was John Gielgud's. Ironically, when Olivier, sensing perhaps that 'no-buddy talks like dat', produced something closer to 'real' speech for Romeo opposite Gielgud in 1935 he was universally slated. (By 'real' he meant nothing more radical than speaking verse 'the way you speak naturally', where 'naturally' naturally meant Rugby PSP.[34])

---

[30] As Jonathan Rose's excellent *Intellectual Life of the British Working Classes* (New Haven, 2001) shows, *reading* Shakespeare remained a feature of British working-class culture throughout the nineteenth century and beyond; however, that same culture by and large assumed that the 'proper' way to *perform* Shakespeare involved 'posh' accents. See pp. 31–5 and 49–52.

[31] Taylor, *Reinventing Shakespeare*, p. 230.

[32] Quoted by Taylor, *Reinventing Shakespeare*, p. 239.

[33] See Michael Holroyd, *Bernard Shaw: The Lure of Fantasy*, vol. 3 (London, 1991), p. 500. At RADA the endowment is known affectionately as the 'Pygmalion Fund'. Shaw's tart thoughts on actors, accents, aspirants, and speech training are recorded in the final paragraph to his *Pygmalion* Preface (1916) where he ends: 'Finally, and for the encouragement of people troubled with accents that cut them off from all high employment, I may add that the change wrought by Professor Higgins in the flower girl is neither impossible nor uncommon. The modern concierge's daughter who fulfils her ambition by playing the Queen of Spain in Ruy Blas at the Théâtre Français is only one of many thousands of men and women who have sloughed off their native dialects and acquired a new tongue. But the thing has to be done scientifically, or the last state of the aspirant may be worse than the first. An honest and natural slum dialect is more tolerable than the attempt of a phonetically untaught person to imitate the vulgar dialect of the golf club; and I am sorry to say that in spite of the efforts of our Academy of Dramatic Art, there is still too much sham golfing English on our stage, and too little of the noble English of Forbes Robertson'.

[34] Laurence Olivier, *Confessions of an Actor* (London, 1982), pp. 75–6. In fact, Olivier was educated at St Edward's School, Oxford. 'But father, what about Rugby?' he remembers asking wistfully as he was sent off to 'the sort of school' that 'in

Jimmy Porter did nothing to liberate Shakespeare either. Indeed, the vox pop revolution John Osborne's Romeo-retread set off in the theatre in 1956 with *Look Back in Anger* may have made things worse for Shakespeare. For Shakespeare was considered the cultural property (and cultural trophy) of a privileged class astonished to find itself on the defensive in post-war Britain, and needing hostages to prerogatives suddenly under siege. And privilege *was* under siege. The post-war labour shortage ('solved' by the Windrush project, importing labour from former Caribbean colonies), post-war rationing (finally phased out in 1954), the Suez crisis (1956), CND and popular political activism, the 'wind of change' that Harold Macmillan, in his famous speech of 1957, saw turning the tide of history in a post-colonial Empire: all this combined to democratize Britain, to empower the working classes and end automatic class deference if not, finally, to level out the class system. Theatre's grand old men and their grand old cut-crystal voices were 'out' – or capitulated as Olivier did;[35] the Jimmy Porter brigade of ragged-arsed youth radiating aggro and commitment in scruffy bed-sits – and in non-U accents – was 'in'. The axis of theatrical power shifted from the West End to the Royal Court and Stratford East. Rattigan gave way to Delaney, and drawing rooms to settings on council estates (in John Arden's *Live Like Pigs*, 1957), London's East End (in Arnold Wesker's *The Kitchen*, 1959, and *Chips With Everything*, 1962), and Northern industrial slums (in Shelagh Delaney's *A Taste of Honey*, 1958). Popular culture's new badge of status was a working-class background, and Romeo (or what passed for him) in 1960s Britain had a working-class accent – in Joe Orton, Harold Pinter, Edward Bond. But not in Shakespeare. Shakespeare belonged to high culture; in 1960s parlance, Establishment culture. Shakespeare was the site in contemporary British culture where elitism held out against the philistine, order against the slide into anarchy, standards against slovenliness. Shakespeare both stood for and guaranteed what Britain wanted to say about itself in the voice it wanted to say it in.

In Stratford, a new generation of university men were running the show: the theatre, made 'Royal' in 1961, had a Cambridge graduate as Artistic Director and a Cambridge don to look after the company's verse-speaking.[36] But the company itself, paradoxically, internalized a schism between elitism and the popular. Actors of this revolutionary generation by and large saw themselves as workers and identified with the working classes. But speaking Shakespeare promoted them into the middle-class elite. A graphic display of this schism is laid out across the pages of the Summer 1965 edition of the company's in-house 'Theatre Club Newspaper', 'Flourish'.[37] On the letters page, Marghanita Laski played devil's advocate to arguments for mass public subsidy for the arts (including what Peter Hall continually lobbied for, an appropriately subsidized Royal Shakespeare Company), on the grounds that art served not 'the many' but 'the few'. For, Laski wrote, 'the capacity to respond to art' was 'confined only to people of a certain temperament and mind…the educated, the refined, the neurotic classes'; 'with the best will in the world, most people cannot respond to art, even after ten years of conditioning in childhood'. In contrast, on the features page, six company members, styling themselves 'Actor's Commando' (in language indebted to political activism's current lingo), talked about a class-conscientious RSC project to take theatre to the working classes, to play 'canteens, halls or social clubs, during lunch-hours or after work', to

---

those days' one was not 'inclined to boast about' (*Confessions*, p. 14).

[35] He went to the Royal Court in 1957 to play the on-the-skids vaudevillian Archie Rice in John Osborne's *The Entertainer*.

[36] Peter Hall took over as Artistic Director in 1960; the Memorial became the Royal Shakespeare Theatre in 1961; John Barton joined Hall from Cambridge in the same year and became an Associate Director in 1964. Trevor Nunn arrived from Cambridge via the Coventry Belgrade in 1965, taking over as Artistic Director three years later.

[37] 'Flourish: Royal Shakespeare Theatre Club Newspaper', Summer 1965 (no. 4), pp. 2, 12. Laski's observations are put hypothetically, not programmatically; her reference to 'the neurotic classes' is quoting Sir James Crichton-Browne. The extract in 'Flourish' was taken from her article in *The Listener*, 8 April 1965.

perform 'in a tone of voice that was friendly but not falsely chummy, forceful but not paternal', a manifesto that unwittingly un-did socialist ideology in its own forms of expression.[38] Their anthology piece, 'How to Stop Worrying and Love the Theatre' – a title intended to end the anxiety of ignorance – was given a first try-out in an electronics works. In a follow-up discussion at a school venue, however, 'a boy who'd only recently left school' 'movingly explained' 'why the actors were wasting their time', why taking Shakespeare 'out to factories' was doomed: 'A programme like this is all right among people like us', he said, including, it seems, the actors among 'us'. 'We're used to thinking. But they don't think'. 'Them' and '[ʌs]', it appears, were going to resist the blandishments of the RSC's leftish gestures, its democratizing 'right on'-ism.

So while the Royal Court Theatre was privileging, even glamorizing working class accents, the Royal Shakespeare Theatre went on assuming RP, even from 'Commandos'. And drama schools went on 'correcting' regional accents.[39] Thus, a generation of actors, contemporaries of Tony Harrison, grew up in the profession in the 1960s bi-lingual, speaking the restricted speech of elitism on one stage; on another stage (and on film), what Harrison calls the 'language that I spoke at home':[40] Albert Finney (*Billy Liar*, *Saturday Night and Sunday Morning* vs. Edgar in *King Lear*); Tom Courtenay (*Billy Liar*, *For King and Country* vs. *Hamlet*); Peter O'Toole (Private Bamforth in *The Long and the Short and the Tall* vs. Petruchio in *The Taming of the Shrew*); Anthony Hopkins (moving from his debut at the Royal Court to spear-carrying in Shakespeare at the National, then *Coriolanus* in 1971); Alan Bates (Cliff in *Look Back in Anger*, Mick in *The Caretaker* vs. *Hamlet* at Nottingham Playhouse and *The Taming of the Shrew* at the RSC). Audiences heard Edward Petherbridge's (otherwise completely erased) 'home' voice in *The Rivals* at the National (1983); Ian McKellen's, as Iago in Trevor Nunn's *Othello* (RSC, 1989); Patrick Stewart has never used his real Northern voice on the professional stage.[41] Actors in Barrie Rutter's generation went the same way, adopting vocal camouflage:

Ian Charleson, Polly Hemingway, Maureen Lipman, Peter Bowles, the Cusack sisters, Brian Cox, Jack Shepherd, Alison Steadman. Did it matter, this alienating, this de-naturing of the actor's voice? *How* did it matter? One act of reminiscence, Peter Brook's, can speak to this entire history. Brook, looking back thirty years to account for the failure of his *Romeo and Juliet* at the RSC in 1947, remembered a time, he said, when 'young actors were all in the RADA image' – that is, 'stiff, conventional, and boring, either genuinely upper class or stilted working class'. The actor Brook cast as Romeo was, by birth, a Cockney. But there was no question of his using his 'real' voice. Made over in the 'RADA image', he'd 'had to learn to talk like a gentleman'. 'And so', said Brook, 'he could not speak from his heart'.[42]

Unexamined, automatic, even 'natural', the prejudice directed against non-RP Shakespeare that continued throughout the 1970s reveals staggering class assumptions, displayed, for example, in Bernard Levin's patrician review of the RSC's 1977 *Henry VI* trilogy. 'I finally lost my temper at Alfred Lynch's Edward', he snapped.

---

[38] In a personal communication, Alan Rivett suggests that 'the post-war revolution' probably 'really started in the regions' and that the 'RSC's commandos were reacting to what was happening in TIE [Theatre in Education], community theatre, etc'. He asks, 'Is this where the reversal started? In Bolton, Newcastle, Leeds, Coventry? Then taken up enthusiastically by the establishment – RSC, Royal Court?'

[39] According to Ali Troughton, whose father, John Finlayson Groves, was Deputy Principal of the Royal Scottish Academy of Music and Drama, 1953–1975, 'corrective' elocution classes remained on the RSA syllabus until the late 1970s.

[40] Tony Harrison, 'Them & [uz]'.

[41] When extracts from *Dear Tom*, Courtenay's memoirs, were broadcast on BBC Radio 4 in October 2000, Courtenay used his acquired RP voice to play himself; Sîan Thomas played his mother in Mrs Courtenay's native Hull accent.

[42] Quoted in Sally Beauman, *The Royal Shakespeare Company: A History of Ten Decades* (Oxford, 1982), p. 184, from an interview with Brook in 1979. In *The Actor and his Text*, Cicely Berry, the RSC's voice coach, describes the voice as 'our sound presence', 'the means by which we commit our private world to the world outside': we 'make a statement with our voice' (London, 1987), p. 16. Arguably, installing RP falsifies that statement and misrepresents that privacy, rendering the commitment spurious.

IV

[W]hat on earth is this slovenly Cockney doing on the throne of England? With the style of a disc-jockey and the diction of a barrow-boy (he gives us, among other hideousnesses, 'presummtion' for presumption and 'watchew' for what you, and even calls his own house 'Yawk,' with the w clearly audible), he would hardly have been accepted as an ally by Cade, let alone proud Warwick.[43]

More depressingly, the same protocols, and the stereotypes they revive and circulate, appear to be fully operational at the RSC at the millennium. In a season that saw the company casting the first black actor ever to play an English king, David Oyelowo as Henry in the *Henry VI* trilogy, thereby officially discarding race as a category discriminating representation, it preserved predictable discriminations fixed on accent. Aristos talked 'posh'; plebs were 'othered' in regional accents. Thus, Des Barritt's Falstaff spoke RP; so did William Houston's Hal and Fiona Bell's (French) Queen Margaret. But Bell used her native Scots accent for her double in *1 Henry VI*, the 'baddie' upstart, Joan la Pucelle. Barritt was suppressing his 'real' Welsh voice, which he'd used for the first time at the RSC a couple seasons back for a Malvolio the production wanted marked as a priggish outsider (1992). So was Houston: in 1998 he played Trojan Troilus in his native Irish accent. Stereotypically, in the same RSC season, cod-rusticity marked the yokels in Arden in *As You Like It* and Gloucestershire and the Boar's Head in *Henry IV*, evidence enough that regional accent remained alive and well at the RSC as 'comic relief'.[44]

This 400-year-long refining of William Shakespeare into elitist writer and darling of the universities has a piquant irony, given early academic opinion pronounced upon him circa 1592 by one of the 'University wits', Robert Greene. For Greene, the grammar school educated arriviste from the provinces was 'an upstart Crow' 'beautified' in poetic 'feathers' plucked from his betters – an early modern version of the class aspirant. By 1992 another 'oop-start' judged it was high time to reclaim Shakespeare for the 'rude', to knock politeness off

the poet and return the playwright to a theatre Peter Brook called 'rough' – in short, to give him back to the groundlings.[45]

V

'So right, yer buggers, then! We'll occupy
your lousy leasehold Poetry.

('Them & [uz]')

Northern Broadsides' theatrical signature is unmistakable. Its boldest features – the driving pace the company sets in performance and their visual inventiveness – derive first from the company's attitude toward the presentational quality of the

---

[43] *The Sunday Times*, 23 April 1978. It is perhaps the persistence of this same prejudice that Barbara Hodgdon hears in review discourse from critics who fault actors on their 'verse speaking', coded language, in some cases, for accents they find inappropriate to Shakespeare. See *The Shakespeare Trade* (Philadelphia, 1998), pp. 56, 179–80.

[44] Signs are that both performance practice and culture are changing. Trailing his 'Appalachian' *Winter's Tale* on Radio 4's 'Front Row' in April 2002, the RSC director Matthew Warchus defended his decision to play Shakespeare in an American accent. 'Actually', he said, 'it's RP that's the anachronism – because it's so recent'. In an issue of *The Independent* magazine (6 April 2002) entirely devoted to identifying what is 'posh' in everything from handbags to railway eateries, Rose George analysed the English obsession with 'talking posh'. While 'linguistic experts have learnt that children start distinguishing between accents at the age of three and a half', in England, she quipped, 'they probably develop perfect accent pitch in the womb' (p. 25). For 'Nowhere, not even the most rigid of Hindu caste systems, is as obsessed by accent as this small island. Or part of it – the Scottish and Welsh were too busy (fighting the English, probably) to develop as complex and damning an accent hierarchy as ours. Only here do so few words reveal so much – background, gender, sexuality, schooling – and generate such contempt so concisely'. But she also quoted Professor David Crystal, who calculates that the number of posh-speakers has halved in one generation, commenting, 'This is grand. If accent has denoted class, then accents breaking down mean class boundaries crumble too'.

[45] Michael Bogdanov's work as director with the English Shakespeare Company (active, 1986–92) needs to be mentioned here as a forerunner to Northern Broadsides, for although the ESC did not aim to popularize a regional voice, it certainly claimed access to Shakespeare for 'uz'.

Northern voice matched to the formal demands of Shakespeare's text, and second, from poverty.

As Irving Wardle observed, 'extraordinary things' happen to Shakespeare when he comes into 'Yorkshire close-up'. To begin with, this company refuses to apologize for Shakespeare's poetry, to treat it naturalistically as though it were a slightly odd version of prose or to divorce poetry from reality and treat poetry as no different from rhetoric. (One recalls, here, Peter Hall's lament dating back to the 1960s, that actors 'had forgotten that there was shape, and form' to poetry: 'verse-speaking was *dying* of naturalism'.[46]) Instead, Northern Broadsides sees the formal structures of the verse as *enabling* performance, the 'compulsive art' of the actor making poetry immediate, and making poetry a 'natural' discourse. Rutter has shown that Northern speech, with its short vowels and concrete consonants, produces 'a great travelling language', a heavy-duty theatre language geared for urgent storytelling on an open stage.[47] 'With' becomes 'w', 'him' becomes ''em', 'to do', 't'do', 'you're', 'y'a': collapsing pronouns and connectives accelerates the verse line, throwing weight upon nouns and verbs, the formal stress points of the line that not only drive the argument of the speech but the pace of the play as a whole, effectively (in Gillian Reynolds' phrase) 'speeding the mind to meaning'.[48] In Broadsides productions, Robert Butler has observed, 'No one lingers': characters speak verse 'because it's the fastest way to make themselves understood', punching out 'big arguments with the urgency of ticker-tape'. 'No Acting' he takes to be the company's motto − or rather, 'no acting' that interrupts the verse line, the iambic rope the poet plays out, releasing the story as it goes. 'If we have to wait for it', Rutter tells actors in rehearsal about bits of business they want to insert, 'out it goes'. This sort of presentational theatre, in which story reveals character, not character story, and in which the text is spoken, not 'delivered', allows 'no room for displays of sensibility, which so often slide in, like double-glazing, between us and the play'.[49]

One effect of this performance style is the reduction of playing times: texts the RSC regularly performs in three and a half hours − *King Lear, Antony and Cleopatra* − Northern Broadsides turns in, with minimal cuts, under two hours forty-five minutes.[50] (Broadsides' *Dream* runs 130 minutes − very close to the 'two-hours' traffic of our stage' critics pooh-pooh as a mere figure of speech in *Romeo and Juliet*.) Hearing Shakespeare played full tilt is a revelation, like hearing Mozart at tempo after a lifetime listening to him performed half speed. At speed, the line for line trade-offs between hunchback Richard and the women he intends sequentially to seduce are not Lyly-esque flourishes but lightning jabs between heavy-weight sluggers; Titania's 'forgeries of jealousy' speech leaps for Oberon's jugular; Ford's incredulous stuttering − '"cuckold", "wittol"!' − stampedes into comically hysterical dementia: 'cuckold, cuckold, cuckold!'; and *King Lear* crashes over the audience as relentlessly, as unpityingly as breakers slamming upon Dover beach, leaving the audience unsheltered, without respite to regroup emotion, simulating for them in the theatre the experience the King and his daughters suffer in the narrative.

Barrie Rutter has observed, 'We Northerners know how to have a good rammy − and so did

---

[46] Quoted in Beauman, *The Royal Shakespeare Company*, p. 268.

[47] Sarah Hemming, *Independent*, 10 June 1992.

[48] Writing about Broadsides' BBC Radio 3 recording of *Richard III* she observed, 'The accents did not distract from the lines but drew the ear towards them. And to great effect − here, for once, every line got proper metric measure. The rhythm of what was being said mattered . . . All the listener had to do was hang on to the rope of [Richard's] words and see, with him, how far he could climb' ('A Northern Richard with the accent on power', *Stage*, 8 September 1995, p. 23).

[49] *Independent on Sunday*, 15 October 1995; *Independent*, 13 December 1992; *Independent*, 20 June 1993.

[50] The performance time for *Richard III* was 2 hours 25 minutes; *King Lear*, 2 hours 25 minutes; *The Merry Wives*, 2 hours 20 minutes; *King John*, 2 hours 10 minutes; *Antony and Cleopatra*, 2 hours 45 minutes. As long ago as 1977 Peter Hall complained, 'RSC Shakespeare is getting slower and slower', writing in his diary of Donald Sinden's *King Lear*. 'Again there was this slow, over-emphatic line-breaking delivery of the text. The actors are so busy telling us the ambiguities and the resonances that there is little or no sense of form. You cannot play Shakespeare without a sense of line'. See John Goodwin, ed., *Peter Hall's Diaries* (London, 1983), p. 302.

Shakespeare'.[51] Indeed, Northern Broadsides' aggressive energies celebrate the pleasures of the verbal punch-up in Shakespeare – its ubiquity, wit, and essential theatricality, and what, rhetorically, it makes available to put emotionally at stake (Antony v. Cleopatra, Capulet v. his daughter; Beatrice v. Benedick; Helena v. Demetrius v. Lysander v. Hermia; Titania v. Oberon; Lear v. his family, court, kingdom, creation). The 'rammy', more or less hyperbolized, is the standard currency of exchange in Shakespeare's theatrical discourse. But the Northern voice also savours language – in Paul Taylor's memorable phrase, it 'makes a sensual meal of language, quite unlike the picky snacking gone in for by some of the more clipped Southern dialects'.[52] Take a line like Mistress Ford's as she plots Falstaff's comeuppance – 'entertain him with hope, till the wicked fire of lust have melted him in his own grease' (2.1.68) – or Enobarbus's, remembering purple sails, a poop of beaten gold, and 'The barge she sat in . . .' (2.2.198). Working her outraged mouth around the different vowels in 'hope', 'lust' and 'grease', Liz Estensen's feisty domestic fury on the warpath made the words, as Jeffrey Wainwright put it, 'little worlds of anticipation in themselves'.[53] It was because Dave Hill's dour veteran of too many campaigns (and too many fag ends dropped in too many pints) told the story of Cydnus in a voice like mud that his audience heard it as wonder. Producing words like 'blood', 'love', 'dote', 'body', 'hungry' from the bowels, not the throat, the Northern voice shifts the centre of gravity of the spoken text from the head, the intellectual, to the visceral, and it makes phrases – 'a lass unparallel'd'; 'Take her or leave her'; 'Mine own and not mine own'; 'Not till God make men of some other mettle than earth' – sound like current colloquialisms: indeed, audiences regularly imagine that Broadsides has modernized Shakespeare's text. The surprise, to some, is that the voice typecast for comic relief finds as true expression, relief-less, in tragedy: Lear howling for his dead daughter, Cleopatra keening for her Herculean Roman; Helena betrayed by love's optical illusions; blind Gloucester stranded on the beach, trying to make sense of man's relationship to the gods. At such moments the primitive darkness the Northern voice taps connects Shakespeare to Aeschylus.

If 'No Acting' is Broadsides's first rule, 'No Production' comes close second. This company travels on a shoestring; production costs money. Besides, 'production', like 'acting', gets in the way of the story. To begin with Rutter – more thieving magpie than upstart crow, his production budget for *Richard III* a mere £2000 – salvaged from Saltaire's derelict millrooms industrial junk for Cinderella make-overs into theatrical props. A rusted First Aid gurney became a morgue on wheels for King Henry's corpse; later, recycled, a mobile fairy bower; recycled again, a parody stand-in for Cleopatra's promiscuous bed. A pair of porter's trolleys on metal wheels, manoeuvred like dodg'ems, were thunderous war horses at Bosworth. Lengths of industrial fencing backed Richard's reign. As traitors and innocents died their redundant effects – the princes' school caps, Rivers's nouveau riche jacket – were hung on the mesh which grew into a spooky memorial rood screen: instead of subjects, lost property, empty objects. On this near-empty stage, single objects signify much: the fur coat, for example, that passed from queen to queen like a white elephant in a royal jumble sale, Elizabeth helping Anne into it, Richard later sliding it off Anne's shoulders with one hand as, with the other, he shoved her, dazed, into oblivion, then tossing her shed skin carelessly on to the throne where it draped, convenient for handing back to Elizabeth to offer the *next* queen, her daughter.

Ten years on, Northern Broadsides continues to live on its wits, carrying practically no baggage except what the actors bring on stage with them. Actors produce the scenic effects: a somersaulting fairy unrolled a diagonal strip of green carpet – the 'woods near Athens'; Puck held out a bunch of silk – the purple flower which magically separated as Oberon grasped it; her women,

[51] *The Glasgow Herald*, 19 December 1992.
[52] *Independent*, 10 December 1992.
[53] Jeffrey Wainwright, *Independent*, 26 June 1993.

answering Cleopatra's 'immortal longings', set her inside a corona of candlelight then gently clasped a jewelled necklace around her throat – the 'asp'; child-changed Lear in a sweat-stained singlet bowled an industrial-sized cotton reel along Dover sands, whipping it like a top; Fenton and Anne, new-married, entered through a white cloud, in front of them an attendant, fanning handfuls of confetti into a swirling storm; Dogberry in Napoleon's hat and Verges as General Montgomery inspected the watch, a drill closer to line-dancing than military parade. Stunning sequences are produced minimalistically. In *Richard III*, the battle of Bosworth Field was staged as a war dance: the full company, two armies changed into boiler suits and clogs, advanced upon each other, the clatter of their wood-shod feet accelerating into a thunderous choreographed din that ended with Richard's abrupt death. One after another, the actors unlaced their clogs and threw them in a heap, silence not triumph the herald of peace. In *Antony and Cleopatra*, the opposing armies – Rome in blue, Egypt in orange – squared up for Actium, facing front, behind oil drums. The battle was all sound, percussion answering percussion in deafening drumming, defectors from Antony, sorely conspicuous, crossing sides, doubling Rome's noise. The rout, too, was acoustic. Cleopatra dropped her sticks, broke rank; Antony, faltering, followed. The Egyptian drums, thrown off beat, tried to recover rhythm, then fell silent. In *King John*, kettle drums mounted on trolleys stood in for the armies, sound again simulating battle while the two great drums, wheeled in formation, took on, uncannily, the juddering movements of galloping horses.

Like props, Broadsides' music is portable, produced by actors from inside the narrative where it is never merely decorative, but like language, works to play.[54] Lear's Fool performed his gags as patter songs to a (nostalgic? or futuristic? – this Fool was both pre- and post-Merlin) George Formby ukulele; the revellers on Pompey's galley backed 'Plumpy Bacchus' with a skiffle band; 'Sigh No More, Ladies' was a barbershop quartet and Beatrice played jazz saxophone at her cousin's (second) wedding. Falstaff, surprised at Herne's oak in his

get-up as the horned Hunter – the 'antlers', bicycle handlebars, complete with bell, fixed to an upside down colander on his head – by a crew of unisex goblins in white tutus and lurex leggings, quailed as they circled him, prancing to the prim refrain, 'Trip, trip, fairies!', then launching into a hissing, punching, pinching song of truly menacing ferocity (5.4). In *Romeo and Juliet*, the town oom-pah band playing Dixieland was heard long before it arrived, Paris in front, at Capulet's door, to discover them weeping and Juliet dead. Perhaps most enchanting was the music the company produced for *A Midsummer Night's Dream*, a musical score for impromptu instruments, voices in close harmony, and the syncopated noise of clogs on cobbles. This *Dream* was the mechanicals' very North of England vision, and it dignified both their work and working-class voices. It opened with the workers sitting at their benches, loom and tailor's dummy. They picked up the tools of their trade – saw, hammer, shuttle, spools – and from banging and rasping produced a kind of industrial music of the spheres. Doubling as Titania's hairy-arsed attendants, working-class fairies-with-attitude, they made her lullaby the choral equivalent of insect repellent. When the fairy world was reconciled, their king and queen 'rock[ed] the ground' – literally, for once – with a clog dance that acoustically celebrated the work-a-day world. Finally, after Puck's epithalamium – a little aria, in Andy Cryer's rendition – the fairies crowded back on stage, singing the newlyweds into their futures with close harmony doo-wop – accompanied on kazoos.

Clearly, the Bard Northern Broadsides works with they can treat cheekily (John Branwell's Bottom sang 'The ousel cock' to the tune of 'Ilkley Moor Ba'tat'). Or even with vulgar irreverence. *Antony and Cleopatra* opened with a front-of-cloth scene, a sleazy musical hall burlesque played to a single spectator, dead-eyed Octavius, who came on in a business suit, collar and tie, standing ramrod straight, his back to the audience, throughout

---

54 The company's music director and composer is Conrad Nelson who, in this company, is also, of course, an actor.

21 Falstaff as Herne the Hunter intent on seduction caught between Mistress Page and Mistress Ford in *The Merry Wives*. The Viaduct Theatre 2001 (l to r: Maggie Ollerenshaw, Barrie Rutter, Joanna Swain).

what was, evidently, his daily 'fix' of black comedy, watching the lovers' story played out in Roman travesty, as if anticipating and fulfilling Cleopatra's premonition: 'The quick comedians / Extemporally will stage us . . . / Some squeaking Cleopatra [will] boy my greatness . . .' (5.2.212–16). After a circus drum roll and a clash of cymbals, on bounded a down-at-heels cabaret artiste in a bowler hat and string vest with salacious patter: 'Nay, but this dotage of our general's . . .' 'Look where they come', he invited lubriciously (1.1.1–10). To hysterical giggles, in careened a rickety trolley, a banner over it proclaiming 'Egypta Capta'. On it reclined a raddled transvestite Cleopatra in suspender belt and panties, a high camp drama queen shrilling, 'If it be love . . .' (1.1.14). When Antony's parody Hercules in peplum and fake chest fur announced, 'Here is my space', he dived for her

crotch, and the shabby spectacle was wheeled out, Cleopatra shrieking laughter, just as, upstage, the real Cleopatra entered, teasing in a voice as dark as molasses, 'If it be love . . .' As prolepsis, this outrageous parody placed Octavius politically: 'Egypta Capta' was his object of desire, and to achieve it he would prepare himself mentally, before militarily moving one cohort eastward, by possessing, colonizing, and subjugating Eastern mythography. It also placed him privately: publicly austere, he was a closet decadent. But it did more: framing the inimitable lovers, the 'illimitable livers' – Plutarch's phrase – with scepticism, Northern Broadsides showed how dangerously close their magnificence, their extravagance was to buffoonery.

Unafraid to explore the ridiculous in Shakespeare ('I'm dying, Egypt, dying' was a laugh line: Ishia Bennison's Cleopatra wouldn't shut up long

22   Prince Arthur trapped between the armies of France and England in *King John*. The Viaduct Theatre 2001 (l to r: Andrew Vincent, Adam Sunderland, Conrad Nelson).

enough to let Antony speak his death speech; but it was also poignant: maybe if she kept talking he *couldn't* die) Northern Broadsides earns its precious moments of sentiment. In the *Dream,* the newly-wed lovers, back-chatting the tradesmen's performance, fell into subdued silence, so heartstricken by Pyramus's dying lament for his lost Thisbe that they gathered up Bottom in their arms and laid him beside Flute. In *King John*, hardened Hubert broke as young Arthur pleaded for his eyes then wept, his whole body shaking, over the boy's mangled body. In *Much Ado*, Claudio lifted the veil – and found Hero alive.

Recently, Peter Holland has urged spectators of Shakespeare to 'see better'.[55] 'Seeing better' is the challenge Northern Broadsides offers. Working as the kind of actor-based permanent ensemble that was Peter Hall's dream for the RSC in the

1960s (and that Adrian Noble officially abandoned in 2001), the company approximates some aspects of early modern performance, putting spectators back in touch with something like 'original' ways of seeing. The budget affords just sixteen actors, like Shakespeare's company. This means that over the ten years, actors touring with the company, leaving and returning, have developed the kind of ensemble relationships that must have characterized the Chamberlain's Men and that today define Olympic class relay teams or high-wire circus performers who know each other's limits and how to stretch them, trust each other on the trapeze catch, and time the baton handover exactly. In this

---

[55] 'Inaugural Address: Seeing Better' (Birmingham, 26 October 1999).

23 'Howl, howl, howl': Lear carries Cordelia into a family reunion of dead daughters in *King Lear*. Salts Mill 1999 (l to r: Barrie Rutter holding Rachel Jane Allen, Craig Cheetham, Deborah McAndrew, Clare Calbraith. Behind: Andy Wear, Jason Furnival, Tom Kennedy, Lawrence Evans, Kjeld Clark).

company, whoever directs performs – like Peter Quince. Actors must carry the set – as Snout, playing Wall, discovers. And make the music – like Feste, travelling with his drum and tabor. Actors must fill the space, with voice, text, and precious little else – impromptu spaces offering not just challenges to performance but real theatrical gains. At Manor Mill in Oldham, Theseus's first entrance was a fifty-metre sprint, hot foot on Hippolyta's tail; at Saltaire, which houses the longest – 150 metres – millroom in Europe, it took Lear a seeming lifetime to cover the distance, carrying Cordelia's corpse. In this company, as in Shakespeare's, everybody doubles – principals in bit parts that allow them to flex different theatre muscles, second-stringers in a sequence of roles that leave them rarely off stage. Thus, the patterns Shakespeare is always writing with actors' bodies across his

performance texts are available to be seen by spectators raised on reading Shakespeare-the-poet, not play-wright. For this company, 'seeing better' means putting spectators close to actors, letting them focus on bodies doing text, seeing the *work* of play, and its detail. Deborah McAndrew's Octavia, transfixed by her brother's solicitous sarcasm, 'You are come / A market maid to Rome', stood stock still; she heard his recriminations – 'He hath given his empire / Up to a whore' – not as political analysis but the end of her marriage, tears sliding silently down her expressionless face (*Antony and Cleopatra* 3.6.50–1, 66–7). Francis Lee's Snug, a sweetly stupid little joiner who asked for 'the lion's part written' because he was 'slow of study' and was greatly relieved by Quince's puzzled assurance that he could do it 'extempore, for it is nothing but roaring', listened, knees pressing tighter and tighter, shoulders hunching, eyes widening in silent terror, as Bottom at the first rehearsal fantasized speech after speech for the hapless Lion, turned from roaring into a major speaking role.

Above all, for Northern Broadsides seeing better means hearing better – or if not better, then *different* – language brought into the kind of close-up that permits spectators to see past the Shakespeare myth, the official Bard, the mystified poet of restricted class access, to a playwright who is so much one of [uz] – *whoever [uz] is* – that he is not even recognized as the Bardbiz icon. As a mother in Halifax wrote on her Customer Questionnaire, what she liked best about Northern Broadsides' *Much Ado About Nothing* in the Viaduct at Dean Clough was watching 'my daughter (aged eleven) enjoy Shakespeare' in her 'own language', not in 'a "Southern" version'. Or as a local 'yoof' in Wandsworth, aged about fifteen, was overheard saying to his girlfriend as they left a London performance of Broadsides' *Dream*, 'That's a lot better than all that old Shakespeare rubbish, in'it?'[56]

---

[56] *Wandsworth Borough News*, July 1995.

SHAKESPEARE PERFORMANCES IN ENGLAND, 2002

MICHAEL DOBSON

The year 2002 has been busy and eventful for the Shakespearian theatre in England, with important and much-publicized productions in each of the Folio's generic categories. Conveniently for a year in which *Shakespeare Survey* has focused on Shakespearian comedy, the overwhelming majority of these have been of comedies. Early in the year Mark Rylance's Globe company performed *Twelfth Night* in the Hall at Middle Temple, in honour of the 400th anniversary of John Manningham's seeing the same play there in 1602. Lucy Bailey's joyous *A Midsummer Night's Dream* played at the Royal Exchange in Manchester in the spring, while Greg Doran's stylish but unsurprising *Much Ado About Nothing* was opening at the Royal Shakespeare Theatre. In the early summer another detachment of the RSC performed a season of three late romances at the Roundhouse in London, including an appealing *Pericles* directed by Adrian Noble; and the autumn saw Sam Mendes's valedictory *Twelfth Night* and Michael Grandage's magisterial *The Tempest* sell out the Donmar in London and the Crucible in Sheffield respectively.

So there has been plenty to laugh at all around the country, but in Stratford there has been plenty, too, over which one sometimes did not know whether to laugh or cry. It is telling that only one of the shows that I have just cited, and intellectually the least stimulating at that, began life at the Royal Shakespeare Theatre: after the alarums and excursions of 2001, with its momentous announcement of Project Fleet, this has been a thoroughly uncertain year for the Royal Shakespeare Company. Although the phrase from the company's official blurb which quietly vanished from its programmes last year – 'Despite continual change, the RSC today is still at heart an ensemble company' – has now been just as quietly reinstated, the scrapping of the repertory system in fact went ahead as threatened, so that in 2002 the Royal Shakespeare Theatre played host to a series of disparate productions rather than to an array of work produced on the premises by a single ensemble. Meanwhile the Barbican has been forsaken, and the Other Place has been dark for most of the year, used only by the company's new designated apprentice division, the RSC Academy, in the autumn (with whose first production, a *King Lear* directed by Declan Donnellan, I shall be concluding). However, the stated aim of Fleet's drastic switch to stand-alone short-run productions – to make it easier for the company to attract internationally famous leading actors – has so far not been achieved. Michael Attenboroughs' production of *Antony and Cleopatra*, for example (produced back-to-back with Doran's *Much Ado About Nothing* by a hand-picked team which took both shows to the gilded Haymarket in the late summer), so far from recruiting a Meryl Streep or a Catherine Deneuve from outside the usual RSC pool to play Cleopatra, was built around Sinead Cusack, who as not just an RSC Associate Artist but one of the Board of Governors surely has to count as the insider's insider. Furthermore, instead of effortlessly signing up Harrison Ford or Gerard Depardieu or whoever to play opposite her for the duration of the run, the company had no end of trouble finding an Antony at all, winding up with the little-known Stuart Wilson, who hadn't otherwise acted on stage in more than a decade. Alongside this show, the *Much Ado* starred another Associate Artist, Harriet Walter, still best-known for the work she has done within the RSC ensemble system over the last twenty years; and two out of the three leads in the Roundhouse season of late romances were, similarly, taken by RSC repertory veterans – Prospero by Malcolm Storry, Pericles by Ray Fearon. The other, Leontes in *The Winter's Tale*, was originally played by Douglas Hodge, an ex-National Theatre actor known outside this country almost exclusively to people who have seen the BBC's adaptations of *Middlemarch* and *The Way We Live Now* on cable, and even he only accepted the role on condition that someone else would take it over when the show transferred to Stratford. With the exception of Anthony Sher, who played in the ensemble company which Greg Doran assembled to perform a small season of Elizabethan and Jacobean plays at the Swan in the summer, the cross-media celebrities were in 2002 performing Shakespeare everywhere but at the RSC: Kenneth Branagh playing Richard III and Derek Jacobi Prospero to packed houses at the Crucible in Sheffield; Emily Watson and Simon Russell Beale adorning *Twelfth Night* at the Donmar; Sean Bean and Samantha Bond selling out the Albery as the Macbeths. On the whole, the RSC's future is if anything less clear now than it was at this time last year. Adrian Noble's resignation as Artistic Director in April, without either making Fleet work or cancelling it, resolved nothing, and it became clear during the selection process for his successor that staying substantially loyal to his so far thoroughly unpopular and unsuccessful set of policies was to be a condition of the appointment. (The few candidates from outside the company's existing hierarchy – notably Michael Pennington, and the attractive-looking team of Simon Russell Beale and John Caird – withdrew their applications accordingly). Michael Boyd got the job, in the event, but at the time of going to press he had clarified little, leaving the Royal Shakespeare Theatre itself under a sort of suspended death sentence, and the company's ability to transfer shows to London in some jeopardy. (A London run for Doran's non-Shakespearian mini-season was eventually negoti-

ated with the Gielgud only at the eleventh hour). Boyd has, however, announced that there will again be a repertory season in Stratford in 2003, quaintly called 'The Summer Festival Season' as per recent practice, so however disoriented the RSC may be next year it should at least be slightly more obvious where to find it.

COMEDIES

Let me turn, however, from the depressing arena of theatrical politics – to leave the role of Mr Dangle, perhaps, and adopt the more familiar one of Mr Sneer – to the far pleasanter task of describing the year's major productions of Shakespearian comedy. These began one cold week in February with the Globe company's *Twelfth Night* at Middle Temple, directed by Timothy Carroll, a show which was revived in the summer at the Globe itself.

This was a beguiling and expensive evening, shrewdly pitched to the wealthier segment of the Globe's regular clientele, as if the reconstructed Globe were temporarily borrowing a quasi-Blackfriars. The hall proper was laid out with a long rectangular acting area down its centre and most of the audience on chairs in tiered rows along three sides of it: these seats cost £50 and upwards each, and even the small number of standing places available in the gallery at the lower end of the hall were priced at £15 a head, three times as much as a place in the Globe's yard in the summer. For these higher admission prices one did get a certain amount of extra pre-show Elizabethan hospitality: each spectator was allowed several welcome helpings of mulled wine and given a sort of Elizabethan airline meal in a cardboard box (mainly a manchet and some spiced dried fruit), and in an antechamber a nine-piece broken consort performed most of the usual sixteenth-century hit parade – 'Packington's Pound', 'The Earl of Essex's Galliard' and such; I wouldn't swear that they didn't throw in 'Greensleeves' for good measure. (This consort played for the show itself from the gallery, accompanying in particular a rather funereal song-and-dance, 'Hey Robin, jolly Robin', transferred from 4.2.73 to be performed by the whole company at

24   *Twelfth Night*, directed by Timothy Carroll for Shakespeare's Globe, at Middle Temple Hall, February 2002. Mark Rylance as Olivia, receiving Eddie Redmayne as Viola.

the start of the second half). We were allowed, furthermore, to watch the actors getting made-up and laced and sewn into their Elizabethan costumes, filing into the hall via their communal dressing room. There was an unusual bonus at the end of the evening, too, when each spectator was given a handsome envelope on the way out containing a thick, beautifully printed card soliciting donations of £1,000 and above towards the completion of the Globe's own projected indoor theatre back in Southwark.

Given the return to the play's first recorded venue and all the authenticity-hungry Elizabethan trimmings, one might have expected the production itself to try harder to conform as far as possible to what we know of the theatrical conventions of 1602, but Rylance's programme note admitted

that his company would be using 'some original playing practices and some modern', and this was certainly the case. It seems very unlikely, for one thing, that theatrical performances in the halls of the Inns weren't a good deal more end-on than the almost traverse arrangement adopted on this occasion, with much smaller stages: but what was most striking about this production was the composition of its company. This was all-male, and as such quite unlike the sort of company one would normally expect to see performing *Twelfth Night* in 2002; however, it was also quite unlike the sort of all-male company that one would have expected to see performing *Twelfth Night* in 1602, since as well as being racially mixed (apparently sexual discrimination can be permitted in the name of historical authenticity, but not racial), it cast a younger actor for only one of the play's three female roles, Viola (and not that much younger, either; a Cambridge undergraduate, Eddie Redmayne). As Maria, Paul Chahidi was more like a nineteenth-century pantomime Dame than either an Elizabethan or a modern Maria, and as Olivia Mark Rylance was – well, was Mark Rylance, further developing the special, anachronistic, and in its own way rather charming species of drag act which he tried out as Cleopatra at the Globe in 1997. In common with actor-managers of every period, Rylance had once again put together a company in which no other performer was half as interesting as he is, and the result was a *Twelfth Night* dominated, unusually, neither by the shipwrecked heroine nor by the steward, a production which instead revolved around the sombrely dressed mistress of Illyria's second household. With an ensemble who were for the most part inconspicuously competent, in a solid, slightly amateur-dramatic manner, the *mise-en-scène* for this show carried an unusual amount of weight: the melancholy music, the dark wood panelling of the hall itself, the large solid table that dominated the scenes at Olivia's house, and above all the costumes. Oliver Cotton's Malvolio was a senior, tall, heavy figure in long black robes – but for his steward's chain, just like a picture of Lord Burleigh – who in 1.3 brought Olivia a large pile of what might have been state papers to look over and sign as she sat solemnly at the head of the table; all his inferiors in the household were also in black, in conformity with their mistress's grief, and there was a strong sense that this was the normal state of affairs in Illyria, here a rather grave country throughout rather than a fantastical realm in which one particular countess was temporarily wearing a black veil as an affectation. His face made-up almost pure white, and wearing a large farthingale under which he took artificially tiny and rapid steps so as to arrive on the stage like a waxwork travelling on invisible wheels, Rylance as Olivia looked something like a well-built Tudor geisha girl and something like the portrait of Elizabeth I visible at the far end of the hall, but he was more dignified than either, and more pained, reproving Malvolio's uncharity towards Feste with a sort of sad absent

generosity (as if Feste's joke about not mourning that her brother was in Heaven hadn't amused Olivia in the present but had just succeeded in awakening some poignant memory of past laughter now gone forever). The whole play became principally the story of how this orderly, dutiful world was comprehensively disrupted by the incursion of Viola and Sebastian, neither of whom gave very vibrant or engaging performances, but who achieved their considerable impact by wearing the same comparatively light-hearted-looking clothes, based on that famous Hilliard miniature of the youth in the hat with the cape on one shoulder. Even Redmayne's Viola did little to upstage this outfit (quietly and sorrowfully effeminate throughout), and so one was left with a rather sinister sense of two eerily identical and only partly inhabited white silk outfits invading the decorous hall and deluding poor Olivia into betraying herself. In the final scene the histrionics of Terence Maynard's Othello-like Orsino, the reunion of the parted siblings and the return of Malvolio very much took second place to Rylance's wonderful rendition of Olivia's sheer mortification at the public exposure of her misguided pursuit of Cesario and its sequels: undoubtedly the best and most painfully funny single moment of the production came when an insensitively jubilant Sebastian, his tactless delight at the situation clearly not shared by his new wife, blurted out 'So comes it, lady, you have been mistook' (5.1.257), to be answered only by a half-wincing little shake of the head, eyes cast down, and a little waving-away gesture of one hand. If one *is* to deny the role of Olivia either to an actress or to a boy, Rylance is certainly the actor to cast, able to turn in a remarkable performance that achieves its comedy by being so overwhelmingly vulnerable that one is too embarrassed not to laugh: but it would be nice to see him for once taking on some other actors capable both of giving him a run for his money and of keeping the scenes in which he doesn't appear rather more alive than they were here.

At the other end of the year, Sam Mendes's Donmar Warehouse production of the same play had by contrast an almost absurdly strong company throughout, and was emphatically a director's

25 *Twelfth Night*, directed by Sam Mendes, Donmar Warehouse. Mark Strong as Orsino, Emily Watson as Viola.

ensemble piece rather than a showcase for a single star. The design, executed by Anthony Ward, revolved around a conceit apparently borrowed from the proxy wooing scenes in Michael Boyd's *Henry VI* sequence for the RSC the previous year: apart from candles and small lamps suspended from ropes above the actors' heads, the Donmar's tiny acting area was usually dominated by a single large gilded empty picture-frame, behind which absent members of the cast being imagined or described could pose, motionless, sometimes for whole scenes at a time. To cite only a few instances, the performance opened with Mark Strong's appealingly Byronic Orsino, seated on a single chair directly in front of this frame, contemplating what appeared to be a three-dimensional portrait of the veiled Olivia; implausibly fierce incarnations of Viola and

Aguecheek respectively appeared while Sir Toby was exaggerating the valour of each to the other in 3.4, and Sebastian appeared like a mirror-image of his twin when Antonio rebuked Cesario for denying his acquaintance after the ensuing duel (3.4.350-62); and, in the sole instance of a character being made visible in this way despite being largely forgotten by those onstage, Malvolio could be seen beyond the frame throughout most of his imprisonment. This may sound tricksy and intrusive, but it worked remarkably well, both to underline the extent to which this play's characters are trapped in their own and one another's fantasies, and simply to articulate its structure, since with this convention in place many scenes turned out, conveniently, to begin as the character last brooded over stepped forward out of the frame and into action.

In keeping with a familiar sense of this play as melancholy and autumnal, Mendes directed *Twelfth Night* in tandem with Chekhov's *Uncle Vanya*, with certain definite consequences. One was a cast which in some areas seemed slightly old for *Twelfth Night*: in particular David Bradley, who in *Vanya* played the insufferable retired academic Serebryakov to perfection, had to make Sir Andrew Aguecheek resemble one of those elderly suitors who bore their way through the comedies of Molière, supposedly funny just for wanting to dance with the ingenue despite their rheumatism, and this rather commonplace reading wasted many of Aguecheek's best lines. Casting an older actor as Feste has in recent times grown more common; Anthony O'Donnell here managed to be a definitely sour middle-aged entertainer without forgetting that part of his job was to make people smile, though his singing of George Stiles's excellent settings of the lyrics (particularly 'O mistress mine', here permitted far more melody than has been customary in Stratford for years) was affectingly melancholy. The main effect of the twinning with *Vanya*, though, was a cast as alive to the social nuances of the Olivia household as they had learned to be to that of the Voynitskys. In inter-war costumes faintly reminiscent of *Mapp and Lucia* (again, a highly conventional choice for this play nowadays), these people, too, belonged to a social order on the wane. Paul Jesson's pepper-and-salt Sir Toby could in moments of crisis fall back on the dignity of an ex-Army man, albeit a disgraced one, stiffening his backbone for 'Art any more than a steward?' (2.3.109) as if remembering how to carpet an NCO from Boer War days; Selina Cadell's Maria, first seen artfully arranging a vase of expensive lilies to keep her mistress's mourning as modish as possible, modulated perfectly between a formidable gentility above stairs and a vengeful giggliness below; and Luke Jardine made Fabian work splendidly as the archetypal insolent young footman in livery.

Simon Russell Beale, meanwhile, was simply the best and most closely observed Malvolio I have ever seen, at once the funniest and the most heartbreak-

26 *Twelfth Night*, directed by Sam Mendes, Donmar Warehouse. 'And so the whirligig of time brings in his revenges': Anthony O'Donnell as Feste, Simon Russell Beale as Malvolio.

ing: the awards he garnered for this performance and his Vanya are almost enough to restore one's faith in prize juries. He managed to combine prissiness, profound earnestness and an underlying sense of insecurity, to a whole range of effects, all of them beautifully highlighted by a visibly cherished Hercule Poirot moustache and an Edward VII beard which struggled in vain to confer an air of distinction on his dumpy chin. He had a specially unctuous, slow-spoken, would-be suave tone of voice in which to show off his judiciousness to a bored Olivia in 1.5, which was abruptly replaced on receipt of the command 'Call in my gentlewoman' (1.5.157) by the manner he reserved for his inferiors. The first word of his 'Gentlewoman, my lady calls' (1.5.158) became a deafeningly imperious, harsh, petulant, contemptuous squawk; on the comma he looked affectedly at his watch, tut-tutting until Maria arrived, and then 'my lady calls' was performed for Olivia's benefit as a condescending and undeserved reproof. The sources not only of Maria's exasperation with the steward but of her sense that he was 'a time-pleaser, an affectioned ass' (2.3.141) were entirely clear from this single tiny encounter: this Malvolio, it transpired when he came downstairs in tightly tied dressing gown and pyjamas to rebuke the revellers in 2.3, even had enough anxious self-regard to sleep in a hairnet, his sense of his own identity apparently depending, in isolation from anyone he could regard as a social equal, on a preening solitary personal vanity. The full ghastly intimate horror of Maria's ensuing vengeance was enhanced by a bold and highly effective change of location for the letter scene, 2.5: instead of lurking behind a potted shrub in an imagined garden, Sir Toby, Sir Andrew and Fabian were covertly ushered by Maria into what was clearly Malvolio's private room in the servants' quarters (a narrow single bed was placed stage left beside the single chair), where 'the box-tree' had dwindled into a screen ornamented with a horticultural design (stage right). As the three trespassing conspirators looked on from behind the screen (and as the veiled Olivia once more appeared as image in the gilded frame, stage centre), Malvolio returned to his room for a short interlude from his duties, the whole audience transfixed with a kind of delighted horror at this artfully intensified violation of his privacy. In 2002, this scene of transgressive voyeurism has suddenly become reminiscent of the agonies of reality TV, and Russell Beale rose to the occasion with a magnificent fussy naturalism: he carefully removed his jacket and meticulously hung it over the back of the chair to avoid creases, and then sniffed each armpit of his shirt to check their freshness before lying on his back on the little bed to console himself with his pathetic daydream of being Count Malvolio. He had a small black book to read – perhaps a Bible – but it turned out that this prop was of less use to him as a source of wisdom than as a repository for the flimsy evidence with which he shored up his sustaining erotic fantasy of upward mobility: on 'There is example for't: the Lady of the Strachey married the yeoman of the wardrobe' (2.5.37–8) he at once furtively and triumphantly produced a treasured press cutting from between its pages and held it up towards the audience, nodding wide-eyed as if demanding our reassuring assent. As he read the forged letter, he came to occupy exactly the position before Olivia's framed image earlier adopted by Orsino, and at the climax of his joyous faith in its contents – 'every reason excites to this, that my lady loves me' (2.5.160) – she lingeringly removed her veil before his rapt gaze, just as she had earlier removed it in person for Cesario. After his departure, Sir Toby's already half-appalled 'Why, thou hast put him in such a dream that when the image of it leaves him, he must run mad' (2.5.186–8) seemed only a literal statement of the case. Malvolio's subsequent cross-gartering was the funnier for being invisible beneath his sober suit (save for its effect on his gait), indicated on the relevant lines by smiling, eminently misunderstandable gestures, and his confinement – seated on the same wooden chair from his little room, but in a straitjacket – seemed crueller than ever. In the final scene, his suddenly immobile face, as the deception was explained to him, seemed at once to age and, beard and moustache already ruined, to empty of all its characteristic expression: everything that had earlier supported Malvolio's precariously maintained sense of himself had been taken away, and the voice that

27 *Twelfth Night*, directed by Sam Mendes, Donmar Warehouse. 'To one of your discerning, enough is shown': Helen McCrory as Olivia.

spoke the line 'I'll be revenged on the whole pack of you' as he stalked hastily off in shame and defiance, though it retained something of the harshness earlier directed at Maria, was quite unlike that of the early acts' oily upper servant. The underlying pain and aggression were no longer filtered through deference and self-consciousness, and they sounded altogether more frightening.

It is a great tribute to this production that Russell Beale's performance never looked like overbalancing it, largely because Emily Watson, Mark Strong and Helen McCrory, as Viola, Orsino and Olivia, though more conventional, were just as good. The arrival of the pony-tail in the 1980s as an item of male coiffure compatible with the wearing of a business suit turns out to have done this play a favour: with most of the men in the cast, especially around Orsino, wearing slightly gangsterish three-piece pinstripes with their shirt collars undone, Watson's Viola could, as Cesario, simply rely on her waistcoat to obscure her bustline, and could, like her brother, just tie back her hair instead of having it cropped. In this production's world it was the suit that spoke of masculinity: otherwise Watson was unusually feminine as Cesario – it wasn't altogether surprising that Feste saw through her disguise while singing the last line of 'Come away, come away, death' in 2.4 – but her eyes always have such a twinkling expression, even in repose, that it was very easy to see how Olivia might misread her unwilling but intrigued performance as Orsino's ambassador in 1.5 as a series of sly come-ons. This early admission of the penetrability of Viola's disguise helped alter the impact of one apparently well-nigh mandatory cliché of recent *Twelfth Nights* to which this production succumbed, namely the customary interpolated kiss between Orsino and the still-disguised Viola, which in most productions is followed by a standard 'o my goodness, I've just kissed a boy!' look on Orsino's face for the sake of a cheap laugh. The text won't obviously support this piece of business anywhere, but it has to be admitted that Mendes placed and used it well, and that Watson and Strong got a good deal more mileage from it than just a facile giggle. Here the kiss took place just after Viola's 'and yet I know not' at 2.4.121, so that the combination of 'I am all the daughters of my father's house . . .' with the subsequent kiss could be read as Viola's deliberate if tentative confession of her real sex. Her ensuing 'Sir, shall I to this lady?' could have been taken by Orsino either as an embarrassed changing of the subject, or as a direct challenge to him as to whether, his relations with his favourite servant having started to take this turn, he still wished to court Olivia: discomfited, Orsino for the moment instinctively clung to what he already knew, replying 'Ay, that's the theme' as if grateful to be prompted back into the usual script.

It was easy to see, too, why the pursuit of this Olivia might be difficult to give up all at once. Helen McCrory was a deliciously kittenish mourner, in her own way just as self-regarding

as Malvolio, her Louise Brooks bob just as impeccably maintained as her steward's beard and moustache. It was the role's potential for conscious self-indulgence to which McCrory's performance responded best (she was already congratulating herself on anticipated pleasures even as she watched herself falling for the just-departed Cesario, reserving a quietly wicked little smile for 'Well, let it be', 1.5.288), though she fell far deeper than she at first anticipated, finding her own confident sophistication inadequate to the situation in which she found herself. For her second encounter with Cesario, 3.1, though still wearing her black mourning overcoat, she had changed into an expensively diaphanous black lace dress underneath, less evening wear than lingerie, so that, when she seductively slipped off the coat, the line 'To one of your discerning, enough is shown' (3.1.119-20) became something of an understatement, as well as comically inappropriate in its attempt to flatter Cesario's presumed male sexual connoisseurship. Olivia was both dismayed and abashed to find that Cesario seemed to find this outfit embarrassing as well as ineffectual, and by the time of their next meeting she was remarking that 'youth is bought more oft than begged or borrowed' (3.4.3) not only as if drawing on past casual experience but with a sudden wistful regret that this cynically unromantic state of affairs should be the case. It is true, alas, that McCrory threw a good deal of this interesting reading of Olivia as a covertly sensual worldling converted by unrequited desire away by falling back on what has become another conventional cheap laugh in 5.1, when Cesario and Sebastian first appear together, where in defiance of all psychological plausibility she spoke the line 'Most wonderful!' (5.1.223) as if merely in salacious delight at having apparently married a self-cloning prodigy able to service her either in a threesome or in shifts: but this was still an expert piece of work, which, placed opposite Watson's simple and appealing goodness as Viola, made the scenes between the two women both sexy and richly comic across a wide emotional range. This was in many respects a deeply conventional *Twelfth Night* for its time, a studio production played for psychological and social depth until if anything it risked stifling under the weight of its own nuances, but it was a thoroughly satisfying one nonetheless. Mendes couldn't have left the Donmar on a higher note: he'll be a hard act even for Michael Grandage, of whom more later, to follow.

The other current favourite for revival among the comedies, *A Midsummer Night's Dream*, had more mixed fortunes in 2002. Richard Jones directed a production for the RSC in the spring, in the Royal Shakespeare Theatre, which rates as the least funny and least charming I can remember, though since the show was clearly more interested in the cleverness of its own sets than in being either I don't suppose that either Jones or his designer, Giles Cadle, would regard this as a criticism. There was a post-Brook white box; for some scenes there were abstractly painted shutters through which actors were visible via a round central aperture; the mechanicals first met on a train; in the wood the lovers stripped, for no obvious reason, to spotless white underwear, and Puck and Oberon feigned to remove their eyes while enchanting them, and large artificial bees appeared in increasing numbers on the walls of the box; some poor devil was on stage dressed as a tree throughout the second half – this play may be pretty much actor-proof, but it turns out that a really determined director, given his head, can still make it surprisingly tedious if he really puts his mind to it. Mike Alfreds's production at the Globe in the summer was funnier, but shrilly and monotonously so, as only Globe productions can be: as if parodying his silk-pyjamas *Cymbeline* in the previous season, Alfreds had all the cast in modern nightwear throughout (they arrived on stage before the start of 1.1 as if putting themselves to bed in a collective public dormitory, and then woke one by one to join the action of the first scene), and Alfreds had employed much puerile ingenuity in restricting them to the use of props associated, however tenuously, with bedtime. Bottom's ass-ears were slippers; Lysander and Demetrius duelled with the antennae of small transistor radios; Moonshine's bush was a lavatory brush; and so on. More damagingly, the mechanicals were encouraged to paraphrase their lines: John Ramm's Bottom, for example, imagining himself

as Lion, characteristically reassured his fellows not with the customary 'I will aggravate my voice so that I will roar you as gently as any sucking dove' but with a rewrite which he himself presumably found more satisfactorily hilarious, 'I will constipate my voice so that I will roar you as gently as any turtle pigeon'. As is usual with performances of comedies at the Globe, this show received almost continuous strenuous laughter, but nothing else: it certainly proved that it is quite possible to direct all of *A Midsummer Night's Dream* at the mentality of a twelve-year-old boy, but it still seems a bit of a waste to do so.

Lucy Bailey's production for the Royal Exchange in Manchester in the Spring, though often just as vulgar, was gloriously and intelligently so throughout, a wholehearted and brilliantly successful exercise in reimagining the play in the terms of contemporary Mancunian life and contemporary mass art. Rae Smith's set was neither a post-modern empty space nor a would-be Elizabethan one, but a mimetic representation of a present-day disused stretch of road, still boasting a single streetlight, on the edge of scrubby woodland. Here, beside an abandoned car, in the disreputable hinterland between city and country, Bailey's cast were free to pick up, play with and discard the miscellaneous debris of popular culture. In an interpolated sequence, as if before the opening credits, Paul McEwan's Oberon vanquished Hilary Maclean's leather-catsuited Titania at the culmination of a pastiche 007 car-chase around the back of the Exchange's circular auditorium; in another nod to post-war pop culture as the first scene developed, Egeus was clearly an ex-Teddy Boy, favouring the soberly drape-suited Demetrius over the shoulder-length-haired Lysander's 1970s would-be cool; later Fenella Woolgar's Helena stomped sullenly onto the stage in purple platform boots and made a pretend-self-induced-vomiting gesture, fingers in mouth, when speaking of Hermia's rival charms, as if fully inhabiting the genre of teenaged girls' fiction, and she later proved to own a mobile phone which as a ringing tone played the signature tune to the Manchester soap-opera *Coronation Street*. So far all this may just sound flippantly opportunistic, but the production's more serious translation of the play's concerns into present-day terms emerged at the start of the second act, when Robin Laing's Puck first appeared – a diminutive figure in army surplus combat fatigues, his face camouflaged with mud, who before speaking a single line had adroitly levered the safety cover from the streetlamp's wiring and put it out of action with a crowbar, reclaiming this edgeland for its native darkness. Apart from his Scots accent, Laing's performance was clearly based on the elfin persona of the self-styled 'eco-warrior' Swampy, who in the 1990s protested against the building of the Newbury by-pass by living in trees in its path and against the building of a new runway at Manchester airport by sitting-in underground in a tunnel dug under its projected course. Impishly destructive in the cause of the forest, Laing's Puck perfectly shared both Swampy's underlying gravitas and his eerily innocent delight in mischief, and the conceit of identifying Shakespeare's supernatural Pan-figure with this local green outlaw made perfect intellectual and theatrical sense. Hippolyta's fairies, meanwhile, similarly on the edge of things, were spectral bag-ladies, moving dreamlike through the wood as if gathering rubbish; and the changeling boy was impersonated by the uncanny black British actor Franky Mwangi (who interestingly doubled as a Clitheroesque Philostrate), a performer who, though clearly much older, looks and sounds about nine (the one line his interpolated character was given was a barely-audible childish goodnight to his stepmother at the end of 'You spotted snakes', at 2.2.31, 'Ni-night, Tit'). The play's parallel realms provided ample scope for present-day visions of the other-worldly and the repressed, as well as for immediately intelligible kitsch.

This was an inventive, supple piece of work throughout, beautifully and wittily managing, for example, the common doubling of Theseus and Hippolyta with Oberon and Titania. In 4.1 Titania's first response to the revelation of her enchanted fling with Bottom (at 'There lies your love', 4.1.77) was an immediate recognition that the gloating Oberon must have caused it and a desire for physical vengeance on him, but, in a reprise of the cinema-cliché at-first-enforced-but-then-welcome kiss with which Theseus had subdued Hippolyta at the opening of the show, her aggression modulated into part of an erotic game, and 'Come, my lord' (4.1.98) beckoned Oberon not offstage but into the abandoned car. This opaque-windowed vehicle's ensuing vigorous rocking suggested that the fairy king and queen were energetically consummating their reconciliation, but both actors then suddenly emerged from the opposite door, having merely completed a dazzlingly quick change into their Theseus and Hippolyta suits for 'Go, one of you, find out the forester' (4.1.102). The other point at which this doubling is physically tricky was managed just as smoothly: McEwan and Maclean simply remained onstage for Puck's 'Now the hungry lion roars' at the start of 5.2, then switched on concealed fairylights all over their costumes where the entrance of Oberon and Titania is marked at 5.2.21, to be joined by Hippolyta's troupe, similarly lit-up. This concluding admission that the king and queen of the forest were identical with the swaggering Duke and his erstwhile Emma-Peel-lookalike duchess, and the participation of Puck the eco-warrior in the marital blessing of these two mellowed motorists, gave the final reconciliation (which can sometimes come across as merely a quaint Merry English cop-out) a special topical poignancy.

Elsewhere the mechanicals, like Puck and the forest, were very much seen in local terms: they entertained fantasies less of being classical lovers than of being cowboys, their scenes based on a detailed and affectionate understanding of the enthusiasm entertained by many members of Northern working-men's-clubs for country-and-western and all that goes with it. As Bottom, Tom Hodgkins was a very Lancastrian weaver who wore heavy horn-rimmed glasses (the only articles of his clothing not stolen by Puck before the hempen homespun awoke naked from his 'dream' of a liaison with Titania), which looked magnificently incongruous with the stetson he donned as Pyramus. The bergo-mask given in lieu of an epilogue was here an energetic line-dance, in which the whole cast and

28   *A Midsummer Night's Dream*, directed by Lucy Bailey, Royal Exchange, Manchester. 'Ni-night, Tit': Hilary Maclean as Titania, Franky Mwangi as the Changeling Boy.

many delighted members of the downstairs audience were more than happy to participate. All in all Bailey's *Dream* was populist Shakespeare *par excellence*, its ingenious contemporary glosses on a well-nigh uncut text profoundly faithful to its spirit, and it provided a welcome demonstration that making this play very funny for a very broad audience is not incompatible either with offering an intelligent reading of its politics or with doing justice to its wonders – the lovers' awakening in 4.1, for example, was extraordinarily moving, and I would challenge any more purist rendering of the play to elicit a more rapt audience response to 'And I have found Demetrius like a jewel,/Mine own and not mine own' (4.1.190-1) than Fenella Woolgar earned here.

The year's other revivals of non-late comedies, all of them far less striking and original, need detain us only briefly. Loveday Ingram's *The*

Merchant of Venice for the RSC, which opened at the Swan late in 2001 and toured extensively in 2002, slavishly followed the interpretative choices made by Trevor Nunn's National production a couple of years earlier (central European 1930s setting, closet gay gentleman's-club Antonio, penitent imperfectly converted Jessica, joke Spanish accent for Aragon, the lot), but though Hermione Gulliford made an interestingly serene and creamy Portia, Ian Bartholomew – to praise with a very faint damn – proved unable to give as complex or powerful a performance as Shylock as had Henry Goodman at the National. Rachel Kavanaugh's *As You Like It* in Regent's Park, adorned by woolly stuffed sheep which might have been left over from Greg Doran's last production of the play for the RSC, was remarkable only for John Hodgkinson's surprisingly well-spoken Touchstone, who insisted, despite the text's failure to encourage or make sense of any such reading, on playing the Fool as hopelessly and tragically in love with Celia throughout, marrying Audrey only on the rebound out of spite and self-loathing. (Poor Celia was even made to appear at the end of 3.3, early for her entrance at the start of 3.4, so that Touchstone's 'I will not to wedding with thee' could be directed bitterly at her instead of at Sir Oliver Martext.) Jonathan Petherbridge directed a highly respectable small-scale *Measure for Measure* for the National's education department, using only eight actors (notably Charles Abomell, an intense Angelo), in a promenade format which turned out to suit this play very well. With so much of the play revolving around courtrooms and the prison, and so many questions under consideration about the everyday experience of authority, being repeatedly shepherded around the Cottesloe by uniformed orderlies made perfect sense, though the production kept interrupting the smooth flow of ideas between scenes which this way of using the space should have favoured to ask its student audience disappointingly inane questions about which characters they liked best so far. This simplification of the play's moral issues, however, was nowhere near as drastic as that perpetrated by Phil Wilmott's adaptation *Measure for Measure Malay* at the Riverside Studios in Hammersmith, in which the Duke and Angelo were uniformly wicked British colonial administrators of the 1930s, presiding over a plot glibly part-hybridized with *The Jewel in the Crown* to supply an English Julietta impregnated by a Eurasian Claudio.

There ought to be far more to say about Greg Doran's RSC *Much Ado About Nothing*, certainly one of the most consistently assured and enjoyable productions of the year: after all, it boasted star-quality performances from its Beatrice and Benedick, Harriet Walter and Nicholas le Prevost, a fine Leonato in Gary Waldhorn, an unusually good pair of juveniles in John Hopkins and Kirsten Parker (he a convincingly callow and prickly Claudio, reminiscent of a young Mike Gwilym, she more of a minx than Hero is often allowed to be), and a terrific Don John in Stephen Campbell-Moore. But the production had nothing new to say about the play whatsoever: setting it visually in the Italy of the 1930s made for elegance and clarity but little more (simply licensing all concerned to enjoy the piece as a Merchant-Ivory exercise in poignant escapism, spared any uncomfortable contemporary resonances), and, for all the programme's extensive notes about Sicilian *omertà* and Mussolini and Mediterranean misogyny, this was a show which never looked or sounded as if it really belonged anywhere except in the West End. *Much Ado About Nothing*, certainly, is the nearest thing Shakespeare ever wrote to the perfect well-made play, and it is no mean feat to give the impression that he must have written it specifically as a vehicle in which le Prevost could do his crusty, nervy, spluttering middle-aged bachelor act opposite Walter's latter-day Katherine Hepburn, but the production as a whole remained glossily empty, much finely polished ado about nothing in particular. (There is probably already a promptbook shorthand for annotating the precise series of variations on the usual pieces of comic business employed in 2.3 and 3.1, the successive gullings of Benedick and Beatrice, in any given production – perhaps a wavy dash to indicate when a bent-double Benedick makes the mandatory implausible sprint from one bush to another so as to remain within earshot of the staged conversation, or, for this production, a smudged asterisk to indicate when Hero drenches the supposedly concealed Beatrice with a garden hose while feigning to concentrate on the shrubs, thereby explaining her subsequent cold.) The sole point at which the 1930s setting woke up any unexpected detail of the text came when Claudio agreed to accept Leonato's fictitious niece: coming from someone apparently just back from invading Abyssinia, and in the presence of an offended black Ursula (the excellent Noma Dumezeni), the line 'I'll hold my mind, were she an Ethiope' (5.4.38) seemed even more crass than usual. But there seemed little compelling overall reason for reviving this play at this moment in this décor, and the production's only conspicuous novelty seemed wholly incidental, an arrestingly eccentric Don Pedro from Clive Wood. Played as an amiable closet case who concealed his depression beneath the exterior of a well-meaning Wodehousean silly ass in pursuit of vicarious jollity,

29 *Much Ado About Nothing*, directed by Gregory Doran for the Royal Shakespeare Company. Nicholas Le Prevost as Benedick, Harriet Walter as Beatrice.

he was forever bending his knees and striking his boot with a riding crop as he barked out another forced 'Ha!' of a laugh. It was all very diverting and very impressive, but the production left one pining, however ungratefully, for some rougher edges and a bit more engagement.

To turn to the late comedies, the RSC's season of romances at the Roundhouse – *The Winter's Tale*, *The Tempest* and *Pericles* – deserves rather closer attention, as it was both more ambitious and a good deal less predictable, even if on the whole much less successful (financially as well as artistically: in London these three shows were said to be playing at only 40 percent of capacity). It was surprising enough that this company should try to use this particular venue at all: the RSC's management, as I've mentioned already, are still threatening to demolish or at least substantially rebuild the Royal Shakespeare Theatre on the grounds that it is uneconomical and overlarge and has poor acoustics, so perhaps they hired the Roundhouse for these three plays so as to be sure that their London-based away team would feel at home. The Roundhouse is an immense, perfectly round brick shed, with a conical wooden roof, at the Chalk Farm end of Camden High Street: it was built in 1846 for the repair of railway engines, and no one has really known what to do with it, except marvel at it, since the end of the great age of steam. It is still best-remembered for its glory days as a hippy venue in the 1960s, when be-ins and Rolling Stones concerts alternated with theatre events including the Nicol Williamson/Marianne Faithfull *Hamlet* in 1969. Those years of miscellaneous experimentation demonstrated above all that it takes a very big act to fill the Roundhouse, whether in terms of scale of performance or of bringing in a sufficient crowd: putting on theatre in the Roundhouse is a bit like putting on opera in Earl's Court or the Albert Hall. But whatever or whoever is using the Roundhouse, for whatever purpose, its true identity as a disused railway building is always vividly evident, since its acoustics are powerfully reminiscent of those which prevail in the average disused railway tunnel. Bands like the Stones used to solve this problem, in so far as they did, by turning up their amplifiers in the hope of drowning all the echoes, and the RSC too used their fair share of electronic assistance. It wasn't just for dramatic effect that Anastasia Hille's Hermione, in what was easily the most powerful scene of Matthew Warchus's *The Winter's Tale*, the first of the romances to open, was not only given a live microphone for her trial – placed in the very centre of the acting area – but was chained by one ankle to a ring set in the floor beside the base of its stand, so that however she circled in her attempts to meet the pacing Leontes' eyes she couldn't get too far away from it.

Nor was this the first microphone to appear in this production. The show opened in a setting which appeared to represent a night club: the round floor of the temporary scaffolding grandstand which filled most of the shed was set with candlelit tables and chairs, and before the performance began ushers moved nervously around this notional club explaining which chairs were available, for the time being, to those members of the audience who had been sufficiently impoverished, curious or prone to exhibitionism to buy cheap 'promenade' tickets and see the show from within the acting arena instead of in the raised seating all around it. Presently the house lights began to dim and a party in 1930s evening dress, resembling that worn by Mafia families on big nights out in American gangster films, arrived to occupy the most desirable tables in the club. For several minutes before a word of Shakespeare's script was spoken, these people, appropriately enough to this brick-built Big Top of an auditorium, watched a magic show: this was principally conducted at the top of a double wrought-iron staircase at one edge of the arena by what I at first took to be a dwarf in a black top hat but which turned out to be a Mamillius of the precocious variety. A lady was placed into a coffin, seemed to disappear, and then, among fireworks and applause, she was made to reappear. For those who didn't know the play and thus weren't equipped to recognize this as the director's obligatory Introductory Thematic Moment, the main point which emerged from the magic show's trad-jazz accompaniment and voodoo props and motifs, along with the general *mise-en-scène*, was that we appeared to be in a filmic version of inter-war New Orleans. This hypothesis was more or less confirmed when Rolf Saxon, as Polixenes, took the microphone stand to make an elaborate speech of thanks for the hospitality of which this display of magic by Mamillius had been the latest specimen, and did so in an American accent belonging to somewhere south of the Mason–Dixon line. Anxiously studying notes on a small card held in one hand, a shaven-headed Leontes made a comparable speech in reply, also in an American accent: this speech was just as elaborate but rather more halting, as if this white-tuxedoed figure were one of those screen mobsters more comfortable with decisive and violent action than with public speaking, even among family and close business associates.

This gambit involved a fairly heavy rewriting of Shakespeare's script, since Polixenes and Leontes gave, as formal, public speeches, recast versions of lines which in the script are formal, private conversation enjoyed before their arrival by the diplomats Archidamus and Camillo. This conspicuous freedom with the text – which extended to a good deal of paraphrase here and there, especially during the first two acts, and later on to the cutting of Time's chorus speech altogether – seemed to advertise, along with the novel venue and the novel American setting, that this first major new production of a Shakespeare play since the dawn of Project Fleet was intended to mark a fresh beginning for the RSC, emancipated from the Barbican and unfettered by tradition. Warchus is still routinely described as a young director, and his *Winter's Tale*, from this literally flashy, firework-assisted opening onwards, provided a classic specimen of what French theatre critics call 'jeunisme' – in other words, it flaunted a rather deliberate brashness and insouciance as if these qualities were prescribed by dogma. In the event, however, this production's continual straining after big visual effects with big musical accompaniments, as if these constituted the only way of engaging an audience's attention in any venue larger than a sitting room, was perfectly familiar from many productions seen in the more usual setting of the RST at any time over the last couple of decades. Hence Leontes's first soliloquy received a lighting change and the sort of cinematic shorthand incidental music intended to spell 'paranoia'; Cleomenes and Dion, spectacularly enough, were a black nun and a visionary blind boy who read the oracle in Braille; and the news of Hermione's supposed death mandated a deafening thunderstorm and gallons of simulated rain being pumped onto the stage, rain which nearly drowned Antigonus's description of the storm in the following scene as well as rendering it superfluous. Fully at the mercy of all these rather literal-minded special effects down in the arena, like a Christian wondering what would come next in the Coliseum, I had by this stage already been wondering for some minutes whether I was about to meet the RSC's first ever real bear, and the creature that became just visible through clouds of dry ice kept me guessing for several anxious moments: a very mimetic sort of bear indeed, a piece of method-acting in a bear-suit that really merited a credit in the programme. But this disappointed expectation of a real predatory animal getting released into the auditorium was then fulfilled in a different manner a couple of scenes later, by a stunning effect which seemed entirely typical of Warchus's production as a whole. Florizel's fleeting recollection in Act 4 that he first met Perdita when his falcon flew across her father's ground here demanded an immediately pre-interval tableau of their dumbstruck first encounter, complete with a real hawk swooping magnificently from one side of the auditorium's great circle to the other. The sight of the bird traversing the windless air above the acting area was surprising, dazzling, beautiful, and entirely irrelevant to the business of involving the audience in the events of the play. One more disconnected circus turn among many, the flight of the falcon only served to emphasize the overarching hollowness both of the building and of the production. (It was reiterated, bathetically enough, by a toy 1930s aeroplane at the end of Act 4, which retraced the hawk's trajectory in reverse along a wire: this was a production desperate enough for novelty to have its Florizel and Perdita, despite the script's references to a ship, travel to Leontes's court by air.)

Whatever Warchus's chosen American setting did or didn't do for *The Winter's Tale* at the level of interpretation – and the sheep-shearing scene, admittedly, worked very pleasantly as an Appalachian hoedown, with Lauren Ward's guitar-strumming Perdita, almost professionally in control of her own cuteness like a young Dolly Parton, spared some of the problems of class-specific diction usually associated with that role – it has to be said that from a purely practical point of view it well-nigh sabotaged it at the level of sheer intelligibility. Softening-off final consonants almost to inaudibility may be a necessary part of imitating American pronunciation, but the combination of the dense, knotty verbal style of late Shakespeare with a simulation of the diction of late Elvis is very hard to follow. This was particularly fatal to the audience's relationship with Leontes: the idea of having Douglas Hodge start his performance reading his lines hesitantly from a card was a disastrous miscalculation, suggesting that the only context in which one could really imagine this gangster speaking Shakespearian English was one in which he was doing so only with extreme difficulty for a special occasion. This suggestion, alas, was only underlined by the rest of Hodge's performance, which seemed to be about nothing more interesting than sheer blank incomprehension. Ranting and pacing monotonously through his performance, Hodge never found a register in which he could just seem to be talking to us, any more than did the production. He looked and sounded like Albert Finney's Daddy Warbucks in the film version of *Annie*, but somehow never achieved the same emotional depth: the only thing this Leontes was able to tell us, over and over again, was that he just didn't get it. Amazingly, he went on not getting it too, even to the very end of the statue scene: 'What, look upon my brother' (5.3.148), instead of marking the final reconciliation between Leontes, Hermione and Polixenes, became a momentary paranoid repetition of Leontes' original jealousy – 'What, look upon my brother??!' – rapidly laughed off in the manner of a Jimmy Cagney psychopath. The dumb cluck had gained nothing from the entire experience of the play, and, left outside the whole empty

and shouting spectacle despite a very moving performance by Anastasia Hille, neither had the audience. This production was an interesting and showy and worthwhile experiment, pushing most of the current repertoire of devices for translating Shakespeare into spectacular, cinematic-cum-circus entertainment to their limits and sometimes beyond: but it undoubtedly failed.

In the Roundhouse schedule, this *Winter's Tale* was followed in May by Michael Boyd's *The Tempest*, which, revealingly, suffered from some of the same problems. Directing for this arena, it seemed easier to achieve incidental circus tricks than very much in the way of human intimacy or mimesis: this production, for example, placed the cast of 1.1 on a mechanized and increasingly unstable deck, its revving hydraulics drowning much of their dialogue. Malcolm Storry's Prospero lapsed into loudly actorish declamation in a bid to cope with the Roundhouse acoustic – using that special stage accent in which the 'o' sounds in 'Antonio' sound more like 'awe' – and for most of the evening he was pushed to the edges of a circle otherwise dominated by Kananu Kirimi's sour, ethereal trapeze artist of an Ariel, visibly jealous of Sirine Saba's Miranda much as Tinkerbell is of Wendy. By the end of this *Tempest* it was clear that the Roundhouse could do masque very well – a drag Ceres punningly dressed in the manner of *Carmen* Miranda would have stolen the entire show had s/he not been succeeded by an unforgettable erotic aerial ballet between nymph and reaper – but it remained to be seen whether this venue could be brought down to earth for the purposes of straight drama. This was finally achieved only when Adrian Noble's production of *Pericles* opened at the end of June, providing, in the wake of his controversial resignation as artistic director, a reminder of what a talented director he can still be whatever he may have done and undone as a manager. Surprisingly, the Roundhouse proved an ideal venue for this least-revived of the romances, perhaps because of all these plays it is the least interested in anything so trivial as psychological realism.

There was nothing very new about this *Pericles*, no mistaking it for anything other than a fine and

30 *Pericles*, directed by Adrian Noble for the Royal Shakespeare Company. Ray Fearon as Pericles, Kananu Kirimi as Marina.

typical specimen of Noble's late manner: here again were the quantities of wind-blown silk, the bright plain pastel nursery colours, the unspecifically and inoffensively orientalist costume designs, the large, graceful, storytelling gestures. Here too was Noble's tendency to present Shakespeare as if alongside Charles and Mary Lamb, through the lens of classic children's literature, an aspect of his recent work which produced such an interesting *Midsummer Night's Dream* and such a disastrous *Twelfth Night*. The difference here was that all of these mannerisms fitted *Pericles* like a glove in a way that they didn't quite fit either of the other romances which Noble has directed in recent seasons, *Cymbeline* and *The Tempest*. The overall conceit, such as it was, was to have Peter McKintosh design *Pericles* as if it were a tale from Edmund Dulac's illustrated edition of the *Arabian Nights* – and, efficiently and

undistractingly, it just worked. The notion of this being a 'promenade' production in any very developed sense, never really achieved by its two predecessors, was largely abandoned: most of the action took place on a flat circular island in the middle of the arena, reached by a single ramp, rather than directly among any of the audience. (As a result, incidentally, this production transferred rather more successfully to the end-on RST than did its two fellows.)

This raised acting area, coupled with some elegant aerial work, proved more than adequate to the needs of this deliberately faux-naive, mock-medieval play: a single billowing sheet of silk, for example, easily transformed it into a ship for the great storm scene, without any of the noisy fairground machinery which Boyd's *Tempest* had employed to simulate a heavy swell. The happy combination of this play's willingly childish story-telling method and Noble's correspondingly arch simplicity of method was beautifully exemplified at the end of this scene by the handling of Thaisa's funeral at sea. Once she had been placed in her coffin, that coffin was simply slid backward out of the way along the ramp below and beyond the billowing sail: then at the scene's close the sail fell onto it, rippling like the sea; then in the next scene, where Thaisa is washed ashore, the coffin was simply drawn forward back into the acting area from under the sail by Cerimon's helpers. There was no straining after effect, no overdone real rainfall, just exactly what was needed to tell the story and to remind the audience to be in the mood to be told such a story. The décor, similarly, gave just enough information about the settings of scenes and about the pleasures of its own elegant tact without intruding: hanging Byzantine lamps to suggest eastern Mediterranean palaces; cushions; turbans; coloured robes; scimitars.

The performances, meanwhile, perverse as it sounds to say it, were just perfectly not too good, worlds away from the suspect slick perfection on display in Doran's *Much Ado*. Fearon was beautiful, and fit, and human, and you could understand every word he said, and he was the protagonist, and you wanted very much to see what happened to him next: anything much more than that would have thrown the whole show out of kilter. If the problem of psychological motivation even arises with *Pericles*, something has gone wrong, and here it didn't. Lauren Ward's Thaisa was dignified and lovely: Kananu Kirimi's Marina was waif-like and affecting: Olwen May's Bawd was twisted and nasty and human; and that's all that was needed. (Sirine Saba – a conspicuously good Mopsa in *The Winter's Tale*, part schoolmarm, part vixen – characteristically and enjoyably gave slightly more than was needed to her series of cameos as Antiochus's daughter, Lychorida, and 'the little baggage', 16.21, at the Mytilene brothel.) As Gower, Brian Protheroe told the story without ever getting in its way or appearing to think that the play was really about either him or the harmless moralizing with which he punctuated it. Such showy

touches as this production did display were exactly where they should have been, in the inset spectacular set-pieces: a good display of severed heads in Antioch, mockingly kissed by Geoff Francis's Antiochus; a very enjoyable and agile martial-arts contest for Thaisa's birthday; above all, a stunning effect for Pericles's dream-vision after the reunion with Marina, when a tiny scrap of white cloth fluttering rapidly down towards the stage from what seemed like miles above his head suddenly turned out to be Fiona Lait as a white-robed Diana, tumbling delicately down a rope – a benign, supernatural revision of the earlier swashbuckling descent on ropes made by the Sinbad-like pirates who abducted Marina from Tharsus. A sometimes excessive use of incidental music (including a sadly banal song, used both for Pericles's serenade to Thaisa and Marina's initial attempt to revive him in the reunion scene) seemed typical of the failure of nerve which the RSC has been suffering about productions for large spaces since even before *Les Misérables*, but this was otherwise an exquisitely judged account of an unfairly neglected and mysteriously powerful play.

The year's other major production of a romance, Michael Grandage's forceful *The Tempest* at the Crucible, also boasted some tremendous designs and effects, courtesy of Grandage's usual designer Christopher Oram. These began with a real *coup de théâtre* at the end of 1.1, when the ship's billowing sail, blocking an ornate and hitherto invisible proscenium, magically disappeared, pulled backwards and downwards at speed down a hole onto which Prospero, suddenly revealed behind the forestage that had been the ship's deck on what looked like the stage of the crumbling opera house in the jungle at Manaos, slammed the cover of a heavy book, and then picked the book up as if he had crammed the entire storm tidily back into its pages. If anything, though, it was not this severe, authoritative Prospero who set this production's tone, but Daniel Evans's slight, desiring Ariel, of whose balletic persona Julian Philips's excellent Debussy-like score (mainly for flute, viola and harp) seemed to speak even in his absence. Derek Jacobi, returning to the role of Prospero twenty years after playing it for the RSC, may well have been struck by how much more receptive the play has become to gay readings since the early 1980s: here again, as in Boyd's production, Act 4's play-within-the-play was performed *en travestie* by male spirits, but here the central relationship of the play proper was also between males, the asymmetrical bond between the enchanter and his chief spirit. Ariel clearly yearned, achingly, for far more of Prospero's attention than he was ever able to get, whether by making a dazzling first appearance as a butterfly centre-stage rear at 1.2.190 (with the help of two fellow-spirits, one to support each paper wing), or by solicitously trying to cheer up Prospero, depressed after giving away his daughter, with his comic account of the drenching of Caliban, Stephano and Trinculo at 4.1.171–84. The keynote for Evans's Ariel was his reading of 4.1.48, 'Do you love me, master? No?', where he paused anxiously for a reply to the initial question and then, to his surprise and horror, took Prospero's failure immediately to provide one as a negative, so that the line became 'Do you love me, master? – *No?*' After this terrible realization, Prospero's gentle but slightly reproving 'Dearly, my delicate Ariel' could not possibly give him adequate reassurance. This Ariel appeared to want his freedom only in the hope of entering into a new, equal partnership with his erstwhile master: in this production, unusually, it was Prospero who was ready for the relationship to end, not Ariel, so that the spirit was left desolate at the end of the play, and the jubilant 'Where the bee sucks' was cut entirely.

But his master, too, was left empty and dissatisfied at the play's ending. The knack of playing Prospero in a production heavily invested in characterization and motive seems to be to make sure that something definitely happens to him over the course of the action, and Jacobi's achievement here stands in marked contrast to that of Richard Briers (in another *Tempest* which by an unfortunate accident of timing this one wholly eclipsed, a touring production by the Plymouth Theatre Royal, with a set which for some reason was designed to resemble the inside of a swimming pool), who spent most of the play beaming genially on all concerned, as if nothing were at stake at all. Jacobi, for all

his authority, never looked complacent: in Act 5 he seemed to be taken aback both by Ariel's pity for his enemies and by his own feeling of being morally obliged to follow its example – this was something he hadn't anticipated at all – and he was clearly shocked to find himself trying to forgive his brother and his associates (he could barely pronounce the word 'forgive' to Antonio at 5.1.78, and he welcomed Alonso at 5.1.113 through clenched teeth, embracing him more aggressively than amicably). His recognition of what the cost would be to himself of this apparent change of plan from vengeance to virtue gave 'Ye elves of hills, brooks, standing lakes and groves' (5.1.33–57), a towering set-piece, the force of a suicide. If anything this was a darker reading of the role than Jacobi gave in 1982, though still enlightened by typical naturalistic touches of humour. At the close of his neurotic lecture to Ferdinand before the masque, for instance, proscribing pre-marital sex, it suddenly occurred to Prospero, to his comical discomfiture, that not only his future son-in-law but his daughter might have dangerous desires, so that the sentence in question, here given an extra full-stop just before its usual close, ran

> [*to Ferdinand, angrily*] If thou dost break her virgin-
> knot before
> All sanctimonious ceremonies may
> With full and holy rite be ministered,
> No sweet aspersion shall the heavens let fall
> To make this contract grow; but barren hate,
> Sour-eyed disdain, and discord, shall bestrew
> The union of your bed with weeds so loathly
> That you shall hate it. [*turns abruptly upstage as if to walk away: stops in his tracks after a couple of paces and raises his head, his back still to the audience: turns and points, nodding rapidly and emphatically at Miranda, and almost stammers*] Both.
>
> (4.1.15–22).

Brooding magus or situation comedy father-in-law, Jacobi, for all the screen work which nowadays fills much of his time, has lost none of his stage technique or his stage presence over the years since his last Prospero, and his slow final exit up the centre aisle of the theatre, after giving the epilogue with

31 *The Tempest*, directed by Michael Grandage, Crucible Theatre, Sheffield. Derek Jacobi as Prospero.

the house lights already up (assisted by some un-forgiving side-lighting that deliberately showed his age), amply deserved the ovation it received.

This production's director, Michael Grandage, will now take over Sam Mendes's artistic director-ship of the Donmar Warehouse, in one of those reshufflings of established middle-aged male per-sonnel so familiar in the English classical theatre, just as the RSC's Michael Attenborough is tak-ing over at the Almeida (and just as Michael Boyd is promoted internally to the artistic directorship of the RSC and Nicholas Hytner to that of the National). Whether the kinds of productions they sponsor at their new respective venues will be sig-nificantly different to the ones they have backed with their current companies, even in terms of per-sonnel, has yet to be seen: certainly this *Tempest*, design-led, psychology-based and star-cast, would have been perfectly at home at the Donmar if scaled down for the smaller auditorium, and for that mat-ter it wasn't obviously different in kind to Jonathan Kent's *Tempest* at the Almeida the previous year. The increasingly freelance nature of the theatre business in England is if anything making for a more homogenous version of top-level professional Shakespeare instead of a more varied one.

HISTORIES

Moving into the Folio's next category, the most conspicuous production of a history this year was also directed by Grandage at the Crucible, *Richard III*, with Kenneth Branagh in the title role (an event which, given Branagh's habit of making films of Shakespeare plays in which he has appeared in the theatre, has fuelled speculation about the pos-sibility of a Branagh *Richard III* movie to com-plete his homage to the Shakespearian cinematic precedents set by Olivier). But for the presence in the cast of Branagh as Richard and Barbara Jefford as Margaret, one might, by comparison with the expensive-looking visual flair of *The Tem-pest*, have called this production penny plain rather than twopence coloured: certainly it was for the most part drab to look at, with Oram confining most of the cast to monochromatic more-or-less

modern dress for most of the time. (One sometimes wonders whether productions of Shakespeare's his-tories and tragedies don't nowadays account for a significant proportion of the annual sales of black leather greatcoats.) The cast of twenty, though probably larger than that used at this play's pre-miere, was comparatively small for a modern pro-duction of *Richard III*, necessitating, along with a few doublings (Rivers with the Lord Mayor, Grey with Richmond), some striking conflations of roles (which, together with some heavy cuts, kept the performance time down to little more than two and a half hours). The murderers of Clarence turned out to be Lovel and Ratcliffe, who also posed as bishops to impress the Lord Mayor in 3.7, and who later reappeared at Bosworth Field to be hastily en-nobled and rechristened for the occasion with hasty touches on the shoulder from an evidently desper-ate and déclassé Richard's sword at 5.6.26 – 'John Duke of Norfolk ['*knights' Lovel*], Thomas Earl of Surrey ['*knights' Ratcliffe*], / Shall have the leading of this multitude.'

The production's opening might have tempted one to suggest that one explanation both for the low-key costumes and for the small cast might be the percentage of the budget that had clearly been invested in staging Richard's deformity – or rather, in this reading, his disability. This at first looked like an expensively over-elaborate bid to achieve some novelty for a dangerously familiar piece of the text. As the lights came up, Branagh began delivering 'Now is the winter of our discontent . . .' a good way towards the rear of the stage, on his back, with his feet towards the audience, while two white-coated assistants methodically detached his wrists and ankles from the extraordinary contraption that was his bed – something like a medieval rack, in which, we gathered, this Richard had to sleep in traction every night. The inexpressive automatic weariness with which Branagh was pronouncing the first paragraph of the speech was not, as it first appeared, the zombie-like trance of a patient un-dergoing long-term treatment in Monty Python's hospital for over-acting, but the sound of Richard painfully and reluctantly getting himself up in the morning by going through his usual mantra to

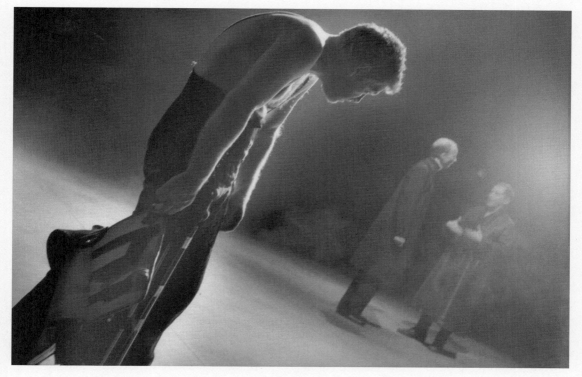

32 *Richard III*, directed by Michael Grandage, Crucible Theatre, Sheffield. Kenneth Branagh as Richard.

himself yet again. It was only when he had managed to bind himself into the stiff straitjacket-like waist-coat which alone could brace his spine sufficiently to keep him upright, and had trussed his inert right leg into its caliper (taking his first unwieldy step, lifting his right leg with his hands, on the word 'lamely' in 'And that so lamely and unfashionable', 1.1.22), that he could bring himself downstage to-wards the audience and start establishing any sort of eye-contact and rapport with them.

Once he did, though, Branagh's performance – low-key as it sometimes seemed for this role, de-spite the virtuoso physical work that went into the minute medical depiction of his disabilities – never looked back. Like Jacobi (one member, inciden-tally, of the most celebrity-strewn press-night au-dience I have ever known drive all the way from London to Sheffield for a single show), Branagh has lost nothing of his touch in the live theatre

despite his long absence in film studios and, though his was a Richard who was less of a satanic practical joker than any I have seen before, he was still in in-timate contact with the audience throughout, able to indicate which lines were modulating into half-asides, which were to be heard in a different sense by his confidants in the auditorium than by his on-stage interlocutors, with the lightest gestures of face or intonation. In some ways this was a nuanced, subtle, close-up, studio-theatre Richard brilliantly communicated to a full-scale house. What Branagh seemed to have decided to do was internalize the play's moral complexities – usually located in our own mixed response to the delightful and only very belatedly conscience-stricken tyrant at its cen-tre – within Richard himself. The Gloucester he played was no gleefully cocky Mr Punch, forever laughing behind the backs of his dupes, but a self-abasing man in continual physical pain who was so good at expressing remorse, penitence and helplessness (especially to Lady Anne in 1.2, and later to Queen Elizabeth, in whose kneeling lap he wound up cradled and weeping for 'Plead what I will be, not what I have been', 4.4.345) that it was almost as if we were watching an essentially moral person who was only experimenting with evil when away from the stronger people around him, rather than following the fortunes of a ruthless predator who only gave sarcastic and perfunctory imitations of virtue when in company. It was Danny Webb's black-coated Buckingham who looked like the cast's professional Machiavel, a hardened career politician who appeared to be leading this conveniently vulnerable member of the royal family astray rather than vice versa. Richard was clearly in awe of Barbara Jefford's silver-haired, almost silver-breastplated Queen Margaret (mind you, anybody would have been), and he reserved his more spiteful lashings-out for his inferiors, as if in sudden vicious frustration that they were enduring less physical suffering than himself. (He abruptly banged the murderers' heads together and threw them to the ground before telling them 'I like you, lads', 1.3.352, and struck Catesby in the face on an anxious 'Call them again!' at 3.7.214, obliging him painfully to conceal his left eye from the returning Lord Mayor and his party.) But he usually dominated the stage physically only by the spectacularly passive display of his weaknesses, particularly during the reception of the little princes, 3.1, when the princes mischievously robbed him of his spine-bracing waistcoat, leaving him humiliatingly slumped-forward, to the paralyzing embarrassment of all the other characters. Even an interpolated coronation procession (as in Bill Alexander's famous RSC production, with Anthony Sher, in 1984) had its brief triumphalism upstaged by the further exposure, for anointing, of Richard's crooked spine. When at last collapsing back into conscience the night before Bosworth Field – a development which here had looked inevitable all along – this Richard looked as much like a misguided victim as like a cornered mass-murderer: strapped back into his orthopaedic rack for the night, the ghosts whirled him cruelly around

the stage on its castors. His outfit for the battle, suddenly and flamboyantly shunning black-and-white naturalism, looked like a prosthetic musculature, with padded armour scarlet and striated as if he were wearing someone else's powerful and half-dissected torso, complete with a line of exposed vertebrae naked down its back: a horribly flayed live boar, finally done to death only by a squad of myrmidons under Richmond's orders, who trapped him in a net and killed him with spears.

The result of all this was a *Richard III* which shared a surprising amount of tone and spirit, rather than just structure, with *Macbeth*: the overall effect was not that this production was a crude piece of special pleading for a Richard who couldn't really be held fully responsible for his crimes because he was disabled, but that it credited its protagonist with much more gradated and complex kinds of self-consciousness than are usual in this play, letting him half-see that the murderous privileging of his ego represented by his lethal and duplicitous passage to the throne began at some level as a lonely and inadequate strategy of self-consolation. The mocking, engaging humour was still there – a lovely dip into modern idiom, for example, when asking Buckingham to hint only delicately that King Edward was illegitimate on the 'you know' of 'Because, my lord, you know my mother lives' (3.5.92) – but there was no contempt for his victims (if anything, there was envy): the shade of Olivier was invoked only when Richard seemed to be consciously forcing himself to stay naughty, snarling a nasal and deliberate 'Tear-falling pity dwells not in this eye' at 4.2.67, and dismissing Buckingham with a blow along with an equally Olivier-like 'Thou-troublest-me. I am not in the vein!' at 4.2.121. This was an original, impressive, intricate and for the most part convincing reading of the play, consonant with *Richard III*'s main performance tradition only in that most of the cast, though never less than competent, were completely overshadowed by the star performance at its centre.

Little else of note happened to Shakespeare's histories on the stages of England in 2002 – history, this year, seemed to be elsewhere. There was an at-best mediocre rendition of *Henry IV Parts 1 and 2* at the Old Vic in Bristol, but the showiest stab (sometimes literally) at putting two or more plays together came from Edward Hall, who brought a two-part redaction of the three *Henry VI* plays, cornily rechristened *Rose Rage* after a phenomenon which the newspapers stopped talking about five years ago, from the Watermill theatre in Newbury to the Haymarket in the summer. A cast of thirteen young men wore dark, approximately Victorian costumes, and when not in the action the players remained around the edges of the stage in stained white coats, brandishing large knives in an implausibly actorish imitation of abattoir employees: what with the interpolated singing of favourite school hymns during transitions between scenes, and the inept caricatures on offer as female impersonations (as Margaret, forever fiddling with lipstick, hand on hip, Robert Hands gave the impression that he'd seen *Some Like It Hot* a lot more often than he'd ever talked to girls), the effect was rather like watching a boys' public-school play pretentiously directed by a teacher who preserved vague memories of early Deborah Warner. To cap it all, a clumsy adaptation (by Roger Warren) left the script deadeningly heavy with exposition, and even those spectators more comfortable than I was with the notion of a director's freedom to deny work to actresses on an interpretative whim (for which, amazingly, the programme notes offered no attempted justification whatsoever) are unlikely to have found these two evenings half as rewarding as Michael Boyd's productions of the same plays for the RSC the previous year.

One rarity demands comment before I pass on to the tragedies, Anthony Clark's RSC production of *Edward III*, staged as part of Gregory Doran's season of Elizabethan and Jacobean plays at the Swan and advertised without qualification as a work by William Shakespeare. I came to this show with an open mind about this play's authorship, and I left it very grateful to have at last been given the chance to evaluate its claims for canonical status in the live theatre. Whoever wrote this script would have found little to complain of in Clark's production, which gave a lucid and attractive account of

the play: David Rintoul was clear and elegant in his portrayal of Edward as a suave but tarnished executive getting over a mid-life crisis, and Jamie Glover showed how good he is at fully inhabiting the blank-verse action-hero mode as his son the Black Prince (helped by some nicely stylized fight sequences, complete with Peking Opera percussion sounds). Caroline Faber made an agreeably soft-voiced Countess of Salisbury, gamely resisting the assaults of a phallic Scottish battering-ram and of the King's set-piece rhetoric with equal grace, and Patrick Connellan's designs established a clear visual style, reminiscent in general effect of Doran's *King John* in 2001. In some details, though, this show seemed deliberately reminiscent of a more celebrated, much earlier production. With its love of textiles, such as the cloak on which the French king picnicked while awaiting news of the battle, its mixture of modern costumes and medieval, and above all the occasions on which its soldiers in the wars against France moved about behind the leading players to fasten guy-ropes to the stage suggestive of tents and pavilions, it seemed to be alluding purposefully to Terry Hands's triumphant *Henry V* of 1975.

Certainly *Henry V* is the Shakespearian history that this one connects with most closely, notably via its quite unhistorical claim that King David of Scotland was captured while Edward III was campaigning in France, a fictitious incident, apparently invented by this play, to which Shakespeare refers when the Archbishop of Canterbury is reassuring Henry V in 1.2 that he needn't be too worried about the weasel Scot attacking England while he is away chastising the Dauphin. It isn't surprising that someone eager to be thought to be directing a long-neglected Shakespearian play should deliberately play up the possible resemblances between the two plays – those besieged and threatened French citizens, those hopelessly outnumbered English forces surrounded by taunting and over-confident French nobles. But the relation in which this play stands to *Henry V*, on this showing, is surely more that of a minor source than that of a first draft. It is abundantly clear that Shakespeare knew *Edward III*, certainly, but then it's equally clear that he knew

The Famous Victories of Henry V, and even Eric Sams doesn't claim that Shakespeare wrote that. In performance, there seemed to be a stiffness about *Edward III* utterly remote from Shakespeare's histories, while its reliance on scenes between only two or three characters at a time is unparalleled in the Shakespeare canon beyond what was probably his first play, *The Two Gentlemen of Verona*. To think even of the first two parts of *Henry VI*, even as revised as *Rose Rage*, is immediately to be reminded of a kind of chronicle play in which different plots and different motifs are interwoven far more fluently than are any of the different strands in *Edward III*, and in which verbal images and staged action are interrelated much more thoroughly. There is a sort of moral certainty and singleness of vision about *Edward III* which even the earliest of Shakespeare's plays never share, a po-faced quality profoundly alien even to Shakespearian tragedy. The characters in *Edward III* all seem congenitally unable to get their tongues even fleetingly into their cheeks, and despite their superficial and temporary disagreements they all inhabit exactly the same earnestly cardboard mental world. I can't think of anything in Shakespeare that is presented with the unqualified solemnity with which this play treats the chivalric arming of the Black Prince, and it is striking, I think, that in his determination to make Lodowick the poet into a sceptical Shakespearian side-commentator or clown, Wayne Cater continually had to invent visual jokes of his own not remotely suggested by this play's script. Clark seemed to me to blow the gaffe on the deeply un-Shakespearian nature of this play's genre when he finally appeared to lose patience with its unremitting straightness and offer a comment of his own about the formulaic inevitability of its ending: very aptly, he turned Lodowick's final messenger speech announcing the triumphant survival of the Black Prince into a piece of *opera seria*, sung to a pastiche Handel accompaniment – '*Rejoice my lord, ascend the imperial throne . . .*' This fitted the moment perfectly, and it also imported some long-desired irony, though again from well outside the script as written. This is a very entertaining play as far as it goes, but to advertise it as unquestionably by Shakespeare is surely to risk the invocation of the Trades Description Act. On this showing, *Edward III* is worlds away from what Keats calls 'the bitter-sweet of this Shakespearian fruit': it sounded here much more like an unusually chewy piece of George Peele.

TRAGEDIES

The year 2002, with the apocalypse of September 11th 2001 just behind it and the prospect of a senseless war with Iraq just ahead, saw something of a boom in productions of *King Lear*. I shall be citing three, though not before mentioning single revivals of five other tragedies. Two of these took place in the North, while two belonged very much to the West End. In Ian Brown's production of *Hamlet*, a shaven-headed Christopher Ecclestone held the attention of predominantly young audiences at the Quarry theatre in West Yorkshire: this was yet another production in costumes suggestive of the 1930s, played in a no-nonsense and to me disappointingly uninvolving and unmetrical manner on a spare, bare-wood set. Braham Murray's *Othello* at the Royal Exchange had so little set as to be almost minimalist – there was less a design than a colour-scheme, predominantly khaki – and it supplied little in the way of intellectual context to distract from two very accomplished, large-scale performances from Paterson Joseph as Othello and Andy Serkis as an inverted-snob Iago.

Back in London, and predictably attracting more media attention than either, Edward Hall's *Macbeth* at the Albery in the autumn provided a good example of how to launder box-office populism with a few directorial ideas. Some of these were mannerisms re-used from *Rose Rage* (in particular, the interpolated singing of hymns as the cast reassembled for a new scene), but this was a show much more colourfully eager to please the largely teenaged audience which it attracted. It can't have escaped the attention of the boys in the audience that they were in the presence not just of the villain from *Goldeneye* (Sean Bean, here playing Macbeth), but the current Miss Moneypenny (Samantha Bond, his Lady) and even the villain from *For Your Eyes Only*

(Julian Glover, doubling Duncan and a shakily Glaswegian Porter who knowingly played with a toy crown), and there was plenty more to appeal to such sensibilities too: shunning Shakespeare's allusions to beards in favour of Holinshed's nymphs, Hall made the witches into seductive, red-haired Gaelic sirens rather than crones, and he filled the modern-dress battle scenes with smoke effects and big guns, with Bean swaggering half-naked to the front of the stage at his first interpolated entrance (defeating Cawdor and setting a rubber head on a spike, between 1.1 and 1.2) to be cheered like a professional wrestler. Bean was very much one of those Macbeths more convincing as a warrior than as a tormented introvert (though his transition into a deskbound dictator, in yet another black leather trenchcoat, after another interpolated coronation, was nicely marked). In this fairly simple-minded reading – the soliloquies taken rapidly and unmusically, in Bean's native Sheffield accent – he became a murderer more as a result of a susceptibly laddish libido than from ambition. Lady Macbeth welcomed him steamily onto a bed to discuss the killing of Duncan in 1.5, where after some enthusiastic initial kissing and tumbling his 'We will speak further' (1.5.70) was pronounced with a heavy overtone of 'sure, whatever you say, but let's not waste any more time talking . . .' Later, rejected at the end of 3.4 by a Lady Macbeth already horrified and disgusted by what he had become, he returned to this bed alone for 'strange and self abuse' that seemed at first a solitary erotic fantasy – the three silk-clad witches, who in daylight scenes doubled as non-speaking castle staff in impeccable Scottish Tourist Board tweed dresses, emerged suddenly from beneath the covers to drape themselves all over him like succubi, conjuring the apparitions in whispers as if adding incongruously gothic special effects to a porn film.

This was almost as tacky as it sounds, if at least as enjoyable, but this production did show considerable intelligence as well as a certain ruthless willingness to cater to the lowest common denominator. The political plot was handled well: the usual point was made about the ominous similarity between Macduff's position at the end of the play

and Macbeth's at the beginning, here by Macduff impaling Macbeth's rubber head on the same spike which had earlier played host to his predecessor as Thane of Cawdor, but Hall had also noticed the extent to which Malcolm seems to have become king at the expense of making Scotland a puppet province of England. Adrian Schiller's chilly, bespectacled Malcolm, whose only display of feeling was, spectacularly, his onstage vomiting after sneaking a quick unscripted offstage peek at his murdered father in 2.3, met Macduff in exile in a cosy establishment clubroom in Westminster, to the audible chiming of Big Ben, and the sinister troops who re-took Scotland not only bore banners in which the Scottish lion rampant occupied only a quarter of the cross of St George but arrested a stunned Ross and Lennox as 'cruel ministers / Of this dead butcher and his fiend-like queen' in response to a nodded command at 5.11.35. Perhaps more importantly, the production achieved poignancy and pain as well as, at times, the texture of an efficient cinematic thriller. Lady Macduff's killing was as excruciating as ever (complete with Young Macduff mockingly dandled on the murderer's dagger, as per Trevor Nunn's famous RSC production of 1976). Banquo's ghost – whose appearances and reappearances at the banquet startled the audience as much as Macbeth thanks to some skilled directorial sleight-of-hand to distract their attention at crucial moments – sadly followed Fleance, unseen, across the stage at his final appearance, and both he and Duncan made unscripted posthumous appearances in the final battle (an increasingly prevalent directorial trick, this, familiar both from *Rose Rage* and from Boyd's *Henry VI*). Above all, Samantha Bond made a terrific Lady Macbeth: she is always so poised, so liable to sound like a good girl giving a good audition speech very well, that her appearance at the start of the sleepwalking scene with her make-up all smudged was shocking enough in itself, but her performance here had a rawness and intensity – especially in its final awful, half-strangled, long moaning sigh – of which I hadn't known her capable. This was superior West End celebrity Shakespeare for schools: the ideas were never wholly subordinated to the flash, and the performances were all a good deal better than they strictly needed to be.

Two Roman plays were revived this year (the RSC's touring *Coriolanus*, which opened late in the year, will be described in the next *Survey*), in very contrasting styles. *Julius Caesar* appeared as *SeZar*, an adaptation written and directed by Yael Farber, first performed at the Grahamstown Main Festival in 2001 and brought over from South Africa for a six-week tour by the Oxford Playhouse. On a bare stage overshadowed by what appeared to be radio transmitter masts made of scaffolding (appropriately, given the taped international media bulletins which punctuated the scene changes), eight African actors gave a heavily cut and incidentally rewritten version of Shakespeare's text (occasional isolated passages were replaced by translations into different African languages), with the play's action transposed to a fictitious modern-day African state called 'Azania'. To risk a dangerous cliché when talking about black African theatre, it was all highly physical (Menzi 'Ngubs' Ngubane and Nomakhosi Masala made a gloriously unstoical and unascetic Brutus and Portia, the strain of holding anything back from his wife almost visibly killing Brutus in the orchard scene), and overall the play was much more depressing than Farber's upbeat programme notes implied – in this version SeZar was murdered not only for wanting to be a dictator but for refusing to admit that AIDS was a virus, and the rest of the story offered the sorry spectacle of fledgling democrats turning into rival warlords. The adaptation was sometimes crude, but the performance undeniably had more life than did the RSC's showily staged production of this play's sequel, Michael Attenborough's *Antony and Cleopatra*, brought from the RST to the Haymarket along with Doran's *Much Ado* in the summer. This text, too, was to a lesser extent cut and rearranged: Pompey, for example, had disappeared entirely, so that the party in 2.7 (here with a butch pseudo-Maori chant substituted for 'Come, thou monarch of the vine') had to celebrate the marriage alliance agreed at Rome in 2.2. Strikingly, some phrases felt to be beyond the comprehension of a modern audience had been replaced (a slippery slope, this!): at 2.5.22 Antony

was reported to have worn not Cleopatra's 'tires and mantles' but her 'robes and sandals', and even Enobarbus's much-quoted account of the lovers' first meeting was at one point similarly dumbed-down, ruining one line's rhythm: 'And for his ordinary, pays his heart' (2.2.232) became 'And for his nourishment, pays his heart'. The central performances were toned-down to match, or at very least off-centre and off-balance. Stuart Wilson looked suitably Herculean as Antony but his scratchy, constrained voice seemed to have no bass frequencies at all, less rattling thunder than crackling parchment, and Sinead Cusack was simply miscast as Cleopatra: lithe as she proved herself to be, her style of beauty is still that of an ingenue, and in her transparent Egyptian robes she seemed less like a femme fatale than like an anxious Sunday school teacher who had forced herself to dress like a tart in the hopes of retaining Antony's interest. Her performance spoke only of desperate and sincere neediness throughout: there wasn't a playful or dissimulating bone in her body. All the worldliness in this show belonged to Octavius, beautifully and convincingly played as an insecure but ruthless and manipulative goody-goody by Stephen Campbell-Moore: in the unheroic age of Tony Blair, this is clearly the role in this script which most readily makes contemporary sense, but it isn't in itself sufficient to sustain a whole production.

I have decided to end with *King Lear*, not only because as a play it is so suitably terminal (is this the promised end?) but because a short account of 2002's three different productions, all of them in their own ways very strong, will allow me to end on a note of optimism which, admittedly, seems perhaps incongruous in the context of this text. Two of these shows were very much in the main line of modern productions of *King Lear*. This is a play which usually gets performed nowadays not because a company feel they have something to say about it, but because a particular actor is at last felt to have earned the title role: productions of *Lear*, consequently, are often as much about the central performer's own endurance and his own emotional hold on his long-term audience as about the various kinds of experience outlined in the text, and much of the emotional impact of the play in performance is usually concerned with the star's own mortality – indeed, given how long actors nowadays have to work before they get cast in this role (which Garrick played at forty), there is often considerable suspense as to whether he will even survive to the final curtain call. Jonathan Kent's production for the Almeida company in the Spring, performed at a temporary auditorium in King's Cross during the theatre's refurbishment, and Stephen Unwin's for English Touring Theatre in the autumn, both fitted this pattern: one will be remembered primarily as Oliver Ford-Davies's Lear, the other as Timothy West's.

Ford-Davies must rate as one of the only actors ever to be awarded this role because everyone thinks him so nice: his was very much a Lear of the second half of the play, far more convincing as a redeemed and affectionate father than as an egotistical tyrant. With the play built as ever around this big piece of characterization at its centre, the rest of the cast played for psychological naturalism throughout (James Frain was particularly successful at making Edmund an unswaggering estuary boy concealing his ambition behind a gauchely demure manner, more Julien Sorel than Heathcliff, and Hugh Simon's Curan was a plausible butler), and Paul Brown's elaborate designs only provided distraction rather than illumination. The first scene seemed to take place in an oak-panelled Edwardian country hotel, with the sisters gathering nervously as if for the reading of a will, and Lear's first two dispositions of his estate were revealed, rather irrelevantly, by his cuing a videotape of himself describing them (on a television monitor that was never used again). Frustratingly, the set's wooden walls were never wholly removed until after the storm, during which enormous quantities of real water were rained onto the stage as if via a cataclysmically leaky roof – this effect was so distracting that it even affected the bar takings during the interval, with many of the audience staying in their seats to watch an army of stagehands remove the resulting near-lake with enormous waterproof vacuum cleaners. Stephen Unwin's production sensibly avoided this – given that it was a touring show,

any such potentially destructive storm was probably out of the question anyway – by having no set at all, just a bare stage, on which the cast's Elizabethan costumes, when one noticed them, looked faintly incongruous. (It is a sign of how far the reconstructed Globe has cornered the market in ye olde doublet and hose that apart from the Globe's *Twelfth Night* this is the only production mentioned here to have used sixteenth-century dress at all.) Timothy West can make a much more convincing bully than Oliver Ford-Davies any day, but even his performance was largely in the event about personal pathos: his voice seemed frail even in the storm scenes, and he spoke so slowly that one wondered whether the heavy cuts to the text had been made specifically to allow him to do so. While his madness was often quirkily and eloquently rendered – especially in a radiant 4.5 – he too died less as a king than as a very foolish, fond and by now touchingly harmless old man.

Both of these productions were extremely moving, in a slightly predictable manner – in both, the impossible old devil was allowed to do his utmost in the way of emotional manipulation to make us pity him unbearably yet again – but neither, to my surprise, has left half as vivid a series of impressions as Declan Donnellan's version for the RSC Academy, performed first at the Swan and then at the Young Vic in the autumn. *King Lear* might seem the last play to direct with a cast of sixteen actors just out of drama school this year, but in fact the liberation of its central role from the naturalistic depiction of old age turned out to enable the whole play to be woken up in all sorts of directions.

This was open-ended direction with a vengeance, much more like the dress rehearsal of an unnaturally good and inventive student production than the sacrament of yet another sacrificial professional *Lear*. There was no set to speak of (though an upper level was used, perhaps controversially for a play in which Shakespeare seems deliberately to confine all this characters to the potential egalitarianism of the platform), and the modern costumes were adopted and discarded ad lib rather than used to suggest a single, realistic, minutely rendered social context for the play's events. The

33   *King Lear*, directed by Stephen Unwin, English Touring Theatre. Timothy West as King Lear.

storm was a billowing piece of white canvas, before which all three sisters appeared as Lear wandered. Gloucester's blinding was an abrupt, shocking, total blackout. Kent disguised himself as a seedy Archie Rice, to compete with a microphone-wielding Fool wearing the shiny jacket of the gameshow host. Edgar started out as a retarded adolescent forever playing childish wargames with toy swords before learning to kill in earnest. Ideas were seized and used (sometimes for too long, sometimes not for long enough), then dropped; characterization was subordinate to them throughout.

The king himself was never the sole key to this production, however central his power and prestige were to the situations in which the play placed him. In the first scene Goneril and Regan, in black evening gowns, stood nervously on the upper level awaiting their respective turns to speak while their dinner-suited menfolk waited obsequiously on Lear around a table below, applauding his gifts on cue with scared-looking enthusiasm. They had every reason to look scared, too. As Lear, Nonso Anozie, the only black actor in the production (he pronounced the phrase 'our darker purpose' with a smug smile and a gesture towards his face, as if asserting a sense of racial superiority), was easily the biggest member of the cast and the most dangerous-looking, capable of lifting Kirsty Besterman's green-clad Cordelia furiously onto the table in a moment to display her to France and Burgundy as

34 *King Lear*, directed by Declan Donnellan for the Royal Shakespeare Company Academy. Nonso Anozie as Lear, Kirsty Besterman as Cordelia.

if conducting a spontaneous slave auction. By contrast to the characterizations given by his seniors, Anozie was a Lear of the first half, an impulsive monomaniac whose ego shattered in the storm but whose personality was never subsequently reconstituted along more acceptably pitiable lines: there was no palliating evidence in the early scenes to suggest that there had ever been a tender side to his fatherhood to which he might ultimately revert at the last minute. He made an obviously impossible guest at Goneril's house, prone to terrifying bouts of high spirits – his entourage, dressed in Blues Brothers dark suits and sunglasses, trashed the premises and chanted mindless catchphrases in response to the Fool's promptings – and, later, a disconcertingly giggly madman, who even died on a sort of grim practical joke, decoying the onlookers

to concentrate on Cordelia's body with 'Look there – look there!' so that he could spring nimbly behind them and die of a choking attack produced as if by willpower without the risk of being revived. It wasn't about pathos; it was about power asserted one last time, if only the power to die.

This small-scale, in its own way unassuming production wasn't to everyone's taste, but it was undeniably faithful to aspects of *King Lear* which more conventional productions can often miss or smoothe out in the pursuit of emotional intensity – it managed to convey something of this text's own incoherence, its alarming willingness to risk making its own events seem meaningless or formless, its juxtapositions of aborted attempts at some sort of human closure with the utter arbitrariness of most of its depicted deaths. Alongside all the productions in 2002 which were bent on making Shakespeare's plays into smoothly oiled pieces of entertainment – whether holy tragic rituals, or circuses, or musicals, or television-drama-style studies in individual psychology – this one was always listening to someone who remains the oddest and most wilfully eccentric playwright in the world as well as the greatest. Above all, it obliged its audience to go on thinking. It's as good a place as any for me to end, and for the RSC to start reinventing itself all over again.

PROFESSIONAL SHAKESPEARE PRODUCTIONS IN THE BRITISH ISLES JANUARY–DECEMBER 2001

JAMES SHAW

Most of the productions listed are by professional companies, but some amateur productions are included. The information is taken from *Touchstone* (http://www.touchstone.bham.ac.uk), a Shakespeare website maintained by the Shakespeare Institute Library. *Touchstone* includes a monthly list of current and forthcoming UK Shakespeare productions from listings information. *The Traffic of the Stage* database, also available on *Touchstone*, archives UK Shakespeare production information since January 1999, correlating information from listings with reviews held in the Shakespeare Institute Library. The websites provided for theatre companies were accurate at the time of going to press.

All's Well that Ends Well
Stamford Shakespeare Company. Tolethorpe Hall, Stamford: 1 June – 28 July
http://www.stamfordshakespeare.co.uk
Amateur Shakespeare production.

As You Like It
Royal Shakespeare Company. The Pit, London: 2 January – 7 February 2001. http://www.rsc.org.uk
Transfer from Royal Shakespeare Theatre: March 2000
Director: Gregory Doran
Designer: Kaffe Fassett, Niki Turner
Rosalind: Alexandra Gilbreath

British Touring Shakespeare Company. Open-air touring production: 23 June – 3 August 2001.
http://www.btsc.homestead.com
Director: Miles Gregory

Creation Theatre Company and Oxford Stage Company. Magdalen College School Grounds, Oxford: 16 July – 1 September 2001. Open-air production. http://www.creationtheatre.co.uk
Director: Charlotte Conquest

The Comedy of Errors
Royal Shakespeare Company. Barbican Centre, London: 29 November 2000 – 3 February 2001
http://www.rsc.org.uk. Transfer of Royal Shakespeare Theatre production, April 2000
Director: Lynne Parker
Designer: Bell Helicopter

West Yorkshire Playhouse, Leeds: 3 March – 7 April 2001. http://www.wyplayhouse.co.uk
Director: Ian Brown
Designer: Peter McKintosh

Abbey Shakespeare Company. St Dogmael's Abbey: 8–11 August 2001
Annual production by amateur Shakespeare company.

Royal Lyceum, Edinburgh: 20 October – 17 November 2001
Director: Tony Cownie
Designer: Hayden Griffin

Southend Shakespeare Company. Palace Theatre, Westcliff: 13–17 November 2001
Amateur company.

Adaptation
Gli Equivoci (the Twins) Bampton Classical Opera, Bath Theatre Royal: 5–17 March 2001

Composer: Stephen Storace
Libretto: Lorenzo da Ponte
Performed as part of the Bath Shakespeare Festival.

The Kyogen of Errors Mansaku Company. Shakespeare's Globe Theatre, London: 18–22 July 2001
Adaptor: Yasunari Takahashi
Performed in Japanese.

Coriolanus
Shakespeare at the Tobacco Factory Theatre Company. The Tobacco Factory, Bedminster: 22 March – 21 April 2001
http://www.shakespeareatthetobaccofactory.co.uk
Director: Andrew Hilton
Coriolanus: Gyuri Sarossy
Well received by critics. Formed in 2000, Shakespeare at the Tobacco Factory have quickly established a reputation for clear, ensemble productions with a detailed attention to the text.

Teatr Heleny Modrzejewskiej. Touring international production, performed at the Edinburgh Festival, August 2001
In Polish.

Adaptation
Plebeians Rehearse the Uprising Arcola Theatre, London: 5 June – 23 June 2001
http://www.arcolatheatre.com
Playwright: Günter Grass
Director: Mehmet Ergen
Translation: Ralph Manheim
Brecht's rehearsal of his adaptation of *Coriolanus* is interrupted by a workers' uprising. Performed as part of the Vintage Shakespeare season at the Arcola Theatre.

Cymbeline
Shakespeare's Globe, The Rose Company: 20 June – 23 September 2001
http://www.shakespeares-globe.org
Director: Mike Alfreds
Posthumus/Cloten/Cornelius: Mark Rylance

Theatre for a New Audience. The Other Place, Stratford-upon-Avon: 19 November – 8 December

2001. http://www.tfana.org
Director: Bartlett Sher
Imogen: Erica Tazel
New York based theatre company. First American company to play at the Royal Shakespeare Company.

Hamlet
Royal National Theatre. International touring production, visiting Elsinore, Stockholm, Belgrade and Boston, Minneapolis, Phoenix and New York. Originally staged at Lyttleton Theatre: September 2000 http://www.nationaltheatre.org.uk
Director: John Caird
Designer: Tim Hatley
Hamlet: Simon Russell Beale
Jonathan Croall gives an account of the production and rehearsal process in *Hamlet Observed: The National Theatre at Work* (London: National Theatre Publications, 2001).

Brunton Theatre Company. Brunton Theatre, Musselburgh: 2–17 February 2001
Director: David Mark Thompson
Hamlet: Liam Brennan

Creation Theatre Company. BMW Group, Oxford Plant: 3 February – 10 March 2001
http://www.creationtheatre.co.uk
Director: Zoë Seaton
Promenade production, performed in the Oxford BMW factory.

Royal Shakespeare Company. Royal Shakespeare Theatre, Stratford-upon-Avon: 31 March – 13 October 2001. Transferred to Theatre Royal, Newcastle-upon-Tyne, November 2001, and Barbican Centre, London: December – April 2002
http://www.rsc.org.uk
Director: Steven Pimlott
Designer: Alison Chitty
Hamlet: Sam West

Horla Productions, Rose and Crown, Hampton Wick, Outer London: 3–21 July 2001
http://www.horla.co.uk
Director: Alistair Green
Hamlet: Sally Orrock

Northcott Theatre Company. Rougemont Gardens, Exeter: 17 July – 11 August 2001
Director: Ben Crocker
Hamlet: Mark Healy

British Touring Shakespeare Production, Westminster Theatre, London: December 2001 – February 2002. http://www.btsc.homestead.com
Director: Miles Gregory
Hamlet: Tom Mallaburn

Adaptation
Kanadehon Hamlet Kiyama Theatre Company. Battersea Arts Centre, London: 23–28 March 2001
Playwright: Harue Tsutsumi
Director: Toshifumi Sueki
Designer: Mitsuru Ishi
Based on Hamlet and the Kanadehon Cushingura Tale of 47 samurai.

Rosencrantz and Guildenstern are Dead Arcola Theatre Company. Arcola Theatre, London: 11 April – 5 May 2001. http://www.arcolatheatre.com
Playwright: Tom Stoppard
Director: William Galinsky
Designer: Miriam Buether
Performed as part of the Vintage Shakespeare season at the Arcola Theatre.

Hamlet Young Shakespeare Company. Orange Tree Theatre, Richmond: Saturday 19 May – Saturday 23 June 2001
Adaptor: Sarah Gordon
Director: Christopher Geelan
Production for children, with four actors in the cast. Performed as part of the Orange Tree Theatre's annual Primary Shakespeare project.

The Secret Love Life of Ophelia King's Head, London: 4–21 July 2001, transferred to the Edinburgh Fringe Festival, August 2001
Playwright: Steven Berkoff
Two-hander consisting of Hamlet, Ophelia, and the voice of Gertrude.

Humble Boy Royal National Theatre Company, Cottesloe Theatre: August 2001
http://www.nationaltheatre.org.uk

Playwright: Charlotte Jones
Director: John Caird
Felix Humble: Simon Russell Beale
A reworking of Hamlet.

The Tragedy of Hamlet The Young Vic, London: 22 August – 8 September 2001. Transfer from Théâtre des Bouffes du Nord, Paris
Director: Peter Brook
Hamlet: Adrian Lester

Barbecuing Hamlet Stageworks Productions. The Rosemary Branch Theatre, London: 12–29 September 2001
Playwright: Pat Cook
Farce about an amateur production of Hamlet.

Hamlet – the Panto Oddsocks Theatre Company. Touring production: January 2001

Ophelia SPID Theatre Company. Jackson's Lane, London: 9–11 November 2001
Playwright/Director: Helena Thompson

Opera
Hamlet Chelsea Opera Group. Queen Elizabeth Hall, London: February 2001
Composer: Ambroise Thomas

Henry IV Part 1
Royal Shakespeare Company. Barbican Centre, London: 21 February – 18 April 2001
http://www.rsc.org.uk. Transfer from Swan Theatre production, 2000
Director: Michael Attenborough
Designer: Es Devlin
Henry IV: David Troughton
Falstaff: Desmond Barrit
Prince Hal: William Houston.
Produced as part of the RSC's Millennium season: *This England: The Histories.*

Henry IV Part 2
Royal Shakespeare Company. Barbican Centre, London: 21 February – 18 April 2001
http://www.rsc.org.uk. Transfer from Swan Theatre production, 2000
Director: Michael Attenborough

Designer: Es Devlin
Henry IV: David Troughton
Falstaff: Desmond Barrit
Prince Hal: William Houston
Produced as part of the RSC's Millennium season:
This England: The Histories.

Henry V
Royal Shakespeare Company. Barbican, London:
22 March – 21 April 2001. http://www.rsc.org.uk
Transfer of Royal Shakespeare Theatre production,
August 2000
Director: Edward Hall
Designer: Michael Pavelka
Prince Hal: William Houston
Produced as part of the RSC's Millennium season:
This England: The Histories.

Festival Players Theatre Company. Touring pro-
duction: June – August 2001
Director: Trish Knight-Webb and Michael Dyer
Touring Shakespeare company.

Bournemouth Shakespeare Players. Priory House
Garden, Chichester: 17–28 July 2001
Amateur company.

Henry VI Part 1
Royal Shakespeare Company. Swan Theatre,
13 December – 10 February 2001, transferred to
The Young Vic, London, 24 April – 25 May
2001
http://www.rsc.org.uk
Director: Michael Boyd
Designer: Tom Piper
Henry VI: David Oyelowo
Joan la Pucelle: Fiona Bell
Part 1 retitled *The War Against France*, and produced
as part of the RSC's Millennium season: *This Eng-
land: The Histories.*

Adaptation
*The Thoughts of Joan of Arc on The English as She
Burns at The Stake* The Young Vic, London: 20
April – 31 May 2001
Written/Director: David Farr
Monologue, loosely based on *Henry VI, pt 1.*

Rose Rage (Parts 1 and 2) Propeller Productions.
The Watermill Theatre, Newbury: 3 February –
16 March 2001. Revived for a UK tour Septem-
ber – October 2001
Director: Edward Hall
Adaptor: Edward Hall and Roger Warren
Designer: Michael Pavelka
Adaptation of the Henry VI trilogy, with all male
cast. Script published by Oberon Books, London,
2001.

Henry VI Part 2
Royal Shakespeare Company. Swan Theatre: De-
cember – February 2001, transferred to The Young
Vic, London, April – May 2001
http://www.rsc.org.uk
Director: Michael Boyd
Designer: Tom Piper
Henry VI: David Oyelowo
Queen Margaret: Fiona Bell
Part 2 retitled *England's Fall*, and produced as part
of the RSC's Millennium season: *This England: The
Histories.*

Adaptation
Rose Rage (Parts 1 and 2) Propeller Productions.
The Watermill Theatre, Newbury: 3 February –
16 March 2001. Revived for a UK tour Septem-
ber – October 2001
Director: Edward Hall
Adaptor: Edward Hall and Roger Warren
Designer: Michael Pavelka
Adaptation of the Henry VI trilogy, with all male
cast. Script published by Oberon Books, London,
2001.

Henry VI Part 3
Royal Shakespeare Company. Swan Theatre: De-
cember – February 2001, transferred to The Young
Vic, London, April – May 2001
http://www.rsc.org.uk
Director: Michael Boyd
Designer: Tom Piper
Henry VI: David Oyelowo
Queen Margaret: Fiona Bell
Part 3 retitled *The Chaos*, and produced as part of

the RSC's Millennium season: *This England: The Histories.*

Adaptation
Rose Rage (Parts 1 and 2) Propeller Productions. The Watermill Theatre, Newbury: 3 February – 16 March 2001. Revived for a UK tour September – October 2001
Director: Edward Hall
Adaptor: Edward Hall and Roger Warren
Designer: Michael Pavelka
Adaptation of the Henry VI trilogy, with all male cast. Script published by Oberon Books, London, 2001.

Julius Caesar
Royal Shakespeare Company. Royal Shakespeare Theatre: 13 July – 13 October 2001
http://www.rsc.org.uk
Director: Edward Hall
Designer: Michael Pavelka
Julius Caesar: Ian Hogg
Mark Antony: Tom Mannion
Brutus: Greg Hicks
Played without an interval.

King John
Northern Broadsides. Touring production, March – May 2001
http://www.northern-broadsides.co.uk
Director: Barrie Rutter; Conrad Nelson
Designer: Jessica Worrall
King John: Fine Time Fontayne
Bastard: Conrad Nelson

Royal Shakespeare Company. Swan Theatre, Stratford-upon-Avon: 21 March – 13 October 2001, transferred to the Pit: December 2001 – February 2002. http://www.rsc.org.uk
Director: Gregory Doran
Designer: Stephen Brimson Lewis
King John: Guy Henry
Bastard: Jo Stone-Fewings

King Lear
Clwyd Theatr Cymru. Theatr Clwyd, Mold, 8 February – 10 March 2001.
http://www.clwyd-theatr-cymru.co.uk
Director: Terry Hands
Designer: Mark Bailey
King Lear: Nicol Williamson

Shakespeare's Globe: 12 May – 21 September 2001. http://www.shakespeares-globe.org
Director: Barry Kyle
Designer: Hayden Griffin
King Lear: Julian Glover

Adaptation
The Executive Lear New Route Theatre Company. Edinburgh Fringe Festival, Edinburgh: 2–27 August 2001

The Yiddish Queen Lear Pascal Theatre Company, Bridewell, London: 2–20 October 2001
Adaptor/Director: Julia Pascal
Esther Laranosvska, an ageing Yiddish actress, gives her theatre company to her three daughters.

Film
The King is Alive
Film by Dogme 95
Director: Kristian Levring
UK release 2001. A group of stranded tourists rehearse *King Lear.*

Love's Labour's Lost
English Touring Theatre. Touring production: 5 February – 28 April 2001.
http://www.englishtouringtheatre.co.uk
Director: Stephen Unwin
Designer: Neil Warmington
Updated to a modern City of London setting.

New Shakespeare Company. Regent's Park Open-Air Theatre, London: 6 June – 8 September 2001
Director: Rachel Kavanaugh
Designer: Kit Surrey

British Touring Shakespeare Company. Open-air touring production, May – August 2001

http://www.btsc.homestead.com
Director: Miles Gregory

Macbeth
Derby Shakespeare Theatre Company. Derby Playhouse, 30 January – 3 February 2001
Director: Alan Smith
Amateur company.

Nitra in Slovakia. Andreja Bagar Theatre Company, Slovakia. Theatre Royal, Bath: 15–17 March 2001
Director: Vladimir Moravek
In Czech, performed as part of the Bath Shakespeare Festival.

Salisbury Playhouse Theatre Company. Playhouse, Salisbury: 16 March – 7 April 2001
Director: Joanna Read
Macbeth: Adrian Lukis

Shakespeare's Globe, The Red Company: 27 May – 22 September 2001
http://www.shakespeares-globe.org
Director: Tim Carroll
Macbeth: Jasper Britton
Lady Macbeth: Eve Best

Ludlow Festival. Ludlow Castle, Ludlow: 23 June – 7 July 2001. http://www.ludlowfestival.co.uk
Director: James Roose-Evans
Macbeth: Peter Lindford
Lady Macbeth: Cathy Owen

Cutting Edge Theatre Company. Touring production: July 2001, venues including Cawdor Castle
Director: Suzanne Lofthus
Macbeth: Christopher Duffy
Lady Macbeth: Shona McIntosh

Lincoln Shakespeare Company. Museum of Lincolnshire Life, Lincoln: 8–17 November 2001
Amateur company.

Adaptation
Macbeth – a Reworking Peregrine Theatre Company. Touring production: January – May 2001.

http://www.peregrinetheatre.co.uk
Director: Miles Foster and Ingrid Statman
Small cast of six actors.

Macbeth: Son of the Grave The Cornish Theatre Collective. Touring production: 3–6 January 2001
Director: Dominic Knutton
Included some translation into Cornish.

Umabatha: the Zulu Macbeth Johannesburg Civic Theatre production, Shakespeare's Globe, London, 18 April – 22 April 2001
http://www.shakespeares-globe.org
Adaptor: Welcome Msomi
Performed in Zulu, and set in nineteenth-century Africa.

A Cumbrian Macbeth Theatre by the Lake, Keswick: 19–21 April 2001 Translated into Cumbrian by Alan Butler.

Lady Macbeth Rewrites the Rulebook Broads With Swords Theatre Company. Warehouse, Croydon: 7–30 September 2001
Adaptor/Director: Renny Krupinski
Tara Loft travels back in time to rewrite Shakespeare in favour of the heroines.

Opera
Macbeth Kirov Opera Royal Opera House, Covent Garden, London: 9–21 July 2001
Director: David McVicar
Opera by Verdi.

Lady Macbeth of Mtsensk English National Opera. Coliseum, London: 15 June – 5 July 2001
Director: David Pountney; Lynn Binstock
Opera by Shostakovich

Measure for Measure
Shakespeare at the Tobacco Factory Theatre Company. The Tobacco Factory, Bristol: 7 February – 17 March 2001.
http://www.shakespeareatthetobaccofactory.co.uk
Director: Andrew Milton
Designer: Andrea Montag
Isabella: Lucy Black
Angelo: John Mackay

Duke Vincentio: Peter Clifford
A well-received production, which included new scenes between the Duke and Mariana, and Angelo and Mariana.

British Touring Shakespeare Company in conjunction with Catdoghorse Theatre Company. Baron's Court Theatre, London, 6 – 25 March 2001.
http://btsc.homestead.com
Director: Tom Mallaburn
Duke Vincentio: Miles Gregory
Isabella: Pennie Crocker
Angelo: Tom Mallaburn

Adaptation
Measure for Measure – restructured Seige Perilous Project. Swan Theatre, High Wycombe, 3–20 October. Performed as part of *The Play's the Thing* Shakespeare season.

The Merchant of Venice
Kiklos Teatro Theatre Company. International touring production. Theatre Royal, Bath: 5–9 June 2001. http://www.kiklos-teatro.it
Italian theatre company.

Heartbreak Productions. Touring production: June – August 2001.
http://www.heartbreakproductions.co.uk
Director: Barry Stanton
Touring Shakespeare company.

Royal Shakespeare Company. The Pit, London: 6–24 November 2001, transferred to the Swan Theatre, Stratford-upon-Avon, November 2001 – January 2002, then touring. http://www.rsc.org.uk
Director: Loveday Ingram
Designer: Colin Falconer
Shylock: Ian Bartholomew
Portia: Hermione Gulliford.

Theatre du Sygne and Haiyuza Company, International tour. UK venues: The Watermill Theatre, Newbury. 4–6 October 2001, The Other Place, Stratford-upon-Avon 25–27 October 2001
Director: Ion Caramitru
Performed by a company of Japanese actors.

Adaptation
Shylock: Shakespeare's alien West Yorkshire Playhouse: 22 June – 7 July 2001.
http://www.wyplayhouse.co.uk
Solo show performed by Patrick Stewart, including recollections of his role of Shylock in John Barton's 1978 RSC production at the Other Place.

The Merry Wives of Windsor
Northern Broadsides. Touring production: March – May 2001.
http://www.northern-broadsides.co.uk
Director/Falstaff: Barrie Rutter

Opera
Falstaff Royal Opera House, London: January 2001. Revival of 1999 production
Director: Graham Vick
Falstaff: Paolo Gavanelli
Opera by Verdi.

Falstaff Opera North/ENO. Coliseum, London: 10–26 May 2001
Director: Matthew Warchus
Falstaff: Andrew Shore
Opera by Verdi.

A Midsummer Night's Dream
Royal National Theatre, Education Department. Touring production: February – April 2001
http://www.nationaltheatre.org.uk
Director: Sean Holmes
Designer: Anthony Lamble
Bottom/Egeus: Martin O'Brian

Albery Theatre, London 16 March – 12 May 2001
Director: Matthew Francis
Designer: Lez Brotherston
Bottom: Dawn French
Oberon/Theseus: Michael Siberry
Titania/Hippolyta: Jemma Redgrave
Set in a country manor house during the Second World War.

Southend Shakespeare Players. Palace Theatre, Westcliff: 9–12 May 2001
Amateur Company.

New Shakespeare Company. Regent Park's Open-Air Theatre, London: 4 June – 8 September 2001.
http://www.openairtheatre.org.uk
Director: Alan Strachan
Designer: Kit Surrey

Arcola Theatre Company: 26 June – 21 July 2001.
http://www.arcolatheatre.com
Director: Jack Shepherd
Performed as part of the Vintage Shakespeare season at the Arcola Theatre.

Chapterhouse Theatre Company. Touring production, July – September 2001
http://www.chapterhouse.org
Director: Richard Main

Illyria Company. Open-air touring production: summer 2001. http://www.illyria.uk.com
Director: Oliver Gray
Open-air touring Shakespeare company with a cast of five actors.

Theatre Royal Company. Theatre Royal, York, 14 September – 17 November 2001
Director: Damian Cruden and Lucy Pitman-Wallace

Citizens Theatre Company. Citizens' Theatre, Glasgow: 26 October – 17 November 2001.
http://www.citz.co.uk
Director/Designer: Giles Havergal
Bottom: John Kazek
Oberon/Theseus: Greg Powrie
Titania/Hippolyta: Helen Devon

Principal Theatre Company. Touring production 2001. http://www.principal-theatre.org.uk
Director: Christopher Geelan

Adaptation
The Dreaming National Youth Musical Theatre, Linbury Studio, Royal Opera House: 18–29 December 2001
Book and lyrics: Charles Hart

Music: Howard Goodall
Musical adaptation.

Ballet
The Dream Royal Ballet, Royal Opera House: 19–31 May and on tour
Libretto: Frederick Ashton

A Midsummer Night's Dream Independent Ballet Wales. Touring production, June – July 2001.
http://www.welshballet.co.uk
Director/Choreographer: Darius James
Ballet based on *A Midsummer Night's Dream* with music by Mendelssohn.

Opera
A Midsummer Night's Dream Glyndebourne: May 2001. Revival of Peter Hall and John Bury's 1981 staging.
Opera by Benjamin Britten.

A Midsummer Night's Dream Royal College of Music. Britten Theatre: 23–25 November, Festival Theatre, Edinburgh: 28–29 November 2001
Director: John Copley
Opera by Benjamin Britten.

Film
The Children's Midsummer Night's Dream
Produced by Sand Films: 2001
Director: Christine Edzard
Music: Michel Sanvoism
Feature film, performed by 350 primary school children from the London borough of Southwark.

Get Over It
Director: Tommy O'Haver
American teen comedy about a high school boy determined to win back his girlfriend by auditioning for the school play, *A Midsummer Night's Dream*.

Much Ado About Nothing
Notos Theatre Company. Riverside 2, London: 1–3 February 2001
Director and Adaptor: Thomas Moschopoulos

Performed in Greek, the cast swapped roles for each performance, and the audience were segregated by gender.

Stamford Shakespeare Festival. Rutland Open-Air Theatre, Stamford: 3 July – 24 August 2001
http://www.stamfordshakespeare.co.uk

Principal Theatre Company. Grovelands House, Southgate, London: 2001
Open-air production.
http://www.principal-theatre.org.uk
Director: Christopher Geelan

Tremor Cordis, Yvonne Arnaud Theatre, Guildford: 22–24 November 2001

Opera
Beatrice and Benedict
Welsh National Opera. Touring production: March – April 2001
Director: Elijah Moshinsky
Berlioz opera, sung in English.

Othello
Dark Side Theatre Company. The Courtyard Theatre, London: 16 October – 4 November 2001
Director: David Keller.

Adaptation
Desdemona – A Play About A Handkerchief Just My Luck Productions. Baron's Court, London: 24 July – 12 August 2001
Playwright: Paula Vogel
Director: Josh Leukhardt

Othello Oddsocks Theatre Company. Touring production: July 2001
Touring company, specializing in comic Shakespeare adaptations: 'Oddsocks proudly presents the newlyweds. Iago reveals how to win friends and influence people'.

Opera
Otello Royal Opera House, London: 19 April – 3 May 2001
Director: Elijah Moshinsky

Otello: Jose Cura
Opera by Verdi.

Otello Glyndebourne Opera, Lewes: 21 July – 25 August 2001
Director: Sir Peter Hall
Otello: David Rendall
Opera by Verdi.

Otello Kirov Opera. Royal Opera House, London: 16 – 18 July 2001. http://www.royalopera.org
Director: Yuri Alexandrov
Otello: Vladimir Galuzin
Opera by Verdi.

Films
O Lions Gate Films: 2001
Director: Tim Blake Nelson
Screenplay: Brad Kaaya
Feature film, updating Othello to a US high school.

Othello Broadcast on ITV: Autumn 2001
Screenplay: Andrew Davies
Film made for television, updating the play to modern London with Othello as a metropolitan police commissioner.

Richard II
Royal Shakespeare Company. The Pit, London: 21 December – 17 April 2001
Transfer from the Swan, Stratford-upon-Avon, 2001. http://www.rsc.org.uk
Director: Steven Pimlott
Richard: Samuel West
Bolingbroke: David Troughton

Richard III
River Styx Company. St George's Theatre, Tufnell Park, London: 4–7 April 2001
Director: Daniel Kramer

Royal Shakespeare Company. The Young Vic, London: 25 April – 26 May 2001
http://www.rsc.org.uk
Director: Michael Boyd
Designer: Tom Piper
Richard III: Aidan McArdle

Produced as part of the RSC's Millennium season: *This England: The Histories.*

Wildcard Theatre Company. Swan Theatre, High Wycombe: 3–20 October and on tour.
http://www.wildcardtheatre.org.uk
Director: Andrew Potter
Performed as part of *The Play's the Thing* Shakespeare season.

Romeo and Juliet
Royal Shakespeare Company. Barbican, London: 17 January – 8 March 2001. http://www.rsc.org.uk
Transfer from the Royal Shakespeare Theatre, June 2000
Director: Michael Boyd
Designer: Tom Piper
Romeo: David Tennant
Juliet: Alexandra Gilbreath

Wilde Thyme Theatre Company. Touring production: April – June 2001
Director: Guy Retallack
Designer: Anthony Lamble
Romeo/Gregory: Joseph Murray
Juliet: Karina Fernandez
Set in sixteenth-century Ireland.

Creation Theatre Company and The Oxford Stage Company. Magdalen College School Grounds, Oxford: 16 July – 1 September 2001
http://www.creationtheatre.co.uk
Director: Richard Beecham
Designer: Soutra Gilmour.

Stamford Shakespeare Festival. Rutland Open-air Theatre, Stamford: 31 May – 30 June; 31 July – 25 August 2001.
http://www.stamfordshakespeare.co.uk

Rattlestick Theatre, Crescent Theatre, Birmingham: July 2001
Director: Nick Fogg
A production exploring homosexual themes, with Romeo played by a woman, which generated debate in the UK tabloid newspapers.

Mu-Lan Theatre Company and Haymarket Theatre Company. Haymarket Basingstoke: 10–27

October 2001
Director: Alasdair Ramsey, Paul Courtenay Hyu
Set in 1920s Shanghai.

New Victoria Theatre, Newcastle-under-Lyme: 26 October – 17 November 2001
Director: Gwenda Hughes

Adaptation
Rome and Jewels Puremovement. Touring US production, October – November 2001
Choreographer: Rennie Harris
A hip-hop dance adaptation.

Ballet
Romeo + Juliet Independent Ballet Wales. Touring production: April – July 2001
http://www.welshballet.co.uk
Director/Choreographer: Darius James
Score: Hector Berlioz

Romeo and Juliet Royal Ballet. The Royal Opera House, London: 2 February – 16 April 2001
Choreographer: Kenneth MacMillan
Prokofiev score

Romeo and Juliet English National Ballet. Royal Albert Hall: 13–23 June 2001
Director: Derek Deane

Opera
I Capuleti e i Montecchi Royal Opera House, London, 31 March – 20 April 2001
Opera score by Vincenzo Bellini and Felice Romani.

Radio
Fatal Loins
BBC Radio 4: 29 October 2001
Playwright: Perry Pontac
A comic retelling of *Romeo and Juliet.*

The Taming of the Shrew
Royal Exchange Theatre Company. Royal Exchange, Manchester: 1 February – 14 April 2001

http://www.royalexchange.co.uk
Director: Helena Kaut-Howson
Designer: Johanna Bryant
Katherine: Tanya Ronder
Petruchio: Lloyd Hutchinson
Played without the Induction scenes. Specially commissioned Induction scenes, written by Snoo Wilson, were discarded after the first preview.

Heartbreak Productions. Touring production: June – August 2001
http://www.heartbreakproductions.co.uk
Director: Peter Mimmack

Bold and Saucy Theatre Company. Touring production: 2 July – 4 August 2001
Director: Sarah Davey

The Court Theatre Training Company. Courtyard Theatre, London: 20 November – 16 December 2001. http://www.thecourtyard.org.uk
Director: June Abbott
Designer: Timothy Meaker

Adaptation
Shrew'd Group K Theatre Company. Arcola Theatre, London: 8 May – 2 June 2001
http://www.arcolatheatre.com
Director/Adaptor: Patrick Kealey and Janine Wunsche
A conflation of *The Taming of the Shrew* and John Fletcher's *The Tamer Tamed*. Performed as part of the Vintage Shakespeare season at the Arcola Theatre.

Kiss Me, Kate Victoria Palace: October 2001
Director: Michael Blakemore
Cole Porter Musical.

The Tempest
Almeida Theatre, London: 14 December 2000 – 17 February 2001
http://www.almeida.co.uk
Director: Jonathan Kent
Designer: Paul Brown
Prospero: Ian McDiarmid

Royal Shakespeare Company. Touring Production: 2000–2001. First performed at The Pit, October 2000. http://www.rsc.org.uk
Director: James McDonald
Designer: Jeremy Herbert
Prospero: Philip Voss
Set on a curving white plywood floor and using video projections to suggest location.

Mercury Theatre, Colchester: 20 April – 12 May 2001
Director: Dee Evans and Craig Bacon
Prospero: Gregory Floy

AandBC Theatre Company. Touring production: August 2001.

Theatre Set-up. Touring production: July – August 2001. http://www.ts-u.co.uk
Director: Wendy Macphee
Prospero: James Clarkson
Open-air Shakespeare company.

Adaptation
The Tempest Arcola Theatre, London: 28 June – 14 July 2001
Adaptor/performer Thaddeus Phillips
A one-man adaptation, first presented at La MaMa Experimental Theatre Club, New York. Prospero alone floating on a trunk, creates his universe, his life, his revenge with water, sand, ropes, pullies shadows and reflections. Performed as part of the Vintage Shakespeare season at the Arcola Theatre.

Return to the Forbidden Planet Savoy Theatre: 13 December 2001 – 19 January 2002
Director: Bob Carlton
Musical adaptation by Bob Carlton.

Titus Andronicus
BAC Development Theatre Company. Battersea Arts Centre, London, 18–28 April 2001
Director: Cal McCrystal and Paul King
Condensed the play into 45 minutes.

Battersea Arts Centre, London, 17 July – 5 August 2001
Director: Phil Wilmott
Designer: Fiona Hankey
Titus: Gary Ross

Twelfth Night
Liverpool Everyman and Playhouse Production. Liverpool Playhouse, 1–17 February 2001
Director: James Kerr
Designer: Colin Falconer
Modern dress production, played on a bare stage and against the backdrop of a thunderstorm.

Perth Theatre Company. Perth Theatre, Perth: 23 February – 10 March 2001
Director: Michael Winter.

Over The Edge Company. Touring production, Theatre Royal, Bath: 13–16 March, Edinburgh Festival: 7–27 August 2001
Touring company from Zimbabwe, setting the play in Africa.

Logos Theatre Company. Wimbledon Studio Theatre, Wimbledon, Outer London: 10–28 April 2001
Director: Melissa Holston

Royal Shakespeare Company. Royal Shakespeare Theatre, Stratford-upon-Avon: 13 April – 13 October 2001. http://www.rsc.org.uk
Director: Lindsay Posner
Designer: Ashley Martin-Davis
Malvolio: Guy Henry
Viola: Zoe Waites

Tremor Cordis Theatre Company. Upstairs at the Gatehouse, London: 5–30 June 2001
Director: Lisa Kendall
Designer: Tracy Curtis
Set in the 1930s with the songs replaced by popular blues numbers.

British Touring Shakespeare Company. Touring production: 23 June – 3 August 2001
http://www.btsc.homestead.com
Director: Miles Gregory

The Rude Mechanical Theatre Company, Theatre of the Green Tour 2001 July – August 2001

New Palace Theatre Company. Palace Theatre, Westcliff, 8–27 October 2001
Director: Roy Marsden

British Touring Shakespeare Company. Touring production: 9 December 2001–2 February 2002
http://www.btsc.homestead.com
Director: Miles Gregory
Revival of June–August 2001 summer touring production.

Adaptation
Malvolio Kaboodle Productions. Theatre Royal, Bath: 5–6 March 2001 and on tour
Playwright/Director: Lee Beagley
Performed as part of the Bath Shakespeare Festival. A reworking of the asylum scene in *Twelfth Night*.

Malvolio's Revenge Everyman Theatre, Cheltenham: 6–8 September 2001
Playwright: Jonathan Shelley

The Winter's Tale
Royal National Theatre. Olivier Theatre, London: May 2001. http://www.nationaltheatre.org
Director: Nicholas Hytner
Designer: Ashley Martin-Davis
Leontes: Alex Jennings
Hermione: Clare Skinner

Dundee Repertory Theatre, Dundee: 14 June – 4 July 2001. http://www.dundeereptheatre.co.uk
Director: Dominic Hill
Designer: Gregory Smith

Poems and Sonnets
The Rape of Lucrece Act V Theatre Company. The Rondo Theatre, Bath: 8 March – 10 March 2001
Performed as part of the Bath Shakespeare Festival.

Miscellaneous
Jubilee Royal Shakespeare Company. Swan Theatre, Stratford-upon-Avon: 12 July – 13 October 2001

http://www.rsc.org.uk
Playwright: Peter Barnes
Director: Gregory Doran
Based on the events of the Garrick Jubilee of 1769.

Prospero – the Rough Magic of Doctor Dee. Playhouse, Salisbury: 26–30 June 2001

Playwright: Stephen Davies
Was Dr Dee the model for Prospero?

Shakespeare's Women Touring production: August 2001
Solo show by Susannah York, linking Shakespeare's women through the theme of love.

THE YEAR'S CONTRIBUTIONS TO SHAKESPEARE STUDIES

1. CRITICAL STUDIES

reviewed by RUTH MORSE

Becoming a contributor to this section of *Shakespeare Survey* after years of being an appreciative user of it has only increased my admiration passing admiration for the fair-minded comprehensiveness and steady *Sitzfleisch* of my predecessors. Like them, no doubt, I have remarked – as the books piled higher – which presses are most efficient at ensuring attention for their books, and how much more alert are North American and British publishers (than publishers elsewhere) to the utility of a notice in these pages, because so much of the world conversation in Shakespeare studies is tacitly a function of those books and periodicals, those conferences, lecture-circuits, and concerns. Let me continue with some observations on the material conditions of publication.

Increasing numbers of university presses are now reluctant to publish first books based on doctoral dissertations, or monographs which do not address central (read 'popular with university teachers for their courses') subjects. The pressure which this puts on scholars to write about Shakespeare or to attach whatever they are writing to Shakespeare, need not be emphasized; there is a self-fulfilling prophecy here, in which 'hegemonic Shakespeare' becomes indirectly a product of refusal – above all the reluctance of individual readers, and then libraries, to buy books, so that publishers then decline to print and booksellers to stock them any more. This offers a new twist to arguments about

cultural control, with 'resistance' becoming a matter of marketing titles. Small presses often suffer from small budgets for publicity. Direct mail is no solution if books are not reviewed, and extracts in publishers' websites do not adequately address this problem. This is a worrying trend, particularly when the field is flourishing.

At the same time, this year's catch was particularly marked, in the Northeast Atlantic, by the stimulus of the Research Assessment Exercise, that scourge of British universities. The requirement to publish in a four-year cycle, in order to keep one's department in the 'excellent' category of research league tables, is responsible for a number of publications which might not otherwise have seen daylight. Some of the weaker contributions this year look like pressured productions – although, in the event, whether they 'produced' or not the government provided no more money.

Previous annualists have worked to encompass other countries, other languages, other conversations, and I am abashed by their inclusiveness. As a contributor who teaches outside the anglophone world, I must be sensitive to the assumptions of colleagues in continental Europe and elsewhere; within the limits of my linguistic competence I shall be trying to articulate something of other points of view. It is hard to be consistent. I am well aware that native speakers can sometimes notice less, hear less, read more cursorily than those who come to Shakespeare from another language; this is no simple matter of 'translating', or intellectual formation, but of nerves, a becoming fear of misunderstanding the text which should be more widespread. As Edward Pechter asked recently in these pages, Does it matter who is speaking? Yes, and it matters who is listening. At the very least I can emphasize the difficulties which hamper access to journals and books in countries ill-endowed with libraries and good bookshops (though this is clearly becoming a problem everywhere). This 'Who is listening' can account for variations in publication style and scholarly orientation which invite explanation. In much of continental Europe, for example, some form of personal subsidy publishing is a fact of applying for higher degrees or competitive posts (because of regulations which insist that work must be 'published' and publicly available for consultation), but such books can then languish as publishers do little by way of sending books out for review. Let me name and shame: Peter Lang Verlag are particularly unreliable in this respect, as if once they had the money they were exonerated from further effort.

In this regard, and in France, for example, as well as in Eastern Europe or India, the world-made-gain of the internet cannot be underestimated: for the first time, students and their teachers, hitherto starved of information about what is being published, can have some sense of what is going on elsewhere, but also 'here', closer to home – since it is part of the difficulty that internal distribution can be limited. For breadth of reference to Net resources, see Werner Habicht's surveys in *Shakespeare Jahrbuch*; I shall try to include addresses of individual research groups whose main method of publication is to collect their proceedings. If desk-top publishing of periodicals has enlarged possibility, it has done little to solve the problem of stocking, browsing, or ordering in particular national currencies, not even for ready money.

It is part of the ambition of annualists to spot trends, or, at least, remark patterns. I was pleased to notice in the review essays published in last year's *Studies in English Literature* a meta-trend of concern with misreading texts ascribed at least in part to

changes in education and the loss of familiarity with periods before or adjacent to 1600, or in languages other than English (let us all say Amen to Heather Dubrow's self-styled 'sermon' in vol. 41.1, 2001, pp. 191–233). Other recent review-essays have also turned attention to criticism published for the general public or for school and undergraduate readers, which otherwise suffers an automatic neglect on the grounds of an expectation that it can only represent a scholarly or critical trickle-down. Writers at all levels write about Shakespearian aftershocks: adaptation, off-shoot, or appropriation, post-colonial or otherwise. But the biggest trend must surely be the historical turn, old, new, or neo; sometimes the new old historicist readings are a reaction to post-colonial readings, and some have sparked a lively emphasis on 'presentism' forever; topical reference and religion, too, occupy us. I shall have much more to say about this below, particularly because I think that 'history' threatens to replace 'theory' as a neoshibboleth of Credentialism. Early Modern English language, followed by rhetoric, then genre, also make recognizable groups, which ought to be, but are not yet, central to historically informed writing about historiography. There were fewer books or articles on text and image than I expected, but there was a welcome resurgence in studies on or of character. And then, as always, there is *Hamlet*.

To begin with a modest book, written for school teachers, Megan Lynn Isaac's survey of children's books which use Shakespearian plots, characters and themes, as well as Shakespeare himself, opened a new seam in this rich area, which includes offshoots of different kinds. *Heirs to Shakespeare* is classroom orientated, and her judgements focus on the ambition of the proposed lessons, on what will go down well with adolescents; it is all the more fascinating for that. *Heirs to Shakespeare* is a useful compendium of such recyclings, with an introductory historical sketch of Shakespeare-for-children which reaches back to the Lambs. As well as the inevitable *Romeo and Juliet*, Isaac concentrates on *Hamlet*, *Macbeth*, *A Midsummer Night's Dream*, *Othello*, *Richard III*, *The Tempest*, and historical fiction which includes Shakespeare the man. Her juxtapositions are original, and likely to spark further research among specialists, as well as further reading – even pleasure. There is nothing like this available – if it remains available. Julie Sanders's university-based *Novel Shakespeares* grew from a course she taught at Keele on 'Shakespearian appropriation in the twentieth century'. Despite its feminist subtitle, it is less agenda-driven than simply descriptive, and the few notes show very little engagement with questions of 'feminist' appropriation beyond quoting the well-known work of Marianne Novy and Peter Erickson. More surprisingly at this level, there is little judgement about the quality of the novels discussed, either in themselves or as appropriations: Barbara Trapido, Angela Carter, Kate Atkinson, Iris Murdoch, Marina Warner, Leslie Forbes, Gloria Naylor, Jane Smiley, as well as shorter sections on other authors. Margaret Laurence is a surprising omission. This question of aesthetic judgement was constantly remarked this year, largely for its absence. Both these books are valuable for their mapping.

Other books for students belong here, not only because they are books for teaching, but because they tell us about trickle *up* – what we can expect to see in students' presuppositions. To start again with young students, Rex Gibson, who has done so much to change the teaching of Shakespeare in British schools, can sometimes seem to propose lists of schematic definitions; but anyone who looks at his 'assignments' and 'activities' will find constant emphasis on questions, on ways of combining criticism and performance of *Shakespearean and Jacobean Tragedy*, of using one's reading: 'is a character in tragedy like a real person? . . . write about the advantages and disadvantages of seeing them as living persons' – not so easy. 'You are about to direct a tragedy. . . . Write the talk you will give to your cast at your first rehearsal meeting'. On criticism: 'show how the interpretation has made you think about your own views'. This is a book which students will use, rather than pillage for the answers, by contrast to the kinds of 'introduction' which reads plays for them, such as Joe Nutt's *Introduction to Shakespeare's Late Plays*. He approaches four

plays (not *Henry VIII* or *The Two Noble Kinsmen*) by close attention to the verse, but without much context, either in period or in Shakespeare's own career. It is too easy to imagine students substituting his words for their own thought. The 'close readings' in Patsy Rodenburg's book are much better argued and convincing. *Speaking Shakespeare* offers a model of practitioner-interpretation, including the late plays. This latest manual for actors is full of insights about character-in-playing. She combines a technical approach to verse-speaking with a very practical criticism: understanding the words, why the characters say them, here at this moment, and what they contribute to the play as a whole. Her practice passages, with their accompanying analysis, consistently read the example in the context of the play as a whole, with its structures of poetry as well as feeling for structures. The book comes with its own professional jargon, and lots of bullet points, but readers should not be put off by its technicalities. I thought it one of the best books I read this year, and one of the least expected. Bernice Kliman's MLA 'Approaches to Teaching' volume on *Hamlet* offers teachers at many levels an efficient anthology of exemplary essays, bibliographies, electronic and film resources, plus the generous sharing of classroom-tested questions, exercises and approaches. It includes an essay on the second-language situation, where Hispanophone students use bilingual editions as an entry into interpretation, a familiar situation outside the Anglophone world.

Teachers *and* students will already be using the successful Oxford Shakespeare Topics series; they are consistently at a high standard. There is no resemblance between Joe Nutt's style of redescription and Russ McDonald's exploratory explanations. *Shakespeare and the Arts of Language* offers an initiation into Shakespeare's English, his rhetoric, and his verbal art. McDonald argues that increased knowledge increases pleasure, sensitivity, and accuracy of analysis; to read without listening is a kind of deafness. Here, too, Shakespeare stands in for wider subjects which have become harder to teach: figurative language, unfamiliar Englishes, poetry, always poetry. McDonald's examples call attention to chronological and stylistic changes within Shakespeare's development. Like a good musician leading us beyond merely humming the tunes, he helps us hear even Shakespearian unclarity, revealing just how expression in late Shakespeare sometimes transcends ordinary verbal meaning. McDonald's approach is particularly recommendable as a corrective to those who treat Shakespeare's *Opera* as if The Works were one undifferentiated compendium. Robert S. Miola uses a distinction between different kinds of reading, the 'textual' and the 'traditional', to make us think better about relations to books in *Shakespeare's Reading*, which also offers his own readings of the plays. Martin Wiggins' *Shakespeare and the Drama of his Time* reminds readers of the plays which Shakespeare might have acted in, attended, even read, and of how he and his competitors learned and stole from each other. A date chart might have helped, but there are clear references to help readers find one. At greater length, not surprisingly, Michael Taylor's assessment of *Shakespeare Criticism in the Twentieth Century* is also harder going, because the issues are often so complex, but his clarity of exposition is a triumph. Along the way he maps the hinterlands of a 'long' century's criticism, helping to explain what has counted as convincing, and why. The strengths and weaknesses of arguments are often clearer at a distance, as he shows by beginning from what Bradley might have been reacting to, and by coming up to yesterday, to show us the history of what *we* react to. Just as Bruce Smith's *Shakespeare and Masculinity* in the same series (praised here last year by Edward Pechter) could be used in a course on gender, so Taylor's book would be exemplary in introducing students to the conversations of criticism. It is another exceptionally good book in an outstanding series.

I want to add a book for the much-touted general reader here. In fact, I want to urge readers of *Shakespeare Survey* who have not yet bought a copy to do so – for pleasure. If the recreative imitations we now call 'appropriations' or 'offshoots' are criticism, so are other writers' appropriative commentaries, the kind of criticism-with-attitude which is neither and both anxiety and/or influence,

part of the writerly work of reading. John Gross's thoughtful, writerly, editorial work for *After Shakespeare: Writing Inspired by the World's Greatest Author*, must have occupied him for years – this is not a young man's anthology. It's too sympathetic. It presents extracts from surprising sources in surprising ways, so that musicians and film-makers, politicians and poets, seem involved in a 400-year-old conversation, not only with Shakespeare, but with each other, and with their editor. The sections range from biographical imaginings about 'The Man and the Legend' and 'The Poet', to ideas of history, to particular 'Plays and Characters'. Here is Gustave Flaubert, writing to Louise Colet about King Lear on the heath, and there is Jean-Paul Sartre reproaching Flaubert with misreading, while imposing his own interpretations on Flaubert and on Shakespeare, too: 'the metamorphoses and correspondences are not meant to lead to philosophical conclusions; they are not symbols of anything but give the whole scene an obscure, profound unity of meaning'. Ivan Turgenev tries to persuade Leo Tolstoy to try just once more to understand Shakespeare, with the result that Tolstoy writes his famously furious diatribe against Shakespeare's unnaturalness. Political prisoners of Robben and Devil's Islands find solace, signalling their individual selections of key passages. Gross knows Shakespeare so well that he is able to identify allusions which might otherwise pass unnoticed. Emily Dickinson permutes the distance between Claribel in Tunis and her kingly father in Naples into a hummingbird's flight – and Gross's explanation turns what has been obscure into a powerful reminiscence of *The Tempest*. Just as certain writers returned again and again to favourite Shakespearian moments, so the same names reappear in different contexts, telling us about Gross's own habits of reading: Heinrich Heine, D. H. Lawrence, Boris Pasternak, and George Bernard Shaw. The acts of remembrance that this book celebrates are, by and large, due to reading, and to the memorization, deliberate and accidental, accurate and approximate, of phrases and passages. Readers of *Shakespeare Survey* are bound to find some of the choices familiar, but all of us will find surprises (Duke

Ellington) – as no doubt disagreements about who's in (at too great length) and who's out altogether. Gross, a former editor of the *Times Literary Supplement*, and a theatre critic of many years' standing (as well as the author of a book on the afterlife of Shylock), must have been keeping notes for decades, and the charms of this collection arise from his arrangements, so that within his own organization, his 'uncommon readers' seem to be in dialogue with each other, as well as with Shakespeare, and not least in this company is Gross's own accompanying voice. There are two good indices.

Also for the general reader, but a pretty grown-up one, is David Bevington's *Shakespeare*, which is unusual not least by virtue of its arrangement by stages of life, or life-problems, above all those which belong to the family at its moments or periods of crisis – not quite a 'seven ages', and resolutely attempting to be more than 'of man'. Individual plays come up in different contexts, so there is no sense of the usual trawl from biography to a chronology of the work. Like Anne Barton's comprehensive introduction to the new Pléiade translations, Bevington thinks about all of Shakespeare, how Shakespeare continually returned to problems, situations, characters he had previously used – but wrote them new. Bevington's prose is accessible American vernacular, but he pulls no punches about his ideas, and this is not an introduction for the completely uninitiated, nor for the very young. It assumes the twentieth-century advances in psychology, anthropology, feminism and cultural decentring which have changed so much; but it conveys Shakespeare's constant source in families and their terrors. Although both book and 'Préface' touch on the poetry, they rather emphasize character and plot, the traditional ways readers read and continue to read. I hope my colleagues over the page will forgive my including here the criticism these books contain.

Character is certainly back this year. The combination of violence and character can be seen especially in work on the vulnerability of women characters. Two articles this year concentrated on rape. Emily Detmer-Goebel looks at Lavinia's silent suffering through an unmodulated feminist lens which reveals only patriarchal suppressions in 'The Need for Lavinia's Voice: *Titus Andronicus* and the Telling of Rape'. The author confuses shame and embarrassment, avoids any question of whether or not Lavinia might *want* to be carried off by her affianced husband or that 'rape' in the mouth of Saturninus might be interpreted according to his evident character (an early distortion). Concentrating with such intensity on Lavinia's 'silencing', she seems not to consider that Lavinia's plight includes being widowed by a murder for which her brothers are framed; claims that her rape is 'undetected'; has difficulties with English legal history, and herself erases the recognition by a male child of Lavinia's attempt to communicate. Rape is an extreme case, and a horrible one, and one needs to remember that the reactions of men whose children, siblings, or loved ones have suffered assaults may include guilt over their own failure to protect, their helplessness in the face of ruined lives, complex combinations of shame. The return of character-based criticism continues in Jessica Slights's, 'Rape and the Romanticization of Shakespeare's Miranda'. Resuscitating Anna Jameson's ethical approach to character, above all female characters, is an adventurous, and welcome, project. Slights reconsiders 'sentimentalist' readings of the play before rebuking more recent critics for doing to Miranda just what earlier criticism did: making her a mere pawn in her father's strategy of revenge and recuperation – as perhaps Lavinia is more important to Tamora's family's revenge against Titus than in herself. If Jameson's 'natural' Miranda seems derived from ideals of innate human goodness, she *is* finding a way to argue that women might legitimately say what they want and act accordingly. There is a problem here: this 'natural' love that Miranda feels negotiates a *social* dynastic ambition which she seems to know and not to know in the course of the play. Slights finds it understandable that Miranda does not want to be raped – whether as part of an attack on her father or not. How curious that this appears a striking thing for a critic to say.

Not all violence is rape. Not everyone would begin a consideration of the ethics of black comedy by analysing the style of Tarantino's screen-play for *Pulp Fiction*, but that is how David Ellis begins 'Black Comedy in Shakespeare', deriving Samuel L. Jackson's hitman from the murderers of Clarence. His point is the killers' double disjunction in style: the satiric misapplication of the demotic to the morally charged subject of murder and the coercive and self-conscious wit of the killing comic. Surveying other film killers (the omission of *Prizzi's Honor*, with its extraordinary moral blank, is surprising), and juxtaposing them to his reading in renaissance drama (and Martin Wiggins's broad survey, *Journeymen in Murder* [1991]), Ellis turns his attention towards the incompetent murderers of *Arden of Feversham*, the mixture of would-be wit and mutilation in *Titus*, the 'stooge' routines in *Jew of Malta*, then edges towards his real subject, which is the failure of our critical language in talking about the tragic grotesque, especially in recent introductions to *Titus*. Character here approaches stereotype at the same time as it engages with ethics, and resistant as we might wish to be about the clichés of rape and murder, there is much worth pondering here. And while we are considering filmic grotesque, memories of Hammer horror movies inspire Paul Goetsch to a curious counter-factual: a Ghost-less *Hamlet*. The idea of 'The Monstrous in *Hamlet*', in *Historicizing/Contemporizing Shakespeare*, is to look once more on what the ghost is doing there. It is a monster, full of contradictions, both 'substitute' and 'supplement'. It is infectious, in the infected court, and creates murderers around itself, including Hamlet, whose own ambivalence saves him from the monstrosity he has confronted.

Power over other individuals, power which is abused, underlies an article on the stripping of Griselda – a public humiliation close to violence or the domestic tyranny of Petruchio over Kate. It must have seemed a good idea to look at Kate's taming in the light of Griselda's patience, her unspeaking patience, as does Margaret Rose Jaster in 'Controlling Clothes, Manipulating Mates: Petruchio's Griselda', but it might have helped to have read J. Burke Severs on the *The Literary Relationships of Chaucer's Clerkes Tale* (New Haven, 1942) or Anna Baldwin's essay on Griselda in *Chaucer Traditions* (Cambridge, 1991) before

making any generalizations about continuities between medieval fiction and early-modern practice, include clothing and unclothing. In the tellings of this tale it is often Griselda who leaves her wealth behind, not necessarily Walter who strips her. Nor does Jaster ever acknowledge that in the Griselda stories, from Petrarch onwards, the behaviour of the offending husband is *always* and *universally* condemned, and her evident goodness remarked by everyone (including the narrating Clerke – not Chaucer-the-author), who recognize that Griselda's exceptional worthiness is complemented by her clothes, not made by them. There is no implication of physical violence here or elsewhere in the originals – unlike the story of Kate the curst. What looks like an illumination through analogues is an unfortunate series of misreadings.

The unsatisfactoriness of male behaviour is the subject of '*The World Must be Peopled*': *Shakespeare's Comedies of Forgiveness*, in which Michael D. Friedman proposes a model narrative to replace supposedly rigid genre expectations, but his own strong distinction between silent 'Griseldas' and talking 'Shrews' creates its own difficulties, as he acknowledges. His readings of difficult moments in the plays are fascinating in themselves, and do not require an early sub-genre of 'forgiveness'. Comedies do end by accepting male misbehaviour (Bertram/Helena *and* Diana, Claudio/Hero, Proteus/Julia *and* Silvia, Angelo/Mariana *and* Isabella, but also, perhaps, Petruchio/Kate) for the sake of procreation, but not these only. Although his frame attempts to find a stageable modern solution which removes the problem of marriage-reconciliation from its double context of imitating divine mercy and conforming to legality (making marriage vows into possible marriages), what it achieves is a way of explaining to contemporary audiences (for whom romantic love trumps arguments from economic dependence, social status, or comic genre) the necessity to accept flawed men. His analyses of productions which make behaviour credible avoids the choicelessness of a world between the loss of nunneries and the invention of the 'respectable professions' of teaching or nursing. Shakespeare's four early plays are indeed hard to stage, and his studies of performances indicate ways in which practitioners have approached the difficulties of making the forgivings credible. He is particularly good on the importance of cutting and rearranging, and on the importation of silent characters.

This might be a good place to notice the emphasis on character which informs Philip Armstrong's *Shakespeare in Psychoanalysis*. Although it is mainly taken up with descriptions of psychoanalytic theories, and is rather short on applications, it demonstrates yet another area where Shakespeare's characters have come to provide examples, common places, of personality types which became available in languages other than English – a striking point when one thinks of the emphasis on the word in most forms of psychoanalytic work. How else is an inner self to manifest its latency, how otherwise can subjectivity find expression? This question of character as an individual subject, particularly a 'bourgeois subject', has occupied criticism for some years now, sometimes as if Shakespeare were the onlie begetter of consciousness.

Hugh Grady has another look at this problem in 'Falstaff: Subjectivity Between the Carnival and the Aesthetic', in which character turns toward subjectivity. Based on his earlier, philosophically orientated 'interrogation' of recent literary analyses of early modern subjectivity (in John Joughin's *Philosophical Shakespeare*, 2000), in which he criticized the reductionism of reading 'characters' as determined apologists for ideology, here he is particularly concerned with Foucault's powerful insistence on centralized repression. This essay attempts a positive contribution to an alternative analysis by reconsidering the variety of Falstaff, and will be useful for its survey of other approaches to Falstaff, as to ideas of early modern subjectivity. It carries the reminder that many European social theorists – like analysts – have had recourse to Shakespearian characters in order to illustrate and argue their own ideas of an emerging modern. Grady's Falstaff, poised between the carnival past and the aestheticized future, is a master of resistance. But even in the theatre, or, perhaps, especially there, we are aware of Falstaff's ambitions for his Hal's future: endless pocket money without responsibility, but with the power of future revenge upon his enemies, such as the Lord Chief Justice. In reconsidering Falstaff as a kind of containment of Carnival by the fictional constraints of production in the London theatre, Grady rereads old interpretations with a Frankfurt accent.

In an older accent, character is still being read in terms of inherited types, such as the Vice (or distinctions about Griseldas). Pauline Blanc attempts to look at continuities in traditional characters in 'La Fonction du rire carnavalesque dans le théâtre des Tudor'. She juxtaposes Shakespeare's use of 'the' Vice figure in *The Winter's Tale* with both *Mankind* and Fulwell's *Like Will to Like* to argue that the comedy of 'mischief' always has greater risk attached than we may, with hindsight, realize. Like the other essays in the same collection on Tudor theatre, this one stresses continuities in the theatre and in other kinds of public entertainment. In addition to the problem of whether or not Shakespeare's audiences could have known the earlier plays, the question arises how far any 'Vice' would be recognizable to an early seventeenth-century audience, and whether, by that time, the heritage of comic rogues plotting in theatrical plots had rather taken on a picaresque, or trickster colouring. Her observation works better in the late-medieval religious context than in Shakespearian late romance, where no one worries that Autolycus will succeed in doing serious harm; the discovery of a traditional 'type' is neither a demonstration that that type continues two hundred years later nor an explanation of how it might have changed in the interim.

Violence and laughter also occupy François Laroque in 'Slaughter and Laughter: Cruel Comedy in fin-de-siècle Tudor Drama'. Like Pauline Blanc, Laroque considers the potential threat of Autolycus, and opens by suggesting that we see him as a comic Leontes, whose 'verbal tyranny' arises from his ability to engender anxiety in Perdita's peasant family by threatening them with imagined tortures which, presumably, Laroque thinks parallel Leontes's potential in the opening scenes of the play. If this seems a bit tenuous, it is there to open up a series of examples of comic horrors, the kinds of grotesque moments when violence is framed by sarcasm, such as Marlowe's murder of Ramus or Shakespeare's of Cinna the poet – or David Ellis's witty murderers. Like Blanc, Laroque assumes a 'carnivalized violence', but he also wants it to be both 'fin de siècle' and allied in some undefined way with the experience of plague. There are some undigested ideas here, with period, other dramatists, the grotesque, and pre-christian folk culture jostling for attention. As one expects from Laroque, there is a fine display of verbal fireworks, but it remains unclear either that Shakespeare followed Marlowe in 'evolving a type of macabre, plaguelike laughter' or that his humour is 'gallows' or 'perverse' or 'mannerist'. Less convincing, still in the same collection, is Marie-Hélène Besnault's vicefigure, '"Richard III" et le rire'. This is a close reading of the development of Richard through the histories, in the context of the Vice, with an eye to the question of just what kinds of reactions audiences have today, might have had, might be expected to have, to Richard, to Richard's laughter at the other characters, and to grotesque situations in the plays. Besnault doesn't talk explicitly about satire as a corrective, rather stressing Richard's own desire, and our collusion with it, and the ways that history provided the corrective, since whatever happens, we know that Richard will be punished. It is striking that here and in Laroque's essay Baudelaire's presence makes itself felt, as a comparative example of multivalent perversity which he found already in the story of the apple of good and evil in Eden.

Claire McEachern wants to be writing about reformation epistemology in 'Figures of Fidelity: Believing in *King Lear*', but I think this ambitious essay is actually also about character and stereotype. She shifts attention from the more familiar study of politics to explore ways that 'the characters and tropes of female identity' might be understood to address beliefs which depend upon ideas about keeping faith. This has the virtue of proposing a problem more nuanced than the either/or approach to atheism or Catholicism, but founders on its discovery that attitudes to women, even when they are daughters rather than sexual partners, are neither new nor changed. Opening from Lear's

tirade against female unchastity, McEachern sees male vulnerability as itself a trope for fidelity in the largest sense: betrayal by misrepresentation, deceit as a kind of seduction which itself recapitulates the Great Deceiver. Lear curses his daughters instead of himself, revealing both family similarity and parental disappointment that children are not better than their parents. This does seem to cross traditional and widespread views of inexorable decline with a very modern ameliorism. It is hard to argue the usual case backwards: Lear's loss of faith, in this reading, precedes his discovery that his daughters have deserted him. Although the parallel with predestinarian thought and the lack of epistemological certainty is attractive, the vocabulary of appearance, doubt, proofs, and reality returns us to older ways of asking how we might know. Women, here as elsewhere, figure the problem in traditional and widespread analyses of their essence: ambivalent, contradictory depictions of their virtues and vices.

Speech has been acknowledged to be imperfect, at least since we lost the Paradisal first tongue, and perhaps before, since the serpent inaugurated its use to deceive. Saying what we mean is as fraught as meaning what we say. In 'The Reclamation of Language in *Much Ado About Nothing*', Maurice Hunt seems to want to stress that since one can hear only what is said, arguments which have concentrated upon 'noting' have almost of necessity emphasized listeners over speakers. He works from a familiar paradigm of 'patriarchal language' and control, in which characters are 'forced' by patriarchal 'dictators' (Leonato is a 'linguistic autocrat' when he tries to save his daughter's marriage), a kind of linguistic violence. Hunt makes heavy weather of what is usually taken to be comedy: the men 'capitalize upon inherent disjunctions between expression and meaning' to ensure that 'patriarchal speech almost always triumphs by mandating its construction of the truth', though that does cause some difficulties for the play's resolution. Is it really true that other people's words 'cause' Beatrice and Benedick to fall in and out of love? or do their friends trick them out of pride into admission – to themselves as much as each other or the world – that they have loved unavowedly for a long time? Women, according to Hunt, have a moral superiority, because their speech is not patriarchal. The essay is written at a high level of abstraction, is restrictive in its interpretations, without always remembering that sometimes, in performance for example, a joke is understood by its auditors (not its targets) as precisely that, *playing* on language.

This year Spenser made a slight comeback, and in 'Laughter Chastened or Arden Language: A Study of Comic Languages in *As You Like It*', in *Tudor Theatre*, Raphaëlle Costa de Beauregard emphasizes the importance of bawdy language in the mouths of the cross-dressed as a source of comedy, especially in a homosexual context (I seem to be credited with responsibility for this view, which I hasten, modestly, to decline); explores euphuized doubleness through disguise (so that characters speak simultaneously from the court and the forest); then finds an unconvincing reinterpretation of Spenser's heroines, especially the cross-dressed Britomart. In addition, she claims that the play invokes the 'language' of miniaturist painters of the period, a claim I am sure I cannot follow, since it appears to render Orlando, at least, naked.

Where traditional stereotypes are evident, and the evidence is used with conviction, is in Laurie Shannon's *Sovereign Amity: Figures of Friendship in Shakespearean Contexts*. This is hardly a new subject, but it is eloquently treated: friendship is the king of loving relations but the relation most difficult for kings. The need, in traditional analyses, for the friends to be equals and similar, must be impossible at the lonely pinnacle of hierarchical societies. It was never clear, or perhaps it was always unclear, how well the picture of possibility worked, since in theory neither women nor children were capable of the free gift of disinterested love which was the defining characteristic of the exchange of amity. The insulation of English is relevant here, for this exceptionally good book could have built upon foundations established first by Jean-Claude Fraisse, in his *Philia: la notion d'amitié dans la philosophie antique; essai sur un problème perdu et retrouvé* (Paris, 1974), and, if I may be allowed a less disinterested reference, by *Shakespeare, la Renaissance et l'amitié*, ed. R. Marienstras and D. Goy-Blanquet

(Amiens, 1998). I mention these books not to fault Shannon's scholarship, but to emphasize the problems of distribution which I mentioned at the outset, of chronological-thinness which Heather Dubrow raised in her *SEL* survey, and of linguistic parochialism.

In the course of the high middle ages in western Europe, friendship was treated most widely in imaginative literature, not in philosophical texts. It would have buttressed this book's argument to be able to refer to long traditions of treating friendship *literature* as posing problems, not solutions; Shannon refers briefly to the survey by Laurens Mills, but really begins in the early modern period. The opening substantive essay on *Mariam* is followed by one on *Two Noble Kinsmen*, before she turns her attention to royal prerogatives – or the lack of them. I want to be clear: this is an outstanding book, and a short one, but, even so, generalizations which leave a thousand years out of account must be the poorer for it. At the very least, the evolution in hierarchical kingship uprooted the baronial obligation of advice to the king from its basis in *amicitia*, not unlike Portia's claim to a kind of equality with Brutus which includes a share in discussion. Still, having registered this ungracious cavil, let me hasten to say that the argument over friendship and kingship, where one soul in bodies twain meets two bodies inhabited by one royal soul, is persuasive. Here the adoption of a new term, or a French term, 'mignonnerie', to indicate the ruler's necessary loss of equality-based friendship, is useful (although one has to remember that in theory, again, friendship between monarchs could be envisaged, however difficult it must be to maintain the parallel of friendship and public peace). As one would expect, there are chapters on *Edward II* and on the *Henries*, and on the Sicily/Bohemia challenge of *Winter's Tale*. Always aware of forms of political life in America, the book ends not with the institutional obligation to 'advise and consent' but with a more Shakespearian attitude to the impossibility for great rulers, including presidents, to maintain a private self.

The concatenation of character shading into ethics through speech is Adrian Poole's subject in

'*Macbeth* and the Third Person'. Not what one expects, this entry into the play via pronouns, and yet
the combination of detailed attention to what is
said and detailed observation of what is performed,
gives us a nuanced and new reading of this play,
with implications well beyond it. The grammatical category of the third person has less precision, either of bodily placement or action, than
has the 'you' of direct address, immediate relation, like the 'this' and 'that' he deals with at the
end of the essay. The potential move from 'he' to
'you' enables Poole to absorb those unaddressed,
unplaced 'attendants' into ontology on the point
of action, danger, complicity. We have all noticed
the ambiguous 'he' who has no children, but not
how frequently the address of one character to another may reveal their relations, how the move from
pronoun to proper noun may function as emphasis – as readers, of course, we have their names
constantly before us. Third persons move out to
encompass heaven as looker-on; the stage lookers-
on often dismissed as characterless spear-carriers –
Cornwall's servant, say, or Timon's. Poole transforms grammar into ethics, 'he' becomes 'you' and
spectators become witnesses. This combination of
linguistically alert close reading and performance
might reconcile performance practitioners and literary critics: Patsy Rodenburg would surely approve. Performance and performatives, language
and linguistics – these new combinations of skills
reread Shakespeare in ways which make a renewed
attention to rhetoric appear moving and persuasive.

Emphasis on particular figures of rhetoric has
often seemed to offer answers to the style and tone
of particular plays. George T. Wright was an early
critic who attended to some of them. In his essays
collected from twenty-five years' practice, *Hearing
the Measures: Shakespearean and other Inflections*, two,
on hendiadys in *Hamlet* and the (verse) measures of
Measure, focus on Shakespeare. Wright emphasizes
the sounds and structures of poetry, building from
linguistics or rhetoric to explain what makes poets –
and sometimes characters – sound characteristically themselves. Shakespeare is present throughout
the whole collection, and English verse informs
the essays on Shakespeare. Auden's question about

'how the verbal contraptions work', which Wright
takes as his text, alerts readers (more than listeners) to the effects of style, and reveals the language
evolving – writers changing it by their adaptations
from Latin or their innovations to create effects.
The much-quoted study of 'hendiadys' reminds us
that we forget at our peril to hear what Shakespeare's characters and plays are saying, because style
speaks, and we risk wrenching their sentences to
our own interpretations.

Wright is not mentioned by Stefania d'Agato
d'Ottavi, 'Tragicomedy and Laughter: The Case
for *Measure for Measure*', who finds the technical
use of chiasmus and oxymoron at the heart of ambivalent reactions to tragicomedy, and argues that
these rhetorical figures enable Shakespeare to depart from earlier renaissance theory (of surprise
happy endings which rescue comedy from tragedy)
in order to create worrying uncertainties all the way
through his plays. Her key plot device for the exercise of rhetorical ambivalence is disguise, and she
concentrates on the Duke's deceptions in *Measure*,
because disguise functions to stress the paradoxes
of power and the instability of government. In addition, she argues for an unrecognized source for
the play which combines the ambivalence she describes, in a poem by the young Thomas More, 'A
mery jest how a sergeant would learn to play the
frere' (there is, however, no demonstration of how
Shakespeare could have known it). Whether or not
this is convincing, it asks us to consider habits in
narratives which use comic approaches to serious
themes such as powerlessness, and reminds us that
such multivalent work existed in English from the
late middle ages.

Not all such reading is ethical – this is one of
the traditional complaints, after all, about rhetoric,
that constantly rediscovered subject. Perhaps in a
longer study it might be possible to argue that the
actual cloth industry and its travails contributed to
linguistic metaphors of misused rhetorical 'colours'
and sumptuary offences, but given how old were
ideas of words 'clothing' underlying reality or 'currency' as a figure of 'exchange', María O'Neill's 'Of
Clothing and Coinage', in *The Anatomy of Tudor
Literature* can only be impressionistic and suggestive.

I'm afraid that this is the kind of chronologically challenged essay which has provoked Graham Bradshaw's distempered lecture, 'Shakespeare's Peculiarity'. Like Brian Vickers, Bradshaw is increasingly concerned with anachronistic projections of current preoccupations onto Shakespeare. This lecture amounts to a rant about current politicized criticism of Shakespeare which is present-minded and misses what is great about Shakespeare – the poetry.

For all the gains in recent innovations in Shakespeare studies, it could not be clearer that one of the great losses in recent education is, bluntly, the ability to read carefully and understand where Shakespeare's language and rhetoric come from. Three contributions to Shakespeare's language and how to read do go right back to consider English before Early Modern English. Last year's review of the collection *Reading Shakespeare's Dramatic Language* reminded us just how careful one has to be about 'who is speaking'. One might think that a manual from Norman Blake would become a basic tool, but *A Grammar of Shakespeare's Language* is dense, detailed, and very difficult to use, although excellent indices help. Not for beginners, but more and more important as students and editors lose experience of early forms of English and of the history of the language. The old problem remains, however, as Blake treats Shakespeare's language as one repertoire, that is, not a variety which changes over the twenty years of his career, nor language which is moulded by metre. There is a methodological difficulty here which contrasts with the approach through the poetry as represented by Russ McDonald or Adrian Poole. Blake does look briefly at characterized speech and at some distinctions of address, and, if you're still reading, his book has the great advantage of quoting directly from Q and F, thus looking afresh at the layout of the language. One would still recommend Barber's *Early Modern English* (1976), which remains the best introduction to the subject, or Manfred Görlach's *Introduction to Early Modern English* for advanced students (available in English translation, 1991), but this is likely to be consulted, with whatever frustrations follow. Nobody

now pays a great deal of attention to phonology, so let me recommend Matthew Giancarlo's fascinating (no, really) 'The Rise and Fall of the Great Vowel Shift? The Changing Ideological Intersections of Philology, Historical Linguistics, and Literary History'. It might seem strange to refer to a study of a controversy among linguists, except that 'Early Modern English', as a periodizing category, intersects with 'Early Modern' as a historical category, and, in both, Shakespeare is a pivotal figure. When we cross disciplinary boundaries we are all too prone to believe what we read, and this is a fine demonstration of the perils of innocence. A quick look at how Shakespeare's contribution to English, Englishes, national standards and RP is a useful way of thinking about thinking through the questions of historical language change and our own categories. Equally enlightening is Hugh Craig's 'Grammatical Modality in English Plays from the 1580s to the 1640s'. It may not be immediately evident from the title, but the implications for any history of the 'modern', for ideas about dramatic dialogue as mimesis of contemporary speech, for authorial self-consciousness, are fascinatingly revealed in this study. It is not news that Jonson, for example, not only imitated contemporary speech for his characters (Marie-Thérèse Jones-Davies discussed this a generation ago), but here is rich, varied, and widespread evidence of changes across a range of dramatists. Attention to 'can', 'could', 'may', 'must' and 'should' may indeed reveal increasing subjectivity in characterization in this period; Craig's analysis of the evidence is modest, cautious, and alert to the ambiguities in what he has surveyed.

If it seems that Shakespeare's poems have been neglected this year, except in collections of essays, there is a timely piece, almost a review-essay, by Peter Robinson which considers the critical positions of editors of *The Sonnets*. Robinson, a poet, writes not only about the difficulties of reading the sonnets as narrative, as autobiographical narrative, as sonnets with a hypothesized narration implied outside them; but equally about recent criticism of these options, Katherine Duncan-Jones's, but especially Helen Vendler's. The title, 'Pretended Speech Acts in Shakespeare's Sonnets', identifies his concern with the limits of speech-act theory as a way of understanding the poetry's claim to do something. Like Vendler, Robinson is committed to contemporary poetry, and what he has learned from long study of Geoffrey Hill makes itself felt here. By contrast, Patrick Cheney argues in 'Shakespeare's Sonnet 106, Spenser's National Epic, and Counter-Petrarchism', that 'Chronicle of wasted time' engages specifically and pointedly with Spenser. To make the link to *The Faerie Queene* he brings up barrages of scholarship to argue for a possible, but ultimately speculative, association in a style of 'topical' reference. It is not clear what we would gain by assuming that one and only one narrative is meant, nor that the use of 'petrarchism' which he finds in the sonnet is aimed at one particular Petrarchan. He hangs an immense argument on details of one sonnet. By contrast, *Neo-Historicism* reprints Heather Dubrow's '"In thievish ways": Tropes and Robbers in Shakespeare's Sonnets and Early Modern England' (revised from *JEGP*, 96 [1997]). This exemplary demonstration of how one might use historical records to illuminate the range of meaning and implications of literature moves from sixteenth-century court records (as indicators of what people were afraid of) to Shakespeare's 'thieves' and 'theft', using some sonnets as a kind of test case – but by the end of the essay Dubrow is casting light on *King Lear*. She explores the questions of categories of crime, anxiety about crime, and blame for crime before looking at literary evocations of 'thievery' (including burglary, robbery, night-attacks, violence and intimidation). Of course she is able to show that Shakespeare's employment of 'thievery' is nuanced, and that our reading benefits from cultural knowledge, but there is a further benefit to this essay, in a focus on issues of place (intrusion into a house, for example). She illustrates the reversal of our usual expectations that while theft is sometimes sexualized, it is just as important to notice that sexual advances might be assimilated to a kind of theft. One thing 'is' not the other, but interchange between the two can reveal complex anxieties about stable ownership of property and values in Shakespeare's texts and in his culture.

In addition to George T. Wright's, collected essay volumes this year include John Kerrigan's and Susan Snyder's. Collection is one method of overcoming difficulties of distribution; it also, of course, reveals the critic's characteristics. A good half of Kerrigan's essays are 'on Shakespeare'; all have been published before, and are well known, much quoted, and often set for undergraduates. 'Shakespeare the Reviser' certainly circulated for years in illegal photocopies, and two essays on tragedy and tragicomedy are of immediate interest to Shakespearians. Kerrigan begins with a commitment to textual bibliography, and builds from a strong base towards constantly revealing readings with unexpected juxtapositions (the essay on Keats reading Shakespeare is worth the price of admission). Kerrigan's work never makes easy reading, but his prose is always worth the struggle because he hears more than many contemporary readers of Shakespeare – or modern poetry, come to that. Take one at bedtime as an antidote to more simplistic pronouncements. Kerrigan is still young, and one can look forward to another such volume in the course of time. But there will be no more new work from Susan Snyder. The acknowledgments which preface *Shakespeare: A Wayward Journey* are a tribute to the author's intellectual tenacity while dying of cancer, and to the love evidenced by her friends' assistance in seeing the book through the press. These fifteen essays span thirty years, developing the penchant of New Criticism for verbal and structural elucidation into generic criticism which was quietly feminist before Feminist was an identity. Three are hitherto unpublished, the others reprinted, and rereading them one is reminded that good readers, accurate readers, see more, see differently; in addition, they absorb the intellectual movements around them while remaining themselves. Like John Kerrigan's collection, this one makes surprising juxtapositions: Kate and Freud's Dora, for example, or the contradictory attitudes to war inherent in challenges to single combat. They range from *Romeo and Juliet* to *The Winter's Tale*, via biblical theology and Lacan. As Meredith Skura acutely notices in her preface, these essays often begin with rupture, move via multiple perspectives, question binary oppositions, and emphasize process; they always argue her ideas with unpretentious wit. Ordinary language criticism has more to be said for it than 'useful for undergraduates'; these essays are based on broad as well as learned reading, and know the exigencies of textual editing and performance. They only look easy.

In applauding combinations of skills, I must commend Jeffrey Masten's, '*More* or Less: Editing the Collaborative', which begins, like Kerrigan on 'revision', from textual bibliography. The idea that we should look at whole plays, not at part-authors, and consider collaborations by starting with the end-product, may not seem a revolutionary idea. But, as Masten points out, approaches to Hand D (viz., in Shakespeare's own) in *The Booke of Sir Thomas More*, have – as with many other presumed Shakespearian collaborations – argued over exactly which bits are from the hand of the Master rather than how collaborators might have worked. His arguments, including the idea that we might look again at the editorial interventions of Hand C, have implications for criticism of Shakespeare, including the Hecate additions to *Macbeth*. Masten's reading of *More* and issues of a self, of society, of the problems of 'strangers' who are 'aliens' here but at home elsewhere, asks us to take the whole play with a seriousness it has not hitherto enjoyed, and to think about its collaborative attention to a serious social problem. I must add, however, that this article, like others in *Shakespeare Studies*, 29, has been inadequately copy-edited, and one has to be alert to errors which have unaccountably crept in.

Emrys Jones's 'Reclaiming Early Shakespeare' is a partly autobiographical account of assessing the style and structures of *Titus*, *John*, and the first English history tetralogy. Jones's acknowledgement of the ways that performances have reassessed them leads to his own reconsideration of their dates and the authorship controversies which surround them: he now accepts Peele's hand in *Titus* (thus reclaiming an early date) but finds Shakespeare's style (Mortimer's death scene in particular) and structures (repeated later in his career) in *1 Henry VI*.

Two contributions by Peter Holland also demonstrate cross-over criticism. 'Seeing Better' belongs to the genre of 'Inaugural Lecture', which commands the new professor to set out his wares, and to demonstrate his expertise. In this rich survey, Holland reminds us all of the need to listen, to watch, to observe – the actual business of moving and persuading of which we all write so confidently in the abstract – and of the history of authors complaining about us, who merely look without concentrated listening. He stresses the need for 'close hearing' without ever losing the requirement for strenuous attention, for 'close seeing', and works in a programme about performance study within academic work, study which might yet discover who hears what, and when. He finds in plays by Jonson and by Shakespeare the distinction between passive spectators and active audiences, then moves to the moral status of acting-upon, or not, what we hear, bringing Hamlet closer to Volumnia than one might expect, and demonstrating how ambiguities about what kind of 'audition' is meant can turn upon themselves in witty verbal play which requires over-hearing as well as observing the observers on stage. He does not neglect the special problems of film-going, or seeing again, perhaps better. As Gombrich put it many years ago, about the difficulties of seeing art, we are always 'learning to look'; without ears in attendance the alternative is mere closed reading. In 'Beginning in the Middle' he extends performance analysis to intervals (in US English, intermissions) in performance; the implication for Shakespeare is that one break in effect creates a two-act organization in audience experience of a play and asks us to think again about the five-act divisions in editions of Shakespeare, about audience attention and directorial shaping. This lecture has the best curtain line in the year's round-up.

Levity, levity, I defy levity. Andreas Höfele's 'Sackerson the Bear' must be the year's funniest essay, but its brilliance lies in its manipulations of style, approach and content, in a series of Chinese boxes in order to make a series of serious points. It begins in pastiche of Greenblatt, with James Joyce's use of Brandes's style of scholarship; moves to the 'old' historicism with which Joyce, among others, was so impatient, then uses its own performance of new historicist approaches to the Elizabethan theatre to move through performance, kingship, spectacular entertainment of ominous character, finally, and convincingly, to a consideration of the place of 'aesthetics', the pleasures of literature and literary judgement – and the retreat from both which, as he elegantly demonstrates, is one of the problems which unites the New Historicism to the Old. He presses at Greenblatt's own evasions of literary judgement, to align the old 'literature and society' to 'society and text' and demonstrate how very close they can seem. And he offers real illumination about the bear.

Wittily titled, 'Pre-loved Partners in Early Modern Comedy' focuses mainly on cast-off mistresses. T. G. A. Nelson surveys pre-marital sex from Roman to contemporary continental comedies, and he finds an English specificity in the emphasis on the fatality of the female slip. Shakespeare is only briefly present, but 'second loves', both male and female, is not the usual view of the permanence and exclusivity of romantic love. Though not Nelson's interest, his subject offers us a different point of view on the Claudios and Juliets of the time, who anticipated consummation; on companionate marriages, with their claims to a new kind of equality; and another wrinkle, too, on the friendship trope whereby one man gives up his beloved to his best friend. It would be good, eventually, to see the asymmetry extended to men, to test the question of whether a male slip irrevocably makes a man a rake. 'Marrying Down: Negotiating a More Equal Marriage on the English Renaissance Stage', by Marliss C. Desens, makes a kind of companion piece. Shakespeare is only one playwright to make an appearance in this essay about social inequalities in marriages in English drama, but I want to call attention to it because its range (Margery Kempe makes a fleeting bow) and balance yield a variety of solutions (and failed solutions) to the problem of marrying within one's own status group. Everyone wants to marry up, but there are obvious limitations to the possibility. Anyone who has looked at the family trees in English country houses will have been struck by the challenge of arranging matches satisfactory to family ambition where there

are daughters in abundance, or too many younger sons. Desens has a keen eye for social history, and her ability to move between it and previous feminist criticism makes for a convincing nuancing of earlier generalizations. Small but telling correctives to the work of Ann Jennalie Cook and Lisa Jardine carry weight as she demonstrates how far women remained from abject submission, and she looks at male dissatisfactions with equal attention. By the time we get to Desdemona the idea that a woman might marry down to gamble on getting a more equal marriage seems an obvious trade. How far changes in post-Shakespearian drama were due to Shakespeare, and how far to other causes, remains a question, but this is a fine essay which looks afresh at an apparently old subject.

Social history is also the base for Jeffrey Theis's 'The "ill kill'd" Deer: Poaching and Social Order in *The Merry Wives of Windsor*'. This intelligent, slightly wilful, essay considers the multiple inversions in the play through metaphors of hunting/poaching, moving through the regulation of forests, social cohesion and coercion, and, of course, current scholarly preoccupations with the uses of socio-cultural history to reread the play. It may be that previous scholarship has noted occasional references to poaching because they are occasionally relevant. Theis argues that a dance of social regulation and escape weaves its way around the idea of geo-spatial control and regulation. Despite his affiliation to Patricia Parker's work, he arguably falls into the patriarchal bias he is unmasking when he extends the meaning of 'poaching', and allows himself to apply it to Fenton's courtship of Anne Ford – surely she has more autonomy and initiative than a doe. One might better try to reconsider how far the old arguments about true nobility might counter the older generation's sociological imperatives about marriage: neither Theis nor Desens looks at the way that the rhetoric of 'true nobility' first creates claims to desert, then, by extension, turns 'deserving' into a kind of ethical defence. That is, Fenton's 'right' to Anne Ford turns on his superiority, to her loving recognition of that superiority, and to their joint appeal to cap any arguments over good matches by substituting 'moral' for money or position in the rhetoric of marrying 'up'.

Post-Shakespearian Shakespeares continue to attract attention. Barbara A. Murray's 'Performance and Publication of Shakespeare, 1660–1682: "Go see them play'd, then read them as before"' starts from the difficulties of reading Shakespeare when Folios were scarce and stage adaptations far from those scarce reading texts. She considers in detail what books were available, and just how confusing adaptations might be. This latter point raises important questions for Restoration culture, which was increasingly alert to the problems inherent in imitation and adaptation in a world beginning to worry about plagiarism. Contemporary play quartos signed by Durfey or Dryden might be unacknowledged adaptations of Shakespeare, as well as vice versa. She questions generalizations by Michael Dobson and Gary Taylor by looking at what allusion or adulation could have been based upon, and suggests intriguing implications about 'who owned Shakespeare', in a period when being able to read Shakespeare was so limited. One of those adaptations is the subject of Margaret Maurer's 'Constering Bianca: *The Taming of the Shrew* and *The Woman's Prize, or The Tamer Tamed*'. Bianca returns in this early 'sequel' attributed to Fletcher, to rewrite her own and her sister's story; changes that we find in this play accord with changes made not only by other 'improvers' of Shakespeare in the course of the eighteenth century, but with other adaptations of other plays, including *Sauny the Scot*. The kind of literary criticism which we find in these sincere forms of flattery restores Bianca's dignity (while hiding her husband), and suggests, for example, that Kate only pretended to be docile. In replaying the taming, Maria, a new wife, is provided for Petruchio, with the impossible mission of reversing the civilising mission and making a man out of Kate's widower. Maurer derives the changes from an Ovidian Penelope, whose wit the new Byancha imitates in a multiply intertextual reinterpretation of the joys that lie in marriage. Such a variation on Shakespeare's theme is less interested in gender issues, and more in the pleasures of imitation. Theatrical traditions also occupy

Heinz Kosok, in 'Making Short Work of the Bard: Shakespeare's Character and Shakespearean Characters in the British Amateur Theatre', in *Historicizing/Contemporizing Shakespeare*. This modest essay presents a rich haul of discoveries in the repertory of British amateur theatricals which referred to or reinterpreted Shakespeare – surely an extract from a much longer, and intriguing, book. It is largely descriptive, with a list of plays and a bibliography likely to be very useful to students of performance and adaptations.

Still looking at women, Rüdiger Ahrens' 'Female Awareness(es) in *The Merchant of Venice*: Shakespeare, Marowitz, Wesker' considers two modern recyclings. The strengths of careful reading call our attention to aspects of text and performances which we might otherwise miss; the risks include overdescription, as well as the accusation of 'big hammer/little nail'. I was surprised by the assurance with which Antonio's melancholy was attributed to the disintegration of traditional economic structures, and the view that *Merchant* 'reflects' Xenophon, a view shared by Christiane Damlos-Kinzel in the same collection; I should have liked to hear more about the ways that the study of Marowitz or Wesker illuminate a return to Shakespeare. Ahrens attributes the importance of the 'appropriated' female characters to the energy with which they are 'debunked', although Wesker's Portia has great self-awareness, just as do his two merchants.

Much depends upon whether one calls one's subjects 'offshoots' (following Ruby Cohn's pathbreaking *Modern Shakespeare Offshoots* of 1976) or 'appropriations' (with its assertions of motivated redemption). This remains a growth area, beyond the flurry of books on *The Tempest*, such as *Constellation Caliban* ed. D'Haen and Lie (Rodopi, 1997), '*The Tempest' and its Travels*, eds. Peter Hulme and William Sherman (noticed in these pages last year), as well as one of those subsidized theses I mentioned above from Peter Lang Verlag, Anja Müller's *Produktive Rezeption von William Shakespeares The Tempest in englischsprachiger Erzählliteratur* (2000), a copy of which repeated letters and e-mails have failed to extract from the publishers. I had better luck with Bärbel Krömer's very useful *Embellished with Beautiful Engravings: Visualisierungen von Shakespeares Tempest in Grossbritannien, 1790–1870*. This generously illustrated history of illustrations to *The Tempest* is a kind of *catalogue raisonné*: it brings together theatrical and artistic interpretations to fill in the pre-post-colonial phase of the play's life. It has the self-effacing virtues of a well-curated exhibition, and is a store of good reproductions.

The themed issue of *Shakespeare Jahrbuch*, 137 (2000) on metamorphoses and afterlives includes an address by Mirjam Pressler about her novel, *Shylocks Tochter: Venedig im Jahre 1568 – Ghetto von Venedig 5327/8* (1999) – (not yet translated into English); Renata Häublein's report of a surviving promptbook from an eighteenth century adaptation of *Merchant*; Klaus Reichert on a contemporary Belgian adaptation of the English histories; Ton Hoenselaars on Wagner's Rossini-esque 'Das Liebesverbot'; Enno Ruge on Robert Nye; Marianne Novy on Kingsolver's *Poisonwood Bible*; Nele Abels-Ludwig, Wanda G. Klee, and Anja Müller on the German gay cartoonist Ralf König (with illustrations), an article which uses its subject to test recent pronouncements about uses of Shakespeare; Johann N. Schmidt on Shakespeare on screen and internet-marketing-derivatives; Manfred Pfister on a doubly comparative quest to see if Sonnet 66 is adapted for political subjects in Eastern Europe as in Germany; and Christoph Schöneich on comparative interpretations of Iago, from Schiller to Peter Szondi. And in the collection *Historicizing/Contemporizing Shakespeare* Isabel Martin gives the best description of the 'Poems for Shakespeare' which I have read; in addition, she reads Peter Reading reading Shakespeare, in 'Postmodernizing Shakespeare: A Palimpsest Poem'.

A number of books and articles deliberately set themselves to look at our cultural moment. Looking back using lenses framed by current technological breakthroughs can be exciting. In Arthur F. Kinney's *Lies Like Truth: Shakespeare, Macbeth, and the Cultural Moment* the basic idea is to use an extended analogy with recent neuro-science, artificial intelligence, and computer technology to offer a model of interpretation. If I have understood the analogy correctly, literary texts necessarily depend upon smaller units of meaning, which themselves in turn combine already assembled blocks of data: strings, or images, or recognized word-associations which communicate old and new combinations in perpetual motion. Our ability to 'recognize' depends upon a mix ('sequencing' and 'instability' are two useful terms) of familiar and unfamiliar words, ideas or images within a field. The term he borrows for these associative blocks is 'lexia', which is his way of avoiding the unavoidable hierarchies which arise from metaphors of geometry. His 'parallels' are 'hypertexts'; his sources or analogues arise where 'nodes' of meaning in *Macbeth* become juxtaposed. This offers interpretation as a kind of 'mise en fenêtres', with windows infinitely extendable. If the complete arbitrariness of the virtual archive is at some distance from the archives which are our textual past, nonetheless the analogy is a fertile one: Kinney proposes that Shakespeare is 'like' information when we have converted it to understanding by a process of assimilation. What controls the simultaneity of images or metaphors is their availablity in the culture: theatrical, royal, political, economic, military, familial, puritan, diabolical . . . It is that mysterious 'conversion' which escapes us: why is this category or explanation more powerful than that? why this argument or that claim to re-cognition? How do we explain explanation? Kinney finds an answer in the combined force of the imaginations, the plural plausibilities of characters and audiences, each of whom has an explanation which can be tested, and will be modified in the course of a performance or reading.

Imagining is not our current cultural focus on the dialogue between verbal and visual representation. There were, however, two books which, although not perhaps meant to be read in the category 'text and image', certainly combine literature and art. Alison Thorne's ambitious project is to take seriously the way that the discourse of painting, beginning with Alberti, uses the discourse of rhetoric, with the strong overlap in the vocabulary of 'colour' and the Erasmian approach to *copia*. She has a series of interesting, rhetorically informed discussions of the reading of seeing, but there does seem to be an insuperable problem in the discussion of *ut pictura poesis* that you can juxtapose the two kinds of analyses and note the similarities of their problems and propositions, but that you cannot get much further than noting, or perhaps seeing, that the similarities exist. That is, Shakespeare's multivalency is not really the same as single- or multi-point perspective, if only because the viewer looking at a painting, whether standing (certainly not reading) in one place or not, is not the same as spectators at a play, where roles are interpreted by multiple actors. An *ekphrasis* remains a verbal description which does not resemble, but evokes, a description of a scene seen. Changing one's mind, seeing things from a different angle or perspective are just as metaphorical in one direction as the rhetoric of visual art in the other. The final, and weakest, chapter seems discordant, as if it had come well after the rest of the book. As analysis of Shakespeare's language of perception, however, the book is full of insight.

By contrast, Christopher Pye appears to use 'art' or 'perspective' theory as one of his entries to what I think he intends as an explanation of the end of feudal and the beginning of modern 'perception'; he quotes a long roll of contemporary critics, and he 'reads' the past, including 'its' gaze, with a Lacanian/Žižekian lens. I am sorry to find that many of his examples from texts of the period appear to retell the story with such assertions as that 'Talbot' is a theatrical construction, though Pye also seems to think that 'a few scenes and a few skirmishes' take no time. This is the Don Armado approach. Quite how he has managed to persuade himself that there is a 'demonism' which corresponds to a shift in the symbolic order, or how an early modern subjectivity might be distinctly, or even distinctively, economic, remains puzzlingly implicit. The move from his curious analyses of a series of paintings of Annunciations to the wooing scene in *Henry V* to Edgar on Dover cliff is a triumph of moving swiftly on. His distinctive steps are either assertion, as in 'it is no coincidence', for example, that 'matter' is material to early modern subjectivity; or, he juxtaposes critics in a se-

ries of conditionals: ' . . . one might consider the wonder cabinet in relation to another moment in the Lacanian analytic, a passage in which he describes the signifying dimension not in its relation to metonymy and desire but in relation to what Freud describes as the incorporative function of mourning'. Or he bombards the reader with rhetorical questions: 'If the early modern "rarity" is something like a fetish, is it of a piece with the commodity, that most famous of modern fetishes?' Pye writes with as much magisterial confidence of 'high humanism' as he does of 'new historicism', but he writes at such a level of abstraction that it is hard to find matter in his art. It is not only in the Atlantic's eastern reaches that books are cobbled together from disparate papers.

I mentioned the specific British pressure to publish in time for the Research Assessment Exercise in my opening paragraphs on this year's cultural moment. I cannot help thinking that Cartmell and Scott's *Talking Shakespeare: Shakespeare into the Millennium*, was such a book. This collection purports to assess Shakespeare's position in 'our' 'culture' (singular) at the turn of the millennium, as a putative popular Shakespeare separates itself from an equally putative academic one. The introduction claims that it is the emphasis on plays as verbal constructs which unites the contributions (the poems are not considered). The essays are indeed united, but often by a demonization of public enemies in the form of conservative politicians, producers, and academics. By and large, the essays are more traditional than the editors announce, and tend to focus on familar moments and scenes: the Chorus in *Henry V*, the ending of *Hamlet*, the garden scene in *Richard II*. Peter Davison's piece on touring practices emphasizes the continuities of actors' experiences on the road. The essays which attempt a revisionist or demystifying stance are not always convincing: to argue that Peter Hall's emphasis on verse speaking created or imposed an idea of English essentialism is to equate 'Shakespeare' with performances in London, and to beg the question (as does Colin Chambers). Speaking verse is hard, requires physical and mental stamina, breath control and syntax, and a lot of spit. The attempts of the Conservative party to 'appropriate' Shakespeare were neither successful in shutting other ideas out nor in keeping the Conservatives in. They were constantly derided and opposed, not least by teachers, who like teaching Shakespeare because students come to like reading and watching Shakespeare. The idea that the British 'national curriculum' stops students noticing, or discussing, seems improbable at best, and certainly parochial. This mix of authoritarian pronouncement and focus on southern England seems at odds with the editors' declared intents. Their contributors describe an author who is complex and equivocal, capable of being enlisted in any number of causes, but who continues to appeal because his plays give pleasure. In fact, this book is an institutionally subventioned miscellany of articles of very varied quality. Nigel Wood reviews *Hamlet*'s endings to consider editing as interpretation; Emma Smith falls into the same pit as the 'league tables' by which British education is currently so abused to 'prove' how far down Shakespeare came in his own time; Dermot Cavanagh demonstrates presentism in his interpretation of Shakespeare's common men and elites; Janice Wardle Chambers considers performance and 'benchmark' performance; Miles Thompson and Imelda Whelehan write about critical responses to criticism of Shakespearian homoeroticism, and then Deborah Cartmell moves into homo*sexuality* in the necessary chapter on race. At this point there is some arguing about what happens in 'dominant' forms of communication, and Cartmell argues that an Othello played by a black actor (e.g. Parker's Laurence Fishburne) may reinforce racial stereotyping (presumably like antisemitism in depictions of Shylock?); then Bernice Kliman moves into Branagh's unfortunate flashcuts in his film *Hamlet*. There are some hard truths here: portraying villains or murderers who belong to 'minorities', say, or Branagh's limitations as a director. Gabriel Egan's essay offers a sequence of examples of the hard business of deciding what to show on stage or on film. Kiernan Ryan offers a Janus-like view of the past and the future as we find them in Shakespeare criticism: is he early-modern (and therefore the beginning of 'us') or distanced

by history, and asks us to think how far Shakespeare might himself be out of his own time, both in the plays and in the sonnets. The closeness of this binary polarity to other works on history this year reinforces my sense that there is a trend. Michael J. Collins ends the collection with a reminder that we like going to the theatre, and there is a coda by Josephine Webb which supplements the yearly website updates by Werner Habicht in *Shakespeare Jahrbuch*.

My most significant observation this year is the appearance and reappearance of the historical turn. Shakespeare in *his* cultural moment includes its diseases: the plague has attracted more attention in the last decade. In '"Disease and Contamination": Reading Shakespeare and Ben Jonson from the Margin', one of the essays in *Historicizing/Contemporizing Shakespeare*, Wolfgang Klooss builds upon Leeds Barroll's work to look at the plague as disease and as metaphor. In the same collection, Christiane Damlos-Kinzel emphasizes the risks of reading 'economics' back into Shakespeare's time. In 'The Tension between Oeconomics and Chrematistics in William Shakespeare's *The Merchant of Venice*', she reads *Merchant* as dealing with the English economic situation, contrasting kinds of what we might call 'economics' in 'household government' rather than in markets or even in money, for which she uses the period word 'chrematistics'. The victory in the play is that the private recuperates the anonymous threats of the public, making Shylock, already distanced from his own associates, a member of the larger community. One may wonder if Shakespeare really had read Xenophon, or thought of himself as contributing to discussions of what we would call economic ideas, but it is no bad thing to have 'households' emphasized once more.

The 'Italian space' is the subject of Jack D'Amico's *Shakespeare and Italy: the city and the stage*. D'Amico argues that Shakespeare's idea of 'Italy' is 'openness', defined broadly as outdoor settings such as the piazza, where people can congregate; a society where 'exchanges' are possible; a danger for foreign travellers. His opening chapter considers Italy as a densely urbanized country, in which contemporary ideas of the city-state take precedence over modern ideas of a nation-state, and he emphasizes the possibility of communication between and among them. D'Amico wants the idea of the physical Italian city, with its public spaces, to offer a parallel to the stage, which, after all, allows characters to congregate in its 'outdoor' places, especially for the final scenes of comedies. There are, as he recognizes, more private moments; life cannot always be lived in public. At that point, however, the analogy of life outside breaks down. The theatrical space is neither inside nor outside; it is permeable as the author decides, for exits and entrances, over-hearing and spying. Outdoor settings are obviously convenient for meetings, since characters can bump into each other; but it is also worth remembering that, historically, church was a convenient place for assignations – and always safer and more convenient for women. It is not always clear how particular actions are specific to their Italian-ness, in the plays he mentions, often in swift passing. He asserts that Shakespeare characterizes the cities variously, but it is not clear that Shakespeare's Milan or his Sicilia are really orientated towards courtly interiors (he recognizes elsewhere that Prospero's city seems to have a port). His ideas of exchange range from ideas to trade to objects. It's curious that D'Amico doesn't turn his ideas about Machiavelli upside down, and explore the ways that the moral counsel of the Italian advisers he notices reaches back to the personal ethics underlying earlier treatises on statecraft which Machiavelli was at such pains to displace. The categories of his analysis enable him to remark the mixture of stereotype (lawyers come from Padua) and anti-type (the honest Diana is just as Italian as the corruptors of youth). He draws Illyria into Italy, by virtue of its Italianate names, as he is also tempted to do with *Measure*'s Vienna. Most generalizations about the cities immediately require modification, and he gives us little analysis of ancient and modern Italy. There is less historical analysis (Venice, for example, was past its prime when Shakespeare was writing, but one would not know that from the city he evokes) than in the essays collected as *Shakespeare's Italy* (1993).

Religion, of course, is at the heart of many considerations of cultural moment (in both senses). It is striking how much 'religion' has been forgotten, and requires restatement. In the many books and articles which came across my desk this year there was a speaking silence about sixteenth-century views that reform meant cleaning up a tarnished act, that it was not the reformers who were doing anything new, but the straying, corrupt followers of the decadent Bishops of Rome. The archaizing language of Bible translations is only one testament to the conservatism, the inertia, of liturgical change; Christians (as we might now say) clung to the same word of God, even if sometimes that word came in differing worldly languages. And if, in a word, we are all Catholics now where the Shakespeare family are concerned, we must constantly remind ourselves that that is what many reformers said and continued to say, while what constituted 'old' or 'new' style or national confession – as we might also now label identities of Christianity – steadily (or, perhaps better, unsteadily) changed. Current controversies sometimes turn around the slipperiness of what constituted which kind of -ism and exactly when. Two articles and a book address ideas of 'religion'. First, Walter S. H. Lim's 'Knowledge and Belief in *The Winter's Tale*', which uses the terminology of Christianity a little insecurely. If Hermione had died, then we might discuss resurrection, but the magical moment in Sicilia turns out to be not magic at all; the statue is not only not an idol, it is not a statue, and the 'chapel' turns out to have been useful only as a place of refuge – not of worship. Lim calls up great resources in background, but the 'faith' Paulina exhorts from her audience really only sets a mood, reverence for reconciliation, not for miracle. To try to make the mood difficult for Protestants is to miss the theatricality of Paulina's 'un-vanishing Lady'. And yet it is clear that what and how we believe does indeed inform the play, if only as a trick on our accepting Antigonus's presumed vision (which is false, and a trick on us all – though we live to discover it). But dreams were always problematic, and this one no more authoritative, in the event, than many. Lim makes such terms as 'wonder' or 'belief' too dark, and forgets the context of a play which draws more upon the reunion of a family than on religious doctrines. There is a tell-tale moment at the end of his essay when it becomes clear that he is thinking of a reader, not a theatrical spectator. There is important work to be done, given our tendencies to generalize about the Jacobethan theatrical space, about churches and chapels: the rarity of such locations as Paulina's evidently pagan place of retreat ought to attract attention.

The controversies about religion cross other controversies, and Tom McAlindon's 'The Discourse of Prayer in *The Tempest*' uses the subject to react to anti-colonialist readings of the play. McAlindon uses careful analysis to offer a discourse of prayer as part of the providentialist tendencies of the Last Plays; his island is a place of ethical interdependence and mutual reciprocity within, necessarily, a hierarchical model of society. It all depends, of course, on how you weight what you listen to and to how you assess the various claims of the plays' competing points of view. McAlindon's 'good guys' are seriously 'Good', which does not imply soft, or undisciplined, or even easy to live with. Learning to curse involves understanding that one may also bless, and that both exist as unstable categories in an animate world in which words have power to harm as well as charm. As patriotism to the scoundrel, so, perhaps, cursing to the impotent, who have to hand no other weapon. McAlindon's point, in an old historicist mode, is that we have forgotten the whole system of spiritual invitation, from bidding prayer to commination; he has a strong point in the connection between the boatswain's blasphemy in the face of destruction and his silence at the play's end. The im-pious presupposes piety, as a value even if not a position. I think McAlindon sometimes pushes the evidence further than it will go, and that not all virtues are necessarily Christian or religious, but his point is well taken without insisting that he necessarily proves anything about Shakespeare.

More worrying is Jeffrey Knapp's *Shakespeare's Tribe: Church, Nation, and Theater in Renaissance England*. The tribe of the title is a loose gathering of playwrights and their associates, loosely over

about a hundred years. The strengths of the book lie in Knapp's reopening – for students of literature – issues such as secularization (one of the many ways in which we have found the roots of the modern in protestantizing England) and internationalism (pan-Protestant national alliances, but also the idea that the continuing threat of Infidel invasion continuously required haunting Europe with the spectre of pan-Christian Crusade). But intellectual history requires, as historians are always telling us, more attention to history. Hidden in the notes are too many shaky authorities, such as A. L. Rowse on Shakespeare's life and religion. In the period which includes Shakespeare's life, the public language of secularization itself would have had to be 'religious', because the presuppositions of morality and ethics would only hold where they were addressed in accepted discourses. From the outset the binary polarity insists on camps, unified by shared 'projects', facing each other from pulpit and press to arena and audience. Church historians would be very surprised by the assumption of education, dignity, commitment, and vocation which Knapp ascribes to the variety of men who took holy orders (and so would many practising Christians). He seems surprised by how many of them aspired to poetry, playwrighting and translation. As earlier generations of scholars have established, not least through the Records of Early English Drama, it was part of the statutes of their schools and colleges to produce plays. It was part of their education as well as part of their attempts at advancement (often from the difficult position of younger sons) to compose verses, trying to make something of themselves in London. That many 'sons of Ben' turned sooner or later to the curacy or benefice has never been thought to be problematic: they could not have foreseen the little local difficulties which were to make the middle of the century interesting times.

In private one could always philosophize. The 'classical' education from which young men benefited (or suffered) continuously offered an orientation which was either not Christian, or was, at least, Christian only insofar as Nature and Revelation revealed the same book. Public discourses of philosophy, however, were less readily available outside a vocabulary which Knapp labels 'religion'. With what other vocabulary could one discuss 're-ligion' than the 'religious', and, within that large discursive field, Christian religious? Knapp moves back and forth over texts taken from Erasmus to the late seventeenth century to describe a rather static broad church which tolerated tolerance, and found sympathy and support in theatrical examinations of ethics and morality. But he wants there to be a 'religion' of what he calls 'theatre people', whom he opposes to 'anti-theatricals'. As with all binary polarities, this one elides the huge and changing range of views among Anglican clergy; the prob-lem of employment for younger sons; the evolution of the Church in the course of the sixteenth and seventeenth centuries (a common problem in the historically orientated books reviewed this year); as well as the available public discourses for moral ar-gument. In addition, it similarly lumps together all kinds of writers, players, pro-theatrical polemicists, over the same long period.

The historical turn is all to the good: we do need more history, better used. But we shall have to listen to historians, and remember that they themselves argue about their interpretations and the arguments of their trade. It will be a pity if we have out-lived a theory/anti-theory split only to refight a similar battle over the uses and abuses of history. There is a risk of a belated reaction, which extends from co-ercive insistence upon only subjects (the public tes-timony of affiliation to New Historicism, say) to a too-casual dismissiveness in the name of where our scholarly conversation appears to be now. There is, perhaps, a certain inevitable windmill-tilting, even dead-horse flogging, as we absorb and move beyond once-new approaches or methodologies. Andreas Höfele's pastiche of Greenblatt strikes me as marking the flight of Minerva's owl – the kind of balanced summary which comes at dusk. And his calm assessment of different 'historicizing' ap-proaches reveals just those similarities which the original ebullient scholarly self-fashioning denied. The difficulties of disciplinary self-definition in-clude revolutionary revisionism, which in turn masks, occludes, denies lines of descent. We are not the only immigrants to have changed our name,

and 'Pre-modern' is a danger as well as an eman-cipation. For many different kinds of texts identi-fied themselves as histories, or historical, and even 'romances' often presupposed a historical substra-tum (not just because they took place in a legendary period). Like our own, the 'new' historiography of the sixteenth century was much less new than its practitioners insisted.

E. M. W. Tillyard has been a whipping boy in these arguments for so long that I would like to propose a moratorium on pillorying him unless we agree to historicize the mid-century challenges to which he was responding, two pan-European wars with their particular arguments about jus-tice. Stefani Brusberg-Kermeier seems to take for granted the existence of a 'Tudor myth' in her 'The Role of Body Images in the Tudor Myth and its Subversion in Shakespeare's History Plays' (in *The Anatomy of Tudor Literature*). This paper must be an extract from her German-language dissertation, but there is not much 'body' here; rather, it gives the impression of the kind of essay against which Tom McAlindon inveighs. It takes 'the' myth as given, then leaps to scholarship at the end of the twentieth century, describes some descriptions, and finds that Shakespeare is subversive. In the same collection, Tracey Hill takes *1 Sir John Oldcastle*, *Thomas Lord Cromwell*, and *The Book of Sir Thomas More* to con-sider the relations between the historical moment of production and the historical moment depicted. '"Since Forged Invention Former Time Defaced": Representing Tudor History in the 1590s' asks that we take these plays more seriously, and Hill makes some interesting suggestions, including the impor-tance of the absent presence of the monarch in the plays and their struggles to negotiate the dangerous shifts from heretic/rebel to English freedom fighter without over-valuing those appeals to conscience which legitimate individual disobedience. Further along, Carol Banks explores what must be part of a much longer argument about attitudes to women in the Quarto and Folio versions of *Henry V*, opening from an idea that 'Tudor' is more and 'Jacobean' less welcoming to women. On the face of it this seems a throwback to a less interesting age: 'Shakespeare's *Henry V*: Tudor or Jacobean'? By contrast, Anthony

Martin's 'The British Myth in Tudor Drama' (in the same volume) looks at depictions of the legendary past as invented by such luminaries of historical responsibility as Geoffrey of Monmouth, examining the pageants presented to Elizabeth before her coronation, of legendary characters in British history. In private poetry and in public performance these 'literary' uses bunch in the late sixteenth century, although they had long been present in prose histories. It all depends on what you call 'literary', of course, but it does seem to be true that insular, indigenous history (as we might call it, to avoid the ambiguity in 'vernacular' history) does not seem to have had the requisite dignity for treatment in free-standing compositions. The absence of King Arthur from Shakespeare's work, except as popular reference (Falstaff sleeping in Arthur's bosom, for example) has always intrigued me, and I'm sure there is something important going on in the ambivalence to historical romance which appears throughout this period. Martin surveys 'the matter of Britain' from Geoffrey's egregious inventions, mentions the emulatory 'histories' of Scotland, but then squanders his concentration on the question of what counts by jumping to *Gorboduc* as the first 'history' play.

Similar generic problems occur in J. Clinton Crumley's 'Questioning History in *Cymbeline*'. To understand how a 'romance' might be 'historical' or 'historiographical', Crumley argues that 'Rome' breaks down under the pressure of popular history (not identified). He explains that if the most repellent characters are most patriotic, it is to reveal the subjectivity of histories such as Caesar's, or even Holinshed's, and offers the sensible counterproposal that if the rejection of Rome had come from Imogen, that would have endorsed the traditional historical view. The wicked step-mother thus becomes a kind of historiographer on the verge of a Baconian inductive method. We cannot believe what we read, as the letters of the play also indicate. Romance may be in a historical style, but that only calls the styles of history into question. But there's a more obvious difficulty with Crumley's apparent sensibleness, for if Imogen had suddenly spouted patriotism, her intervention would have

created three new problems: talking over her father, the king; interfering in a public occasion in which she has no standing as, say, a Prince of Wales (which will be important for her later displacement); masculinizing a character who is always feminine.

Not that the historians, or the political philosophers, have things their own way, or necessarily give us an example of how we might read better. Leon Harold Craig's *Of Philosophers and Kings: Political Philosophy in Shakespeare's Macbeth and King Lear*, a self-proclaimedly 'old-fashioned' book, is perplexing in its own disregard of history. It isn't really about political philosophy at all. Rather, it is a reading, by a teacher of political science who has previously written about Plato, of two plays. It is resolutely a book about Shakespeare as a book, and an old-fashioned book at that, with little respect for the complexities of where theatre texts come from, or performance, or how one might distinguish a script from a novel. It makes a straightforward use of the conflated *Lear* on grounds of personal preference – though how a book with this focus can manage to avoid discussing the change to the final political arrangements in the revisions between Q and F is a puzzle. Craig takes up numerous 'loose ends' as if they were subterranean signals toward the true subjects of the plays; these 'unconformities', which have been the subject of Kristian Smidt's work, require a reader of prodigious memory and alertness. Craig's Shakespeare is for all time: he is unworried about interpreting Elizabethan emotions or motivations, or the poetry. More surprisingly still, the political situations of England, or Europe, at the time the plays were written, make no appearance, so that, for example, anxieties about succession after Elizabeth do not seem to interest him at all. Craig tells the stories, and treats the characters as if they were people to whose motives he has special access, and whose lives, outside the plays, he can elucidate. There is a battle of sorts going on in the extremely lengthy footnotes, which indicate distaste for a list of modern-isms, but which also put in their places a succession of critics, from Coleridge to Cavell. There is an inescapable feel of a Great Books course, including great philosophy books, where the books hover above the plays in immateriality; asserted resemblances to Plato abound and, although Machiavelli makes repeated appearances, it is only to find his recommendations juxtaposed with those of Shakespeare's characters. There is no sense of how Shakespeare might have had access to, or have read, or heard discussed, the 'philosophers' of politics. A final chapter suggests interpretations of a variety of other plays, including *Measure*, *Othello* and *The Winter's Tale*. This book was published with the aid of subventions from three different Canadian public bodies; its blurb rightly calls it 'unconventional in its approach'.

Crossing disciplinary boundaries always brings with it the recognizable problem of how we read each other's sources and each other's scholarly conversations. But there is another problem, which follows from my observations about getting published: the need to put a 'central' topic or author in our titles. It has to be recognized that a scholar who becomes interested in, say, weighing sin against crime, or interested in different kinds of courts, or in whether or not one might consider the theatre as having a religious orientation which we may have lost sight of, has to find a Shakespearian hook. So one turns to Debora Kuller Shuger with high expectations. However, *Political Theologies in Shakespeare's England: The Sacred and the State in Measure for Measure* begins from question-begging presuppositions (which Shuger explicitly recognizes), and is bound to raise reservations throughout. *Measure* is not quite the subject, though its departures from *Promos and Cassandra* are asked to bear a lot of weight; nor is politics, nor theology; nor (in some ways more intriguingly) is current American intolerance of sexual peccadilloes in its rulers; nor, for that matter, South Africa's Truth and Reconciliation movement. Yet they are all integral to this ambitious meditation. The style ranges from the folksy ('my spell checker made me do it') to the high abstract, and the argument is not always clear: if this is a book about our categories of 'offence' (on which depend either penitential or punitive treatment), then it is a problem that there is (confessedly) so little treatment of what a stage 'Vienna' might be. It is hard to believe that Shakespeare's city 'reflects on the post-Reformation crossover of the

sacred from ecclesial to temporal polity . . . [in] an attempt to imagine what Christianity might look like as a political praxis'. I think that underneath the manifest subject there is a not-very-latent search for the origins of the separation of church and state. More worrying, modern American presuppositions about constitutionalism hamper Shuger in her search for an explanation of 'penitential justice'. She jumps from one primary source to another without seating them in the particular cultures or argumentative contexts out of which they came: too sure about 'sacral kingship', too confident about her ability to distinguish puritan, protestant, and catholic attitudes. Nonetheless, here is another reminder that we are 'recovering' religion, that religious attitudes are integral to sixteenth-century politics, and that there is work to be done.

The 'how-to' contributions this year ranged in many directions. Two of the contributors to *Historicizing/Contemporizing Shakespeare* offer philosophically orientated suggestions. Claus Uhlig goes right back to Hegel in 'Memory and Appropriation: Shakespeare in Aesthetic Thought'. He points out how far 'appropriation' has been a substitute for 'memory', and if his enthusiasm for finding everything in Hegel seems a little excessive, his insistence on thinking back historically even as far as character criticism seems increasingly forward-looking. This theoretically informed and thoughtful reconsideration of Hegel's engagement with Shakespeare both contextualizes some current trends in Shakespeare studies (e.g. Performance) and suggests ways forward in interdisciplinary study. In 'Reading Shakespeare Historically: "Postmodern" Attitudes and the History Plays', Christoph Reinfandt focuses on history in the history plays to consider postmodernity and recent historiography. He sensibly reminds us that however 'historical' the plays, they are full of 'fictional' characters, which further complicates the kind of narrative Shakespeare proposes. The application of 'modern' ideas of 'modernizing' leads him to characterize Henry IV as proposing a 'culturally retrogressive attempt at atonement by mounting a crusade'. This attitude to pan-national, or pan-confessional Christian alliances intersects with Knapp's and Hillman's rather different concerns. This trend also suggests that there is still plentiful room for debate in our discussions of periodizing and historical change, interests which seemed perhaps to peak during the celebrations which surrounded the millennium – or not-the-millennium, depending on one's taste in chronological styles. Reinfandt's article was not the only moment this year when the Crusades reappeared as a challenge to our appreciation of just how much we ought to take seriously the sixteenth-century assessment of late-medieval investments in the Holy Places. Above all, the use of a period label such as 'late-medieval' raises once more the problem that Shakespeare would not have, because he could not have, used 'middle ages' for the period which encompassed his English history plays.

Historiography readily leads to analysis of rhetorical styles of writing, though it is just as important to reverse this point in order to understand that the history/literature split which tempts us may be more usefully defined by thinking how far rhetoric and rhetorically informed habits of writing organized the invention of the past. Ruth Lunney emphasizes the rhetorical style of characterization through represented argument in 'Rewriting the Narrative of Dramatic Character, or, Not "Shakespearean" but "Debatable"'. We seem always to be rediscovering rhetoric. Here the argument is that the shift in characterization associated with the 1590s should be orientated toward the rhetorical relationship between speaking personae and interpreting audience. Marlowe remains the architect of the change because his characters argue their positions to themselves, and, therefore, to us, in what I take to be a kind of individualized *psychomachia*. The problem with the term suggested is that it is a truism that speeches invented for characters, in all kinds of narratives, were organized to represent the arguments which such a person (historical or imaginary) might have used to move and persuade, rhetorically, an audience or reader. Such speeches were of their nature 'debatable', because they urged courses of actions, or defended things done, or represented moments of extreme passion. What changed, culturally, was surely something to do with those additional touches, those gratuitous idiosyncrasies, which give us the feeling not of an argument, or even a representative individual, but an individual *tout court*. Individuating argument comes not from 'rhetoric', nor from Protestantism, as the possibilities had already been used from time to time, but from widespread changes in expected styles which coincided in art, in historical and fictional writing. Not only is there debatable gain in the suggested term, there is certain loss. This approach is becoming more popular, and most popular this year in analyses of the English history plays.

In Ronald Knowles's *Shakespeare's Arguments with History*, the history plays speak once again as arguments, persuading and moving; imitating, parodying, and satirizing styles and positions articulated elsewhere. 'Argument' also takes its meaning as 'the plot', rightly encompassing the thrust of the plot's contents, as with Shakespeare's critical interpretation of his sources. Knowles sees Shakespeare in the light of humanist historiography, but, in the circumstances of publicly performed plays, as an author whose multivocality and multivalency suspend, question and contradict the epideictic mood in historical celebration. Shakespeare certainly deserves a place among imaging and imagining historians of his time (whose own commitment to 'new' history was often less radical than they claimed). Knowles has some familiar difficulties as he generalizes about the history of historiography, taking the rhetoric of prefaces and positions perhaps too much at their words, and if 'argument' sometimes threatens to cover everything, it is nonetheless good to see the ethical arts of language taken so seriously.

Two contrasting approaches to the English history plays indicate something of the similarities in differences this year. Nicholas Grene's *Shakespeare's Serial History Plays* might be thought of as an 'impure' book. In his search for structures, Grene begins with narrative sources, then considers the availability of ideas and habits of writing linked plays in Elizabethan London, before moving to performance history, and then to recent productions, because he is trying to find a way around our habitual approaches to the English histories. The ground bass of Tillyard's ideas can be heard, of course, but this is a serious attempt to come at the question of 'link' in a different key, though it is simply impossible to escape the plays as political, unifying, 'nation-building' – even if you are not English. Marlowe, too, is a recurring theme here as elsewhere this year, but so are authors of historical sequences, or cycles, which have not survived. Benjamin Griffin's work supplies some of the missing pieces, though both Grene and Griffin run up against the question of why the production of such plays seems to have stopped when it did. Once again, actors' and directors' discoveries in the plays help us all rethink them, as the sequences produced since the 1960s aptly demonstrate. The RSC's early 'Wars of the Roses' (as a look at the published script still allows one to 'see'), showed just how much conversation there is among them (as did their recent millennium productions, 'This England'). If one wants to object that actors find consistency, or create it, and that therefore the so-called 'test' of through-casting proves nothing beyond their skill, Grene has a strong case in his illustrations of character development – not inconsistency, since the changes are motivated by events ('deeds worthy to be done') or stimulated by reaction (not just 'defences of a course taken') within individual plays. In the absence of surviving play-texts by other dramatists, it would be worth speculating about the possibility that secular English history might have offered a celebration to replace the outmoded 'mystery' cycles; about the adoption of neo-classical forms and classical subjects; or about sprawling structures for legendary ones. Is it remotely possible that *Lear* and *Cymbeline* were part of some huge, never-accomplished project? Grene's arguments reach toward Jeffrey Masten's ideas about taking 'hands' C and D together in 'Editing the Collaborative', where the team looks increasingly cooperative.

What has been missing in accounts of the history plays is a deep and broad study of previous histories; Benjamin Griffin's *Playing the Past: Approaches to English Historical Drama 1385–1600* goes right back to the mystery cycles, to folk plays, to religious celebrations of different kinds to find the different ways people staged pasts which were English,

what I earlier called 'insular indigenous' history. He studies genre, that is, by finding a way around it. This has the great advantage of avoiding the pitfall of ancestor-hunting and looking for an originary history play in a recognizable shape. Griffin also makes good use of misattribution to Shakespeare of non-Shakespearian histories. By reaching out in careful readings of Heywood's *The Royal King and the Loyal Subject*, the collaborative *Sir Thomas Wyatt*, and *1 Sir John Oldcastle*, by alertness to the Henslowe companies as well as to the Chamberlain's Men, Griffin allows himself a detailed corrective to such descriptions of an upwardly mobile Shakespeare alone creating a prince of all common hearts (as in Richard Helgerson's *Forms of Nationhood*) with evidence of just what the representations were elsewhere in London. Griffin's Shakespeare looks more like his contemporaries, with their derision of low-born rebels, with their demands for representation – despite a widespread approval of popular proto-protestantism. He is equally severe on previous explanations for the decline in new history plays: he shows how little available was the supposedly 'new' historiography of Bacon, Camden or Selden, how unconvincing are the arguments for a new audience scepticism about history. Another historiographical old chestnut (the 'revolution' in humanist historical writing) takes another salutary bashing; one should never take claims for the 'new' of the New at their words – whether it be restoration, reform or revival of learning. His suggestion that the eminence of certain plays created the impression of 'definitive' interpretations (viz., not treating something Shakespeare had treated because it would be thought less good) is buttressed by a series of statistical Appendices showing the subjects of history plays. And he has a convincing argument from belatedness about traditional ideas of a recognizable genre created in retrospect (and his tables of 'reprintings' are persuasive). He is unconvinced by arguments that neo-classical expectations elsewhere may have worked against the sprawl of history plays. Rather, he has an interesting speculation that the 1590s offered a rare period of suspension: the ageing queen still ageing; foreign invaders threatening, but receding. Nostalgic continuity in the chain of English monarchs offered a kind of civil order. Disorder, in this description, moved from what Grene might call serial history to the independent (and formally more coherent) tragedy. And, if I may once again point out what is going on in publishing, this is a book-of-the-thesis, supported, without subvention, by a small press (D. S. Brewer) which is still willing to take a chance on a young scholar.

Claus Uhlig's worries about memory and appropriation are voiced at much greater length in Tom McAlindon's *Shakespeare's Tudor History: A Study of Henry IV, Parts 1 and 2*. This self-styled 'historicist' study has a polemical insistence on the need for memory; in addition to the manifest argument in the text, there is a manifesto running throughout the notes. McAlindon, here, as always in his work, has read hugely in primary sources so as not to succumb to second-hand arguments and scholarship. Like Grene, he is aware of the belief that a kind of parody labelled 'Tillyard' seems to have erased knowledge of the variety of earlier critical interpretations of the plays, and his rebukes to self-styled 'radical' criticism are made from a strong position. Thus his emphasis on forgetting as falsification becomes integral to a study of Tudor experiences of rebellion, both political and religious, which informed historical memory in the sixteenth century, and integral to a demonstration of how a historicized study might be made. In this sense it would matter less whether we now think that social changes indeed arose from a feudalism associated with Catholicism to a powerful, centralizing, monarchic Protestantism, than that those ideas or beliefs were current in Shakespeare's England (thus far I think we all agree on the principle that common contemporary beliefs about history often matter more than anything some more 'accurate' historical demonstration might reveal). McAlindon's interpretation of the history plays depends upon the view that the historians Shakespeare read projected their own interpretations of recent rebellion onto the middle ages (not, of course, then so labelled). He thus links anxious memory of the internal rebellions of 1536, 1547 and 1569 to late sixteenth-century drama. Getting from Henry IV

to the Pilgrimage of Grace assumes memory and recognition in his theatre-goers which runs just short of danger for the playwright. There can be no doubt that one of the constants of historiography is the question of repetition, and Christian historiography, with its emphasis on linearity, always had to deal with the evidence that experience might also be cyclical. In that sense rebellion is always with us, as are the ways of dealing with it: Harrington's epigram about treason is a witty recognition, not a new thought.

I want to repeat the caveat about the hazards of interpretation in all work which moves from 'history' (as writing) to the categories we think of as 'literary', that necessary category-crossing which sends us from our own disciplinary formation to history (as a study). I do not think that this is a point about scholarship v. criticism, or a claim that if we only knew more interpretation would be easier, or more conducive to agreement. When we read histories, chronicles, or annals, we are all susceptible to believing that the sections we think are convincing must therefore be true. They are not. They are plausible, persuasive, beautifully written, moving – but not thereby *either* true or false. Rhetoric – as a study – is indispensible here, and must itself also be historicized. Among other things, it reveals that one quotes direct or reported direct speech as true at one's peril. Falsification must come otherwise. McAlindon, like the rest of us, sometimes believes that 'History' says something; he refers to 'feudal ideology'; to 'the Tudor propaganda machine'; to Tudor government as a successful centralizing body; he sometimes forgets that the publication of a book is neither its reception nor its influence. His alertness to the special circumstances of 'oaths' and 'honour' in Shakespeare is persuasive, and, I believe, likely to be true; but the idea that obedience and loyalty were once to be trusted has *always* been a nostalgia placed at some point in the past. The *encomia* for our ancestors, those 'great men', were always built upon this position. If McAlindon wanted to argue that the experience or memory of rebellions led historiographers to recognize similarities in the behaviour of men (and women) which in turn supported ideas that there might just be cycles in historical events, I would follow him with pleasure. I think his emphasis on an England informed by religion and not just power-politics is salutary (although it is also salutary to remember those contradictory varieties within Christianities which were protected, even encouraged – not just tolerated – by magnates such as John of Gaunt). But I think he does himself a disservice by his insistence that he has recognized specific reminiscences, that they were evident to Shakespeare and to his audience, and that we have somehow forgotten them. It will be a pity if this energetically argued book is dismissed because of its weaknesses, when its virtues in identifying the subjects of history in history's subjects are so strong.

This question of memory and reference in the large context of rebellion and political instability informs Richard Hillman's thoughtful work on continental politics, *Shakespeare, Marlowe, and the Politics of France*, where he makes some of the same claims about audience recognition as does McAlindon. By contrast to the 'old-fashioned' mode, his work absorbs a Lacanian model of development which underpins his discovery of pattern. If I have understood him, he proposes a new historical contextualization in what seems to be three layers. First, there is the question of intertextuality, understood as something happening between certain French historiographical texts and Shakespeare's English history plays. Second, there is something happening between contemporary English playgoers' anxieties about civil wars, past and potentially future, and their awareness of the bloody dynastic and religious conflicts which rendered France unstable for so long. Third, there is an appeal to a Lacanian Other/Absence/Lack to explain, or perhaps only to find a possible pattern for, a proposed relationship between a developing sense of English nationhood and an 'Imaginary' (in the Lacanian sense) 'France', a France both receding from the English grasp as a possession and looming as a once and future fate. This last point results in an increasing concentration, as the book proceeds, on the feminizing and demonizing figure of Jeanne d'Arc, but it also depends upon a historical homophobic assumption that kings who love men are weak. There are timely reminders in the course of this book about the ways that religious affiliations could continue to contradict national contestation (Protestant loyalties should over-ride the nation state). Hillman's work has always raised serious questions about audience reception, and about Shakespeare's plays as texts intended to be read as well as seen (Barbara A. Murray's article makes an interesting companion piece in this regard). I remain unsure, however, how far perennial questions of the role of the 'strong' governor in the prevention of civil disorder necessarily depended upon specific topicalities, or how far particular events were regularly assimilated to ideas that cycles of history include the clear and present dangers of anarchic collapse. Nonetheless, the book's contribution to thinking about the ways that late-sixteenth-century authors and audiences remembered the middle ages is a timely one.

Any hope that a better example would be set by a professional historian falls before Keith Dockray's chatty *William Shakespeare The Wars of the Roses and the Historians*. Long on description and narrative, but short on analysis, this is a popular, and puzzling, introduction to Shakespeare's Wars of the Roses which either describes Shakespeare's plots and characters or narrates the historians' versions, but creates no real bridge between the two. There are some potentially interesting illustrations, but they are not discussed. A wasted opportunity, particularly this year when history in the history plays is so current. One would do better to use a manual, such as Dominique Goy-Blanquet's *Shakespeare et l'Invention de l'histoire*, which identifies the agents of history, the sources, and Shakespeare's treatment of them in the English history plays. And sometimes 'history' intrudes like King Charles's remembered head. *Quoting Shakespeare* is not just about how Shakespeare quoted, nor how he has been quoted – the title is one of those attempts I mentioned to tag an eccentric book with an enticing label. Bruster's passionate argument is with the failure of New Historicism to think deeply enough about how texts 'position' themselves by quotation, both explicit and implicit. I find the polemic something of a distraction, but it seems to be part of this year's trend.

He doesn't mean just 'quotation', but also 'allusion' and the use of recognizable reference which we sometimes call 'intertextuality'. The book begins with an essay about Marlowe's passionate shepherd's subsequent appearances. But it ends in America, with the 'creation' of an 'English Renaissance' in order to 'justify' the creation of an American renaissance, by way of a Harlem renaissance, and, in the course of these large claims, 'quotation' begins to spread itself far beyond the book's title. In between there are substantive chapters on how Shakespeare quotes, especially in comedy; on *The Tempest*; and on *The Two Noble Kinsmen* and the language of madwomen.

After a group of books resolutely trying to grapple with the recovery of context, there is one which is energetically present-minded, *Shakespeare in the Present*. Hillman's care with his reading, McAlindon's detailed return to his sources, or Griffin's analyses of plays written and performed make a striking contrast to the freewheeling polemic of Terence Hawkes. Based on unidentified earlier publications (your reviewer can reveal that one chapter also appears without acknowledgement in Kinney's *Hamlet: New Critical Essays*), Hawkes collects, or, perhaps, revises them with an opening claim for 'presentism' as the best, and, indeed, the only, coherent approach to Shakespeare by re-inventing Mr Gradgrind as his Other, in order to parody an enemy who only wants facts, a straw positivist who must be condemned. But it is a striking feature of Hawkes's approach that his own claim to command the high ground of self-conscious analysis of history rests on the authority of scholarship, of his superior deployment of history. And here, it has to be said, his high-handed, careless, inaccuracies; his clever, meretricious rhetorical juxtapositions; and his self-serving insistence on an anachronistic idea of Ireland as soul, saviour, and sump of an eternal England invite reservations at every step. I give one example, trivial, but typical: he wants to figure Eliot as the stranger within, prone to emphasize certain kinds of rigidities because of his own New England Puritanism. Now, if someone else allegorized one of Hawkes's Irish

underdogs that way he would be up in arms about hegemonic readings. I do not think it gradgrindery to point out that Eliot was not a New Englander, that 'puritan' is a category urgently in need of historicizing. But the function of Eliot-bashing actually turns out to be part of a line-up of the usual critical suspects who are the challenge to be met. Hawkes's 'readings' are tendentious, constantly – as he would perhaps agree with pride – turned toward current arguments about nationalism, about Britain's own belated, repressed return to dismantling the colonizing project of Union. If I were reading this book in the Indian subcontinent I would not like to be told I was a subjected colonial suffering from an infliction of English and speaking in a despised accent. I cannot see that Welsh readers will be grateful for his reinscriptions of Welsh exoticism, celtic magic and all. What are, say, American readers to make of the claim that the only way to read Shakespeare now is in the shadow of Westminster constitutionalism? Or that American censors in post-war Berlin heralded a New World Order – which in fact imitated Old World Anglo-Saxon belligerence? What is implicitly, profoundly, self-referentially, 'at stake' in this book is the status of criticism, and there is a not-very-implicit claim, projected onto both Arnold and Eliot, that the true intellectual hero is the critic; that a great criticism is and must be the acknowledged legislator of contemporary cultural politics. Hawkes wants it to be disturbing that we do not think better about authorities (read the perennial Stubbes, who has had a lot of publicity this year) fulminating about bear-baiting and the theatre. I would rather be disturbed by the exception of public assemblies at church as any kind of threatening assembly, especially in times of plague – something one never sees discussed. The 'legislation' in these essays uncovers multiple occult associations. Chapters open or close with a kind of non-argued non-logic: Freud's 'unheimlich' with posters in American restaurants illustrating the 'Heimlich' manoeuvre (how to dislodge food from the throat of someone who is choking) or the association of the port of Milford Haven, Standard Oil's suspiciously named 'Sea Empress' whose oil spill devastated the Welsh coast, Milford Haven as the ancestral geographical origin of Folger of the Library and, finally, Folger's employer, Standard Oil; Shakespeare (and his father) resisting sameness (and thereby unified subjectivity) with various spellings of their name. A disturbing number of unsurprising coincidences and sinister associations inform this book. This is parochial, authoritarian work, which mimics the very all-encompassing hegemonic grip it purports to unmask.

The big subjects, the current trends, always leave space for criticism of single plays, or of small groups of plays. A quick guide to some of this year's articles, then. Jerald Spotswood argues in '"We are Undone Already": Disarming the Multitude in *Julius Caesar* and *Coriolanus*' that Shakespeare disarms his plebians by associating them with animals, creating a 'socially indistinct mass' which, because he has levelled its manifold differences, further emphasizes the individually distinguished high-status characters. Two more from the *Tudor Theatre* collection. In '*As You Like It, Rosalynde*, and Mutuality', Nathaniel Strout finds a parallel between courtship's relationship of mutuality and the experience of audience approval marked by applause. He contrasts the play to Lodge's prose narrative, which is closed to the sense of possibility, presumably because we cannot applaud a book. He emphasizes the importance of the presence of speaking female characters as a means of underwriting a point of view stifled by Lodge's misogyny. An odd reading of *The Tempest* by Martine Y. Gamaury in the French style of playing with a keyword in a text, which can be a great imaginative liberation, but here manages to attribute to characters ideas and opinions which I cannot find in the play, to ignore criticism which might have been relevant, and to misread and misinterpret as if the author had no experience of plays or this period. Maria Katarzyna Greenwood lists garlands and laureations in 'Garlands of Derision: The Thematic Imagery in Chaucer's *The Knight's Tale* and Shakespeare's *A Midsummer Night's Dream*'. If the examples are asked to carry more weight than they perhaps can bear, nonetheless, Greenwood asks us to attend to props. These French articles often arise from the

structures of the national qualifying examinations for entry into the teaching profession. The articles sometimes appear in Shakespeare bibliographies, on-line and off-, so non-French readers intrigued by their titles might want to be aware that their orientation may surprise. François Laroque's '*Antoine et Cléopâtre* ou l'esthétique du vide' therefore exemplifies the kinds of word-play with (sometimes floating) concepts which attract approbation in that examination. It also has the characteristic French view that the play is mannerist, almost baroque, and that its surface richness hides an aesthetic of uncertainty, making noise, as it were, over a void, its hyperbole and binary polarity revealing, in the end, a *Macbeth*ian nothing. This is a reader's play, and a text for the imagination, since the brilliant display of inversions and variations assume an ability to think in both in terms of painterly equivalents and of textual antecedents. Still French, but from a different generation, is a short book which combines a meditation on reading Shakespeare after the horrors of the twentieth century's atrocities with a gentle introduction to the tragedies. Originally intended for the huge new translation project of the Pléiade Shakespeare, Richard Marienstras's *Shakespeare aux XXIe Siècle: Petite introduction aux tragédies* is a rare offering from the foremost French critic of his generation.

European Shakespeares don't always look like British or North American ones, and it is salutary to think about different points of view, which offer alternative places to stand when thinking about how we think about Shakespeare now. In *Translating Traduire Tradurre Shakespeare*, Neil Forsyth offers a short introductory essay, 'Shakespeare the European' to a collection of essays about the problems of translating Shakespeare which may appear to appeal only to specialists – but there is more here than technical discussions, since reading translators reading often reveals assumptions which are profoundly in period. In addition to an extract from Jean-Michel Déprats's long essay from the Pléiade, John E. Jackson discusses 'What's in a Sonnet? Translating Shakespeare'; Martine Hennard Dutheil de la Rochère looks in detail at one sonnet four ways in 'Le Sonnet 18 de

Shakespeare en français'; and Simona Gorga reads three Italian translators, including Montale.

There is a fine collection of criticism in that new Pléiade (which includes essays by Anne Barton and Lois Potter elegantly translated into French). The volumes' individual critical essays resume and re-produce a French tradition in Shakespeare criti-cism, where he is often characterized as 'baroque'. There is an important link here to cultural habits which continue to teach rhetoric, and to take it very seriously. Beyond the term's origin with the beauty of the irregular pearl, the received use of 'baroque' indicates the unruly cornucopia of his creation. But it is already an evaluative de-scription which implies that the superabundance is 'super', decorative; by analogy with art history, ex-crescent; by analogy with the implicit presuppo-sitions of classicism, extravagant; and, rhetorically, translated, 'coloured' from an underlying reality. 'Baroque Shakespeare' implies a traditional view that language covers or clothes something else, some thing – innate, original, *authentic* – which the words 'carry over' to us. 'Baroque' also implies an authenticity which is elsewhere. If Shakespeare *is* the complex tissue of permutation and combina-tion (in which character, incident, and image re-call, repeat, and vary themes, situations, historical and mythical intertexts), then the poetry the plays speak (often through their unwitting speakers), es-pecially in the context of the necessary partialities of translation, requires extra elucidation.

It is the quest for an authentic (baroque) Shake-speare which unifies a sequence of different criti-cal approaches to the plays. Three generations of established French scholars are represented, and they combine Anglo-Saxon and French criticism, particularly the anthropologically informed in-sights first developed by French classicists exploring Greek tragedy, which Richard Marienstras intro-duced to Shakespeare studies. Robert Ellrodt com-bines reflection on the bibliographical revolutions of the last twenty-five years with a character-based approach to *Lear*; Marienstras himself writes con-cisely and trenchantly on Shakespeare the politi-cal writer, offering his own corrective to Anglo-Saxon *idées reçues* about class wars; and, above all,

Yves Peyré introduces *Titus Andronicus* and *Macbeth* in two exceptional, wide-ranging essays which do succeed in conveying the complex solidity of Shakespeare's language and structures of thought, demonstrating the limitations of 'baroque' in their analyses of the ways the plays speak through their characters.

Lois Potter's essay is on *Hamlet*, and thinks seri-ously about *Hamlet* in France, and what Hamlet has meant in French (I'm afraid it must be reported that in translating her essay, the editors have rewritten it in several places, not always felicitously). For there is always *Hamlet*. In addition to the stimulating col-lection by Bernice Kliman already mentioned, or the similarly useful essay by Paul Goetsch, there was '"Things standing thus unknown": The Epis-temology of Ignorance in *Hamlet*' by Eric P. Levy. Levy treats *Hamlet* on a literal 'need-to-know' basis. Sometimes it is helpful to redescribe something fa-miliar in a new vocabulary, and here the attempt is to emphasize a world in which certainty is pos-sible, even if apparently often out of reach: the philosophical term exploited is 'prior sequence'. 'In this context, *Hamlet* emerges as an epistemo-logical tragedy in which the need to know collides with the need to maintain the security of igno-rance which, in turn, intensifies the turmoil caused by unexpected knowledge' – not quite Hamlet's prophetic soul reaction. Like Othello's preference for unwitting cuckoldom, or Oedipus's ignorance that he was always unhappy, there is a problem that the tragic situation traditionally seemed to depend upon an acknowledgement that the sudden wreck of life is in fact a recognition that one was always wrecked. The reassessment in hindsight was not a simple corrective, but a complete revision of the story which underlay the drama. But Othello is wrong, and Hamlet, although he discovers that he is right that his father has been murdered, still has choices to make. Nor is it clear that ignorance is safety. If the conclusion is that Hamlet's search for knowledge must turn on self-knowledge and 'epis-temological self-control', then it is not clear that the new terminology has increased understanding; per-haps it is significant that this is another emphatically readerly interpretation, and that it is based on the last great conflated edition, Jenkins's Arden. The 23rd volume of *Hamlet Studies* contains a review of other periodicals' work on the play (mid-1999 to 2000) as well as five essays: Dowling Campbell on how issues of 'honour' might take us to contemporary thought on royal marriage policy; Bryan N. S. Gooch on delay; Paul J. Voss on 'praying' and 'preying'; Joseph B. Wagner on Hamlet's identification with his dead father; and Yoshiko Kawachi, 'Translating *Hamlet* into Japanese'. I cannot give a more detailed description, as I received a defective copy.

Arthur Kinney's collection of new essays, by contrast, is impeccably presented. His long introduction surveys the history of *Hamlet*-interpretation in 68 pages, mainly in Europe and America; it is a sensible overview, which opens and closes with performance, a welcome accent of our times. He includes film and television, and some attention to non-English language *Hamlets* and Hamlets (German romanticism takes pride of place). This is a thankless task which almost inevitably becomes a chronological list, with emphasis on the innovations of the last generation or two. E. Pearlman's essay, 'Shakespeare at Work: The Invention of the Ghost', studies ghosts, not just the literary prehistory, but the evolution of Shakespeare's own apparitions; he demonstrates how multiply new is *Hamlet*'s: in his silences, his failure to behave like a Nuntius come from the grave to tell us of it (including his undignified molery in the cellarage), and his reticent ambiguity. It thus makes a good companion piece to Goetsch's monster. In similarly contextualizing vein, R. A. Foakes considers Hamlet as not-a-revenge-play, starting from an observation of John Kerrigan's that Hamlet promises to 'remember' not to 'revenge'. 'Hamlet's Neglect of Revenge' thus joins Kerrigan in asking us to rethink what we have always thought fundamental to the play. The interpretation runs into difficulty when Hamlet runs Polonius through, but it is no less stimulating for that. Philip Edwards finds the poet's concentration on writing poetry as a search for a moment of perfection as a starting place for reflections on revision in 'The Dyer's Infected Hand: The Sonnets and the Text of Hamlet'. Paul Werstine writes from his authority as a tex-

tual bibliographer to criticize the presuppositions of the editing tradition and, in a closely argued essay, offers his own historical contextualization to illuminate the genesis of play-scripts. This is a teasing piece, whose positive side must appear in a new edition of *Hamlet*. Ann Thompson, another editor whose *Hamlet* is awaited with trepidations of all kinds, looks all too briefly at the play's place in the appreciation of Shakespeare, and along the way takes issue with the question of Shakespeare's place in a multitudinous Globe. *Hamlet* without the prints would certainly be less visually familiar. Opening with some well- and less-well-known paintings, and sculptures, Catherine Belsey goes on to remind us of the question about Hamlet's 'feminine' qualities (his gentle introspection, his apparent failure of testosterone), in '"Was Hamlet a Man or a Woman?": The Prince in the Graveyard, 1800–1920'. It is good to have this material assembled here. No such collection would be complete without an essay on 'early-modern subjectivity', which Jerry Broton provides in 'Ways of Seeing *Hamlet*', where he argues that one of the most signifying material ways of seeing is in a mirror. It helps the argument not at all to depend upon Lisa Jardine's misreading of 'closets', or what might hang here and there in Elsinore (ah, it's the fall of Troy), and Lacan's distortions of the play. Race, too, could hardly be absent from an American collection, and Peter Erickson provides it, focusing on the 'transition' from Hamlet to Othello. And Richard Levin ends the book with a very personal, grumpy, insistence that he likes Hamlet and *Hamlet* and thinks that Shakespeare meant us to think about the prince, too. That he also dismisses Laertes because a man concerned with family honour could not also love his father, but is 'a nice young man' in any case, is something of a disappointment coming from a well-known critic. Haste, perhaps.

WORKS REVIEWED

Armstrong, Philip, *Shakespeare in Psychoanalysis*. Accents on Shakespeare (London, 2001).

Barton, Anne, 'Préface', in *Oeuvres Complètes*, ed. Jean-Michel Déprats, pp. x–lxxviii.

Besnault, Marie-Hélène, '"Richard III" et le rire', in *Tudor Theatre*, pp. 177–96.

Banks, Carol, 'Shakespeare's *Henry V*: Tudor or Jacobean', in Pincombe, *The Anatomy of Tudor Literature*, pp. 174–88.

Belsey, Catherine, '"Was Hamlet a Man or a Woman?": The Prince in the Graveyard, 1800–1920', in Kinney, *Hamlet*, pp. 135–60.

Bevington, David, *Shakespeare: An Introduction* (Oxford, 2002).

Blake, N. F., *A Grammar of Shakespeare's Language* (Basingstoke, 2002).

Blanc, Pauline, 'La Fonction du rire carnavalesque dans le théâtre des Tudor', in *Tudor Theatre*, pp. 61–80.

Bradshaw, Graham, 'Shakespeare's Peculiarity', *Proceedings of the British Academy*, 111: Lectures and Memoirs (Oxford, 2001), 99–126.

Brotton, Jerry, 'Ways of Seeing *Hamlet*', in Kinney, *Hamlet*, pp. 161–76.

Brusberg-Kermeier, Stefani, 'The Role of Body Images in the Tudor Myth and its Subversion in Shakespeare's History Plays', in Pincombe, *The Anatomy of Tudor Literature*, pp. 189–94.

Bruster, Douglas, *Quoting Shakespeare: Form and Culture in Early Modern Drama* (Lincoln, Nebraska and London, 2000).

Campbell, Dowling G., 'The Double Dichotomy and Paradox of Virtue in Hamlet', *Hamlet Studies* 23 (2001), 13–48.

Cheney, Patrick, 'Shakespeare's Sonnet 106, Spenser's National Epic, and Counter-Petrarchism', *English Literary Renaissance*, 31 (2001), 331–64.

Costa de Beauregard, Raphaëlle, 'Laughter Chastened or Arden Language: A Study of Comic Languages in *As You Like It*', in *Tudor Theatre*, pp. 211–31.

Craig, Hugh, 'Grammatical Modality in English Plays from the 1580s to the 1640s' *English Literary Renaissance*, 30 (2000), 32–54.

Craig, Leon Harold, *Of Philosophers and Kings: Political Philosophy in Shakespeare's Macbeth and King Lear* (Toronto, 2001).

Crumley, J. Clinton, 'Questioning History in Cymbeline' *Studies in English Literature 1500–1900*, 41 (2001), 297–316.

D'Amico, Jack, *Shakespeare and Italy: The City and the Stage* (Florida, 2001).

Desens, Marliss C., 'Marrying Down: Negotiating a More Equal Marriage on the English Renaissance Stage', *Medieval and Renaissance Drama in England*, 14 (2001), 227–55.

Dockray, Keith, *William Shakespeare The Wars of the Roses and the Historians* (Charleston and Stroud, 2002).

Dubrow, Heather, '"In thievish ways": Tropes and Robbers in Shakespeare's Sonnets and Early Modern England', reprinted (revised) in Headlam Wells et al., *Neo-Historicism*, pp. 219–39.

Dutheil de la Rochère, Martine Hennard, 'Le Sonnet 18 de Shakespeare en français', Irene Weber Henkin, *Translating Traduire, Tradurre Shakespeare*, pp. 75–96.

Edwards, Philip, 'The Dyer's Infected Hand: the Sonnets and the Text of *Hamlet*', in Kinney, *Hamlet*, pp. 101–14.

Ellis, David, 'Black Comedy in Shakespeare', *Essays in Criticism*, 51 (2001), 385–403.

Erickson, Peter, 'Can we Talk about Race in Hamlet?', in Kinney, *Hamlet*, pp. 207–14.

Foakes, R. A., 'Hamlet's Neglect of Revenge', in Kinney, *Hamlet*, pp. 85–101.

Friedman, Michael D., *"The World Must be Peopled": Shakespeare's Comedies of Forgiveness* (Madison, 2002).

Giancarlo, Matthew, 'The Rise and Fall of the Great Vowel Shift? The Changing Ideological Intersections of Philology, Historical Linguistics, and Literary History', *Representations*, 76 (2001), 27–60.

Gibson, Rex, *Shakespearean and Jacobean Tragedy* (Cambridge, 2000).

Gooch, Gryan N. S., 'Hamlet as Hero: The Necessity of Virtue', *Hamlet Studies*, 23 (2001), 50–8.

Gorga, Simona, 'Il Secondo mestiere del poeta: Eugenio Montale traduce Shakespeare: *Julius Caesar*, *Timon of Athens*, *The Winter's Tale* e *The Comedy of Errors*. Un confronto con le traduzioni di Cesare Vico Lodovico e Gabrielle Baldini' in Irene Weber Henkin, *Translating Traduire, Tradurre Shakespeare*, pp. 97–135.

Goy-Blanquet, Dominique, *Shakespeare et l'Invention de l'histoire* (Brussels, 1997).

Grene, Nicholas, *Shakespeare's Serial History Plays* (Cambridge, 2002).

Griffin, Benjamin, *Playing the Past: Approaches to English Historical Drama 1385–1600* (Woodbridge, Suffolk, 2001).

Hackett, Helen, *Women and Romance Fiction in the English Renaissance* (Cambridge, 2000).

Hawkes, Terence, 'The Old Bill', in Kinney, *Hamlet*, pp. 177–92.

Shakespeare in the Present (New York and London, 2002).

Headlam Wells, Robin, 'An Orpheus for a Hercules: Virtue Redefined in "The Tempest"', in Headlam Wells et al., *Neo-Historicism*, pp. 240–62.

Headlam Wells, Robin, Glenn Burgess, and Rowland Wymer, eds., *Neo-Historicism: Studies in Renaissance Literature, History and Politics* (Woodbridge, Suffolk, 2000).

Hill, Tracey, '"Since Forged Invention Former Time Defaced": Representing Tudor History in the 1590s', in Pincombe, *The Anatomy of Tudor Literature*, pp. 195–210.

Hillman, Richard, *Shakespeare, Marlowe, and the Politics of France* (Basingstoke, 2002).

Höfele, Andreas, 'Sackerson the Bear', *REAL: Yearbook of Research in English and American Literature*, 17 (2001), 161–77.

Holland, Peter, 'Seeing Better' (Birmingham, 1999).

'Beginning in the Middle', *Proceedings of the British Academy: Lectures and Memoirs* (Oxford, 2000), 127–55.

Hunt, Maurice, 'The Reclamation of Language in *Much Ado About Nothing*', *Studies in Philology*, 97 (2000), 165–91.

Isaac, Megan Lynn, *Heirs to Shakespeare: Reinventing the Bard in Young Adult Literature* (Portsmouth, New Haven and London, 2000).

Jackson, John E., 'What's in a Sonnet? Translating Shakespeare', in Irene Weber Henkin, *Translating Traduire, Tradurre Shakespeare*, pp. 57–74.

Jaster, Margaret Rose, 'Controlling Clothes, Manipulating Mates: Petruchio's Griselda', *Shakespeare Studies*, 29 (2001), 93–108.

Jones, Emrys, 'Reclaiming Early Shakespeare', *Essays in Criticism*, 51 (2001), 35–50.

Kawachi, Yoshiko, 'Translating *Hamlet* into Japanese', *Hamlet Studies*, 23 (2001), 93–102.

Kerrigan, John, *On Shakespeare and Early Modern Literature: Essays* (Oxford, 2001).

Kinney, Arthur F. *Lies Like Truth: Shakespeare, Macbeth, and the Cultural Moment* (Detroit, 2001).

ed., *Hamlet: New Critical Essays*, Shakespeare Criticism, vol. 27 (New York and London, 2002).

Knapp, Jeffrey, *Shakespeare's Tribe: Church, Nation, and Theater in Renaissance England* (Chicago and London, 2002).

Knowles, Ronald, *Shakespeare's Arguments with History* (New York and Basingstoke, 2002).

Laroque, François, 'Slaughter and Laughter: Cruel Comedy in fin-de-siècle Tudor Drama', in *Tudor Theatre*, pp. 161–76.

Antoine et Cléopâtre ou l'esthétique du vide', *Etudes Anglaises*, 53 (2000), 400–12.

Levin, Richard, 'Hamlet, Laertes, and the Dramatic Function of Foils', in Kinney, *Hamlet*, pp. 215–30.

Levy, Eric P., '"Things standing thus unknown": The Epistemology of Ignorance in *Hamlet*', *Studies in Philology*, 97 (2000), 192–209.

Lim, Walter S. H., 'Knowledge and Belief in *The Winter's Tale*', *Studies in English Literature 1500–1900*, 41 (2001), 317–34.

Lunney, Ruth, 'Rewriting the Narrative of Dramatic Character, or, Not "Shakespearean" but "Debatable"', *Medieval and Renaissance Drama in England*, 14 (2001) 66–85.

McAlindon, Tom, *Shakespeare's Tudor History: a study of Henry IV, Parts 1 and 2* (Aldershot, 2001).

'The Discourse of Prayer in *The Tempest*', *Studies in English Literature 1500–1900*, 41 (2001), 335–56.

McDonald, Russ, *Shakespeare and the Arts of Language*. Oxford Shakespeare Topics (Oxford, 2001).

McEachern, Claire, 'Figures of Fidelity: Believing in *King Lear*', *Modern Philology*, 98 (2000) 211–30.

Marienstras, Richard, *Shakespeare aux XXIe Siècle: Petite introduction aux tragédies* (Paris, 2000).

Martin, Anthony, 'The British Myth in Tudor Drama', in Pincombe, *The Anatomy of Tudor Literature*, pp. 157–65.

Martin, Isabel, 'Postmodernizing Shakespeare: A Palimpsest Poem', in Bode and Klooss, *Historicizing/Contemporizing Shakespeare*, pp. 185–200.

Miola, Robert S., *Shakespeare's Reading*, Oxford Shakespeare Topics (Oxford, 2000).

Murray, Barbara A., 'Performance and Publication of Shakespeare, 1660–1682: "Go see them play'd, then read them as before"', *Neuphilologische Mitteilungen*, 102 (2001), 435–49.

Nelson, T. G. A., 'Pre-loved Partners in Early Modern Comedy', *Studies in Philology*, 97 (2000), 362–78.

Nutt, Joe, *An Introduction to Shakespeare's Late Plays* (Basingstoke, 2002).

O'Neill, María, 'Of Clothing and Coinage', in Pincombe, *The Anatomy of Tudor Literature*, pp. 166–73.

Pearlman, E., 'Shakespeare at Work: The Invention of the Ghost', in Kinney, *Hamlet*, pp. 71–84.

Pincombe, Mike, ed., *The Anatomy of Tudor Literature: Proceedings of the First International Conference of the Tudor Symposium (1998)* (Aldershot, 2001).

Poole, Adrian, 'Macbeth and the Third Person', *Proceedings of the British Academy: Lectures and Memoirs*, 109 (Oxford, 1999), pp. 73–92.

Pye, Christopher, *The Vanishing: Shakespeare, the Subject, and Early Modern Culture* (Durham and London, 2000).

Robinson, Peter, 'Pretended Speech Acts in Shakespeare's Sonnets', *Essays in Criticism*, 51 (2001), 283–307.

Rodenburg, Patsy, *Speaking Shakespeare* (London, 2002).

Sanders, Julie, *Novel Shakespeares: Twentieth-Century Women Novelists and Appropriation* (Manchester, 2001).

Shannon, Laurie, *Sovereign Amity: Figures of Friendship in Shakespearean Contexts* (Chicago, 2002).

Shuger, Debora Kuller, *Political Theologies in Shakespeare's England: The Sacred and the State in Measure for Measure* (New York and London, 2001).

Slights, Jessica, 'Rape and the Romanticization of Shakespeare's Miranda', *Studies in English Literature 1500–1900*, 41 (2001), 357–80.

Snyder, Susan, *Shakespeare: A Wayward Journey* (Newark and London, 2002).

Spotswood, Jerald, '"We are undone already": Disarming the Multitude in *Julius Caesar* and *Coriolanus*', *Texas Studies in Language and Literature*, 42 (2000), 61–78.

Strout, Nathaniel, '*As You Like It*, *Rosalynde*, and Mutuality', *Studies in English Literature 1500–1900*, 41 (2001), 277–96.

Taylor, Michael, *Shakespeare Criticism in the Twentieth Century*, Oxford Shakespeare Topics (Oxford, 2001).

Theis, Jeffrey, 'The "ill kill'd" Deer: Poaching and Social Order in *The Merry Wives of Windsor*', *Texas Studies in Language and Literature*, 43 (2001), 46–73.

Thorne, Alison, *Vision and Rhetoric in Shakespeare: Looking through Language* (Houndmills, Basingstoke, 2000).

Thompson, Ann, 'Hamlet and the Canon', in Kinney, *Hamlet*, pp. 193–206.

Voss, Paul J., 'To Prey or not to Prey: Prayer and Punning in *Hamlet*', *Hamlet Studies*, 23 (2001), 59–74.

Wagner, Joseph B., 'Hamlet Rewriting *Hamlet*', *Hamlet Studies*, 23 (2001), 75–92.

Wiggins, Martin, *Shakespeare and the Drama of his Time*. Oxford Shakespeare Topics (Oxford, 2000).

Wright, George T., *Hearing the Measures: Shakespearean and other Inflections* (Madison, Wisconsin, 2001).

Collections (by title)

After Shakespeare: Writing Inspired by the World's Greatest Author, ed. John Gross (Oxford, 2002).

The Anatomy of Tudor Literature: Proceedings of the First International Conference of the Tudor Symposium (1998), ed. Mike Pincombe (Vermont, 2001).

Approaches to Teaching Shakespeare's Hamlet, ed. Bernice W. Kliman (New York, 2001).

Hamlet: New Critical Essays, ed. Arthur F. Kinney, Shakespeare Criticism, vol. 27 (New York and London, 2002).

Historicizing/Contemporizing Shakespeare: Essays in Honour of Rudolf Böhm, ed. Christoph Bode and Wolfgang Klooss (Trier, 2000).

Neo-Historicism: Studies in Renaissance Literature, History and Politics, eds. Robin Headlam Wells, Glenn Burgess and Rowland Wymer (Woodbridge, Suffolk, 2000).

Shakespeare, *Oeuvres Complètes: Les Tragédies* (Pléiade), ed. Jean-Michel Déprats (Paris, 2002).

Talking Shakespeare: Shakespeare into the Millennium, ed. Deborah Cartmell and Michael Scott (Basingstoke, 2001).

Translating Traduire Tradurre Shakespeare, ed. Irene Weber Henkin. *Théorie* 40 (2001), available from Le Centre de traduction littéraire, Université de Lausanne (www.unil.ch/ctl).

Tudor Theatre: For Laughs?/Pour rire? Puzzling Laughter in Plays of the Tudor Age / Rires et problèmes dans le théâtre des Tudor (Tours, Centre d'études supérieures de la Renaissance, Collection Theta, 6) published by Peter Lang, 2002.

2. SHAKESPEARE'S LIFE, TIMES AND STAGE

reviewed by LESLIE THOMSON

Judging from the selection of books that have arrived for review this year, the practice of Shakespeare and related criticism is ever more diverse, seemingly without a clear direction, even miscellaneous. This is of course not altogether a bad thing, since the opportunities for new and innovative approaches are necessarily plentiful at such a time. Certainly 'variety' is the byword of this year's review: variety in topics, in quality, in critical approach, and in the media discussed.

The evidence of publishers' lists and tables at conferences suggests that those planning to undertake studies of Shakespeare's contemporaries might want to think twice before beginning a project without that magic name in its title. The same evidence also indicates that one publisher in particular is making a concerted effort to broaden the range of criticism on early modern subjects. Ashgate is noteworthy for both the quantity and quality of its offerings on a broad selection of such topics, a good example being *Marlowe's Soldiers: Rhetorics of Masculinity in the Age of the Armada*, by Alan Shepard. It offers an ambitious treatment of all Marlowe's plays; indeed, its scope is rather wider than the title and subtitle seem to advertise. Central to his argument is the idea that 'under the stresses of war, counterfeiting the guise of a soldier in the streets could bring a death sentence, while in the theatre it could bring modest celebrity to a player and, in rare circumstances, wealth to shareholders. Or, if the anti-theatricalists were to be believed, counterfeiting a soldier could unravel the nation's military resolve if not the structure of society itself'. In this context, his particular concern is 'how and why Marlowe's plays make entertainment of a wealth of historically and geopolitically divergent fantasies about martial law and its discontents' (p. 2). Not surprisingly, this being about Marlowe, Shepard sees the plays as 'engag[ing] in deeply ambiguous, sometimes subtle acts of resistance to the explicit endorsements of martial law' (p. 3) expressed elsewhere in Elizabethan society. To 'provide a contemporary context for understanding Marlowe's own dialectical treatments of militarism' (p. 7), Shepard quotes from many of the treatises, pamphlets and monographs with a military focus that were published during the period. He deals especially with *Tamburlaine* and *Doctor Faustus*, but also gives extended attention to *Dido Queen of Carthage*, *Edward II*, *The Jew of Malta*, and *The Massacre at Paris*, the latter described as 'Marlowe's study of the use of the rhetorics of masculinity as weapons in the French wars of religion in his own time' (p. 16). The chapter on

the two-part *Tamburlaine* is centred on the murders of Calyphas, Olympia and Agydas as incidents when 'the exigencies of war offer no defense of the soldiers' brutality' (p. 35), despite the martial law imposed by Tamburlaine and his deputies. *Dido*, in Shepard's view, offers a 'scrutiny of the fictions of epic masculinity that are implicitly resident in the Dido–Aeneas myth' (p. 55). In *Edward II*, he argues, 'Marlowe creates the contrast between the Mortimers in part to help establish that the question of whether a man's martial nature is possessed or performed is a root conflict of the play' (p. 91). *The Jew of Malta* he sees as a tragi-comedy that 'presents an oblique pageant of the contemporary rivalry between a cohort of English war hawks and an ever-growing accumulation of merchants, who have gradually become a threat to the chivalric code that still sustained even ordinary veterans, and who come to vie for control of the ethos of London in the wake of the Armada' (p. 113). Shepard concludes his reassessment of Marlowe by contrasting *Doctor Faustus* with the other plays: 'Without perceptible irony', he says, both the A and B texts 'revel in war fever' (p. 175). Taking the subplot material at face value, he treats it as '*magical realism*', with 'magically real phenomena' that 'transport us back and forth across "certain frontiers" that are variously geographical, visceral, cosmological, ontological. The two *Faustus* plays ask spectators to imagine a series of border-crossings that have the potential to reshape not the geography of Europe or its religious landscape, but more fundamentally the relationship of the fabulous to ordinary civic life, and so the roles of art in defining and securing a state' (pp. 175–6). Shepard's broader purpose is to show that 'the Marlowe plays present zero-sum universes, peopled by absolutists and despots of all kinds who exact their pounds of flesh from the more visibly complex beings in their midst who are trying desperately to inhabit a more symphonic universe' (p. 217). Whether you agree or disagree depends in part on whether or not you concur with his interpretations of the characters (always an iffy business), but he carefully establishes the premises of his argument, and presents his evidence in such a way as to make one willing to reconsider some of the Elizabethan theatre's most troubling figures.

A playwright long virtually ignored is John Marston, and after reading through *The Drama of John Marston*, edited by T. F. Wharton, it isn't difficult to understand why. Given Marston's emphasis on physical and verbal violence, sexual obsession and obscene puns, together with the anti-heroes who dominate his plays, it is probably inevitable that the cumulative effect of this book is to inundate the reader with the unpleasantness of its subject's characteristic mode. Indeed, because Marston's world is not easily shared for too long, these twelve essays might best be read separately; nevertheless, because recent work on this controversial author is rare, this collection warrants attention. On offer here are many different, sometimes conflicting, views and approaches – a reflection of the contradictions that typify the Marston canon. In his introduction Wharton calls Marston 'a relentless self-publicist', who 'sought out – or created – moral *dis*order and made it his medium'; he suggests that postmodern criticism's tendency 'not to valorize moral rectitude' (p. 3) can permit new evaluations of Marston's work. In the first essay, Rick Bowers focuses on the Antonio plays, especially *Antonio's Revenge*, described as 'Rude, crude, and theatrically unglued' (p. 15). Because he views Marston as the 'theatrical bad boy of his time' (p. 17), this description is more positive than negative. Bowers argues that Marston deliberately mocks and undermines conventional expectations; he 'is interested in local theatrical effect, in comic inflation/deflation, in absurd and discontinuous action critically self-conscious of the very genre of revenge' (p. 20). Furthermore, 'The admittedly outrageous energies of the play are parodic, melodramatic, and satirical. And they are to be enjoyed as such' (p. 24). W. Reavley Gair follows with a rather unfortunate piece that would have benefited from more careful editing. He tries to explain virtually all aspects of Marston's plays as largely determined by the theatrical space for which they were written and by Marston's desire to please an audience: 'Even his famed – even notorious – device of making his characters fall to the ground in passion may be seen

as a technique for minimizing stage movement' (p. 34). When discussing *Antonio and Mellida* at St Paul's playhouse, Gair both repeats and offers a spirited defence of his earlier study establishing the location of this venue, but seems unaware that at least two recent essays (by Roger Bowers and Herbert Berry – see last year's review) have pretty well negated his argument. On page 34 there seems to be a problem with notes and numbers. More troubling, however, is Gair's claim that 'In the side aisles of Paul's there were numerous shops' (p. 36). He is, of course, completely wrong: the shops were built against the *outside* of the cathedral.

Two essays in the collection deal specifically with Marston as a satirist. Patrick Buckridge applies Annabel Patterson's ideas of 'a hermeneutics of "reading between the lines" and of a poetics of "writing between the lines"' as products of censorship (p. 61) to his consideration of several plays, primarily *The Scourge of Villainy*, *Jack Drum's Entertainment*, and *Antonio and Mellida*. Buckridge advances the theory that instead of using 'traditional encrypting devices – allegory, emblem, typology and the like', Marston directed attention 'away from the possibility of "real-world" applications and correspondences . . . towards an alternative form of literary pleasure and profit'. This kind of satire Buckridge calls 'recreation' (p. 61), a usage he contextualizes with examples from Marston's contemporaries. His plays are therefore 'recreative rather than persuasive in their dramatic and rhetorical techniques' (p. 79). What we are left with is a defanged Marston on the one hand, but on the other, new reasons to see his plays as cohesive wholes with a purpose. In her essay, Janet Clare also addresses the related issues of satire and censorship by 'tracing the inter-relationship between Marston's plays and the vagaries of Elizabethan and Jacobean censorship, to examine how tropes of the latter insistently figure in the dramatist's work, formulating a discourse on poetic liberty, censure and censorship' (p. 194). Her departure point is the 1599 bishops' ban on satires and epigrams, which, Clare argues (against others, including Linda Boose), must be understood 'in the context of the political instabilities of the *fin de siècle*, of which Essex's rebellion was the culmination but not the sole cause' (p. 197). Clare examines the playtexts for evidence of moderating changes necessitated by external circumstances. Her purpose is to show how Marston's 'experience of the suppression of the satires, the textual interferences with *The Malcontent*, reactions to *The Fawn* contributing to the company's loss of royal patronage, and finally the reception of *Eastward Ho*, all serve to indicate how censure could lead to censorship' (p. 209).

In other pieces, Matthew Steggle considers *What You Will*, a play probably few know well enough to agree or disagree with his complex analysis of it as a 'fantasy' (p. 48) that 'celebrates the imperfectly articulated, the irrational, and the playful' (p. 57). Richard Scarr's interest is the use of *double entendres* and sexual puns (is there a difference?) in Marston's 'courtesan plays', *The Dutch Courtesan* and *The Insatiate Countess*. Although Scarr acknowledges parenthetically that the latter play is 'possibly co-authored' (p. 90), he discusses its puns as if they are as much Marston's as those in *Dutch Courtesan*. Puns of a previous age are notoriously difficult to explicate meaningfully; Scarr errs on the side of over-explaining. His rather repetitive technique is to quote a passage, give a straightforward reading, then follow with his interpretations of the bawdy innuendo. William Slights examines 'Marston's take on the notion of *Nosce teipsum*, especially as the Renaissance discourse of self has come to be newly understood'. He argues that following 'Montaigne and the neo-sceptics' Marston 'debunks excessive self-regard in a sustained series of grotesque images of inward filth and masturbatory self-gratification' (p. 101). In this context, *The Fawn* is examined as an early response to 'James's *self*-promoting era' (p. 102). In assessing Marston's challenge to ideas popular in his day, Slights questions the view 'of so many academic lectures on the self in connection with everything from Hooker to hookers' that to see sexual identity as a product of either nature or culture is to set up a 'false dichotomy' (pp. 123 note 45, 116). Next, in a series of detailed analyses, Sukanya B. Senapati examines Marston's treatment of his female characters to argue against the assumption that his plays are

largely misogynist. Her belief is that he shows 'patriarchal misogyny, yet only within the context of showing the absurdities of anxious male competition'. Senapati offers examples of how Marston created 'powerful female counter-voices to patriarchal assumptions' (p. 125). Those who know his plays well will find much with which to agree and disagree here.

At about the mid-point of this collection, Kiernan Ryan begins his essay, 'There is a mystery at the heart of Marston's drama' (p. 145). This, of course, is not merely an innocuous observation made in passing but the lead-in to a solution. For Ryan, the answers lie in modern psychoanalytic theories about hysteria, which he proceeds to apply to *The Malcontent*. 'Marston's genius, and his curse', he reports, 'was to voice through his drama and enshrine in *The Malcontent* the inherent hysteria of capitalist culture at the point when that culture had just coalesced in its early modern form' (p. 159). Montaigne's influence on Marston is again the subject in David Pascoe's study of how the playwright 'adulterates' (p. 171) the message of Florio's Montaigne in *The Dutch Courtesan*. Next, Wharton discusses how, in *The Malcontent*, 'both political failure and success are verified in terms of potency and sexual dominance' (p. 182). This he connects to the world outside the theatre: 'Marston produces a parody-version of James's theories of the monarchy-amorous' (p. 184). The final piece is Michael Scott's assessment of why Marston's plays are rarely staged or taught today. He asks why 'hostility by Marston to social convention, to norms of moral codes, and to dominant ideologies does not attract contemporary historicist, cultural materialists or feminist critics?' (p. 216). Scott surveys the work of several prominent critics fitting these descriptions to show how none has got Marston right, then (no surprise) offers his own angle. He sees the plays as 'apolitical', to be 'understood precisely in their reflection of a landscape that is the human condition. The dramatic form reflected such a landscape, not in the context of the dramatist's life but in relation to the forms, structure, juxtaposing, and performance of the dramatic artefacts' (p. 222). Scott ends with an observation with which most of the contributors to (and readers of) this collection would probably agree: 'Marston will not conform to criticism nor to theatrical fashion. He confronts both and, in doing so, will probably always remain at the margins of English cultural activity' (p. 228).

The material world within which Marlowe, Marston and their contemporaries wrote has recently been scrutinized in a number of fruitful studies. This productive emphasis on the places, possessions, and practices of that world continues in several new works. The first of these, *Tudor London: A Map and a View*, is a London Topographical Society publication edited by Ann Saunders and John Schofield. The two items referred to in the title are the so-called Copperplate Map, of which a third section (an area including St Paul's Cathedral) has been discovered, and the View of the city of London from the North, of which a second, more complete copy has emerged. The Copperplate Map receives the most attention here, with Schofield on the three extant sheets of the map, Stephen Powys Marks on the map's date, and Peter Barber on its context. In the final section Schofield returns to discuss the View, and he is particularly concerned with questions about its date and where the artist stood when drawing it. This View famously shows one and perhaps two theatres – thought to be the Curtain and/or the Theatre – making it particularly interesting to theatre historians. One of Schofield's chief purposes here is to respond to articles by James Lusardi and Herbert Berry, who have most recently undertaken to answer both questions.[1] All three agree on some matters, but about others Schofield disagrees with both. His evidence and reasoning are too detailed and specialized to summarize here, but essentially he agrees with Lusardi rather than Berry about where the artist stood and disagrees with Berry's dating of 1600 and therefore with his conclusion that the Curtain is the theatre in question. Schofield dates the drawing between 1577 and 1598, thus confirming that it is 'a panorama of London in the time of John Stow'; consequently, he 'must disappoint Shakespearean scholars, since we have made no headway in the debate about which theatre is shown . . . The remarkable building

on the left of the View could be either the Theatre or the Curtain' (p. 45).

As its rather oblique title might indicate, Russell West's *Spatial Representations and the Jacobean Stage from Shakespeare to Webster* is a book that uses a lot of big words to say not very much, or at least not a lot new about the plays that are ostensibly its focus. West describes his purpose as being to 'outline some of the ways in which the Jacobean theatre, as an ostentatiously spatial art-form, interacts with the context of early modern society' (p. 3). He will 'endeavour to make the notion of space concrete by situating it in quite specific areas of historical social practice, thereby avoiding the perils of excessive metaphoricity, while maintaining the conceptual flexibility inevitably necessary to deal with very diverse aspects of human action'. These 'areas' are 'spaces of exchange', of 'social mobility', of 'demographic mobility', 'geographical spaces' and 'spaces of thought' (p. 5). His method of argument and proof consists of making statements rather than suggesting possibilities – and consultation of the many notes reveals that a large number of his premises are in fact paraphrases of other critics. These statements accumulate into long strings of information with little supporting analyses of actual playtexts. Despite the title, when there are examples they are disproportionately from Thomas Middleton. Repeatedly, only one example is used to illustrate a central point. Elsewhere the pseudo-technical language, heavy with the terminology of theory, obscures West's argument and seriously reduces his chances of being read, let alone understood, by many readers. His 'Coda' begins, 'The emergence of a localized mode of thought and of a form of subjectivity predicated upon operative, pragmatic action is the culmination of the diverse aspects of changing spatial experience considered in the preceding chapters: money as a catalyst for

---

[1] James P. Lusardi, 'The Pictured Playhouse: Reading the Utrecht Engraving of Shakespeare's London', *Shakespeare Quarterly*, 44 (1993), 202–27; Herbert Berry, 'The View of London from the North and the Playhouses in Holywell', *Shakespeare Survey 53* (2000), pp. 196–212.

spatial transformation, social and demographic mobility, and overseas travel' (p. 240). *Caveat lector*.

Masks and Masking in Medieval and Early Tudor England, by Meg Twycross and Sarah Carpenter, is one of the first offerings in the recently launched and most welcome Ashgate series devoted to Studies in Performance and Early Modern Drama. The authors' purpose is 'to historicise and contextualize the moments and patterns of mask-wearing in the Middle Ages'; in particular, their focus is on 'performance masking, whether in drama or in other kinds of game' (pp. 3, 7). However, they face problems of both definition and evidence. In the pre-Shakespearian period with which the book is concerned, *mask* usually 'designated a particular kind of court entertainment, the forerunner of what later became known as the Stuart *masque*' – although Twycross and Carpenter do not use that spelling because of its seventeenth-century associations. Further complicating matters is that 'the term *mask* did not acquire our primary sense of "an object used to cover the face"' until the later sixteenth century (p. 2). As to the second problem, the authors note that 'the sources of evidence on which we depend, though rich, are partial, ambivalent, and sometimes contradictory' (p. 6). Nevertheless, with a source of information such as REED to draw from, they have much more to work with than did earlier scholars. The book is divided into four parts: the first three, Popular, Courtly and Theatrical Masking, deal with virtually every kind of performance masking, while the fourth, Theory and Practice, considers the possible meanings of masking on the one hand, and on the other, the practical business of mask-making and the terminology used to describe all aspects of masking. Helpful illustrations, some by Twycross, are interspersed throughout, and an extensive bibliography and notes update older studies.

Among the reasons to value this book is that it provides what is surely the most comprehensive analysis of the Feast of Fools and similar early festivals since E. K. Chambers's *Medieval Stage*, published in 1903. As the authors acknowledge, 'Carnival as such never reached England', but they devote a chapter to it 'Partly because it demonstrates various aspects of masks and masking behaviour in their most intense form' (p. 55). Nevertheless, as they also admit, here and elsewhere they often must extrapolate from European customs because there is little evidence of what happened in England. The section on courtly masking (with chapters on tournaments, disguisings, courtly mumming and amorous masking) is perhaps the most successful, at least partly because the evidence of court practices is more plentiful. Here they also deal with a confusing mix of kinds not easily distinguished today: 'it is not only the boundaries of genre, but those between game and performance that are blurred: masks are worn in a whole spectrum of activities, from tournaments to pageants to dances, in which the demarcation between "performer" and "spectator" becomes thoroughly elusive and sometimes non-existent'. Central to Twycross and Carpenter's discussion of courtly masking is that 'where faces were hidden, questions of power combine and often interact with questions of identity and its role in courtly communities' (p. 102). Henry VIII naturally receives considerable attention.

Ironically but inevitably, when finally the authors turn to masking in a specifically theatrical context, the imbalance between speculation and evidence increases. They explain the difficulty of matching the random information found in records – of props and costumes, for example – with the extant plays. In addition, there is 'almost no contemporary comment or criticism directly about mystery-play masks' (p. 194). One feature of medieval theatre considered at length is that 'since only some of the characters appear to have been masked, masked and unmasked performers share the same stage' (p. 199). We learn that devils seem to have been the only characters who were always masked in medieval theatre: many accounts include the costs of making devils' black 'heads'. As to whether human characters wore masks, there is almost no certain evidence, although it seems that wicked figures such as Herod either did so or had their faces painted. At the other extreme, God was either masked or had his face painted gold. As for morality plays, they 'use masks freely to contribute particular moral and theatrical effects; but they do not appear to be plays in which allegorical characters are masked most or all of the time' (p. 233). Despite the paucity of evidence for theatrical masking, Twycross and Carpenter undertake an extended discussion of possibilities, which seems excessive, especially since it comes nearer the end of the book than the beginning. This impression is also created by the tendency to repetitiousness, not only in the possibly necessary re-use of examples, but also in the repetition of points already made. All in all, unless you are a keen devotee of medieval entertainments this study is probably more suitable for consulting than for reading through. There is a detailed index – but a note format that uses virtually no punctuation and which seems to have been invented for the nonce, inconveniently turns what should be a quick glance for information into a rather longer task of interpretation.

In *Banquets Set Forth: Banqueting in English Renaissance Drama*, Chris Meads surveys an even more specific element of early drama. This latest addition to the Revels Plays Companion Library deals with 'ninety-nine plays, containing 114 scenes for which banquets provide the setting' (p. 1). On the positive side, the book is clearly the product of assiduous research; anyone interested in banquet scenes probably need look no further. It demonstrates the advantages of detailed analysis of one kind of scene: the conventions and the important similarities and differences in their use become apparent. On the negative side, the book is essentially a long list which with the benefit of aggressive editing probably could have been shortened by a third. In the first few chapters Meads discusses the real-life banqueting practices of the time, the literary and cultural sources of banquet scenes, and the staging of banquets and food. The bulk of the book is a chronological survey of, it seems, every one of the 114 scenes, with particular attention given to Heywood, Middleton, and Fletcher. In addition, an appendix provides a detailed list of all the plays and scenes. Meads discerns 'two main types of banquet scene, the more intimate banquets and the banquets intended as public display' (p. 41). He traces the use and development of certain elements common to

many stage banquets including 'the triumvirate of lust, appetite, and vengeance' (p. 27), which produce what he terms the 'love-banquet' (p. 32). Also prominent, especially in Jacobean plays, is the use of disguise in these scenes. The topic requires extensive quotation of the stage directions that introduce and describe banquets, but Meads strangely does not reproduce them in italic, making it difficult to distinguish dialogue from direction. The best known banquet scenes are analysed, including those in *The Spanish Tragedy*, *Titus Andronicus*, *Macbeth*, *Timon of Athens*, *The Tempest*, *No Wit No Help Like a Woman's*, *The Revenger's Tragedy*, *Henry VIII*, and *The Maid's Tragedy*; but the more obscure plays with such scenes are given equal attention, often because they include the most spectacular instances of the potent mix of the symbolic and physical that occurs when appetites are foremost.

Elucidating original meanings and contexts is also Natasha Korda's purpose in her extremely interesting study, *Shakespeare's Domestic Economies: Gender and Property in Early Modern England*. Her particular concern is 'household stuff' – the moveable objects of a house – and her purpose 'to illuminate both the symbolic dimension of household things and the historical dimension of household words' (p. 2), or 'the rhetorical dimension of property relations' (p. 4). Describing her approach as that of a materialist feminist, Korda examines the real-world restrictions on women's property rights and how those conditions helped to determine the male-female relations in *The Taming of the Shrew*, *The Merry Wives of Windsor*, *Othello*, and *Measure for Measure*. She explains that 'in focusing on women's relations to moveables [she is] intentionally moving away from traditional accounts of the commodification of women, which maintain that throughout history women have been "trafficked," as passive objects of exchange between men' (p. 11). Korda argues persuasively that 'women's de facto and de jure control over household property became important sites of struggle and resistance to England's patrilineal property regime' (p. 12). In the first very informed and informative chapter Korda develops this idea with reference to numerous both recent and early modern non-dramatic sources dealing with questions of women's property rights in Shakespeare's day. She ranges from the etymology of specific words – for example, oeconomy, household, keeper – to discussions of the place of goods in domestic life. Among other significant conclusions, which Korda applies to her subsequent considerations of the plays, is that 'During the long period of transition from feudal to nascent capitalist modes of production, the residual ideal of the self-sufficient housewife who produces what she consumes competed with the emergent ideal of the passive and obedient keeper who mothers the goods her husband provides' (p. 38).

Korda's interpretation of *The Shrew* rests on the definition of *cates* as 'exchange-values – commodities properly speaking – as opposed to mere use-values, or objects of home production' (p. 52). With the shift from production for home consumption to production for the market, women were freed from producing their own household stuff. Thus in this play 'Petruchio's taming strategy is . . . aimed not at his wife's productive capacity – not once does he ask Kate to brew, bake, wash, card, or spin – but at her consumption. He seeks to educate Kate in her new role as a consumer of "household cates"' (p. 54). In *Merry Wives*, 'the "disquietnesse" surrounding the housewife's supervisory role with respect to marital property is fully explored, and ultimately dispelled, by the wives' consummate self-discipline' (p. 83). At several points Korda bravely undertakes to explain and apply the complex law of 'coverture' (which regulated a wife's right to property); when she does so in relation to *Merry Wives*, for instance, her argument may seem complex and arcane, but clearly no more so than the law Korda seeks to apply to Mistress Page's Act 5 speech. These two chapters appeared first as articles, which have been revised for publication here, and possibly they benefited from the suggestions and comments of readers; whatever the reason, they are rather more polished and persuasive than the two that follow. But Korda has aimed very high in attempting to first interpret many different kinds of writing on legal and domestic topics, then to apply those interpretations to the plays. Certainly there is much of value in her suggestive and innovative treatments of *Othello* and

Measure for Measure, two more difficult works. Not surprisingly, the handkerchief is the object of attention in chapter 4, in which Korda argues that 'English ambivalence toward the extravagant importance of household stuff is manifested in the pivotal role of the handkerchief, a domestic "trifle" that brilliantly weaves together the familiar civility of the luxury commodity or status-object and the alienating strangeness of the African fetish' (p. 116). *Measure for Measure* is treated differently from the other three plays: Korda's analysis centres 'on key-silences, rather than key-words, within the textual economy of the play' because such silences point to 'women's property relations outside of both marriage and the familial household'. As she notes, '*Measure for Measure* manifests a marked absence of familiar, familial forms of domesticity; no one is "at home" in this play, and virtually no one is married' (p. 160). Korda's particular concern, therefore, is 'the effects of nascent capitalism . . . on women living outside familial households, including both impoverished and propertied singlewomen' (p. 161), among whom are the almost silent Sisters of the Order of St. Clare. The subsequent discussion of the play, like the book as a whole, clearly reflects Korda's careful and extensive research, analysis, and thought – work to which it is impossible to do justice here. I look forward to more from her, especially on some of the issues she raises in the final chapter, which moves forward to a discussion of stage properties as 'material artifacts of production, consumption, and exchange' (p. 194).

The idea that each age creates its own Shakespeare is certainly not new, but it is unlikely that any age before ours has been as attentive to such recreations and what they can tell us about the times that produced them. *Restoration Shakespeare: Viewing the Voice*, by Barbara A. Murray, looks at the first period of recreation. She examines 'seventeen versions of sixteen of Shakespeare's plays made over a period of twenty years' (1660–82), to show that 'for quite complex theoretical and theatrical reasons, the adapters' driving motive was to develop the visual and metaphorical coherence of the originals for entertainment and to enhance their didactic function' (p. 199). Murray explains how staging, special effects, sets, and music were used by adapters to emphasise or enhance the visual elements. Her analyses are detailed and straightforward, focussing on comparisons between the original play and its Restoration version(s). The notes section seems excessively long at sixty pages, with some notes running to three pages. Despite this, however, Murray typically cites not the original sources but later works that have either reproduced or referred to the originals. For those with an interest in either Shakespeare adaptation or Restoration theatre this book offers much to consider; for others, whose knowledge of the mostly long forgotten adaptations is minimal, Murray's method of close study will probably be wasted.

Shakespeare's plays have also been recreated in the service of a political ideology different from his own, a fact well illustrated in *Painting Shakespeare Red: An East-European Appropriation*, by Alexander Shurbanov and Boika Sokolova. Both Bulgarians with degrees and publications in English, the authors are probably better able than most to appreciate and interpret what was done to Shakespeare in the service of communism. Their study is in two parts: context and appropriation; they lived the first and saw for themselves the results of the second. They present a fascinating array of evidence to show how 'Shakespeare was given a place of distinction as an artistic forerunner of the communist future and was consequently reduced to yet another Byzantine icon, as stylized and deprived of life as were Marx and Engels. A stiff ideological narrative, largely derived from a mythology already existent but remodeled to meet new requirements, was imposed on the richly dialogical Shakespearean legacy' (pp. 20–1). Attention is given to other communist countries, especially of course Russia, but the emphasis is on the uses to which Shakespeare was put in Bulgaria between 1944 and 1989. The first part of the book gives a history of Bulgarian theatre before communism and describes both indigenous drama and interest in Shakespeare from about 1858. The development of the country's National Theatre is described here and referred to throughout. A Bulgarian school of Shakespeare criticism is another focus, with special

praise given to Marco Mincoff at Sofia University. Shurbanov and Sokolova highlight some controversial early stagings of such plays as *The Merchant of Venice*, *Macbeth*, *Henry IV*, and *Coriolanus*. They also chart the gradual but inexorable process by which Bulgarian culture and the arts generally, but theatre in particular, were brought under Communist Party control. A problem the authors faced when researching productions was the lack of extant material. They note that, 'though between 1947 and 1953 there were over twenty productions of [Shakespeare's] plays throughout the country, it has proved impossible to find more than one review for the whole of 1947 and a mere handful for the remaining six years' (p. 127). Shakespeare's relatively 'less didactic stance' and the plays' 'much less transparent meaning' created a problem for reviewers: 'He was a must, according to all prescriptions, and was also very much alive in the theater, but it was far from clear how to interpret the concrete achievements or failures of a specific production in ideological terms' (pp. 127–8).

The second part of this study concentrates on how the 'tug-of-war between the theater and the authorities' (p. 130) affected the appropriation of Shakespeare. Shurbanov and Sokolova provide telling examples of how the plays were tailored to fit communist ideals. An unintentional irony is that these crude attempts to make Shakespeare one of the workers' party are not markedly different from what results when Western critics and directors try to interpret the plays according to one or another particular ideology. The stakes were higher behind the Iron Curtain, but the aims and techniques were much the same, it seems. An important factor determining which plays were staged was that 'at a time of stiff hierarchical thinking, literary and dramatic genres were neatly arranged in a hierarchy with tragedy on top'. Furthermore, 'Shakespeare's creative career, like the entire history of literature, was perceived as being fully in the control of a sociopolitical evolutionary determinism' (p. 144). Nevertheless, a special concern of this section is to show how Shakespeare was 'naturalized in a markedly subversive way' (p. 249). Productions of *Romeo and Juliet*, *Julius Caesar*, and especially

Hamlet are described and analysed from this viewpoint. The authors have managed to find an excellent selection of thirty black and white photographs of the various productions they discuss. They also provide detailed notes and an extensive bibliography of works in five languages, a good place to start for those who want to know more about Shakespeare under communism.

Performance studies continue to appear, although this year's selection is especially varied, with everyone from critics to directors to actors having their say about Shakespeare on both stage and film. The first group can be found in *Shakespeare and the Modern Theatre: The Performance of Modernity*, edited by Michael Bristol and Kathleen McLuskie, with Christopher Holmes. According to the introductory blurb, these eight essays (from a 1997 conference at McGill University) address the question of whether there is 'any reason to ask people to read Shakespeare's plays' in an age of film, video and live performance; and they explore 'the institutional practices that shape [those] contemporary performances'. Included is Hugh Grady, who traces 'the production of a modernist and then a postmodernist Shakespeare over the course of the twentieth century' (p. 21). Paul Yachnin looks at several late twentieth-century works that 'talk back' to Shakespeare, asserting that 'In so far as the structure of the literary field seems to compel oppositional writers to celebrate Shakespeare's kingship, modern bardicide can be seen as an expression of the strain of nostalgic royalism or social élitism that survives within modern democratic political culture, especially in the United States' (p. 51). In her piece, Catherine Graham uses productions starring Olivier and Gielgud as evidence that 'For the twentieth-century actor, playing Hamlet may be the crucial test of professionalism not only because the role requires superior acting skills, but because it allows the performer to confront the contradictory demands of professionalism and of acting' (p. 57). Translation is the concern of Jean-Michel Déprats, who delineates two approaches to the task: 'The historic approach emphasizes what is over, what is unique and discontinued. The actualizing [or 'modern'] approach, on the contrary, empha-

sizes underlying affinities; it underlines things that are permanent, and describes History as the return of the past, in a different guise' (p. 77). A version of Sarah Werner's essay on the RSC Women's Group is in her own book, discussed below. In his heavily theorized discussion of 'Shakespearean performativity', W. B. Worthen states that to understand it 'principally as a mode of textual transmission surprisingly limits the theater's capacity to evoke history – the true Shakespearean subject, like or unlike "us" – because stage acting isn't determined by textual meanings, but uses them to fashion meanings in the fashions of contemporary behavior' (pp. 131–2). Irena Makaryk looks at a 1924 production of *Macbeth* by the Soviet Ukrainian director Les Kurbas, 'who, more than anyone else in Ukrainian theatrical history, is associated with the performance of Shakespeare' (p. 143). Makaryk's analyses of this production and of responses to it provide ample evidence for her description of Kurbas's methods and effects: 'Rather than foreground the audience–actor connection, Kurbas's modernist productions presumed that the audience wished to co-create a new ground for interpretation and communion while creating a semiotic earthquake where nothing remained stable or certain' (pp. 156–7). In the final essay, Maarten van Dijk explores 'the aesthetics of cheek', or 'how the spirit of commedia' on the modern stage 'has served consistently as a multifaceted, irreverent, oppositional utopia, where ebullient artifice could interrogate entrenched structures of power, genre, taste, and tradition' (p. 161). In keeping with the predominant mode of this collection, it concludes with a substantial theory-oriented bibliography.

At the opposite end of the critical spectrum is Steven Adler's *Rough Magic: Making Theatre at the Royal Shakespeare Company*, a generally favourable profile which was finished just as the most recent problems of that institution were beginning. Although Adler starts with a brief history of the company, his focus is the more recent past and includes virtually every aspect of 'making theatre' at the RSC. He begins in Stratford-upon-Avon, describing not only the theatres and how they evolved but also the other company properties and their uses.

The stories of how Frederick Koch came to finance the building of the Swan and of the first and second versions of the Other Place make especially interesting reading. The London venues come next, with a detailed discussion of the Barbican theatres and the problems related to their use being the main concerns. Adler then charts the development of the company's repertory season and of its touring schedule. The business side is the focus of chapters on administration and finances (including sources of income), followed by a look at the education and marketing departments. Having established these contexts, Adler turns to the production process, with a lengthy and detailed discussion of such matters as casting in a repertory system; the roles of producers, stage managers, technicians; and the particular functions of directors (including Katie Mitchell) and voice coaches (especially Cecily Berry). The final chapter focuses on acting at the RSC with particular reference to four actors, Simon Russell Beale, Kate Duchêne, David Troughton and Robert Bowman. Especially here, but throughout the book, Adler quotes at length from his extensive interviews with RSC figures, most of whom are more positive than otherwise about an institution that has more critics than this book suggests. Nevertheless, for those who know little about the inner – or outer – workings of this famous company, Adler provides a clearly written, straightforward study well worth a look.

Some of the issues only glanced at in Adler's book are at the forefront of *Shakespeare and Feminist Performance: Ideology on Stage*, by Sarah Werner. Again the focus is the RSC, but the conclusions are much less happy. Werner argues that the company's 'practices are built on and create specific ideological readings that limit both the possible meanings of the plays and the role of Shakespeare in our world'. Her examination of 'actor training at the RSC, the company's corporate structure and the reactions of reviewers to performances' is intended to show 'that no performance of Shakespeare can be understood as neutral'. The breadth this suggests is actually narrowed to 'one aspect of the company's theatrical practice, that of feminist performance' as a representative example of the larger

point because, 'Women's work on the plays as actors and directors has continually been measured by whether or not it lives up to expectations of universality' (p. 18). The subsequent chapters deal with diverse topics only loosely connected by the feminist point of view established at the start. First comes a consideration of especially Cecily Berry's but also Patsy Rodenburg's influence on performance at the RSC. Werner quotes from books by both voice teachers to question their 'link between voice and self' (p. 26). In her view, 'By reading a play's language as revelatory of a character's feelings and thought processes, voice work ignores the representational and dramaturgical strategies of the text and withholds from actors the tools to deconstruct patriarchal character readings. It focuses on the character at the expense of the play' (p. 34).

Werner's severest criticism comes in her chapter on the short-lived RSC Women's Group, organized in 1985 by Fiona Shaw, Juliet Stevenson and others to protest the absence of women in power at the company. Drawing on magazine articles and interviews with some of the participants, she describes the group's dealings with Terry Hands and comments, 'In many ways, the relationship between Hands and the Women's Group played itself along the lines of a *paterfamilias* and his rebellious adolescent children'. Furthermore, 'For the members of the group, their status as actors defined them as children and their status as women within the patriarchal structure doubly reinforced their distance from the source of power'. Hands nevertheless invited the women to do a production, and they in turn involved Susan Todd who 'had a long history with feminist theatre' (p. 56). For her part Todd apparently felt that 'the group's lack of feminist theatre experience was a hindrance to their effectiveness in creating a feminist project' (p. 58). Werner explains how they first hoped to do an all-female *Macbeth*, but Hands rejected the idea. She argues that when the group 'came back to Hands with something completely removed from the realm of classical theatre, they became "girly" at the expense of making Shakespeare a legitimate arena for women's work' (p. 62). In the end, Deborah Levy's *Heresies* was adapted for performance at

The Pit in 1986, after which the group disbanded. Werner brings the story of women at the RSC into the '90s, noting that while there is 'still a dearth of female administrators at the company' (p. 66), the number of women directors has increased; overall, though, the Women's Group changed virtually nothing.

The final chapter is what Werner calls a 'case study in the process of writing performance criticism'. Since, however, the production in question is the RSC's 1995 *Taming of the Shrew*, directed by Gale Edwards, 'feminist performance criticism' would be more accurate – a description Werner doubtless would not deny. Her study considers 'textual and performance history, production analysis, reviewer response, [and] critical interpretation' (p. 70). She argues that having a woman direct the play 'sets up oppositional ideologies: the female director's presence legitimizes women's interpretations of Shakespeare, while the playscript's patriarchal thrust silences women' (p. 78). This problem is central to the subsequent analysis of a production which by Werner's account confronted audiences and reviewers with 'incompatible endorsements and critiques of the taming plot' (p. 86). The book's epilogue then moves away from the RSC to a University of Pennsylvania Theatre Arts staging of *The Two Gentlemen of Verona* with an all-female cast, about which everything except the script seems to have been non-Shakespearean. In concluding, Werner returns to Shakespeare, seduced by arguments that Ferdinand actually says 'So rare a wondered father and a wife' (rather than 'wise'); being a feminist but not a bibliographer or expert in seventeenth-century printing she believes what she prefers to believe. She might, however, want to consult the Arden 3 edition of *The Tempest* for an explanation of why the word in the Folio is really *wise*.[2]

The title of Patrick Tucker's book – *Secrets of Acting Shakespeare: The Original Approach* – is certainly attention-getting. It is also rather sly, since the 'secrets' are, as he proudly says in the introduction, 'all [his] own opinion', and the 'original approach' actually refers to the methods used by his Original Shakespeare Company. This book is aimed at actors not academics, and the latter are likely to be exasperated by the conclusions that arise from Tucker's 'research' and 'evidence'. He first explains that when he realised from studying Henslowe's performance calendar that the playing companies had virtually no time for rehearsal, he decided to see how modern actors would perform under similar conditions. He 'found the results to be startling and gratifyingly refreshing' (p. 9). Tucker tells of how he developed the idea of a 'Cue Script' from the actor's 'part' (consisting of lines and cues), and adapted the 'Platt (or plot) hanging in the wings' (pp. 9, 12). Most of the book is devoted to Tucker's enthusiastic impartation of his 'discoveries directly resulting from putting on a Cue Script production, with the preparation restricted to one-on-one verse sessions and a simple full-company meeting to settle entrances and exits' (p. 38). Among these 'discoveries' are the idea that the bookholder or prompter sat on the stage, that the use of *thee* and *you* differentiates between 'the public pronouncements and the private moments' (p. 27), and that 'the Elizabethans had a touring balcony cum truck that was used for *all* their structures' (such as balconies and walls; p. 174). After the lengthy section of performance examples (pp. 43–187), Tucker has a chapter on 'The Folio Secrets', which begins with his working premise: 'If you twisted my arm, and asked me if I *really* believed that the Folio is correct in every variation, I would reply no, but that if it is actable, then it is worth trying, and anyway, with my actors striding out onstage with nothing to guide them except the text, I find that using the "original" text allows them to act and make theatrical decisions with great confidence' (p. 229). 'Folio capitalization' therefore signals meaning, as do what Tucker calls 'Folio lineage' (seemingly unaware that his word does not mean *lineation*), punctuation, and spelling. For actors or companies interested in trying his system there is an 'OSC Checklist', a point-form summary of the opinions and practices Tucker has spelled out in the book.

2 William Shakespeare, *The Tempest*, eds. Virginia Mason Vaughan and Alden T. Vaughan (Walton-on-Thames, Surrey, 1999), pp. 136–8.

The non-academic market is also the target of *Actors on Shakespeare*. The general editor, Colin Nicholson, explains that this new series 'asks contemporary performers to choose a play of particular interest to them, push back any formal boundaries that may obstruct channels of free communication and give the modern audience a fresh, personal view' (p. vi). These criteria are certainly satisfied in the first five short texts to appear, each expressing the ideas of one actor but otherwise being very different in format and approach. Simon Callow discusses *Henry IV, part 1*, although he has only played Falstaff in a stage production of *Chimes at Midnight*. Nevertheless, his aim is 'to take the reader through the play from the point of view of a practitioner, not becoming entangled in the tricky logistics of the actual staging, but presenting a practical view of the play, a sort of groundwork for a production, which may bring out some of the ways in which the play works' (p. 2). After a brief discussion of 'carnival', Callow goes through the play by act and scene. Emma Fielding chose *Twelfth Night*, which she knows from playing Viola in the 1994 RSC production. Her focus is the lovers and how she came to deal with the Viola-Cesario duality. Of the soliloquies it produces, she comments: 'The complicity with the audience, after initially being the most terrifying part of the performance – you're so exposed as an actor and character – became the most relaxing part to play. She is entirely herself, Viola not Cesario, and can talk to the audience who know her more thoroughly than does anyone in the play, except Sebastian. They let some steam out of the pressure cooker for her. If she didn't have this relief, she'd be an entirely different girl' (p. 15). Corin Redgrave's analysis of *Julius Caesar* is governed by his politics. Indeed, although his study is ostensibly based on his involvement with three different productions, it is as much a manifesto for change in today's Britain as it is a one-sided discussion of the play. His view is that 'one feels instantly in *Julius Caesar* the birth pangs of a new England, confident of its own resources, anxiously searching its own conscience, trying to do what is right, reaching out towards science and away from superstition. After 400 years, that England has exhausted

itself, and waits for a new revolution' for which the play 'might yet turn out to be . . . very timely' (p. 61). Surprisingly, perhaps, Vanessa Redgrave's focus in her treatment of *Antony and Cleopatra* is not explicitly political. This is the shortest of the five booklets, and includes the longest passages of quotation from its play. Redgrave's interest is Antony, a man who for her both is and is not the man he was in the earlier play discussed by her brother. In Vanessa Redgrave's view, the later Antony is an alcoholic who is not in love with Cleopatra, who, on the other hand, is 'quintessentially an English Elizabethan, and a unique one at that: Elizabeth Tudor' (p. 42). Redgrave also insists that Cleopatra is 'a "good" woman, a constant woman' saying that this is a conclusion she 'arrived at too late for any performance' (p. 44). The best of the five so far in this series is on *Macbeth*, by Harriet Walter, who draws on her experience playing Lady Macbeth with the RSC in 1999. While centred on that figure, this analysis also deals with the relationship between husband and wife. Particularly illuminating is the explanation of how she dealt with the implications of Lady Macbeth's 'I have given suck'. Walter discovered that Holinshed says she had a son by an earlier marriage, which she felt would both make sense of the couple's childlessness and 'fuel Lady Macbeth's taunts about her husband's manhood'. Her practical approach is apparent in what she says about using this idea: 'I have to emphasize at this point that I am not claiming to know Shakespeare's intentions. He left much unexplained and we can only assume that he meant to leave it that way. However, for each performer or director the questions need to be addressed. A playable path must be found' (p. 27). Similarly, she later comments, 'I concentrated on finding the extremes to which a "normal" person can be driven, rather than personifying an "abnormal" psychopath. In the context of our production that was the coherent path. There are many others' (p. 63).

Reworkings of *Hamlet* by three modern (or postmodern) directors are the concern of Andy Lavender in *Hamlet in Pieces*, which offers detailed analyses of Peter Brook's *Qui Est Là*, Robert Lepage's *Elsinore*, and Robert Wilson's *Hamlet:*

A Monologue. Lavender says his interest is 'less in the object of textual surgery, and more in the techniques by which the surgeons carved it up, and in the new bodies which they produced' (p. 11). All three directors 'in different ways, trade in a phenomenological theatre, exploiting qualities of space, sound, movement, rhythm, visual image and the body of the performer' (p. 44). Having seen all three productions, Lavender can report, for example, that '*Qui Est Là* was a bracing two hours long. Around a fifth of its eventual script was composed of fragments of writings by the historical figures [Edward Gordon Craig, Stanislavsky, Meyerhold, Zeami, Artaud, Brecht].... This meant that the *Hamlet*-material took up just over an hour and a half – a series of glances rather than the full picture' (p. 67). In concluding his analysis of this production Lavender observes that 'It stages *possibility*, not certitude. In doing so it offers an extremely subtle response to one of the dominating themes of the play (the effect of doubt) and marks itself as the product of an era in which uncertainty and relativity have been central modes' (p. 89). He also describes each director's production company, working methods, and rehearsal process. For *Elsinore*, he begins with details about Ex Machina, Lepage's company, and its base in Quebec City where his experiments in technical wizardry originate. Lepage actually mounted two different productions of the play, which Lavender describes and compares. In both versions, 'The frisson of opening with the words "To be or not to be" underlines *Elsinore*'s bravura sense of (the) play. The production is luminously Shakespearean – and it is definitely *not* Shakespeare's *Hamlet*' (p. 120). As to Lepage's use of 'machinery', Lavender says it produces 'not only an articulation of *Hamlet*, but an articulation of the meeting between theatre and electronic technology. The production is about – it *stages* – the interface between the human and the technological' (p. 145). At the opposite extreme is Wilson's minimalist adaptation, which nevertheless demanded, as all this director's productions do, complex sound and lighting design. Lavender observes that 'Wilson's theatre always *looks* like theatre – illuminated, displayed, staged' (p. 173). This production gave Shakespeare's text 'a good stir': Wilson began with three repetitions of 'Had I but time' after which 'All the action is located in Hamlet's memory, desire and psyche' (pp. 174, 175). Drawing on his evidently considerable knowledge of Wilson's previous work, Lavender says that 'His Hamlet distils over thirty years' worth of Wilsonian performance into the one iconic rendition' (p. 179). After his detailed analyses, he moves to a more general discussion of what he calls the 'theatreness' (p. 44) of the three shows; they are, he says, 'less interested in Hamlet as a single character, and a lot more interested in how he is a device for metatheatre' (p. 214). The book concludes by returning to Peter Brook, but to his subsequent production of *Hamlet*, in which the play is 'remade from within' (p. 230). A selection of good black and white photographs of each production Lavender discusses provides evidence of his detailed descriptions.

Visual Shakespeare is a collection of Graham Holderness's 'essays in film and television' written between 1984 and 1993, with one from 1998. It begins with a section of two pieces dealing with the Shakespeare on the BBC. Holderness first summarizes the different but (to him) essentially conservative approaches of Cedric Messina and Jonathan Miller. He then gives examples of some productions, notably Jane Howell's of the *Henry VI* plays, which demonstrate the 'radical potentialities of television Shakespeare' (p. 22) that he believes were not sufficiently exploited by others. His dismissive and damning verdict is that 'The BBC Shakespeare series is in fact the most perfect consummation to date of a process which commenced in Shakespeare's own time, with the Tudor government's systematic destruction of the national religious drama, the professionalising of theatre by the licensing of a few acting companies and the building of the first purpose-built playhouses; the privileging of metropolitan over national culture, and the incorporation of the drama into the culture structure of an emergent bourgeois nation-State' (pp. 22–3). Not for nothing does Simon Callow refer to Holderness as 'a neo-marxist firebrand writing in the 1980s'.[3] The second of the two essays in this section (written with Carol Banks) is the most recent, but judging from it his opinions have not changed. The next group of two, which look at Shakespeare on film, show their age because since they were written so many more films have appeared. In Holderness's view, Akira Kurosawa's *Throne of Blood* 'is the most complete translation of Shakespeare into film' (p. 64); it 'is self-evidently *not* Shakespeare; and therein lies its incomparable value for strategic use in a radical exploration of the play. If the text can be reproduced in a virtually unrecognisable form, then the plurality of the text is proved beyond reasonable doubt. This bastard offspring, the play's *alter ego*, can then be brought back into conjunction with the text, to liberate some of its more radical possibilities of meaning' (p. 68). In the following piece, Holderness develops his belief that there are 'within the histories of theatre and film, as well as within the methodologies of contemporary post-structuralist criticism, resources for the production of an alternative "Shakespeare-on-film"' (p. 76). The final section consists of three 'case studies' – of Olivier's *Henry V*, and Zeffirelli's *Taming of the Shrew*, and *Romeo and Juliet* – the last of which I found the most satisfying because its tone is the least didactic and strident.

The increasing heft of filmed Shakespeare is evident in *Spectacular Shakespeare: Critical Theory and Popular Cinema*, edited by Courtney Lehmann and Lisa S. Starks. From the title, subtitle and cover through to the final essay, this collection hypes the importance of recent Bard-dependent films. On the one hand, the writers here take the films they discuss seriously as works of art (which is sometimes a bit of a reach); but on the other, these essays constitute a good introduction to criticism of Shakespeare on film for academics who have previously shunned it as irrelevant slumming. 'Media Imperialism: Appropriating Culture, Race, and Authority' is the banner for the first three essays. Marguerite Hailey Rippy's 'All Our *Othellos*: Black Monsters and White Masks on the American Screen' focuses on

film and television uses of the play as 'a problem of white male identity' (p. 41). Lisa Hopkins's title, '"How very like the home life of our own dear queen": Ian McKellen's *Richard III*', pithily conveys her amusing argument. And in '(Un)doing the Book "without Verona walls": A View from the Receiving End of Baz Luhrmann's *William Shakespeare's Romeo + Juliet*', Alfredo Michel Modenessi considers 'how the provocatively uncertain text of Mexican culture is brought to bear on the "certain text" of Shakespeare's play' (p. 73). The next three essays are grouped under the heading 'Reframing Romance: Sex, Love, and Subjectivity'. Laurie Osborne's 'Cutting up Characters: The Erotic Politics of Trevor Nunn's *Twelfth Night*' looks at how the film editor's 'radical use of crosscutting and intercutting' produces 'cinematic fragments that paradoxically "fill up" the subjectivity of early modern characters' (p. 89). She pays particular attention to the way this film 'reveals our twentieth-century investment in character as a complex weave of gender identity and erotic alliance' (p. 106). Next, Samuel Crowl analyses 'the Marriage of Shakespeare and Hollywood: Kenneth Branagh's *Much Ado about Nothing*'. Crowl calls the film 'Branagh's greatest achievement' because it links 'the ideas in Shakespeare's play with the witty Hollywood comedies of the 1930s that have come to be labeled as "screwball"' (p. 112). In '*Shakespeare in Love*: Romancing the Author, Mastering the Body', Courtney Lehman applies Slavoj Žižek's ideas about 'enjoyment' in 'late capitalistic society' to 'Shakespeare's latest incarnation as a cinematic romance hero' (p. 126). If theory is your preference, enjoy. The final section, titled 'The Politics of the Popular: From Class to Classroom', begins with Douglas Lanier's '"Art thou base, common and popular?": The Cultural Politics of Kenneth Branagh's *Hamlet*'. In this thoughtful examination of the relationships among the Branagh film, 'its cinematic paratexts *Swan Song* (1992) and *A Midwinter's Tale* (1995)', and details from

---

[3] In his booklet on *Henry IV, Part 1*, reviewed earlier here, p. 345.

Branagh's biography, Lanier argues that 'Branagh's Shakespeare films thematize the conditions of their own reception; they constitute an extended meditation on the idea of Shakespeare (re)integrated into the cultural life of the common man, a meditation conducted from within the institutional imperatives of the contemporary stage and screen' (p. 149). Elizabeth A. Deitchman's 'From the Cinema to the Classroom: Hollywood Teaches *Hamlet*' considers some minor filmed and televised Shakespeare. Then comes Annalisa Castaldo's 'The Film's the Thing: Using Film in the Shakespearean Classroom', which sees film as a way of illustrating 'ideas of textual variation, multiple authorship, source material, and cultural alteration of the text's meaning' (p. 190). The last piece in this collection is titled 'Afterword: Te(e)n Things I Hate about Girlene Shakesploitation Flicks in the Late 1990s, or, Not-So-Fast Times at Shakespeare High'. In it, Richard Burt coins even more words as he looks at 'Shakesploi flicks' as 'instances of conservative feminism' (p. 206).

As the numerous references in the above collection and others indicate, Kenneth Branagh is the actor-director most closely identified with Shakespeare on stage and film today. Not long ago, however, Orson Welles would have been a contender for this designation. In *Orson Welles: interviews*, Mark W. Estrin presents conversations between Welles and various interviewers from 1938 (with Richard O'Brien in the *New York Times*) to 1989 (with Gore Vidal in the *New York Review of Books*). Estrin provides an introduction, a chronology of Welles's life, and a filmography. As his helpful index makes apparent, in many of these interviews Welles is asked about and refers to Shakespeare, sometimes in passing, other times in greater detail. The longest discussion – two hours in 1974 with Richard Marienstras for a French television series – is translated for this collection by Alisa Hartz as 'Shakespeare, Welles, and Moles'. Among the topics is Peter Brook; of his *Midsummer Night's Dream* Welles says, 'I am one of the two or three people in the world who don't like that production. As a production it's remarkable, but it's an insult to the play!' (p. 147). Of *Macbeth* he observes, 'It's the story of a weak man. This is why Macbeth has never been the great role of a great actor. To play it requires an actor of great physical strength and intellectual power, capable of incarnating a weakling' (p. 152). Welles's staging of this play in Harlem is discussed at length. Later he is challenged but doesn't back down after saying of Falstaff: 'I think that in all of Shakespeare, he's the only good man' (p. 161). And in a moment of 'what might have been' they turn to *The Tempest* and Welles says 'I would love to stage that play or make a film of it. I think it could be a marvelous film' (p. 171). Others since have thought so too, of course, and made their own films of the play. Similarly, as the work discussed here demonstrates, there is always someone to continue where others have left off in the analysis, criticism, staging, adaptation or appropriation of 'Shakespeare'.

WORKS REVIEWED

Adler, Steven, *Rough Magic: Making Theatre at the Royal Shakespeare Company* (Carbondale and Edwardsville, IL, 2001).

Bristol, Michael and Kathleen McLuskie, with Christopher Holmes, eds., *Shakespeare and Modern Theatre: The Performance of Modernity* (London and New York, 2001).

Callow, Simon, *Henry IV, Part 1*, Actors on Shakespeare (London, 2002).

Estrin, Mark W., *Orson Welles: Interviews* (Jackson, MS, 2002).

Fielding, Emma, *Twelfth Night*, Actors on Shakespeare (London, 2002).

Holderness, Graham, *Visual Shakespeare: Essays in film and television* (Hatfield, 2002).

Korda, Natasha, *Shakespeare's Domestic Economies: Gender and Property in Early Modern England* (Philadelphia, 2002).

Lavender, Andy, *Hamlet in Pieces* (London, 2001).

Lehmann, Courtney and Lisa S. Starks, eds., *Spectacular Shakespeare: Critical Theory and Popular Cinema* (Madison, NJ, 2002).

Meads, Chris, *Banquets set forth: Banqueting in English Renaissance Drama* (Manchester and New York, 2001).

Murray, Barbara A., *Restoration Shakespeare: Viewing the Voice* (Madison, NJ, 2001).

Redgrave, Corin, *Julius Caesar*, Actors on Shakespeare (London, 2002).

Redgrave, Vanessa, *Antony and Cleopatra*, Actors on Shakespeare (London, 2002).

Saunders, Ann and John Schofield, eds., *Tudor London: A Map and a View* (London, 2001).

Shepard, Alan, *Marlowe's Soldiers: Rhetorics of Masculinity in the Age of the Armada* (Aldershot, Hants and Burlington, VT, 2002).

Shurbanov, Alexander and Boika Sokolova, *Painting Shakespeare Red: An East-European Appropriation* (Newark, NJ, 2001).

Tucker, Patrick, *Secrets of Acting Shakespeare: The Original Approach* (London and New York, 2002).

Twycross, Meg and Sarah Carpenter, *Masks and Masking in Medieval and Early Tudor England* (Aldershot, Hants, 2002).

Walter, Harriet, *Macbeth*, Actors on Shakespeare (London, 2002).

Werner, Sarah, *Shakespeare and Feminist Performance: Ideology on Stage* (London and New York, 2001).

West, Russell, *Spatial Representations and the Jacobean Stage from Shakespeare to Webster* (Houndmills, Hants and New York, 2002).

Wharton, T. F., ed., *The Drama of John Marston* (Cambridge, 2000).

3. EDITIONS AND TEXTUAL STUDIES

reviewed by ERIC RASMUSSEN

When Harold Bloom talks, people listen. In *Shakespeare: The Invention of the Human*, Bloom gave his imprimatur to one series ('I recommend the Arden Shakespeare') while dismissing another edition out of hand ('I have avoided the New Oxford Shakespeare'). Although Bloom's *ex cathedra* pronouncements have occasioned some spirited responses,[1] I'm not particularly anxious about their influence – save that my review of this year's additions to the Arden and Oxford series coincidentally confirms Bloom's prejudices: whereas I can highly recommend the new Arden 3 editions of *1 Henry IV* and *Richard II*, I would advise serious students to approach with caution the new Oxford edition of the poems.

The Oxford *Complete Sonnets and Poems*, edited by Colin Burrow, is one of the most error-riddled critical editions of Shakespeare in recent memory. All told, there are twenty-six substantive errors in the text, including several that could significantly affect interpretation: for 'breathes' read 'breeds' (*Venus* 742), for 'reweaves' read 'unweaves' (*Venus* 991; a mistake that not only weakens the Penelope allusion but invents a word, *reweaves*, that does not appear in the Shakespeare canon), for 'sweet' read 'swift' (*Venus* 1190), for 'will' read 'ill' (*Lucrece* 91; the slip is exacerbated by a substantial commentary note on *will*), for 'wretch' read 'wench' (*Lucrece* 1273), for 'ringing' read 'hanging' (*Lucrece* 1493). I should make it clear that these are not intentional emendations, but unintended errors that often render the lines in question nonsensical.

Transpositions abound in Burrow's text – 'could I' for 'I could' (*Venus* 805), 'she hath' for 'hath she' (*Passionate Pilgrim* 7.7), 'and sad' for 'sad and' ('Let the bird of loudest lay', i.e., *The Phoenix and Turtle* 3), 'be from you' for 'from you be' (Sonnet 75.12), 'might well' for 'well might' (Sonnet 83.6), 'I am' for 'am I' (Sonnet 134.14) – along with a host of minor errors: 'eyes' for 'eye' (*Venus* 400), 'a' for 'the' (*Venus* 416), 'hath' for 'have' (*Venus* 775), 'others' for 'other' (*Venus* 1102), 'looks' for 'look' (*Lucrece* 403), 'man' for 'men' (*Lucrece* 1252), 'takes' for 'tak'st' ('Let the bird of loudest lay',19), 'these' for 'those' (Sonnet 68.9), 'loves' for 'love' (Sonnet 93.10), 'did' for 'didst' (Sonnet 99.2), 'my' for 'mine' (Sonnet 110.3), 'Those' for 'These' (Sonnet 110.7), 'bosom' for 'bosoms' (Sonnet 120.12, and quotation on page 136), and 'court and city' for 'court, of city' (*A Lover's Complaint* 59).

Transcriptional error seems endemic to this edition. In transcribing the twenty-five words on the title-page of Q1 *Lucrece*, for instance, Burrow

---

My thanks to Arthur Evenchik for his invaluable assistance, as always, with this review essay.

[1] See especially the essays by Terence Hawkes, William W. Kerrigan, and Gary Taylor in the recent collection of responses to Bloom, *Harold Bloom's Shakespeare*.

gets three of them wrong ('John' for 'Iohn', 'Grehound' for 'Greyhound', 'Churchyard' for 'Churh-yard'); in transcribing the famous title-page of the 1609 quarto of the Sonnets, Burrow makes a remarkable six errors; and there are similar errors in his transcriptions of the title-pages from *The Passionate Pilgrim* and *Loves Martyr* and in the collations throughout.[2] There's even a mistake in Francis Meres's well-known reference to Shakespeare's 'Sonnets among his private friends', rendered here as 'Sonnets to his private friends' – a minor slip, to be sure, but one that subtly changes the meaning by implying that the poems were presented *to* the friends rather than circulated *among* them.

The edition is not without compensatory strengths. Burrow has a talent for discerning overarching patterns in Shakespeare's lyric and narrative poetry, as when he writes that both the early sonnets and *Venus and Adonis* 'recurrently explore how even the most elaborate rhetoric can fail to persuade its addressee'. The introductory essay surveys the editorial tradition that has long viewed the poems as 'supplemental' to, and lesser than, the plays (a judgement reflected in 'the dire privative prefix of the *non*-dramatic works'). Burrow's discussion of the poems' reception history is equally admirable, though I remain unpersuaded by the logic which sees the few surviving copies of the early editions of *Venus and Adonis* as evidence that 'many eager readers read their copies to pieces'; virtually no one would make the claim that most copies of the first quarto of *Hamlet* – of which there are now only two extant – were similarly read to bits.

Burrow is a tremendously helpful guide to historical and cultural matters. His extended analysis of early modern views of rape provides an essential context, it seems to me, for understanding and appreciating *Lucrece*. He provides new information about such matters as the precipitous downfall of Southampton's financial fortunes in 1594. In pointing out that 'Wriothesley' is pronounced 'Risely', Burrow performs a considerable service to American readers, many of whom (myself included) are often clueless about British pronunciation. Burrow writes with style and wit, ac-

knowledging and undermining the grail-quest for Mr W. H. by wryly suggesting 'Who He?'

This imposing volume will have a claim to being one of the best critical editions of Shakespeare's poetry once its textual errors are corrected in subsequent printings. For the moment, however, users of *The Complete Sonnets & Poems* will, somewhat ironically, have to supplement it by consulting the text of another edition.

A growing number of talented literary critics have recently turned to editing. As David Scott Kastan, one of these critics, has observed, 'everyone seems to be doing it these days . . . editing has suddenly become hot'.[3] Within the editorial establishment, there were concerns that the newcomers might not have the temperament for editing – which, as Kastan acknowledges, involves 'a lot of very tedious, numbingly cold work' – and would ultimately produce editions with trendy introductory essays but abysmal texts. In his own editorial debut, Kastan has done much to disarm these concerns. In his Arden 3 edition of *King Henry IV Part One*, the introduction and commentary are predictably engaging, trenchant, and urbane; but Kastan, it turns out, is an outstanding textual editor as well. I have collated Kastan's edited text against the early quartos and can report with some confidence that it is error-free. (For textual scholars, the facsimile of the 1598 Q0 fragment included in an appendix is worth the price of the whole volume.)

---

[2] *The Sonnets* title-page: 'Shake-Speares' for 'SHAKE-SPEARES', 'Sonnets' for 'SONNETS', 'At London' for 'AT LONDON', 'G. Eld' for 'G. Eld', 'T.T.' for 'T.T.', 'John' for 'Iohn'; *The Passionate Pilgrim* 1599: 'Churchyard' for 'Churchyard'; separate title-page on C3r: 'to' for 'To'; 1612 title-page: 'THE PASSIONATE' for 'THE | PASSIONATE', 'mented' for 'mented', 'By W. Shakespere' for 'By W. Shakespere', 'first from' for 'first | from'; *Loves Martyr* 1601: 'In' for 'in', 'FOLLOW' for 'FOLLOVV', 'love' for 'loue'. In the *Venus and Adonis* collation at 185 'souring' for 'Souring' in lemma and 'so' for 'So' in quotation from Q; 466 'love' for 'loue'; 645 'down' for 'downe'; 680 'over-shut' for 'ouer-shut'; *Passionate Pilgrim* 14, line 17, O2 reading 'sits and' is adopted without collation; *Passionate Pilgrim* 14, line 24, O2 reading 'sighed' is again adopted without collation.

[3] *Shakespeare after Theory* (New York and London, 1999), p. 59.

Instead of offering a tiresome string-cite of previous commentary, Kastan has mined the vast amount of commentary on *1H4* and arranged its essential insights into a narrative that should appeal to first-time readers and seasoned scholars alike. His own close readings are smart and perspicacious, as when he observes that 'the royal "we" that Henry publicly uses cannot truthfully speak the mutuality of King and country that it is designed to articulate; and face to face with the refractory northerners, he tellingly begins in the first person "my blood hath been too cold . . . "'. After expertly ranging over the historical background, Kastan aptly reminds his readers 'how much of the play is given over not to subtly restructured history but to conspicuously invented fiction'.

A thought-provoking section of the introduction adjudicates between 'the drama's understanders, in its intellectual sense' and 'the physical understanders', i.e., those who stood in the yard at the Globe: 'From above', the play seems to be, as critics from Tillyard to Greenblatt have argued, about 'the authorization of power and the assumption of rule'. But 'seen, we might say, from below', the play is 'less a production of power than a challenge to it' in which 'the comic plot may seem indeed to give compelling voice to what aristocratic history would repress'.

To cite all the perceptive readings from Kastan's introduction would be to reproduce the essay itself. Still, the superb explication of the homonymic nuances in the play's final line deserves mention. In 'And since this business so fair is done, / Let us not leave till all our own be won' (5.5.43–4), Kastan suggests that 'won' might well be heard as 'one', which would 'exactly enact the process of unification the play imagines, verbally reconciling what can usually only be coerced . . . the process of incorporation inevitably involves a more violent repression of difference than can comfortably be admitted in a complex society; too often only what is "won" is "one"'.

In his account of the play's performance history, Kastan is sometimes hasty in asserting an absence of evidence. For instance, the claim that there is 'no evidence that the plays [*1H4* and *2H4*] were ever played together in Shakespeare's time' gives insufficient weight to the possibility that the Dering manuscript (*c.* 1613), which, as Kastan notes, is 'a conflation of the two parts of *Henry IV* into a single play designed for an amateur performance', may reflect an early practice of performing the two parts together. Moreover, the assertion that 'there is no evidence that before the middle of the nineteenth century the plays [of the tetralogy] were ever performed sequentially' is refuted by the theatrical records: In 1738, John Rich's acting company at Covent Garden performed *Richard II* on 11 February, *1 Henry IV* on 13 February, *2 Henry IV* on 16 February, and *Henry V* on 23 February. The experiment of performing the plays sequentially apparently proved successful, since the company repeated it in the following winter season, staging *Richard II* on 1 December, *1 Henry IV* on 2 December, *2 Henry IV* on 4 December, and *Henry V* on 5 December.[4]

Kastan has obviously devoted a great deal of care and attention to his immaculate text of the play: every emendation has been thought through and defended in a commentary note. In a number of key places, Kastan breaks with tradition by unemending; these decisions, too, are always supported by cogent arguments (see especially the note on retaining Q1's 'Supposition' at 5.2.8).

There is, however, one editorial task to which, it seems to me, Kastan has not sufficiently attended: tracking down sources of emended readings in the text. Kastan's textual notes claim that the added stage directions at 1.3.14, 1.3.70, 1.3.123, 1.3.208, 1.3.210, 1.3.296, 2.4.169, 5.1.30 and 5.3.62 are unique to '*this edn*' whereas, in fact, they all appear verbatim in the Oxford Complete Works, which also anticipates the placement of 3.1.186.1; the SDs at 1.2.115, 2.4.268, 3.1.187, and 3.3.204 are all substantially the same in Oxford. The emendations at 1.2.35, 1.2.105, 1.3.221, 1.3.223, 1.3.250, 1.3.251, 2.2.0.1, 2.3.49, 2.4.16, 2.4.24–5, 2.4.25–6, 2.4.30, 2.4.31, 2.4.102,

---

4 See Charles Beecher Hogan, *Shakespeare in the Theatre 1701–1800: A Record of Performances in London 1701–1750* (Oxford, 1952), pp. 166, 196, 187, and 377.

2.4.102–3, 2.4.103–4, 2.4.104, 2.4.105, 2.4.105–6, 2.4.108, 3.1.154, 3.1.245, 3.1.246, 3.1.250, 3.2.48, 3.2.49, which are all attributed to later editors, should properly be attributed to Alexander Dyce.

Although Kastan does not follow the Oxford editors in changing Falstaff to Oldcastle, he does alter another sanctioned name. Whereas most previous editors have followed the Folio spelling of 'Bardolph', Kastan restores 'Bardoll', the form in which the name appears (along with 'Bardol') in the early quartos. No one would question this adherence to the copy-text were it not for the complicating factor that in *2 Henry IV*, *Henry V*, and *Merry Wives*, the character invariably appears as 'Bardolfe' or 'Bardolph'. It seems likely that Shakespeare originally called the character 'Russell' (the family name of the Earls of Bedford): a vestigial 'Rossill' appears in the quarto at 1.2.154, and '*Ross.*' speech headings occur at 2.4.168, 170, and 174. Kastan argues that Shakespeare probably changed the name 'at the same time he changed Oldcastle to Falstaff'. Apparently someone went through the manuscript that lies behind the *1H4* quarto and changed all appearances of 'Oldcastle' to 'Falstaff' and 'Rossill' to 'Bardoll' (albeit missing a few). The same process occurred with the manuscript that lies behind the *2H4* quarto, in which there's a vestigial '*Old.*' speech heading and a fossil name '*sir Iohn Russel*'. Thus, the name change seems to have been made *after* the composition of *2H4*. Kastan, who maintains that '*1 Henry IV* should be thought of as imaginatively prior to and independent of *2 Henry IV*', writes, 'it seems clear that once Shakespeare settled on a name for the character he called him "Bardoll"'. But this may not be quite as clear as Kastan suggests. If the changes to the *1H4* and *2H4* manuscripts were made at the same time, there is no compelling reason to privilege *1H4*'s 'Bardoll' over *2H4*'s 'Bardolfe'. Doing so sacrifices consistency with the other plays in the interest of being faithful to the quartos of *1H4*. However, Kastan's fidelity to copy-text names is inconsistently applied: the Q 1 spellings 'Blunt' and 'Westmerland' are rendered 'Blount' and 'Westmoreland' in Kastan's text (apparently because the names appear in the latter forms in the *DNB*; per-

haps the historical model for the fictional Bardolph might somewhere have an entry there as well?).

The modernization of 'Holmedon' to 'Humbleton' also strikes me as questionable. Despite Kastan's cultural-linguistic discovery that 'the modern Humbleton' is 'often pronounced by local residents with a collapse of the three medial consonants to produce a word (almost) of two syllables', the place name will almost certainly appear trisyllabic to readers and actors, in which case it clearly wrecks the meter: 'Betwixt that Humbleton and this seat of ours' (1.1.65), 'On Humbleton's plains. Of prisoners Hotspur took' (1.1.70), 'Which Harry Percy here at Humbleton took' (1.3.24), 'O Douglas, hadst thou fought at Humbleton thus' (5.3.14). Kastan concludes that little is to be gained 'by retaining an idiosyncratic form of a place-name in an edition which otherwise is committed to modernization'. I confess that I have never understood the logic behind modernizing obscure place names and personal names while retaining older forms of other words. By analogy, shouldn't an editor modernize Lady Percy's 'Come, come, you paraquito, answer me' (2.3.82) to 'parakeet'?

Overall, my objections to some of Kastan's textual decisions are trivial, and certainly pale before the many things that are done supremely well. My filial piety to David Bevington (the editor of the single-text Oxford *1H4*) notwithstanding, it seems to me that Kastan's is now arguably the best critical edition of *1 Henry IV* currently available.

Even in the field of burgeoning Arden 3 editions, Charles R. Forker's *Richard II* stands out: at 593 pages, it is the longest Arden 3 to date, nearly a hundred pages longer than the previous record-holder, Gordon McMullan's monumental *Henry VIII*. The sheer mass of Forker's edition may have the unintended consequence of putting off potential readers; and it certainly raises the question of what should be considered an (in)appropriate length for a critical edition of a single play. Much of this edition's exceptional size is attributable to the substantial quotations from Shakespeare's sources that appear in the commentary notes. Forker argues that 'it is important to make immediately present to readers as rich a historical context as possible for the understanding and interpretation of a drama that exploits nuanced or conflicting attitudes and that portrays ambiguities of motive'. Indeed, having extended extracts from Hall and Holinshed on the same page as the relevant text of the play, rather than in an appendix, is a valuable feature that distinguishes this edition from others currently available. For users with even a passing interest in Shakespeare's handling of the chronicle source material, the utility of this feature should outweigh any inconvenience posed by a thick volume.

The single slip I found in Forker's superlative text of the play is the most inconsequential error imaginable ('contrived' at 1.1.96 should have a syllabic è). A few added stage directions are erroneously claimed to be original to this edition (the SD at 1.1.186 should be credited to Bevington; those at 1.3.248, 2.2.105, 2.2.106, 2.2.139, and 4.1.182 to the Oxford Complete Works). But these are rule-proving exceptions to what is otherwise a textually perfect edition.

Forker, the editor of the magisterial Revels edition of Marlowe's *Edward II*, is an inspired choice to edit *Richard II*: His trenchant analysis of the relationship between the two plays is one of the highlights of this edition. Other sections of the introductory essay are somewhat less successful, and might have benefited from rigorous editing. In Forker's discussion of imagery, for instance, several of the more densely written paragraphs are three pages long, and the transitions are often formulaic: 'Another significant pattern...Additional image patterns...Another antithesis...Additional antitheses...'. The next section provides an elaborate catalogue of the play's rhetorical tropes and figures – *accumulatio, divisio, auxesis, asyndeton, synonymia, polyptoton, epizeuxis, anadiplosis, epistrophe, anaphora, parison, isocolon, antimetabole, chiasmus, paronomasia, catachresis, aphorismus, anthimeria, significatio,* and *prosopopoeia* – each illustrated by multiple examples from the text. Forker's introduction is a model of *accumulatio* in its own right, but this renders it more a resource to be consulted than an essay to be read.

Forker is especially attuned to the ways in which the rhyme and rhythms of the play are tailored to individual characters. He points out that metrical irregularity in York's speeches often suggests agitation or confusion. The gloss on Gaunt's speech at 2.1.5–16 draws attention to 'the weighty sententiousness of these lines, slowed down by three couplets and a quatrain, [which] not only suggests old age, but also Gaunt's laboured utterance'. One wonders if a further connection could be drawn between Richard's 'liberal use of feminine endings' and, as Forker observes in another context, 'Richard's gift for female-style intimacy'.

Forker offers a rich discussion of the play's pertinence to the contemporary political scene. The Chamberlain's Men's commissioned performance of *Richard II* on 7 February 1601, the day before Essex staged his abortive rebellion, has figured prominently in recent studies of the early appropriation of Shakespeare as political propaganda. Although Forker may be right that 'Shakespeare and his fellows were innocent of any seditious design' (since they escaped punishment and were playing at court only days after Essex's trial), they surely must have understood – if after the fact – that the performance was intended to get the public in the mood to overthrow a monarch. The so-called deposition episode (4.1.155–318) had, of course, been subjected to some form of censorship several years earlier when it was omitted from the early quartos; the scene of Richard's dethronement, as Forker notes, 'had apparently been considered too dangerous to print in 1597'.

The deposition appears for the first time in Q4 (1608), the title-page of which advertises the 'new additions of the Parliament scene and the deposing of King Richard'. Forker speculates about the nature of the printers' copy that may lie behind the 'inferior' version of the scene in Q4 ('a manuscript of dubious origin') and behind the 'fuller and more satisfactory' version in the First Folio (a 'transcript of these lines from the promptbook'), but his introduction offers no insight into the political and cultural changes that had apparently made the printing of the deposition scene less dangerous by 1608. Given the considerable attention that Forker devotes to the play's topicality, it is surprising that he makes no mention of a seemingly crucial fact about *Richard II*'s publication history: The three quartos that omit the deposition – Q1 (1597), Q2 (1598), and Q3 (1598) – were all published during Elizabeth's reign. In contrast, the scene appears in all three editions of the play – Q4 (1608), Q5 (1615), and F1 (1623) – published under James I.

Cyndia Susan Clegg's *Press Censorship in Jacobean England* argues that the practice of censorship under James varied significantly from Elizabethan practice. Clegg presents her book as a corrective to previous studies of Jacobean censorship which have, she argues, 'perpetuated among literary scholars the image of Stuart political culture as authoritarian and abusive'. Clegg hopes to replace the 'outmoded historical model of unified and repressive state censorship' with a model of censorship as a practice involving complex cultural negotiation. In this account, James's decision not to suppress a libellous book 'so as not to give it importance or cause it to be sought' appears not as a departure from the usual rigour of Jacobean censorship, but rather as an example of its subtlety. Readers hoping to understand why publication of the deposition scene was impossible under Elizabeth but apparently acceptable under James might well begin their investigation with Clegg's important new study.

David Scott Kastan's *Shakespeare and the Book* – which had its origins in the Lord Northcliffe Lectures that Kastan delivered at University College, London in 1999 – revolves around the remarkable fact, hitherto unnoted, that 'at the time of his death, the total number of editions of Shakespeare's plays far exceeded that of any other contemporary playwright'. Although Kastan is mistaken in one of his subsidiary claims – that 'no single play to that time had sold as well as *1 Henry IV*' (by 1616, *1H4* had appeared in six quarto editions, but there were also six editions of *Mucedorus* and *seven* editions of *The Spanish Tragedy* in print by that date) – his larger claim is certainly true, and it's a bombshell. Kastan's book brilliantly sheds light on an area of Shakespeare's reception history that has been unaccountably unexplored; despite the detailed attention that has been lavished upon individual quartos of Shakespeare's plays, we have clearly failed to see the forest for the trees: 'While he lived, Shakespeare arguably had some competitors for theatrical pre-eminence, but what has often been overlooked is that as a published dramatist he had none'.

Even as he calls attention to Shakespeare as 'the period's leading published playwright', Kastan perpetuates some old ideas about Shakespeare's reticent attitude toward print, characterizing him as a dramatist who 'never sought his success as in [sic] print' and 'never asserted any proprietary right over his scripts or expressed any anxiety about their printed form'. This may not be true. Many scholars believe that Shakespeare (and/or his company) provided authorized copy of *Romeo and Juliet* in 1599 to replace the apparently unsanctioned printing of 1597, and authorized copy of *Hamlet* in 1604 to replace the unsanctioned printing of 1603. As Kastan notes, such provision was virtually all that early modern writers who *did* assert proprietary rights could do when defective versions of their work found their way into print.

One of the more striking textual observations from Kastan's lectures concerns the much-maligned 'Aye, there's the point' in 'To be or not to be' in Q1 *Hamlet*, which Kastan identifies as a perfectly uncorrupt Shakespearian line that appears in *Othello* (3.3.232). To my knowledge, no previous commentator has noticed that the theatrical authorizations ('as it was played') which feature so prominently on the title-pages of the quartos of Shakespeare's plays have no place in the First Folio, a text in which, as Kastan points out, the acting companies are nowhere mentioned by name. Other scholars have suggested that the compilers of the First Folio may have purposefully excluded plays they knew to be collaborations (e.g., *Pericles* and *The Two Noble Kinsmen*), as Ben Jonson had done in his 1616 Folio. Kastan, however, is the first to argue for the corollary of this view: that Heminge and Condell's *inclusion* of *Henry VIII* attests to 'their belief that it satisfied the conditions of single authorship'.[5]

---

[5] There are only a few slips in Kastan's book worth noting: Henry Condell was *not* one of 'the original shareholders in the company' (p. 54); for 'title page' read 'table of contents page' (p. 71); for 'Henningman' read 'Herringman' (p. 98).

An observation from Lukas Erne's incisive 'Shakespeare and the Publication of Plays' nicely complements Kastan's lectures: Of the first dozen plays that Shakespeare wrote for the Lord Chamberlain's Men, 'not a single one that could legally have been printed remained unprinted by 1602'. Moreover, Erne believes he has found a fairly consistent pattern in the publication histories. As a rule, the Lord Chamberlain's Men 'seem to have sold Shakespeare's manuscripts to a publisher approximately two years after the plays reached the public stage'. In presenting his thesis, Erne acknowledges that dates of composition and first performance for these plays are often conjectural. Still, his article poses a significant challenge to the traditional narratives about the players' supposed reluctance to publish their playscripts. In fact, Erne argues, the company may have viewed performance and print 'as not only compatible but synergetic'.

In 'Scribe or Compositor: Ralph Crane, Compositors D and F, and the First Four Plays in the Shakespeare First Folio', Paul Werstine demonstrates that an understanding of Crane's spelling habits in the probable manuscripts that served as printer's copy for quires A–G of the Folio, combined with a close examination of the practices attributed to Compositors D and F as compared with those of B and C, 'casts serious doubt on the possibility that Compositor F can be distinguished as an individual from Compositor D'. Werstine acknowledges that this may not create 'a state of crisis in compositor studies', since the individual identities of the major compositors in the Folio (A, B, C, and E) remain intact. And yet, Werstine's findings reveal the extent to which the peripheral compositors such as F, H, I and J are 'precarious inferential constructions in which it is hard to have much confidence'.

In a provocative article on 'Act Divisions in the Shakespeare First Folio', James Hirsh initiates what may come to be known as 'divider studies'. Hirsh argues that the act divisions in the First Folio were added specifically for publication and 'were created by two persons': Divider A and Divider B. According to Hirsh, Divider A's method was to count off approximately one-fifth of the play and then insert the 'Act 2' heading at the nearest scene break at which the stage was cleared; he would then count off another one-fifth and add 'Act 3' at the most convenient scene break, and proceed similarly to mark the beginning of Act 4. 'Act 5', however, would be located at a scene break at the point approximately midway between the beginning of Act 4 and the end of the play. Hirsh finds that seventeen Folio plays conform fairly closely to this pattern. Divider B, by contrast, was less concerned with proportionality, but placed a high priority on locating act divisions so that a new act would begin with the entrance of a large number of characters. Hirsh finds that nine Folio plays conform to this pattern. Hirsh also points out that the pattern of act division in Ralph Crane's manuscripts tends to follow Pattern A. But the fact that several of the Folio plays for which Crane prepared the printer's copy conform to Pattern A does not support the absolute confidence of Hirsh's assertion that 'Ralph Crane is the only individual who could have been Divider A' – especially since one of the Folio plays thought to be based on a Crane transcript, *Cymbeline*, is one of the anomalous plays which does not conform to either Pattern A or Pattern B.

The dramaturge for a major Shakespeare festival occasionally e-mails me to ask whether a given semi-colon or question mark in the First Folio is italic or roman. My knee-jerk response is to ask, 'What difference does it make?' However, I temper my reply because I know that it makes a difference to him. Although most textual scholars believe that punctuation in early modern texts is generally compositorial rather than authorial, a number of theatre professionals remain convinced that the Folio's punctuation is key (if not 'the key') to understanding the way in which Shakespeare's lines should be articulated onstage.

Neil Freeman's new Applause edition of the First Folio admonishes actors to 'trust F1's punctuation. Because if you don't, you might do as much damage to the character and scene as modern editors'. Actors are encouraged to 'make sure the breath is over-emphasised a little after each piece of punctuation, and *feel* what happens'. In a (literally) bold move, Freeman gives punctuation pride of place in his diplomatic transcript of the First Folio. The 'minor punctuation' (commas, dashes, and the like) is set normally, but 'major punctuation' (colons, semi-colons, and periods) is set in bold face, and extra space is inserted before and after each major punctuation mark. By this means, Freeman hopes to provide actors with 'a reminder that this may allow for a momentary pause' which 'in acting terms, allows for a greater transition after such punctuation'. Indeed, the punctuation marks in this edition – bold, free-floating signifiers – are impossible to miss: 'Stay : speake ; speake : I Charge thee, speake.'

Potential users of Freeman's text might want to consider the final page of Folio *Romeo and Juliet*, signature gg3r, a page that had to be reset during the course of printing when it was decided that *Timon of Athens* rather than *Troilus and Cressida* would follow *Romeo and Juliet*. By the time this change was decided upon, a sheet had already been printed with the final page of *Romeo and Juliet* on the recto and the first page of *Troilus and Cressida* on the verso. Both the original and the reset page are extant, and both are reproduced in Hinman's Norton facsimile. The compositor who was responsible for resetting the seventy-seven lines of type on this page made wholesale changes to the punctuation: commas are changed to semi-colons (TLN 3108, 3126, 3167), commas are changed to colons (3110, 3156, 3161, 3169, 3173), commas are changed to periods (3127, 3134), commas are added (3112, 3121, 3135, 3163, 3164), commas are deleted (3147, 3164), a period is added (3148), a bracket is added (3132), a bracket is changed to a comma (3133), a period is changed

to a comma (3149), colons are changed to commas (3116, 3138, 3182), a colon is changed to a period (3121), a colon is changed to a semi-colon (3181), and question marks are changed to commas (3165, 3166). Thus, there is manifest proof that most of the punctuation on this Folio page originated with the typesetter. For actors contemplating the bold-faced marks in Freeman's edition, *this* should give them pause.

WORKS REVIEWED

Clegg, Cyndia Susan. *Press Censorship in Jacobean England* (Cambridge, 2001).

Erne, Lukas. 'Shakespeare and the Publication of His Plays', *Shakespeare Quarterly*, 53 (2002), 1–20.

Freeman, Neil, ed. *The Applause First Folio of Shakespeare in Modern Type* (New York and London, 2002).

Harold Bloom's Shakespeare, ed. by Christy Desmet and Robert Sawyer (New York, 2002).

Hirsh, James. 'Act Divisions in the Shakespeare First Folio', *Papers of the Bibliographical Society of America*, 96 (2002), 219–56.

Kastan, David Scott. *Shakespeare and the Book.* (Cambridge, 2001).

Shakespeare, William. *The Complete Sonnets and Poems*, ed. by Colin Burrow, Oxford Shakespeare (Oxford, 2002).

   King Henry IV, Part 1, ed. by David Scott Kastan, Arden 3 (London, 2002).

   King Richard II, ed. by Charles R. Forker, Arden 3 (London, 2002).

Werstine, Paul. 'Scribe or Compositor: Ralph Crane, Compositors D and F, and the First Four Plays in the Shakespeare First Folio', *Papers of the Bibliographical Society of America*, 95 (2001), 315–39.

BOOKS RECEIVED

This list includes all books received between September 2001 and September 2002 which are not reviewed in this volume of *Shakespeare Survey*. The appearance of a book in this list does not preclude its review in a subsequent volume.

Aspinall, Dana E., ed., *The Taming of the Shrew: Critical Essays* (London, 2002).

Baker, William, ed., *The Year's Work in English Studies 1999* (Oxford, 2001).

Castagno, Paul C., *New Playwrighting Strategies – A Language-Based Approach to Playwrighting* (London, 2002).

Corbin, P. and D. Sedge, eds., *Thomas of Woodstock, or King Richard the Second, Part One* (Manchester, 2002).

Dillon, Janette, *Performance and Spectacle in Hall's Chronicle* (London, 2002).

Hadfield, Andrew, ed., *Literature and Censorship in Renaissance England* (Basingstoke, 2001).

Holderness, Graham, *The Prince of Denmark* (Hertfordshire Press, 2002).

Honigmann, E. A. J., *Shakespeare: Seven Tragedies Revisited. The Dramatist's Manipulation of Response* (1976; 2nd edn, Basingstoke, 2002).

Kruszewska, Felicja, *A Dream* (London, 2002).

Levin, Carole, *The Reign of Elizabeth I* (Basingstoke, 2002).

Lowenstein, Joseph, *The Author's Due: Printing and the Prehistory of Copyright* (Chicago, 2002).

Lunney, Ruth, *Marlowe and the Popular Tradition* (Manchester, 2002).

McDonald, Russ, *The Bedford Companion to Shakespeare* (1996; 2nd edn, Boston, 2001).

McManus, Clare, *Women on the Renaissance Stage: Anne of Denmark and Female Masquing in the Stuart Court* (Manchester, 2002).

Minois, Georges, *History of Suicide* (1995; 1st paperback edn, Baltimore, 2001).

Quennell, Peter and Hamish Johnson, *Who's Who in Shakespeare* (1973; 3rd edn, London, 2002).

Rose, Mary Beth, *Gender and Heroism in Early Modern English Literature* (Chicago, 2002).

Schneider, Rebecca and Gabrielle Cody, eds., *Re:direction – A Theoretical and Practical Guide* (London, 2002).

Schormann, Vanessa, *Shakespeare's Globe, Repliken, Rekonstruktionen, und Bespielbarkeit* (Heidelberg, 2002).

Weimann, Robert, *Zwischen Performanz und Repräsentation: Shakespeare und die Macht des Theaters. Aufsätze von 1959–1995* (Heidelberg, 2000).

Wilson, Richard, ed., *Macmillan New Casebooks: Julius Caesar* (Basingstoke, 2002).

INDEX

No book titles are included in this index, but the names of the authors are given. Book titles in the review articles are listed alphabetically at the end of each article.

INDEX

INDEX

INDEX

INDEX

INDEX

INDEX

INDEX

INDEX